Lecture Notes in Computer Science   9681

Commenced Publication in 1973
Founding and Former Series Editors:
Gerhard Goos, Juris Hartmanis, and Jan van Leeuwen

Editorial Board

More information about this series at http://www.springer.com/series/7408

Erika Ábrahám · Marieke Huisman (Eds.)

Integrated Formal Methods

12th International Conference, IFM 2016
Reykjavik, Iceland, June 1–5, 2016
Proceedings

 Springer

Editors
Erika Ábrahám
RWTH Aachen University
Aachen
Germany

Marieke Huisman
University of Twente
Enschede
The Netherlands

ISSN 0302-9743   ISSN 1611-3349   (electronic)
Lecture Notes in Computer Science
ISBN 978-3-319-33692-3   ISBN 978-3-319-33693-0   (eBook)
DOI 10.1007/978-3-319-33693-0

Library of Congress Control Number: 2016937350

LNCS Sublibrary: SL2 – Programming and Software Engineering

© Springer International Publishing Switzerland 2016

Printed on acid-free paper

This Springer imprint is published by Springer Nature
The registered company is Springer International Publishing AG Switzerland

Preface

Applying formal methods may involve the usage of different formalisms and different analysis techniques to validate a system, either because individual components are most amenable to one formalism or technique, because one is interested in different properties of the system, or simply to cope with the sheer complexity of the system. The iFM conference series seeks to further research into hybrid approaches to formal modeling and analysis; i.e., the combination of (formal and semi-formal) methods for system development, regarding both modeling and analysis. The conference covers all aspects from language design through verification and analysis techniques to tools and their integration into software engineering practice.

These proceedings document the outcome of the 12th International Conference on Integrated Formal Methods, iFM 2016, on recent developments toward this goal. The conference was held in Reykjavik, Iceland, during June 1–5, 2016, hosted by Reykjavik University. Previous editions of iFM were held in York, UK (1999), Schloss Dagstuhl, Germany (2000), Turku, Finland (2002), Kent, UK (2004), Eindhoven, The Netherlands (2005), Oxford, UK (2007), Düsseldorf, Germany (2009), Nancy, France (2010), Pisa, Italy (2012), Turku, Finland (2013), and Bertinoro, Italy (2014).

The conference received 99 submissions of authors from 34 countries. Papers were submitted in four categories: research papers, regular tool papers, short tool papers, and case study papers. All papers were reviewed by at least three members of the Program Committee. After careful deliberations, the Program Committee selected 30 papers for presentation.

In addition to these papers, this volume contains contributions of three invited keynote speakers: Reiner Hähnle, TU Darmstadt, Germany; Laura Kovács, Chalmers University of Technology, Sweden, and TU Wien, Austria; and Marsha Chechik, University of Toronto, Canada:

- Martin Hentschel, Reiner Hähnle, and Richard Bubel: "Can Formal Methods Improve the Efficiency of Code Reviews?"
- Laura Kovács: "Symbolic Computation and Automated Reasoning for Program Analysis"
- Marsha Chechik, Michalis Famelis, and Rick Salay: "Perspectives of Model Transformation Reuse"

Invited presentations are always the highlights of a conference; these contributions are therefore gratefully acknowledged.

iFM was accompanied by the following satellite events, managed by the workshop chairs, Marcel Kyas, University of Reykjavik, Iceland, and Wojciech Mostowski, Halmstad University, Sweden:

- The 6th International Symposium on Unifying Theories of Programming (UTP 2016)
- Workshop on Pre- and Post-Deployment Verification Techniques (PrePost)

- Workshop on Formal Methods for and on the Cloud (iFMCloud 2016)
- Workshop on Verification and Validation of Cyber-Physical Systems (V2CPS)
- PhD Symposium at iFM 2016 on Formal Methods: Algorithms, Tools and Applications (PhD-iFM 2016)

The conference would not have been possible without the enthusiasm and dedication of the iFM general chair, Marjan Sirjani, and the support of the School of Computer Science at Reykjavik University, Iceland. For the work of the Program Committee and the compilation of the proceedings, Andrei Voronkov's EasyChair system was employed; it freed us from many technical matters and allowed us to focus on the program, for which we are grateful. Conferences like iFM rely on the willingness of experts to serve on the Program Committee; their professionalism and their helpfulness were exemplary. Finally, we would like to thank all the authors for their submissions, their willingness to continue improving their papers, and their presentations!

March 2016   Erika Ábrahám
                                                                   Marieke Huisman

Organization

Program Chairs

Erika Ábrahám	RWTH Aachen University, Germany
Marieke Huisman	University of Twente, The Netherlands

Steering Committee

Erika Ábrahám	RWTH Aachen University, Germany
Elvira Albert	Complutense University of Madrid, Spain
John Derrick	University of Sheffield, UK
Marieke Huisman	University of Twente, The Netherlands
Einar Broch Johnsen	University of Oslo, Norway
Dominique Méry	Université de Lorraine, France
Luigia Petre	Åbo Akademi University, Finland
Steve Schneider	University of Surrey, UK
Emil Sekerinski	McMaster University, Canada
Marjan Sirjani	University of Reykjavik, Iceland
Helen Treharne	University of Surrey, UK
Heike Wehrheim	University of Paderborn, Germany

Organizing Committee

Marjan Sirjani	University of Reykjavik, Iceland
Marcel Kyas	University of Reykjavik, Iceland
Wojciech Mostowski	Halmstad University, Sweden

Program Committee

Wolfgang Ahrendt	Chalmers University of Technology, Sweden
Elvira Albert	Complutense University of Madrid, Spain
Bernd Becker	Albert-Ludwigs-Universität Freiburg, Germany
Clara Benac Earle	Universidad Politecnica de Madrid, Spain
Borzoo Bonakdarpour	McMaster University, Canada
Ferruccio Damiani	Università di Torino, Italy
Frank de Boer	CWI, The Netherlands
Delphine Demange	University of Rennes 1/IRISA, France
Jan Friso Groote	Eindhoven University of Technology, The Netherlands
Dilian Gurov	KTH Royal Institute of Technology, Sweden
Holger Hermanns	Saarland University, Germany
Einar Broch Johnsen	University of Oslo, Norway

Peter Gorm Larsen   Aarhus University, Denmark
Martin Leucker   University of Lübeck, Germany
Dominique Méry   Université de Lorraine, LORIA, France
Rosemary Monahan   National University of Ireland Maynooth, Ireland
Nadia Polikarpova   MIT, USA
Cesar Sanchez   IMDEA Software Institute, Spain
Sriram   University of Colorado, Boulder, USA
  Sankaranarayanan
Ina Schaefer   Technische Universität Braunschweig, Germany
Gerardo Schneider   University of Gothenburg, Sweden
Emil Sekerinski   McMaster University, Canada
Armando Tacchella   Università di Genova, Italy
Mark Utting   University of the Sunshine Coast, Australia
Heike Wehrheim   University of Paderborn, Germany
Kirsten Winter   University of Queensland, Australia

Additional Reviewers

Alborodo, Raul Nestor Neri   Dezani-Ciancaglini, Mariangiola
Aliakbary, Sadegh   Din, Crystal Chang
Antignac, Thibaud   Doménech, Jesus
Arenas, Puri   Díaz, Gregorio
Avanzini, Martin   Faghih, Fathiyeh
Balliu, Musard   Filali-Amine, Mamoun
Bartocci, Ezio   Flores Montoya, Antonio E.
Baumann, Christoph   Fontaine, Pascal
Berardi, Stefano   Fredlund, Lars-Ake
Berger, Christian   Furia, Carlo A.
Besson, Frédéric   Ganty, Pierre
Bijo, Shiji   Garavel, Hubert
Bodeveix, Jean-Paul   Giachino, Elena
Bubel, Richard   Gomez-Zamalloa, Miguel
Burchard, Jan   Gordillo, Pablo
Burton, Eden   Guanciale, Roberto
Cardone, Felice   Gómez-Martínez, Elena
Cheng, Zheng   Hallerstede, Stefan
Chimento, Jesus Mauricio   Harder, Jannis
Coppo, Mario   Heckl, Istvan
Cordy, Maxime   Isabel, Miguel
Correas Fernándcz, Jesús   Isenberg, Tobias
De Carvalho Gomes, Pedro   Itzhaky, Shachar
De Frutos Escrig, David   Jacobs, Bart
De Gouw, Stijn   Jakobs, Marie-Christine
De Vink, Erik   Jensen, Thomas
Decker, Normann   Keshishzadeh, Sarmen

Kromodimoeljo, Sentot
Krämer, Julia Désirée
Kuraj, Ivan
Lachmann, Remo
Lago, Patricia
Lhotak, Ondrej
Liang, Hongjin
Lienhardt, Michael
Lity, Sascha
Liu, Tianhai
Lucanu, Dorel
Luttik, Bas
Löding, Christof
Malavolta, Ivano
Mariño, Julio
Markin, Grigory
Martin-Martin, Enrique
Mauro, Jacopo
Medhat, Ramy
Meijer, Jeroen
Mennicke, Stephan
Merz, Stephan
Milicevic, Aleksandar
Mogren, Olof
Nanevski, Aleksandar
Neubauer, Felix
Nicolaou, Nicolas
Oortwijn, Wytse
Owe, Olaf
Palmskog, Karl
Paolini, Luca
Petri, Gustavo
Power, James
Pozzato, Gian Luca
Pun, Ka I
Quilbeuf, Jean
Rafnsson, Willard
Reimer, Sven
Rezine, Ahmed
Robillard, Simon
Román-Díez, Guillermo
Sanchez, Alejandro
Sauer, Matthias
Scheffel, Torben
Scheibler, Karsten

Schewe, Sven
Schlatte, Rudolf
Schmaltz, Julien
Schmitz, Malte
Schwarz, Oliver
Scozzari, Francesca
Serbanescu, Vlad Nicolae
Siddique, Umair
Singh, Neeraj
Smith, Graeme
Sproston, Jeremy
Steffen, Martin
Stoller, Scott
Stolz, Volker
Stümpel, Annette
Summers, Alexander J.
Swartjes, Lennart
Talebi, Mahmoud
Tamarit, Salvador
Tapia Tarifa, Silvia Lizeth
Testerink, Bas
Thoma, Daniel
Thorn, Johannes
Thüm, Thomas
Toews, Manuel
Tran-Jørgensen, Peter
Travkin, Oleg
Trivedi, Ashutosh
Ulbrich, Mattias
Walther, Sven
Wasowski, Andrzej
Weng, Min-Hsien
Westman, Jonas
Wille, David
Willemse, Tim
Wimmer, Ralf
Winterer, Leonore
Wong, Peter
Wouda, Sanne
Yang, Fei
Zalinescu, Eugen
Zantema, Hans
Zavattaro, Gianluigi
Zutshi, Aditya

Contents

Concurrency

Safety and Liveness

Model Learning

Invited Contributions

Can Formal Methods Improve the Efficiency of Code Reviews?

Martin Hentschel, Reiner Hähnle$^{(\boxtimes)}$, and Richard Bubel

Department of Computer Science, TU Darmstadt, Darmstadt, Germany
{hentschel,haehnle,bubel}@cs.tu-darmstadt.de

Abstract. Code reviews are a provenly effective technique to find defects in source code as well as to increase its quality. Industrial software production often relies on code reviews as a standard QA mechanism. Surprisingly, though, tool support for reviewing activities is rare. Existing systems help to keep track of the discussion during the review, but do not support the reviewing activity directly. In this paper we argue that such support can be provided by formal analysis tools. Specifically, we use symbolic execution to improve the program understanding subtask during a code review. Tool support is realized by an Eclipse extension called Symbolic Execution Debugger. It allows one to explore visually a symbolic execution tree for the program under inspection. For evaluation we carefully designed a controlled experiment. We provide statistical evidence that with the help of symbolic execution defects are identified in a more effective manner than with a merely code-based view. Our work suggests that there is huge potential for formal methods not only in the production of safety-critical systems, but for any kind of software and as part of a standard development process.

Keywords: Code review · Symbolic execution · Empirical evaluation

1 Introduction

Writing and reading source code is the daily business of software developers. Whenever the behavior of a program is not well understood or a program does not behave as expected, then an interactive debugger becomes an important tool. In interactive debugging, first concrete input values must be found that bring program execution to a point of interest, for example, by setting suitable breakpoints. Now the developer interactively controls execution and studies each execution step until the program behavior is fully understood.

Suitable input values are sometimes provided by failed test cases or by bug reports. In general, however, it can be challenging to determine input conditions under which the code under inspection exhibits faulty behavior. Another limiting factor in conventional interactive debugging is the fact that only one particular execution path is inspected per debugging session. To inspect a different execution path, debugging needs to start over with different input values.

© Springer International Publishing Switzerland 2016
E. Ábrahám and M. Huisman (Eds.): IFM 2016, LNCS 9681, pp. 3–19, 2016.
DOI: 10.1007/978-3-319-33693-0_1

In addition to debugging and testing, source code can be studied in a (static) code review. Goals of a review include to find defects or to improve design and code quality. A review can be performed either by a team or by a single person. An important category of team review is an inspection [1,2] where people with different roles study the source code according to aspects defined by their role. Even a single developer can review source code as part of his or her personal software process (PSP) [3,4] to ensure that he or she is satisfied with the achieved quality. Checklists are often used to guide a review and to define the criteria under which the source code is reviewed.

Reviews can be performed on all kinds of documents without the need for tool support. However, we believe that symbolic execution [5–8] nurtures program understanding and that its use for bug finding is promising. To validate this claim we take an empirical approach that is standard in experimental software engineering [9]. We compare source code reviews with and without having a symbolic execution tree available. For tool support we use the Symbolic Execution Debugger (SED) [10], an Eclipse extension for interactive symbolic execution of Java into which any symbolic execution engine for Java can be integrated. In our work we use KeY [11] as the underlying symbolic execution engine.

The SED visualizes a symbolic execution tree representing all possible behaviors of a given program until a certain point. The SED's visual output is a tree where each node represents an execution step of the program under inspection. The user can interact with the visualization, for example, one can inspect and visualize the symbolic state at an execution point to help comprehension of program behavior. Standard symbolic execution explores only finite fragments of an execution which is a serious limitation in the presence of loops with symbolic bounds, method calls with unknown implementations, and recursive calls. The SED is able to process formal specifications in the form of method contracts and loop invariants during symbolic execution. This guarantees that the full program behavior is explored for *any* possible execution path of the program [12].

The purpose of our experiment is to evaluate the effectiveness and efficiency of a source code review with and without the SED. Traditional debugging is explicitly allowed in a direct code review (DCR) without the SED. The experiment is run from the research perspective to find out if the SED significantly improves the review quality. During the evaluation Java source code is shown to the participants and they are asked questions about it to measure their performance. Each code example realizes a small, but functionally complete program and is inspired by the literature or other interesting problems. The expected behavior is always described by comments and sometimes additionally by Java Modeling Language (JML) [13] specifications. The questions asked are a form of checklist used to review the source code. The experiment was performed with engineers at Bosch Engineering GmbH and was announced in public on the KeY website, also on the JML and KeY mailing lists. We summarize the scope of the experiment:

Analyze *code review with and without the SED*
for the purpose of *evaluation*
with respect to *effectiveness and efficiency*
from the point of view of the *researcher*
in the context of *Java developers in industry and research.*

The paper is organized as follows: Sect. 2 discusses related work. Then we describe the planning and setup of the experiment. The measured variables are determined in Sect. 3, the hypotheses to test in Sect. 4. Section 5 lays out the design of the experiment and Sect. 6 presents the instrumentation. We conclude experiment planning by discussing threats to validity in Sect. 7. The execution of the experiment is presented in Sect. 8. Collected data are analyzed in Sect. 9 before discussing the results in Sect. 10. We conclude the paper with Sect. 11.

2 Related Work

In [1,2] software inspection is introduced and its impact is confirmed by experience reports. The effectiveness of inspections has been confirmed in many case studies and experience reports, for example, [14,15].

Systems like Gerrit[1] organize the information that is accumulated during a review such as comments. A comparison of early computer support systems for software inspection is in [16]. For some roles assumed during a team review tool support exists. For instance, the moderator can be assisted by decision support facilities [17]. The defect detection step itself is targeted by [18]: they realize learning from the experience encoded in checklists and automatic scans of the source code for violations of checklist items.

To the best of our knowledge, no tool support targeting the interactive defect detection step in a source code review exists. In addition, the effectiveness of reviews is usually confirmed by experience reports whereas in this paper a controlled experiment is performed to draw conclusions with statistical relevance.

3 Variable Selection

First we need to determine and classify the variables of the experiment. We distinguish two kinds of variables: *independent variables* and *dependent variables*. The independent variables are those which can be varied or at least controlled by us and whose influence and effect on the outcome of the experiment we intend to study. Dependent variables are those that are measured during the course of the experiment and which we want to study. A value of an independent variable that was changed during the experiment is called *treatment*.

Table 1 lists the variables of our experiment. The independent variables which can be varied by us are M (with treatments SED and DCR) and S (with the six code examples to review). The subset of independent variables that are merely

---

[1] www.gerritcodereview.com.

Table 1. Variables of the experiment

	Name	Value domain	Description
Independent Variable	M	{SED, DCR}	The compared methods
	S	{BankUtil, MathUtil, IntegerUtil, Stack, ValueSearch, ObservableArray}	The reviewed source code example and related questions
Controlled Variable	E_{Java}	{*none*, < 2, ≥ 2}	Years of experience with Java
	E_{JML}	{*none*, < 2, ≥ 2}	Years of experience with JML
	E_{SE}	{*none*, < 2, ≥ 2}	Years of experience with symbolic execution
	E_{SED}	{*none*, < 1, ≥ 1}	Years of experience with SED
Dependent Variable	Q_{tm}	Integer	Number of correctly answered questions per treatment *tm* of M
	QS_{tm}	Real	Correctness score per treatment *tm* of M
	C_{tm}	Integer	Confidence score per treatment *tm* of M based on Q
	CS_{tm}	Real	Confidence score per treatment *tm* of M based on QS
	T_{tm}	Integer	Time needed to answer questions of a treatment *tm* of M in seconds

controlled are called $E_{Java|JML|SE|SED}$. Their values provide an answer to the question about a participant's experience level. The separation between less and more than two years is made to separate beginners from experienced users assuming that this is roughly the time needed to master Java, JML and symbolic execution well enough for the evaluation. As the SED is rather new, it is assumed that participants have not much experience with it. For this reason, the separation between beginners and experienced users is set to one year.

The dependent variables are used to quantify *efficiency* and *effectiveness* of the different methods. Efficiency is measured by the time T_{tm} spend to answer the questions using method $tm \in M$. Effectiveness is measured in the number of correctly answered questions and the confidence in the given answers. Questions are single or multiple choice questions to enable an automatic analysis. Each question lists a number of correct and wrong answers from which the participant has to choose. For a given method tm, a multiple choice question is answered correct (measured by Q_{tm}) if all and only the correct answers are selected.

A correctness score is used to give credit for partially correct answers. The correctness score $QS_{tm} = \sum_{q \in tm} qs(q)$ is the sum of the scores over all questions of treatment *tm*. For a single question q the score $qs(q)$ is defined as:

$$qs(q) = \begin{cases} \frac{\#corSelAnsw(q) - \#wrgSelAnsw(q)}{\#corSelAnswers} & \text{if } \#corSelAnsw(q) > \#wrgSelAnsw(q) \\ \frac{\#corSelAnsw(q) - \#wrgSelAnsw(q)}{\#wrgSelAnswers} & \text{if } \#corSelAnsw(q) \leq \#wrgSelAnsw(q) \end{cases}$$

Intuitively, the question score $qs(q)$ is the difference between the number of selected correct answers $\#corSelAnsw(q)$ and the number of selected wrong

Table 2. Confidence ratings $c(q)$, $cs(q)$ of a single question q

	Correct answer of q or $qs(q) > 0$	Wrong answer of q or $qs(q) \leq 0$
Sure	2	-2
Educated Guess	1	-1
Unsure	-1	1

answers $\#wrgSelAnsw(q)$ of question q. But each question has a different number of correct (wrong) answers. To achieve comparability between questions, the difference between correct and wrong answers is divided by the total number of correct (wrong) answers.

For each question we asked the participants about the confidence in their answers. Available confidence levels are *sure (My answer is correct!)*, *educated guess (As far as I understood the content, my answer should be correct.)* and *unsure (I tried my best, but I don't believe that my answer is correct.)*.

For each question q (each question score $qs(q)$) a confidence rating $c(q)$ ($cs(q)$) is computed according to Table 2. A participant who is sure the answer is correct when it is actually correct (the confidence score is positive) obtains maximal points. If the answer is wrong, but the participant was sure that it is correct (the confidence score is positive), he or she gets the lowest possible rating. If the answer is based on an educated guess, which is weaker than certainty, the participant gets less (or loses less) points. If the participant is unsure and thinks the answer is wrong, and it is actually wrong (the confidence score is not positive), then still one score point is assigned, because the intuition was correct. If the participant thinks the answer is wrong but it is right (the confidence score is positive), he or she loses one score point for the same reason. Finally, the confidence score $C_{tm} = \sum_{q \in tm} c(q)$ is the sum of the confidence ratings over all questions answered for treatment tm. The confidence score based on question scores $CS_{tm} = \sum_{q \in tm} cs(q) \cdot qs(q)$ takes partially correct answers into account.

4 Hypothesis Formulation

From our experiment we want to gain statistical evidence that the SED increases effectiveness and efficiency of a code review. To this extent we formulate for each dependent variable (see Table 1) an alternative hypothesis $H_{1_Q} - H_{1_T}$ (see Table 3). As usual [9] the claims of these hypotheses are confirmed by ruling out each corresponding null hypothesis $H_{0_Q} - H_{0_T}$.

5 Choice of Experiment Design Type

An important design decision of the experiment is to ensure that participants benefit from their participation. To achieve this, each participant uses both methods resulting in a paired comparison design (see Table 4). In case participants are

Table 3. Hypotheses

Name	Hypothesis	Def. of $\mu_{V_{tm}}$ for dependent variable V, treatment tm
H_{0_Q}	$\mu_{Q_{SED}} = \mu_{Q_{DCR}}$	with $\mu_{Q_{tm}} = \frac{Q_{tm}}{\#questionsOfTmnt} \in \{x \in \mathbb{Q} \mid 0 \leq x \leq 1\}$
$H_{0_{QS}}$	$\mu_{QS_{SED}} = \mu_{QS_{DCR}}$	with $\mu_{QS_{tm}} = \frac{QS_{tm}}{\#questionsOfTmnt} \in \{x \in \mathbb{Q} \mid 0 \leq x \leq 1\}$
H_{0_C}	$\mu_{C_{SED}} = \mu_{C_{DCR}}$	with $\mu_{C_{tm}} = \frac{C_{tm}}{\#questionsOfTmnt} \in \{x \in \mathbb{Q} \mid -2 \leq x \leq 2\}$
$H_{0_{CS}}$	$\mu_{CS_{SED}} = \mu_{CS_{DCR}}$	with $\mu_{CS_{tm}} = \frac{CS_{tm}}{\#questionsOfTmnt} \in \{x \in \mathbb{Q} \mid -2 \leq x \leq 2\}$
H_{0_T}	$\mu_{T_{SED}} = \mu_{T_{DCR}}$	with $\mu_{T_{tm}} = \frac{T_{tm}}{timeOfAllTmnts} \in \{x \in \mathbb{Q} \mid 0 \leq x \leq 1\}$
H_{1_Q}	$\mu_{Q_{SED}} > \mu_{Q_{DCR}}$	
$H_{1_{QS}}$	$\mu_{QS_{SED}} > \mu_{QS_{DCR}}$	
H_{1_C}	$\mu_{C_{SED}} > \mu_{C_{DCR}}$	
$H_{1_{CS}}$	$\mu_{CS_{SED}} > \mu_{CS_{DCR}}$	
H_{1_T}	$\mu_{T_{SED}} < \mu_{T_{DCR}}$	

Table 4. Paired comparison design

	Example 1	Example 2	Example 3	Example 4	Example 5	Example 6
SED	Subject$_n$	Subject$_n$	Subject$_n$	Subject$_{n+1}$	Subject$_{n+1}$	Subject$_{n+1}$
DCR	Subject$_{n+1}$	Subject$_{n+1}$	Subject$_{n+1}$	Subject$_n$	Subject$_n$	Subject$_n$

unfamiliar with the SED, this allows them to try it out and to decide whether it is helpful for their work.

We applied the general experiment design principles *randomization, blocking* and *balancing* [9] to avoid biases, to block out effects in which we are not interested in, and to simplify and strengthen hypothesis testing. We randomized the order of code examples presented to the participants to avoid that, for instance, differences in the level of difficulty can influence the result of the experiment.

The first three code examples are always to be reviewed using the same method and the next three code examples with the other one (recall that we have six code examples to review). The decision which method is used for the first three code examples is random. This avoids multiple switches between methods which could confuse the participant. Additionally, a participant who is not familiar with a reviewing method has more experience in the later tasks. The server used to collect evaluation results guarantees that all possible permutations of example orders will be evaluated equally often as well as all other constraints.

The performance of the participants may depend on their experience with Java which is used for blocking. Grouping the participants according to their experience level with Java allows us to interpret the results for the different groups separately. Balancing is automatically achieved by the chosen design, because each participant uses both methods and reviews all six code examples. Thus the number of participants is the same for each treatment. The number of participants who reviewed a source code example might be not balanced in case participants decided not to review all of them.

6 Instrumentation

We did not want to limit the group of participants to people familiar with symbolic execution, JML or the SED. The only hard requirement on the participants was basic knowledge in Java (or a similar language). To accommodate this decision, the evaluation had to be self-explanatory. We achieved this by showing three instructional videos: an introduction to the evaluation itself and one to each method. A brief textual introduction was given on how to read and write JML specifications (the JML specifications used in the evaluation do not use advanced concepts).

During the evaluation participants reviewed source code with and without using the SED. As the SED is available within Eclipse, the evaluation itself is implemented as an Eclipse wizard which is opened in an additional window so that the functionality of Eclipse is not impaired.

The evaluation setup consists of two phases during which information is collected and sent to the server. The first phase collects background knowledge on the participant and determines the order of code examples and the method assignment. The actual evaluation is performed in the second phase. A participant who cancels the evaluation during the second phase is asked to send partial results to the server. When that participant opens the evaluation wizard the next time, he or she is offered to recover the previous state to continue the already started evaluation. The evaluation workflow in detail is as follows:

1. Initialization Phase
   (a) *Terms of Use*: Terms of use need to be accepted.
   (b) *Background Knowledge*: Information about background knowledge is gathered (Java, JML, symbolic execution, SED).
   (c) *Extent*: Participant chooses between reviewing four or six code examples.
   (d) *Sending Data*: Data is sent and order of code examples is received.
2. Evaluation Phase
   (a) *Evaluation Instructions*: A video explaining how to answer questions.
   (b) *JML*: A textual documentation introducing the features of JML necessary for the evaluation.
   (c) *SED/DCR Instruction*: A video explaining needed features and best practices to review a code example with and without the SED (depending on order).
   (d) *Code Examples 1 and 2 (and 3)*: The first two/three code examples and the questions that test the understanding.
   (e) *The complementary SED/DCR Instruction*: The remaining video.
   (f) *Code Examples 4 and 5 (and 6)*: As above
   (g) *Feedback about SED and Evaluation*: The participant is asked to rate the usefulness of SED features (mentioned in the videos).
   (h) *Sending Data and Acknowledgment*: Data is sent and the successful completion of the evaluation is acknowledged.

We summarize the six code examples[2] to be reviewed and the defects the participants were supposed to identify:

---

[2] Available at http://www.key-project.org/eclipse/SED/ReviewingCodeEvaluation/examples.

BankUtil implements a stair-step table lookup, inspired by [19, p. 427]. The source code does not adhere to its documentation because a wrong value is returned for an age above 35.

IntegerUtil is inspired by [20, p. 255]. The challenge is to find the mistake that in one case y is returned instead of x.

MathUtil can throw an uncaught ArrayIndexOutOfBoundsException caused by overflow. Such an overflow was present in Java's binary search implementation, see bug item JDK-5045582[3].

ValueSearch contains unreachable code, namely statement return false. The surrounding method accept is only called within the loop in method search. The loop guard already ensures that the then branch of accept is never taken. Such issues are difficult to detect by test case generation tools based on symbolic execution: when unrolling the loop further there might be a future loop iteration in which the then branch will be taken after all. Further, there is a defect in method find. The parameter value is never used. Finally, in case the array is null, an uncaught NullPointerException is thrown.

ObservableArray is inspired by [21, p. 265]. The class constructor and the method setArrayListeners behave according to the documentation. But method set has several problems: (i) in case the index is outside the array bounds an uncaught ArrayIndexOutOfBoundsException is thrown, (ii) in case the element is not compatible to the component type of the array an ArrayStoreException is thrown, (iii) not all observers that exist at call time are informed about the change in case an observer changes the available observers during the event, and (iv) if an observer sets arrayListeners to null, an uncaught NullPointerException is thrown.

Stack is inspired by [21, p. 24]. The first constructor which creates a new stack throws an uncaught NegativeArraySizeException if the maximal size is negative. The second constructor which clones a stack does not behave as documented, because the clone shares the same elements array and is thus not independent. Further, it throws a NullPointerException if the existing stack is null. Method push behaves as documented, but method pop does not remove the top element from the stack which violates the class invariant.

We designed questions and answers for each code example according to the following schema: The participant is asked (i) for each method/constructor to review whether the implementation behaves as documented, (ii) in case a class invariant is present to review whether it is preserved/established, (iii) for methods with a return value to choose which claims from a given list are valid and (iv) to determine which statements can be reached. In case a participant answers that the source code does not behave as documented, all applicable reasons why this is the case from a predefined list of potential causes had to be chosen. In case an undocumented exception is thrown, the participant is asked which one. When a participant answers that an invariant is violated, the invalid parts have to be identified. Entering free text with additional reasons is always possible.

---

[3] http://bugs.java.com/bugdatabase/view_bug.do?bug_id=5045582.

For the code examples to be reviewed with the SED we asked participants to rate the helpfulness of the symbolic execution view. For DCR, we asked whether the conventional Java debugger was used and if so, how helpful debugging was.

In every review using the SED the fully explored symbolic execution tree is shown. Interactive symbolic execution is avoided to ensure that all participants review the source code under the same conditions. In DCR a main method with a call of the code to review is provided. Required values of parameters are missing and have to be provided by the participant. The code is there to help participants without or little Java experience to start a debugging session.

7 Validity Evaluation

In this section we discuss threats to the validity of our experiments and the drawn conclusions. For each threat we provide a mitigation strategy.

"*Conclusion validity* concerns the statistical analysis of results and the composition of subjects." [9, p. 185] The hypotheses of this experiment are tested with well known statistical techniques. Threats to conclusion validity are the low number of samples and the quality of the answers. Subjects may fake answers to compromise the experiment. However, several participants are people we know (colleagues, project partners, students, etc.), in addition, some were monitored during the evaluation. We consider the motivation of subjects to compromise the experiment to be very low.

"*Internal validity* concerns matters that may affect the independent variable with respect to causality, without the researcher's knowledge." [9, p. 185] Reviewing source code is time intensive and the participation time is up to 90 min; hence, participants may get tired or bored. There is a risk that participants lack motivation and thus answer questions not seriously. However, participation is voluntary and can be done at any time convenient for the subject.

Maturation is a threat to internal validity as each method is applied to three code examples and participants may learn how to use it, which is desired. We consider this non-critical as randomization is applied to the order of treatments. Participants have most likely no experience with the SED which is uncritical as the instrumentation introduces all relevant features and best practices of both review methods. There might be a threat that some participants are not willing to learn how to use the SED. However, SED is designed to support the reviewing process. A potential bias about the experience with the SED would only contribute against our claim that SED improves upon efficiency and effectiveness and not in its favor. Other threats are considered to be uncritical.

"*Construct validity* concerns generalisation of the experiment result to concept or theory behind the experiment." [9] A threat to construct validity is that the chosen code examples are not be representative. To mitigate the code examples were chosen from the standard literature or from widely discussed problems. Other threats to construct validity are considered uncritical. Even though a participant might guess the expected outcome from the general motivation of the experiment (a comparison between a code review with and without the SED) and that SED is a new tool, we consider it uncritical as the exact hypotheses and related measurements are unknown to them. In addition, the participants do not have any advantage or disadvantage from the outcome of the experiment.

"*External validity* concerns generalisation of the experiment result to other environments than the one in which the study is conducted." [9, p. 185] A threat to external validity is that the source code is kept to a minimum—in some cases only one method. This is required to reduce the time participants need to review the source code and to read its documentation. Real Java code is much more complex. On the other hand, symbolic execution with specifications is modular, only a small part of the source code needs to be considered. The participants are selected randomly and their experience varies from none to expert. Consequently, the selection of participants is not a threat to external validity.

We state that there are threats to the validity of the experiment, and hence, the drawn conclusions are valid within the limitations of the threats.

8   Execution

The experiment started in September 2015 with the staff of the Software Engineering group at TU Darmstadt. It included students, PhD students and post-docs. Each participant was monitored during the evaluation to improve the instructions and answers. Questions and answers remained stable after the first participant. For this reason, the results of the first participant were excluded, but the others were kept.

The evaluation was then performed with engineers at Bosch Engineering GmbH. None of the engineers use Java in their daily business and the Java experience was none or less then a year. However, participants were interested in new methods and liked to try out the SED. In total, 11 engineers started the evaluation. One participant canceled the evaluation and three participants did not submit the answers. Additionally, one participant did not follow the instructions and used the SED for all code examples. Consequently, the results of six participants are considered as valid.

The evaluation went public in October 2015. It was announced on the KeY website, as well as the KeY and JML mailing lists. The evaluation is available as a preconfigured Eclipse product. Installation instructions and download links are available on the KeY website.[4] Main steps are to download and run the Eclipse product and to perform the evaluation. An installation is not required, the participants' system is unaffected. Until mid January 2016, 27 participants started the evaluation, of these 19 completed it. Twelve of the participants were monitored during the evaluation (with their approval).

The distribution of background knowledge of participants is shown in Fig. 1. The experience of participants with knowledge in JML and symbolic execution is fairly distributed. Most of the participants had more than two years of Java experience and none with the SED.

---

[4] http://www.key-project.org/eclipse/SED/ReviewingCode.html.

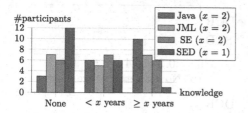

Fig. 1. Knowledge of participants

Table 5. Java vs SED experience

		SED		
		None	< 1 year	≥ 1 year
	None	3	0	0
Java	< 2 years	6	0	0
	≥ 2 years	3	6	1

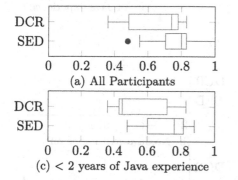

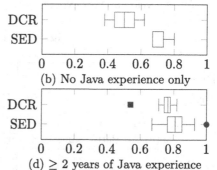

Fig. 2. Correct Answers

The relation between the Java and the SED experience is shown in Table 5. It shows that all participants with SED experience have at least two years of Java experience.

9   Analysis

Now we visualize the collected data to get a first impression about their distribution and to identify possible outliers, before we test our hypotheses. Interpretation and discussion of the results is done in Sect. 10.

To visualize data we use boxplots (Figs. 2, 3, 4, 5 and 6). The middle vertical bar in the rectangle of a boxplot indicates the median of the data. The left border represents the lower quartile lq and the right border represents the upper quartile uq. The left and right whiskers indicate the theoretical bounds of the data assuming a normal distribution. Data points outside the whiskers are outliers. The left whisker is defined as $lq - 1.5\,(uq - lq)$ and the right whisker as $uq + 1.5\,(uq - lq)$. Additionally, whiskers are truncated to the nearest existing value within the bounds to avoid meaningless values. The constant 1.5 is chosen following [22].

The boxplots in Fig. 2 show the distribution of the correctly answered questions with the lower bound 0 meaning that no question was answered correctly and the upper bound 1 attained when all answers were correct. The boxplots

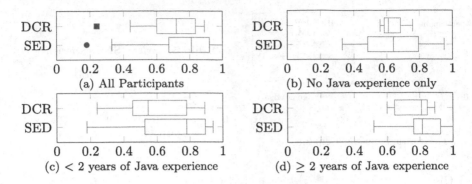

Fig. 3. Correctness Score

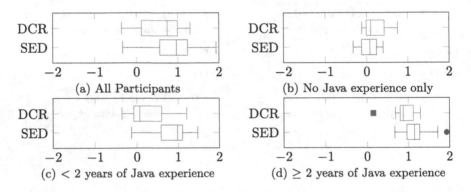

Fig. 4. Confidence Score

in Fig. 2a show the distribution for all participants for the treatments SED and DCR, whereas Fig. 2b–d show the distribution of correct answers broken down to different levels of Java experience. In all boxplots, the achieved correctness is better using SED.

The distribution of the measured correctness scores (taking partially correct answers into account, see Sect. 3) is shown in Fig. 3. In each case the correctness score is at least as high as in the distribution of correct answers (Fig. 2). Again, the achieved correctness is always better using SED. In the class of participants without Java experience, the achieved correctness using SED varies considerably.

The distributions of the confidence score are similar to those of the correctness score. As Figs. 4 and 5 show, the confidence is higher with SED. An exception is the class of participants without Java experience which achieved slightly better confidence without using the SED. In each case the confidence score increases (the boxplot "moves right") when taking partially correct answers into account.

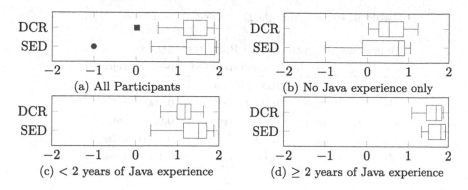

Fig. 5. Confidence Score of Partially Correct Answers

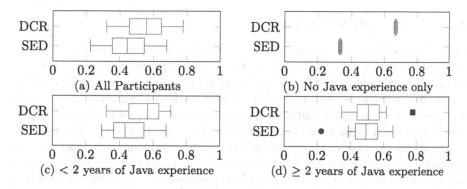

Fig. 6. Time

The measured time[5] is shown in Fig. 6. A value of 1 means that a participant spent all the time using one reviewing method. The opposite is 0 when a participant spent no time with a reviewing method. In all boxplots, the review time is less using SED.

The null hypotheses of Table 3 can be rejected without assuming a normal distribution using a one sided *Wilcoxon Signed Rank Test* or a one sided *Sign Test*, see [9]. As basis for the tests we used the results of *all* participants and did not test each experience level separately, because there are too few participants in each class to apply any test method. The significance level is set to 0.05 meaning that there is a 5 % chance at which a hypotheses is wrongly rejected. The results of the tests are shown in Table 6.

All tests reject the correctness-related hypothesis H_{0_Q} and the Wilcoxon Signed Rank Test rejects in addition the confidence-related hypothesis H_{0_C}. Looking at the promising boxplots we expect to reject the other hypotheses as well once more people participate in the experiment.

---

[5] The times measured for three of the participants were invalid and, therefore, excluded.

Table 6. Results from the One Sided Tests with $\alpha = 0.05$

Hypothesis	Wilcoxon Signed Rank Test			Sign Test	
	W-value	p-value	rejected	p-value	rejected
H_{0_Q}	176,5	0,0002	true	0,0012	true
$H_{0_{QS}}$	119,5	0,1660	false	0,5000	false
H_{0_C}	151	0,0115	true	0,0835	false
$H_{0_{CS}}$	119	0,1762	false	0,1796	false
H_{0_T}	82	0,1147	false	0,1509	false

10   Interpretation

10.1   Correctness of Answers

The analysis of our experiment permits to conclude that participants performed significantly better in code reviewing tasks when the SED is used. Also the participant's confidence in the given answers is higher when the SED is involved.

To answer the question whether the SED performs universally better or only in a specific code reviewing situation, we look at how often an expected correct answer was given using each of the methods. We summarize now the results.[6]

Questions whether the implementation behaves as documented and whether a constructor establishes an invariant were answered more often correctly in a direct code review without using the SED, particularly, in the examples `Stack` and `ValueSearch`. In traditional debugging sessions the explored execution path shows only symptoms of a defect. This is also true for symbolic execution paths visualized by the SED. To locate the defect in the program logic causing the observed symptom (at runtime) the source code needs to be reviewed. This relation between debugging and reviews is also discussed in [3]. However, the SED shows source code and symbolic execution tree at the same time.

Questions about the reason for a misbehavior were only answered by participants when they had realized before that something is wrong. As participants using the SED often failed to identify a problem, it is not surprising that the correct reasons were also more often identified in a direct code review. Interestingly, participants identified more often that an exception is thrown and the correct type of the thrown exception using the SED. Thrown exceptions are explicitly visualized in the SED by special symbolic execution tree nodes.

In addition to the symbolic execution tree, the SED highlights the statements that were reached during symbolic execution. This seems to be helpful as the reachable statements were more often correctly identified using the SED.

Participants were also asked to identify valid claims about a method's return value from a given list of options. The SED visualizes symbolic values that can be potentially returned as part of the method return node. In the `MathUtil`

---

[6] Detailed results are available at http://www.key-project.org/eclipse/SED/Reviewing CodeEvaluation/results.

and `ValueSearch` example the correct answers were more often selected using SED, whereas in the `BankUtil`, `Stack` and `IntegerUtil` example the direct code review achieved better results.

In total correct answers were more often identified in the classes of participants with Java experience using the SED. In the class without Java experience correct answers were more often selected in a direct code review. Taking into account that only three participants are in that class and that many questions are never answered with both methods, no meaningful conclusions can be drawn. Overall, a few more correct answers were identified in a direct code review.

We conclude that the SED helps to answer questions about aspects that are represented in the symbolic execution tree. According to the given answers, the SED seems not to increase the understanding of the program logic.

10.2   Perceived Usefulness of Features

For the SED, nearly all participants considered the symbolic execution tree view and the highlighting of source code reached during symbolic execution as helpful or very helpful. The variable view used to visualize the symbolic state of a symbolic execution tree node as well as the properties view showing additional information like path conditions were in many cases not used by the participants. But those who used them considered them mostly as (very) helpful.

Participants had the opportunity to use the Java debugger in a direct code review. But the source code required to do so was often not written and if it was, its helpfulness varies from very to somewhat helpful.

Several participants provided constructive suggestions for improvement: first, source code reached in the currently selected execution path as well as the corresponding symbolic execution nodes should be highlighted. Following further suggestions we plan to visualize additional information, including the path condition and selected memory locations within symbolic execution tree nodes.

Participants were also asked whether they prefer a code review with or without using the SED (as the SED is designed to support a review and not to replace it). Our evaluation shows, that the SED effectively helps to discover information about feasible execution paths. Studying a symbolic execution tree, however, is not sufficient to understand the program logic. It is, therefore, not surprising that roughly two thirds of the participants would consider the SED depending on the nature of the given source code.

11   Conclusion

We described an experiment comparing the effectiveness and efficiency of a code review with and without using the SED. The result provides statistically significant evidence for increased effectiveness when a symbolic execution tree view is used during code reviews.

Very few formal methods are evaluated with user studies. Usually, perceived advantages are simply claimed or, in the best case, validated against a case study.

As far as we know, this is the first comparative experimental user case study of its kind. We strongly believe that more work like it is needed to convince industrial stakeholders about the value of formal methods. The advantages of case studies are obvious: effectivity claims get empricially substantiated which is a solid basis for decision makers. In addition, researchers obtain valuable feedback from the field and can make better usage of resources.

One must also clearly state that user studies mean a lot of work. Statistical techniques most researchers in formal methods are unfamiliar with have to be mastered. Designing and carrying out the actual study is very time consuming. To sustain further studies, participants must be reimbursed. But we think that the increased credibility of our claims and the insights we gained are well worth the effort.

Acknowledgment. We thank all participants of the evaluation for their valuable time and feedback.

References

1. Fagan, M.E.: Design and code inspections to reduce errors in program development. IBM Syst. J. **15**(3), 182–211 (1976)
2. Fagan, M.E.: Advances in software inspections. IEEE Trans. Softw. Eng. **12**(7), 744–751 (1986)
3. Humphrey, W.S.: A Discipline for Software Engineering. Addison-Wesley Longman Publishing Co., Inc, Boston (1995)
4. Humphrey, W.S.: Introduction to the Personal Software Process. Addison-Wesley Longman Publishing Co., Inc, Boston (1997)
5. Boyer, R.S., Elspas, B., Levitt, K.N.: SELECT–a formal system for testing and debugging programs by symbolic execution. ACM SIGPLAN Not. **10**(6), 234–245 (1975)
6. Burstall, R.M.: Program proving as hand simulation with a little induction. In: Information Processing 1974. Elsevier/North-Holland (1974)
7. Katz, S., Manna, Z.: Towards automatic debugging of programs. In: Proceedings of the International Conference on Reliable Software, pp. 143–155. ACM Press, Los Angeles (1975)
8. King, J.C.: Symbolic execution and program testing. Commun. ACM **19**(7), 385–394 (1976)
9. Wohlin, C., Runeson, P., Höst, M., Ohlsson, M.C., Regnell, B.: Experimentation in Software Engineering. Springer, Heidelberg (2012)
10. Hentschel, M., Bubel, R., Hähnle, R.: Symbolic execution debugger (SED). In: Bonakdarpour, B., Smolka, S.A. (eds.) RV 2014. LNCS, vol. 8734, pp. 255–262. Springer, Heidelberg (2014)
11. Beckert, B., Hähnle, R., Schmitt, P.H.: Verification of Object-Oriented Software: The KeY Approach. LNCS, vol. 4334. Springer, Heidelberg (2007)
12. Hentschel, M., Hähnle, R., Bubel, R.: Visualizing unbounded symbolic execution. In: Seidl, M., Tillmann, N. (eds.) TAP 2014. LNCS, vol. 8570, pp. 82–98. Springer, Heidelberg (2014)

13. Leavens, G.T., Poll, E., Clifton, C., Cheon, Y., Ruby, C., Cok, D., Müller, P., Kiniry, J., Chalin, P., Zimmerman, D.M., Dietl, W.: JML Reference Manual. Draft Revision 2344, 31, May 2013
14. Doolan, E.P.: Experience with Fagan's inspection method. Softw. Pract. Exper. **22**(2), 173–182 (1992)
15. Russell, G.W.: Experience with inspection in ultralarge-scale development. IEEE Softw. **8**(1), 25–31 (1991)
16. Macdonald, F., Miller, J.: A comparison of computer support systems for software inspection. Autom. Softw. Eng. **6**(3), 291–313 (1999)
17. Miller, J., Macdonald, F., Ferguson, J.: Assisting management decisions in the software inspection process. Inf. Technol. Manag. **3**(1–2), 67–83 (2002)
18. Nick, M., Denger, C., Willrich, T.: Experience-based support for code inspections. In: Althoff, K.-D., Dengel, A.R., Bergmann, R., Nick, M., Roth-Berghofer, T.R. (eds.) WM 2005. LNCS (LNAI), vol. 3782, pp. 121–126. Springer, Heidelberg (2005)
19. McConnell, S.: Code Complete, 2nd edn. Microsoft Press, Redmond (2004)
20. Zeller, A.: Why Programs Fail–A Guide to Systematic Debugging, 2nd edn. Elsevier, San Francisco (2006)
21. Bloch, J.: Effective Java, 2nd edn. Prentice Hall, Upper Saddle River (2008)
22. Frigge, M., Hoaglin, D.C., Iglewicz, B.: Some implementations of the boxplot. Am. Stat. **43**(1), 50–54 (1989)

Symbolic Computation and Automated Reasoning for Program Analysis

Laura Kovács[1,2]([⊠])

[1] Chalmers University of Technology, Gothenburg, Sweden
laura.kovacs@chalmers.se
[2] TU Wien, Vienna, Austria

Abstract. This talk describes how a combination of symbolic computation techniques with first-order theorem proving can be used for solving some challenges of automating program analysis, in particular for generating and proving properties about the logically complex parts of software. The talk will first present how computer algebra methods, such as Gröbner basis computation, quantifier elimination and algebraic recurrence solving, help us in inferring properties of program loops with non-trivial arithmetic. Typical properties inferred by our work are loop invariants and expressions bounding the number of loop iterations. The talk will then describe our work to generate first-order properties of programs with unbounded data structures, such as arrays. For doing so, we use saturation-based first-order theorem proving and extend first-order provers with support for program analysis. Since program analysis requires reasoning in the combination of first-order theories of data structures, the talk also discusses new features in first-order theorem proving, such as inductive reasoning and built-in boolean sort. These extensions allow us to express program properties directly in first-order logic and hence use further first-order theorem provers to reason about program properties.

1 Introduction

The successful development and application of powerful verification tools such as model checkers [3,18], static program analyzers [5], symbolic computation algorithms [2], decision procedures for common data structures [16], as well as theorem provers for first- and higher-order logic [17] opened new perspectives for the automated verification of software systems. In particular, increasingly common use of concurrency in the new generation of computer systems has motivated the integration of established reasoning-based methods, such as satisfiability modulo theory (SMT) solvers and first-order theorem provers, with complimentary techniques such as software testing [8]. This kind of integration has however imposed new requirements on verification tools, such as inductive reasoning [13,15], interpolation [9], proof generation [7], and non-linear arithmetic symbolic computations [6]. Verification methods combining symbolic computation and automated reasoning are therefore of critical importance for improving software reliability.

© Springer International Publishing Switzerland 2016
E. Ábrahám and M. Huisman (Eds.): IFM 2016, LNCS 9681, pp. 20–27, 2016.
DOI: 10.1007/978-3-319-33693-0_2

In this talk we address this challenge by automatic program analysis. Program analysis aims to discover program properties preventing programmers from introducing errors while making software changes and can drastically cut the time needed for program development, making thus a crucial step to automated verification. The work presented in this talk targets the combination of symbolic computation techniques from algorithmic combinatorics and computer algebra with first-order theorem proving and static analysis of programs. We rely on our recent *symbol elimination method* [13]. Although the symbol elimination terminology has been introduced only recently by us, we argue that symbol elimination can be viewed as a general framework for program analysis. That is, various techniques used in software analysis and verification, such as Gröbner basis computation or quantifier elimination, can be seen as application of symbol elimination to safety verification of programs.

In a nutshell, symbol elimination is based on the following ideas. Suppose we have a program P with a set of variables V. The set V defines the language of P. We extend the language P to a richer language P_0 by adding functions and predicates, such as loop counters. After that, we automatically generate a set Π of first-order properties of the program in the extended language P_0, by using techniques from symbolic computation and theorem proving. These properties are valid properties of the program, however they use the extended language P_0. At a last step of symbol elimination we derive from Π program properties in the original language P, thus "eliminating" the symbols in $P_0 \setminus P$.

The work presented in this talk describes symbol elimination in the combination of first-order theorem proving and symbolic computation. Such a combination requires the development of new reasoning methods based on superposition first-order theorem proving [14], Gröbner basis computation [2], and quantifier elimination [4]. We propose symbol elimination as a powerful tool for program analysis, in particular for generating program properties, such as loop invariants and Craig interpolants. These properties express conditions to hold at intermediate program locations and are used to prove the absence of program errors, hence they are very important for improving automation of program analysis.

Since program analysis requires reasoning in the combination of first-order theories of data structures, the talk also presents new features in first-order theorem proving, such as inductive reasoning and built-in boolean sort. These extensions allow us to express program properties directly in first-order logic and hence use further first-order theorem provers to reason about program properties.

The algorithms described in this talk are supported by the development of the world-leading theorem prover Vampire [14], and its extension to support program analysis. Thanks to the full automation and tool support of our work, researchers and software engineers/developers are able to use our results in their work, without the need to become experts in first-order theorem proving and symbolic computation.

The work presented here is structured as follows. We first describe the use of symbol elimination in symbolic computation for generating polynomial program properties (Sect. 3). We then extend symbol elimination to its use in first-order theorem proving and present how arbitrarily quantified program properties can be inferred using symbol elimination (Sect. 4).

2 Motivating Example

Let us first motivate the work described in this talk on a small example. Consider the program given in Fig. 1, written in a C-like syntax. The program fills an integer-valued array B by the positive values of a source array A added to the values of a function call h, and an integer-valued array C with the non-positive values of A. In addi-

```
a := 0; b := 0; c := 0; s :=0;
while (a < n) do
    if A[a] > 0
        then B[b] := A[a] + h(b); b := b + 1;
        else C[c] := A[a]; c := c + 1;
    a := a + 1; s := s + a * a;
end do
assert((∀p)(0 ≤ p < b ⟹ B[p] − h(p) > 0) ∧
        6 * s = n * (n + 1) * (2 * n + 1))
```

Fig. 1. Motivating example.

tion, it computes the sum s of squares of the visited positions in A. A safety assertion, in first-order logic, is specified at the end of the loop, using the assert construct. The program of Fig. 1 is clearly safe as the assertion is satisfied when the loop is exited. However, to prove program safety we need additional loop properties, i.e. invariants, that hold at any loop iteration. It is not hard to derive that after any iteration k of the loop (assuming $0 \le k \le n$), the linear invariant relation $a = b+c$ holds. It is also not hard to argue that, upon exiting the loop, the value of a is n. However, such properties do not give us much information about the arrays A, B, C and the integer s. For proving program safety, we need to derive that each $B[0], \ldots, B[b-1]$ is the sum of a strictly positive element in A and the value of f at the corresponding position of B. We also need to infer that s stores the sum of squares of the first n non-negative integers, corresponding to the visited positions in A. Formulating these properties in first-order logic yields the loop invariant:

$$(\forall p)(0 \le p < b \implies$$
$$(\exists q)(0 \le q < a \ \wedge \ A[q] > 0 \ \wedge \ B[p] = A[q] + h(p)) \ \wedge \qquad (1)$$
$$6 * s = a * (a + 1) * (2 * a + 1))$$

The above property requires quantifier alternations and polynomial arithmetic and can be used to prove the safety assertion of the program. This loop property in fact describes much of the intended behavior of the loop and can be used to analyze properties of programs in which this loop is embedded. Generating such loop invariants requires however reasoning in full first-order logic with theories, in our example in the first-order theory of arrays, polynomial arithmetic and uninterpreted functions. Our work addresses this problem and proposes symbol elimination for automating program analysis.

3 Symbol Elimination in Symbolic Computation

The first part of this talk concerns the automatic generation of loop invariants over scalar variables. This line of research implements the general idea of symbol

$$\begin{cases} a^{(k+1)} = a^{(k)} + 1 \\ s^{(k+1)} = s^{(k)} + a^{(k)} * a^{(k)} \end{cases}$$

$$\begin{cases} a^{(k)} = a^{(0)} + k \\ s^{(k)} = s^{(0)} + \\ \quad \frac{k*(k+1)*(2*k+1)}{6} \end{cases}$$

$$6 * s^{(k)} = a^{(k)} * (a^{(k)} + 1) * (2 * a^{(k)} + 1)$$

(i)   (ii)   (iii)

Fig. 2. Symbol Elimination in Symbolic Computation on Fig. 1.

elimination by using techniques from symbolic computation, as follows. Given a loop, we first extend the loop language by a new variable n, called the loop counter. Program variables are then considered as functions of n. Next, we apply methods from algorithmic combinatorics and compute the values of loop variables at arbitrary loop iterations as functions of n. Finally, we eliminate n using computer algebra algorithms, and derive polynomial relations among program variables as loop invariants.

In our work, we identified a certain family of loops, called P-solvable loops (to stand for polynomial-solvable) with sequencing, assignments and conditionals, where test conditions are ignored [11]. For these loops, we developed a new algorithm for generating polynomial loop invariants. Our method uses algorithmic combinatorics and algebraic techniques, namely solving linear recurrences with constant coefficients (so-called C-finite recurrences) or hypergeometric terms, computing algebraic relations among exponential sequences, and eliminating variables from a system of polynomial equations. More precisely, the key steps of using symbol elimination in symbolic computation are as follows. Given a P-solvable loop with nested conditionals, we first rewrite the loop into a collection of P-solvable loops with assignments only. Next, polynomial invariants of all sequences of P-solvable loops with assignments only are derived. These invariants describe polynomial relations valid after the first iteration of the P-solvable loop with nested conditionals, however they might not be valid after an arbitrary iteration of the P-solvable loop with nested conditionals. Therefore, from the ideal of polynomial relations after the first iteration of a P-solvable loop with nested conditionals, we keep only those polynomial relations that are polynomial invariants of the P-solvable loop with nested conditionals. In the process of deriving polynomial invariants for a (sequence of) P-solvable loop(s) with assignments only, we proceed as follows. We introduce a new variable n denoting the loop counter. Next, recurrence equations over the loop counter are constructed, describing the behavior of the loop variables at arbitrary loop iterations. These recurrence relations are solved, and closed forms of loop variables are computed as polynomials of the initial values of variables, the loop counter, and some new variables in the loop counter so that we infer polynomial relations among the new variables. The loop counter and variables in the loop counter are then eliminated by Gröbner basis computation to derive a finite set of polynomial identities among the program variables as invariants. From this finite set any other polynomial identity that is an invariant of the P-solvable loop with assignments only can be derived.

To illustrate the workflow proposed above, consider Fig. 2. Figure 2(i) describes the system of recurrence equations corresponding to the updates over a and s in Fig. 1, where $s^{(k)}$ and $a^{(k)}$ denote the values of s and a at the kth loop iteration of Fig. 1. That is, program variables become functions of loop iterations k. The closed form solutions of Fig. 2(i) is given in Fig. 2(ii). After substituting the initial values of a and s, Fig. 2(iii) shows a valid polynomial identity among the values of a and s at any loop iteration k.

Our invariant generation method using symbol elimination in symbolic computation is proved to be complete in [12]. By completeness we mean that our method generates the basis of the polynomial invariant ideal, and hence any other polynomial invariant of the P-solvable loop can be derived from the basis of the invariant ideal. For doing so, we generalised the invariant generation algorithm of [11] for P-solvable loops by iteratively computing the polynomial invariant ideal of the loop. We proved that this generalisation is sound and complete. That is, our method infers a basis for the polynomial invariant ideal of the P-solvable loop in a finite number of steps. Our proof relies on showing that the dimensions of the prime ideals from the minimal decomposition of the ideals generated at an iteration of our algorithm either remained the same or decreased at the next iteration of the algorithm. Since dimensions of ideals are positive integers, our algorithm terminates after a finite number of iterations.

4 Symbol Elimination in First-Order Theorem Proving

In the second part of our talk, we describe the use of symbol elimination in first-order theorem proving. The method of symbol elimination using a first-order theorem prover has been introduced in [13]. Unlike all previously known techniques, our method allows one to generate first-order invariants containing alternations of quantifiers for programs with arrays.

When using symbol elimination for generating loop invariants of programs with arrays, the method is based on automatic analysis of the so-called update predicates of loops. An update predicate for an array expresses updates made to the array. We observe that many properties of update predicates can be extracted automatically from the loop description and loop properties obtained by other methods such as a simple analysis of counters occurring in the loop, recurrence solving and quantifier elimination over loop variables. In the first step of loop analysis we introduce a new variable n denoting the loop counter, and use the symbolic computation framework from Sect. 3 to generate polynomial invariants over the scalar loop variables. Scalar and array variables of the loop are considered as functions of n and the language P of the loop is extended by these new function symbols. Further, the loop language is also extended by the update predicates for arrays and their properties are added to the extended language too. The update predicates make use of n and essentially describe positions at which arrays are updated, iterations at which the updates occur and the update values of the arrays. For example, we may write $upd(B, k, p, x)$ to express that an array B was updated at loop iteration k and array position p by the value x. For our running example from Fig. 1, $upd(B, k, p, x)$ is defined as:

$$upd(B,k,p,x) \iff 0 \le k \le n \wedge A^{(k)}[a^{(k)}] > 0 \wedge p = b^{(k)} \wedge x = A^{(k)}[a^{(k)}] + h(b^{(k)}),$$

expressing that k is a loop iteration value at which the array B was updated (the true-branch of the conditional of Fig. 1 was visited). As before, $A^{(k)}$ denotes the value of the array A at the kth loop iteration (A is actually unchanged throughout the loop of Fig. 1).

As a result of this step of symbol elimination, a new, extended loop language P_0 is obtained, and a collection Π of valid first-order loop properties expressed in P_0 is derived. For example, a first-order property of Fig. 1 in the extended loop language P_0 derived by our work is:

$$(\forall i, j, p, x)\big(upd(B, i, p, x) \wedge (upd(B, j, p, x) \implies j = i) \implies B^{(n)}[p] = x\big) \quad (2)$$

Property (2) expresses that if the array B is updated only once at a position p, the value x associated with this update is the final value in B.

Formulas in Π cannot be used as loop invariants, since they use symbols not occurring in the loop, and even symbols whose semantics is described by the loop itself. Note that, while the property (2) is a valid loop property, it is not yet a loop invariant as it uses the update predicates $upd(B, i, p, x)$ and $upd(B, j, p, x)$ and $B^{(n)}$ to express the final value of array B as function of n. These symbols are in P_0 but are not part of the loop language P; and hence a loop invariant expressed in the loop language P cannot make use of them, Nevertheless, the formulas in Π, such as (2), are valid properties of the loop and have a useful property: all their consequences are valid loop properties too. The second phase of symbol elimination therefore tries to generate logical consequences of Π in the original language of the loop. Any such consequence is also a valid property of the loop, and hence an invariant of the loop. Logical consequences of Π are generated by running a first-order saturation theorem prover on Π in a way that it tries to eliminate the newly introduced symbols $P_0 \setminus P$ from the extended loop language P_0. As a result of symbol elimination, a loop invariant generated for Fig. 1 is the first-order formula expressed in (1).

The main obstacle to the experimental evaluation of symbol elimination lied in the fact that all existing first-order theorem provers lacked several features essential for implementing our procedure for invariant generation. These features included reasoning with various theories and procedures for eliminating symbols. In our work we addressed these limitations as follows: we changed the term ordering used by theorem provers to make symbol elimination generate loop invariants and we added incomplete, but sound axiomatizations of first-order theories to first-order theorem provers, in particular to the Vampire theorem prover. To this end, Vampire has now built-in support for the first-order theories of integers, rationals and rationals. We have also extended Vampire with the polymorphic theory of arrays with extensionality and added the boolean sort as first-class sort in Vampire [10]. With these new features at hand, Vampire now supports automatic program analysis and invariant generation for programs with arrays [1]. We believe the new extension in Vampire increase the expressivity of first-order reasoners and facilitate reasoning-based program analysis and verification.

Acknowledgments. The work described in this talk is based on joint work with a number of authors, including Tudor Jebelean (RISC-Linz), Evgeny Kotelnikov and Simon Robillard (Chalmers University of Technology), and Andrei Voronkov (The University of Manchester and Chalmers University of Technology).

The author acknowledges funding from the ERC Starting Grant 2014 SYMCAR 639270, the Wallenberg Academy Fellowship 2014, the Swedish VR grant D0497701 and the Austrian research project FWF S11409-N23

References

1. Ahrendt, W., Kovács, L., Robillard, S.: Reasoning About Loops Using Vampire in KeY. In: Davis, M., Fehnker, A., McIver, A., Voronkov, A. (eds.) LPAR-20 2015. LNCS, vol. 9450, pp. 434–443. Springer, Heidelberg (2015). doi:10.1007/978-3-662-48899-7_30
2. Buchberger, B.: An algorithm for finding the basis elements of the residue class ring of a zero dimensional polynomial ideal. J. Symbolic Comput. **41**(3–4), 475–511 (2006)
3. Clarke, E.M., Emerson, E.A.: Design and synthesis of synchronization skeletons using branching-time temporal logic. In: Kozen, D. (ed.) Logic of Programs. LNCS, pp. 52–71. Springer, Heidelberg (1981)
4. Collins, G.E.: Quantifier elimination for real closed fields by cylindrical algebraic decomposition. In: Brakhage, H. (ed.) ATFL. LNCS, pp. 134–183. Springer, Heidelberg (1975)
5. Cousot, P., Cousot, R.: Abstract interpretation: a unified lattice model for static analysis of programs by construction or approximation of fixpoints. In: POPL, pp. 238–252 (1977)
6. de Moura, L., Passmore, G.O.: Computation in real closed infinitesimal and transcendental extensions of the rationals. In: Bonacina, M.P. (ed.) CADE 2013. LNCS, vol. 7898, pp. 178–192. Springer, Heidelberg (2013)
7. de Moura, L.M., Bjorner, N.: Proofs and refutations, and z3. In: CEUR Workshop Proceedings (2008)
8. Hamon, G., de Moura, L., Rushby, J.M.: Generating efficient test sets with a model checker. In: SEFM, pp. 261–270 (2004)
9. Jhala, R., McMillan, K.L.: A practical and complete approach to predicate refinement. In: Hermanns, H., Palsberg, J. (eds.) TACAS 2006. LNCS, vol. 3920, pp. 459–473. Springer, Heidelberg (2006)
10. Kotelnikov, E., Kovács, L., Reger, G., Voronkov, A.: The Vampire and the FOOL. In: Proceedings of CPP, pp. 37–48. ACM (2016)
11. Kovács, L.: Reasoning algebraically about P-solvable loops. In: Ramakrishnan, C.R., Rehof, J. (eds.) TACAS 2008. LNCS, vol. 4963, pp. 249–264. Springer, Heidelberg (2008)
12. Kovács, L.: A complete invariant generation approach for P-solvable loops. In: Pnueli, A., Virbitskaite, I., Voronkov, A. (eds.) PSI 2009. LNCS, vol. 5947, pp. 242–256. Springer, Heidelberg (2010)
13. Kovács, L., Voronkov, A.: Finding loop invariants for programs over arrays using a theorem prover. In: Chechik, M., Wirsing, M. (eds.) FASE 2009. LNCS, vol. 5503, pp. 470–485. Springer, Heidelberg (2009)
14. Kovács, L., Voronkov, A.: First-order theorem proving and vampire. In: Sharygina, N., Veith, H. (eds.) CAV 2013. LNCS, vol. 8044, pp. 1–35. Springer, Heidelberg (2013)

15. McMillan, K.L.: Quantified invariant generation using an interpolating saturation prover. In: Ramakrishnan, C.R., Rehof, J. (eds.) TACAS 2008. LNCS, vol. 4963, pp. 413–427. Springer, Heidelberg (2008)
16. Nelson, G., Oppen, D.C.: Fast decision procedures based on congruence closure. J. ACM **27**(2), 356–364 (1980)
17. Robinson, J.A., Voronkov, A.: Handbook of Automated Reasoning (in 2 Volumes). Elsevier and MIT Press, Cambridge (2001)
18. Sifakis, J.: A unified approach for studying the properties of transition systems. Theor. Comput. Sci. **18**, 227–258 (1982)

Perspectives of Model Transformation Reuse

Marsha Chechik[1(✉)], Michalis Famelis[2], Rick Salay[1], and Daniel Strüber[3]

[1] University of Toronto, Toronto, Canada
{chechik,rsalay}@cs.toronto.edu
[2] University of British Columbia, Vancouver, Canada
famelis@cs.ubc.ca
[3] Philipps-Universität Marburg, Marburg, Germany
strueber@mathematik.uni-marburg.de

Abstract. Model Transformations have been called the "heart and soul" of Model-Driven software development. However, they take a lot of effort to build, verify, analyze, and debug. It is thus imperative to develop good reuse strategies that address issues specific to model transformations. Some of the effective reuse strategies are adopted from other domains, specifically, programming languages. Others are custom developed for models. In this paper, we survey techiques from both categories.

Specifically, we present two techniques adoped from the PL world: subtyping and mapping, and then two techniques, lifting and aggregating, that are novel in the modeling world. Subtyping is a way to reuse a transformation for different - but similar - input modelling languages. Mapping a transformation designed for single models reuses it for model collections, such as megamodels. Lifting a transformation reuses it for aggregate representations of models, such as product lines. Aggregating reuses both transformation fragments (during transformation creation) and partial execution results (during transformation execution) across multiple transformations.

We then point to potential new directions for research in reuse that draw on the strengths of the programming and the modeling worlds.

1 Introduction

Model-Driven Engineering (MDE) is a powerful approach used in industry for managing the complexity of large scale software development. MDE helps manage this complexity by using *models* to raise the level of abstraction at which developers build and analyze software and *transformations* to automate the various engineering tasks that apply to models. Model Transformations have been called the "heart and soul" of Model-Driven software development [30], and they are used to perform various manipulations on models, such as adding detail, refactoring, translating to a different formalism, generating code, etc. They have certain particular characteristics: (1) They are aimed, at least in principle, to accomplish a well-defined one-step "task" with a specific intent. Transformations are often chained together to form more complex tasks, much like pipelining processes in Unix. (2) They are also strongly typed, by the types of models they

© Springer International Publishing Switzerland 2016
E. Ábrahám and M. Huisman (Eds.): IFM 2016, LNCS 9681, pp. 28–44, 2016.
DOI: 10.1007/978-3-319-33693-0_3

take as input and produce as output. (3) Since models are essentially typed graphs, transformations are often implemented using specialized languages that allow easy manipulation of graphs.

Because transformations are central to success of MDE, it is imperative to develop good reuse strategies for them. Since transformations are specialized programs, any attempt to study transformation reuse must answer the question: *how is transformation reuse different from or similar to program reuse?* This implies two perspectives of model transformation reuse. On the one hand, we can approach it as a problem of adapting, generalizing and/or "reinventing" techniques already understood in the context of program reuse. On the other hand, we can identify areas in which the MDE setting provides opportunities for creating novel reuse techniques, specific to the kinds of abstractions and usage scenarios found in modelling.

In this paper, we attempt to study transformation reuse from both of these perspectives, by illustrating examples of reuse mechanisms in each one. We show two examples of techniques, namely *subtyping* and *mapping*, that are adapted from program reuse. Specifically: (1) subtyping is a way to reuse a transformation for different – but similar – input modelling languages; and (2) mapping a transformation designed for single models reuses it for model collections, such as specialized model collections used in MDE called *megamodels*. We then show two MDE-specific reuse techniques, namely, *lifting* and *aggregating* that leverage the unique way in which MDE represents variability. Specifically: (3) lifting a transformation reuses it for aggregate representations of models, such as product lines; and (4) aggregating reuses both transformation fragments (during transformation creation) and partial execution results (during transformation execution) across multiple transformations. To our best knowledge, these techniques do not have any correspondences in programming.

A detailed survey of the state of the art in model transformation reuse can be found in [16]. Our specific aim is to explore the different ways of approaching the problem of transformation reuse and to study its differences and similarities from well-understood approaches in program reuse. We assume that the reader is familiar with standard MDE concepts such as models, meta-models and transformations. For a good reference on these, please see [27].

The rest of this paper is organized as follows: In Sect. 2, we describe an example transformation which will be used to illustrate the different reuse strategies. In Sect. 3, we describe approaches that are adapted from program reuse. In Sect. 4, we describe novel reuse approaches that arise from the unique characteristics of MDE. We conclude in Sect. 5 with a discussion of how further progress can be achieved in research on transformation reuse.

2   Example Transformation

We begin with the following example transformation called "Fold Entry Action" [23] referring to it as FoldEntry. Figure 1(a) shows the *signature* of the transformation. It takes a state machine as input and refactors it by moving

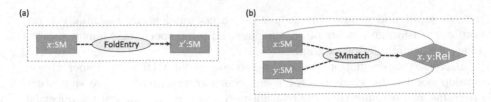

Fig. 1. (a) The signature of transformation FoldEntry; (b) The signature of transformation SMmatch.

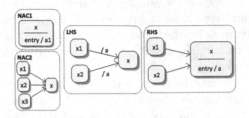

Fig. 2. The rule implementing the FoldEntry transformation to refactor a state machine.

common actions on incoming transitions to a state into the entry action for the state to produce the output state machine. Figure 2 shows a *graph transformation rule* that implements FoldEntry. Specifically, the rule is applied to a state machine by attempting to match it to the location where some state, x, has two incoming transitions with a common action, a, as depicted in the LHS of the rule in the middle of Fig. 2. Then the matched portion is replaced with the RHS of the rule (on the right of the figure) which deletes action a from the transitions and makes it the entry action of state x. The *negative application conditions* (NACs, on the left of Fig. 2) prevent the rule from being applied when state x already has an entry action (NAC1) or when there are more than two incoming transitions to it (NAC2)[1]. The transformation is executed by applying the rule R_F to the given state machine G until it can no longer be applied, resulting in a new state machine H; we symbolize this as $G \xRightarrow{R_F} H$.

FoldEntry is the simplest type of model transformation – it takes only a single model and produces a single model; however, more complex transformation signatures are possible. For example, Fig. 1(b) shows the signature of SMmatch (implementation not shown) that takes two state machines as input as produces a model relationship (i.e., a mapping) between them as output. In the rest of this paper, we illustrate transformation reuse scenarios using these example transformations.

3 Reuse from Programming Languages

In this section, we describe reuse mechanisms that are well understood for programs and were adapted for model transformations.

---

[1] The general case allows moving the action if it is present in all incoming transitions but we limit it to two transitions for simplicity.

3.1 Subtyping

In this section, we discuss model transformation reuse through subtyping.

Subtyping is common a reuse mechanism defined through programming type theory [19]. For example, Int is a subtype of Real, so any function written to accept Reals should also work for Ints. The simplest form of subtyping semantically defines a subset of values. This is the case with Int and Real. A more sophisticated form of subtyping is called *coercive subtyping*. Here, one type can count as a subtype of another if there exists an implicit type conversion function. For example, using an Int expression directly in a print statement may be possible by coercing the Int into a String using a conversion.

The adaption of simple subset-based approaches for model subtyping to support transformation reuse has been studied. Given a transformation $F : T \to T'$, if we know that another type S is a subtype of T then F should be reusable for inputs of type S. Generally speaking, this works whenever an S model contains all information that F relies on to operate correctly. Interestingly, S need not be a subset of T and we illustrate this below. With model types, we require a relation $\mathbf{S} <: \mathbf{T}$ between metamodels (metamodel of a type is indicated by bold font) that ensures that S is a subtype of T.

Kuehne [14,15] has studied the subtype relation from a theoretical perspective. Several works provide practical definitions for the subtype relation. Steel [31] was the first to propose a set of syntactic matching rules between metamodels. To maximize reuse, Sen *et al.* [28,29] recognized the importance of identifying the *effective model type* of a transformation: the minimal subset of the elements of the input metamodel that is needed for the transformation to function correctly. They present an algorithm for deriving effective model types through static analysis of a model transformation's code. In later work, Guy et al., [12] improved on Steel's matching rules as well as defining a number of variants of the subtype matching relationship (which they call *isomorphic model subtyping*). *Non-isomorphic sub-typing* allows the definition of an explicit model adaptation function to translate instances of $\mathbf{S}$ into instances of $\mathbf{T}$. Of particular interest are bi-directional model adaptations. The paper further distinguishes (on a separate dimension) *total* and *partial* sub-typing. Total subtyping corresponds to the usual case. Partial subtyping allows the subtype to reuse only a subset of transformations by satisfying the subtyping relation only for the effective model types of these transformations.

To illustrate transformation reuse through simple subtyping, consider the state machine metamodels shown in Fig. 3. We define subtyping matching rules as follows: $\mathbf{S} <: \mathbf{T}$ iff (1) all component (i.e., element, attribute and edge) types in $\mathbf{S}$ are also found in $\mathbf{T}$; and (2) the multiplicities on component types in $\mathbf{S}$ are no less constraining than those in $\mathbf{T}$.

Rule (1) means that S models have all components of T models but may have more. Rule (2) means that the number of occurrences of components in S models conforms to the constraints on the number of occurrences of these components allowable in T models. The intuition is that if $\mathbf{S} <: \mathbf{T}$ and a transformation written for T inputs is given an S model, it will still run since it has access to

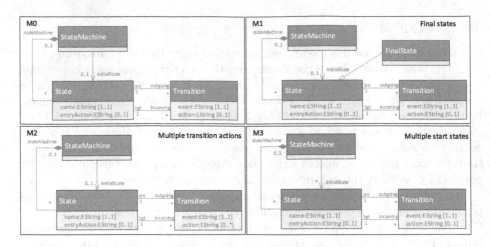

Fig. 3. A state machine metamodel M0 and three variants.

all component types it expects (Rule 1) and the number of occurrences of these components it expects (Rule 2).

If we check these rules on Fig. 3, we find that M1 is a valid subtype of M0 while neither M2 (violates Rule (2) on number of transition actions) nor M3 (violates Rule (2) on number of start states) are valid subtypes of M0. Indeed, our example transformation FoldEntry (written for M0) works for M1 models but not for M2 models because the rule (see Fig. 2) assumes at most a single transition action and will behave unpredictably when faced with multiple transition actions. Interestingly, FoldEntry would work correctly on an M3 model despite that fact that it violates the subtyping rules. This is because it doesn't "care" about the number of start states. This points to a weakness of the simple subtyping approach – it is overly conservative and may disallow reuse for transformations that can tolerate specific violations.

Coercive Model Subtyping. The existing work on model subtyping focuses on a simple notion of subtype in which the subtype can be directly substituted for the supertype in a transformation. In our work [10], we have developed the more general notion of coercive model subtyping.

Definition 1 (Coercive Model Typing System). *A model typing system is coercive iff it contains a distinguished subset of unary operators called* conversion operators *satisfying the following properties:*

1. *For every type T, the identity operator $id_T : T \rightarrow T$ defined as $\forall x \in T \cdot id_T(x) = x$ is a conversion operator.*
2. *For every pair $F : T \rightarrow T'$ and $G : T' \rightarrow T''$ of conversion operators, the sequential composition $(F; G) : T \rightarrow T''$ is a conversion operator.*

In any coercive subtyping scheme, there may be different sequences of conversions that can lead from one type to another. Thus, a set of conversion functions

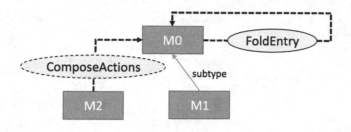

Fig. 4. A coercive subtyping scenario.

is desired to be *coherent*, i.e., yielding the same outcome regardless of which conversion sequence is taken. In general, coherence is defined for pairs $F : T \rightarrow T'$, $G : T \rightarrow T'$ of conversion transformations, requiring that F is behaviorally equivalent to G, that is, $\forall x : T \cdot F(x) = G(x)$.

For example, in Fig. 4 we show the three model types from Fig. 3. Type M1 is related to M0 by the subtyping relation discussed above, and FoldEntry is shown as taking M0 both as input and output. In addition, the transformation ComposeActions takes M2 models as input and produces M0 models. The transformation composes the set of actions on each transition into a single combined action. The dashed ovals are used to indicate that this is a designated conversion transformation, to be used for type coercions. Specifically, this means that FoldEntry can be used directly with inputs of type M2 because the coercion system will precompose it with ComposeActions. Coherence is not an issue in this small example since there is only one way coerce M2 into M0. This example illustrates how coercive subtyping can allow for more transformation reuse opportunities than simple subtyping alone. In fact, simple subtyping can be viewed as a special case of coercive subtyping where the conversion transformation is automatically generated from the subtyping relation. In the case of M1, this means that the conversion retypes FinalState elements as State elements.

We have implemented a coercive model typing system within our type-driven interactive model management tool called Model Management INTeractive (*MMINT*) [10]. The tool assists the user in reusing transformations by providing a dynamically generated list of usable transformations for a given input model by computing all possible coercions using conversion transformations. In addition, runtime checking for coherence is performed by ensuring that all possible coercion paths produce the same output for the given input.

3.2 Mapping

In this section, we show how the map (sometimes called fold) operator provided in many modern programming languages to reuse functions for collections such as lists can also allow the reuse of transformations in MDE [24].

A *megamodel* [3] is a kind of model that is used to represent collections of models and their relationships at a high level of abstraction. Here the nodes

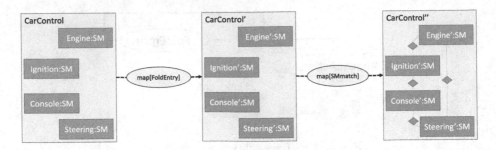

Fig. 5. Mapping `FoldEntry` and then `SMmatch` over the megamodel `CarControl` of state machines.

represent models, and edges represent relationships between the models. For example, the bottom left box in Fig. 5 is the megamodel `CarControl` of state machine models in a hypothetical automotive system. Megamodels are used in the activity of Model Management [2] – a field that has emerged to help deal with the accidental complexity caused by the proliferation of models during software development.

The usual behaviour of the `map` operation is to traverse a collection (e.g., list, tree, etc.) and apply a function to the value at each node in the collection. The result is a collection with the same size and structure as the original with the function output value at each node. For example, given the list of integers $L = [10, 13, 4, 5]$ and the function *Double* that takes an integer and doubles it, applying map with *Double* to L yields the list $[20, 26, 8, 10]$. If the function has more than one argument, the mapped version can take a collection (with the same size and structure) for each argument, and the function is applied at a given node in the collection using the value at that node in each argument in the collection.

We have adapted this operator to allow model transformations to be reused for megamodels [24]. Since a transformation signature is a graph, applying a transformation to each node of a megamodel is not possible. Instead, the `map` operator for megamodels applies the transformation for every possible binding of the input part of the signature in the input megamodel(s). The collection of outputs from these applications forms the output megamodel.

When the transformation signature consists of a single input and output type and uses a single input megamodel which happens to be a set (i.e., no relationships) of instances of the input type, then our `map` produces the same result as a "programming language" map operator applied to a set.

However, in the general case, `map` is more complex and differs from the behaviour of the standard map. In particular,

(1) The output megamodel may not have the same structure as the input megamodel since the structure is dependent on the output signature of the transformation.

(2) The size of the output may not be equal to the size of the input. For example, if a transformation takes two models as input and produces one as its

output, applying map to it on a megamodel with n models will produce as many as $n \times (n - 1)$ output models since each pair of input models may be matched in a binding. At the other extreme, if no input models form a binding then the output will be the empty megamodel.

(3) When there are multiple input megamodels, each binding of the input signature is split across the input megamodels in a user-definable way.

(4) When the transformation is *commutative* (i.e., the order of inputs does not affect the result), we want to avoid replication in the output due to isomorphic bindings.

Some of these principles are illustrated in Fig. 5 showing the use of map to first apply FoldEntry and then SMmatch to megamodel CarControl. Mapping FoldEntry binds to each of the four state machines in CarControl and produces a new megamodel CarControl' with corresponding refactored state machines. Then mapping SMmatch over CarControl' binds it to every pair of state machines to produce CarControl''. Although there are twelve possible ways to bind the inputs of SMmatch to the content of CarControl', the result shows only four relationships. This is because SMmatch is commutative (eliminating six possible bindings), and only four of the remaining six applications produced a non-empty result.

We have implemented map for megamodels in our *MMINT* model management tool [10] along with two other common operators: filter for extracting subsets of a megamodel satisfying a given property and reduce for aggregating the models in a megamodel using a given *model merge* transformation. We have shown that many common model management scenarios can be accomplished using these three operators in different combinations. The details are given in [24].

3.3 Other Approaches

Generic programming [18] is a technique in which parts of a concrete algorithm are abstracted as parameters to an abstract algorithm. This way, the same algorithm can be reused in many contexts with minimal variation. A classical example is an abstract Sort routine that can sort any type of object as long as it implements a lessThan operator.

De Lara *et al.* [7] and Rose *et al.* [21] proposed an idea they call *model concepts*. The idea of this model transformation reuse approach, inspired by generic programming, is to first define an abstract version of a transformation on a generic metamodel that represents the minimal context in which the transformation could possibly be defined. Then the transformation can be reused for specific concrete metamodels by mapping the concrete metamodel to the generic metamodel and using this mapping to automatically specialize the abstract transformation.

4   Novel Reuse Mechanisms

In this section, we describe reuse mechanisms that were created specifically for model transformations.

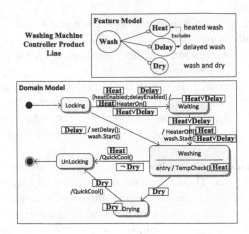

Fig. 6. Example washing machine controller product line W.

4.1   Lifting

In this section, we discuss the approach of reusing transformations for different products within a software product line.

Software Product Line Engineering (SPLE) is an approach to manage large sets of software product variants. This is done by modelling explicitly the variants' commonalities and variabilities as a single conceptual unit [4]. Most existing transformations (refactoring, code generation, etc.) are developed for individual product models, not taking SPLE variability constructs into account.

Consider the example product line W for washing machine controllers, shown in Fig. 6. W is an *annotative* product line [5,13,22], defined using three parts:

(a) The *feature model* defines the set of features in W. Specifically, it defines three optional features that can be added to a basic washing machine: **Heat** adds hot water washing, **Dry** adds automatic drying, and **Delay** adds the ability to delay the start time of the wash. In addition, the feature model defines relationships between features, which determine the set of valid *configurations* ρ of W, denoted by Conf(W). In W, **Heat** and **Delay** are mutually exclusive (shown by the Excludes constraint), and so $\rho_1 =\{$**Wash, Heat, Dry**$\}$, $\rho_2 =\{$**Wash, Dry**$\}$ and $\rho_3 =\{$**Wash**$\}$ are some of its valid configurations. Formally, the semantics of the feature model of W is a propositional formula Φ_W over the feature variables [6], specifically the formula $\Phi_W =$**Wash**$\wedge \neg($**Heat**$\wedge$**Delay**$)$.

(b) The *domain model* of W is a UML state machine which specifies that after initiating and locking the washer, a basic wash begins or a waiting period is initiated, either for heating the water or for a delayed wash. Then the washing takes place, followed, optionally, by drying. If drying or heating was used, the clothes are cooled and the washer is unlocked, terminating the process.

(c) Depending on which of the features have been selected, only some parts of this process are available. The propositional formulas in boxes throughout the domain model indicate the *presence conditions* [5] for different model elements, i.e., the configurations of features under which the element is present in a product. For example, the transition from `Locking` to `Waiting` is only present if **Heat** or **Delay** is selected; it is guarded by `heatingEnabled` and has action `HeaterOn()` only when **Heat** is selected, while it is guarded by `delayEnabled` only if **Delay** is selected. A particular product can be *derived from* W by setting the variables in the presence conditions according to some valid configuration and discarding any elements for which the presence condition evaluates to *false*. For example, the product derived using only the feature **Wash** will go through the states `Locking`, `Washing` and `Unlocking`, while the product derived using the features **Wash** and **Dry** will go through the states `Locking`, `Washing`, `Drying` and `Unlocking`.

In [23], we proposed a method of *lifting* transformations, in order to make them variability-aware. The method applies to arbitrary transformations and model-based product lines. Adapting a transformation R, such as the one in Fig. 2, so that it can be applied to product lines, such as W, results in its lifted version, denoted by $R^\uparrow$. Applying $R^\uparrow$ to a source product line should result in a target product line with the same set of products as it would if R were applied separately to each product in the source product line. Formally:

Definition 2 (Correctness of lifting). *Let a rule R and a product line P be given. $R^\uparrow$ is a* correct lifting *of R iff (1) for all rule applications $P \xrightarrow{R^\uparrow} P'$, $\mathsf{Conf}(P') = \mathsf{Conf}(P)$, and (2) for all configurations ρ in $\mathsf{Conf}(P)$, $M \xrightarrow{R} M'$, where M is derived from P, and M' is derived from P' under ρ.*

Transformations are lifted *automatically*, i.e., no manual changes are required to enable them to apply to entire product lines. Instead, we *reinterpret* the semantics of the transformation *engine*. Lifting is described in detail in [23]. Here, we illustrate it by applying the lifted version $R^\uparrow_F$ of the rule in Fig. 2 to the example product line W. The result is shown in Fig. 7, with shading indicating changed presence conditions. There are two matching sites for the rule: K_1 is the match on the two incoming transitions to state `Washing` with common action `wash.Start()` and K_2 matches on the incoming transitions to state `UnLocking` with common action `QuickCool()`.

Given a matching site, the first step is to check the *applicability condition*, i.e., to make sure that at least one product can be derived from W such that the non-lifted transformation can be applied at K. For example, there is no valid configuration of W that contains the entire matching site K_2 since `QuickCool()` cannot appear on both incoming transitions to `Unlocking` at once. Therefore, even though there exists a match, the lifted rule is not applied.

For K_1, the applicability condition is satisfied only in those products that have **Wash**, **Delay** and *not* **Heat**. This is because when **Heat** is selected, the entry action `TempCheck()` occurs, and this triggers NAC1, so the rule is not applicable. Since **Delay** and **Heat** are mutually exclusive, the configurations of W that satisfy the above condition are uniquely characterized by the formula Φ_{apply} =**Delay**. In other words, the transformation is applicable for those configurations where Φ_{apply} is *true*. Thus, elements added by the transformation,

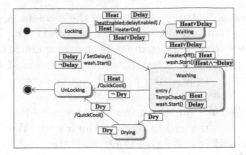

Fig. 7. The result of applying the lifted rule $R_F^\uparrow$ from Fig. 2 to the product line W in Fig. 6.

i.e., the new entry action wash.Start() for state Washing, should have Φ_{apply} as their presence condition, i.e., **Delay**. Conversely, elements deleted by the transformation should only be deleted in configurations where Φ_{apply} is *true* and kept for others. Thus, the presence condition of the action on the transition out of Locking when **Delay** is changed to $\neg\Phi_{apply}$, i.e., to $\neg$**Delay**. Similarly, the presence condition of the one out of Waiting becomes **Heat**$\wedge\neg\Phi_{apply}$, i.e., **Heat**$\wedge\neg$**Delay**. The resulting domain model is shown in Fig. 7.

Lifting has been implemented for transformations expressed in the Henshin graph transformation language [1], using the Z3 SMT solver [9] to do the applicability condition checks. Moreover, we have lifted a subset of DSLTrans, a full-fledged model transformation language that combines graph-rewriting with advanced language constructs and is rich enough to implement real-world transformations [17]. Using the lifted version of the DSLTrans engine, we were able to execute an industrial-grade model transformation of product lines from the automotive domain [11].

4.2   Aggregating

In this section, we discuss the approach of reusing transformation fragments to create transformations with variability, and show how variability-based transformation can reuse intermediate execution artifacts [32,33].

While lifting addresses variability at the transformation's inputs and outputs, aggregating helps capture and leverage variability in the transformation itself. We distinguish two points in time where variability in transformations is encountered: (a) during transformation creation, and (b) during transformation execution.

When building large transformation systems to perform tasks such as refactoring and code generation, developers often end up creating rules that are similar but different to each other. SPLE techniques offer a typical solution for effectively managing and maintaining such sets of transformation rules, representing them in a single conceptual artifact. Individual variants can then be obtained by configuring this artifact. We illustrate this using the example of a

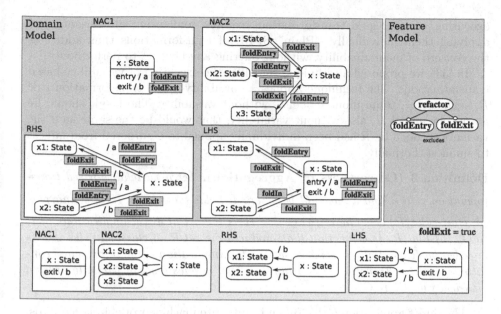

Fig. 8. Variability-based transformation $\hat{R}_F$, encoding two refactoring variants: `foldEntry`, shown in Fig. 2, and `foldExit`, shown in the bottom.

team that wants to create a transformation system for refactoring UML state machines. Among other refactorings, the team wants to create the transformation `foldEntry`, described in Sect. 2, that moves common actions on incoming transitions to a state into the entry action for the state. The team also wants to create the transformation `foldExit`, that moves common actions on *outgoing* transitions from a state into the *exit* action for the state. The two transformations are similar enough to be considered variants of each other. In order to reuse their common parts, the team can thus employ SPLE techniques to create the transformation $\hat{R}_F$ in Fig. 8, expressed using the annotative approach described in Sect. 4.1. Its feature model defines two mutually exclusive features: **foldEntry** and **foldExit**. The two variants are then encoded using presence conditions on the elements of the domain model of $\hat{R}_F$. Configuring $\hat{R}_F$ for $\rho_1 = \{\textbf{foldEntry}\}$ results in the transformation `foldEntry`, shown in Fig. 2, whereas configuring it for $\rho_2 = \{\textbf{foldExit}\}$ results in the transformation `foldExit`, shown at the bottom of Fig. 8.

SPLE techniques thus allow developers to reuse model fragments across transformation variants at creation time. For example, the pattern made up of the states x, x1, x2 is reused in both variants encoded by $\hat{R}_F$. Transformations with variability, such as $\hat{R}_F$, are called *variability-based* transformations.

However, variability can be also leveraged at transformation execution time. To motivate the need for this, consider an aggregate rule such as $\hat{R}_F$ used with an arbitrary input. In order to execute $\hat{R}_F$, each variant must be matched and applied individually, using the classic graph-rewriting approach. Effectively, executing an aggregate transformation requires configuring all variants and applying them individually. "Plain" SPLE of transformations thus addresses the concern of maintainability, without offering any benefits to performance.

In [33], we proposed a technique that lifts the execution of variability-based transformations. The technique applies a variability-based transformation rule $\hat{R}$, such as $\hat{R}_F$, to an input model G without variability. The result should be an output model H, also without variability, that would be the same as if the variants encoded by $\hat{R}$ had been individually applied to G, ordered from largest to smallest. Formally:

Definition 3 (Correctness of Aggregation). *Let a variability-based transformation rule $\hat{R}$ and a model G be given. It holds that $G \overset{\hat{R}}{\Longrightarrow} H$ is isomorphic to Trans(Flat($\hat{R}$),G), where: (a) $G \overset{\hat{R}}{\Longrightarrow} H$ is the set of direct applications of $\hat{R}$ to G, (b) Flat($\hat{R}$) is a function that produces the set $\mathcal{R}$ of classical rules that is encoded by $\hat{R}$, partially ordered based on the implication of their presence conditions, and (c) Trans($\mathcal{R}, G$) is a function that applies a set of partially ordered classical rules $\mathcal{R}$ to G.*

The direct application of $\hat{R}_F$ on an input state machine works in three steps. First, application sites for the *base rule* are determined. The base rule comprises all parts of $\hat{R}_F$ without annotations, that is, nodes x1, x2, and x without their adjacent edges. Consequently, all combinations of three states in the input state machine are application sites for the base rule. Second, configurations are enumerated systematically, which allows augmenting the original application sites with the variant-specific nodes and edges, yielding full matches. A full match for the **foldEntry** variant would bind its two edges, in addition to the node bindings of a base application site. Third, these full matches are filtered to yield largest ones. Since both variants of $\hat{R}_F$ are equally large, this set is trivial to obtain. Applying $\hat{R}_F$ at all of these largest matches yields the set of direct applications. Note that the NACs of $\hat{R}_F$ cannot be evaluated incrementally. Since their partial checking would lead to false negatives, they have to be checked on the full matches after the second step (systematic enumeration of configurations).

This application process can offer considerable performance savings since it considers shared patterns just once. In the case of $\hat{R}_F$, first binding the state nodes without considering their interrelating edges may produce a potentially large set of base matches that have to be extended individually. In more sizable examples, the benefit of considering large common patterns becomes more significant. In our experiments on larger rule sets, we were able to show speed ups between a factor of 4 and 158 [32].

Aggregate rules such as $\hat{R}_F$ do not have to be created from scratch. They can also be derived automatically, using a technique called *rule merging*. Rule merging takes a set of rules, identifies similar variants among these rules and unifies each set of variants into an aggregate rule. In the example, $\hat{R}_F$ is the result of merging the FoldEntry and FoldExit rules. To create $\hat{R}_F$, the common state nodes from these rules are unified, whereas variant-specific edges and attributes are annotated with presence conditions using names derived from the input rules. The details for this process are described in [32].

We have implemented variability-based rules and their application as an extension to the Henshin model transformation language [1]. In addition, in our recent work [34], we have devised a tool environment to address the usability of variability-based rules. As known from the SPLE domain, the use of annotative representations poses challenges at design time. Rules with annotations tend to be larger and contain a greater amount of visual information, which may impair their readability. Editing presence conditions manually might also give rise to an increased proneness to errors. Inspired by the paradigm of *virtual separation of concerns* [13], our tool environment allows users to view and edit the variants expressed in an aggregate rule individually, allowing us to mitigate these issues.

4.3 Other Approaches

Some other novel approaches to model transformation reuse focus on composing transformations either by chaining [36] or by weaving transformation specifications more invasively [37]. More recently, De Lara *et al.* [8] have defined a way of reusing transformations across families of related domain-specific modeling languages by specifying the transformation at the meta-modeling level used to define these languages. Kusel *et al.* [16] provide a good overview and empirical evaluation of some of these approaches.

5 Discussion and Future Directions

We have explored two perspectives on model transformation reuse: one the one hand, program reuse techniques can be adapted for model transformations; on the other hand, MDE offers opportunities for novel reuse techniques that leverage the specific affordances of its higher level of abstraction. For each perspective, we have discussed two such approaches: subtyping and mapping, and lifting and aggregating, respectively.

How can these two perspectives guide research in the area of model transformation reuse, as well as program reuse in general? Reflection on the four reuse approaches presented in this paper points us to some directions.

Transformation Intent. Since transformations are specialized programs, any attempt to study transformation reuse must answer the question: *how is transformation reuse different from or similar to program reuse?* Programs are clearly more general and thus more complex. But transformations, being Unix-like in the sense that they are typically intended for a one-step "task", typically have clearly identified *intents*. We observe that the *preservation* of intent is a common and central concern for all reuse techniques presented here: (1) subtyping aims to preserve intent when applied to subtypes of the original input/output model types of the transformation, (2) mapping aims to have the same intended effect to a collection of models, (3) lifting affects a set of variants in the same way, while (4) the main goal of aggregation is to preserve the intent of individual sub-structures of transformations. In this last case, intent is in fact explicitly captured in the aggregate rule's feature model. We have investigated the effect of intent for subtyping-based reuse in [26]. We are currently developing a general strategy for analyzing the soundness and completeness of a given transformation reuse mechanism with respect to the preservation of transformation intent [25].

Domain Specificity. Progress in model transformation reuse research can also be achieved by considering the specific requirements for reuse in different software engineering disciplines. The techniques presented earlier follow this pattern. Specifically, subtyping and mapping are reuse techniques inspired by the requirements for reuse in the field of model management [2]; lifting and aggregating specifically tackle issues arising from the need to model variability and make extensive use of software product line theory [20]. New reuse strategies can therefore be identified by combining model transformations with the concerns of other software engineering disciplines. An excellent recent work in this direction is from Juan De Lara *et al.* [8], where domain-specificity is used to reuse transformations defined at the meta-modeling level.

Adapting MDE Techniques to Programs. Some of the special-purpose techniques developed for model transformation reuse can be ported back to the world of programming languages. For example, Christian Kästner and his colleagues (see, e.g., [35]) extended static and dynamic program analysis techniques to handle programs with variability. Yet correctness of the approach needs to be established for each extension. It would be tremendously exciting to be able to lift a variety of program analyses (with minimal modifications to their implementations!) developed for individual projects to apply to product families.

A Parting Thought. Interdisciplinary research can yield interesting insights and we hope we have demonstrated it somewhat in the exciting field of model transformation reuse.

References

1. Arendt, T., Biermann, E., Jurack, S., Krause, C., Taentzer, G.: Henshin: advanced concepts and tools for in-place EMF model transformations. In: Petriu, D.C., Rouquette, N., Haugen, Ø. (eds.) MODELS 2010, Part I. LNCS, vol. 6394, pp. 121–135. Springer, Heidelberg (2010)
2. Bernstein, P.A.: Applying model management to classical meta data problems. In: Proceedings of CIDR 2003, pp. 209–220 (2003)
3. Bézivin, J., Jouault, F., Valduriez, P.: On the need for megamodels. In Proceedings of OOPSLA/GPCE Workshops (2004)
4. Clements, P.C., Northrop, L.: Software Product Lines: Practices and Patterns. SEI Ser. in SE. Addison-Wesley, Reading (2001)
5. Czarnecki, K., Antkiewicz, M.: Mapping features to models: a template approach based on superimposed variants. In: Glück, R., Lowry, M. (eds.) GPCE 2005. LNCS, vol. 3676, pp. 422–437. Springer, Heidelberg (2005)
6. Czarnecki, K., Wasowski, A.: Feature diagrams and logics: there and back again. In: Proceedings of SPLC 2007, pp. 23–34 (2007)
7. de Lara, J., Guerra, E.: From types to type requirements: genericity for model-driven engineering. SoSyM **12**(3), 453–474 (2013)

8. de Lara, J., Guerra, E., Cuadrado, J.S.: Model-driven engineering with domain-specific meta-modelling languages. SoSyM **14**(1), 429–459 (2015)
9. De Moura, L., Bjørner, N.: Satisfiability modulo theories: introduction and applications. Commun. ACM **54**(9), 69–77 (2011)
10. Di Sandro, A., Salay, R., Famelis, M., Kokaly, S., Chechik, M.: MMINT: a graphical tool for interactive model management. In: Proceedings of MODELS 2015 (Demo Track) (2015)
11. Famelis, M., et al.: Migrating automotive product lines: a case study. In: Kolovos, D., Wimmer, M. (eds.) ICMT 2015. LNCS, vol. 9152, pp. 82–97. Springer, Heidelberg (2015)
12. Guy, C., Combemale, B., Derrien, S., Steel, J.R.H., Jézéquel, J.-M.: On model subtyping. In: Vallecillo, A., Tolvanen, J.-P., Kindler, E., Störrle, H., Kolovos, D. (eds.) ECMFA 2012. LNCS, vol. 7349, pp. 400–415. Springer, Heidelberg (2012)
13. Kästner, C., Apel, S.: Integrating compositional and annotative approaches for product line engineering. In: Proceedings of GPCE 2008, pp. 35–40 (2008)
14. Kühne, T.: An observer-based notion of model inheritance. In: Petriu, D.C., Rouquette, N., Haugen, Ø. (eds.) MODELS 2010, Part I. LNCS, vol. 6394, pp. 31–45. Springer, Heidelberg (2010)
15. Kühne, T.: On model compatibility with referees and contexts. SoSyM **12**(3), 475–488 (2013)
16. Kusel, A., Schönböck, J., Wimmer, M., Kappel, G., Retschitzegger, W., Schwinger, W.: Reuse in model-to-model transformation languages: are we there yet? SoSyM **14**(2), 537–572 (2015)
17. Lúcio, L., Barroca, B., Amaral, V.: A technique for automatic validation of model transformations. In: Petriu, D.C., Rouquette, N., Haugen, Ø. (eds.) MODELS 2010, Part I. LNCS, vol. 6394, pp. 136–150. Springer, Heidelberg (2010)
18. Musser, D.R., Stepanov, A.A.: Generic programming. In: Gianni, P. (ed.) ISSAC 1988. LNCS, vol. 358, pp. 13–25. Springer, Heidelberg (1988)
19. Pierce, B.C.: Types and Programming Languages. MIT Press, Cambridge (2002)
20. Pohl, K., Böckle, G., Van Der Linden, F.: Software Product Line Engineering: Foundations, Principles, and Techniques. Springer Verlag New York Inc., Secaucus (2005)
21. Rose, L., Guerra, E., de Lara, J., Etien, A., Kolovos, D., Paige, R.: Genericity for model management operations. SoSyM **12**(1), 201–219 (2011)
22. Rubin, J., Chechik, M.: Combining related products into product lines. In: de Lara, J., Zisman, A. (eds.) FASE 2012. LNCS, vol. 7212, pp. 285–300. Springer, Heidelberg (2012)
23. Salay, R., Famelis, M., Rubin, J., Di Sandro, A., Chechik, M.: Lifting model transformations to product lines. In: Proceedings of ICSE 2014, pp. 117–128 (2014)
24. Salay, R., Kokaly, S., Di Sandro, A., Chechik, M.: Enriching megamodel management with collection-based operators. In: Proceedings of MODELS 2015 (2015)
25. Salay, R., Zchaler, S., Chechik, M.: Correct Reuse of Transformations is Hard to Guarantee (submitted, 2016)
26. Salay, R., Zschaler, S., Chechik, M.: Transformation reuse: what is the intent? In: Proceedings of AMT@MODELS 2015, pp. 1–7 (2015)
27. Schmidt, D.C.: Model-driven engineering. IEEE Comput. **39**(2), 25–31 (2006)
28. Sen, S., Moha, N., Baudry, B., Jézéquel, J.-M.: Meta-model pruning. In: Schürr, A., Selic, B. (eds.) MODELS 2009. LNCS, vol. 5795, pp. 32–46. Springer, Heidelberg (2009)
29. Sen, S., Moha, N., Mahé, V., Barais, O., Baudry, B., Jézéquel, J.-M.: Reusable model transformations. SoSyM **11**(1), 1–15 (2010)

30. Sendall, S., Kozaczynski, W.: Model transformation: the heart and soul of model-driven software development. IEEE Softw. **20**(5), 42–45 (2003)
31. Steel, J., Jézéquel, J.-M.: On model typing. SoSyM **6**(4), 401–413 (2007)
32. Strüber, D., Rubin, J., Arendt, T., Chechik, M., Taentzer, G., Plöger, J.: Rule-Merger: automatic construction of variability-based model transformation rules. In: Stevens, P., Wasowski, A. (eds.) FASE 2016. LNCS, vol. 9633, pp. 122–140. Springer, Heidelberg (2016). doi:10.1007/978-3-662-49665-7_8
33. Strüber, D., Rubin, J., Chechik, M., Taentzer, G.: A variability-based approach to reusable and efficient model transformations. In: Egyed, A., Schaefer, I. (eds.) FASE 2015. LNCS, vol. 9033, pp. 283–298. Springer, Heidelberg (2015)
34. Strüber, D., Schulz, S.: A Tool Environment for Managing Families of Model Transformation Rules (submitted, 2016)
35. Thum, T., Apel, S., Kastner, C., Schaefer, I., Saake, G.: A classification and survey of analysis strategies for software product lines. ACM Comput. Surv. **47**(1), 1–45 (2014)
36. Vanhooff, B., Ayed, D., Van Baelen, S., Joosen, W., Berbers, Y.: UniTI: a unified transformation infrastructure. In: Engels, G., Opdyke, B., Schmidt, D.C., Weil, F. (eds.) MODELS 2007. LNCS, vol. 4735, pp. 31–45. Springer, Heidelberg (2007)
37. Wagelaar, D., van der Straeten, R., Deridder, D.: Module superimposition: a composition technique for rule-based model transformation languages. SoSyM **9**, 285–309 (2010)

Program Verification

On Type Checking Delta-Oriented Product Lines

Ferruccio Damiani$^{(\boxtimes)}$ and Michael Lienhardt

University of Torino, Torino, Italy
{ferruccio.damiani,michael.lienhardt}@unito.it

Abstract. A Software Product Line (SPL) is a set of similar programs generated from a common code base. Delta Oriented Programming (DOP) is a flexible approach to implement SPLs. Efficiently type checking an SPL (i.e., checking that all its programs are well-typed) is challenging. This paper proposes a novel type checking approach for DOP. Intrinsic complexity of SPL type checking is addressed by providing early detection of type errors and by reducing type checking to satisfiability of a propositional formula. The approach is tunable to exploit automatically checkable DOP guidelines for making an SPL more comprehensible and type checking more efficient. The approach and guidelines are formalized by means of a core calculus for DOP of product lines of Java programs.

1 Introduction

A *Software Product Line* (SPL) is a set of similar programs, called *variants*, with a common code base and well documented variability [6]. *Delta-Oriented Programming* (DOP) [5,18,19] is a flexible transformational approach to implement SPLs. A DOP product line is described by a *Feature Model* (FM), a *Configuration Knowledge* (CK), and an *Artifact Base* (AB). The FM provides an abstract description of variants in terms of *features*: each feature represents an abstract description of functionality and each variant is identified by a set of features, called a *product*. The AB provides language dependent code artifacts that are used to build the variants: it consists of a *base program* (that might be empty or incomplete) and of a set of *delta modules*, which are containers of modifications to a program (e.g., for Java programs, a delta module can add, remove or modify classes and interfaces). The CK connects the code artifacts in the AB with the features in the FM (thus defining a mapping from products to variants): it associates to each delta module an *activation condition* over the features and specifies an *application ordering* between delta modules [19]. DOP supports the automatic generation of variants based on a selection of features: once a user selects a product, the corresponding variant is derived by applying the delta

The authors of this paper are listed in alphabetical order. This work has been partially supported by: project HyVar (www.hyvar-project.eu), which has received funding from the European Union's Horizon 2020 research and innovation programme under grant agreement No. 644298; by ICT COST Action IC1402 ARVI (www.cost-arvi.eu); and by Ateneo/CSP D16D15000360005 project RunVar.

© Springer International Publishing Switzerland 2016
E. Ábrahám and M. Huisman (Eds.): IFM 2016, LNCS 9681, pp. 47–62, 2016.
DOI: 10.1007/978-3-319-33693-0_4

modules with a satisfied activation condition to the base program according to the application ordering.

DOP is a generalization of *Feature-Oriented Programming* (FOP) [4,9,22]: the artifact base of a FOP product line consists of a set of *feature modules* which are delta modules that correspond one-to-one to features and do not contain remove operations. Hence FOP product line development always starts from base feature modules corresponding to mandatory features. Instead, DOP allows to use arbitrary code as a base program. For example, the base program can be empty and different variants can be used as base delta modules with pairwise disjoint activation conditions [20]. Therefore, DOP supports both proactive SPL development (i.e., planning all products/variants in advance) and extractive SPL development [15] (i.e., starting from existing programs). Moreover (see, e.g., [5]), the decoupling between features and delta modules allows to counter the optional feature problem [13], where additional glue code is needed in order to make optional features to cooperate properly. Due to the additional flexibility, in DOP it is more challenging than in FOP to efficiently type check a product line [5]. Type checking approaches for DOP have already been studied [5,8], and implemented [1] for the ABS modeling language [12]. Although these approaches do not require to generate any variant, they involve an explicit iteration over the set of products, which becomes an issue when the number of products is large (a product line with n features can have up to 2^n products).

In this paper we propose a novel type checking approach for DOP by building on ideas proposed for FOP [9,22]. Our approach represents an achievement over previous type checking approaches for DOP [5,8] since it provides earlier detection of some type errors and does not require to iterate over the set of products. Like the techniques in [9,22], our approach requires to check the validity of a propositional formula (which is a co-NP-complete problem) and can take advantages of the many heuristics implemented in SAT solvers (a SAT solver can be used to check whether a propositional formula is valid by checking whether its negation is unsatisfiable)—[9,22] report that the performance of using SAT solvers to verify the propositional formulas for four non-trivial product lines was encouraging and that, for the largest product line, applying the approach was even faster than generating and compiling a single product. Moreover, our approach is designed to be tunable to take advantage of automatically checkable DOP guidelines that make a product line more comprehensible and type checking more efficient. We formalize the approach and guidelines by means of IMPERATIVE FEATHERWEIGHT DELTA JAVA (IFΔJ) [5], a core calculus for DOP product lines where variants are written in an imperative version of FEATHERWEIGHT JAVA (FJ) [11].

Section 2 introduces an example that will be used through the paper and recalls IFΔJ. Section 3 introduces two DOP guidelines (*no-useless-operations* and *type-uniformity*). Section 4 gives a version of the approach tuned to exploit type-uniformity. Section 5 outlines a version that exploits no guidelines. Section 6 proposes other guidelines. Section 7 discusses related work. Section 8 concludes the paper by outlining planned future work. Proofs of the main results and a prototypical implementation are available in [2] (currently only the version of the approach in Sect. 4 is supported).

2 Model

In this section we introduce the running example of this paper and briefly recall the IFΔJ [5] core calculus. A product line L consist of a feature model, a configuration knowledge, and an artifact base. In IFΔJ there is no concrete syntax for the feature model and the configuration knowledge. We use the following notations: L.features is the set of features; L.products specifies the products (i.e., a subset of the power set $2^{L.\text{features}}$); L.activation maps each delta module name d to its activation condition; and L.order (or $<_L$, for short) is the application ordering between the delta modules. Both the set of valid products and the activation condition of the delta modules are expressed as propositional logic formulas Φ where propositional variables are feature names φ (see [3] for a discussion on other possible representations):

$$\Phi ::= \text{ true } \mid \varphi \mid \Phi \Rightarrow \Phi \mid \neg\Phi \mid \Phi \wedge \Phi \mid \Phi \vee \Phi.$$

As usual, we say that a propositional formula Φ is *valid* if it is true for all values of its propositional variables. To avoid over-specification, the order $<_L$ can be partial. We assume *unambiguity* of the product line, i.e., for each product, any total ordering of the activated delta modules that respects $<_L$ generates the same variant. We refer to [5,16] for a discussion on an effective means to ensure unambiguity.

The running example of this paper is a version of the *Expression Product Line* (EPL) benchmark [17] (see also [5]) defined by the following grammar which describes a language of numerical expressions:

```
Exp ::= Lit | Add    Lit ::= <non-negative-integers>    Add ::= Exp ''+'' Exp
```

Each variant of the EPL contains a class Exp that represents an expression equipped with a subset of the following operations: toInt, which returns the value of the expression as an integer (an object of class Int); toString, which returns the expression as a String; and eval, which in some variants returns the value of the expression as a Lit (the subclass of Exp representing literals) and in the other variants returns it as an Int. The EPL has 6 products, described by two feature sets: one concerned with data—fLit, fAdd—and one concerned with operations —fToInt, fToString, fEval1, fEval2. Features fLit and fToInt are mandatory. The other features are optional with the two following constraints: exactly one between fEval1 and fEval2 must be selected; and fEval1 requires fToString. The EPL is illustrated in Fig. 1. The partial order L.order is expressed as a total order on a partition of the set of delta modules. To make the example more readable, in the artifact base we use the JAVA syntax for operations on strings and sequential composition —encoding in IFΔJ syntax is straightforward (see [5] for examples). Note that, in the method Test.test (in the base program), the

```
EPL.features  =  {fLit, fAdd, fToInt, fToString, fEval1, fEval2}
EPL.products  =  fLit ∧ fToInt ∧ (fEval1 ⇒ fToString) ∧ (fEval1 ∨ fEval2) ∧ ¬(fEval1 ∧ fEval2)
```

```
EPL.order      =  {dAdd} <_L {d_notTostr, dAdd_notTostr} <_L {dEval1, dEval2}
EPL.activation =  dAdd ↦ fAdd,
                  d_notTostr ↦ (¬fToString),  dAdd_notTostr ↦ (fAdd ∧ ¬fToString),
                  dEval1 ↦ fEval1,  dEval2 ↦ fEval1
```

```
// Base program
class Exp extends Object { // To be used only as a type (i.e., not to be instantiated)
  Int toInt() { return new Int(); }
  String toString() { return ""; }
}
class Lit extends Exp {
  Int val;
  Lit setLit(Int x) { this.val=x; return this; }
  Int toInt() { return this.val; }
  String toString() { return this.val.toString(); }
}
class Test extends Object {
  String test(Exp x) { return x.eval().toString(); }
}
// Delta Modules
delta dAdd {
  adds class Add extends Exp {
    Exp a;   Exp b;
    Int toInt() { return this.a.toInt().add(this.b.toInt()); }
    String toString() { return this.a.toString() + "+" + this.b.toString(); }
  }
}
delta d_notTostr {
  modifies class Exp { removes toString; }
  modifies class Lit { removes toString; }
}
delta dAdd_notTostr {  modifies class Add { removes toString; }  }
delta dEval1 {  modifies class Exp { adds Lit eval() {return (new Lit()).setLit(this.toInt());} }  }
delta dEval2 {  modifies class Exp { adds Int eval() {return this.toInt();} }  }
```

Fig. 1. Expression Product Line: FM (top), CK (middle), AB (bottom)

expression x.eval() has type Lit if feature fEval1 is selected (for this reason feature fEval1 requires feature fToString) and type Int otherwise.

In the following, we first introduce the IFJ calculus, which is an imperative version of FJ [11], and then we introduce the constructs for variability on top of it. The abstract syntax of IFJ is presented in Fig. 2 (top). Following [11], we use the overline notation for (possibly empty) sequences of elements: for instance $\overline{e}$ stands for a sequence of expressions. Variables x include the special variable this (implicitly bound in any method declaration MD), which may not be used as the name of a method's formal parameter. A program P is a sequence of class declarations $\overline{CD}$. A class declaration class C extends C′ { $\overline{AD}$ } comprises the name C of the class, the name C′ of the superclass (which must always be specified, even if it is the built-in class Object), and a list of field and method declarations $\overline{AD}$. All fields and methods are public, there is no field shadowing, there is no method overloading, and each class is assumed to have an implicit constructor that initializes all fields to null. The subtyping relation <: on classes, which is the reflexive and transitive closure of the immediate subclass relation

$$P \quad ::= \overline{CD} \qquad\qquad\qquad\qquad\qquad\qquad\qquad\qquad \text{Program}$$
$$CD ::= \textbf{class C extends C } \{ \ \overline{AD} \ \} \qquad\qquad\qquad\qquad \text{Class}$$
$$AD ::= FD \ | \ MD \qquad\qquad\qquad\qquad \text{Attribute (Field or Method)}$$
$$FD ::= \texttt{C f} \qquad\qquad\qquad\qquad\qquad\qquad\qquad\qquad \text{Field}$$
$$MD ::= \texttt{C m}(\overline{\texttt{C x}}) \ \{\textbf{return } e; \} \qquad\qquad\qquad\qquad \text{Method}$$
$$e \quad ::= \texttt{x} \ | \ e.\texttt{f} \ | \ e.\texttt{m}(\overline{e}) \ | \ \textbf{new } \texttt{C}() \ | \ (\texttt{C})e \ | \ e.\texttt{f} = e \ | \ \textbf{null} \qquad \text{Expression}$$

$$L \quad ::= FM \ \ CK \ \ AB \qquad\qquad\qquad\qquad\qquad \text{Product Line}$$
$$AB ::= P \ \ \overline{\varDelta} \qquad\qquad\qquad\qquad\qquad\qquad\qquad \text{Artifact Base}$$
$$\varDelta \quad ::= \textbf{delta } \texttt{d} \ \{ \ \overline{CO} \ \} \qquad\qquad\qquad\qquad \text{Delta Module}$$
$$CO ::= \textbf{adds } CD \ | \ \textbf{removes } \texttt{C} \ | \ \textbf{modifies } \texttt{C } [\textbf{extends } \texttt{C}'] \ \{ \ \overline{AO} \ \} \quad \text{Class Operation}$$
$$AO ::= \textbf{adds } AD \ | \ \textbf{removes } \texttt{a} \ | \ \textbf{modifies } MD \qquad \text{Attribute Operation}$$

Fig. 2. Syntax of IFJ (top) and of IF$\varDelta$J (bottom)

(given by the **extends** clauses in class declarations), is assumed to be acyclic. Type system, operational semantics, and type soundness for IFJ are given in [5].

The abstract syntax of the language IF$\varDelta$J is given in Fig. 2 (bottom). An IF$\varDelta$J program L comprises: a feature model FM, a configuration knowledge CK, and an artifact base AB. Recall that we do not consider a concrete syntax for FM and CK and use the notations L.features, L.products, L.activation, and L.order ($<_L$ for short) introduced above. The artifact base comprises a possibly empty or incomplete IFJ program P, and a set of delta modules $\overline{\varDelta}$.

A delta module declaration $\varDelta$ comprises the name d of the delta module and class operations $\overline{CO}$ representing the transformations performed when the delta module is applied to an IFJ program. A class operation can add, remove, or modify a class. A class can be modified by (possibly) changing its super class and performing attribute operations $\overline{AO}$ on its body. An *attribute name* a is either a field name f or a method name m. An attribute operation can add or remove fields and methods, and modify the implementation of a method by replacing its body. The new body may call the special method `original`, which is implicitly bound to the previous implementation of the method and may not be used as the name of a method. The class operations in a delta module must act on distinct classes, and the attribute operations in a class operation must act on distinct attributes. The operational semantics of IF$\varDelta$J variant generation is given in [5].

We conclude this section with some notations and definitions. First, in the rest of the document, we will use the term *module* to refer to the base program or a delta module: we denote with p the name of the base program, and extend L.activation by convention, stating that L.activation(p) = **true**. Second, the *projection* of a product line on a subset S of its products is the product line obtained by restricting the L.products formula to describe only the products in S and by ignoring delta modules that are never activated. Third, the following definitions introduce auxiliary structures and getters that are useful to type check an IF$\varDelta$J product line.

Definition 1 (FCST). *A Class Signature (CS) is a class declaration deprived of the bodies of its methods, it comprises the name of the class and of its* *superclass, and a mapping from attribute names to types. A* Family Class Signature *(FCS) is a more liberal version of class signature that may extend multiple classes and associate more than one type to each attribute name. A* Family Class Signature table *(FCST) is a mapping that associates to each class name* C *an FCS for* C*. The subtyping relation* <: *described by an FCST can be cyclic. A* Class Signature Table *(CST) is a FCST that contains only class signatures and has an acyclic subtyping relation.*

To simplify the notation, except when stated otherwise, we always assume in the following a fixed product line $L = FM\ CK\ AB$. The FCST of L, denoted by $L.$FCST, contains for each class C declared in AB all superclasses of C and all types of all attributes of C. Note that the FCST of L is defined only in terms of AB and it can be computed by a straightforward inspection of it. The FCST of a set of IFJ programs (or of a subset of AB) is defined similarly.

Definition 2 (Getters on AB). add(C) *is the set of modules that* add *the class* C*;* remove(C) *is the set of modules that* remove *the class* C*;* modifyWEC(C) *is the set of modules that modify the class* C without changing its **extends** clause*;* modifyAEC(C) *is the set of modules that modify the class* C also by changing its **extends** clause*;* modify(C) *is* modifyWEC(C) ∪ modifyAEC(C)*;* add(C.a) *is the set of modules that* add *the attribute* C.a*;* remove(C.a) *is the set of modules that* remove *the attribute* C.a*;* modify(C.a) *is the set of modules that* modify *the attribute* C.a*;* replace(C.m) *is the set of modules that modify the method* C.m *without using calls to* original *(i.e., replace its body); and* wrap(C.m) *is the set of modules that modify the method* C.m *by also using calls to* original *(i.e., wrap its body).*

Definition 3 (Getter on FM and CK). *Let Φ be extended to include module names* d *as propositional variables. The formula* $L.$FMandCK $\triangleq$ $L.$products $\wedge$ $\bigwedge_{d}$(d $\Leftrightarrow$ $L.$activation(d)) *specifies the products and binds each variable* d *to the activation condition of module* d *(i.e., it specifies which modules are activated for each product).*[1]

3   Two Delta-Oriented Programming Guidelines

The first guideline is to avoid *useless operations*, i.e., declarations in P and **adds** or **modifies** in $\overline{\Delta}$ that introduce code that is never present in any of the variants.

G1. Ensure that the product line does not contain useless operations.

For instance, in the product line obtained by projecting the EPL on the products described by ¬fToString, the declarations of the methods with name toString in the base program and in the **adds** class operation in the delta module dAdd are useless. The notion of useless operation is formalized as follows (thus making Guideline G1 automatically checkable).

---

[1] The last occurrence of d in $L.$FMandCK is not used as a variable: it is used as argument of the map $L.$activation to obtain the activation condition of module d.

Definition 4 (Useless operation and module). *The declaration, addition or modification of an attribute* C.a *in a module* d *is* useless *iff the formula* $(L.\text{FMandCK} \wedge \text{d}) \Rightarrow \bigvee_{\text{d}'} \text{d}'$ *(with* $\text{d}' \in$ remove(C.a) $\cup$ remove(C) $\cup$ replace(C.a) *and* $(\text{d} <_L \text{d}'))$ *is valid. An* **extends** *clause introduced in a class* C *by a module* d *is* useless *iff the formula* $(L.\text{FMandCK} \wedge \text{d}) \Rightarrow \bigvee_{\text{d}'} \text{d}'$ *(with* $\text{d}' \in$ remove(C) $\cup$ modifyAEC(C) *and* $(\text{d} <_L \text{d}'))$ *is valid. A module* d *is* useless *iff* $L.\text{products} \Rightarrow \neg L.\text{activation}(\text{d})$ *is valid.*

The second guideline is to have consistent declarations over the whole SPL (the FOP case-studies presented in [22] adhere to this guideline). For IFΔJ (since IFJ has no method overloading and field shadowing), this means that two declarations of the same attribute (of the same class) in two different modules must have the same type.[2] We call this property *type-uniformity*. It can be straightforwardly formalized by exploiting the family class signature table of the product line.

Definition 5 (Type-uniformity). *A FCST FCST is* type-uniform *iff:*

- $\forall \text{C} \in \text{dom}(\text{FCST}), \forall \text{a} \in \text{dom}(\text{FCST}(\text{C}))$ *the set* FCST(C.a) *is a singleton; and*
- $\forall \text{C}_1, \text{C}_2, \text{C}_3 \in \text{dom}(\text{FCST})$ *such that* $\text{C}_1 <: \text{C}_2$ *and* $\text{C}_1 <: \text{C}_3$, *we have:*
  $\forall \text{a} \in \text{dom}(\text{FCST}(\text{C}_2)) \cap \text{dom}(\text{FCST}(\text{C}_3)), \text{FCST}(\text{C}_2.\text{a}) = \text{FCST}(\text{C}_3.\text{a})$

An IFΔJ product line (or a subset of its artifact base, or a set of IFJ programs) is type-uniform *iff its FCST is type-uniform.*

Our second guideline is thus stated as follows (and it can automatically be checked by a straightforward inspection of the FCST).

G2. Ensure that the product line is type-uniform.

The EPL is not type-uniform, because of the method eval of class Exp, that is added with two different types by delta modules dEval1 and dEval2, respectively. Instead, both its two projections respectively described by the mutually exclusive features fEval1 and fEval2 are type-uniform.

We say that an IFΔJ product line is *variant-type-uniform* to mean that: (i) its variants can be generated; and (ii) the FCST of the set of its variants is type-uniform. The following proposition illustrate how type-uniformity relates to variant-type-uniformity.

Proposition 1. *Let L be an IFΔJ product line such that its variants can be generated. If L is type-uniform, then it is variant-type-uniform. If L satisfies Guideline G1 and is variant-type-uniform, then it is type-uniform.*

4   Type Checking for Type-Uniform IFΔJ

This section presents a version of the type checking approach tuned to exploit Guideline G2 and states its correctness and completeness. Type-uniformity makes type checking more efficient. The approach is modularized in three independent parts: *partial typing*, *applicability*, and *dependency*. All the parts rely on the FCST of the product line (see Definition 1).

---

[2] Note that, since the type system of IFJ is nominal, a class may have different sets of attributes in different variants.

Product Line Partial Typing. Partial typing checks that all fields, methods and classes in AB type-check with respect to the product line FCST (i.e., with respect to declarations made in AB). Partial typing does not use any knowledge about valid feature combinations (it does not use FM and CK), so it does not guarantee that variants are well-typed, as delta modules may be activated or not. However, it guarantees that variants that have their inner dependencies satisfied (i.e., all used classes, methods and fields are declared) are well-typed.

The IFΔJ partial-type-system is a straightforward extension of the (standard) IFJ type system [5] that: (i) includes rules for the new syntactic constructs of IFΔJ; (ii) checks well-typedness with respect to the product line FCST (instead of the program CST); and (iii) allows to introduce a same class or attribute in different modules of AB (e.g., a class of name C may be added by different delta modules).

The projection of the EPL described by feature fEval1 is type-uniform. Its artifact base (which is obtained from the EPL artifact base in Fig. 1 by dropping the delta module dEval2) is accepted by partial typing, even if the method Exp.eval might not be available in some variant (in principle the delta module dEval1 might not be selected). This is because the way the method Exp.eval is used in the method Test.test in the base program is correct with respect to its definition in the delta module dEval1 (it takes no parameters and returns a Lit object).

Product Line Applicability. Applicability ensures that variants can actually be generated (variant generation fails if, e.g., a delta module that adds a class C is applied to an intermediate variant that already contains a class named C). It is formalized by a constraint ensuring that, during variant generation, each delta operation is applied to an intermediate variant on which that operation is defined. For instance, for adding a class C, this class must not be present in the intermediate variant (either it never was added, or it was removed at some point). The applicability constraint comprises three validation parts: element addition (either a class or an attribute), element removal, and element modification.

In the following we use ρ to denote either a class name C or a fully qualified attribute name C.a. The constraint for checking that an element ρ can be added is as follows:

$$\texttt{appADD}(\rho) \triangleq \bigwedge_{\mathsf{d} \neq \mathsf{d}'} \mathsf{d} \wedge \mathsf{d}' \Rightarrow \bigvee_{\mathsf{d}''} \mathsf{d}'' \quad \text{with} \quad \begin{cases} \mathsf{d}, \mathsf{d}' \in \texttt{add}(\rho),\ \mathsf{d}'' \in \texttt{remove}(\rho) \\ \text{and } \mathsf{d} <_L \mathsf{d}'' <_L \mathsf{d}' \end{cases}$$

It ensures that all **adds** operations are performed on a partial variant that does not contain the added element: basically, it requires that if two delta modules d and d' add the same element, then there must be another delta module d'' in between that removes it.

The constraint for removal of an element ρ is slightly more complex:

$$\texttt{appRM}(\rho) \triangleq \bigwedge_{\mathsf{d}} \mathsf{d} \Rightarrow \left(\bigvee_{\mathsf{d}_1} \mathsf{d}_1 \wedge \bigwedge_{\mathsf{d}'} (\mathsf{d}' \Rightarrow \bigvee_{\mathsf{d}_2} \mathsf{d}_2) \right) \quad \text{with} \quad \begin{cases} \mathsf{d}, \mathsf{d}' \in \texttt{remove}(\rho),\ \mathsf{d}_1, \mathsf{d}_2 \in \texttt{add}(\rho) \\ \mathsf{d}_1 <_L \mathsf{d} <_L \mathsf{d}_2 <_L \mathsf{d}' \end{cases}$$

In comprises two parts: the first part $(\mathtt{d} \Rightarrow \bigvee_{\mathtt{d}_1})$ ensures that the element ρ is added to the partial variant (by some $\mathtt{d}_1$) before it is removed (by $\mathtt{d}$); the second part ensures that if two delta modules $\mathtt{d}$ and $\mathtt{d}'$ remove ρ, then there is another delta module $\mathtt{d}_2$ in between that adds it.

The constraint for modification of an element ρ simply ensures that ρ is present for the modification:

$$\mathtt{appMOD}(\rho) \triangleq \bigwedge_{\mathtt{d}} \mathtt{d} \Rightarrow \left(\bigvee_{\mathtt{d}'} \mathtt{d}' \wedge \bigwedge_{\mathtt{d}''} \neg \mathtt{d}'' \right) \quad \text{with} \quad \begin{cases} \mathtt{d} \in \mathtt{modify}(\rho), \ \mathtt{d}'' \in \mathtt{remove}(\rho) \\ \mathtt{d}' \in \mathtt{add}(\rho), \ \mathtt{d}' <_L \mathtt{d}'' <_L \mathtt{d} \end{cases}$$

Basically, it checks that there is a delta module $\mathtt{d}'$ that adds the element before it is modified by $\mathtt{d}$, and that there is no delta module $\mathtt{d}''$ in between that removes it.

The formula $\mathtt{app}(L) \triangleq \bigwedge_{\rho \in \mathtt{add}(L)} \mathtt{appADD}(\rho) \wedge \mathtt{appRM}(\rho) \wedge \mathtt{appMOD}(\rho)$ combines the constraints described above, and the formula $\mathtt{ac}(L) \triangleq L.\mathtt{FMandCK} \Rightarrow \mathtt{app}(L)$ associates to each product of L its applicability constraints. Applicability-consistency (i.e., the fact that variants of L can be generated) is therefore formalized as follows.

Definition 6 (Applicability-consistency). *A product line L is* applicability-consistent *iff the formula* $\mathtt{ac}(L)$ *is valid.*

Product Line Dependency. Dependency ensures that no generated variant has a missing dependency, which can be straightforwardly expressed by means of constraints on attributes and classes. For instance, the dependencies induced by "class C extends class C'" could be encoded with the constraint $\mathtt{decl}(\mathtt{C}) \Rightarrow (\mathtt{decl}(\mathtt{C}') \wedge \neg\mathtt{sub}(\mathtt{C}', \mathtt{C}))$, as the declaration of C requires that the declaration of C' is present and that C' is not a subtype of C (to ensure that the inheritance graph has no loops). In DOP, since each declaration is made in a module that can be activated or not, dependency constraints must be lifted at the module level. For instance, if the fact that C extends C' is declared in the module $\mathtt{d}$, then the previous constraint becomes: $\mathtt{d} \Rightarrow \neg\mathtt{rm}(\mathtt{d}, \mathtt{C}) \Rightarrow \neg\mathtt{modifyEC}(\mathtt{d}, \mathtt{C}) \Rightarrow (\mathtt{decl}(\mathtt{C}') \wedge \neg\mathtt{sub}(\mathtt{C}', \mathtt{C}))$, basically stating that if the module $\mathtt{d}$ is activated and no other module that removes C or changes its **extends** clause is activated afterward, then the class C' must be present in the generated variant and must not be a subtype of C.

The product line dependency constraint is generated by exploiting the rules in Figs. 3 and 4, which infer a dependency constraint for each expression and declaration, respectively. It is based on the following atomic constraints: $\mathtt{rm}(\mathtt{d}, \mathtt{C})$ (resp. $\mathtt{rm}(\mathtt{d}, \mathtt{C}.\mathtt{a})$) ensures that the class C (resp. attribute C.a) added by the delta module $\mathtt{d}$ will be removed afterward; $\mathtt{modifyEC}(\mathtt{d}, \mathtt{C})$ ensures that the class C added or modified by the delta module $\mathtt{d}$ will have its **extends** clause modified by another delta module afterward; $\mathtt{replace}(\mathtt{d}, \mathtt{C}.\mathtt{m})$ ensures that the method C.m added or modified by the delta module $\mathtt{d}$ will be replaced by another delta module afterward; $\mathtt{sub}(T, \mathtt{C}')$ ensures that T (either a class or **null**) is a subtype of C'; $\mathtt{decl}(\mathtt{C})$ (resp. $\mathtt{decl}(\mathtt{C}.\mathtt{a})$) ensures that the class C (resp. the attribute a)

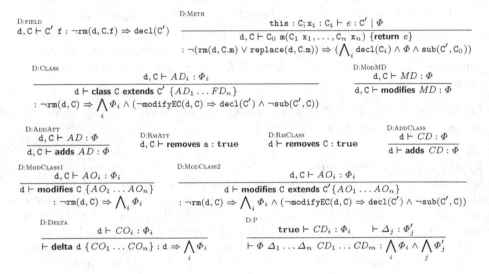

$$\frac{\Gamma(\mathtt{x}) = \mathtt{C}}{\Gamma \vdash \mathtt{x} : \mathtt{C} \mid \mathbf{true}} \quad \text{E:VAR}$$

$$\frac{\Gamma \vdash e : \mathtt{C} \mid \Phi \qquad \mathtt{FCST}(\mathtt{C.f}) = \mathtt{C}'}{\Gamma \vdash e.\mathtt{f} : \mathtt{C}' \mid \Phi \land \mathtt{decl}(\mathtt{C.f})} \quad \text{E:FIELD}$$

$$\frac{}{\Gamma \vdash \mathbf{null} : \bot \mid \mathbf{true}} \quad \text{E:NULL}$$

$$\text{E:METH} \quad \frac{\Gamma \vdash e : \mathtt{C} \mid \Phi \qquad \mathtt{FCST}(\mathtt{C.m}) = \mathtt{C}'(\mathtt{C}_1, \ldots, \mathtt{C}_n)}{\Gamma \vdash e_i : T_i \mid \Phi_i \qquad \Phi_i' = \mathtt{sub}(T_i, \mathtt{C}_i)}{\Gamma \vdash e.\mathtt{m}(e_1, \ldots, e_n) : \mathtt{C}' \mid \bigwedge_i (\Phi_i \land \Phi_i') \land \Phi \land \mathtt{decl}(\mathtt{C.m})}$$

$$\frac{}{\Gamma \vdash \mathbf{new}\ \mathtt{C}() : \mathtt{C} \mid \mathtt{decl}(\mathtt{C})} \quad \text{D:NEW}$$

$$\text{E:CAST} \quad \frac{\Gamma \vdash e : T \mid \Phi}{\Gamma \vdash (\mathtt{C})e : \mathtt{C} \mid \Phi \land (\mathtt{sub}(T, \mathtt{C}) \lor \mathtt{sub}(\mathtt{C}, T))}$$

$$\text{E:ASSIGN} \quad \frac{\Gamma \vdash e.\mathtt{f} : \mathtt{C} \mid \Phi_1 \qquad \Gamma \vdash e' : T \mid \Phi_2}{\Gamma \vdash e.\mathtt{f} = e' : \mathtt{C} \mid \Phi_1 \land \Phi_2 \land \mathtt{sub}(T, \mathtt{C})}$$

Fig. 3. Dependency generation for expressions

$$\text{D:FIELD} \quad \mathtt{d}, \mathtt{C} \vdash \mathtt{C}'\ \mathtt{f} : \neg\mathtt{rm}(\mathtt{d}, \mathtt{C.f}) \Rightarrow \mathtt{decl}(\mathtt{C}')$$

$$\text{D:METH} \quad \frac{\mathtt{this} : \mathtt{C}; \mathtt{x}_i : \mathtt{C}_i \vdash e : \mathtt{C}' \mid \Phi}{\mathtt{d}, \mathtt{C} \vdash \mathtt{C}_0\ \mathtt{m}(\mathtt{C}_1\ \mathtt{x}_1, \ldots, \mathtt{C}_n\ \mathtt{x}_n)\ \{\mathbf{return}\ e\}}{: \neg(\mathtt{rm}(\mathtt{d}, \mathtt{C.m}) \lor \mathtt{replace}(\mathtt{d}, \mathtt{C.m})) \Rightarrow (\bigwedge_i \mathtt{decl}(\mathtt{C}_i) \land \Phi \land \mathtt{sub}(\mathtt{C}', \mathtt{C}_0))}$$

$$\text{D:CLASS} \quad \frac{\mathtt{d}, \mathtt{C} \vdash AD_i : \Phi_i}{\mathtt{d} \vdash \mathbf{class}\ \mathtt{C}\ \mathbf{extends}\ \mathtt{C}'\ \{AD_1 \ldots FD_n\}}{: \neg\mathtt{rm}(\mathtt{d}, \mathtt{C}) \Rightarrow \bigwedge_i \Phi_i \land (\neg\mathtt{modifyEC}(\mathtt{d}, \mathtt{C}) \Rightarrow \mathtt{decl}(\mathtt{C}') \land \neg\mathtt{sub}(\mathtt{C}', \mathtt{C}))}$$

$$\text{D:MODMD} \quad \frac{\mathtt{d}, \mathtt{C} \vdash MD : \Phi}{\mathtt{d}, \mathtt{C} \vdash \mathbf{modifies}\ MD : \Phi}$$

$$\text{D:ADDATT} \quad \frac{\mathtt{d}, \mathtt{C} \vdash AD : \Phi}{\mathtt{d}, \mathtt{C} \vdash \mathbf{adds}\ AD : \Phi}$$

$$\text{D:RMATT} \quad \frac{}{\mathtt{d}, \mathtt{C} \vdash \mathbf{removes}\ a : \mathbf{true}}$$

$$\text{D:RMCLASS} \quad \frac{}{\mathtt{d} \vdash \mathbf{removes}\ \mathtt{C} : \mathbf{true}}$$

$$\text{D:ADDCLASS} \quad \frac{\mathtt{d} \vdash CD : \Phi}{\mathtt{d} \vdash \mathbf{adds}\ CD : \Phi}$$

$$\text{D:MODCLASS1} \quad \frac{\mathtt{d}, \mathtt{C} \vdash AO_i : \Phi_i}{\mathtt{d} \vdash \mathbf{modifies}\ \mathtt{C}\ \{AO_1 \ldots AO_n\}}{: \neg\mathtt{rm}(\mathtt{d}, \mathtt{C}) \Rightarrow \bigwedge_i \Phi_i}$$

$$\text{D:MODCLASS2} \quad \frac{\mathtt{d}, \mathtt{C} \vdash AO_i : \Phi_i}{\mathtt{d} \vdash \mathbf{modifies}\ \mathtt{C}\ \mathbf{extends}\ \mathtt{C}'\{AO_1 \ldots AO_n\}}{: \neg\mathtt{rm}(\mathtt{d}, \mathtt{C}) \Rightarrow \bigwedge_i \Phi_i \land (\neg\mathtt{modifyEC}(\mathtt{d}, \mathtt{C}) \Rightarrow \mathtt{decl}(\mathtt{C}') \land \neg\mathtt{sub}(\mathtt{C}', \mathtt{C}))}$$

$$\text{D:DELTA} \quad \frac{\mathtt{d} \vdash CO_i : \Phi_i}{\vdash \mathbf{delta}\ \mathtt{d}\ \{CO_1 \ldots CO_n\} : \mathtt{d} \Rightarrow \bigwedge_i \Phi_i}$$

$$\text{D:P} \quad \frac{\mathbf{true} \vdash CD_i : \Phi_i \qquad \vdash \Delta_j : \Phi_j'}{\vdash \Phi\ \Delta_1 \ldots \Delta_n\ CD_1 \ldots CD_m : \bigwedge_i \Phi_i \land \bigwedge_j \Phi_j'}$$

Fig. 4. Dependency generation for declarations

is present in the generated variant (resp. is an attribute of the class C, possibly through inheritance).

Dependency generation rules for expressions perform a type analysis to know what is the type of each expression, which is used to compute the appropriate dependency. They have judgments of the form $\Gamma \vdash e : T \mid \Phi$, where: Γ is an environment giving the type of each variable; e is the parsed expression; T is its type; and Φ is the generated dependency constraint. The rules for expressions are quite direct: accessing a variable (rule (E:VAR)) does not raise any dependency, while accessing a field requires for this field to be accessible (rule (E:FIELD)); method calls (rule (E:METH)) require that the method is accessible and that the parameters have a type consistent with the method's declaration; object creation requires for the class of the object to be defined (rule (E:NEW)); and **null** does not raise any dependency (rule (E:NULL)), while casting and assignment generate constraints ensuring that the right inheritance relation holds (rules (E:CAST) and (E:ASSIGN)).

Dependency generation rules for declarations have judgments of the form $\Omega \vdash A : \Phi$ where Ω can either be empty, d (meaning that we are parsing the content of the module d), or d, C (meaning that we are parsing the content of the class C inside d); A is the parsed declaration (e.g., an attribute, a class operation); and Φ is the generated constraint. Rules (D:FIELD) for field and (D:METH) for method declarations are quite direct: if the attribute is not removed afterward, the dependencies it generates must be validated. The rule (D:CLASS) for class declaration is similar (if the class is not removed, its inner dependencies must be validated), with an additional clause for the **extends** clauses (as previously discussed). Rules (D:MODMD) for modifying methods and (D:ADDATT) and (D:ADDCLASS) for adding attributes and classes simply forward the constraints generated from the inner declaration, while removing an attribute or a class (rules (D:RMATT) and (D:RMCLASS)) does not generate any dependency. The rules (D:ADDCLASS1) and (D:ADDCLASS2) for modifying a class are simple variations on the rule for class declaration. Finally, the dependencies of a delta module body are activated only if the delta module is activated (rule (D:DELTA)), and the dependencies of a whole program is the conjunction of the dependencies of all its parts (rule (D:P)). The resulting constraint thus has the form $\bigwedge_i \mathsf{d}_i \Rightarrow \Phi_i$, giving for all module d_i its dependencies Φ_i. Let then $\mathsf{dep}(L)$ be the constraint generated for the product line L. The formula $\mathsf{dc}(L) \triangleq L.\mathsf{FMandCK} \Rightarrow \mathsf{dep}(L)$ associates to each product of L its dependency constraints. Dependency-consistency (i.e., variants of L have all their dependencies fulfilled) is therefore formalized as follows.

Definition 7 (Dependency-consistency). *A product line L is* dependency-consistent *iff the formula* $\mathsf{dc}(L)$ *is valid.*

Correctness and Completeness of the Approach. The following theorem states that, if the product line follows Guideline G2, then the presented IFΔJ product line type checking approach is correct with respect to generating variants and checking them using the IFJ type system. The approach is complete (i.e., if the check performed by the approach fails then at least one variant is not a well-typed IFJ program) if also Guideline G1 is followed.

Theorem 1. *Let L be a type-uniform product line. Consider the properties:*

i. L is well partially-typed, applicability- and dependency-consistent.
ii. Variants of L can be generated and are well-typed IFJ programs.

Then: (i) implies (ii); and if L has no useless operations then (ii) implies (i).

5 Type Checking for IFΔJ Without Guidelines

In this section we outline how the type checking approach presented in Sect. 4 can be tuned to non type-uniform product lines (i.e., not to exploit any guidelines). This modification is quite straightforward, although it involves many technical details. Partial typing must be adapted since the product line FCST maps attribute names to sets of types with possibly more than one element, and expressions can have more than one type. E.g., a method call expression $e.\mathtt{m}(\overline{e'})$ can use any declaration of the method $\mathtt{C.m}$ (considering that e is typed $\mathtt{C}$) whose type accepts a combination of types of the call's arguments. So partial typing may carry a combinatorial explosion.

Applicability does not need any modification to analyze non-uniform programs. This is due to the fact that the applicability criteria focuses on the interplay between delta operations and do not consider attribute types.

Dependency is the part that changes more: it now has to be type-aware, and thus subsumes partial typing. We illustrate it on the rule that generates the dependency for field usage (second rule in Fig. 3). This rule must be extended in two ways to manage non-uniform programs: (i) e can have more than one type; (ii) the field type lookup $\mathtt{FCST(C.f)}$ can return different possible types for $\mathtt{C.f}$, depending on which modules are activated. Consequently, the dependency generation judgment for expressions now has the form $\Gamma \vdash e : [\Phi_i \mapsto T_i]_{i \in I}$ where T_i are the possible types of e, and Φ_i is the condition (i.e. which module must or must not be activated) for e to have the type T_i in the final product.

Hence, the rule becomes as displayed on the right,

$$\frac{\Gamma \vdash see : \Phi_i \mapsto \mathtt{C}_i]_i \cup [\Phi_{i'} \mapsto \bot]_{i'} \, \mathtt{FCST(C}_i.\mathtt{f)} = [\Phi_{i,j} \mapsto \mathtt{C}_{i,j}]_j}{\Gamma \vdash see. : [\Phi_i \wedge \Phi_{i,j} \mapsto \mathtt{C}_{i,j}]_{i,j}}$$

where $\Phi_{i,j}$ is the formula that enforces that the field $\mathtt{f}$ accessible from the class $\mathtt{C}_i$ has the type $\mathtt{C}_{i,j}$ in the final product.

Correctness and completeness are stated as in Theorem 1 by dropping the assumption that the product line is type-uniform.

6   Three Other Guidelines

Our type-checking approach is modularized in three parts: (i) partial typing performs a preliminary type analysis that can be exploited by an IDE for prompt notification of type-errors and auto-completing code; (ii) applicability ensures that variants can be generated; and (iii) dependency completes the analysis done by the partial typing. The approach is tunable to exploit DOP guidelines that enforce structural regularities in product line implementation. In Sect. 4 we have presented a version tuned to exploit type-uniformity. In this section we briefly discuss three other automatically checkable guidelines (other useful guidelines could be devised).

First, whenever it is possible to enforce the following guideline (satisfied by the EPL), the dependency analysis can be simplified, as it is no longer needed to check the absence of inheritance loop in the generated variant (cf. dependency generation for class declaration and modification in Fig. 4).

G3. Ensure that the product line FCST subtyping relation is acyclic.

If a product line cannot be made variant-type-uniform, then guideline G2 cannot be enforced (see Proposition 1), and understanding the structure of the SPL may become an issue. The following guideline (satisfied by the EPL) aims at helping the understanding of an SPL implementation by decoupling the sources of non type-uniformity.

G4. Ensure that, for all distinct modules d_1 and d_2, if the set comprising d_1 and d_2 is not type-uniform then their activation conditions are mutually exclusive.

Consider for instance a module d that declares an attribute C.a with a type t. Then, if the SPL follows G3, we are sure that each variant using d in its construction will have C.a typed t when it contains this attribute.

We introduce our final guideline with the following consideration: implementing or modifying a product line involves editions of the feature model, the configuration knowledge and the artifact base that may affect only a subset of the products. For example, adding, removing or modifying a delta module d and its activation condition will affect only the products that activate d. Therefore, only the projection of the product line on the affected products needs to be re-analyzed. If such a projection is type-uniform, then the more efficient type checking technique of Sect. 4 can be used (even if the whole product line is not type-uniform). The following guideline naturally arises.

G5. (i) Ensure that the set of products is partitioned in such a way that: each part S is type-uniform (i.e., the projection of the SPL on S is type uniform), and the union of any two distinct parts is not type-uniform.
(ii) If the number of parts of such a partition is "too big", then merge some of them to obtain a "small enough" partition where only one part is not type-uniform.

The goal of this guideline is to allow to use as much as possible the version of the approach presented in Sect. 4. For the EPL the partition that satisfies Guideline G5.i is unique: the two products with feature fEval1 and the four products with feature fEval2. However, in general, such a partition may be not unique and tool support for identifying a partition that satisfies G5.i and further conditions (e.g., having a minimal number of parts) or G5.ii and other conditions (e.g., the number of products in the non type-uniform part is as small as possible) would be valuable.

7 Related Work

Product line analysis approaches can be classified into three main categories [23]: *Product-based* analyses operate only on generated variants (or models of variants); *Family-based* analyses operate only on the AB by exploiting the FM and the CK to obtain results about all variants; *Feature-based* analyses operate on the building blocks of the different variants (feature modules in FOP and delta modules in DOP) in isolation (without using the FM and the CK) to derive results on all variants. We refer to [23] for a survey on product line type checking. Here we discuss previous type checking approaches for DOP [5,8] and the two approaches for FOP that are closets to our proposal [9,22].

The type checking approach for DOP in [5] comprises: a feature-based analysis that uses a constraint-based type system for IFJ to infer a type abstraction for each delta module; and a product-based step that uses these type abstractions to generate, for each product of the SPL, a type abstraction (of the associated variant) that is checked to establish whether the associated variant type checks. The approach of [5] is enhanced in [8] by introducing a family-based step that builds a product family generation tree which is then traversed in order to perform optimized generation and check of type abstractions of all variants. The approach proposed in this paper, which is feature-family-based, represents an achievement over [5,8] since it does not require to iterate over the set of products (cf. Sect. 1) and supports earlier detection of errors via partial typing.

The paper [22] informally illustrates the implementation of a family-based approach for the AHEAD system [4]. The approach comprises: (i) a family-feature-based step that computes for each class a stub (all stubs can be understood as a type-uniform FCST for the product line) and compiles each feature module in the context of all stubs (thus performing checks corresponding to our type-uniformity and partial-typing); and (ii) a family-based step that infers a set of constraints that are combined with the FM to generate a formula (corresponding to our type-uniform applicability and dependency) whose satisfiability should imply that all variants successfully compile.

The paper [9] formalizes a feature-family-based approach for the LIGHT-WEIGHT FEATURE JAVA (LFJ) calculus, which models FOP for the LIGHT-WEIGHT JAVA (LJ) [21] calculus. The approach comprises: (i) a feature-based step that uses a constraint-based type system for LFJ to analyze each feature module in isolation and infer a set of constraints for each feature module; and (ii) a family-based step where the FM and the previously inferred constraints are used to generate a formula whose satisfiability implies that all variants type check. The applicability and dependency analyses presented in Sect. 5 provide an extension to DOP of these two steps. Moreover, our approach provides partial typing for early error detection and is tunable to exploit different programming guidelines.

8   Conclusions and Future Work

We have proposed a modular and tunable approach for type checking DOP product lines. A prototypical implementation is available [2] (currently only the version of the approach exploiting type-uniformity is supported).

In future work we plan to: implement our approach for both DeltaJ 1.5 [14] (a prototypical implementation of DOP that supports full Java 1.5) and ABS [12] (this would allow experimental comparison with the approaches of [5,8], which have been implemented for ABS [1]); to develop case studies to evaluate the effectiveness of the approach and of the proposed guidelines; to investigate further DOP guidelines; and to develop tool support to allow the programmer to choose the guidelines to be automatically enforced. We also plan to investigate whether the proposed DOP guidelines (or other guidelines) could be useful for other kind of product line analyses. In particular, we would like to consider formal verification (proof systems for the verification of DOP product lines of Java programs have been recently proposed [7,10]).

Acknowledgements. We are grateful to Don Batory for clarifications about previous work on type checking FOP, and to Ina Schaefer and Thomas Thüm for discussions about how to classify SPL type checking approaches. We also thank the iFM 2016 anonymous reviewers for insightful comments and suggestions.

References

1. https://github.com/abstools/abstools/tree/master/frontend/src/abs/frontend/delta
2. https://github.com/gzoumix/IFDJTS
3. Batory, D.: Feature models, grammars, and propositional formulas. In: Obbink, H., Pohl, K. (eds.) SPLC 2005. LNCS, vol. 3714, pp. 7–20. Springer, Heidelberg (2005)
4. Batory, D., Sarvela, J.N., Rauschmayer, A.: Scaling step-wise refinement. In: 2003 Proceedings of ICSE, pp. 187–197. IEEE (2003)
5. Bettini, L., Damiani, F., Schaefer, I.: Compositional type checking of delta-oriented software product lines. Acta Informatica **50**(2), 77–122 (2013)
6. Clements, P., Northrop, L.: Software Product Lines: Practices and Patterns. Addison Wesley Longman, Boston (2001)
7. Damiani, F., Owe, O., Dovland, J., Schaefer, I., Johnsen, E.B., Yu, I.C.: A transformational proof system for delta-oriented programming. In: 2012 Proceedings of SPLC, vol. 2, pp. 53–60. ACM (2012)
8. Damiani, F., Schaefer, I.: Family-based analysis of type safety for delta-oriented software product lines. In: Margaria, T., Steffen, B. (eds.) ISoLA 2012, Part I. LNCS, vol. 7609, pp. 193–207. Springer, Heidelberg (2012)
9. Delaware, B., Cook, W.R., Batory, D.: Fitting the pieces together: a machine-checked model of safe composition. In: 2009 Proceedings of ESEC/FSE. ACM (2009)
10. Hähnle, R., Schaefer, I.: A Liskov principle for delta-oriented programming. In: Margaria, T., Steffen, B. (eds.) ISoLA 2012, Part I. LNCS, vol. 7609, pp. 32–46. Springer, Heidelberg (2012)
11. Igarashi, A., Pierce, B., Wadler, P.: Featherweight Java: a minimal core calculus for Java and GJ. ACM TOPLAS **23**(3), 396–450 (2001)
12. Johnsen, E.B., Hähnle, R., Schäfer, J., Schlatte, R., Steffen, M.: ABS: a core language for abstract behavioral specification. In: Aichernig, B.K., Boer, F.S., Bonsangue, M.M. (eds.) Formal Methods for Components and Objects. LNCS, vol. 6957, pp. 142–164. Springer, Heidelberg (2011)
13. Kästner, C., Apel, S., ur Rahman, S.S., Rosenmüller, M., Batory, D., Saake, G.: On the impact of the optional feature problem: analysis and case studies. In: Proceedings of SPLC 2009, pp. 181–190 (2009)
14. Koscielny, J., Holthusen, S., Schaefer, I., Schulze, S., Bettini, L., Damiani, F.: Deltaj 1.5: delta-oriented programming for Java 1.5. In: 2014 Proceedings of PPPJ, pp. 63–74. ACM (2014)
15. Krueger, C.: Eliminating the adoption barrier. IEEE Softw. **19**(4), 29–31 (2002)

16. Lienhardt, M., Clarke, D.: Conflict detection in delta-oriented programming. In: Margaria, T., Steffen, B. (eds.) ISoLA 2012, Part I. LNCS, vol. 7609, pp. 178–192. Springer, Heidelberg (2012)
17. Lopez-Herrejon, R.E., Batory, D., Cook, W.: Evaluating support for features in advanced modularization technologies. In: Gao, X.-X. (ed.) ECOOP 2005. LNCS, vol. 3586, pp. 169–194. Springer, Heidelberg (2005)
18. Schaefer, I.: Proceedings of VaMoS 2010. In: International Workshop on Variability Modelling of Software-intensive Systems (2010)
19. Schaefer, I., Bettini, L., Bono, V., Damiani, F., Tanzarella, N.: Delta-oriented programming of software product lines. In: Bosch, J., Lee, J. (eds.) SPLC 2010. LNCS, vol. 6287, pp. 77–91. Springer, Heidelberg (2010)
20. Schaefer, I., Damiani, F.: Pure delta-oriented programming. In: 2010 Proceedings of FOSD, pp. 49–56. ACM (2010)
21. Strniša, R., Sewell, P., Parkinson, M.: The Java module system: core design and semantic definition. In: 2007 Proceedings of OOPSLA, pp. 499–514. ACM (2007)
22. Thaker, S., Batory, D., Kitchin, D., Cook, W.: Safe composition of product lines. In: Proceedings of GPCE 2007, pp. 95–104. ACM (2007)
23. Thüm, T., Apel, S., Kästner, C., Schaefer, I., Saake, G.: A classification and survey of analysis strategies for software product lines. ACM Comput. Surv. **47**(1), 6:1–6:45 (2014)

Modelling and Verifying a Priority Scheduler for an SCJ Runtime Environment

Leo Freitas[1]([⊠]), James Baxter[2], Ana Cavalcanti[2], and Andy Wellings[2]

[1] Newcastle University, Newcastle upon Tyne, UK
leo.freitas@ncl.ac.uk
[2] University of York, Heslington, UK
jeb531@york.ac.uk

Abstract. Safety-Critical Java (SCJ) is a version of Java suitable for programming real-time safety-critical systems; it is the result of an international standardisation effort to define a subset of the Real-Time Specification for Java (RTSJ). SCJ programs require the use of specialised virtual machines. We present here the result of our verification of the scheduler of the only SCJ virtual machine up to date with the standard and publicly available, the icecap HVM. We describe our approach for analysis of (SCJ) virtual machines, and illustrate it using the icecap HVM scheduler. Our work is based on a state-rich process algebra that combines Z and CSP, and we take advantage of well established tools.

Keywords: Java · SCJ · *Circus* · Process algebra · FDR

1 Introduction

There has been an international effort to make Java and its Runtime Environment (RTE) suitable for safety-critical systems. All proposed extensions to Java have an associated Java Specification Request (JSR), a Reference Implementation (RI) and a Technology Compatibility Kit (TCK). The Safety-Critical Java (SCJ) specification (JSR 302) is an Open Group Standard [20], based on a subset of the Real-Time Specification for Java (RTSJ) [35]. It defines Java services designed for applications requiring certification. It replaces Java's memory model with support for memory regions [34], and its execution model is based on missions and event handlers with a predictable scheduler.

The goal of an RI is to demonstrate the feasibility of implementing a proposed JSR and to illustrate its impact on the standard Java RTE. The RI for JSR 302 consists of the addition of the `javax.safetycritical` package and a modified JVM. Together these make up the SCJ RTE.

The TCK is a suite of test programs that check that an implementation conforms to a JSR. The SCJ TCK, when available, will provide a degree of confidence in the correctness of an SCJ RTE. It is unlikely, however, that this will be adequate for systems with the highest certification level. For SCJ to become a viable technology, certified runtime environments must become available.

© The Author(s) 2016
E. Ábrahám and M. Huisman (Eds.): IFM 2016, LNCS 9681, pp. 63–78, 2016.
DOI: 10.1007/978-3-319-33693-0_5

The constraints embedded in the SCJ design makes programs amenable to formal analysis. Schedulability analysis techniques [3] can be used to provide evidence that programs meet their deadlines. Ongoing effort to support development, validation, and verification of SCJ programs has already produced results [6,7,16,24,33]. The work presented here uses formal methods to increase confidence and provide evidence that an SCJ RTE satisfies its requirements.

SCJ programs cannot run on a standard JVM; they require specialised support for memory regions and preemptive priority-based scheduling. The SCJ RI is under development and will be based on JamaicaVM [18]. To our knowledge, there are currently five SCJVM (virtual machines that support SCJ): Fiji VM [28], icecap HVM (Hardware near Virtual Machine) [32], Ovm (Open Virtual Machine) [1], HVM$_{TP}$ [21] and PERC Pico [2,29]. Of these, Fiji VM and Ovm are not specific for SCJ, PERC Pico does not conform to the current version of SCJ, and HVM$_{TP}$ is based on the icecap HVM.

As far as we know, the only SCJVM that is up to date with the SCJ standard and publicly available is the icecap HVM. Here, we consider the verification of its single-processor scheduler, a core component of an SCJVM. We present a formal model, and establish some of its properties by model checking and theorem proving. This is part of a larger effort to produce a completely verified SCJ RTE. We also present the general approach to construct and analyse formal models of an SCJVM that we use in the verification of the icecap HVM scheduler.

An identification of requirements for an SCJVM and an associated formal model are presented in [4]. The modelling uses *Circus* [26], a state-rich process algebra that combines Z and CSP. *Circus* is a notation for refinement and can be used to compare the requirements in [4] with models of implementation.

In our work, we use *Circus* processes to specify components of the icecap tools and their integration. *Circus* has an extension to deal with object-orientation [5]; it is helpful here, since the icecap tools are implemented in Java. We pursue a close match to the implementation structure to provide accurate low-level *Circus* models. In our approach, the *Circus* processes define the boundaries of each component of an SCJVM implementation, and their dependencies. Due to the compositionality of refinement, we can analyse these components in isolation. We tackle here a central component of an SCJVM, the scheduler, and identify the assumptions it makes about management of SCJ processes.

In summary, our contributions in this paper are a modelling and analysis technique tailored for an SCJVM, and its application to the scheduler of the only up to date SCJVM publicly available. The discussion of the technique summarises the lessons we have learned in carrying out this case study. In addition, the *Circus* model itself is of interest for documentation of the icecap tools and for fostering reuse of the icecap scheduler in the implementation of other SCJVMs.

Next, we present background material for our work: SCJ and the icecap tools, and *Circus*. Section 3 describes our modelling approach. Sections 4 and 5 present our scheduler model and its analysis. We consider related work in Sect. 6, and conclude in Sect. 7 considering also future work.

2   Preliminaries

We present SCJ and the icecap tools in Sect. 2.1, and *Circus* in Sect. 2.2.

2.1   SCJ and the Icecap Tools

SCJ places restrictions on the features of Java that can be used, and defines different scheduling and memory models. SCJ has three compliance levels of increasing complexity; the icecap tools support all levels.

An SCJ program is structured as a series of missions, executed sequentially in an order determined by a program-supplied mission sequencer. Each mission manages various schedulable objects: asynchronous event handlers (at levels 0 and 1), and real-time threads and nested mission sequencers (at level 2). A mission execution goes through several phases shown in Fig. 1. First, each of the schedulable objects and any data that may be required for the duration of the mission are initialised. Afterwards, the mission runs until requested to terminate, and then each of the schedulable objects are terminated, any required cleanup is performed, and the mission sequencer runs the next mission.

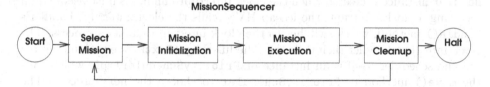

Fig. 1. A diagram showing the phases of mission execution

Asynchronous event handlers can be released periodically at set intervals or aperiodically in response to software requests. Schedulable objects are managed by a priority-based preemptive scheduler. Priority ceiling emulation, whereby a thread has its priority elevated upon taking a lock, prevents problems arising from priority inversion in locking [35]. Support for multiprocessor systems allows schedulable objects to be associated with allocation domains that define the processors in which they are allowed to run.

The icecap tools target embedded systems and precompiles Java bytecode to C, in addition to supplying a lightweight bytecode interpreter. The running of SCJ programs is supported by an implementation of the SCJ API, tightly coupled to the SCJVM. The API implementation and the code that supports it are written in Java, with only the most low-level components written in C and assembly. In the scheduler, only the task of process switching is written in C and assembly, with the code to determine which process should run written in Java.

The structure of the scheduler implementation is shown in Fig. 2. The scheduler is triggered by the clock interrupt handler, a singleton instance of Clock-InterruptHandler, which implements the interfaces InterruptHandler and

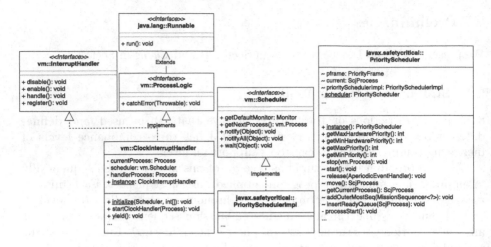

Fig. 2. UML class diagram showing the classes that make up the icecap HVM scheduler

Runnable. A process executing the `run()` method of the `ClockInterrupt-Handler` instance is created when the clock interrupt handler is initialised. Upon receiving a clock interrupt, the icecap HVM calls the clock interrupt handler's `handle()` method, which switches to the clock interrupt handler's process. The clock interrupt handler then calls the scheduler's `getNextProcess()` method.

The scheduler itself is an instance of `PrioritySchedulerImpl`, which calls the `move()` method of `PriorityScheduler` to choose the next process. The `move()` method wakes any sleeping processes that have passed their wake-up time and pops the next process from a priority queue of processes that are ready to run. The work of switching to the new process is then performed via a native method call to the low-level virtual machine (written in C, rather than Java).

In Sect. 4, we present a model of this scheduler: a network of *Circus* processes interacting with the SCJ API implementation and the operating system.

2.2   Circus

Circus [26] is a formal notation that combines the style for data modelling of the Z [36] notation with that for process specification of CSP [17,30]. Like a CSP model, a *Circus* specification defines processes that communicate over channels, but that, unlike CSP processes, may contain internal state defined in Z. The internal state is encapsulated so that it can only be updated and accessed via communication on the channels of the process.

A *Circus* process is defined as a series of Z paragraphs and *Circus* actions, which are written using a combination of CSP constructs and Z operations. The process definition ends with a main action that defines the behaviour of the process using the actions defined previously in the process. Most CSP operators can be used in *Circus* actions, including external and internal choice, parallel

Table 1. A summary of the *Circus* notation used in this paper

Operator	*Circus* Symbol
Prefixing of signal on channel c to action A	$c \longrightarrow A$
Prefixing of input on c of value x to A	$c?x \longrightarrow A$
Prefixing of output on c of value of expression e to A	$c!e \longrightarrow A$
Guarding of A with predicate g	$g \ \& \ A$
Termination	**Skip**
External choice of actions A and B	$A \ \square \ B$
Sequential composition of A and B	$A \ ; \ B$
Interrupt of A by B	$A \ \triangle \ B$
Parallel composition A and B synchronising on the intersection of channel sets $cs1$ and $cs2$	$A \ _{cs1}\|_{cs2} \ B$
Parallel interleaving of A and B	$A \ \|\|\| \ B$
Hiding of channel set cs in A	$A \setminus cs$

composition, sequential composition, and the interrupt operator. Additionally, *Circus* includes assignment, if statements, loops, and variable declarations, as well as permitting the use of Z schema data operations in *Circus* actions. Processes can also be combined using CSP operators: parallelism, hiding, and so on.

Circus has several extension, to cater for time, mobility, synchronicity and so on. Here, we use classes, included the object-oriented extension *OhCircus* [5].

A detailed account of *Circus* can be found in [26]. Examples are presented in Sect. 4. Table 1 summarises the action notation that we use here.

3 Verification Approach

In this section, we present our approach to verification of an SCJVM. This arises from previous experiences on modelling and verification of large existing systems [9–11]. It is, however, tailored for the needs of a VM and of an SCJVM, in particular. In this respect, this is our distillation of the lessons learned in applying *Circus* to reason about the icecap HVM and its scheduler. The application of the approach presented here to the scheduler is the subject of the next section.

Our technique, first of all, creates a model for a piece of code implementing a VM or a component of a VM, like a scheduler, written in any imperative or object-oriented language. Having identified the modules or classes that implement the component, our **approach to modelling** is in three phases: (a) data, (b) control-flow, and (c) integration modelling. These are described below.

a. Define a Z Data Model.i In this phase, we formalise the data types used in the program, via the four steps below. The data types may be in the program in one of three forms: types available in the programming language, types available via a library, like the collection API of Java, or just as pieces of data not necessarily identified as a data type in the program. For the latter, identification of data types in the model is a matter of convenience for verification.

1. *Define the state to capture the variables used in the program, creating appropriate datatypes where necessary.*
2. *Capture invariants that are expected.* These are properties of the data model we expect the program to satisfy, even if not explicitly checked (but see b.4).
3. *Define the procedures (methods, functions, and so on) of the program that manipulate the data types defined above.*
4. *Identify their error cases and totalise the data operations.* We use theorem proving to reveal the preconditions of the operations, and extend the model to totalise those whose precondition are not just true.

   By modelling errors to totalise the operations, we achieve a better understanding of the data types of the program. Its precise behaviour, which may not include checking error conditions, is captured in the next phase.

The model may be seen as a suggestion for improving the code structure (like error checking). Information from the environment of the component may also need to be identified as a type whose values are communicated in channels.

b. Capture the Control Flows Through the VM. Using the Z model, we construct a *Circus* model following the steps below. Roughly, each module (that is, a class, in the case of a Java program) is modelled by a *Circus* process or class, and its procedures by actions and methods in *Circus*.

1. *Define channels corresponding to the services of the component.* For each provided or internal service, we define a pair of channels to model calls and returns of invocations. For each required external service, we have a single channel, because we do not model its behaviour.
2. *Use processes and classes to capture the modular structure of the program.* A Java class should be modelled by an *OhCircus* class, if it includes only passive methods, that is, methods that can be modelled using only data operations without the use of channel communications, and by a process, otherwise.
3. *Define the actions for the services corresponding to the channels above.* In this step, we use the data operations defined in the previous phase, and capture the control flows in the definition of each action.
4. *Eliminate the error cases in the Z data operations that are not handled in the code, transforming the remaining cases to guards in order to enable identification of mistakes in use of data operations via deadlock checks.* In this way, we ensure that the model is not more robust than the code, and any invalid assumptions about the use of the data can be revealed by analysis.
5. *Define in the main action how the services are to be provided.* In principle, all actions could be combined in an external choice, so that their services are available for use one at a time. A call graph, however, may identify services that are needed in parallel because they are part of different lines of execution.

c. Generate a Circus model of the component. We use the processes defined in phase **(b)** to produce a model of the component as a network of processes.

1. *Introduce processes to reflect the parallel design (if any) of the code.*
2. *Combine the various processes to define the component.*

In this phase, we need to make the case that the model is closely related to the program. The argument should explain how the program modules are reflected in the structure of the Z data model and of processes in the network of phase **(b)**. We need to explain how the model can be refined back to the code, and that needs to be relatively simple. For Java programs, a strong argument includes a class diagram and a mapping from the *Circus* processes to that diagram.

A truly faithful model defines the modelled procedures of the program as actions in *Circus* using programming constructs (assignments, loops, and so on) just like in the code. For reasoning, however, it is convenient to use a predicative specification of the procedures in Z. This is the reason for the abstraction in phase **(a)**, followed by the argument constructed here. As a consequence, we catch integration problems via formal analysis, but not necessarily programming errors. The modelling effort, however, may well reveal programming errors in phases **(a)** and **(b.4–5)**. In our case study, we found missing error checks.

With a model produced as described above, we open the possibility of the use of a multitude of **analysis techniques**. We distinguish the following possibilities as particularly useful in the case of SCJVM analysis.

1. *Prove that the Circus model is deadlock free*
2. *Use refinement to prove more general properties.*

For the icecap case study, we carry out proof of properties of the Z data model using Z/Eves [25], and translate the *Circus* model to CSP to use the FDR3 model checker [14]. In the translation, we lose the expressiveness of Z, but gain the ability to use automatic analysis of the process network.

More details about our approach to modelling and analysis are in [12].

4   Formal Model Overview

We next give an overview of our model of the icecap HVM scheduler. The complete model can be found in [12, Ch. 5]; its components are shown in Fig. 3. There is a *Circus* process for each Java class in Fig. 2. The environment includes the low-level virtual machine written in C, the operating system, and other components of the SCJVM, including the SCJ API. These components communicate with the scheduler to initialise it and to obtain information. *PrioScheduler*, corresponding to the **PriorityScheduler** class, receives requests to move and stop SCJVM processes from *PrioSchedulerImpl*. It also communicates with the *ClockInterruptHandler* to enable and disable interrupts, and to register and start the clock handler. *ClockInterruptHandler* communicates with *PrioSchedulerImpl* to obtain the next SCJVM process to run. *PrioSchedulerImpl* is a bridge between *ClockInterruptHandler* and *PrioScheduler*, using services of *PrioScheduler* to

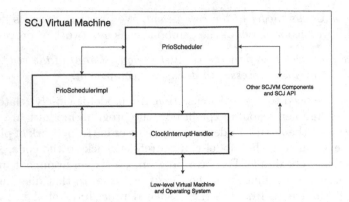

Fig. 3. SCJ VM components

determine the next process. *ClockInterruptHandler* also sends requests to transfer between processes to the low-level virtual machine.

Next, we describe how our model is obtained using the approach in the previous section. In phase **(a)**, we define a Z data model. The most interesting types come from the class `PriorityScheduler`. Its state **(a.1)** has four parts: (i) the current time, the identifier of a `ClockInterruptHandler`, and a reference to an unique instance of `PriorityScheduler` itself ; (ii) the references to the processes managed by the scheduler; (iii) the scheduling queues containing the processes that are ready, sleeping/blocked, locked/waiting, and so on; and (iv) the SCJ event handlers managed by the scheduler. The managed processes are identified by unique elements of a set *PID* of identifiers used by the operating system.

The managed event handlers are modelled by the schema *HandlerSet*. It contains *PID* sets representing the different categories of handlers: periodic (*peh*), aperiodic (*aeh*), and one shot (*oseh*), as well as sets of allocated (*meh*) and free (*freeHS*) handlers. It also includes a dummy identifier *idle*, used to avoid management of empty queues: it is queued, when the ready queue is emptied.

$$
\begin{array}{l}
\rule{4cm}{0.4pt}\ HandlerSet \rule{7cm}{0.4pt} \\
\quad peh, aeh, oseh, meh, freeHS : \mathbb{P}\ PID \\
\quad idle : PID \\
\rule{13cm}{0.4pt} \\
\quad idle \in peh \wedge \langle peh, aeh, oseh \rangle\ \text{partition}\ meh \\
\quad \langle meh, freeHS \rangle\ \text{partition}\ PID
\end{array}
$$

The state invariant **(a.2)** establishes that the *idle* process is a periodic event handler, and that the allocated managed event handlers partition the different categories. Similarly, all values in *PID* correspond to managed processes: the allocated (*meh*) and free (*freeHS*) identifiers partition *PID*.

The methods corresponding to *HandlerSet* operations are captured as Z operations **(a.3)**. They are simple and involve adding and removing various handlers from the corresponding sets, for example. Proving that the state invariant is preserved by these operations shows whether or not they are feasible. This is part of the totalisation process (a.4) that identifies error conditions to be dealt with. For example, there are operations in the scheduler that take a handler as input. There is, however, no check in the code that the input is a handler managed by the scheduler. This is an example of where we have uncovered possible issues, or hidden assumptions, of the code through modelling and proof.

In phase (b), the SCJVM-specific control-flow is captured using *Circus* processes. We cater for the scheduling-specific features. For illustration, we describe below the *Circus* basic process representing the `PriorityScheduler` class.

To identify the services (b.1), we perform a call-graph analysis of the non-private methods and create corresponding channels. As shown in Fig. 3, the scheduler interacts with the SCJ API and the operating system. A path in the call graph involving the public method `transfer` is as follows. Although `transfer` is a method of `Process`, because we model `Process` as a data type, conceptually, we regard `transfer` as a method of `ClockInterruptHandler`.

```
ClockInterruptHandler.run, PrioritySchedulerImpl.getNextProcess,
ClockInterruptHandler.disable, PriorityScheduler.move,
PriorityScheduler.stop, ClockInterruptHandler.transfer
```

The path above is part of a line of execution (and is public). So, we have a channel *transfer* corresponding to uses of this service. The types of the channels depend on the associated method's parameter and return types.

We follow a naming convention to identify what method call and return we are capturing. For instance, the channel *KPSreleaseCall* represents the package (K) method of the `PriorityScheduler` class (PS) named *release* that is being called. Public methods follow a similar naming, and private methods are represented with subsidiary actions, so there are no channels associated with them.

As already mentioned, for each class of the scheduler, we define a process (b.2). In defining actions (b.3), we also take advantage of the call graph. As an example, we present below the action for the `release` method.

$$Release \mathrel{\widehat{=}} KPSreleaseCall?\,apeh \longrightarrow$$
$$PCIHdisableCall \longrightarrow PCIHdisableRet \longrightarrow$$
$$(\textbf{pre}\ ReleaseHandler\ \&\ ReleaseHandler);$$
$$PCIHenableCall \longrightarrow PCIHenableRet \longrightarrow$$
$$KPSreleaseRet \longrightarrow \textbf{Skip}$$

It is triggered by a call via *KPSreleaseCall*, and concludes with a synchronisation on *KPSreleaseRet*. Its body contains a call to `disable` followed by a data operation *ReleaseHandler* of *HandlerSet* and by a call to `enable`. The precondition pre *ReleaseHandler* of *ReleaseHandler* is used as a guard (b.4); the input *apeh* is used in *ReleaseHandler* and its guard pre *ReleaseHandler*.

Another example is the action *SCJStop* corresponding to the method `Stop`. It takes an input *curr*, with the guard $curr \neq nullpid$, which corresponds to the precondition of the method.

$$SCJStop \; \widehat{=} \; KPSstopCall?\,curr : (curr \neq nullpid) \longrightarrow$$
$$PVMtransfer!\,curr!\,mainProcess \longrightarrow$$
$$KPSstopRet \longrightarrow \mathbf{Skip}$$

The input $curr$ is passed on, along with the state component $mainProcess$ corresponding to an inherited field of the class $\texttt{PriorityScheduler}$, to the lower-level virtual machine using a channel $PVMtransfer$.

To conclude phase (b), we identify the services of the API that are provided in choice and in interleaving (b.5). Following the structured indicated in Fig. 3, we define that the $\texttt{PriorityScheduler}$ API has three separate groups, which we name $SCJApi$, $SCJRTE$, and $CIHApi$, containing services provided to the SCJ infrastructure, the runtime environment and the $\texttt{ClockInterruptHandler}$. The three groups of services are combined in interleaving, with each of its constituent services in external choice. Thje choice is external, since it provides to the environment of the $PriorityScheduler$ (see Fig. 3) the choice of which service to execute. The interleaving defines an action Run.

$$CIHApi \; \widehat{=} \; Move \; \Box \; SCJStop$$
$$SCJRTE \; \widehat{=} \; Start \; \Box \; Release \; \Box \; AddOuterMostSeq \cdots$$
$$SCJApi \; \widehat{=} \; GetHWPrio \; \Box \; GetPrio$$
$$Run \; \widehat{=} \; SCJApi \; ||| \; SCJRTE \; ||| \; CIHApi$$

In the main action of $PriorityScheduler$, which is distinguished below by a preceding • symbol, after an initialisation using an action $Init$, another action $Execute$ uses Run to provide the services of the scheduler.

$$Catch \; \widehat{=} \; PCIHcatchError?\,e \longrightarrow \mathbf{Skip}$$
$$Execute \; \widehat{=} \; Run \; \triangle \; Catch$$
$$\bullet \; Init \; ; \; Execute$$

Low-level (VM) exceptions might interrupt the control flow. These exceptions may occur as a result of user-code runtime exceptions, VM-generated exceptions from environmental assumption violations (like out of memory), or residual design errors. They are indicated via a channel $PCIHcatchError$ as defined in the action $Catch$, used in $Execute$ to define the possible interruption of Run.

Finally, in phase (c) we define the $Circus$ processes network linking together all processes representing classes from Fig. 2; it is as follows.

$$\mathbf{process}\; IcecapVM \; \widehat{=} \; \left(\begin{array}{l} ClockInterruptHandler\ CihPsInterface \\ || \\ PrioScheduler\ PSIInterface \\ || \\ PrioSchedulerImpl\ ScjPInterface \\ || \\ ScjProcess\ ScjInterface \end{array} \right) \setminus csSCJRTE$$

Channel sets *CihPsInterface*, *PSIInterface*, *ScjPInterface*, and *ScjInterface* are defined to include all channels used in each process. A final set containing the internal channels identified in **(b.1)** is used in a hiding: *csSCJRTE* above.

5   Evaluation

The icecap classes `PrioScheduler` and `ClockInterruptHandler` are modelled as processes. For other infrastructure classes, like `PriorityFrame`, for example, only a data model is provided, because their provided services are support operations over such data, rather than active lines of execution or SCJ provided services.

The icecap Java code associated with the component in Figs. 2 and 3 amounts to about 1600 lines of code. Following the modelling technique in Sect. 3, and illustrated in Sect. 4, we obtain a *Circus* model presented in its entirety in [12]. There, we also find Z/Eves proofs of the totalisation of various Z schema operations, as well as a CSP version of the *Circus* model used for refinement and deadlock freedom checks. Table 2 provides a summary of numbers of definitions and proofs, to provide an overall total of 755. The nature of the actual proofs using Z/Eves and FDR3 is discussed in the sequel.

Table 2. Summary of all *Circus* declarations.

Z Declarations	Total	*Circus* Declarations	Total
Unboxed items	84	Channel declarations	51
Axiomatic definitions	28	Channel set declarations	13
Generic axiomatic definitions	2	Process declarations	12
Schemas	77	Actions	83
Generic schemas	1		
Theorems	202		
Proofs	202		

5.1   Z/Eves Proofs

We have used the CZT tools [23][1] to develop the *Circus* model. These tools include *Circus* as an extension of Z within its Eclipse interface. CZT also integrates the Z/Eves theorem prover [31] and its proof language as an extension.

Within CZT, we have typeset (in LaTeX), typechecked and proved well-formedness conditions of the whole model. This involves theorems about functions being applied within their domain, axiomatic definitions soundness, type non-emptiness, and so on. These proofs ensure that the model is consistent.

---

[1] See also http://czt.sourceforge.net.

The CZT tools also have a verification-condition generator for Z and *Circus*. These include well-formedness checks (for instance, functions are called within their domains), and other consistency checks like feasibility of Z schema operations and race-freedom of *Circus* parallel actions. We have performed mechanised proofs in Z/Eves of each of these generated verification conditions.

Of greater interest are the (21) precondition proofs: they are directly related to the totalisation of operations as described by our approach (**a.4**). It is useful to discover the various conditions to feature in the *Circus* model as guards for communications. As explained, this introduces deadlocks whenever they are not satisfied. Other proofs are for well-formedness (12) and various lemmas (169) about involved types to make the precondition proofs viable.

5.2 FDR Refinement Checks

The *Circus* model is translated to CSP for automatic analysis using FDR3 [14]: a powerful refinement checker for CSP enabling automatic checking for deadlock and livelock freedom, as well as other properties of interest.

The translation strategy from *Circus* to CSP is beyond the scope of this paper; details about it can be found in [27]. It involves representing the Z data model within FDR's rich functional language, whereas the *Circus* CSP constructs are almost in one-to-one correspondence with those of CSP-M. Access to process state is done via channel communication and appropriate parallelism with its corresponding process main action representation in CSP.

Details about this translation for the icecap HVM scheduler model can be found in [12]. Key decisions about data abstraction and simplification of type domains are necessary to avoid state explosion. Even so, FDR can handle quite complex processes and enabled us to perform important consistency checks.

We have checked for deadlock and livelock freedom the processes related to components in Figs. 2 and 3. As expected, deadlock counterexamples occur on either events external to the components, for example, required services from the operating system, or failed precondition proofs modelled as CSP guards. The required services are for handling exceptions thrown by design or at runtime. The guards highlight hidden assumptions the icecap HVM scheduler code makes. For instance, the priority scheduler implicitly expects all processes to be known to the scheduler, and yet we can call the scheduler with "rogue" processes.

The CSP model has 540 lines excluding comments, and contains 4 top-level processes with a total of around 100 implicitly declared processes through `let` expressions. We use such expressions to encode *Circus* actions as well as state. We are still working on the process network to deal with complex state invariants, and prove more specific properties of a scheduler and of SCJ.

6 Related Work

There are other works on verification of real-time schedulers. Ferreira et al. [8] have worked on formal verification of the FreeRTOS scheduler using HIP/SLEEK.

They use separation logic to verify memory safety as the FreeRTOS scheduler uses a lot of pointers, which make the use of more traditional formal verification techniques difficult. In our work, memory safety is partially guaranteed by Java's memory model and our challenges arise instead from the complex control flow of the icecap HVM scheduler. On the other hand, it has to be shown that icecap tools generate C code that is memory safe. This is a separate problem of compiler correctness, which is part of our agenda for future work.

A comprehensive verification of the seL4 microkernel is reported in [19]. This includes verification of the scheduler and other areas of the kernel, and a proof that the binary code of the kernel correctly implements the C source code. The verification of the functional properties of the system is machine-checked using a C semantics in Isabelle/HOL. While we focus on the icecap HVM scheduler, we expect that the icecap tools can be completely verified in the future.

For larger kernels, a major challenge in verification is the complex interdependency between the scheduler and the rest of the kernel. Gotsman and Yang [15] have developed an approach for verifying such kernels modularly using separation logic. It is also relevant to embedded systems where size and speed constraints necessitate tight coupling between operating system components. Indeed, Klein et al. [19] note that the call graph of seL4 shows high levels of interdependency between components. Gotsman and Yang demonstrate their approach by verifying a scheduler based on the Linux 2.6.11 scheduler.

We face similar challenges as the icecap tools also target embedded systems, leading to tight coupling between components, but, as said before, our challenges concern the communication between components rather than sharing of pointers. We tackle our challenges by identifying the components and specifying their interfaces. We define them as *Circus* processes and specify their interaction via parallel networks. Compositional reasoning and refinement can then be used.

The work of Ludwich and Fröhlich [22] verifies a system-level model of a scheduler by annotating its functions with preconditions and postconditions. These annotations constitute a formal specification that the scheduler must fulfil, which is checked using the C/C++ model checker CMBC. This work is perhaps most similar to ours due to its use of preconditions and postconditions, but our approach involves constructing a formal model from the code rather than presenting the requirements as annotations to the code.

Finally, the great value of applying formal methods in the area of scheduling is shown in [13], which reports a verification of the GCC scheduler using a model in Isabelle/HOL. This effort has uncovered a bug in the GCC Itanium scheduler that caused programs to be compiled incorrectly.

7 Conclusion

For SCJ to become a viable technology for use in safety-critical systems, certified runtime environments are essential. The most advanced implementation of an SCJ RTE is provided by the icecap tools. The implementation is complex. A formal model is a major step in the development of a verified RTE for SCJ.

Developing a formal model of existing software is a major challenge. This is made more difficult with the SCJ RTE as we have to model both high and low-level abstractions. We have presented an approach that produces a *Circus* model for Java and C source code. Automatic construction of models is not possible, but support can be made available for encoding Java types in Z, calculation of preconditions of data operations, and extraction of call graphs, for instance.

Our experience with the icecap tools implementation has been largely positive. Although the code can be hard to fathom in places, we have found just a few bugs, mainly as the result of studying the code in sufficient depth to produce the model. There are also places where there appears to be unreachable code and where more defensive programming techniques can be employed to catch errors that can be introduced during development and maintenance.

Our experience with *Circus* has also been largely positive. The lack of process inheritance in *Circus*, however, has hindered some of our efforts. For example, for the `ScjProcess` class representing the abstraction for a low-level `vm.Process` within the SCJ paradigm, we need the `gotoNextState` method, which is redefined in subclasses of `ScjProcess` that represent periodic and aperiodic handlers and so on. Since we do not have process inheritance in *Circus*, in our model we have a single process *ScjProcess*, in which the action corresponding to `gotoNextState` uses a conditional to model the dynamic binding.

Our future work includes: (1) more analysis of the scheduler, for example, to show it always dispatches the highest priority SCJ event handler; (2) improvement to the code to take into account our results; (3) the analysis of other components of the icecap tools RTE, in particular the memory management module; and (4) extensions of *Circus* with process inheritance.

Acknowledgements. The authors gratefully acknowledge useful feedback from anonymous referees, and Stephan Erbs Korsholm and Shuai Zhao for their help in understanding the icecap HVM and its rationale. This work is supported by EPSRC Grant EP/H017461/1. No new primary data were created in this study.

References

1. Armbruster, A., et al.: A real-time Java virtual machine with applications in avionics. ACM TECS **7**(1), 5:1–5:49 (2007)
2. Atego: Atego PERC Pico - Products - Atego (2015). www.atego.com/products/atego-perc-pico/
3. Audsley, N., Burns, A., Richardson, M., Tindell, K., Wellings, A.J.: Applying new scheduling theory to static priority pre-emptive scheduling. Softw. Eng. J. **8**(5), 284–292 (1993)
4. Baxter, J.: Requirements for Safety-Critical Java Virtual Machines. Technical report, University of York (2015). http://www.cs.york.ac.uk/circus/publications/techreports/reports/scjvm-requirements.pdf
5. Cavalcanti, A.L.C., Sampaio, A.C.A., Woodcock, J.C.P.: Unifying classes and processes. SoSyM **4**(3), 277–296 (2005)
6. Cavalcanti, A.L.C., Zeyda, F., Wellings, A., Woodcock, J.C.P., Wei, K.: Safety-critical Java programs from Circus models. RTS **49**(5), 614–667 (2013)
7. Dalsgaard, A.E., Hansen, R.R., Schoeberl, M.: Private memory allocation analysis for safety-critical Java. In: JTRES, pp. 9–17. ACM (2012)
8. Ferreira, J., et al.: Automated verification of the FreeRTOS scheduler in Hip/Sleek. STTT **16**(4), 381–397 (2014)
9. Freitas, L., McDermott, J.P.: Formal methods for security in the Xenon hypervisor. STTT **13**(5), 463–489 (2011)
10. Freitas, L., Woodcock, J.C.P.: Mechanising mondex with Z/Eves. FACJ **20**(1), 117–139 (2008)
11. Freitas, L., Woodcock, J.C.P., Fu, Z.: POSIX file store in Z/Eves: an experiment in the verified software repository. SCP **74**(4), 238–257 (2009)
12. Freitas, L., Cavalcanti, A., Wellings, A.: Formal specification of SCJ icecap-implementation. Technical report, Newcastle University (2015). https://www.cs.york.ac.uk/circus/publications/techreports/reports/hvm.pdf
13. Gesellensetter, L., Glesner, S., Salecker, E.: Formal verification with Isabelle/HOL in practice: finding a bug in the GCC scheduler. In: Leue, S., Merino, P. (eds.) FMICS 2007. LNCS, vol. 4916, pp. 85–100. Springer, Heidelberg (2008)
14. Gibson-Robinson, T., Armstrong, P., Boulgakov, A., Roscoe, A.W.: FDR3 — a modern refinement checker for CSP. In: Ábrahám, E., Havelund, K. (eds.) TACAS 2014 (ETAPS). LNCS, vol. 8413, pp. 187–201. Springer, Heidelberg (2014)
15. Gotsman, A., Yang, H.: Modular verification of preemptive OS kernels. JFP **23**, 452–514 (2013)
16. Haddad, G., Hussain, F., Leavens, G.T.: The design of SafeJML, a specification language for SCJ with support for WCET specification. In: JTRES. ACM (2010)
17. Hoare, C.A.R.: Communicating Sequential Processes. Prentice-Hall, Upper Saddle River (1985)
18. aicas realtime.: JamaicaVM User Manual (2014). www.aicas.com/cms/en/reference-material
19. Klein, G., et al.: Comprehensive formal verification of an OS microkernel. ACM TCS **32**(1), 2:1–2:70 (2014)
20. Locke, D., Andersen, B.S., Brosgol, B., Fulton, M., Henties, T., Hunt, J.J., Nielsen, J.O., Nilsen, K., Schoeberl, M., Tokar, J., Vitek, J., Wellings, A.: Safety Critical Java Specification. The Open Group, UK (2010)
21. Luckowe, K.S., Thomsen, B., Korsholm, S.E.: HVMTP: a time predictable and portable java virtual machine for hard real-time embedded systems. In: JTRES, pp. 107–116. ACM (2014)

22. Ludwich, M.K., Frohlich, A.A.: System-level verification of embedded operating systems components. In: SBESC, pp. 161–165, November 2012
23. Malik, P., Utting, M.: CZT: a framework for Z tools. In: Treharne, H., King, S., C. Henson, M., Schneider, S. (eds.) ZB 2005. LNCS, vol. 3455, pp. 65–84. Springer, Heidelberg (2005)
24. Marriott, C., Cavalcanti, A.: SCJ: memory-safety checking without annotations. In: Jones, C., Pihlajasaari, P., Sun, J. (eds.) FM 2014. LNCS, vol. 8442, pp. 465–480. Springer, Heidelberg (2014)
25. Meisels, I.: Software Manual for Windows Z/EVES Version 2.1. ORA Canada, tR-97-5505-04g (2000)
26. Oliveira, M.V.M., Cavalcanti, A.L.C., Woodcock, J.C.P.: A UTP semantics for Circus. FACJ 21(1–2), 3–32 (2009)
27. Oliveira, M., Sampaio, A.: Compositional analysis and design of CML models. Technical report D24.1, COMPASS, March 2013. www.compass-research.eu/Project/Deliverables/D241.pdf
28. Pizlo, F., Ziarek, L., Vitek, J.: Real time Java on resource-constrained platforms with Fiji VM. In: JTRES, pp. 110–119. ACM (2009)
29. Richard-Foy, M., et al.: Use of PERC Pico for safety critical Java. In: ERTS (2010)
30. Roscoe, A.W.: Understanding Concurrent Systems. Texts in Computer Science. Springer, London (2011)
31. Saaltink, M.: Z/Eves 2.0 user's guide. Technical report. TR-99-5493-06a, ORA Canada (1999)
32. Søndergaard, H., Korsholm, S.E., Ravn, A.P.: Safety-critical Java for low-end embedded platforms. In: JTRES, pp. 44–53. ACM (2012)
33. Tang, D., Plsek, A., Vitek, J.: Static Checking of Safety Critical Java Annotations. In: JTRES. ACM (2010)
34. Tofte, M., Talpin, J.P.: Region-based memory management. Inf. Comput. 132(2), 109–176 (1997)
35. Wellings, A.: Concurrent and Real-Time Programming in Java. Wiley, Hoboken (2004)
36. Woodcock, J.C.P., Davies, J.: Using Z-specification, refinement, and proof. Prentice-Hall, Upper Saddle River (1996)

Why Just Boogie?
Translating Between Intermediate Verification Languages

Michael Ameri[1] and Carlo A. Furia[2](✉)

[1] Chair of Software Engineering, Department of Computer Science,
ETH Zurich, Zurich, Switzerland
`mameri@student.ethz.ch`
[2] Department of Computer Science and Engineering,
Chalmers University of Technology, Gothenburg, Sweden
`furia@chalmers.se`

Abstract. The verification systems Boogie and Why3 use their respective intermediate languages to generate verification conditions from high-level programs. Since the two systems support different back-end provers (such as Z3 and Alt-Ergo) and are used to encode different high-level languages (such as C# and Java), being able to translate between their intermediate languages would provide a way to reuse one system's features to verify programs meant for the other. This paper describes a translation of Boogie into WhyML (Why3's intermediate language) that preserves semantics, verifiability, and program structure to a large degree. We implemented the translation as a tool and applied it to 194 Boogie-verified programs of various sources and sizes; Why3 verified 83 % of the translated programs with the same outcome as Boogie. These results indicate that the translation is often effective and practically applicable.

1 Introduction

Intermediate verification languages (IVLs) are intermediate representations used in verification technology. Just like compiler design has benefited from decoupling front-end and back-end, IVLs help write verifiers that are more modular: the front-end specializes in encoding the rich semantics of a high-level language (say, an object-oriented language such as C#) as a program in the IVL; the back-end generates verification conditions (VCs) from IVL programs in a form that caters to the peculiarities of a specific theorem prover (such as an SMT solver).

Boogie [3] and WhyML [6] are prime examples of popular IVLs with different, often complementary, features and supporting systems (respectively called Boogie and Why3). In this paper we describe a translation of Boogie programs into WhyML programs and its implementation as the tool b2w. As we illustrate with examples in Sect. 3, using b2w increases the versatility brought by IVLs: without having to design and implement a direct encoding into WhyML, users can take advantage of some of the best features of Why3 when working with high-level languages that translate to Boogie.

C.A. Furia—Work done mainly while affiliated with ETH Zurich.

© Springer International Publishing Switzerland 2016
E. Ábrahám and M. Huisman (Eds.): IFM 2016, LNCS 9681, pp. 79–95, 2016.
DOI: 10.1007/978-3-319-33693-0_6

Boogie vs. WhyML. While the roles of Boogie and WhyML as IVLs are similar, the two languages have different characteristics that reflect a focus on complementary challenges in automated verification. Boogie is the more popular language in terms of front-ends that use it as IVL, which makes a translation *from* Boogie more practically useful than one into it; it has a finely tuned integration with the Z3 prover that results from the two tools having been developed by the same group (Microsoft Research's RiSE); it combines a simple imperative language with an expressive typed logic, which is especially handy for encoding object-oriented or, more generally, heap-based imperative languages. In contrast, WhyML has a more flexible support for multiple back-end provers it translates to, including a variety of SMT solvers as well as interactive provers such as Coq; it can split VCs into independent goals and dispatch them to different provers; if offers limited imperative constructs within a functional language that belongs to the ML family, which brings the side benefit of being able to *execute* WhyML programs—a feature quite useful to debug and validate verification attempts.

Goals and Evaluation. The overall goal of this paper is devising a translation T from Boogie to WhyML programs. The translation, described in Sect. 4, should preserve correctness and verifiability as much as possible. Preserving correctness means that, given a Boogie program p, if its translation $T(p)$ is a correct WhyML program then p is correct (soundness); the converse should also hold as much as possible: if $T(p)$ is incorrect then p is too (precision). Preserving verifiability means that, given a Boogie program p that verifies in Boogie, its translation $T(p)$ is a WhyML program that verifies in Why3.

The differences, outlined above, between Boogie and WhyML and their supporting systems make achieving correctness and verifiability challenging. While we devised T to cover the entire Boogie language, its current implementation b2w does not fully support a limited number of features (branching, the most complex polymorphic features, and bitvectors) that make it hard to achieve verifiability in practice. In fact, while replacing branching (goto) with looping is always possible [9], a general translation scheme does not produce verifiable loops since one should also infer invariants (which are often cumbersome due to the transformation). Polymorphic maps are supported to the extent that their type parameters can be instantiated with concrete types; this is necessary since WhyML's parametric polymorphism cannot directly express all usages in Boogie, but it may also introduce a combinatorial explosion in the translation; hence, b2w fails on the most complex instances that would be unmanageable in Why3. Boogie's bitvector support is much more flexible than what provided by Why3's libraries; hence b2w may render the semantics of bitvector operations incorrectly.

These current implementation limitations notwithstanding (see Sect. 4 for details), we experimentally demonstrate that b2w is applicable and useful in practice. As Sect. 5 discusses, we applied b2w to 194 Boogie programs of different size and sources; most of the programs have not been written by us and exercise Boogie in a variety of different ways. For 83 % (161) of these programs, b2w produces a WhyML translation that Why3 can verify as well as Boogie can verify the original, thus showing the feasibility of automating translation between IVLs.

Tool Availability. For lack of space this paper omits some details that are available as a technical report [1]. The tool **b2w** is available as open source at: https://bitbucket.org/michael_ameri/b2w/

2   Related Work

Translations and Abstraction Levels. Translation is a ubiquitous technique in computer science; however, the most common translation schemes bridge *different abstraction levels*, typically encoding a program written in a high-level language (such as Java) into a lower-level representation which is suitable for execution (such as byte or machine code). Reverse-engineering goes the opposite direction—from lower to higher level—for example to extract modular and structural information from C programs and encode it using object-oriented constructs [19]. This paper describes a translation between intermediate languages—Boogie and Why3—which belong to *similar abstraction levels*. In the context of model transformations [15], so-called bidirectional transformations [18] also target lossless transformations between notations at the same level of abstraction.

Intermediate Verification Languages. The Spec# project [4] introduced Boogie to add flexibility to the translation between an object-oriented language and the verification conditions. Since its introduction for Spec#, Boogie has been adopted as intermediate verification language for numerous other front-ends such as Dafny [13], AutoProof [21], Viper [10], and Joogie [2]; its popularity demonstrates the advantages of using intermediate verification languages.

While Boogie retains some support for different back-end SMT solvers, Z3 remains its primary target. By contrast, supporting multiple, different back-ends is one of the main design goals behind the Why3 system [6] Why3 also fully supports interactive provers, which provide a powerful means of discharging the most complex verification conditions that defy complete automation.

In all, while the Boogie and WhyML languages belong to a similar abstraction level, they are part of systems with complementary features, which motivates this paper's idea of translating one language into the other.

Other intermediate languages for verification are Pilar [17], used in the Sireum framework for SPARK; Silver [10], an intermediate language with native support for permissions in the style of separation logic; and the flavor of dynamic logic for object-oriented languages [16] used in the KeY system. Another approach to generalizing and reusing different translations uses notions from model transformations to provide validated mappings for different high-level languages [5]. Future work may consider supporting some of these intermediate languages and approaches.

3   Motivating Examples

Verification technology has made great strides in the last decade or two, but a few dark corners remain where automated reasoning shows its practical limitations. Figure 1 provides three examples of simple Boogie programs that trigger incorrect or otherwise unsatisfactory behavior. We argue that translating these programs to WhyML makes it possible to verify them using a different, somewhat complementary verification tool; overall, confidence in the results of verification is improved.

Procedure not_verify in Fig. 1 has a contradictory postcondition (notice N < N, N is a nonnegative constant, and the loop immediately terminates). Nonetheless, recent versions of Boogie and Z3 successfully verify it[1]. More generally, unless the complete toolchain has been formally verified (a monumental effort that has only been performed in few case studies [11,12,14]), there is the need to *validate* the successful runs of a verifier. Translating Boogie to Why3 provides an effective validation, since Why3 has been developed independent of Boogie and uses a variety of backends that Boogie does not support. Procedure not_verify translated to Why3 (Fig. 2) does not verify as it should.

Procedures lemma_yes and lemma_no in Fig. 1 demonstrate Boogie's support for mathematical real numbers, which is limited in the way the power operator ** is handled. Boogie vacuously verifies both properties $2^3 > 0$ and $2^3 < 0$, even though Z3 outputs some unfiltered errors that suggest the verification is spurious. Why3 provides a more thorough support for real arithmetic; in fact, it verifies the translated procedure lemma_yes but correctly fails to verify lemma_no.

The loop in procedure trivial_inv in Fig. 1 includes an invariant asserting that i takes only even values. Even if this is clearly true, Boogie fails to check it; pinning down the precise cause of this shortcoming requires knowledge of Boogie's (and Z3's) internals, although it likely is a manifestation of the "triggers" heuristics that handle (generally undecidable) quantified expressions. However, if we insist on verifying the program in its original form, Why3 can dispatch verification conditions to *interactive* provers, where the user provides the crucial proof steps[2]. Cases such as the loop invariant of trivial_inv where a proof is "obvious" to a human user but it clashes against the default strategies to handle quantifiers are prime candidate to exploit interactive provers.

```
const N: int;                procedure lemma_yes()         procedure trivial_inv()
axiom 0 ≤ N;                   ensures 2.0**3.0 > 0.0;       {
                             { }                              var i: int;
procedure not_verify()                                        i := 0;
  ensures (∀ k, l: int •     procedure lemma_no()             while (i < 10)
    0 ≤ k ≤ l < N ⟹ N < N);    ensures 2.0**3.0 < 0.0;         invariant 0 ≤ i ≤ 10;
{                            { }                               invariant
  var x: int;                                                   (∃ j: int • i = 2*j);
  x := -N;                                                    { i := i + 2; }
  while (x ≠ x) { }                                          }
}
```

Fig. 1. Three simple Boogie programs for which automated reasoning is limited.

---

[1] https://github.com/boogie-org/boogie/issues/25.
[2] Why3 can also check the invariant automatically by relying on the CVC4 SMT solver.

4 Boogie-to-Why3 Translation

Intermediate languages for verification combine programming constructs and a logic language. When used to encode programs written in a high-level language, the programming constructs encode program behavior, and the logic constructs encode specifications, constrain the semantics to conform to the high-level language's (typically through axioms), and support other kinds of annotations (such as triggers).

Both Boogie and WhyML provide, as logic language, a typed first-order logic with arithmetic. Boogie's programming constructs are a simple imperative language with both structured (while loops, procedures) and unstructured (jumps, global variables) statements. WhyML's programming constructs combine an ML-like functional language with a few structured imperative features such as mutable variables and loops.

Correspondingly, we define a translation $T: Boogie \to WhyML$ of Boogie to WhyML as the composition $\mathcal{E} \circ \mathcal{D}$ of two translations: $\mathcal{D}: Boogie \to Boogie$ is a desugaring[3] which rewrites away the Boogie constructs, such as *call-forall*, that have no similar construct in WhyML by expressing them using other features of Boogie. Then, $\mathcal{E}: Boogie \to WhyML$ encodes Boogie programs simplified by $\mathcal{D}$ as WhyML programs. For simplicity, the presentation does not sharply separate the two translations $\mathcal{D}$ and $\mathcal{E}$ but defines either or both of them as needed to describe the translation of arbitrary Boogie constructs.

A single feature of the Boogie language significantly compounds the complexity of the translation: *polymorphic maps*. For clarity, the presentation of the translation initially ignores polymorphic maps. Then, Sect. 4.8 discusses how the general translation scheme can be extended to support them.

```
constant N: int
axiom A0: 0 ≤ N;

val not_verify (): ()
  ensures { ∀ k, l: int .
    0 ≤ k ≤ l < N → N < N }

let not_verify_impl(): ()
  ensures { ∀ k, l: int .
    0 ≤ k ≤ l < N → N < N }
  =(
    let x = ref (any int) in
    x.contents ← -N;
    while
    (x.contents ≠ x.contents)
    do done;
  end )
```

```
val lemma_yes (): ()
  ensures
    { (pow 2.0 3.0) >. 0.0 }

val lemma_no (): ()
  ensures
    { (pow 2.0 3.0) <. 0.0 }

let lemma_yes_impl (): ()
  ensures
    { (pow 2.0 3.0) >. 0.0 }
  =( )

let lemma_no_impl (): ()
  ensures
    { (pow 2.0 3.0) <. 0.0 }
  =( )
```

```
val trivial_inv (): ()

let trivial_inv_impl (): ()
  =(
    let i = ref (any int) in
    i.contents ← 0;
    while (i.contents < 10) do
    invariant
      { 0 ≤ i.contents ≤ 10 }
    invariant
      { ∃ j: int .
        i.contents = 2*j }
    i.contents ← i.contents + 2;
    done;
  )
```

Fig. 2. The translation to WhyML of the three Boogie programs in Fig. 1.

---

[3] This is unrelated to Boogie's built-in desugaring mechanism (option **/print Desugared**).

As running examples, Fig. 2 shows how $\mathcal{T}$ translates the examples of Fig. 1. For lack of space, we focus on describing the most significant aspects of the translation that are also implemented; see [1] for the missing details.

4.1   Types

Primitive Types are `int` (mathematical integers), `real` (mathematical reals), and `bool` (Booleans). $\mathcal{T}$ translates primitive types into their Why3 analogues as shown in Table 1.

Table 1. Translation of primitive types, and Why3 libraries supplying the necessary operations.

T	$\mathcal{T}(T)$	Why3 libraries
`int`	`int`	`int.Int, int.EuclideanDivision`
`real`	`real`	`real.RealInfix, real.FromInt, real.Truncate, real.PowerReal`
`bool`	`bool`	`bool.Bool`

Type Constructors. A Boogie type declaration using the *type constructor* syntax introduces a new parametric type T. $\mathcal{T}$ translates it to an algebraic type with constructor T: $\mathcal{T}($ `type T` $a_1...a_m$ $) =$ `type T'`$a_1...$`'`a_m for $m \geq 0$, where ticks ' identify type parameters in WhyML.

Map Types. A Boogie *map type* M declared as: `type M = [`$T_1, ... T_n$`] U` defines the type of a mapping from $T_1 \times \cdots \times T_n$ to U, for $n \geq 1$. Why3 supports maps through its library `map.Map`; hence, $\mathcal{T}(M) = $ `map` $(\mathcal{T}(T_1), ..., \mathcal{T}(T_n))\,\mathcal{T}(U)$, where an n-tuple encapsulates the n-type domain of M.

4.2   Constants

The translation of constant declarations is generally straightforward, following the scheme:

$$\mathcal{T}(\texttt{const c: T}) = \texttt{constant c:}\ \mathcal{T}(T)$$

$\mathcal{T}$ expresses *unique* constants and *order* constraints by axiomatization.

4.3   Variables

Why3 supports mutable variables through the reference type `ref` from theory `Ref`. Boogie global variable declarations become global value declarations of type `ref`; Boogie local variable declarations become `let` bindings with local scope. Thus, if `v` is a global variable and `l_v` is a local variable in Boogie:

global variable $\mathcal{T}(\texttt{var v: T}) = \texttt{val v: ref}\ \mathcal{T}(T)$
local variable $\mathcal{T}(\texttt{var l\_v: T}) = \texttt{let l\_v = ref (any}\ \mathcal{T}(T)\texttt{) in}$

The expression `any T` provides a nondeterministic value of type T.

4.4 Functions

Boogie function *declarations* become WhyML function declarations:

$$\mathcal{T}(\texttt{function f(}x_1\colon \texttt{T}_1, \ \ldots, \ x_n\colon \texttt{T}_n\texttt{) returns (U))} \tag{1}$$
$$= \texttt{function f } (x_1\colon\mathcal{T}(\texttt{T}_1))\cdots(x_n\colon\mathcal{T}(\texttt{T}_n))\colon \ \mathcal{T}(\texttt{U})$$

WhyML function *definitions* require, unlike Boogie's, a variant to ensure that recursion is well-formed. Therefore, Boogie function definitions are not translated into WhyML function definitions but are axiomatized[4].

4.5 Expressions

Variables. Since a Boogie variable v of type T turns into a value v of type ref $\mathcal{T}(T)$, occurrences of v in an expression translate to v.contents, which represents the value attached to reference v.

Map Expressions. $\mathcal{T}$ translates map selection and update using functions get and set from theory Map. If m is a map of type M defined in Sect. 4.1, then:

	E	$\mathcal{T}(E)$
selection	m[e_1, ..., e_n]	get $\mathcal{T}$(m) ($\mathcal{T}(e_1)$,...,$\mathcal{T}(e_n)$)
update	m[e_1, ..., e_n := f]	set $\mathcal{T}$(m) ($\mathcal{T}(e_1)$,...,$\mathcal{T}(e_n)$) $\mathcal{T}$(f)

Lambda Expressions. The translation desugars lambda expression into constant maps: $\mathcal{D}(\lambda \ x_1\colon \texttt{T}_1, \ldots, x_n\colon \texttt{T}_n \bullet \ \texttt{e}) \ = \ \texttt{lmb}$, where const lmb : $[\texttt{T}_1, \ldots, \texttt{T}_n]\tau(\texttt{e})$ is axiomatized by axiom $(\forall \ x_1\colon \ \texttt{T}_1, \ldots, x_n\colon \ \texttt{T}_n \bullet \texttt{lmb}[x_1, \ldots, x_n] \ = \ \texttt{e})$, and $\tau(\texttt{e})$ is e's type.

4.6 Procedures

Boogie procedures have a declaration (signature and specification) and zero or more implementations. The latter follow the general syntax of Fig. 3 (left). For simplicity of presentation, p has one input argument, one output argument, and one local variable, but generalizing the description to an arbitrary number of variables is straightforward.

The specification of procedure p consists of preconditions requires, frame specification modifies, and postconditions ensures. Specification elements marked free are assumed without being checked.

$\mathcal{T}$ translates a generic procedure p as shown in Fig. 3 (right). The declaration of p determines val p, which defines the semantics of p for clients: the free precondition fR does not feature there because clients don't have to satisfy it, whereas both free and non-free postconditions are encoded as returns conditions. The implementation of p determines let p_impl0, which triggers

---

[4] To take advantage of Why3's well-formedness checks, we plan to offer translations of Boogie functions to WhyML functions as a user option in future work.

```
procedure p(t: T where Wt)              val p (t : T(T)): T(U)
  returns (u: U where Wu);                requires { T(R) }
  requires      R;                        writes    { M }
  free requires fR;                       returns  { | u → T(E) }
  modifies      M;                        returns  { | u → T(fE) }
  ensures       E;                        returns  { | u → T(Wu) }
  free ensures  fE;
                                        let p_impl0 (t: T(T)): T(U)
implementation p(t: T)                    requires { T(R) } requires { T(fR) }
  returns (u: U)                          returns { | u → T(E) }
  {                                     =(
    var l: L where Wl;                    T(var u: U; var l: L;)
    B                                     assume { T(Wg) }  -- where of globals
  }                                       assume { T(Wt) }  -- where of inputs
                                          assume { T(Wl) }  -- where of locals
                                          assume { T(Wu) }  -- where of outputs
                                          try ( T(B) )
                                          with | Return → assume { true } end
                                          T(u)
                                        )
```

Fig. 3. Translation of a Boogie procedure (left) into WhyML (right).

the verification of the implementation against its specification: both free and non-free preconditions are encoded, whereas the free postcondition fE does not feature there because implementations don't have to satisfy it. The body introduces let bindings for the local variable l and for a new local variable u which represents the returned value; these declarations are translated as discussed in Sect. 4.3. Then, a series of assume encode the semantics of Boogie's where clauses, which constrain the nondeterministic values variables can take (Wg comes from any global variables, which are visible everywhere); p's body B is translated and wrapped inside an exception-handling block try, which does not do anything other than allowing abrupt termination of the body's execution upon throwing a Return exception (see Sect. 4.7 for details). Regardless of whether the body terminates normally or exceptionally, the last computed value of u is returned in the last line, and checked against the postcondition in returns. In all, the modular semantics of Boogie's procedure p is preserved.

4.7   Statements

Assignments. Assignments involve variables (global or local), which become mutable references in WhyML: $T(v := e) = v.\text{contents} \leftarrow T(e)$. Boogie parallel assignments become simple assignments using let bindings of limited scope:

$$T(v_1, \ldots, v_m := e_1, \ldots, e_m) = \begin{cases} \text{let } e'_1 = T(e_1), \ldots, e'_m = T(e_m) \text{ in} \\ \quad T(v_1 := e'_1); \cdots; T(v_m := e'_m) \end{cases} \quad (2)$$

Havoc. An abstract function val havoc (): 'a provides a fresh, nondeterministic value of any type 'a. It translates Boogie's havoc statements following the scheme:

$$T(\text{havoc u, v}) = T(u) \leftarrow \text{havoc}(); T(v) \leftarrow \text{havoc}(); \text{assume } \{T(Wu)\}; \text{assume } \{T(Wv)\}$$

where Wu and Wv are the where clauses of u's and v's declarations; the generalization to an arbitrary number of variables is obvious. It is important that the assume statements follow all the calls to havoc: since Wv may involve u's value, havoc u, v is not in general equivalent to havoc u; havoc v; the translation reflects this behavior.

Return. The behavior of Boogie's return statement, which determines the abrupt termination of a procedure's execution, is translated to WhyML using exception handling. An exception handling block wraps each procedure's body, as illustrated in Fig. 3, and catches an exception Return; thus, $\mathcal{T}(\texttt{return}) =$ raise Return.

Loops. Figure 4 shows the translation of a Boogie loop into a WhyML loop. An invariant marked as free can be assumed but need not be checked; correspondingly, the translation adds assumptions that ensure it holds at loop entrance and after every iteration. The exception handling block surrounding the loop in WhyML emulates the semantics of the control-flow breaking statement break : $\mathcal{T}(\texttt{break}) =$ raise Break.

```
                                    assume { T(fI) }
                                    try while T(b) do
   while (b)                          invariant { T(I) }
     invariant I;                     invariant { T(fI) }
     free invariant fI;               T(B)
   { B }                              assume { T(fI) }
                                    done;
                                    with | Break → assume { T(fI) } end
```

Fig. 4. Translation of a Boogie loop (left) into WhyML (right).

4.8 Polymorphic Maps

We now consider *polymorphic map* types, declared in Boogie as:

$$\texttt{type pM} = \langle \alpha \rangle \ [\texttt{T}_1, \dots, \texttt{T}_n] \ \texttt{U} \qquad (3)$$

where α is a vector $\alpha_1, \dots, \alpha_m$ of $m > 0$ type parameters, and some of the types $\texttt{T}_1, \dots, \texttt{T}_n, \texttt{U}$ in pM's definition depend on α. In the next paragraph, we explain why polymorphic maps cannot be translated to WhyML directly. Instead, we replace them with several monomorphic maps based on a global analysis of the types that are actually used in the Boogie program being translated. The result of this rewrite is a Boogie program without polymorphic maps, which we can translate to Why3 following the rules we previously described. The shortcoming of this approach is that it gives up *modularity*: verification holds only for the concrete types that are used (closed-word assumption); this seems to be necessary to express Boogie's extremely liberal polymorphism without resorting to intricate "semantic" translations, which would likely fail verifiability.

Boogie Vs. WhyML Polymorphism. While WhyML also supports generic polymorphism, its usage is more restrictive than Boogie's. The first difference is that *mutable* maps cannot be polymorphic in WhyML. The second difference is that, in some contexts, a variable of polymorphic map type in Boogie effectively corresponds to *multiple* maps. Consider, for example, a type Mix = $\langle\alpha\rangle$ [α]α of maps from generic α to α; Boogie accepts formulas such as axiom ($\forall$ m: Mix • m[0] = 1 $\wedge$ m[true]) where m acts as a map over int in the first conjunct and as a map over bool in the second. WhyML, in contrast, always makes the type parameters explicit; hence, a logic variable of type map 'a 'a denotes a single map of a generic type that can only feature in expressions which do not assume anything about the concrete type that will instantiate 'a.

Besides type declarations and quantifications, polymorphic maps can appear within polymorphic functions and procedures, declared as:

$$\text{function } \mathbf{pF}\langle\alpha\rangle(\mathbf{x}_1: T_1, \ldots, \mathbf{x}_n: T_n) \text{ returns (U)} \qquad (4)$$

$$\text{procedure } \mathbf{pP}\langle\alpha\rangle(\mathbf{x}_1: T_1, \ldots, \mathbf{x}_n: T_n) \text{ returns (u: U)} \qquad (5)$$

Type Analysis. We have seen that a Boogie polymorphic map may correspond to multiple monomorphic maps in certain contexts. The translation reifies this idea based on global type analysis: for every item (constant, program or logic variable, or formal argument) pm of polymorphic map type pM as in (3), it determines the set *types*(pm) of all actual types pm takes in expressions or assignments, as outlined in Table 2. This in turn determines the set *types*(pM) as the union of all sets *types*(p) for p of type pM.

The types in *types*(pM) include in general both concrete and parametric types. For example, the program of Fig. 5 (left) determines *types*(m) = {[int]int, [β]β}, *types*(n) = {[bool]bool}, and *types*(M) = *types*(m) $\cup$ *types*(n), where β is procedure p's type parameter (since p is not called anywhere, that's the only known actual type of x). Let *conc*(pM) denote the set of all *concrete* types in *types*(pM).

```
type M = ⟨α⟩ [α]α;                  type (M_int, M_bool, M_a) = ([int]int, [bool]bool, [a]a);
var m: M;                           var (m_int, m_bool, m_a): (M_int, M_bool, M_a);
axiom (∀ n: M • n[true]);           axiom (∀ (n_int, n_bool, n_a): (M_int, M_bool, M_a) •
                                          n_bool[true]);

procedure p⟨β⟩(x: β)                procedure (p_int, p_bool, p_a)(x: (int, bool, a))
  requires (∀ i: int • m[i] = i);     requires (∀ i: int • m_int[i] = i);
  modifies m;                         modifies (m_int, m_bool, m_a);
{ m[x] := x; }                      { (m_int, m_bool, m_a)[x] := x }
```

Fig. 5. An example of how polymorphic maps (left) translate to monomorphic (right). Procedure p translates to 3 procedures p_int, p_bool, and p_a, each with argument of type int, bool, or a.

Table 2. Each occurrence of an item pm of polymorphic map type pM determines the set *types*(pm) of actual types. (x::*t* denotes that x has type *t*.)

			types(pm) includes $[t_1,\ldots,t_n]u$ such that:
expressions	read	pm	pm :: $[t_1,\ldots,t_n]u$
	select	pm[$e_1,\ldots,e_n$]	e_1 :: $t_1,\ldots,e_n$ :: t_n, pm[$e_1,\ldots,e_n$] :: u
	update	pm[$e_1,\ldots,e_n$]:= f]	e_1 :: $t_1,\ldots,e_n$ :: t_n, f :: u
	function reference	f(it)	it :: $[t_1,\ldots,t_n]u$, where function f(pm: pM)
statements	copy	pm := it	it :: $[t_1,\ldots,t_n]u$
	assignment	pm[$e_1,\ldots,e_n$] := f	e_1 :: $t_1,\ldots,e_n$ :: t_n, f :: u
	havoc	havoc pm	−
	procedure call in	call p(it)	it :: $[t_1,\ldots,t_n]u$, where procedure p(pm: pM)
	procedure call out	call it := p()	it :: $[t_1,\ldots,t_n]u$, where procedure p() returns(pm: pM)

Desugaring Polymorphic Maps. To describe how the translation replaces polymorphic maps by monomorphic maps, we introduce a pseudo-code notation that allows *tuples* (in round brackets) of program elements where normally only a single element is allowed. The semantics of this notation corresponds quite intuitively to multiple statements or declarations. For example, a variable declaration var (x, y): (int, bool) is a shorthand for declaring variables x: int and y: bool; a formula (x, y) = (3, true) is a shorthand for x = 3 ∧ y; and a procedure declaration using the tuple notation procedure (p_int, p_bool)(x: (int, bool)) is a shorthand for declaring two procedures p_int(x: int) and p_bool(x: bool).

We also use the following notation: given an n-vector $a = a_1,\ldots,a_n$ and a type expression T parametric with respect to α, T_a denotes T with a_k substituted for α_k, for $k = 1,\ldots,n$. If $\mathbb{T}$ is a set of types obtained from the same type expression T, such as *types*(pM) with respect to pM's definition, and id is an identifier, let $(\mathbb{T})$ denote $\mathbb{T}$ as a tuple, and $(id\_\mathbb{T})$ denote the tuple of identifiers id_t such that T_t is the corresponding type in $\mathbb{T}$. In the example of Fig. 5, if $T = [\alpha]\alpha$ then $T_{\text{int}} = [\text{int}]\text{int}$, $(types(\text{m})) = ([\text{int}]\text{int}, [\beta]\beta)$, and $(j\_types(\text{m})) = (j\_int, j\_\beta)$. Throughout, we also assume that an uninterpreted type a_k is available for $k = 1,\ldots,n$, that M_a denotes the type expression $[T_1,\ldots,T_n]$ U in (3) with each α_k replaced by a_k, and that $conc^+(\text{pM}) = conc(\text{pM}) \cup \{M_a\}$.

Declarations. Type declaration (3) desugars to several type declarations:

$$\text{type } (\text{pM\_}conc^+(\text{pM}))) = (conc^+(\text{pM})) \tag{6}$$

The declaration of an *item* pm: pM, where pm can be a constant, or a program or logic variable, desugars to a declaration $(\text{pm\_}conc^+(\text{pM}))): (conc^+(\text{pM}))$ of multiple items of the same kind. The declaration of a *procedure* or *function* g with an (input or output) argument x: pM desugars to a declaration of multiple procedures or functions $(\text{g\_}conc^+(\text{pM}))(\text{x}: (conc^+(\text{pM}))$—multiple declarations each with one variant of x ; if g has multiple arguments of this kind, the desugaring is applied recursively to each variant. Figure 5 (right) shows how the polymorphic map type M and each of the items m and n of type M become 3 monomorphic types and 3 items of these monomorphic types.

For every polymorphic function or procedure g with type parameters β, also consider any one of their arguments declared as x: X. If X is a type expression that depends on β, and there exists a map type $[V_1, \ldots, V_n]V_0$ in $types(\text{pM})$ such that $X = V_k$ for some $k = 0, \ldots, n$, then g becomes $(\text{g\_}\mathbb{V}_k)(\text{x}: (\mathbb{V}_k))$—corresponding to multiple g's each with one argument, where $\mathbb{V}_k = \{\overline{V}_k \mid [\overline{V}_1, \ldots, \overline{V}_n]\overline{V}_0 \in conc^+(\text{pM})\}$ is the set of all concrete types that instantiate the kth type component. This transformation enables assigning arguments to polymorphic maps inside polymorphic functions or procedures that have become monomorphic. Figure 5 (right) shows how argument x: β becomes an argument of concrete type int, bool, or a, since $[\beta]\beta \in types(\text{M})$. (As procedure p does not use β elsewhere, we drop it from the signature.)

Expressions. Every occurrence—in expressions, as l-values of assignments, and as targets of havoc statements—of an item w of polymorphic type W whose declaration has been modified to remove polymorphic map types is replaced by one or more of the newly introduced monomorphic types as follows. If w's actual type within its context is a *concrete* type C, then we replace w with w_c such that $W_c = $ C; otherwise, w's actual type is a *parametric* type, and we replace w with the tuple (w_X), including all variants of w that have been introduced. In Fig. 5 (right), n[true] rewrites to just n_bool[true] since the concrete type is bool; the assignment in p's body, whose actual type is parametric with respect to β, becomes an assignment involving each of the three variants of m corresponding to the three variants of p that have been introduced.

5   Implementation and Experiments

5.1   Implementation

We implemented the translation $\mathcal{T}$ described in Sect. 4 as a command-line tool b2w implemented in Java 8. b2w works as a staged filter: (1) it parses and type-checks the input Boogie program, and creates a Boogie AST (abstract syntax tree); (2) it desugars the Boogie AST according to $\mathcal{D}$; (3) it transforms the Boogie AST into a WhyML AST according to $\mathcal{E}$; (4) it outputs the WhyML AST in the form of code.

Stage (1) relies on Schäf's parsing and typechecking library Boogieamp[5], which we modified to support access using the visitor pattern, AST in-place modifications, and the latest syntax of Boogie (e.g., for integer vs. real division). Stages (2) and (3) are implemented by multiple AST visitors, each taking care of a particular aspect of the translation, in the style of [20]; the overhead of traversing the AST multiple times is negligible and improves modularity: handling a new construct (for example, in future versions of Boogie) or changing the translation of one feature only requires adding or modifying one feature-specific visitor class.

---

[5] https://github.com/martinschaef/boogieamp.

5.2 Experiments

The goal of the experiments is ascertaining that b2w can translate realistic Boogie programs producing WhyML programs that can be verified taking advantage of Why3's multiple back-end support. The experiments are limited to fully-automated verification, and hence do not evaluate other possible practical benefits of translating programs to WhyML such as support for interactive provers and executability for testing purposes.

Programs. The experiments target a total of 194 Boogie programs from three groups according to their origin: group NAT (native) includes 29 programs that encode algorithmic verification problems directly in Boogie (as opposed to translating from a higher-level language); group OBJ (object-oriented) includes 6 programs that are based on a heap-based memory model; group TES (tests) includes 159 programs from Boogie's test suite. Table 3 summarizes the sizes of the programs in each group.

Table 3. A summary of the Boogie programs used in the experiments, and their translation to WhyML using b2w. For each program GROUP, the table reports how many programs it includes (#), the minimum m, mean μ, maximum M, and total Σ length in non-comment non-blank lines of code (LOC) of those BOOGIE programs and of their WHYML translations.

GROUP	#	LOC BOOGIE				LOC WHYML			
		m	μ	M	Σ	m	μ	M	Σ
NAT	29	20	73	253	2110	62	128	318	3716
OBJ	6	44	146	385	878	90	208	446	1245
TES	159	3	21	155	3272	36	64	290	10180
Total:	194	3	34	385	6260	36	106	446	15141

The programs in NAT, which we developed in previous work [7,8], include several standard algorithms such as sorting and array rotation. The programs in OBJ include 2 simple examples in Java and 1 in Eiffel, encoded in Boogie by Joogie [2] and AutoProof [21] (we manually simplified AutoProof's translation to avoid features b2w doesn't support), and 3 algorithmic examples adapted from NAT to use a global heap in the style of object-oriented programs. Among the 515 programs that make up Boogie's test suite[6] we retained in TES those that mainly exercise features supported by b2w.

Setup. Each experiment targets one Boogie program b: it runs Boogie with command boogie b and a timeout of 180 seconds; it runs b2w to translate b to w in WhyML; for each SMT solver p among Alt-Ergo, CVC3, CVC4, and Z3, it runs Why3 with command why3 prove -P p w, also with a timeout of 180 seconds. For each run we collected the wall-clock running time, the total number of verification goals, and how many of such goals the tool verified successfully.

---

[6] https://github.com/boogie-org/boogie/tree/master/Test.

Table 4. A summary of how Boogie performs in comparison with Why3. For each program GROUP, the table reports how many programs it includes (#), for how many of the programs Boogie verifies as many goals (B = W), more goals (B > W), or fewer goals (B < W) than Why3 with any of the SMT solvers; for how many of the programs both Boogie and Why3 verify none (0=0), some but not all (50=50), or all (100=100) of the goals; the last column (SPURIOUS) indicates that b2w's translation never introduces spurious goals that are proved by Why3 (that is, if Boogie's input has zero goals, so does WhyML's translation).

GROUP	#	B = W	B > W	B < W	0=0	50=50	100=100	SPURIOUS
NAT	29	19	10	0	1	0	18	0
OBJ	6	5	0	1	1	2	2	0
TES	159	137	21	1	71	21	45	0
Total:	194	161	31	2	73	23	65	0

All the experiments ran on a Ubuntu 14.04 LTS GNU/Linux box with 8-core Intel i7-4790 CPU at 3.6 GHz and 16 GB of RAM, with the following tools: Alt-Ergo 0.99.1, CVC3 2.4.1, CVC4 1.4, Z3 4.3.2, Mono 4.2.2, Boogie 2.3.0.61016, and Why3 0.86.2. To account for noise, we repeated each verification three times and report the mean value of the 95th percentile of the running times.

Results. Table 4 shows a summary of the results where we compare Why3's best performance, with any one of the four SMT solvers, against Boogie's. The most significant result is that the WhyML translation produced by b2w behaves like the Boogie original in 83% (161, B=W) of the experiments. This means that Boogie may fail to verify all goals (column 0=0), verify some goals and fail on others (column 50=50), or verify all goals (column 100=100); in each case, Why3 consistently verifies the same goals on b2w's translation. Indeed, many programs in TES are tests that are supposed to fail verification; hence, the correct behavior of the translation is to fail as well. We also checked the failures of programs in NAT and OBJ to ascertain that b2w's translation preserves correctness. Table 4 does not show this, but we also found another 2 programs in NAT where Why3 proves the same goals as Boogie only by combining the results of multiple SMT solvers.

Boogie verifies more goals than Why3 in 16% (31, B > W) of the experiments, where it is more effective because of better features (default triggers, invariant inference, SMT encoding) or simply because of some language features that are not fully supported by b2w (examples are Z3-specific annotations, which b2w simply drops, and `goto`, which b2w encodes as `assert false` to ensure soundness). In 1% (2, B < W) of the experiments, Why3 even verifies more goals than Boogie. One program in OBJ is a genuine example where Why3's Z3 encoding is more effective than Boogie's; the one program in TES should instead be considered spurious, as it deploys some trigger specifications that are Boogie-specific (negated triggers) or interact in a different way with the default triggers. As this was the only program in our experiments that introduced clearly spurious behavior, the experiments provide convincing evidence that b2w's translation preserves correctness and verifiability to a large degree.

Table 5. For each program GROUP the table reports how many programs it includes (#) and, for both Boogie and Why3 for each choice of SMT solver among ALT-ERGO, CVC3, and Z3: the mean percentage of goals verified in each program (OUTCOME μ), how many programs were completely verified (OUTCOME $\forall$), and how many were not verified at all (OUTCOME $\nexists$), the mean μ and total Σ verification TIME in seconds, and how many programs timed out.

| | | Z3 BOOGIE | | | | | ALT-ERGO WHY3 | | | | | CVC3 WHY3 | | | | | CVC4 WHY3 | | | | | Z3 WHY3 | | | | |
| | | OUTCOME | | | TIME | | | OUTCOME | | | TIME | | | OUTCOME | | | TIME | | | OUTCOME | | | TIME | | | OUTCOME | | | TIME | | |
GROUP	#	μ	$\forall$	$\nexists$	μ	Σ	∞	μ	$\forall$	$\nexists$	μ	Σ	∞	μ	$\forall$	$\nexists$	μ	Σ	∞	μ	$\forall$	$\nexists$	μ	Σ	∞	μ	$\forall$	$\nexists$	μ	Σ	∞
NAT	29	93	25	1	0.4	12	0	61	14	6	20.6	598	0	28	1	12	0.2	5	0	33	2	11	30.1	873	0	73	16	5	12.6	367	0
OBJ	6	52	2	2	3.9	23	0	46	1	2	30.1	181	0	46	1	2	0.2	1	0	52	2	2	28.4	170	0	68	3	1	23.7	142	0
TES	159	45	55	71	0.3	53	0	37	45	85	25.8	4096	1	33	39	91	0.1	18	0	37	45	86	27.4	4360	1	37	44	86	25.9	4121	1
Total:	**194**	60	82	74	0.7	88	0	53	60	93	22.6	4875	1	30	41	105	0.2	24	0	35	49	99	29.7	5403	1	69	63	92	14.5	4630	1

Table 5 provides data about the experiments' running times, and differentiates the performance of each SMT solver with Why3. Z3 is the most effective SMT solver in terms of programs it could completely verify (columns $\forall$), followed by Alt-Ergo. While CVC3 is generally the least effective, it has the advantage of returning very quickly (only 0.2 s of average running time), even more quickly than Z3 in Boogie. CVC4 falls somewhere in the middle, in terms both of effectiveness and of running time. Boogie's responsiveness remains excellent if balanced against its effectiveness; a better time-effectiveness of Why3 with Alt-Ergo and Z3 could be achieved by setting tight per-goal timeouts (in most cases, verification attempts that last longer than a few seconds do not eventually succeed).

6 Discussion

The current implementation of the translation $\mathcal{T}$ has some limitations that somewhat restrict its applicability. As we already mentioned in the paper, some features of the Boogie language are not supported (bitvectors, gotos), or only partially supported (polymorphic mappings); and frame specifications are assumed. All of these are, however, limitations of the current prototype implementation only, and we see no fundamental hurdles to extending b2w along the lines of the definition of $\mathcal{T}$ in Sect. 4.

Since b2w also takes great care to confine the effect of translating Boogie programs that include unsupported features, and to fail when it cannot produce a correct translation, it still largely preserves *correctness* (soundness, in particular). On the other hand, our experiments also demonstrate that the translation $\mathcal{T}$, as implemented by b2w, largely meets the other goal of preserving *verifiability*: even if the experimental subjects all are idiomatic Boogie programs written independent of the translation effort, 83 % of the translated programs behave in Why3 as they do in Boogie.

In future work, we will address the features of Boogie that are still not satisfactorily supported by b2w. We will also devise strategies to take advantage of Why3's multi-prover support. Other possible directions include formalizing the translation to prove that it preserves correctness; and devising a reverse translation from WhyML to Boogie.

References

1. Ameri, M., Furia, C.A.: Why just Boogie? Translating between intermediate verification languages, January 2016. http://arxiv.org/abs/1601.00516
2. Arlt, S., Schäf, M.: Joogie: infeasible code detection for Java. In: Madhusudan, P., Seshia, S.A. (eds.) CAV 2012. LNCS, vol. 7358, pp. 767–773. Springer, Heidelberg (2012)
3. Barnett, M., Chang, B.-Y.E., DeLine, R., Jacobs, B., Leino, K.R.M.: Boogie: a modular reusable verifier for object-oriented programs. In: de Boer, F.S., Bonsangue, M.M., Graf, S., de Roever, W.-P. (eds.) FMCO 2005. LNCS, vol. 4111, pp. 364–387. Springer, Heidelberg (2006)
4. Barnett, M., Fähndrich, M., Leino, K.R.M., Müller, P., Schulte, W., Venter, H.: Specification and verification: the Spec# experience. Commun. ACM **54**(6), 81–91 (2011)
5. Cheng, Z., Monahan, R., Power, J.F.: A sound execution semantics for ATL via translation validation. In: Kolovos, D., Wimmer, M. (eds.) ICMT 2015. LNCS, vol. 9152, pp. 133–148. Springer, Heidelberg (2015)
6. Filliâtre, J.-C., Paskevich, A.: Why3 — where programs meet provers. In: Felleisen, M., Gardner, P. (eds.) ESOP 2013. LNCS, vol. 7792, pp. 125–128. Springer, Heidelberg (2013)
7. Furia, C.A.: Rotation of sequences: Algorithms and proofs. http://arxiv.org/abs/1406.5453
8. Furia, C.A., Meyer, B., Velder, S.: Loop invariants: Analysis, classification, and examples. ACM Comput. Surv. **46**(3), Article 34 (2014)
9. Harel, D.: On folk theorems. Commun. ACM **23**(7), 379–389 (1980)
10. Heule, S., Kassios, I.T., Müller, P., Summers, A.J.: Verification condition generation for permission logics with abstract predicates and abstraction functions. In: Castagna, G. (ed.) ECOOP 2013. LNCS, vol. 7920, pp. 451–476. Springer, Heidelberg (2013)
11. Klein, G., Andronick, J., Elphinstone, K., Heiser, G., Cock, D., Derrin, P., Elkaduwe, D., Engelhardt, K., Kolanski, R., Norrish, M., Sewell, T., Tuch, H., Winwood, S.: seL4: formal verification of an operating-system kernel. Commun. ACM **53**(6), 107–115 (2010)
12. Kumar, R., Myreen, M.O., Norrish, M., Owens, S.: CakeML: a verified implementation of ML. In: Proceedings of POPL, pp. 179–192. ACM (2014)
13. Leino, K.R.M.: Developing verified programs with Dafny. In: Proceedings of ICSE, pp. 1488–1490. ACM (2013)
14. Leroy, X.: Formal verification of a realistic compiler. Commun. ACM **52**(7), 107–115 (2009)
15. Mens, T., Van Gorp, P.: A taxonomy of model transformation. Electr. Notes Theor. Comput. Sci. **152**, 125–142 (2006)
16. Schmitt, P.H., Ulbrich, M., Weiß, B.: Dynamic frames in Java dynamic logic. In: Beckert, B., Marché, C. (eds.) FoVeOOS 2010. LNCS, vol. 6528, pp. 138–152. Springer, Heidelberg (2011)
17. Segal, L., Chalin, P.: A comparison of intermediate verification languages: Boogie and Sireum/Pilar. In: Joshi, R., Müller, P., Podelski, A. (eds.) VSTTE 2012. LNCS, vol. 7152, pp. 130–145. Springer, Heidelberg (2012)

18. Stevens, P.: A landscape of bidirectional model transformations. In: Lämmel, R., Visser, J., Saraiva, J. (eds.) GTTSE 2007. LNCS, vol. 5235, pp. 408–424. Springer, Heidelberg (2008)

19. Trudel, M., Furia, C.A., Nordio, M., Meyer, B.: Really automatic scalable object-oriented reengineering. In: Castagna, G. (ed.) ECOOP 2013. LNCS, vol. 7920, pp. 477–501. Springer, Heidelberg (2013)

20. Trudel, M., Furia, C.A., Nordio, M., Meyer, B., Oriol, M.: C to O-O translation: beyond the easy stuff. In: Proceedings of WCRE, pp. 19–28. IEEE Computer Society, October 2012

21. Tschannen, J., Furia, C.A., Nordio, M., Polikarpova, N.: AutoProof: auto-active functional verification of object-oriented programs. In: Baier, C., Tinelli, C. (eds.) TACAS 2015. LNCS, vol. 9035, pp. 566–580. Springer, Heidelberg (2015)

Probabilistic Systems

Statistical Approximation of Optimal Schedulers for Probabilistic Timed Automata

Pedro R. D'Argenio[1], Arnd Hartmanns[2(✉)], Axel Legay[3], and Sean Sedwards[3]

[1] Universidad Nacional de Córdoba, Córdoba, Argentina
dargenio@famaf.unc.edu.ar
[2] University of Twente, Enschede, The Netherlands
a.hartmanns@utwente.nl
[3] INRIA Rennes – Bretagne Atlantique, Rennes, France
{axel.legay,sean.sedwards}@inria.fr

Abstract. The verification of probabilistic timed automata involves finding schedulers that optimise their nondeterministic choices with respect to the probability of a property. In practice, approaches based on model checking fail due to state-space explosion, while simulation-based techniques like statistical model checking are not applicable due to the nondeterminism. We present a new lightweight on-the-fly algorithm to find near-optimal schedulers for probabilistic timed automata. We make use of the classical region and zone abstractions from timed automata model checking, coupled with a recently developed smart sampling technique for statistical verification of Markov decision processes. Our algorithm provides estimates for both maximum and minimum probabilities. We compare our new approach with alternative techniques, first using tractable examples from the literature, then motivate its scalability using case studies that are intractable to numerical model checking and challenging for existing statistical techniques.

1 Introduction

Probabilistic timed automata (PTA) [17] are a popular modelling formalism for the analysis of real-time systems. As a generalisation of timed automata (TA) [1], they support (discrete) nondeterministic choices as well as (continuous) nondeterministic timing with hard bounds. As a generalisation of Markov decision processes (MDP), they additionally allow (discrete) probabilistic choices. A PTA model can thus combine hard real-time aspects (using fixed or nondeterministic time bounds) with soft real-time features (using probabilistically chosen delays). PTA also permit abstraction, introducing nondeterminism to reduce the model's size, and allow choices between enabled events to be specified as probabilistic if information on the frequency of their occurrence is available, or as nondeterministic otherwise. Examples of verification questions that can be answered with PTA include "what is the worst-case probability of the modelled process meeting its deadline?", "can it terminate with probability greater than p?", and "is the probability to spend more than 2 s in an unsafe state greater than zero?"

© Springer International Publishing Switzerland 2016
E. Ábrahám and M. Huisman (Eds.): IFM 2016, LNCS 9681, pp. 99–114, 2016.
DOI: 10.1007/978-3-319-33693-0_7

All PTA verification questions include a quantification over schedulers, i.e. over resolutions of the nondeterministic decisions: the "worst-case probability" is the lowest probability achievable for any scheduler; when we ask whether something "can happen with probability greater than p", we need to find at least one scheduler that makes the probability greater than p. The key challenge in PTA verification thus lies in finding *optimal schedulers*, i.e. those that maximise or minimise the probability for the question of interest. If all time constraints in a PTA rely on integer bounds, optimal schedulers can be found by analysing an MDP abstraction of the PTA's semantics using probabilistic model checking. Whether using regions [17], digital clocks [16] or zones [17,18] for the abstraction, this approach inevitably fails for large models due to state-space explosion. While the number of extra states needed to capture information about time can be small when using zones, realistic PTA models use compact model descriptions with a parallel composition operator and discrete state variables, both of which already cause the underlying state spaces to be intractably large in practice.

For the analysis of purely stochastic systems, such as Markov chains, an alternative to traditional model checking with exhaustive state-space exploration is *statistical model checking* (SMC, [10,20]): a number of *simulation* runs is performed on the model, generating traces that can be used to statistically *estimate* the probability of a given path formula with some level of confidence. By definition, however, nondeterministic decisions cannot be simulated, so SMC cannot be applied directly to models like MDP or PTA. For the former, some SMC-like approaches have recently been developed. They either work by iteratively optimising the decisions of an explicitly-stored scheduler [4,9], or by sampling from the scheduler space and iteratively improving a *set* of candidate near-optimal schedulers [5]. The former are *heavyweight* techniques because the size of the description of the (memoryless) scheduler is significant, and in the worst case is the size of the state space. The latter is a *lightweight* approach that uses $\mathcal{O}(1)$ memory to represent each (history-dependent) scheduler.

UPPAAL-SMC [7] implements a stochastic model of timed automata that can be used to perform SMC on PTA. By instantiating invariants as either uniform or exponential distributions over time, it can estimate the expected probability of a PTA property under a specific stochastic scheduler. Making use of the same model, UPPAAL STRATEGO [6] handles a more general model than PTA. It combines a scheduler *synthesis* phase with a subsequent SMC analysis of the model under this scheduler, but is limited by an explicit representation of schedulers.

In this paper we develop a lightweight technique to approximate optimal schedulers for PTA, based on the lightweight approach for MDP of [5]. While PTA can be abstracted to MDP, allowing the approach of [5] to be applied directly, the need to explicitly simulate many small delay steps has a catastrophic affect on performance. In addition, the region and digital clocks abstractions are often unnecessarily fine grained, resulting in an explosion of possible schedulers and potentially making near-optimal schedulers very rare. As simulation is inherently a forwards exploration technique, of the zone-based approaches only the one of [17] would be applicable. Unfortunately, it admits unrealistically powerful schedulers, and thus delivers *upper bounds* on maximum and *lower bounds* on minimum probabilities. This is fundamentally incompatible with sampling schedulers as in [5], which delivers *lower* bounds on maximum and *upper* bounds on minimum probabilities. Our technique nevertheless uses zones on-the-fly to perform a forwards exploration, but selects a single target region after each discrete jump. This avoids the problems of [17], while the conceptual blow-up of state space does not affect our technique because it simulates a trace by storing only one state in memory at a time.

We report on a prototype implementation of our new technique. We test it with standard models from the literature that are tractable for probabilistic model checking, in order to compare the near-optimal schedulers that we find with the optimal schedulers computed by PRISM [15]. We then show that our technique works well for some intractably large examples. We also compare our results with those produced by the single-scheduler approach of UPPAAL-SMC.

2   Preliminaries

$\mathbb{N}$ is $\{0, 1, \dots\}$, the set of natural numbers. $\mathbb{R}^+$ is $(0, \infty)$, the set of positive real numbers. $\mathbb{R}_0^+$ is $[0, \infty)$, the set of nonnegative real numbers. $a.b$ denotes the concatenation of two sequences a and b or of two objects interpreted as bitstrings.

Definition 1. *A (discrete)* probability distribution *over a set Ω is a function* $\mu \in \Omega \to [0, 1]$ *such that* $\mathrm{support}(\mu) \stackrel{\mathrm{def}}{=} \{\omega \in \Omega \mid \mu(\omega) > 0\}$ *is countable and* $\sum_{\omega \in \mathrm{support}(\mu)} \mu(\omega) = 1$. $\mathrm{Dist}(\Omega)$ *is the set of all probability distributions over Ω.*

We write $\mathcal{D}(s)$ for the *Dirac distribution* for s, defined by $\mathcal{D}(s)(s) = 1$.

Definition 2. *A uniform* pseudo-random number generator *(PRNG) is a an object $\mathcal{U}$ that, once initialised with a seed $i \in \mathbb{N}$ (denoted $\mathcal{U} := \mathrm{PRNG}(i)$), can be iterated (denoted $\mathcal{U}()$) to produce a new value that is pseudo-uniformly distributed in $[0, 1)$ and pseudo-statistically independent of previous iterates. $\mathcal{U}$ is deterministic if, for a given seed, the sequence of iterates is always the same.*

We only consider deterministic PRNG. Determinism is standard in commonly used PRNG [12]. We denote by $\mathcal{U}(\mu)$ the pseudo-random selection of a value from $\mathrm{support}(\mu)$ according to a value sampled from $\mathcal{U}$ and the probabilities in μ. In what follows, when we write "random" w.r.t. a choice made by a PRNG we implicitly mean "pseudo-random" unless qualified otherwise.

2.1   Markov Decision Processes

Markov decision processes combine nondeterminism and probabilistic choices: to move from one state to another, first a transition is chosen nondeterministically; each transition then leads into a probability distribution over successor states.

Definition 3. *A* Markov decision process *(MDP) is a 4-tuple* $\langle S, A, T, s_{init} \rangle$ *where S is a countable set of states, A is a countable set of transition labels, $T \in S \rightarrow 2^{A \times \mathrm{Dist}(S)}$ is the transition function with $T(s)$ countable for all $s \in S$, and $s_{init} \in S$ is the initial state.*

A triple $\langle s, a, \mu \rangle$ such that $\langle a, \mu \rangle \in T(s)$ is called a *transition*. We also write $s \xrightarrow{a} \mu$ for the transition $\langle s, a, \mu \rangle$.

2.2   Probabilistic Timed Automata

Probabilistic timed automata deal with time through *clocks*: variables whose domain is $\mathbb{R}_0^+$ that advance synchronously with rate 1 over time. Given a set of clocks $\mathcal{C}$, the valuation $\mathbf{0} \in Val$ (with $Val = \mathcal{C} \rightarrow \mathbb{R}_0^+$) assigns zero to every clock $c \in \mathcal{C}$. For $v \in Val$ and $t \in \mathbb{R}_0^+$, we denote by $v + t$ the valuation where all clock variables have been incremented by t, and by $v[X]$ the one where all clocks in $X \subseteq \mathcal{C}$ have been reset to zero. *Clock constraints* are expressions of the form

$$\mathcal{CC} ::= true \mid false \mid \mathcal{CC} \wedge \mathcal{CC} \mid c \sim n \mid c_1 - c_2 \sim n$$

where $\sim \in \{>, \geq, <, \leq\}$, $c, c_1, c_2 \in \mathcal{C}$ and $n \in \mathbb{N}$. The form $c_1 - c_2 \sim n$ is called a *diagonal*, and a clock constraint without diagonals is *diagonal-free*. If all comparison operators used in a clock constraint are in $\{\geq, \leq\}$, it is *closed*. $[\![e]\!]$ for $e \in \mathcal{CC}$ is the set of valuations $v \in Val$ such that e evaluated in v is *true*.

Definition 4. *A* probabilistic timed automaton *(PTA for short) is a 6-tuple* $\langle Loc, \mathcal{C}, A, E, l_{init}, Inv \rangle$ *where Loc is a countable set of locations, $\mathcal{C}$ is a finite set of clocks, A is a countable set of edge labels, $E \in Loc \rightarrow 2^{\mathcal{CC} \times A \times \mathrm{Dist}(2^{\mathcal{C}} \times Loc)}$ is the edge function with $E(l)$ finite for all $l \in Loc$, $l_{init} \in Loc$ is the initial location, and $Inv \in Loc \rightarrow \mathcal{CC}$ is the invariant function.*

A 4-tuple $\langle l, g, a, \mu \rangle$ such that $\langle g, a, \mu \rangle \in E(l)$ is called an *edge*. It consists of the guard g, the label a and the probability distribution μ over sets of clocks to reset and target locations. We also write $l \xrightarrow{g,a} \mu$ for the edge $\langle l, g, a, \mu \rangle$. Using PTA to directly build models of complex systems is cumbersome. Instead, higher-level formalisms such as PRISM's [15] guarded command language are used. Aside from a parallel composition operator, they add to PTA variables that take values from finite domains. In a *PTA with variables* (VPTA), guards and invariants can include Boolean expressions over the variables, the set of clock resets is extended by assignments of new values to variables, and the probabilities of target locations can be computed based on the current valuation. The semantics of a VPTA M is a PTA whose locations are pairs $\langle l, v \rangle$ of a location of M and a valuation v for the variables. VPTA can compactly describe very large PTA.

The semantics of a PTA is as follows: When in location l, time can pass as long as the invariant $Inv(l)$ remains satisfied. An edge $e \in E(l)$ as above can be taken if its guard is satisfied at the current point in time. When this happens, a target $\langle X, l' \rangle$ is chosen according to the probability distribution μ, the clocks in X are reset, and we move to the successor location l'.

Example 1. An example PTA is shown in Fig. 1. It has two clocks x and y. The edge labelled a from location l_0 has guard $x \leq 1$ and leads into the probability distribution $\{ \langle \varnothing, l_1 \rangle \mapsto \frac{1}{2}, \langle \{ y \}, l_2 \rangle \mapsto \frac{1}{2} \}$. The invariant of l_2 is $y \leq 0$, thus no time can pass while the system is in that location.

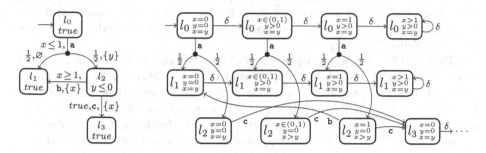

Fig. 1. Example PTA   **Fig. 2.** The region MDP of the example PTA

Definition 5. *A timed probabilistic transition system (TPTS for short) is a 4-tuple $\langle S, A, T, s_{init} \rangle$ where S is a set of states, $A = \mathbb{R}^+ \uplus A'$ is a set of transition labels partitioned into delays in $\mathbb{R}^+$ and jump labels in A', $T \in S \to 2^{A \times \mathrm{Dist}(S)}$ is the transition function, and $s_{init} \in S$ is the initial state. The delay-labelled transitions must lead into Dirac distributions and be time-deterministic and time-additive.*

TPTS can be seen as uncountably infinite-state, uncountably-branching Markov decision processes. We use them to formally define the semantics of PTA:

Definition 6. *The semantics of a well-formed PTA $M = \langle Loc, \mathcal{C}, A, E, l_{init}, Inv \rangle$ is the TPTS $[\![M]\!] = \langle Loc \times Val, \mathbb{R}^+ \uplus A, T_M, \langle l_{init}, \mathbf{0} \rangle \rangle$ where T_M is the smallest function such that the following two inference rules are satisfied:*

$$\frac{l \xrightarrow{g,a}_E \mu \quad v \in [\![g]\!]}{\langle l, v \rangle \xrightarrow{a}_{T_M} \mu_M^v} \; (jump) \qquad \frac{t \in \mathbb{R}^+ \quad \forall t' \leq t \colon (v + t') \in [\![Inv(l)]\!]}{\langle l, v \rangle \xrightarrow{t}_{T_M} \mathcal{D}(\langle l, v + t \rangle)} \; (delay)$$

where $\mu_M^v(\langle l', v' \rangle) = \mu(\langle X, l' \rangle)$ if $v' = v[X]$ and $\mu_M^v(s) = 0$ otherwise.

We refer to the transitions resulting from the respective inference rules as *jumps* and *delays*. It is undesirable to be able to jump into a location l' such that $Inv(l')$ is immediately violated. If this is not possible in a PTA, we say that it is *well-formed*. Non-well-formed PTA need to be rejected as modelling errors.

2.3 Probabilistic Timed Reachability

A behaviour of a TPTS $M = \langle S, A \uplus \mathbb{R}^+, T, s_{init} \rangle$ is a *path* $\pi \in Paths(M)$: an infinite sequence $\langle s_0, a_0 \rangle \langle s_1, a_1 \rangle \cdots \in (S \times A \uplus \mathbb{R}^+)^\omega$ of states and actions or delays. The system starts in the initial state $s_0 = s_{init}$. Assuming that the current state is s_i, the choice of the next transition $s_i \xrightarrow{a_i} \mu_i$ is nondeterministic. Such a choice is made by a scheduler:

Definition 7. *For a TPTS as above, a (memoryless deterministic) scheduler is a function* $\mathfrak{S} \in S \to A \times \mathrm{Dist}(S)$ *s.t.* $\mathfrak{S}(s) \in T(s)$ *for all* $s \in S$.

Once the scheduler has chosen $\mathfrak{S}(s_i) = s_i \xrightarrow{a_i} \mu_i$, the next state s_{i+1} is selected randomly according to μ_i. Using the usual cylinder set construction [17], every scheduler $\mathfrak{S}$ defines a probability measure $\mathbb{P}_\mathfrak{S}$ over the set of all paths. Let $\delta(\pi)$ be the sum of all transition labels in $\mathbb{R}^+$ on path π. Following the standard approach, we restrict to time-divergent schedulers, i.e. we only consider schedulers $\mathfrak{S}$ where $\mathbb{P}_\mathfrak{S}(\{\pi \in Paths(M) \mid \delta(\pi) = \infty\}) = 1$.

Given a PTA M, we are interested in the verification of *probabilistic timed reachability* properties, which are queries of the form "starting from the initial state, what is the maximum/minimum probability of eventually/within time t reaching a location $l \in L$ when c holds" (quantitative form) resp. "is this probability less/greater than or equal to p" (qualitative form) for $L \subseteq Loc$, $c \in \mathcal{CC}$, and $t \in \mathbb{R}_0^+$. The time-bounded questions can be turned into unbounded ones by adding a new clock c_t to M that is never reset, and using the clock constraint $c_t \leq t \wedge c$ in place of c. It thus suffices to consider the time-unbounded questions, which is why we do *not* need history-dependent schedulers. L and c together characterise a set F of states of $[\![M]\!]$. We are thus interested in the extremal probabilities $\sup_\mathfrak{S} \mathbb{P}_\mathfrak{S}(\Pi_F)$ (the maximum probability) and $\inf_\mathfrak{S} \mathbb{P}_\mathfrak{S}(\Pi_F)$ (the minimum probability) where Π_F is the set of paths containing a state in F. If we can compute them, we can also compute e.g. the probabilities of linear-time (safety) path properties by running M in parallel with a finite state machine observer and using its final states for L. If schedulers exist that realise the sup (inf) above (which is always the case for MDP), we call them *optimal* or *maximising (minimising)* schedulers.

Example 2. Two properties of interest on the PTA of Example 1 are (1) the maximum probability to reach l_1 with $x < 1$, which is $\frac{1}{2}$, and (2) the minimum probability to reach a location in $\{l_1, l_2\}$, which is 0 (since we can stay in l_0 forever).

2.4 Digital Clocks, Regions and Zones

To compute reachability probabilities for a (finite) PTA, we cannot construct its semantics since this is an uncountably infinite object. However, three countable (finite) abstractions have been developed to be used for model checking:

Digital clocks. We can replace the clock variables by bounded integers and add self-loop edges to increment them synchronously as long as the location invariant is satisfied. If all clock constraints are closed and diagonal-free, this turns a PTA into a (finite) MDP with variables, while preserving reachability probabilities [16]. The number of states of the underlying *digital clocks MDP* is exponential in the number of clocks and the maximum constants they are compared to. In practice, however, it is often small enough to be amenable to model checking.

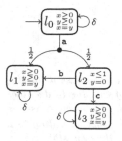

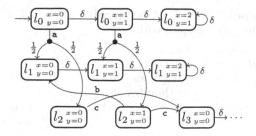

Fig. 3. The zone MDP   **Fig. 4.** The digital clocks MDP of the example PTA

Regions. The *region MDP* is a (finite) abstraction that preserves reachability probabilities for any (finite) PTA [17]. Like the region graph for TA, it is the quotient of the TPTS semantics of a PTA under the equivalence relation that groups the states that cannot be distinguished by any clock constraint (up to the largest value any clock is compared with in the PTA). Its states are thus pairs $\langle l, [v]_C \rangle$ of a location l and a *clock equivalence class* $[v]_C$. In this paper we write *region* to refer to a clock equivalence class, i.e. a set of valuations. The region graph construction suffers from the same blow-up as the digital clocks approach, but region graphs are almost always too large to be useful for model checking.

Zones. A PTA's behaviour often is the same for many regions. This observation has already led to the development of zone-based approaches for TA. A *zone* is a set of valuations characterised by a clock constraint, or equivalently, it is a convex union of regions. Using zones we can construct significantly smaller MDP abstractions of PTA than with individual regions. However, if the standard TA forwards reachability procedure is used for PTA, the resulting *zone MDP* admits schedulers that are too powerful, and thus the reachability probabilities computed in this abstraction are upper/lower bounds on the PTA's respective maximum/minimum probabilities only [17]. To obtain compact zone graphs that do not exhibit this problem, a backwards analysis is needed [18].

In the zone-based algorithms that we present later in this paper, we will write $z_1 \sqcup z_2$ for the convex union of the two zones z_1 and z_2, i.e. the minimal zone that contains both z_1 and z_2, $z{\uparrow}$ for the delay zone $\{ v + t \mid v \in z \wedge t \in \mathbb{R}_0^+ \}$, and $Reg(z)$ for the set of regions in zone z.

Example 3. For the PTA of Example 1, we show the region MDP in Fig. 2, the digital clocks MDP in Fig. 4, and the zone MDP in Fig. 3. Transitions representing delays are labelled δ. If we compute the probabilities of Example 2 on these abstractions, we find that we obtain the correct values with regions and digital clocks. For the former, this was not guaranteed since property (1) contains a non-closed clock constraint. On the zone MDP, however, we obtain probability 1 for property (1). This is because in the original PTA the delay chosen in l_0 determines whether l_1 can be reached from l_2 after the probabilistic jump. In the zone MDP, however, this choice is effectively moved to l_2, giving schedulers extra power.

Input: MDP $\langle S, A, T, s_{init}\rangle$, path property ϕ, scheduler id $\sigma \in \mathbb{Z}$
Output: Sampled path π

```
1  s := s_init, π := s_init
2  while φ(π) = undecided do
3  │   U_nd := PRNG(H(σ.s))              // use hash of σ and s as seed for U_nd
4  │   if T(s) = ∅ then break            // end of run due to deadlock
5  │   ⟨a, μ⟩ := ⌈U_nd() · |T(s)|⌉-th element of T(s)   // use U_nd to select transition
6  │   s' := U_pr(μ)                     // use U_pr to select target according to μ
7  │   π := π.s', s := s'                // append the new state s to π
8  return π
```

Algorithm 1. Path generation for an MDP and a fixed scheduler

3   Lightweight Verification of MDP

We briefly recall the lightweight verification technique for MDP of [5] that underpins our new approach for PTA. As a statistical model checking (SMC) technique, it is based on generating a number of simulation runs through the MDP and then statistically estimating the (reachability) probability of interest. When simulating a fully stochastic model, e.g. a Markov chain, the individual probabilistic decisions are resolved randomly, and thus *a run is sampled* faithfully from the probability measure over all runs of the system. However, in MDP, the nondeterministic choices need to be resolved, too. The lightweight approach of [5] addresses this problem by also *sampling individual schedulers* from the overall space of all schedulers. An adapted SMC analysis is performed for each scheduler, and a set of candidate near-optimal schedulers is iteratively refined by keeping those that deliver the highest (lowest) probabilities. An iterative "smart sampling" technique [5] maximises the probability of finding an optimal scheduler with a finite simulation budget.

   To avoid storing schedulers as explicit mappings, our lightweight approach constructs them on-the-fly using pseudo-random number generators. It uses two independent PRNG U_{pr} and U_{nd} to resolve the probabilistic and nondeterministic choices, respectively. A single integer $\sigma \in \mathbb{Z}$ of b_σ bits identifies and fully specifies a scheduler. At its core, the adapted SMC analysis uses Algorithm 1 to perform simulation runs. We assume that the MDP is given in some compact representation, e.g. as a network of MDP with variables, where a state of the concrete MDP can be seen as a valuation for the system variables v_i with the value of each v_i being represented by a number of bits b_i. A state can thus be represented by the concatenation of the bits of the system variables. In line 3, the scheduler identifier σ is concatenated to the bits representing the current state s (denoted $\sigma.s$). U_{nd} is then initialised using the hash code $h = \mathcal{H}(\sigma.s)$. $\mathcal{H}$ maps $\sigma.s$ to a seed that is deterministically dependent on the state and the scheduler. U_{nd} maps the seed to a value that is uniformly distributed but also deterministically dependent on the trace and the scheduler (line 5). For the fixed σ, this use of U_{nd} thus results in exactly the behaviour of a memoryless scheduler.

In an outer loop, the lightweight approach performs multiple SMC analyses with different sampled values for σ to estimate the property's probability for different schedulers, keeping track of the highest (lowest) overall estimate, which results from the scheduler closest to optimality that has been sampled so far. In a typical implementation on current hardware, a hash function and PRNG may span $\sim 10^{19}$ schedulers. This is usually orders of magnitude more than the number of schedulers sampled. To avoid a cumulative error when choosing a single probability estimate from a number of alternatives, [5] defines a Chernoff bound for multiple estimates. Note that this ensures that the statistical confidence w.r.t. individual estimates is well-defined, but does not provide confidence w.r.t. the optimality of the overall estimate: For maximum (minimum) reachability probabilities, the overall estimate is a lower (upper) bound on the actual probability.

4   Lightweight Verification of PTA

To adapt the lightweight approach described in the previous section to work for PTA, we could use it as-is on the digital clocks or region abstraction. While this works, we find that such a naive adaptation is inefficient: Letting time pass within a location corresponds to a sequence of states and δ-transitions within the digital clocks or region MDP. This makes simulation dependent on the absolute value of delays, reducing performance in models with longer delays because many more transitions need to be simulated. It also means that there are exponentially more schedulers to consider and that they are more likely to pick short delays. These phenomena have the potential to make near-optimal schedulers infeasibly rare.

Example 4. Consider using the region MDP of Fig. 2 with Algorithm 1, and let s be the initial state. $\mathcal{U}_{\mathrm{nd}}$ is used to select one of the outgoing transitions in line 5. Given a fixed σ, i.e. scheduler, this is a deterministic selection. σ is fixed *within* one SMC analysis, but uniformly randomly chosen for each analysis. The probability of using a scheduler that chooses a given transition from s is thus $\frac{1}{2}$, so the probability to pick one that delays up to the top-rightmost state is only $\frac{1}{8}$. However, for property (2) of Example 2, these schedulers are the only ones that lead to the actual minimum probability of 0, while all others (which have probability mass $\frac{7}{8}$) lead to probability 1, a correct but useless upper bound.

The example shows that we would prefer schedulers for every delay to be equally likely. This can be achieved with zones: every state of the zone MDP has an outgoing jump for each edge that ever becomes enabled over time in the corresponding location (cf. Fig. 3). However, as we have already observed, a zone MDP's optimal schedulers may lead to true upper (lower) bounds on maximum (minimum) probabilities. If we were to use the lightweight approach on the zone MDP, we would get lower bounds on upper bounds on maximum probabilities (and vice versa for minimum), i.e. *some* value whose relation to the actual probability is unknown, which is arguably of little use for formal verification.

Input: PTA $M = \langle Loc, \mathcal{C}, A, E, l_{init}, Inv \rangle$, path property ϕ, scheduler id $\sigma \in \mathbb{Z}$
Output: Simulation trace ω

```
1  l := l_init; z := { 0 }; ω := ⟨l_init, z⟩
2  while φ(ω) = undecided do
3  |   if z ∩ [[Inv(l)]] is empty then raise error      // check that M is well-formed
4  |   J := ∅; z_J := z; z' := z↑ ∩ [[Inv(l)]]   // let time pass as the invariant allows
5  |   foreach ⟨g, a, μ⟩ ∈ E(l) where z' ∩ [[g]] ≠ ∅ do
6  |   |   J := J ∪ { ⟨μ, z' ∩ [[g]]⟩ }      // store edge distr., zone where it is enabled
7  |   |_  z_J := z_J ⊔ (z' ∩ [[g]])          // z_J always eventually has an enabled edge
8  |   if J = ∅ then ω := ω.⟨l, z'⟩; break       // can only delay into deadlock
9  |   if z' ≠ z_J then J := J ∪ { D(⟨∅, l⟩), z' \ z_J }  // possible delay into deadlock
10 |   U_nd := PRNG(H(σ.l.z'))                // use hash of σ, l and z' as seed for U_nd
11 |   ⟨μ, z_μ⟩ := ⌈U_nd() · |J|⌉-th element of J   // use U_nd to select one of the edges
12 |   ⟨X, l'⟩ := U_pr(μ)              // use U_pr to select resets, target according to μ
13 |   r := ⌈U_nd()·|Reg(z_μ)|⌉-th element of Reg(z_μ)  // use U_nd to select region in z_μ
14 |   r' := r[X]                              // reset the clocks in X
15 |_  ω := ω.⟨l, z ⊔ r⟩.⟨l', r'⟩, l := l', z := r'   // append delay and jump to trace ω
16 return ω
```

Algorithm 2. Trace generation for a PTA and a fixed scheduler using zones

To avoid this problem, after deciding to perform a particular jump, we also select the concrete region from which the jump takes place, using $\mathcal{U}_{nd}$ again since this is resolving nondeterminism. Doing so *does* conceivably blow up the state space compared to the zone MDP, but this is irrelevant because we only ever construct the state space local to a simulation. Note that it *does not* introduce extra transitions that could lead to the problems we encountered with regions or digital clocks. Furthermore, we distinguish between being allowed to delay into a deadlock situation vs. having an enabled edge at the upper bound of a location's invariant. In effect, we thus simulate the region MDP, but exploit zones to do so in a way suitable for the lightweight approach. Algorithm 2 shows the concrete zone-based simulation that we use for PTA in place of Algorithm 1 for MDP. Otherwise, the lightweight approach remains as described previously.

Algorithm 2 computes the set of edges that become enabled while time passes in the current location, subject to the invariant, in lines 4 to 7. Additionally, the maximum delay after which there is still an enabled edge is computed as z_J. This is necessary to allow the scheduler to choose delaying into a deadlock, like delaying beyond $x = 1$ in l_1 in Fig. 1, when this is possible (line 9, implemented by a self loop into a situation where line 8 will apply). $\mathcal{U}_{nd}$ is then initialised for the current scheduler identifier σ together with the current location l and zone z', and used in line 11 to select one of the edges. Subsequently, a concrete region needs to be chosen out of the range of delays allowed by that edge's guard, which is done by $\mathcal{U}_{nd}$ in line 13. The simulation trace is updated in lines 8 and 15, taking care to include every relevant intermediate state since the property at hand may refer to clocks as described in Sect. 2.3. In our implementation, the trace is never stored explicitly, instead the evaluation of ϕ occurs on-the-fly and incrementally.

In line 13 of Algorithm 2, one region is selected from a zone, using $\mathcal{U}_{nd}$ to choose a region pseudo-randomly with respect to all possible schedulers (the choice made by an individual scheduler is of course deterministic). Since we do not know which region is optimal, we require the choice to be uniformly random. To maintain efficiency, we also require to select directly from the data structure defining the zone, without enumerating all the regions. To achieve this we have implemented two algorithms, one using rejection sampling, to guarantee uniform coverage, the other using conditional sampling, to maximise efficiency.

Both algorithms assume that the increasing integer and fractional values of clocks, corresponding to the division of regions, are represented by a monotonically increasing set of integers. A region is then uniquely identified by a tuple of indices. Some zones are unbounded above, so the maximum region the algorithms consider is the minimum region that exceeds the maximum clock bound in the model. All choices are thus made from a finite range of indices. Neither algorithm considers clocks that are not constrained by bounds within the model, such as the global clock used by the time bounded properties.

The rejection sampling algorithm works by first selecting a value "uniformly at random" (i.e., using $\mathcal{U}_{nd}$) from a cube that encloses the range of indices of the zone. This is achieved by selecting a value uniformly at random from the range of indices corresponding to each clock. As each individual ordinate is chosen, the feasibility of the tentative region is checked against the constraints of the zone. If at any point the region is judged to be infeasible, the sampling process is restarted.

Given that the initial zone is non-empty, the rejection sampling algorithm will eventually terminate with a valid selection, however the execution time scales exponentially with the number of clocks. The conditional sampling algorithm avoids this complexity by ensuring that every choice is made from a feasible interval. Using $\mathcal{U}_{nd}$, the algorithm first chooses a "random" order of clocks. This is necessary because the order in which the clocks are sampled may bias the choices. Then, for each clock in order, an index is chosen uniformly at random with respect to the current range of permissible values. After each choice the data structure representing the zone is updated to reflect the choice, restricting the bounds of the remaining clocks and thus the range of permissible indices.

Note that while our case studies do not motivate the use of the less efficient algorithm (i.e., we found no benefit in terms of optimality), we nevertheless consider efficient uniform region selection a subject of ongoing research.

5   Experiments

We have created a prototype implementation of our new approach for lightweight PTA analysis. It is intended to become part of the PLASMA toolset for statistical model checking [3,11], to take advantage of PLASMA's integrated development environment and distribution algorithms [3]. We use the name PLASMA

SETA (Statistical Estimation of Timed Automata) to identify our results in the figures. The tool is written in Java and uses its own implementation of the standard difference-bound matrix (DBM) data structure to represent invariants, clock constraints, zones and regions in memory. Operations on DBM are used to advance the state of a simulation and check whether the current state satisfies a property. We use a textual modelling language that mirrors the annotated graph-based structure traditionally used to describe timed automata and that facilitates simple conversion between existing graphical and textual formalisms. In contrast to SMC for Markov chain-based models, a state of our simulations represents a set of feasible schedulings (cf. Algorithm 2), whose value with respect to optimality is dependent on the context of whether a minimum or maximum is sought. It is therefore not sufficient to use the standard Monte Carlo estimator and bounded time linear temporal logic. Accordingly, we have implemented a simple continuous time logic that expresses non-nested time-bounded properties of the syntactic forms $\Box_{\leq t}\,\phi$, $\Diamond_{\leq t}\,\phi$ and $\phi\,\mathsf{U}_{\leq t}\,\phi$.

We have applied our implementation to PTA models from the PRISM benchmark suite [13], in order to evaluate its effectiveness (can it solve examples that are intractable to related tools?), its efficiency (what is the performance compared to related tools?), and its usefulness (what is the quality of the results, i.e. the bounds on extremal probabilities that we obtain, and how do these results compare with those of related tools?). Where possible we compare with (a) PRISM's default game-based engine [14] for traditional exhaustive PTA model checking, with (b) UPPAAL-SMCas a statistical model checker that uses a single stochastic scheduler, and with (c) the original lightweight approach (as described in Sect. 3) on a digital clocks abstraction of the PTA.

All experiments were performed on an Intel Xeon 2.8 GHz system running Ubuntu 15.04 with 8 GB of memory. We used PRISM 4.3 with default settings and UPPAAL 4.1.19 with statistical parameter $\epsilon = 0.01$. UPPAAL's estimates are thus given $\pm \leq 0.01$ with probability ≥ 0.95, w.r.t. the value being estimated. For the original lightweight technique and our new approach, we used smart sampling with a per-iteration simulation budget of 3×10^4 and parameters $\epsilon = \delta = 0.01$. This guarantees that the computed results are $\pm \leq 0.01$ with probability ≥ 0.99, w.r.t. the values being estimated.

Firewire. We first look at the `firewire_abst` PRISM PTA benchmark, which models the IEEE 1394 FireWire root contention protocol in an abstract manner. The property we check is $\Diamond_{\leq t}\,done$, for deadline $t \in \{0.4, 0.8, 1.2, \ldots, 10\}\,\mu s$ and where *done* signifies that both stations have completed their transmissions. The results are shown in Fig. 5. The shaded regions denote a ± 0.01 error interval around the values calculated by PRISM, corresponding to our specified confidence. The circles show the probability estimates for the best maximising/minimising scheduler found by our new approach. The crosses mark the single probability estimated by UPPAAL-SMC.

We see that our approach finds schedulers that are very close to the optimal schedulers found by model checking. For deadlines of 5 μs or less, the estimates produced by our approach are within the specified statistical confidence, noting

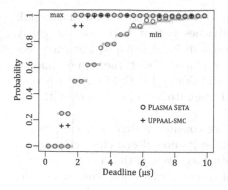 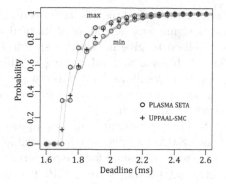

Fig. 5. Firewire results   **Fig. 6.** CSMA-2 results

that this confidence is not with respect to optimality. For greater deadlines our
minimising estimates are less accurate with respect to the true minima, but
are nevertheless clearly discernible from the maximising estimates. By contrast,
the estimates produced by UPPAAL-SMClie arbitrarily between the maxima and
minima. Very approximately, UPPAAL-SMC's results denote the performance of
the "average" scheduler found by our approach.

CSMA-2 and CSMA-3. We now turn to larger and more challenging models.
The first is the csma PRISM PTA benchmark, which models the IEEE 802.3
CSMA/CD protocol for shared medium access with two senders (CSMA-2). The
second is a new model that adds a third sender (CSMA-3). We also consider a
digital clocks version of CSMA-2. For both, we seek the maximum and minimum
probability that all senders successfully finish sending one message within t ms.
The experimental results for CSMA-2 are shown in Fig. 6. Once again our approach finds schedulers that very closely approximate the optima calculated by
PRISM. In this case all the results are within the specified statistical confidence.
As before, the single estimates produced by UPPAAL-SMClie arbitrarily between
minimum and maximum: for deadlines less than ~ 1.9 ms they lie close to the
minimum, while above this deadline they lie close to the maximum.

CSMA-2 is tractable for PRISM using values of t from 0 to 3 ms and well
beyond. With CSMA-3, however, PRISM runs out of memory with even the lowest
interesting deadline. Our approach remains tractable with CSMA-3 and arbitrary
deadlines, albeit with increased running time. We report the following results
for CSMA-3, although we currently have no means to independently verify their
accuracy:

deadline (ms)	2	3	4	6	8
max. prob	0.0	0.544	0.640	0.650	0.671
min. prob	0.0	0.192	0.246	0.249	0.244

Performance. Our results have been produced using a single execution thread, but a significant benefit of statistical approaches is that they may be easily parallelised to give near-linear speedup with additional threads. For the specified confidence and interesting deadlines, we need about the same time to generate a result as PRISM (between 400 and 500 s) for CSMA-2. With parallelisation, we expect one or two orders of magnitude improvement with our statistical approach.

To further motivate our new approach, we consider a digital clocks version of the CSMA-2 model, which is possible because its non-closed clock constraints can be worked around for the property we consider. We can thus use the original lightweight technique for MDP. The use of discrete time, however, incurs the penalty of having to explicitly consider every delay step in the time bound of the property. Our results with CSMA-2 suggest that this penalty leads to at least an order of magnitude increase in computational time.

We have also profiled our implementation using the CSMA-2 model. We find that around 56 % of the total runtime is spent on DBM operations excluding region selection (as described at the end of Sect. 4), which account for a further 10 %. Around 32 % is used by the simulation loop to enumerate choices and compute synchronisations in the model. Profiling with the more challenging CSMA-3 model reveals that DBM operations continue to account for around 55 % of the execution time, while the amount of time dedicated to region selection is approximately doubled to 22 %. Synchronising and selecting actions accounts for a further 22 %. It is clear that optimising all DBM operations, including those for region selection, will be a profitable direction of future work to improve performance.

6   Conclusion

We have provided the first algorithm and implementation for statistical approximation of optimal schedulers for PTA. This enables statistical model checking of PTA with proper consideration of nondeterminism. Our algorithm is built on top of the smart sampling technique [5] using zones first, for selecting an enabled edge, and then regions to define the particular (abstract) moment in which the scheduler determines the execution of a transition. This two-step technique minimises possible bias towards selecting fast or slow schedulers. Using zones improves performance compared to a digital clocks or region-based techniques.

Our experiments have validated our technique, reporting near-optimal estimates that are close to the true optima calculated via probabilistic model checking with PRISM. As a simulation-based tool, our technique can report results when probabilistic model checking runs out of memory, as shown for the CSMA-3 cxample. We have also compared it with UPPAAL-SMC, the only other tool that can simulate PTA. UPPAAL-SMCassumes that the sojourn time at a location is either uniformly distributed, if the invariant limits it, or exponentially distributed otherwise. It thus uses a single fully stochastic scheduler and reports only a single estimated value. As we have seen in the experiments, this value can occur at any point within the interval bounded by the actual minimum and maximum probabilities. We cannot in general quantify how close our approximations are to the true optima, however they must lie within the interval spanned by the true optimal values or else lie outside with quantified statistical confidence. Thus the reported values can always be used to reject the model when the desired maximum (minimum) probability is smaller (greater) than the estimated one.

Future work. This work opens new directions of possible research. We could consider priced PTA to estimate e.g. energy consumption or financial costs. Ideas in this direction have already been reported in [19] for non-timed models. If extended to stochastic timed automata (STA) [2], our approach could be useful in combination with the STA model checking technique of [8], which delivers upper/lower bounds, while we obtain lower/upper bounds on maximum/minimum probabilities. We would also like to reduce the sample space of schedulers to increase the likelihood of choosing near-optimal schedulers in our algorithm.

References

1. Alur, R., Dill, D.L.: A theory of timed automata. Theor. Comput. Sci. **126**(2), 183–235 (1994)
2. Bohnenkamp, H., D'Argenio, P., Hermanns, H., Katoen, J.P.: MoDeST: a compositional modeling formalism for real-time and stochastic systems. IEEE Trans. Softw. Eng. **32**(10), 812–830 (2006)
3. Boyer, B., Corre, K., Legay, A., Sedwards, S.: PLASMA-lab: a flexible, distributable statistical model checking library. In: Joshi, K., Siegle, M., Stoelinga, M., D'Argenio, P.R. (eds.) QEST 2013. LNCS, vol. 8054, pp. 160–164. Springer, Heidelberg (2013)
4. Brázdil, T., Chatterjee, K., Chmelík, M., Forejt, V., Křetínský, J., Kwiatkowska, M., Parker, D., Ujma, M.: Verification of Markov decision processes using learning algorithms. In: Cassez, F., Raskin, J.-F. (eds.) ATVA 2014. LNCS, vol. 8837, pp. 98–114. Springer, Heidelberg (2014)
5. D'Argenio, P., Legay, A., Sedwards, S., Traonouez, L.M.: Smart sampling for lightweight verification of Markov decision processes. STTT **17**(4), 469–484 (2015)
6. David, A., Jensen, P.G., Larsen, K.G., Mikučionis, M., Taankvist, J.H.: Uppaal stratego. In: Baier, C., Tinelli, C. (eds.) TACAS 2015. LNCS, vol. 9035, pp. 206–211. Springer, Heidelberg (2015)
7. David, A., Larsen, K.G., Legay, A., Mikucionis, M., Poulsen, D.B.: Uppaal SMC tutorial. STTT **17**(4), 397–415 (2015)
8. Hahn, E.M., Hartmanns, A., Hermanns, H.: Reachability and reward checking for stochastic timed automata. ECEASST, 70 (2014)
9. Henriques, D., Martins, J.G., Zuliani, P., Platzer, A., Clarke, E.M.: Statistical model checking for Markov decision processes. In: 2012 Ninth International Conference on Quantitative Evaluation of Systems, pp. 84–93. IEEE (2012)
10. Hérault, T., Lassaigne, R., Magniette, F., Peyronnet, S.: Approximate probabilistic model checking. In: Steffen, B., Levi, G. (eds.) VMCAI 2004. LNCS, vol. 2937, pp. 73–84. Springer, Heidelberg (2004)

11. Jegourel, C., Legay, A., Sedwards, S.: A platform for high performance statistical model checking – PLASMA. In: Flanagan, C., König, B. (eds.) TACAS 2012. LNCS, vol. 7214, pp. 498–503. Springer, Heidelberg (2012)
12. Knuth, D.E.: The Art of Computer Programming: Sorting and Searching, 2nd edn. Addison-Wesley, Redwood (1998)
13. Kwiatkowska, M., Norman, G., Parker, D.: The PRISM benchmark suite. In: Proceedings of the 9th International Conference on Quantitative Evaluation of Systems (QEST 2012). pp. 203–204. IEEE CS Press, September 2012
14. Kwiatkowska, M.Z., Norman, G., Parker, D.: Stochastic games for verification of probabilistic timed automata. In: Ouaknine, J., Vaandrager, F.W. (eds.) FORMATS 2009. LNCS, vol. 5813, pp. 212–227. Springer, Heidelberg (2009)
15. Kwiatkowska, M.Z., Norman, G., Parker, D.: PRISM 4.0: verification of probabilistic real-time systems. In: Gopalakrishnan, G., Qadeer, S. (eds.) CAV 2011. LNCS, vol. 6806, pp. 585–591. Springer, Heidelberg (2011)
16. Kwiatkowska, M.Z., Norman, G., Parker, D., Sproston, J.: Performance analysis of probabilistic timed automata using digital clocks. FMSD 29(1), 33–78 (2006)
17. Kwiatkowska, M.Z., Norman, G., Segala, R., Sproston, J.: Automatic verification of real-time systems with discrete probability distributions. Theor. Comput. Sci. 282(1), 101–150 (2002)
18. Kwiatkowska, M.Z., Norman, G., Sproston, J., Wang, F.: Symbolic model checking for probabilistic timed automata. Inf. Comput. 205(7), 1027–1077 (2007)
19. Legay, A., Sedwards, S., Traonouez, L.: Estimating rewards & rare events in nondeterministic systems. ECEASST, 72 (2015)
20. Younes, H.L.S., Simmons, R.G.: Probabilistic verification of discrete event systems using acceptance sampling. In: Brinksma, E., Larsen, K.G. (eds.) CAV 2002. LNCS, vol. 2404, pp. 223–235. Springer, Heidelberg (2002)

Probabilistic Formal Analysis of App Usage to Inform Redesign

Oana Andrei$^{(\boxtimes)}$, Muffy Calder, Matthew Chalmers, Alistair Morrison,
and Mattias Rost

School of Computing Science, University of Glasgow, Glasgow, UK
oana.andrei@glasgow.ac.uk

Abstract. Evaluation and redesign of user-intensive mobile applications is challenging because users are often heterogeneous, adopting different patterns of activity, at different times. We set out a process of integrating *statistical*, longitudinal analysis of actual logged behaviours, *formal, probabilistic discrete state models* of activity patterns, and hypotheses over those models expressed as *probabilistic temporal logic properties* to inform redesign. We employ formal methods not to the design of the mobile application, but to characterise the different probabilistic patterns of actual *use* over various time cuts within a population of users. We define the whole process from identifying questions that give us insight into application usage, to event logging, data abstraction from logs, model inference, temporal logic property formulation, visualisation of results, and interpretation in the context of redesign. We illustrate the process through a real-life case study, which results in a new and principled way for selecting content for an extension to the mobile application.

1 Introduction

Evaluation and redesign of deployed user-intensive mobile applications (apps) is challenging because users are often heterogeneous and adopt different patterns of activity, at different times. Good redesign must support users' different styles of use, and should not be based solely on static attributes of users, but on those styles, which may be dynamic. This raises many questions, including: what characterises the usage of a user, how should we identify the different styles of use, how does that characterisation evolve, e.g. over an individual user trace, and/or over days and months, and how do *properties* of usage inform evaluation and redesign? This paper attempts to answer these questions, setting out a novel process of integrating statistical analysis of logged behaviours, probabilistic formal methods and probabilistic temporal logic with rewards.

Our approach is based on integrating three powerful ingredients: (1) *inference* of *admixture* probabilistic Markov models (called *activity patterns*) from automatically logged data on user sessions, (2) *characterisation* of the activity patterns by probabilistic *temporal logic* properties using model checking techniques, and (3) *longitudinal* analysis of usage data drawn from different time cuts (e.g. the first day, first month, second month, etc.). Our contribution is

© Springer International Publishing Switzerland 2016
E. Ábrahám and M. Huisman (Eds.): IFM 2016, LNCS 9681, pp. 115–129, 2016.
DOI: 10.1007/978-3-319-33693-0_8

defining the whole process from identifying questions that give us insight into an app usage, to event and attribute logging, data pre-processing and abstraction from logs, model inference, temporal logic property formulation using the probabilistic temporal logic PCTL with rewards [1], visualisation of results and interpretation in the context of redesign. Our work provides new insights into app usage and affords new redesign ideas that are solidly grounded in observed activity patterns. We apply *scientific* and *formal* methods in a novel way to the observed *use* of artefacts that have been *engineered*. We illustrate throughout with a case study of AppTracker [2], a freely available mobile, personal productivity app that allows users to collect quantitative statistics about the usage of all apps installed on their iOS devices, i.e., iPhones, iPads, or iPods.

Initially, we *instrument* the app of interest to log usage behaviours and process them into sets of user traces expressed in terms of higher level actions. These actions are carefully selected, jointly by analysts and developers, to relate to the intended analysis: they determine the scope of properties and the dimensions of the state space underlying the model. We segment the sets of traces into different time cuts so that we can determine how activity patterns evolve over time.

For each time cut of user traces we infer *admixture bigram models of activity patterns*, where activity patterns are discrete-time Markov chains. We use admixture models because we are not classifying users into a single prototypical behavioural trait (or usage style), but we have complex behavioural traits where individuals move between patterns during an observed user trace. Bigrams, which provide the conditional probability of an action given the preceding action, are one of the most successful models for language analysis (i.e. streams of symbols) and are good representations for populations of dynamic, heterogeneous users [3]. We characterise each user trace as an admixture of K activity patterns shared within the population of users. K is an important exploratory tool, and rather than assuming or finding an optimal value for K, we use it to explore the variety of usage styles that are meaningful to redesign. We typically start with low K values, but the choice may be dependent on factors intrinsic to the app. For a given K value, the parameters of the inferred model are the probabilities of a given action (from a preceding action), for each activity pattern, as well as the probabilities of transitioning *between* activity patterns. It is important to note that we are not inferring the underlying system topology, which is determined by the functionality of the app. We are investigating an artefact that has been engineered, but there may be differing generating processes of use. We employ a standard local non-linear optimisation algorithm for parameter estimation – the Expectation-Maximisation (EM) algorithm [4]. We use EM, as opposed to say MCMC, because it is fast and computationally efficient for our kind of data. EM converges provably to a local optimum of the criterion, in this case the likelihood function, and as such validation is not an issue. To the best of our knowledge, inferring such temporal structures has not been described outside our group.

We then *hypothesise* temporal probabilistic properties, expressed in PCTL extended with rewards [1,5] to explore the activity patterns, considering various admixture models, values for K, and time cuts. We compare the distribution of patterns in the population of users longitudinally and structurally drawing on all the formal analysis to provide new, grounded insights into possible redesign. In our case study, our analysis mitigates against a simple partitioning of different versions, specific to each activity, but rather offers a new and principled way of selecting glanceable information as an extension of the app.

Three AppTracker designers were involved in this paper, guiding the integration of formal analysis with hypotheses about user behaviours. This is our second application of formal analysis to models of inferred user behaviour: in [6] we defined activity patterns for an individual user as a user metamodel with respect to a population of users, and analysed a mobile game app. This work differs substantially in that here our goal is redesign in the context of a different app, we use the parameter K as an exploratory tool, employ completely different temporal properties (e.g. using rewards) and longitudinal analysis, and analyse the whole population of users, comparing distributions of activity patterns across the user population longitudinally for a fixed and different values for K.

2   Technical Background

We assume familiarity with Markov models, PCTL, PRISM probabilistic model checking, bigram models and Expectation-Maximisation algorithms.

A **Discrete-Time Markov chain** (DTMC) is a tuple $\mathcal{D} = (S, \bar{s}, \mathrm{P}, l)$ where: S is a set of states; $\bar{s} \in S$ is the initial state; $\mathrm{P} : S \times S \to [0,1]$ is the transition probability function (or matrix) such that for all states $s \in S$ we have $\sum_{s' \in S} \mathrm{P}(s, s') = 1$; and $l : S \to 2^{\mathcal{A}}$ is a labelling function associating to each state s in S a set of valid atomic propositions from a set $\mathcal{A}$. A *path* (or execution) of a DTMC is a non-empty sequence $s_0 s_1 s_2 \ldots$ where $s_i \in S$ and $\mathrm{P}(s_i, s_{i+1}) > 0$ for all $i \geq 0$. A transition is also called a *time-step*.

Probabilistic Computation Tree Logic (PCTL) [1] allows expression of a probability measure of the satisfaction of a temporal property. The syntax is:

$$\text{State formulae } \phi ::= true \mid a \mid \neg\phi \mid \phi \wedge \phi \mid \mathrm{P}_{\bowtie p}[\psi]$$
$$\text{Path formulae } \psi ::= \mathsf{X}\phi \mid \phi\,\mathsf{U}^{\leq n}\,\phi \mid \mathsf{F}^{\leq n}\,\phi$$

where a ranges over a set of atomic propositions $\mathcal{A}$, $\bowtie \in \{\leq, <, \geq, >\}$, $p \in [0,1]$, and $n \in \mathbb{N} \cup \{\infty\}$. State formulae are also called *temporal properties*. The usual semantics apply, with U and F standing for *until* and *eventually*, respectively.

PRISM [7] computes a satisfaction probability, e.g. $\mathrm{P}_{=?}[\psi]$, allowing also for *experimentation* when the range and step size of the variable(s) are specified. PRISM supports a *reward*-based extension of PCTL, called *rPCTL*, that assigns non-negative real values to states and/or transitions. $\mathrm{R}\{x\}_{=?}[\mathsf{C}^{\leq N}]$ computes the reward named x accumulated along *all* paths within N time-steps, $\mathrm{R}\{x\}_{=?}[\mathsf{F}\,\phi]$ computes the reward named x accumulated along *all* paths until ϕ is satisfied. Filtered probabilities check for properties that hold from sets of states satisfying given propositions. Here we use `state` as the filter operator: e.g., `filter(state, `ϕ`, `*condition*`)` where ϕ is a state formula and *condition* a Boolean proposition uniquely identifying a state in the DTMC.

Inference of Admixture Bigram Models. Given a vocabulary V of size n, a trace over V is a finite non-empty sequence of symbols from V. Let $S = \{0, 1, \ldots, n\}$ be the set of states and consider a bijective mapping $V \mapsto S$. Let x be a data sample of M traces over V, $x = \{x_1, \ldots, x_M\}$. Each trace x_m can be represented as a DTMC: the set of states $S = \{0, 1, \ldots, n\}$, the initial state is 0, the transition probability matrix is the $n \times n$ *transition-occurrence matrix* such that x_{mij} on position (i, j) gives the number of times the pair (x_{mi}, x_{mj}) occurs in the trace x_m. Consider K $n \times n$ transition matrices denoted Φ_k over the states in S, for $k = 1, \ldots, K$, such that Φ_{kij} denotes the probability of moving from state i to state j. Also consider a $M \times K$ matrix Θ such that at any point in time Φ_k is used by the trace x_m with probability Θ_{mk}. Let $\lambda = \{\Phi_k, \Theta_{mk} \mid k = 1, \ldots, K; \ m = 1, \ldots, M\}$ be the parameters of the statistical model. We use the EM algorithm [4] to find maximum likelihood parameters λ of observing each trace x_m, restarting the algorithm whenever the log-likelihood has multiple-local maxima. The result is an *admixture bigram model*: a Θ-weighted mixture of the K DTMCs Φ_k. The model is bigram because only dependencies between adjacent symbols in the trace are considered.

3   Case Study: AppTracker

AppTracker is an iOS application that provides a user with information on the usage of their device. It operates on iPhones/iPads/iPods, running in the background and monitoring the opening and closing of apps as well as the locking and unlocking of the device. It was released in August 2013 and downloaded over 35,000 times. The interface displays a series of charts and statistics to give insight into how long one is spending on their device, the most used apps, how these stats fluctuate over time, etc. Fig. 1 shows three views from the app. The main menu screen offers four main options (Fig. 1(a)). The first menu item, *Overall Usage*, contains quick summaries of all the data recorded since AppTracker was installed opening the views TopApps and Stats (Fig. 1(b)). The second menu item, *Last 7 Days*, displays a chart limited to the activity recorded over the last 7 days. The third menu item, *Select by Period*, shows statistics for a selected period of time. For example, one could investigate which apps one used the most last Saturday, see how the time one spent on Facebook varied each day across last month, or examine patterns of use over a particular day (Fig. 1(c)). The final menu option, *Settings*, allows a user to start and stop the tracker, or to reset their recorded data. A *Terms and Conditions* screen is shown to a user on first launch that describes all the data that will be recorded during its use and provides contact details to allow the user to opt out at any time.

Preparing Raw Logged Data. Data is collected within the SGLog framework [8]. Each log, stored in a MySQL database, contains information about the user, the device, and the event that took place. For our analysis, we are interested in the events resulting in a switch between views within the app. The raw data is extracted and processed using JavaScript to obtain user traces of views (for each user). A special view denotes when the user leaves the app (UseStop) and we

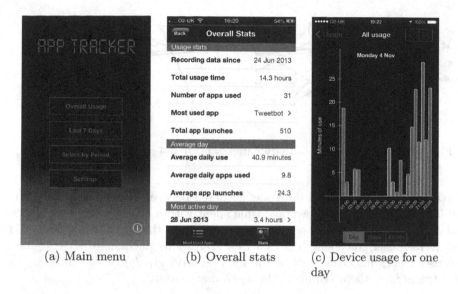

(a) Main menu   (b) Overall stats   (c) Device usage for one day

Fig. 1. Screenshots from AppTracker

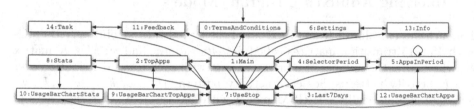

Fig. 2. AppTracker state diagram

define a *session* as the event sequence delimited by two UseStop states, except the initial session which starts from the TermsAndConditions. This results in a total of 15 unique views, with transitions, illustrated in Fig. 2 with the following meaning: (0) TermsAndConditions is the terms and conditions page; (1) Main is the main menu screen; (2) TopApps shows the summary of all recorded data; (3) Last7Days shows the last 7 days of top 5 apps used; (4) SelectPeriod shows app usage stats for a selected time period; (5) AppsInPeriod shows apps used for a selected period; (6) Settings shows the settings options; (7) UseStop stands for closing/sending to background the AppTracker; (8) Stats shows statistics of app usage; (9) UsageBarChartTopApps shows app usage when picked from TopApps; (10) UsageBarChartStats shows app usage when picked from Stats; (11) Feedback shows a screen for giving feedback; (12) UsageBarChartApps shows app usage when picked from AppsInPeriod; (13) Info shows information about the app; (14) Task shows a feedback question chosen from the Feedback view. The 15 views relate directly to the underlying atomic propositions used later in the DTMCs and we map user traces to 15×15 transition-occurrence matrices.

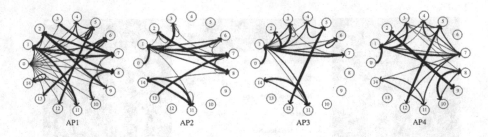

Fig. 3. The DTMCs of the activity patterns for $K = 4$ and first month of usage.

Data for this Study. All data was gathered between August 2013 and May 2014, from 489 users. The average time spent within the app per user is 626 s (median 293 s), the average number times going into the app is 10.7 (median 7), the average user trace length is 73.6 view transitions (median 46). We segment the user traces into time cuts of the interval form $[d_1, d_2)$, which includes the user traces from the d_1-th up to the d_2-th day of usage.

4 Inferring Admixture Bigram Models

For each chosen value of K and time cut of the logged data we obtain K DTMCs with 15×15 transition matrices called *activity patterns* and an $M \times K$ matrix Θ, where M is the number of user traces, and with each row a distribution over the K activity patterns. For each activity pattern APk, for $k = 1, \ldots, K$, we generate automatically a PRISM model with one variable x for the views of the app with values ranging from 0 to 14. For each state value of x we have a PRISM command defining all possible 15 probabilistic transitions where Φ_{kij} is the transition probability from state $x = i$ to the updated state $x' = j$ in activity pattern APk, for all $i, j = 0, \ldots, 14$. For each state value we associate the label corresponding to a higher level state in AppTracker (see the mapping in Fig. 2) as well as a reward structure which assigns a reward of 1 to that state. The PRISM file for each activity pattern also includes a reward structure assigning a rewards of 1 to each transition (or time step) in the DTMC. All our PRISM models have at most 15 states and at most 51 transitions.

We implemented the EM algorithm in Java, applying the algorithm to data sets with 100 iterations maximum and 200 restarts maximum. Running the EM algorithm takes about 119 s for $K = 2$, 162 s for $K = 3$, and 206 s for $K = 4$ on a 2.8 GHz Intel Xeon. Timings are obtained by running the algorithm 90 times. The algorithm is single threaded and runs on one core.

As example, Fig. 3 illustrates state-transition diagrams of all the $K = 4$ activity patterns, the thickness of the transitions corresponding to ranges of probability: the thicker the line, the higher the probability of that transition. Note this illustration does not include the distribution over the activity patterns.

Table 1. rPCTL properties PROP1–PROP5

ID	Formula and informal description
PROP1	$P_{=?}[!\ell\ U^{\leq N}\ \ell]$: Probability of visiting a ℓ-labelled state for the first time from the initial state within N time steps
PROP2	$R\{"r\_\ell"\}_{=?}[C^{\leq N}]$: Expected number of visits to a ℓ-labelled state from the initial state within N time steps
PROP3	$R\{"r\_Steps"\}_{=?}[F\ \ell]$: Expected number of time steps to reach a ℓ-labelled state from the initial state
PROP4	$\mathtt{filter(state,} R\{"r\_Steps"\}_{=?}[F\ \ell_1], \ell_2)$: Expected number of time steps to reach a ℓ_1-labelled state labelled from a ℓ_2-labelled state
PROP5	$\mathtt{filter(state,} P_{=?}[((!\ell_1)\&(!"UseStop"))\ U^{\leq N}\ \ell_1], \ell_2)$: Probability of reaching for the first time a ℓ_1-labelled state from a ℓ_2-labelled state during a session

5 Analysing rPCTL Properties

We have found that most patterns for logic properties (e.g. probabilistic response, probabilistic precedence, etc.) relate to the design of reactive systems and are not generally helpful for evaluation of user-intensive apps. However, a study of which patterns would be useful is beyond the scope of this paper. Table 1 lists the rPCTL properties we used, with state labels ℓ, ℓ_1, ℓ_2. PROP1, PROP2, and PROP3 are the properties we investigated initially; PROP4 and PROP5 were identified later, prompted by designers' hypotheses and inconclusive initial results. PROP4 generalises PROP3 by analysing traces starting with a chosen state, not necessarily the initial one.

We inferred models for $K \in \{2, 3, 4\}$ for various time cuts and performed analysis of rPCTL properties PROP1 – PROP5 on all activity patterns. For brevity, here we show only properties concerning the states: TopApps, Stats, SelectPeriod, Last7Days, UseStop. These five states showed significant results and differences across time cuts and temporal properties and the designers showed particular interest in them when formulating hypotheses about the actual app usage.

We adopt the following interpretations of model checking results for PROP1, PROP2, and PROP3 in our case study for the same value of N. We say that a pair of state and activity pattern (ℓ, APi) scores a better (resp. worse) result than (ℓ', APj), for all $1 \leq i \neq j \leq K$, where either $\ell \neq \ell'$ or $i \neq j$, if: PROP1 returns a higher (resp. lower) value, PROP2 a higher (resp. lower) value, and PROP3 a positive lower (resp. higher) value for (ℓ, APi) than for (ℓ', APj).

Analysing rPCTL Properties for $K = 2$. We verify PROP1, PROP2, and PROP3 on the two activity patterns AP1 and AP2 for six time cuts: first day $[0, 1)$, first week minus the first day $[1, 7)$, the first month minus the first week $[7, 30)$, the first month $[0, 30)$, the second month $[30, 60)$ and the third month $[60, 90)$, and for N ranging from 10 to 150 with step-size 10. Here we only show the results for $N = 50$ in Table 2. The best results with respect to the property checked across the two patterns are in bold font: we can easily see that the two patterns correspond to different behaviours (results) with respect to the

Table 2. PROP1 (the probability of reaching a given state for the first time within N steps), PROP2 (the expected number of visits to a given state within N steps), and PROP3 (the expected number of time steps to reach a given state) checked for different states and time cuts, and for $N = 50$ steps. The best results with respect to the property checked across the two patterns are in bold font.

Property	Time cut	TopApps		Stats		SelectPeriod		Last7Days		UseStop	
		AP1	AP2	AP1	AP2	AP1	AP2	AP1	AP2	AP1	AP2
PROP1	$[0,1)$	0.99	0.99	0.99	0.83	0.47	**0.79**	0.49	**0.96**	0.99	0.99
	$[1,7)$	0.99	0.99	0.98	0.80	0	**0.93**	0	**0.98**	0.99	0.99
	$[7,30)$	0.99	0.99	0.99	0.64	0.01	**0.94**	0.84	**0.96**	0.99	0.99
	$[0,30)$	0.99	0.99	0.99	0.75	0.21	**0.92**	0.44	**0.98**	0.99	0.99
	$[30,60)$	0.99	0.99	0	**0.90**	0.73	**0.83**	0.56	**0.98**	1	0.99
	$[60,90)$	1	0.95	0.96	0.72	0	**0.94**	0	**0.97**	1	0.99
PROP2	$[0,1)$	**13.94**	7.44	**7.63**	2.15	0.79	**1.82**	0.70	**3.13**	**11.41**	6.17
	$[1,7)$	**17.22**	5.77	**4.00**	2.31	0	**3.97**	0	**4.03**	**12.91**	6.30
	$[7,30)$	**14.93**	7.15	**5.43**	1.47	0.01	**4.61**	1.78	**3.41**	**12.86**	5.74
	$[0,30)$	**14.67**	6.48	**5.08**	1.90	0.24	**3.58**	0.58	**3.99**	**11.00**	6.51
	$[30,60)$	**13.40**	6.83	0	**3.76**	4.41	2.04	0.85	**4.54**	**12.46**	5.61
	$[60,90)$	**17.30**	5.83	2.94	2.60	0	**3.26**	0	**4.43**	**13.96**	5.63
PROP3	$[0,1)$	**3.31**	8.41	**8.18**	28.67	79.32	**32.46**	74.87	**15.56**	**4.86**	7.88
	$[1,7)$	**2.05**	10.70	**12.44**	31.90	∞	**19.12**	∞	**12.38**	**3.85**	7.55
	$[7,30)$	**2.52**	9.68	**9.70**	48.61	∞	**17.78**	26.61	**14.58**	**3.88**	8.44
	$[0,30)$	**3.05**	9.73	**11.01**	36.03	209.68	**19.94**	87.54	**12.19**	**4.67**	7.43
	$[30,60)$	**4.04**	10.34	∞	**22.33**	38.21	**28.28**	61.74	**11.08**	1	8.82
	$[60,90)$	**2.02**	15.28	**16.53**	39.68	∞	**17.41**	∞	**11.56**	**3.57**	8.90

five states to be more likely, more often, and more quickly reached. Note that looking at the analysis results for UseStop, on average we see twice as many sessions under AP1 than under AP2 and the average session length in terms of time steps under AP2 is double the average session length under AP1.

If we overlook (for now) the results for the time cut $[30, 60)$, we conclude that there are two distinct activity patterns:

AP1: Overall Viewing pattern corresponds to more likely, more often, and more quickly to reach TopApps and Stats, thus more higher level stats visualisations and shorter sessions.

AP2: In-depth Viewing pattern corresponds to more likely, more often, and more quickly to reach Last7Days and SelectPeriod, thus more in-depth stats visualisations and longer sessions.

Now considering the time cut $[30, 60)$, on Table 2 we note slightly different results for this time cut compared to the more consistent results for the other five time cuts: a high number of visits to and a relative low number of time steps to reach Stats no longer belongs to AP1, but to AP2; PROP1 and PROP2 for SelectPeriod no longer discriminate clearly between AP1 and AP2 due to very close results. As a consequence we analyse the additional rPCTL properties (see Table 3) for the time cut $[30, 60)$. We colour-code the results to correspond to the Overall Viewing pattern in **blue-coloured, bold font** and to the In-depth Viewing

Table 3. Properties PROP4 (expected number of time steps to reach a row state from a column state for each pattern) and PROP5 (probability of reaching for the first time a row state from a column state during a session for each pattern) verified for $K = 2$, time cut $[30, 60)$. **Blue-coloured, bold font results** are characteristic to the **Overall Viewing pattern**, while red-coloured font results to the In-depth Viewing pattern; default text colour means inconclusive.

PROP4		Pattern	TopApps	Last7Days	SelectPeriod	Main
TopApps	AP1		–	**3.62**	**11.09**	**2.22**
	AP2		–	10.56	14.89	9.347
Last7Days	AP1	**61.83**		–	**68.68**	**59.56**
	AP2	14.01		–	15.61	10.08
SelectPeriod	AP1	**38.30**	**36.69**		–	**36.03**
	AP2	31.21	28.77		–	27.28
UseStop	AP1	**1.49**	**3.61**	9.23		**3.33**
	AP2	11.74	6.24	11.51		7.82

PROP5		Pattern	TopApps	Last7Days	SelectPeriod
TopApps	AP1		–	**0.66**	**0.26**
	AP2		–	0.26	0.30
Last7Days	AP1	**0.006**		–	**0.02**
	AP2	0.49		–	0.38
SelectPeriod	AP1	**0.008**	**0.08**		–
	AP2	0.23	0.15		–

in red-coloured font. Except for two inconclusive pairs of results (default text colour), Table 3 tells us that the two activity patterns learned from the time cut $[30, 60)$ are respectively similar to the two activity patterns identified for the rest of time cuts analysed previously. The difference in the behaviour around Stats could be explained by a new usage behaviour of the AppTracker around the 30th day of usage due to approximately a full month worth of new statistics, leading to a spurt of more exploratory usage of AppTracker. We note that for the time cut $[60, 90)$ the results listed in Table 2 make again a clear distinction between the two activity patterns with respect to the states SelectPeriod and Last7Days. We might say that in the third month the exploratory usage of AppTracker settles down and users know exactly what to look for and where. A finer-grained longitudinal analysis based on one-week time cuts could reveal additional insight into the behaviour involving Stats around the 30th day of usage.

Our conclusion concerning the two types of activity patterns meets the developers' hypothesis about two distinct usages of the apps. However they expected also to see one pattern revolving around TopApps and Stats, one around SelectPeriod and another one around Last7Days. Since we analysed the admixture model for $K = 2$, we only got two distinct patterns, the last two patterns conjectured by developers being aggregated into a single one. As a consequence, we investigate higher values for K.

Analysing rPCTL Properties for $K = 3$. We analyse PROP1, PROP2, and PROP3 on the admixture model inferred for $K = 3$, time cut $[0, 30)$ and $N = 50$. For brevity, we omit the details, and based on the results we characterise the three patterns as follows:

– AP1 is an Overall Viewing pattern because TopApps and Stats have best results
  for all three properties. SelectPeriod and Last7Days are absent. The sessions are
  twice as short and twice more frequent than for the In-depth Viewing pattern.
– AP2 is a 'weaker' Overall Viewing pattern than AP1 because TopApps has worse
  results, and better results than Stats and Last7Days; SelectPeriod is absent.
– AP3 is an In-depth Viewing pattern because SelectPeriod has the best results,
  followed closely by TopApps and Last7Days.

Analysing rPCTL Properties for $K = 4$. We analyse PROP1, PROP2, and
PROP3 on the admixture model inferred for $K = 4$, time cut $[0, 30)$ and for
$N = 50$. Again, details are omitted and we characterise the patterns as follows:

– AP1 is mainly a TopApps Viewing activity pattern because it has the best
  results for TopApps, compared to Stats, SelectPeriod, and Last7Days which
  score very low results.
– AP2 is a Stats – TopApps Viewing activity pattern, with very low results from
  Last7Days; SelectPeriod is absent.
– AP3 is an In-depth Viewing pattern with dominant Last7Days followed closely
  by TopApps and SelectPeriod; Stats is absent.
– AP4 is mainly a TopApps Viewing pattern because TopApps has the best
  results, while all other states need on average an infinite number of time
  steps to be reached. The fact that it takes on average an infinite number of
  time steps to reach the end of a session (i.e., the state UseStop) motivated us
  to analyse this pattern with other temporal properties and for other states.
  As a consequence we saw that UsageBarChartTopApps has similar properties
  as TopApps, meaning that this pattern corresponds to repeatedly switching
  between TopApps and UsageBarChartTopApps.

Based on the results obtained for UseStop we observe: twice as many sessions
for AP1 than for AP2 and AP3, only a couple of sessions on average for AP4,
fewer views per session (i.e., shorter sessions) for AP1 than for AP2 and AP3.

Longitudinal Θ-Based Comparison. In addition to analysing rPCTL properties, we also compare how the distribution Θ of the two activity patterns for
the entire population of users changes in time. For each time cut considered for
the rPCTL analysis above and activity pattern AP2, we order non-decreasingly
the second column of Θ and re-scale its size to the interval $[0, 1]$ to represent the
horizontal axis, while the ordered Θ values are projected on the vertical axis.
Figure 4 shows the Θ values for AP1 and AP2 for the population of users across
the first three months of usage. We conclude that during the first day of usage,
up to 40 % of users exhibit exclusive In-depth Viewing behaviour (probability
close to 1 on the y-axis) corresponding to an initial exploration of the app with
significant number of visits to TopApps, Stats, SelectPeriod, and Last7Days. Also,
at most 10 % of the users exhibit exclusive Overall Viewing behaviour maybe
because they feel less adventurous in exploring the app, preferring mostly the
first menu option of looking at TopApps and subsequently at Stats. We note that
the distributions of the two activity patterns in the population of users are similar for the time cuts $[0, 1)$ and $[30, 60)$ – probably because more users exhibit

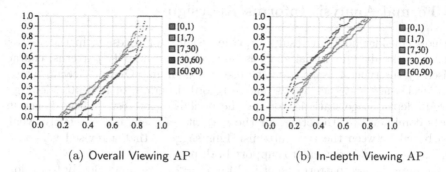

(a) Overall Viewing AP   (b) In-depth Viewing AP

Fig. 4. Longitudinal comparison of the activity pattern distributions Θ over the population of users for $K = 2$ and time cuts $[0, 1), [1, 7), [7, 30), [30, 60), [60, 90)$

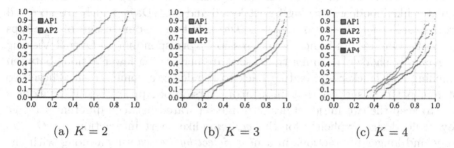

(a) $K = 2$ (b) $K = 3$ (c) $K = 4$

Fig. 5. Pattern distributions for $K = 2$ (Overall Viewing, In-depth Viewing), $K = 3$ (Overall Viewing, weak Overall Viewing, In-depth Viewing,) and $K = 4$ (mainly TopApps Viewing, equally Stats and TopApps Viewing, In-depth Viewing with no Stats, exclusive TopApps and UsageBarChartTopApps), time cut $[0, 30)$.

a more exploratory behaviour during these times (new types of usage statistics become available after one month of usage). At the same time, the plots for the time cuts $[1, 7), [7, 30),$ and $[60, 90)$ are also similar, and we think that they correspond to a settled (or routine) usage behaviour.

Structural Θ-Based Comparison. In Fig. 5 we plot the weightings of all users for each activity patterns for $K \in \{2, 3, 4\}$ and the time cut $[0, 30)$. Figure 5(a) tells us that for $K = 2$ the In-depth Viewing has higher weightings across the user population with almost 25 % of the users using the app exclusively like this, hence either exploring the app or genuinely interested in in-depth usage statistics. Figure 5(b) tells us that almost 10 % of the users are exclusively interested in TopApps, Stats and Last7Days but not SelectPeriod; this behaviour is the most popular among users. From Fig. 5(c) we see that almost 50 % of the users do not behave according to AP4 – switching repeatedly between TopApps and UsageBarChartTopApps. Note that for $K = 3$ and $K = 4$ no pattern stands out as very different from the others.

6   Formal Analysis Informs Redesign

We now consider how our results provide insights for redesign, in the context of the case study. Our initial analysis uncovered two activity patterns, characterised by the type of usage stats the user is examining: Overall Viewing – more high-level usage statistics for the entire recorded period, or In-depth Viewing – more in-depth usage statistics for specific periods of interest. Neither is significantly dominant over the other: for the majority of users, usage is fairly evenly distributed between the two patterns. This suggests that a revised version of AppTracker should continue to support both patterns.

We note the two patterns identified for $K = 2$ correspond closely to options presented on AppTracker's main menu (see Fig. 1(a)), as follows. Overall Viewing indicates a greater likelihood of using TopApps and Stats, which are interface screens accessed through the *Overall Usage* menu item. In-depth Viewing indicates a greater likelihood of reaching SelectPeriod and Last7Days, which are accessed through *Select by Period* and *Last 7 Days*, but also some usage of TopApps and Stats. Our results indicate that sessions corresponding to Overall Viewing are generally shorter: meaning that users are performing fewer actions between launching AppTracker and exiting back to the device's home screen. These two different patterns suggest that, in a future version of AppTracker, if developers want to keep the two major styles of usage separated between different screens, they could design explicitly for the *glancing*-like short interactions in *Overall Usage* and longer interactions in a new *Select by Period* screen along with the initial *Last 7 Days* screen. Also more filtering and querying tools could be added to *Select by Period*.

We wondered if users are simply following the paths suggested by the main menu (Fig. 1(a)). We therefore probed further, considering $K \in \{3, 4, 5\}$ (details are omitted for $K = 5$). For $K = 3$, if the analysis was merely mirroring the menu structure, we might expect to see one pattern centred around each of the first three main menu items. Although we see the pattern AP2 centred around TopApps, Stats, and Last7Days but no SelectPeriod, we do not see a pattern centred around SelectPeriod and not including Last7Days. For $K = 4$ we find Last7Days and SelectPeriod together in a pattern, with the former view slightly more popular than latter one; this combination also occurred for $K = 2$ and $K = 5$. For $K = 4$ we see a distinct new pattern showing users repeatedly switching between TopApps and UsageBarChartTopApps. TopApps is an ordered list of the user's most used apps; selecting an item from this list opens UsageBarChart-TopApps, a bar chart showing daily minutes of use of this app. This persistent switching suggests a more investigatory behaviour, which is more likely to be associated with the In-depth Viewing. Yet this behaviour is occurring under the *Overall Usage* menu item, which we hypothesised and then identified as being associated with more glancing-like behaviour. This suggests that our results are providing more nuanced findings than simple uncovering of existing menu structure. We therefore suggest that if developers want to separate the two types of usage between different menu items even more, they could move the TopApps – UsageBarChartTopApps loop from *Overall Usage* to *Select by Period*.

Glancing Activity Patterns. Discovering a *glancing* activity pattern provides significant benefits for app redesign. Since the release of the iOS 8 SDK in 2014, Apple has allowed the development of *'Today widgets'* – extensions to apps comprising small visual displays and limited functionality appearing in the Notification Centre. Beyond the advice from Apple's Human Interface Guidelines[1], developers struggle to decide which pieces of their app's contents would best suit inclusion in a Today widget: few conventions have built since the release. Developers have to rely on their own judgement to select appropriate content from their app to populate this view. In our analysis, we have uncovered explicitly the specific screens that people look at when they are undertaking short sessions of glancing-type behaviour, i.e. the typical glancing patterns for AppTracker – the Overall Viewing pattern and the TopApps-centred patterns. In identifying such activity patterns, our approach provides a more principled method of selecting content appropriate for an app extension such as a Today widget.

7 Discussion

Related Work. Logging software is frequently used to understand program behaviours, and typically to aid program comprehension – building an understanding of how the program executes [9]. There are various techniques that use logs of running software, such as visualising logs (e.g. [10]) and capture and replay (e.g. [11]), with the aims of failure analysis, evaluating performance, and to better understand the system behaviour (as it executes). In contrast, we are interested in ways users interact with software, and we do so by analysing logs captured during actual use. The difference is important. In the case of program comprehension, log analysis is used to understand better what is going on within the code and how the artefact is engineered (in order to be better prepared for improvements and maintenance). In our case, log analysis provides insights about distinct styles of use and informs improvements of the high-level design. For example, in [12] the authors infer FSMs for modelling a system's behaviour, while we infer DTMC of different actual usage behaviours, and admixtures thereof, to model populations of users. There is complementarity with the approach of [13], which employs usage logs and applies temporal logical analysis, but a key difference is their models are based on static user attributes (e.g. city location of user) rather than on inferred behaviours. Their approach assumes within-class use to be homogeneous, whereas our research demonstrates within-class variation.

Methodological Issues. Our approach is a collaboration between developers familiar with app development and instrumentation, and analysts familiar with statistics and formal modelling. We note some methodological issues.

First, our approach gains from having significant volumes of log data to work on, for reliable application of statistical methods. However, neither the volume

---

[1] https://developer.apple.com/library/ios/documentation/UserExperience/
Conceptual/MobileHIG/AppExtensions.html.

of log data nor number of users is relevant for the probabilistic model checking, only the number of higher level states for analysis selected from the raw data determines the complexity. Therefore *our approach scales* because it does not depend on the number of activity patterns or the number of users/data size, but on the state space of the abstract model of the app. The AppTracker case study involved a vocabulary of 15 views/states, which was comfortably manageable, but our approach would have difficulty with very large vocabularies.

Second, the issue of *what to log* is not trivial. The collection of log entries can include anything from a button press, to the change of WiFi signal of the device, and so on. In the case of AppTracker, we decided to use states corresponding to individual screens possible to transition to within the app. This highlights the rather simple nature of AppTracker – it is essentially a browser of information. In contrast, a game such as Angry Birds allows the user to perform a much more complex set of actions. Even after pruning the logs to include only user actions (rather than lower level device events), one still needs to decide how to model these actions as a state space. The chosen state space will ultimately influence what activity patterns become prominent. We therefore suggest that discussion and preliminary analysis be done early in the development process, so that the decisions about what to log and what the state space should be are made by developers and analysts jointly in a well-informed way.

Third, the activity patterns and their number (i.e. K) are key to analysis. The patterns are inferred by various standard statistical methods based on non-linear optimisation. We do not model for predictability, there is no *true model* of the generating process, but one that is posited based on known characteristics such as the sequential nature of issuing app events. We study the time-series behaviour that has been logged from a probabilistic perspective. The admixture model is important because we are defining a complex behavioural trait where the individual moves between patterns during an observed user trace. The number of patterns K is an important exploratory tool, there is no optimal value for K.

8   Conclusions and Future Work

We have outlined an approach to exploring and gaining insight into usage patterns that informs redesign based on probabilistic formal analysis of actual app usage. Our approach is a combination of bottom up statistical inference from user traces, and top down probabilistic temporal logic analysis of inferred models. We have illustrated this via the mobile app AppTracker, and discussed how the results of this analysis inform redesign that is grounded in existing patterns of usage. A notable conclusion of our work is that, while our analysis of App-Tracker's use identifies several clearly distinct activity patterns, it also reveals the distribution of activity patterns over the population of users and over time. For AppTracker, this mitigates against a simple partitioning of the app into two different versions, each specific to one activity pattern. In addition, our analysis offers a more principled way of selecting glanceable information.

AppTracker developers are currently implementing a redesign based on our analysis, and we eagerly await new data sets of logged behaviours for further analysis. Future work will involve that analysis, as well as patterns for logic properties and generalisation of our approach to a principled way of providing software redesign guidelines as part of a user-centered design process.

Acknowledgements. This research is supported by the EPSRC Programme Grant *A Population Approach to Ubicomp System Design* (EP/J007617/1).

References

1. Baier, C., Katoen, J.P.: Principles of Model Checking. The MIT Press, Cambridge (2008)
2. Bell, M., Chalmers, M., Fontaine, L., Higgs, M., Morrison, A., Rooksby, J., Rost, M., Sherwood, S.: Experiences in logging everyday App. use. In: Proceedings of Digital Economy 2013. ACM (2013)
3. Girolami, M., Kabán, A.: Simplicial mixtures of Markov chains: distributed modelling of dynamic user profiles. In: Thrun, S., Saul, L.K., Schölkopf, B. (eds.) Advances in Neural Information Processing Systems 16 (NIPS 2003), pp. 9–16. MIT Press (2004)
4. Dempster, A.P., Laird, N.M., Rubin, D.B.: Maximum likelihood from incomplete data via the EM algorithm. J. Roy. Stat. Soc. Ser. B (Methodol.) **39**(1), 1–38 (1977)
5. Kwiatkowska, M., Norman, G., Parker, D.: Stochastic model checking. In: Bernardo, M., Hillston, J. (eds.) SFM 2007. LNCS, vol. 4486, pp. 220–270. Springer, Heidelberg (2007)
6. Andrei, O., Calder, M., Higgs, M., Girolami, M.: Probabilistic model checking of DTMC models of user activity patterns. In: Norman, G., Sanders, W. (eds.) QEST 2014. LNCS, vol. 8657, pp. 138–153. Springer, Heidelberg (2014)
7. Kwiatkowska, M., Norman, G., Parker, D.: PRISM 4.0: verification of probabilistic real-time systems. In: Gopalakrishnan, G., Qadeer, S. (eds.) CAV 2011. LNCS, vol. 6806, pp. 585–591. Springer, Heidelberg (2011)
8. Hall, M., Bell, M., Morrison, A., Reeves, S., Sherwood, S., Chalmers, M.: Adapting ubicomp software and its evaluation. In: Graham, T.C.N., Calvary, G., Gray, P.D. (eds.) Proceedings of EICS 2009, pp. 143–148. ACM (2009)
9. von Mayrhauser, A., Vans, A.M.: Program comprehension during software maintenance and evolution. IEEE Comput. **28**(8), 44–55 (1995)
10. Fittkau, F., Waller, J., Wulf, C., Hasselbring, W.: Live trace visualization for comprehending large software landscapes: the ExplorViz approach. In: Telea, A., Kerren, A., Marcus, A. (eds.) Proceedings of VISSOFT 2013, pp. 1–4 (2013)
11. Gomez, L., Neamtiu, I., Azim, T., Millstein, T.D.: RERAN: timing- and touch-sensitive record and replay for Android. In: Notkin, D., Cheng, B.H.C., Pohl, K. (eds.) Proceedings of ICSE 2013, pp. 72–81. IEEE/ACM (2013)
12. Beschastnikh, I., Brun, Y., Ernst, M.D., Krishnamurthy, A.: Inferring models of concurrent systems from logs of their behavior with CSight. In: Jalote, P., Briand, L.C., van der Hoek, A. (eds.) Proceedings of ICSE 2014, Hyderabad, India, pp. 468–479. ACM (2014)
13. Ghezzi, C., Pezzè, M., Sama, M., Tamburrelli, G.: Mining behavior models from user-intensive web applications. In: Proceedings of ICSE 2014, Hyderabad, India, pp. 277–287. ACM (2014)

Extension of PRISM by Synthesis of Optimal Timeouts in Fixed-Delay CTMC

Ľuboš Korenčiak[✉], Vojtěch Řehák, and Adrian Farmadin

Faculty of Informatics, Masaryk University, Brno, Czech Republic
{korenciak,rehak,xfarmad}@fi.muni.cz

Abstract. We present a practically appealing extension of the probabilistic model checker PRISM rendering it to handle fixed-delay continuous-time Markov chains (fdCTMCs) with rewards, the equivalent formalism to the deterministic and stochastic Petri nets (DSPNs). fdCTMCs allow transitions with fixed-delays (or timeouts) on top of the traditional transitions with exponential rates. Our extension supports an evaluation of expected reward until reaching a given set of target states. The main contribution is that, considering the fixed-delays as parameters, we implemented a synthesis algorithm that computes the epsilon-optimal values of the fixed-delays minimizing the expected reward. We provide a performance evaluation of the synthesis on practical examples.

1 Introduction

PRISM [10] is an efficient tool for probabilistic model-checking of stochastic systems such as Markov decision processes (MDPs), discrete-time Markov chains (DTMCs), or continuous-time Markov chains (CTMCs). The PRISM community frequently raises requests to incorporate the possibility to express delays with deterministic durations in a CTMC.[1] The standard PRISM recommendation is to approximate the deterministic durations using a phase-type technique [12] and thus obtaining a CTMC. This works for some models, however there are models for which such approximation can cause either a large error or a state space explosion (see, e.g. [2,7]). However, there is a formalism called fixed-delay CTMCs (fdCTMCs) [1,4,7] that is the requested extension of CTMCs by fixed-delay (fd) events, modeling the deterministic transitions or timeouts. Recent result [1] came up with new synthesis algorithms working directly on fdCTMCs (rather than approximating them with CTMCs). Here we provide the first attempt to experimental evaluation of such synthesis algorithms and show that they are practically applicable. In the following running example we demonstrate the fdCTMC semantics as well as the parameters and objectives of the synthesis.

Example 1. The figure bellow depicts fdCTMC of a slightly modified model of dynamic power management of a Fujitsu disk drive taken from the PRISM case studies[2] [14]. The disk has three modes *idle*, *busy*, and *sleep*. In the *idle* and *sleep* modes the

---

[1] http://www.prismmodelchecker.org/manual/FrequentlyAskedQuestions/PRISMModelling#det_delay.

[2] http://www.prismmodelchecker.org/casestudies/power_ctmc3.php.

© Springer International Publishing Switzerland 2016
E. Ábrahám and M. Huisman (Eds.): IFM 2016, LNCS 9681, pp. 130–138, 2016.
DOI: 10.1007/978-3-319-33693-0_9

disk receives requests, in the *busy* mode it also serves them. The disk is equipped with a bounded buffer, where it stores requests when they arrive. The requests arrive with an exponential inter-arrival time of rate 1.39 and increase the current size of the buffer. The requests are served in an exponential time of rate 12.5, what decreases the buffer size. Note that restricting the model to the *idle* and *busy* modes only, we obtain a CTMC model of an M/M/1/n queue.

Moreover, the disk can move from the *idle* mode to the *sleep* mode where it saves energy. Switching of the disk to the *sleep* mode is driven by timeout. This is modeled by an fd event f_1 moving the state from $(idle, 0)$ to $(sleep, 0)$ when the disk is steadily idle for a specified amount of time (e.g. 1 s). The disk is woken up by another timeout modeled by an fd event f_2, which is active in all *sleep* states. After staying in the *sleep* mode for, e.g. 2 s, f_2 changes the state according to the dashed arrows.

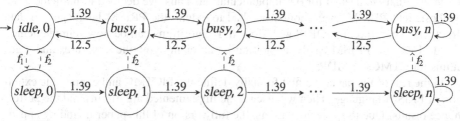

Additionally, every state is given a rate cost that specifies an amount of energy consumed per each second spent there. Optionally, an impulse cost can be specified, e.g., say that the change from $(idle, 0)$ to $(sleep, 0)$ consumes 0.006 energy units instantaneously. Now, one might be interested in how much energy on average is consumed before emptying the buffer, i.e. to compute the expected energy consumed until reaching target that is a new successor of $(busy, 1)$ instead of the initial state $(idle, 0)$. But, being a developer of the disk, can we set better timeouts for f_1 and f_2? Hence, we consider timeouts as parameters and synthesize them in order to minimize the expected amount of consumed energy.

Our Contribution is as follows. 1. We provide an extension of the PRISM language and of the internal data structures to support specification of fdCTMC with impulse and rate costs (or equivalently rewards). Hence, our version of PRISM is now ready for other experiments with fdCTMC algorithms including the possibility to support model-checking options as for CTMCs and DTMCs. 2. We added an evaluation of expected reward until reaching a given set of target states. 3. We analyzed the synthesis algorithm from [1], derived exact formulas and implemented the algorithm. 4. Additionally, we accelerated the implementation by few structural changes, that significantly improved the running time and the space requirements of the synthesis implementation. 5. We provide a performance evaluation proving that current implementation is practically applicable to a complex model from the PRISM case-study.

Related Work. There are many papers that contain models with fd events suitable for synthesis such as deterministic durations in train control systems [16], time of server rejuvenation [3], timeouts in power management systems [14], etc. Some of the models already contain specified impulse or rate costs.

In [15] authors compute the optimal value of webserver timeout using impulse and rate costs. The implementation can dynamically change the optimal value of timeout based on the current inter-arrival times of requests. It works on the exact fdCTMC model and cannot be easily applied to the more general fdCTMC models our implementation can handle.

The formalism of deterministic and stochastic Petri nets (DSPNs) is equivalent to fdCTMCs. DSPNs have been extensively studied and many useful results are directly applicable to fdCTMCs. To the best of our knowledge the synthesis of fd events has not been studied for DSPNs. The most useful tools for DSPNs are ORIS [6] and TimeNET [17].

There was also an option to implement the synthesis algorithm as an extension of ORIS. However, PRISM is much more used in practice and contains solution methods for MDPs, that we needed for our implementation. Thus, we decided to implement the synthesis into PRISM, even thought we had to extend the PRISM language and data structures. Therefore, the ORIS and TimeNET algorithms can be now reimplemented for fdCTMCs in PRISM easily, exploiting its efficient symbolic structures and algorithms for CTMCs or MDPs.

In the rest of the paper we first formally define the fdCTMC and explain the extension of PRISM language. Then we discuss the implemented algorithms and the performance results. Due to space constraints, the full version of this paper including appendices is provided in [8].

2   Preliminaries

We use $\mathbb{N}_0$, $\mathbb{R}_{\geq 0}$, and $\mathbb{R}_{>0}$ to denote the set of all non-negative integers, non-negative real numbers, and positive real numbers, respectively. Furthermore, for a countable set A, we denote by $\mathcal{D}(A)$ the set of discrete probability distributions over A, i.e. functions $\mu : A \to \mathbb{R}_{\geq 0}$ such that $\sum_{a \in A} \mu(a) = 1$.

Definition 1. *A   fixed-delay   CTMC   (fdCTMC)   C   is   a   tuple $(S, Q, F, A, N, d, s_{in})$ where*

- *S is a finite set of states,*
- *$Q : S \times S \to \mathbb{R}_{\geq 0}$ is a rate matrix,*
- *F is a finite set of fixed-delay (fd) events,*
- *$A : S \to 2^F$ assigns to each state s a set of active fd events in s,*
- *$N : S \times F \to \mathcal{D}(S)$ is the successor function, i.e. assigns a probability distribution specifying the successor state to each state and fd event that is active there,*
- *$d : F \to \mathbb{R}_{>0}$ is a delay vector that assigns a positive delay to each fd event,*
- *$s_{in} \in S$ is an initial state.*

Note that fdCTMC C with empty set of fd events is a CTMC. The fdCTMC formalism can be understood as a stochastic event-driven system, i.e. the amount of time spent in each state and the probability of moving to the next state is driven by the occurrence of events. In addition to the fd events of F, there is an *exponential event* $\mathcal{E}$ that is active in all states s where $\sum_{s' \in S} Q(s, s') > 0$. During an execution of an fdCTMC all active events keep one *timer*, that holds the remaining time until the event occurs. The execution starts in the state s_{in}. The timer of each fd event f in $A(s_{in})$ is set to $d(f)$. The timer of the exponential event is set randomly according to the exponential distribution with a rate $\sum_{s' \in S} Q(s_{in}, s')$. The event e with least[3] timer value t occurs and causes change of state. In case e is an fd event, the next state is chosen randomly according to the distribution $N(s_{in}, e)$, otherwise e is an exponential event and the probability of choosing s as a next state is $Q(s_{in}, s)/\sum_{s' \in S} Q(s_{in}, s')$. In the next state s, the timers of all newly active fd events (i.e. $A(s) \setminus A(s_{in})$), the occurred event e, and the exponential event are set in the same way as above. Observe that the timers of the remaining active fd events decreased by time t spent in the previous state. The execution then proceeds in the same manner.

We illustrate the definition on the fdCTMC model from Example 1. The execution starts in $(idle, 0)$. The events f_1 and $\mathcal{E}$ are active and their timers are set to 1 and e.g. 1.18, respectively. Hence, after 1 s f_1 occurs and changes the state to $(sleep, 0)$ with probability 1. The timers of newly active event f_2 and $\mathcal{E}$ are set to 2 and e.g. 1.5, respectively. Now, $\mathcal{E}$ occurs and changes the state to $(sleep, 1)$. Here f_2 is still active and thus its timer holds the original value subtracted by the time spent in $(sleep, 0)$, i.e. $2 - 1.5 = 0.5$. The timer of the exponential event is set, etc.

A *run* of the fdCTMC is an infinite sequence $(s_0, e_0, t_0)(s_1, e_1, t_1) \ldots$ where $s_0 = s_{in}$ and for each $i \in \mathbb{N}_0$ it holds that $s_i \in S$ is the i-th visited state, $e_i \in \{\mathcal{E}\} \cup F$ is the event that occurred in s_i, and $t_i \in \mathbb{R}_{\geq 0}$ is the time spent in s_i. For the formal definition of the semantics of fdCTMC and the probability space on runs see [9].

Total Reward Before Reaching a Target. To allow formalization of performance properties we enrich the model in a standard way with rewards or costs (see, e.g. [13]). For an fdCTMC C with a state space S we additionally define a set of target states T, reward rates $\mathcal{R}$, and impulse rewards $\mathcal{I}$. Formally, the target state T is a subset of $S \setminus s_{in}$, $\mathcal{R} : S \to \mathbb{R}_{\geq 0}$ assigns a reward rate to every state, and $\mathcal{I} : S \times (\{\mathcal{E}\} \cup F) \times S \to \mathbb{R}_{\geq 0}$ assigns an impulse reward to every change of state. Now the reward assigned to a run $(s_0, e_0, t_0)(s_1, e_1, t_1) \ldots$ is the reward accumulated before reaching a state of T, i.e. $\sum_{i=0}^{n-1} (t_i \cdot \mathcal{R}(s_i) + \mathcal{I}(s_i, e_i, s_{i+1}))$ where $n > 0$ is the minimal index such that $s_n \in T$. We set the reward to infinity whenever there is no such n. The reward of a run can be viewed as a random variable, say $Cost_{C,T,\mathcal{R},\mathcal{I}}$. By $E_{C,T,\mathcal{R},\mathcal{I}}$ (or simply E_C) we denote the expected value of $Cost_{C,T,\mathcal{R},\mathcal{I}}$.

Synthesis. Given a delay vector d', let (parametric) fdCTMC $C(d')$ be the fdCTMC C where the delay vector is changed to d'. Our aim is to find a delay vector d such that the expected reward $E_{C(d)}$ is minimal. Formally, given an error bound $\varepsilon > 0$ the synthesis algorithm computes delay vector d, such that $E_{C(d)} \leq Val[C] + \varepsilon$, where $Val[C]$ denotes the optimal reward $\inf_{d'} E_{C(d')}$.

---

[3] For the sake of simplicity, when multiple events $X = \{e_1, \ldots, e_n\}$ occur simultaneously, the successor is determined by the minimal element of X according to some fixed total order on F.

3   PRISM Language and User Interface Extension

Each fdCTMC model file must begin with the keyword `fdctmc`. For the purpose of our synthesis and expected reward implementation, the set of target states has to be specified by label "`target`", e.g.

$$\text{label "target" = s=2;}$$

The exponential event (the matrix Q) is specified the same way as in CTMC models of PRISM. The fd events are local to a module and must be declared immediately after the module name. E.g. the `fdelay f = 1.0` defines the fd event f with delay of a double value 1.0. For an fd event f we specify its set of active states (i.e. $A^{-1}(f)$) and transition kernel (i.e. $N(\cdot, f)$) by PRISM commands where the identifier f is in the arrow, e.g.

$$\text{[L] s=1 --f-> 0.3:(s'=0) + 0.7:(s'=2)}$$

specifies that the fd event f is active in all states where `s=1` and whenever it occurs, the next state is derived from the original one by changing variable s to 0 with probability 0.3 and to 2 with probability 0.7. The probabilities in each command have to sum to one. Observe that fd event commands are similar to DTMC commands in PRISM. The synchronization labels are used only to impose impulse rewards as for CTMC, e.g.

$$\text{rewards   [L] true : 1.0;   endrewards}$$

The rate rewards are specified the same way as for CTMC in PRISM. The PRISM source code for the fdCTMC of Example 1 is in [8]. The implementation details concerning the fdCTMC structure are provided in [8] as well.

Users can run the implemented algorithms from both the graphical and the command-line interfaces of PRISM. The expected reward and synthesis implementations are available in menu `Model -> Compute -> Exp. reachability reward` and `Model -> Compute -> FD synthesis`, respectively or using the command-line option `-expreachreward` and `-fdsynthesis`, respectively. The error bound ε is specified in `Options -> Options -> Termination epsilon` or in the command-line option `-epsilon`.

4   Implementation Issues

Implementation of the expected reward computation was a straightforward application of existing PRISM methods. For the synthesis we implemented the *unbounded optimization* algorithm from [1]. The algorithm is based on discretization, i.e. we provide discretization bounds and restrict the uncountable space of delay vectors into a finite space. Instead of an exhaustive search through the finite space, we use the idea of [1] and transform the parametric (discretized) fdCTMC into an MDP where actions correspond to the choices of fd event delays. Now, the minimal solution of the MDP yields the optimal delay vector.

The discretization bounds consist of the discretization step δ, the upper bound on fd event delay $\overline{d}$ and the precision κ for computation of action parameters. They are computed for each fd event separately from the error bound ε, the number of states, the minimal transition probability, and other fdCTMC model attributes. For more detail see [8]. Note that in every fdCTMC model, the delays for all fd events have to be specified. Applying these delays, we compute the corresponding expected reward $\overline{Val}$ which is used as an upper bound for the optimal reward. Then $\overline{Val}$ is employed when computing the discretization bounds. The lower the $\overline{Val}$ is, the faster the synthesis implementation performs. Thus it is worth to think of good delays of fd events when specifying the model.

Given the discretization bounds one has to compute the transition probabilities and expected accumulated reward for each action in the MDP corresponding to the discretized delay of fd event. This can be done using the transient analysis of subordinated CTMCs [11].

Prototype Implementation. In the first implementation we used straightforward approach to call built-in methods of PRISM to compute the required quantities for each discretized fd event delay separately. This is reasonable since the built-in methods are correctly and efficiently programmed for all PRISM engines and methods of computing transient analysis. However, we experienced that most of the time was spent computing the transient analysis rather than solving the created MDP, e.g. 520 s out of 540 s of total time.[4] One of the reasons is that in each iteration a small portion of memory is allocated and freed by built-in PRISM methods. Since there is a large number of actions, the amount of reallocated memory was slowing down the computation. Thus we decided to reimplement the computation of transient probabilities applying principles of dynamic programming.

Iterative Computation of Transient Analysis. The transient probabilities can be very efficiently approximated up to an arbitrary small error using the uniformization technique. The problem is that we have to compute the transient probabilities for each value of a very large set $\{i \cdot \delta \mid i \in \mathbb{N}_0 \text{ and } 0 < i \leq \overline{d}/\delta\}$ and allow only fixed error κ for each computation. The transient probability vector $\pi(\delta)$ of a CTMC C at time δ can be computed using uniformization by

$$\pi(\delta) = \sum_{j=0}^{J} \mathbf{1}_{s_{in}} \cdot P^j \cdot \frac{(\lambda \cdot \delta)^j}{j!} \cdot e^{-\lambda \cdot \delta}, \tag{1}$$

where $\mathbf{1}_{s_{in}}$ is the initial vector of C, λ is the uniformization rate of C, and P is the transition kernel of the uniformized C. The choice of number J influences the error of the formula. It is easy to compute the value of J such that the error is sufficiently small.

However, for time $i \cdot \delta$ we can use the previously computed transient probabilities as

$$\pi(i \cdot \delta) = \sum_{j=0}^{J} \pi((i-1) \cdot \delta) \cdot P^j \cdot \frac{(\lambda \cdot \delta)^j}{j!} \cdot e^{-\lambda \cdot \delta}. \tag{2}$$

It is again easy to compute J such that the overall allowed error is not exceeded. Instead of performing naïve computation for each number in $\{i \cdot \delta \mid i \in \mathbb{N}_0 \text{ and } 0 < i \leq \overline{d}/\delta\}$ with

---

[4] Computed for the rejuv model and the error bound 0.001, see Sect. 5.

according number of steps $J_1, \ldots, J_{\overline{d}/\delta}$ to cause error bounded by κ in each computation, we compute the transient probabilities iteratively with sufficiently large J to cause small error in all computations. For example, if we have $\delta = 0.1, \overline{d}/\delta = 1000$, rate $\lambda = 1.0$ and $\kappa = 0.01$ using the naïve method we have to do $J_1 + \cdots + J_{\overline{d}/\delta} = 66,265$ steps and using the iterative method $J \cdot \overline{d}/\delta = 3,000$ steps. This is significant difference since a vector matrix multiplication is performed in each step. Thus we hard-programmed the iterative computation of transient probabilities and accumulated rewards in CTMC what caused a dramatic speedup thanks to the smaller number of arithmetic operations and better memory management.

Precomputation. Careful reader may have noticed that (2) can be further simplified to

$$\pi(i \cdot \delta) = \pi((i-1) \cdot \delta) \cdot e^{-\lambda \cdot \delta} \cdot \sum_{j=0}^{J} P^j \cdot \frac{(\lambda \cdot \delta)^j}{j!}. \qquad (3)$$

Hence, the matrix $e^{-\lambda \cdot \delta} \cdot \sum_{j=0}^{J} P^j \cdot (\lambda \cdot \delta)^j / j!$ can be easily precomputed beforehand and used for computation of each $\pi(i \cdot \delta)$ to increase the savings even more. However, this is not true. J is small and the matrix P is sparse for the most reasonable models and error bounds. But $e^{-\lambda \cdot \delta} \cdot \sum_{j=0}^{J} P^j \cdot (\lambda \cdot \delta)^j / j!$ is not sparse for almost each error bound, P, and λ, what is known as "fill-in" phenomenon. Thus using (2) is typically more efficient than using (3). Similar observations were discussed in [5].

Implementing the synthesis algorithm of [1], we inherited the following restrictions on the input fdCTMC models. There is at most one concurrently active fd event in each state, i.e. $\forall s \in S : |A(s)| \leq 1$. For each fd event there is at most one state where its timer is set. Every state has a positive rate reward, i.e. $\forall s \in S : \mathcal{R}(s) > 0$. Moreover, we add that all fd events have positive impulse rewards, i.e. $\forall f \in F \wedge s, s' \in S : N(s, f)(s') > 0 \implies I(s, f, s') > 0$. For the expected reward implementation only the first two restrictions are valid.

5   Experimental Results

We tested the performance of our synthesis implementation on the model from Example 1 for various sizes of the queue (2, 4, 6, and 8) and the rejuvenation model provided in [8]. The considered error bounds are 0.005, 0.0025, 0.0016, 0.00125, and 0.001. The following table shows the expected rewards and the computation times for a given error bound. As the expected rewards are very similar for different error bounds, we show their longest common prefix, instead of listing five similar long numbers.

Note that the computed values of the expected reward are of a much better precision than required. This indicates that there might even be a space for improvements of the synthesis algorithm, e.g. by computation of tighter discretization bounds. It is worth mentioning that the longest computation (dpm8 for error 0.001) took only 1 h and 30 min of real clock time thanks to the native parallelism of Java (the table shows the sum for all threads). Our experiments show that the implementation retains the theoretical complexity bounds saying that the computation time is exponential to the number of states and polynomial to $1/\varepsilon$.

Model	CPU time [s]					Longest
ε: 0.005	0.0025	0.0016	0.00125	0.00100	common prefix
$1/\varepsilon$: 200	400	600	800	1000	of exp. rewards
rejuv	5.87	12.09	14.71	21.60	23.84	0.94431314832
dpm2	58.22	121.15	195.61	234.58	248.52	0.336634754
dpm4	156.02	354.35	509.19	2197.10	2652.05	0.337592724
dpm6	259.76	532.47	2705.45	3026.77	5124.10	0.337583980
dpm8	616.47	3142.44	6362.79	22507.55	27406.62	0.337537611

The computations were run on platform HP DL980 G7 with 8 64-bit processors Intel Xeon X7560 2.26 GHz (together 64 cores) and 448 GiB DDR3 RAM, but only 304 GB was provided to Java. The time was measured by the Linux command `time`.

6 Conclusions and Future Work

In this paper, we incorporated the fdCTMC models into PRISM and implemented the expected reward computation and the synthesis algorithm. The tool is available on http://www.fi.muni.cz/~xrehak/fdPRISM/. We have used the explicit state PRISM engine. Based on the promising results, it is reasonable to (re)implement the synthesis and other model checking algorithms for fdCTMCs in the more efficient PRISM engines. Moreover, new effort can be put to reduce the number of current restrictions on the fdCTMC models. For instance the method of stochastic state classes [6] implemented in ORIS may be applied for computation of transient analysis instead of uniformization.

Acknowledgments. We thank Vojtěch Forejt and David Parker for fruitful discussions. This work is partly supported by the Czech Science Foundation, grant No. P202/12/G061.

References

1. Brázdil, T., Korenčiak, Ľ., Krčál, J., Novotný, P., Řehák, V.: Optimizing Performance of Continuous-Time Stochastic Systems Using Timeout Synthesis. In: Campos, J., Haverkort, B.R. (eds.) QEST 2015. LNCS, vol. 9259, pp. 141–159. Springer, Heidelberg (2015)
2. Fackrell, M.: Fitting with matrix-exponential distributions. Stoch. Models 21(2–3), 377–400 (2005)
3. German, R.: Performance Analysis of Communication Systems with Non-markovian Stochastic Petri Nets. Wiley, New York (2000)
4. Guet, C.C., Gupta, A., Henzinger, T.A., Mateescu, M., Sezgin, A.: Delayed continuous-time Markov chains for genetic regulatory circuits. In: Madhusudan, P., Seshia, S.A. (eds.) CAV 2012. LNCS, vol. 7358, pp. 294–309. Springer, Heidelberg (2012)
5. Haddad, S., Mokdad, L., Moreaux, P.: A new approach to the evaluation of non Markovian stochastic Petri nets. In: Donatelli, S., Thiagarajan, P.S. (eds.) ICATPN 2006. LNCS, vol. 4024, pp. 221–240. Springer, Heidelberg (2006)
6. Horváth, A., Paolieri, M., Ridi, L., Vicario, E.: Transient analysis of non-Markovian models using stochastic state classes. Perform. Eval. 69(7–8), 315–335 (2012)

7. Korenčiak, Ľ., Krčál, J., Řehák, V.: Dealing with zero density using piecewise phase-type approximation. In: Horváth, A., Wolter, K. (eds.) EPEW 2014. LNCS, vol. 8721, pp. 119–134. Springer, Heidelberg (2014)
8. Korenčiak, Ľ., Řehák, V., Farmadin, A.: Extension of PRISM by synthesis of optimal timeouts in fdCTMC. CoRR abs/1603.03252 (2016)
9. Krčál, J.: Formal analysis of discrete-event systems with hard real-time bounds. Ph.D. thesis, Faculty of Informatics, Masaryk University, Brno (2014)
10. Kwiatkowska, M., Norman, G., Parker, D.: PRISM 4.0: verification of probabilistic real-time systems. In: Gopalakrishnan, G., Qadeer, S. (eds.) CAV 2011. LNCS, vol. 6806, pp. 585–591. Springer, Heidelberg (2011)
11. Lindemann, C.: An improved numerical algorithm for calculating steady-state solutions of deterministic and stochastic Petri net models. Perform. Eval. **18**(1), 79–95 (1993)
12. Neuts, M.: Matrix-Geometric Solutions in Stochastic Models: An Algorithmic Approach. The Johns Hopkins University Press, Baltimore (1981)
13. Puterman, M.: Markov Decision Processes. Wiley, New York (1994)
14. Qiu, Q., Wu, Q., Pedram, M.: Stochastic modeling of a power-managed system: construction and optimization. In: ISLPED, pp. 194–199. ACM Press (1999)
15. Xie, W., Sun, H., Cao, Y., Trivedi, K.S.: Optimal webserver session timeout settings for web users. In: Computer Measurement Group Conferenceries, pp. 799–820 (2002)
16. Zimmermann, A.: Applied restart estimation of general reward measures. In: RESIM, pp. 196–204 (2006)
17. Zimmermann, A.: Modeling and evaluation of stochastic Petri nets with TimeNET 4.1. In: ICST, pp. 54–63. IEEE (2012)

Concurrency

Monitoring Multi-threaded Component-Based Systems

Hosein Nazarpour, Yliès Falcone[✉], Saddek Bensalem, Marius Bozga,
and Jacques Combaz

Univ. Grenoble Alpes, Inria, CNRS, VERIMAG, LIG, Grenoble, France
{Hosein.Nazarpour,Ylies.Falcone,Saddek.Bensalem,Marius.Bozga,
Jacques.Combaz}@imag.fr

Abstract. This paper addresses the monitoring of logic-independent linear-time user-provided properties on multi-threaded component-based systems. We consider intrinsically independent components that can be executed concurrently with a centralized coordination for multiparty interactions. In this context, the problem that arises is that a global state of the system is not available to the monitor. A naive solution to this problem would be to plug a monitor which would force the system to synchronize in order to obtain the sequence of global states at runtime. Such solution would defeat the whole purpose of having concurrent components. Instead, we reconstruct on-the-fly the global states by accumulating the partial states traversed by the system at runtime. We define formal transformations of components that preserve the semantics and the concurrency and, at the same time, allow to monitor global-state properties. Moreover, we present RVMT-BIP, a prototype tool implementing the transformations for monitoring multi-threaded systems described in the BIP (Behavior, Interaction, Priority) framework, an expressive framework for the formal construction of heterogeneous systems. Our experiments on several multi-threaded BIP systems show that RVMT-BIP induces a cheap runtime overhead.

1 Introduction

Component-based design is the process leading from given requirements and a set of predefined components to a system meeting the requirements. Building systems from components is essential in any engineering discipline. Components are abstract building blocks encapsulating behaviour. They can be composed in order to build composite components. Their composition should be rigorously defined so that it is possible to infer the behaviour of composite components from the behaviour of their constituents as well as global properties from the properties of individual components.

The problem of building component-based systems (CBSs) can be defined as follows. Given a set of components $\{B_1, \ldots, B_n\}$ and a property of their product state space φ, find multiparty interactions γ (i.e., "glue" code) s.t. the coordinated behaviour $\gamma(B_1, \ldots, B_n)$ meets the property φ. It is however generally

© Springer International Publishing Switzerland 2016
E. Ábrahám and M. Huisman (Eds.): IFM 2016, LNCS 9681, pp. 141–159, 2016.
DOI: 10.1007/978-3-319-33693-0_10

not possible to ensure or verify the desired property φ using static verification techniques, either because of the state-explosion problem or because φ can only be decided with runtime information. In this paper, we are interested in complementary verification techniques for CBSs such as runtime verification. In [9], we introduce runtime verification of sequential CBSs against properties referring to the global states of the system, which, in particular, implies that properties can not be "projected" and checked on individual components. From an input composite system $\gamma(B_1, \ldots, B_n)$ and a linear-time regular property, a component monitor M and a new set of interactions γ' are synthesized to build a new composite system $\gamma'(B_1, \ldots, B_n, M)$ where the property is checked at runtime.

The underlying model of CBSs relies on multiparty interactions which consist of actions that are jointly executed by certain components, either sequentially or concurrently. In the sequential setting, components are coordinated by a single centralized controller and joint actions are atomic. Components notify the controller of their current states. Then, the controller computes the possible interactions, selects one, and then sequentially executes the actions of each component involved in the interaction. When components finish their executions, they notify the controller of their new states, and the aforementioned steps are repeated. For performance reasons, it is desirable to parallelize the execution of components. In the multi-threaded setting, each component executes on a thread and a controller is in charge of coordination. Parallelizing the execution of $\gamma(B_1, \ldots, B_n)$ yields a bisimilar [10] component [1] where each synchronized action a occurring on B_i is broken down into β_i and a' where β_i represents an internal computation of B_i and a' is a synchronization action. Between β_i and a', a new *busy location* is added. Consequently, the components can perform their interaction independently after synchronization, and the joint actions become non atomic. After starting an interaction, and before this interaction completes (meaning that certain components are still performing internal computations), the controller can start another interaction between ready components.

The problem that arises in the multi-threaded setting is that a global steady state of the system (where all components are ready to perform an interaction) may never exist at runtime. Note that we do not target distributed but multi-threaded systems in which components execute with a centralized controller, there is a global clock and communication is instantaneous and atomic. We define a method to monitor CBSs against linear-time properties referring to global states. Our method preserves the concurrency and semantics of the monitored system. It transforms the system so that global states can be reconstructed by accumulating partial states at runtime. The execution trace of a multi-threaded CBS is a sequence of partial states. For an execution trace of a multi-threaded CBS, we define the notion of *witness* trace, which is intuitively the unique trace of global states corresponding to the trace of the multi-threaded CBS if this CBS was executed on a single thread. For this purpose, we define transformations allowing to add a new component building the witness trace.

We prove that the transformed and initial systems are bisimilar: the obtained reconstructed sequence of global states from a parallel execution is as the

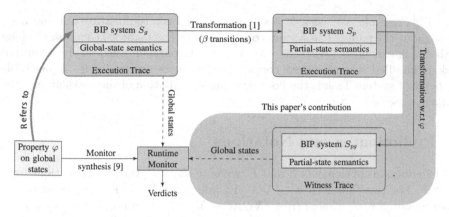

Fig. 1. Approach overview

sequence of global states obtained when the multi-threaded CBS is executed with a single thread. We introduce RVMT-BIP, a tool integrated in the BIP tool suite.[1] BIP (Behavior, Interaction, Priority) framework is a powerful and expressive component framework for the formal construction of heterogeneous systems. RVMT-BIP takes as input a BIP CBS and a monitor description which expresses a property φ, and outputs a new BIP system whose behavior is monitored against φ while running concurrently.

Figure 1 overviews our approach. Recall that according to [1], a BIP system with global-state semantics S_g (sequential model), is (weakly) bisimilar with the corresponding partial-state model S_p (concurrent model) noted $S_g \sim S_p$. Moreover, S_p generally runs faster than S_g because of its parallelism. Thus, if a trace of S_g, i.e., σ_g, satisfies φ, then the corresponding trace of S_p, i.e., σ_p, satisfies φ as well. Naive solutions to monitor S_p would be (i) to monitor S_g with the technique in [9] and run S_p, which ends up with delays in detecting verdicts or (ii) to plug the monitor proposed in [9] in S_p, which forces the components to synchronize for the monitor to take a snapshot of the global state of the system. Such approaches would completely defeat the purpose of using multi-threaded models. Instead, we propose a transformation technique to build another system S_{pg} out of S_p such that (i) S_{pg} and S_p are bisimilar (hence S_g and S_{pg} are bisimilar), (ii) S_{pg} is as concurrent as S_p and preserves the performance gained from multi-threaded execution and (iii) S_{pg} produces a witness trace, that is the trace that allows to check the property φ. Our method does not introduce any delay in the detection of verdicts since it always reconstructs the maximal (information-wise) prefix of the witness trace (Theorem 1). Moreover, we show that our method is correct in that it always produces the correct witness trace (Theorem 2).

An extended version of this paper with more detail and proofs is available as [13].

---

[1] RVMT-BIP is available for download at [12].

Running Example. We use a task system, called Task, to illustrate our approach throughout the paper. The system consists of a task generator (*Generator*) along with 3 task executors (*Workers*) that can run in parallel. Each newly generated task is handled whenever two cooperating workers are available. A desirable property of system Task is the homogeneous distribution of the tasks among the workers.

2   Preliminaries and Notations

For two domains of elements E and F, we note $[E \to F]$ the set of functions from E to F. For two functions $v \in [X \to Y]$ and $v' \in [X' \to Y']$, the substitution function noted v/v', where $v/v' \in [X \cup X' \to Y \cup Y']$, is defined as $v/v'(x) = v'(x)$ if $x \in X'$, and $v(x)$ otherwise. Given a set of elements E, $e_1 \cdot e_2 \cdots e_n$ is a sequence or a list of length n over E, where $\forall i \in [1, n] : e_i \in E$. Sequences of assignments are delimited by square brackets for clarity. The empty sequence is noted ϵ or $[\ ]$, depending on the context. The set of (finite) sequences over E is noted E^*. E^+ is defined as $E^* \setminus \{\epsilon\}$. The length of a sequence s is noted length(s). We define $s(i)$ as the ith element of s and $s(i \cdots j)$ as the factor of s from the ith to the jth element. We also note pref(s), the set of *prefixes* of s s.t. pref$(s) = \{s(1 \cdots k) \mid k \leq \text{length}(s)\}$. Operator pref is naturally extended to sets of sequences. Function $\max_{\preceq}$ (resp. $\min_{\preceq}$) returns the maximal (resp. minimal) sequence w.r.t. prefix ordering of a set of sequences. We define function last : $E^+ \to E$ s.t. last$(e_1 \cdot e_2 \cdots e_n) = e_n$. For a sequence $e = e_1 \cdot e_2 \cdots e_n$ over E, and a function $f : E \to F$, map $f\ e$ is the sequence over F defined as $f(e_1) \cdot f(e_2) \cdots f(e_n)$ where $\forall i \in [1, n] : f(e_i) \in F$.

3   Component-Based Systems with Multiparty Interactions

An action of a CBS is an interaction i.e., a coordinated operation between certain atomic components. Atomic components are transition systems with a set of ports labeling individual transitions. Ports are used by components to communicate. Composite components are obtained from atomic components by specifying interactions.

An *atomic component* is endowed with a finite set of local variables X taking values in a domain Data, and it synchronizes with other components through *ports*. A port $p[x_p]$, where $x_p \subseteq X$, is defined by a port identifier p and some variables in a set x_p.

Definition 1 (Atomic Component). *An atomic component is defined as a tuple* (P, L, T, X) *where P is the set of ports, L is the set of (control) locations, $T \subseteq L \times P \times \mathcal{G}(X) \times \mathcal{F}^*(X) \times L$ is the set of transitions, and X is the set of variables. $\mathcal{G}(X)$ denotes the set of Boolean expressions over X and $\mathcal{F}(X)$ the set of assignments of expressions over X to variables in X. For each transition $\tau = (l, p, g_\tau, f_\tau, l') \in T$, g_τ is a Boolean expression over X (the guard of τ),*

$f_\tau \in \{x := f^x(X) \mid x \in X \wedge f^x \in \mathcal{F}^*(X)\}^*$: *the computation step of* τ, *a sequence of assignments to variables.*

The semantics of the atomic component is an LTS $(Q, P, \rightarrow)$ where $Q = L \times [X \rightarrow \text{Data}]$ is the set of states, and $\rightarrow = \{((l, v), p(v_p), (l', v')) \in Q \times P \times Q \mid \exists \tau = (l, p, g_\tau, f_\tau, l') \in T : g_\tau(v) \wedge v' = f_\tau(v/v_p)\}$ is the transition relation.

A state is a pair $(l, v) \in Q$, where $l \in L$, $v \in [X \rightarrow \text{Data}]$ is a valuation of the variables in X. The evolution of states $(l, v) \xrightarrow{p(v_p)} (l', v')$, where v_p is a valuation of the variables x_p attached to port p, is possible if there exists a transition $(l, p[x_p], g_\tau, f_\tau, l')$, s.t. $g_\tau(v) = \texttt{true}$. As a result, the valuation v of variables is modified to $v' = f_\tau(v/v_p)$.

We use the dot notation to denote the elements of atomic components. e.g., for a component B, $B.P$ denotes the set of ports of the atomic component B, etc. Figure 2 depicts atomic components of system Task.

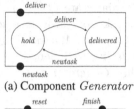

(a) Component *Generator*

Definition 2 (Interaction). *An interaction* a *is a tuple* $(\mathcal{P}_a, F_a)$, *where* $\mathcal{P}_a = \{p_i[x_i] \mid p_i \in B_i.P\}_{i \in I}$ *is the set of ports s.t.* $\forall i \in I : \mathcal{P}_a \cap B_i.P = \{p_i\}$ *and* F_a *is a sequence of assignment to the variables in* $\cup_{i \in I} x_i$.

Variables attached to ports are purposed to transfer values between interacting components. When clear from the context, in the following examples, an interaction $(\{p[x_p]\}, F_a)$ consisting of only one port p is noted p.

(b) Component *Worker*

Fig. 2. Atomic components

Definition 3 (Composite Component). *A composite component* $\gamma(B_1, \ldots, B_n)$ *is defined from a set of atomic components* $\{B_i\}_{i=1}^n$ *and a set of interactions* γ.

A state q of $\gamma(B_1, \ldots, B_n)$ is an n-tuple $q = (q_1, \ldots, q_n)$, where $q_i = (l_i, v_i)$ is a state of atomic component B_i. The semantics of the composite component is an LTS $(Q, \gamma, \longrightarrow)$, where $Q = B_1.Q \times \ldots \times B_n.Q$ is the set of states, γ is the set of all possible interactions and $\longrightarrow$ is the least set of transitions satisfying the following rule:

$$\frac{a = (\{p_i[x_i]\}_{i \in I}, F_a) \in \gamma \qquad \forall i \in I : q_i \xrightarrow{p_i(v_i)}_i q_i' \wedge v_i = F_{a_i}(v(X)) \qquad \forall i \notin I : q_i = q_i'}{(q_1, \ldots, q_n) \xrightarrow{a} (q_1', \ldots, q_n')}$$

X *is the set of variables attached to the ports of* a, v *is the global valuation, and* F_{a_i} *is the restriction of* F *to the variables of* p_i.

A trace is a sequence of states and interactions $(q_0 \cdot a_1 \cdot q_1 \cdots a_s \cdot q_s)$ s.t.: $q_0 = Init \wedge (\forall i \in [1, s] : q_i \in Q \wedge a_i \in \gamma : q_{i-1} \xrightarrow{a_i} q_i)$, where $Init \in Q$ is the initial state. The sequence of interactions is then defined as $\underline{\text{interactions}}(q_0 \cdot a_1 \cdot q_1 \cdots a_s \cdot q_s) = a_1 \cdots a_s$. The set of traces of composite component B is denoted by $\text{Tr}(B)$.

Example 1 (Interaction, Composite Component). Figure 3 depicts the composite component $\gamma(Worker_1,$ $Worker_2,\ Worker_3,\ Generator)$ of system Task. The set of interactions is $\gamma\ =\ \{ex_{12}, ex_{13}, ex_{23}, r_1, r_2, r_3,$ $f_1, f_2, f_3, n_t\}$. For instance, we have $ex_{12} = (\{deliver, exec_1, exec_2\}, [\ ])$.

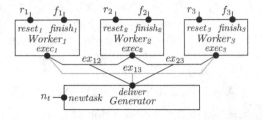

Fig. 3. Composite component of system Task

One of the possible traces[2] of system Task is: $(free, free, free, hold)\cdot$ $ex_{12}\cdot (done,\ done,\ free,\ delivered)\cdot n_t \cdot (done,\ done,\ free,\ hold)$ s.t. from the initial state $(free,\ free,\ free,\ hold)$, where workers are at location $free$ and task generator is ready to deliver a task, interaction ex_{12} is fired and $Worker_1$ and $Worker_2$ move to location $done$ and $Generator$ moves to location $delivered$. Then, a new task is generated by the execution of interaction n_t so that $Generator$ moves to location $hold$.

4   Monitoring Multi-threaded CBSs with Partial-State Semantics

The semantics defined in Sect. 3 is referred to as the global-state semantics of CBSs because each state of the system is defined in terms of the local states of components, and, all local states are defined. In this section, we consider the partial-state semantics where the states of a system may contain undefined local states because of the concurrent execution of components.

4.1   Partial-State Semantics

To model concurrent behavior, we associate a partial state model to each atomic component. In global-state semantics, one does not distinguish the beginning of an interaction (or a transition) from its completion. That is, the interactions and transitions of a system execute atomically and sequentially. Partial states and the corresponding internal transitions are needed for modeling non-atomic executions. Atomic components with partial states behave as atomic components except that each transition is decomposed into a sequence of two transitions: a visible transition followed by an internal β-labeled transition (aka busy transition). Between these transitions, a so-called *busy location* is added. Below, we define the transformation of a component with global-state semantics to a component with partial-state semantics (extending the definition in [1] with variables, guards, and computation steps on transitions).

Definition 4 (Components with Partial States). *The partial-state version of atomic component* $B = (P, L, T, X)$ *is* $B^{\perp} = (P \cup \{\beta\},\ L \cup L^{\perp},\ T^{\perp},\ X)$, *where*

---

[2] For the sake of simpler notation, we represent a state by its location.

$\beta \notin P$ is a special port, $L^{\perp} = \{l_t^{\perp} \mid t \in T\}$ (resp. L) is the set of busy locations (resp. ready location) s.t. $L^{\perp} \cap L = \emptyset$, $T^{\perp} = \{(l, p, g_\tau, [\,], l_\tau^{\perp}), (l_\tau^{\perp}, \beta, \text{true}, f_\tau, l') \mid \exists \tau = (l, p, g_\tau, f_\tau, l') \in T\}$ is a set of transitions.

Assuming some atomic components with partial-state semantics $B_1^{\perp}, \ldots, B_n^{\perp}$, we construct a composite component $B^{\perp} = \gamma^{\perp}(B_1^{\perp}, \ldots, B_n^{\perp})$ where $\gamma^{\perp} = \gamma \cup \{\{\beta_i\}\}_{i=1}^{n}$, and $\{\{\beta_i\}\}_{i=1}^{n}$ is the set of busy interactions. The notions and notation related to traces are lifted to components with partial-state semantics in the natural way. We extend the definition of <u>interactions</u> to traces in partial-state semantics s.t. $\beta_{i \in [1,n]}$ are filtered out.

Example 2 (Composite Component with Partial States). The corresponding composite component of Task with partial-state semantics is $\gamma^{\perp}(Worker_1^{\perp},$ $Worker_2^{\perp},$ $Worker_3^{\perp},$ $Generator^{\perp})$, where each $Worker_i^{\perp}$ for $i \in [1, 3]$ is identical to the component in Fig. 4b and $Generator^{\perp}$ is the component in Fig. 4a. We represent each busy location $l^{\perp}$ as $\perp$.

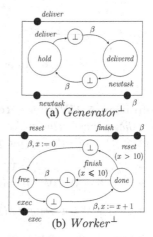

(a) $Generator^{\perp}$

(b) $Worker^{\perp}$

Fig. 4. Atomic components of Task with partial-states

It is possible to show that the partial-state system is a correct implementation of the global-state system, that is, the two systems are (weakly) bisimilar (cf. [1], Theorem 1). Weak bisimulation relation R is defined between the set of states of the model in global-state semantics (i.e., Q) and the set of states of its partial-state model (i.e., $Q^{\perp}$), s.t. $R = \{(q, r) \in Q \times Q^{\perp} \mid r \xrightarrow{\beta^{*}} q\}$. Any global state in partial-state semantics model is equivalent to the corresponding global state in global-state semantics model, and any partial state in partial-state semantics model is equivalent to the successor global state obtained after stabilizing the system by executing busy interactions.

In the sequel, we consider a CBS with global-state semantics B and its partial-state semantics version $B^{\perp}$. Intuitively, from any trace of $B^{\perp}$, we want to reconstruct on-the-fly the corresponding trace in B and evaluate a property which is defined over global states of B.

4.2 Witness Relation and Witness Trace

We define the notion of *witness* relation between traces in global-state semantics and traces in partial-state semantics, based on the bisimulation between B and $B^{\perp}$. Any trace of $B^{\perp}$ is related to a trace of B, i.e., its *witness*. The witness trace allows to monitor the system in partial-state semantics (thus benefiting from the parallelism) against properties referring to the global behavior of the system.

Trace in partial-state semantics

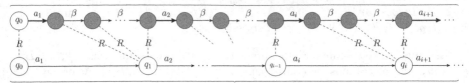

Witness trace in global-state semantics

Fig. 5. Witness trace built using weak bisimulation (R)

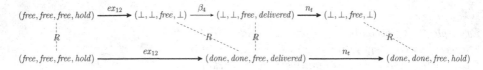

Fig. 6. An example of witness trace in system Task

Definition 5 (Witness Relation). *Given the bisimulation R between B and $B^\perp$, the witness relation $W \subseteq \mathrm{Tr}(B) \times \mathrm{Tr}(B^\perp)$ is the smallest set that contains* $(Init, Init)$ *and satisfies the following rules: For* $(\sigma_1, \sigma_2) \in W$,

- $(\sigma_1 \cdot a \cdot q_1, \sigma_2 \cdot a \cdot q_2) \in W$, *if* $a \in \gamma$ *and* $(q_1, q_2) \in R$;
- $(\sigma_1, \sigma_2 \cdot \beta \cdot q_2) \in W$, *if* $(\mathrm{last}(\sigma_1), q_2) \in R$.

If $(\sigma_1, \sigma_2) \in W$, *we say that* σ_1 *is a* witness trace *of* σ_2.

Suppose that the witness relation relates a trace in partial-state semantics σ_2 to a trace in global-state semantics σ_1. The states obtained after executing the same interaction in the two systems are bisimilar. Moreover, any move through a busy interaction in $B^\perp$ preserves the bisimulation between the state of σ_2 followed by the busy interaction in $B^\perp$ and the last state of σ_1 in B.

Example 3 (Witness Relation and Trace). Figure 5 illustrates the witness relation. State q_0 is the initial state of B and $B^\perp$. In the trace of $B^\perp$, gray circles after each interaction represent partial states which are bisimilar to the global state that comes after the corresponding trace of B.

Let us consider σ_2 as a trace of system Task with partial-state semantics depicted in Fig. 6 where $\sigma_2 = (free, free, free, hold) \cdot ex_{12} \cdot (\perp, \perp, free, \perp) \cdot \beta_4 \cdot (\perp, \perp, free, delivered) \cdot n_t \cdot (\perp, \perp, free, \perp)$. The witness trace corresponding to trace σ_2 is $(free, free, free, hold) \cdot ex_{12} \cdot (done, done, free, delivered) \cdot n_t \cdot (done, done, free, hold)$.

Property 1 states that any trace in partial-state semantics and its witness trace have the same sequence of interactions. Property 2 states that any trace in the partial-state semantics has a unique witness trace in the global-state semantics.

Property 1. $\forall (\sigma_1, \sigma_2) \in W$, $\underline{interactions}(\sigma_1) = \underline{interactions}\ (\sigma_2)$.

Property 2. $\forall \sigma_2 \in \text{Tr}(B^\perp), \exists! \sigma_1 \in \text{Tr}(B), (\sigma_1, \sigma_2) \in W.$

Following Property 2, we note $W(\sigma_2) = \sigma_1$ when $(\sigma_1, \sigma_2) \in W$.

Note that, when running a system in partial-state semantics, the global state of the witness trace after an interaction a is not known until all the components involved in a have reached their ready locations after the execution of a. Nevertheless, even in non-deterministic systems, this global state is uniquely defined and consequently there is always a unique witness trace (that is, non-determinism is resolved at runtime).

4.3 Construction of the Witness Trace

Given a trace in partial-state semantics, the witness trace is computed using function RGT (Reconstructor of Global Trace).

Definition 6 (Function *RGT*). *Function* RGT $: \text{Tr}(B^\perp) \longrightarrow \text{pref}(\text{Tr}(B))$ *is defined as* $\text{RGT}(\sigma) = \text{discriminant}(\text{acc}(\sigma))$, *where:*

- $\text{acc} : \text{Tr}(B^\perp) \longrightarrow Q \cdot (\gamma \cdot Q)^* \cdot (\gamma \cdot (Q^\perp \backslash Q))^*$ *is defined as:*
  - $\text{acc}(Init) = Init$,
  - $\text{acc}(\sigma \cdot a \cdot q) = \text{acc}(\sigma) \cdot a \cdot q$ $\qquad\qquad\qquad$ *for* $a \in \gamma$,
  - $\text{acc}(\sigma \cdot \beta \cdot q) = \text{map} \, [x \mapsto \text{upd}(q, x)] \, (\text{acc}(\sigma))$ $\qquad$ *for* $\beta \in \{\{\beta_i\}\}_{i=1}^n$;
- $\text{discriminant} : Q \cdot (\gamma \cdot Q)^* \cdot (\gamma \cdot (Q^\perp \backslash Q))^* \longrightarrow \text{pref}(\text{Tr}(B))$ *is defined as:*
  $$\text{discriminant}(\sigma) = \max_{\preceq}(\{\sigma' \in \text{pref}(\sigma) \mid \text{last}(\sigma') \in Q\})$$

with $\text{upd} : Q^\perp \times (Q^\perp \cup \gamma) \longrightarrow Q^\perp \cup \gamma$ *defined as:*

- $\text{upd}((q_1, \ldots, q_n), a) = a$, *for* $a \in \gamma$,
- $\text{upd}\left((q_1, \ldots, q_n), (q_1', \ldots, q_n')\right) = (q_1'', \ldots, q_n'')$,

  where $\forall k \in [1, n], q_k'' = \begin{cases} q_k & \text{if } (q_k \notin Q_k^\perp) \wedge (q_k' \in Q_k^\perp) \\ q_k' & \text{otherwise.} \end{cases}$

Function RGT uses sub-functions acc and discriminant. First, acc takes as input a trace in partial-state semantics σ, removes β interactions and the partial states after β. Function acc uses the (information in the) partial state after β interactions in order to update the partial states using function upd. Then, function discriminant returns the longest prefix of the result of acc corresponding to a trace in global-state semantics.

Note that, because of the inductive definition of function acc, the input trace can be processed step by step by function RGT which can incrementally generate the witness trace of a running system by monitoring interactions and partial states of components.

Example 4 (Applying Function RGT*).* Table 1 illustrates Definition 6 on one trace of system Task with initial state $(free, free, free, hold)$ followed by interactions ex_{12}, β_4, n_t, β_2, and β_1. At step 0, the outputs of functions acc and

Table 1. Values of function RGT for a sample input

Step	Input trace in partial semantics, σ	Intermediate step, $\mathrm{acc}(\sigma)$	Output trace in global semantics, $\mathrm{RGT}(\sigma)$
0	$(\mathit{free}, \mathit{free}, \mathit{free}, \mathit{hold})$	$(\mathit{free}, \mathit{free}, \mathit{free}, \mathit{hold})$	$(\mathit{free}, \mathit{free}, \mathit{free}, \mathit{hold})$
1	$(\mathit{free}, \mathit{free}, \mathit{free}, \mathit{hold}) \cdot e x_{12} \cdot$ $(\bot, \bot, \mathit{free}, \bot)$	$(\mathit{free}, \mathit{free}, \mathit{free}, \mathit{hold}) \cdot e x_{12} \cdot$ $(\bot, \bot, \mathit{free}, \bot)$	$(\mathit{free}, \mathit{free}, \mathit{free}, \mathit{hold}) \cdot e x_{12}$
2	$(\mathit{free}, \mathit{free}, \mathit{free}, \mathit{hold}) \cdot e x_{12} \cdot$ $(\bot, \bot, \mathit{free}, \bot) \cdot \beta_4 \cdot$ $(\bot, \bot, \mathit{free}, \mathit{delivered})$	$(\mathit{free}, \mathit{free}, \mathit{free}, \mathit{hold}) \cdot e x_{12} \cdot$ $(\bot, \bot, \mathit{free}, \mathit{delivered})$	$(\mathit{free}, \mathit{free}, \mathit{free}, \mathit{hold}) \cdot e x_{12}$
3	$(\mathit{free}, \mathit{free}, \mathit{free}, \mathit{hold}) \cdot e x_{12} \cdot$ $(\bot, \bot, \mathit{free}, \bot) \cdot \beta_4 \cdot$ $(\bot, \bot, \mathit{free}, \mathit{delivered}) \cdot n_t \cdot$ $(\bot, \bot, \mathit{free}, \bot)$	$(\mathit{free}, \mathit{free}, \mathit{free}, \mathit{hold}) \cdot e x_{12} \cdot$ $(\bot, \bot, \mathit{free}, \mathit{delivered}) \cdot n_t \cdot$ $(\bot, \bot, \mathit{free}, \bot)$	$(\mathit{free}, \mathit{free}, \mathit{free}, \mathit{hold}) \cdot e x_{12}$
4	$(\mathit{free}, \mathit{free}, \mathit{free}, \mathit{hold}) \cdot e x_{12} \cdot$ $(\bot, \bot, \mathit{free}, \bot) \cdot \beta_4 \cdot$ $(\bot, \bot, \mathit{free}, \mathit{delivered}) \cdot n_t \cdot$ $(\bot, \bot, \mathit{free}, \bot) \cdot \beta_2 \cdot$ $(\bot, \mathit{done}, \mathit{free}, \bot)$	$(\mathit{free}, \mathit{free}, \mathit{free}, \mathit{hold}) \cdot e x_{12} \cdot$ $(\bot, \mathit{done}, \mathit{free}, \mathit{delivered}) \cdot n_t \cdot$ $(\bot, \mathit{done}, \mathit{free}, \bot)$	$(\mathit{free}, \mathit{free}, \mathit{free}, \mathit{hold}) \cdot e x_{12}$
5	$(\mathit{free}, \mathit{free}, \mathit{free}, \mathit{hold}) \cdot e x_{12} \cdot$ $(\bot, \bot, \mathit{free}, \bot) \cdot \beta_4 \cdot$ $(\bot, \bot, \mathit{free}, \mathit{delivered}) \cdot n_t \cdot$ $(\bot, \bot, \mathit{free}, \bot) \cdot \beta_2 \cdot$ $(\bot, \mathit{done}, \mathit{free}, \bot) \cdot \beta_1 \cdot$ $(\mathit{done}, \mathit{done}, \mathit{free}, \bot)$	$(\mathit{free}, \mathit{free}, \mathit{free}, \mathit{hold}) \cdot e x_{12} \cdot$ $(\mathit{done}, \mathit{done}, \mathit{free}, \mathit{delivered}) \cdot n_t \cdot$ $(\mathit{done}, \mathit{done}, \mathit{free}, \bot)$	$(\mathit{free}, \mathit{free}, \mathit{free}, \mathit{hold}) \cdot e x_{12} \cdot$ $(\mathit{done}, \mathit{done}, \mathit{free}, \mathit{delivered}) \cdot n_t$

discriminant are equal to the initial state. At step 1, the execution of inter-action $e x_{12}$ adds $e x_{12} \cdot (\bot, \bot, \mathit{free}, \bot)$ to traces σ and $\mathrm{acc}(\sigma)$. At step 2, the state after β_4 has fresh information on component *Generator* which is used to update the existing partial states, so that $(\bot, \bot, \mathit{free}, \bot)$ is updated to $(\bot, \bot, \mathit{free}, \mathit{delivered})$. At step 5, *Worker$_1$* becomes ready after β_1, and the partial state $(\bot, \mathit{done}, \mathit{free}, \mathit{delivered})$ in the intermediate step is updated to the global state $(\mathit{done}, \mathit{done}, \mathit{free}, \mathit{delivered})$, therefore it appears in the output trace.

The following proposition states that applying function RGT on a trace in partial-state semantics produces the longest possible prefix of the corresponding witness trace with respect to the current trace of the partial-state semantics model.

Theorem 1 (Computation of the Witness With RGT). $\forall \sigma \in \mathrm{Tr}(B^{\bot})$:

$$\mathrm{last}(\sigma) \in Q \implies \mathrm{RGT}(\sigma) = \mathrm{W}(\sigma)$$
$$\wedge \, \mathrm{last}(\sigma) \notin Q \implies \mathrm{RGT}(\sigma) = \mathrm{W}(\sigma') \cdot a, \, \textit{with}$$
$$\sigma' = \min_{\preceq} \{\sigma_p \in \mathrm{Tr}(B^{\bot}) \mid \exists a \in \gamma, \exists \sigma'' \in \mathrm{Tr}(B^{\bot}) : \sigma = \sigma_p \cdot a \cdot \sigma'' \wedge \exists i \in [1, n] :$$
$$(B_i.P \cap a \neq \emptyset) \wedge (\forall j \in [1, \mathrm{length}(\sigma'')] : \beta_i \neq \sigma''(j))\}$$

Theorem 1 distinguishes two cases:

- When the last state of a system is a global state ($\mathrm{last}(\sigma) \in Q$), none of the components is in a busy location. Moreover, function RGT has sufficient information to build the corresponding witness trace ($\mathrm{RGT}(\sigma) = \mathrm{W}(\sigma)$).
- When the last state of a system is a partial state, at least one component is in a busy location and function RGT can not build a complete witness

trace because it lacks information on the current state of such components. It is possible to decompose the input sequence σ into two parts σ' and σ'' separated by an interaction a. The separation is made on the interaction a occurring in trace σ s.t., for the interactions occurring after a (i.e., in σ''), at least one component involved in a has not executed any β transition (which means that this component is still in a busy location). Note that it may be possible to split σ in several manners with the above description. In such a case, function RGT computes the witness for the smallest sequence σ' (w.r.t. prefix ordering) as above because it is the only sequence for which it has information regarding global states. Note also that such splitting of σ is always possible as $last(\sigma) \notin Q$ implies that σ is not empty, and σ' can be chosen to be ϵ.

In both cases, RGT returns the maximal prefix of the corresponding witness trace that can be built with the information contained in the partial states observed so far.

5   Model Transformation

5.1   Instrumentation of Atomic Components

Given an atomic component with partial-state semantics as per Definition 4, we instrument this atomic component s.t. it is able to transfer its state through port β, each time the component moves out from a busy location.

Definition 7 (Instrumenting an Atomic Component). *Given an atomic component in partial-state semantics* $B^{\perp} = (P \cup \{\beta\}, L \cup L^{\perp}, T^{\perp}, X)$ *with initial location* $l_0 \in L$, *we define a new component* $B^r = (P^r, L \cup L^{\perp}, T^r, X^r)$ *where:*

- $X^r = X \cup \{loc\}$, *loc is initialized to* l_0;
- $P^r = P \cup \{\beta^r\}$, *with* $\beta^r = \beta[X^r]$;
- $T^r = \{(l, p, g_\tau, [\ ], l_\tau^{\perp}), (l_\tau^{\perp}, \beta, \text{true}, f_\tau; [loc := l'], l') \mid (l, p, g_\tau, [\ ], l_\tau^{\perp}), (l_\tau^{\perp}, \beta, \text{true}, f_\tau, l') \in T^{\perp}\}$.

In X^r, *loc* is a variable containing the current location. X^r is exported through port β. An assignment is added to the computation step of each transition to record the location.

Example 5 (Instrumenting an Atomic Component). Figure 7 shows the instrumented version of atomic components in system Task (depicted in Fig. 4).

5.2   Creating a New Atomic Component to Reconstruct Global States

Let us consider $B^{\perp} = \gamma^{\perp}(B_1^{\perp}, \ldots, B_n^{\perp})$ with partial-state semantics, s.t.:

- γ is the set of interactions in the corresponding composite component with global-state semantics with $\gamma = \gamma^{\perp} \setminus \{\{\beta_i\}\}_{i=1}^n$, and

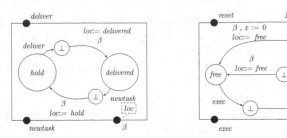

(a) Instrumented component $Generator^r$ (b) Instrumented component $Worker^r$

Fig. 7. Instrumented atomic components of system Task

- the corresponding instrumented atomic components $B_1^r, \ldots, B_n^r$ have been obtained through Definition 7 s.t. B_i^r is the instrumented version of $B_i^\perp$.

We define a new atomic component, called RGT, which is in charge of accumulating the global states of the system $B^\perp$. Component RGT is an operational implementation as a component of function RGT (Definition 6).

Definition 8 (RGT Atom). *Component RGT is defined as (P, L, T, X) where:*

- $X = \bigcup_{i \in [1,n]} \{B_i^r.X^r\} \bigcup_{i \in [1,n]} \{B_i^r.X_c^r\} \cup \{gs_a \mid a \in \gamma\} \cup \{(z_1, \ldots, z_n)\} \cup \{V, v, m\}$, *where $B_i^r.X_c^r$ is a set containing a copy of the variables in $B_i^r.X^r$.*
- $P = \bigcup_{i \in [1,n]} \{\beta_i[B_i^r.X^r]\} \cup \{p_a[\emptyset] \mid a \in \gamma\} \cup \{p_a'[\bigcup_{i \in [1,n]} \{B_i^r.X_c\}] \mid a \in \gamma\}$.
- $L = \{l\}$ *is a set with one control location.*
- $T = T_{\text{new}} \cup T_{\text{upd}} \cup T_{\text{out}}$, *where:* $T_{\text{new}} = \{(l, p_a, \text{true}, \text{new}(a), l) \mid a \in \gamma\}$, $T_{\text{upd}} = \{(l, \beta_i, \bigwedge_{a \in \gamma}(\neg gs_a), \text{upd}(i), l) \mid i \in [1,n]\}$, $T_{\text{out}} = \{(l, p_a', gs_a, \text{get}, l) \mid a \in \gamma\}$.

For space reasons, we only overview the description of atom RGT and do not provide the internal algorithms. Full and formal details can be found in [13]. A global state is encoded as a tuple consisting of the valuation of variables and the location for each atomic component. After a new interaction gets fired, component RGT builds a new tuple using the current states of components. Component RGT builds a sequence with the generated tuples. The stored tuples are updated each time the state of a component is updated. Following Definition 7, atomic components transfer their states through port β each time they move from a busy location to a ready location. RGT reconstructs global states from these received partial states, stores them in variable V and delivers them through the dedicated ports.

Example 6 (RGT Atom). Figure 8 depicts the component RGT for system Task. For space reasons, only one instance of each type of transitions is shown. At runtime, RGT produces the sequence of global states in the right-most column of Table 1.

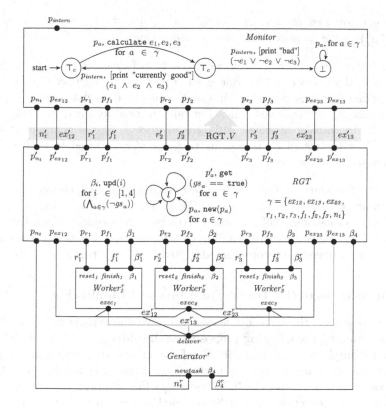

Fig. 8. Monitored version of system Task

5.3   Connections

After building component RGT (see Definition 8), and instrumenting atomic
components (see Definition 7), we modify all interactions and define new interactions to build a new transformed composite component. To let RGT accumulate
states of the system, first we transform all the existing interactions by adding
a new port to communicate with component RGT, then we create new interactions that allow RGT to deliver the reconstructed global states of the system to
a runtime monitor.

Given a composite component $B^\perp = \gamma^\perp(B_1^\perp, \ldots, B_n^\perp)$ with corresponding
component RGT and instrumented components $B^r = (P \cup \{\beta^r\}, L \cup L^\perp, T^r,$
$X^r)$ s.t. $B^r = B_i^r \in \{B_1^r, \cdots, B_n^r\}$, we define a new composite component.

Definition 9 (Composite Component Transformation). *For a composite
component $B^\perp = \gamma^\perp(B_1^\perp, \ldots, B_n^\perp)$, we introduce a corresponding transformed
component $B^r = \gamma^r(B_1^r, \ldots, B_n^r, RGT)$ s.t. $\gamma^r = a_{\gamma^\perp}^r \cup a^m$ where:*

- $a_{\gamma^\perp}^r = \{a^r \mid a \in \gamma^\perp\}$ *is the set of transformed interactions with:*

$$\forall a \in \gamma^\perp, a^r = \begin{cases} a \cup \{RGT.p_a\} & \text{if } a \in \gamma, \\ a \cup \{RGT.\beta_i\} & \text{otherwise } (a \in \{\{\beta_i\}\}_{i=1}^n). \end{cases}$$

- a^m is a set of new interactions s.t. $a^m = \{a' \mid a \in \gamma\}$, where $\forall a \in \gamma, a' = \{RGT.p'_a\}$ is the corresponding unary interaction.

For each interaction $a \in \gamma^\perp$, we associate a transformed interaction a^r which is the modified version of interaction a s.t. a corresponding port of component RGT is added to a. Instrumenting interaction $a \in \gamma$ does not modify sequence of assignment F_a, whereas instrumenting busy interactions $a \in \{\{\beta_i\}\}_{i=1}^n$ adds assignments to transfer attached variables of port β_i to the component RGT. The set a^m is the set of all unary interactions a' associated to each existing interaction $a \in \gamma$ in the system.

Example 7 (Transformed Composite Component). Figure 8 shows the transformed composite component of system Task. The goal of building a' for each interaction a is to enable RGT to connect to a runtime monitor. Upon the reconstruction of a global state corresponding to interaction $a \in \gamma$, the corresponding interaction a' delivers the reconstructed global state to a runtime monitor.

5.4   Correctness of the Transformations and Monitoring

Combined together, the transformations preserve the semantics of the initial model as stated by the following propositions. Intuitively, component RGT (cf. Definition 8) implements function RGT (cf. Definition 6). Reconstructed global states are transferable through the ports $p'_{a \in \gamma}$. If interaction a happens before interaction b, then in component RGT, port p'_a which contains the reconstructed global state after executing a will be enabled before port p'_b: the total order between executed interactions is preserved.

Proposition 1 (Correctness of Component RGT). *For any execution, at any time, variable RGT.V encodes the witness trace of the current execution: RGT.V is a sequence of tuples where each tuple consists of the state and the interaction that led to this state, in the same order as they appear on the witness trace.*

For each trace in partial-state semantics, component RGT produces the witness trace in the initial model, as stated by the following theorem.

Theorem 2 (Transformation Correctness). $\gamma^\perp(B_1^\perp, ..., B_n^\perp) \sim \gamma^r(B_1^r, ..., B_n^r, RGT)$.

Connecting a Monitor. Using [9], one can monitor a system with partial-state semantics with the previous transformations by plugging a monitor to component RGT through the dedicated ports. At runtime, such monitor will i) receive the sequence of reconstructed global states corresponding to the witness trace, ii) preserve the concurrency of the system, and iii) state verdicts on the witness trace.

Example 8 (Monitoring System Task). Figure 8 depicts the transformed system Task with a monitor (for the homogeneous distribution of the tasks among the workers) where e_1, e_2, and e_3 are events related to the pairwise comparison of the number of executed tasks by *Workers*. For $i \in [1,3]$, event e_i evaluates to true whenever $|x_{i \bmod 3+1} - x_{i \bmod 3}|$ is lower than 3 (for this example). Component *Monitor* evaluates $(e_1 \wedge e_2 \wedge e_3)$ upon the reception of a new global state from RGT and emits the associated verdict till reaching bad state $\bot$. The global trace $(free, free, free, hold) \cdot ex_{12} \cdot (done, done, free, delivered) \cdot n_t$ (see Table 1) is sent by component RGT to the monitor which in turn produces the sequence of verdicts $\top_c \cdot \top_c$ (where $\top_c$ is verdict currently good, see [3,8]).

6   Implementation and Performance Evaluation

We present some case studies on executable BIP systems conducted with RVMT-BIP, a tool integrated in the BIP tool suite [2].

Case Study 1: Demosaicing. Demosaicing is an algorithm for digital image processing used to reconstruct a full color image from the incomplete color samples output from an image sensor. The model contains *ca.* 1,000 lines of code, consists of 26 atomic components interacting through 35 interactions. We consider two specifications related to process completion: (i) Internal demosaicing units should finish their process before post-demosaicing starts processing (φ_1). (ii) Internal demosaicing units should not start demosaicing process before pre-demosaicing finishes its process (φ_2).

Case Study 2: Task Management. We consider our running example system Task and a specification of the homogeneous distribution of the tasks among the workers (φ_3).

Evaluation Principles. For each system, and all its properties, we synthesize a BIP monitor following [9] and combine it with the CBS output from RVMT-BIP. We obtain a new CBS with corresponding RGT and monitor components. We run each system by using various number of threads and observe the execution time. Executing these systems with a multi-threaded controller results in a faster run because the systems benefit from the parallel threads. Additional steps are introduced in the concurrent transitions of the system. Note, these are asynchronous with the existing interactions and can be executed in parallel. These systems can also execute with a single-threaded controller which forces them to run sequentially. Varying the number of threads allows us to assess the performance of the (monitored) system under different degrees of parallelism. In particular, we expected the induced overhead to be insensitive to the degree of parallelism. For instance, an undesirable behavior would have been to observe a performance degradation (and an overhead increase) which would mean either

Table 2. Results of monitoring Demosaicing and Task with RVMT-BIP

system	# interactions	no monitor		with monitor					
		thread	time (s)	specification	# extra interactions	events	thread	time (s)	overhead (%)
Demosaicing	8,400	1	67.97	Process completion	φ_1 : 6,800	4,399	1	68.706	1.07
							3	41.245	1.53
							10	29.521	1.24
		3	40.62		φ_2 : 2,200	1,599	1	69.116	1.67
							3	41.235	1.51
		10	29.15				10	29.251	0.31
Task (100,000 tasks)	399,999	1	117.96	Task distribution	φ_3 : 200,198	100,197	1	121.12	2.67
		2	72.32				2	72.85	0.73

that the monitor sequentializes the execution or that the monitoring infrastructure is not suitable for multi-threaded systems. We also extensively tested the functional correctness of RVMT-BIP, that is whether the verdicts of the monitors are sound and complete.

Results (*cf.* Table 2). Each time measurement is an average value obtained after 100 executions. Column *# interactions* shows the number of functional steps of system. Columns *no monitor* reports the execution time of the systems without monitors when varying the number of threads. Columns *with monitor* reports the execution time of the systems with monitors when varying the number of threads, the number of additional interactions and overhead induced by monitoring. Column *events* indicates the number of reconstructed global states (events sent to the associated monitor). As shown in Table 2, using more threads reduces significantly the execution time in both the initial and transformed systems. Comparing the overheads according to the number of threads shows that the proposed monitoring technique i) does not restrict the performance of parallel execution and ii) scales up well with the number of threads.

RV-BIP vs. RVMT-BIP. To illustrate the advantages of monitoring multi-threaded systems with RVMT-BIP, we compared it to RV-BIP [9]. Table 3 shows the results of a performance evaluation of monitoring Demosaicing and Task. RV-BIP induces a cheap overhead of 6.91 % with one thread and a huge overhead of 46.1 % (which is mainly caused by globally-synchronous extra interactions introduced by RV-BIP) with two threads, whereas according to Table 2, the overhead induced by RVMT-BIP with two threads is 0.73 %. The induced overhead is even better than the overhead induced when monitoring the single-threaded version of the system which is 2.67 %. As can be seen in Table 3, RVMT-BIP outperforms RV-BIP when monitoring Demosaicing. The latter does not take any advantage of the parallel execution. This clearly demonstrates the advantages of our monitoring approach over [9].

7   Related Work

Several approaches are related to the one in this paper, as they either target CBSs or address the problem of concurrently runtime verifying systems.

Table 3. Results of monitoring with RV-BIP

system	# interactions	no monitor		with monitor				
		thread	time (s)	specification	# extra interactions	thread	time (s)	overhead (%)
Demosaicing	8,400	1	67.97	Process completion φ_2	3,202	1	175.83	158.6
		10	29.15			10	172.31	491.1
Task (100,000 tasks)	399,999	1	117.96	Task distribution φ_3	177,611	1	126.11	6.91
		2	72.32			2	105.66	46.1

Runtime Verification of Single-Threaded CBSs. In [9], we proposed a first approach for the runtime verification of CBSs. The approach takes a CBS and a
regular property as input and generates a monitor implemented as a component which is then integrated within an existing CBS. At runtime, the monitor
consumes the global trace (i.e., sequence of global states) and yields verdicts
regarding property satisfaction. The technique in [9] only efficiently handles
CBSs with sequential executions: if applied to a multi-threaded CBS, the monitor would sequentialize completely the execution. Hence, the approach proposed
in this paper can be used in conjunction with the approach in [9] when dealing
with multi-threaded CBSs: a monitor as synthesized in [9] can be plugged to
component RGT which is reconstructing the global states of the system.

Decentralized Runtime Verification. The approaches in [4, 7] decentralize monitors for linear-time specifications on a system made of synchronous black-box
components that cannot be executed concurrently. Moreover, monitors only
observe the outside visible behavior of components to evaluate the formulas
at hand. The decentralized monitor evaluates the global trace by considering
the locally-observed traces obtained by local monitors. To locally detect global
violations/satisfactions, local monitors need to communicate, because their trace
are only partial w.r.t. the global behavior of the system.

Monitoring Safety Properties in Concurrent Systems. The approach in [16]
addresses the monitoring of asynchronous multi-threaded systems against temporal logic formulas expressed in MTTL. MTTL augments LTL with modalities
related to the distributed/multi-threaded nature of the system. The monitoring
procedure in [16] takes as input a safety formula and a partially-ordered execution of a parallel asynchronous system, and then predicts a potential property
violation on one of the causally-consistent interleavings of the observed execution. Our approach mainly differs from [16] in that we target CBSs. Moreover,
we assume a central scheduler and we only need to monitor the unique causally-
consistent global trace with the observed partial trace. Also, we do not place
any expressiveness restriction on the formalism used to express properties.

Parallel Runtime Verification of Monolithic Sequential Programs. Berkovich et
al. [5] introduce parallel algorithms to speed up the runtime verification of
sequential programs against complex LTL formulas using a graphics processing
unit (GPU). Monitoring threads directly execute on the GPU. The approach in

[5] is not tailored to CBSs and is a complementary technique that adds significant computing power to the system to handle the monitoring overhead. Note that, as shown by our experiments, our approach preserves the performance of the monitored system. Finally, our approach is not bound to any particular logic, and allows for Turing-complete monitors.

8   Future Work

A first direction is to consider monitoring for fully decentralized and distributed models where a central controller does not exist. For this purpose, we intend to make controllers collaborating in order to resolve conflicts in a distributed fashion. This setting should rely on the distributed semantics of CBSs [6]. A lot of work has been done in order to monitor properties on a distributed (monolithic) systems; e.g., [15] for online monitoring of CTL properties, [11] for online monitoring of LTL properties, [14] for offline monitoring of properties expressed in a variant of CTL, and [17] for online monitoring of global-state predicates. In the future, we plan to adapt these approaches to the context of CBSs. Another possible direction is to extend the proposed framework for timed components and timed specifications as presented in [2].

Acknowledgement. The authors are supported by the Artemis ARROWHEAD project under grant agreement number 332987 (ARTEMIS/ECSEL Joint Undertaking, supported by the European Commission and French Public Authorities). The work reported in this article is in the context of the COST Action ARVI IC1402, supported by COST (European Cooperation in Science and Technology).

References

1. Basu, A., Bidinger, P., Bozga, M., Sifakis, J.: Distributed semantics and implementation for systems with interaction and priority. In: Suzuki, K., Higashino, T., Yasumoto, K., El-Fakih, K. (eds.) FORTE 2008. LNCS, vol. 5048, pp. 116–133. Springer, Heidelberg (2008)
2. Basu, A., Bozga, M., Sifakis, J.: Modeling heterogeneous real-time components in BIP. SEFM **2006**, 3–12 (2006)
3. Bauer, A., Leucker, M., Schallhart, C.: Comparing LTL semantics for runtime verification. J. Log. Comput. **20**(3), 651–674 (2010)
4. Bauer, A.K., Falcone, Y.: Decentralised LTL monitoring. FM **2012**, 85–100 (2012)
5. Berkovich, S., Bonakdarpour, B., Fischmeister, S.: GPU-based runtime verification. IPDPS **2013**, 1025–1036 (2013)
6. Bonakdarpour, B., Bozga, M., Jaber, M., Quilbeuf, J., Sifakis, J.: A framework for automated distributed implementation of component-based models. Distrib. Comput. **25**(5), 383–409 (2012)
7. Falcone, Y., Cornebize, T., Fernandez, J.-C.: Efficient and generalized decentralized monitoring of regular languages. In: Ábrahám, E., Palamidessi, C. (eds.) FORTE 2014. LNCS, vol. 8461, pp. 66–83. Springer, Heidelberg (2014)
8. Falcone, Y., Fernandez, J., Mounier, L.: What can you verify and enforce at runtime? STTT **14**(3), 349–382 (2012)

9. Falcone, Y., Jaber, M., Nguyen, T., Bozga, M., Bensalem, S.: Runtime verification of component-based systems in the BIP framework with formally-proved sound and complete instrumentation. Softw. Syst. Model. **14**(1), 173–199 (2015)
10. Milner, R.: Communication and Concurrency, vol. 84. Prentice Hall, New York (1989)
11. Mostafa, M., Bonakdarpour, B.: Decentralized runtime verification of LTL specifications in distributed systems. IPDPS **2015**, 494–503 (2015)
12. Nazarpour, H.: Runtime Verification of Multi-Threaded BIP. http://www-verimag. imag.fr/~nazarpou/rvmt.html
13. Nazarpour, H., Falcone, Y., Bensalem, S., Bozga, M., Combaz, J.: Monitoring multi-threaded component-based systems. Technical Report TR-2015-5, Verimag Research Report (2015). http://www-verimag.imag.fr/TR/TR-2015-5.pdf
14. Sen, A., Garg, V.: Detecting temporal logic predicates in distributed programs using computation slicing. In: Papatriantafilou, M., Hunel, P. (eds.) OPODIS 2003. LNCS, vol. 3144, pp. 171–183. Springer, Heidelberg (2004)
15. Sen, A., Garg, V.K.: Formal verification of simulation traces using computation slicing. IEEE Trans. Comput. **56**(4), 511–527 (2007)
16. Sen, K., Vardhan, A., Agha, G., Rosu, G.: Decentralized runtime analysis of multithreaded applications. In: Proceedings of the 20th International Parallel and Distributed Processing Symposium (IPDpPS 2006), 25–29 April 2006, Rhodes Island, Greece, IEEE (2006)
17. Tomlinson, A.I., Garg, V.K.: Monitoring functions on global states of distributed programs. J. Parall. Distrib. Comput. **41**(2), 173–189 (1997)

A Generalised Theory of Interface Automata, Component Compatibility and Error

Sascha Fendrich[(✉)] and Gerald Lüttgen

Software Technologies Research Group, University of Bamberg, Bamberg, Germany
{sascha.fendrich,gerald.luettgen}@swt-bamberg.de

Abstract. Interface theories allow systems designers to reason about the composability and compatibility of concurrent system components. Such theories often extend both de Alfaro and Henzinger's *Interface Automata* and Larsen's *Modal Transition Systems*, which leads, however, to several issues that are undesirable in practice: an unintuitive treatment of specified unwanted behaviour, a binary compatibility concept that does not scale to multi-component assemblies, and compatibility guarantees that are insufficient for software product lines.

In this paper we show that communication mismatches are central to all these problems and, thus, the ability to represent such errors semantically is an important feature of an interface theory. Accordingly, we present the *error-aware* interface theory EMIA, where the above shortcomings are remedied by introducing explicit *fatal error states*. In addition, we prove via a Galois insertion that EMIA is a conservative generalisation of the established MIA (Modal Interface Automata) theory.

1 Introduction

Today's software systems are increasingly composed from off-the-shelf components. Hence, software developers desire to detect incompatibilities between components early. This is supported by *interface theories* [1,2,4,6,7,9,17,20,21], which may serve as specification theories for component-based design [2,4,8,15], software product lines [17], web services [5] and the Internet of Things [19]. Interface theories may also be employed as contract languages or behavioural type theories when transitioning from software design to implementation [3,13].

Many interface theories [4,6,17,20,21] extend de Alfaro and Henzinger's *Interface Automata* (IA) [1,2] and Larsen's *Modal Transition Systems* (MTS) [16,18]. In order to express compatibility assumptions of components on the communication behaviour of their environment, IA divides an interface's action alphabet into input ('?'), output ('!') and an internal action τ. A *communication mismatch*, or error, arises between parallelly composed components P and Q, if P may issue an output $a!$ while Q is not ready to receive the input $a?$ in its current state. Orthogonally, MTS permits one to specify required and optional behaviour. Taking stepwise decisions on the optional behaviour allows for a component-based, incremental design, which is supported by a compositional refinement preorder.

Supported by the DFG (German Research Foundation) under grant LU-1748/3-1.

E. Ábrahám and M. Huisman (Eds.): IFM 2016, LNCS 9681, pp. 160–175, 2016.
DOI: 10.1007/978-3-319-33693-0_11

Unfortunately, interface theories combining IA and MTS have several issues that impact their practical use. *Issue (A):* Forbidden inputs are preserved by the resp. refinement preorder but are widely ignored by parallel composition, such that behaviour that is forbidden in one component may be re-introduced in the composed system if another component defies this prohibition. This unintuitive treatment of communication mismatches and, in particular, unwanted behaviour, is dangerous for safety-critical applications. *Issue (B):* Pairwise binary compatibility of multiple components does not guarantee their overall compatibility when being considered as a multi-component assembly, and vice versa, even if parallel composition is associative. To address this, Hennicker and Knapp [14] have introduced *assembly theories* that extend interface theories by a separate level of assemblies where multi-component compatibility is checked. However, these assemblies have to be re-interpreted as interfaces to be of further use. *Issue (C):* Optional behaviour, modelled via may-transitions as in MTS, may be employed to express variability inherent in software product lines. In current interface theories, two product families may be considered compatible only if all products of one family are compatible with all products of the other. However, one would prefer a more detailed set of guarantees, such that one may distinguish if all, some or none of the product lines' products are compatible [17]. *Issue (D):* MTS and MTS-based interface theories have some subtle differences wrt. modalities, resulting in different composition concepts: in MTS, components unanimously agree on transitions of their composition; in interface theories, an error arises if the components' requirements do not match. Each theory makes a global choice of a composition concept, which is tightly bound to a respective compatibility notion and does not allow one to mix different compatibility and composition concepts that are suitable for the application at hand.

This paper shows that communication mismatches are central to Issues (A)–(D) above. Hence, the ability to represent such errors semantically is an important feature that is missing in current interface theories. We illustrate this in Sect. 2 by an example wrt. Issue (A). In Sect. 3 we present our interface theory *Error-aware Modal Interface Automata* (EMIA), for which we remedy Issues (A)–(D) by making communication mismatches explicit in form of *fatal error states* and by employing an *error-aware refinement preorder*. In contrast, current interface theories [1,2,4,6,7,9,17,20,21] remove such information about the causes and possible resolutions of communication mismatches. As is typical for interface theories, EMIA also includes conjunction and disjunction operators, which enables systems designers to combine operational and declarative specification styles. In Sect. 4 we show that a Galois insertion [10] renders our refined semantics a conservative extension of the arguably most general interface theory to date, MIA (Modal Interface Automata) [6]. Section 5 revisits the example of Sect. 2 in terms of EMIA, and discusses how fatal error states solve Issues (A)–(D). The resulting specification theory tightly integrates MTS, interface theories and assembly theories, and allows systems designers to combine the different composition concepts of these theories within a single interface specification. Due to space constraints, the proofs of our results are included in a technical report [12].

2   Motivating Example

In this section we discuss compatibility problems of current interface theories by means of an illustrative example highlighting Issue (A). Consider a driving assistance system that enables a car to drive into and out of a garage autonomously. Such a system must communicate with the garage in order to make it open and close its door. In Fig. 1 we show specifications G and C of the garage's and the car's interfaces, resp. Starting in state g_0, the garage is ready to receive a passage request (rqstPass?). After such a request, the garage opens its door (openDoor!), waits for a car driving in or out (drive?) and, finally, closes the door (closeDoor!) again. The car starts in state c_0 waiting for a user's request (rqstCar?). Upon receiving such a request, the car requests passage from the garage (rqstPass!) and then drives into or out of the garage (drive!), reaching state c_0 again.

Specifications G and C have a communication mismatch due to the drive!-transition at state c_2 and the fact that no drive?-transition is specified at state g_1. Hence, in the parallel product $G \otimes C$ shown in Fig. 2 (left), state $\langle g_1, c_2 \rangle$ is considered illegal. In *pessimistic* theories, e.g., [4,20], the parallel composition of G and C is undefined, because the illegal state $\langle g_1, c_2 \rangle$ is reachable from the initial state $\langle g_0, c_0 \rangle$. *Optimistic* theories, e.g., [1,2,6,7,9,17,20,21], assume a helpful environment that tries to steer away from communication mismatches by controlling the composed system via its input transitions. A state is optimistically illegal if a communication mismatch is reachable via uncontrollable actions, i.e., output- or τ-transitions. Parallel composition $G \parallel C$ is obtained from $G \otimes C$ by

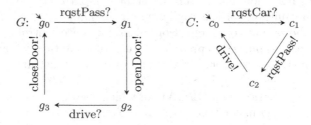

Fig. 1. Example of a driving assistant system including a garage G and a car C.

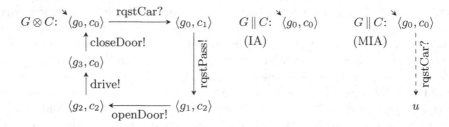

Fig. 2. Parallel product in IA or MIA (left), and parallel composition in IA (middle) and MIA (right) of the components depicted in Fig. 1.

removing all illegal states. In our example, state $\langle g_1, c_2 \rangle$ is illegal, just as state $\langle g_0, c_1 \rangle$ from which $\langle g_1, c_2 \rangle$ is reachable by an output (rqstPass!). This pruning leaves a single state $\langle g_0, c_0 \rangle$ with no transitions; all other states are unreachable. The rqstCar?-transition at state $\langle g_0, c_0 \rangle$, which would allow one to reach illegal states when triggered by the environment, is also removed. However, in order to ensure compositionality of refinement, rqstCar? must be permitted with arbitrary behaviour afterwards (cf. [6]); IA-based refinement [1,2,20] allows this implicitly for all unspecified inputs (Fig. 2, middle). In MTS-based interface theories, where unspecified transitions represent forbidden behaviour, compositionality is achieved by replacing pruned behaviour by an explicit optional transition to a special, universally refineable state u (Fig. 2, right) [6].

Due to this possibility of introducing arbitrary behaviour in case of a communication mismatch, stepwise refinement may re-introduce behaviour that has previously been removed due to the mismatch. Hence, optimistic theories accept a car driving into or out of the garage before the door is opened as a valid implementation of $G \parallel C$. This contradicts G's sensible constraint that driving in or out is only permitted after the door has been opened, i.e., the meaning of a car crashing into the door can simply be 'refined' to not being an error. In other words, the assumptions and guarantees expressible in current interface theories are insufficient for expressing unwanted behaviour.

Bujtor and Vogler [7] have shown that keeping or removing illegal states on a purely syntactic level are equivalent for IA wrt. preserving compatibility. In this spirit, current interface theories [1,2,4,6,7,17,20,21] eliminate erroneous behaviour either by regarding it as undefined (pessimistic) or by pruning (optimistic); all errors are treated semantically equivalent. Due to this equivalence, theories combining IA and MTS cannot remove illegal states completely but must replace them by a special, arbitrarily refinable behaviour as mentioned above. However, because optional transitions (i.e., may-transitions) allow for underspecification in MTS-based interface theories, one may distinguish potential errors that can be resolved by a suitable refinement from actual, unresolvable errors that arise when an output is required and the corresponding input is forbidden. That is, specifications based on MTS contain more information wrt. compatibility, which we make explicit in EMIA. EMIA guarantees that compatible specifications have only compatible implementations, potential errors have both compatible and erroneous implementations, and actual errors have only erroneous implementations (cf. Sect. 5, Issue (C)).

3   Error-Aware Modal Interface Automata

Our interface theory *Error-aware Modal Interface Automata* (EMIA), which we present in this section, is equipped with a *parallel composition operator* modelling concurrency and communication, a *conjunction operator* permitting the specification of a component from different perspectives, and a *compositional refinement preorder* enabling the substitution of an interface by a more concrete version. In addition to these standard requirements on interface theories, EMIA solves Issues (A)–(D) of Sect. 1. We achieve this by introducing *fatal error states*, which represent unresolvable incompatibilities between interfaces. This enables EMIA to deal with errors on a semantic level, since forbidden behaviour can be modelled by input transitions leading to a fatal error state.

Definition 1 (Error-Aware Modal Interface Automata). *An* Error-aware Modal Interface Automaton *(EMIA) is a tuple* $P := (S_P, I_P, O_P, \longrightarrow_P, \dashrightarrow_P, S^0_P, D_P)$, *where S_P is the set of states, I_P, O_P are the disjoint alphabets of input and output actions not including the silent action τ (we define $A_P := I_P \cup O_P$ and $\Omega_P := O_P \cup \{\tau\}$), $\longrightarrow_P \subseteq S_P \times (A_P \cup \{\tau\}) \times \mathfrak{P}(S_P)$ is the disjunctive must-transition relation ($\mathfrak{P}$ denotes the power set operator), $\dashrightarrow_P \subseteq S_P \times (A_P \cup \{\tau\}) \times S_P$ is the may-transition relation, $S^0_P \subseteq S_P$ is the set of initial states, and $D_P \subseteq S_P$ is the set of fatal error states. We also adopt* syntactic consistency *from MTS, i.e., for all $\alpha \in A_P \cup \{\tau\}$ and $p \xrightarrow{\alpha} P'$, we have $\forall p' \in P. p \overset{\alpha}{\dashrightarrow} p'$.*

Our definition of weak transitions that abstract from internal behaviour is adopted from the one in MIA [6]:

Definition 2 (Weak Transition Relations). *Let P be an EMIA. We define weak must- and may-transition relations, $\Longrightarrow$ and $=\!\Rightarrow$ resp., as the smallest relations satisfying the following conditions, where we use $P' \overset{\hat{\alpha}}{\Longrightarrow} P''$ as a shorthand for $\forall p \in P' \exists P_p. p \overset{\hat{\alpha}}{\Longrightarrow} P_p$ and $P'' = \bigcup_{p \in P'} P_p$:*

> WT1. $p \overset{\epsilon}{\Longrightarrow} \{p\}$ *for all $p \in P$,*
> WT2. $p \xrightarrow{\tau} P'$ *and* $P' \overset{\hat{\alpha}}{\Longrightarrow} P''$ *implies* $p \overset{\hat{\alpha}}{\Longrightarrow} P''$,
> WT3. $p \xrightarrow{a} P'$ *and* $P' \overset{\epsilon}{\Longrightarrow} P''$ *implies* $p \overset{a}{\Longrightarrow} P''$,
> WT4. $p =\!\overset{\epsilon}{\Rightarrow} p$,
> WT5. $p =\!\overset{\epsilon}{\Rightarrow} p'' \overset{\tau}{\dashrightarrow} p'$ *implies* $p =\!\Rightarrow p'$,
> WT6. $p =\!\overset{\epsilon}{\Rightarrow} p'' \overset{\alpha}{\dashrightarrow} p''' =\!\overset{\epsilon}{\Rightarrow} p'$ *implies* $p =\!\overset{\epsilon}{\Rightarrow} p'$.

We write $\overset{a}{\longrightarrow}\!\overset{\epsilon}{\Rightarrow}$ for transitions built up according to WT3 and call them trailing-weak *must-transitions. Similarly, $\overset{a}{\dashrightarrow}=\!\overset{\epsilon}{\Rightarrow}$ stands for trailing-weak may-transitions.*

Our *error-aware modal refinement preorder* $\sqsubseteq_{EA}$ corresponds to standard modal refinement from MTS [16,18] but reflects *and* preserves fatal error states. Intuitively, $P \sqsubseteq_{EA} Q$ for an implementation P and a specification Q, enforces that P's may-transitions are permitted by Q while for any of Q's disjunctive must-transitions at least one of the branches is implemented by P. In contrast to DMTS [18], we require that all branches of a disjunctive transition have the same label. This is sufficient for our purposes and does away with technical complications of parallel composition in the presence of τ-transitions (cf. [12]).

Definition 3 (Error-Aware Modal Refinement). *Let P and Q be EMIAs with equal alphabets, i.e., $I_P = I_Q$ and $O_P = O_Q$. A relation $\mathcal{R} \subseteq S_P \times S_Q$ is an* error-aware modal refinement *relation (EA-refinement) if, for all $\langle p, q \rangle \in \mathcal{R} \setminus (D_P \times D_Q)$, the following conditions hold:*

R1. $p \notin D_P$ *and* $q \notin D_Q$,

R2. $q \xrightarrow{i} Q'$ *implies* $\exists P'. p \xrightarrow{i}{\Rightarrow}^{\epsilon} P'$ *and* $\forall p' \in P' \; \exists q' \in Q'. \langle p', q' \rangle \in \mathcal{R}$,

R3. $q \xrightarrow{\omega} Q'$ *implies* $\exists P'. p \xRightarrow{\omega} P'$ *and* $\forall p' \in P' \; \exists q' \in Q'. \langle p', q' \rangle \in \mathcal{R}$,

R4. $p \dashrightarrow^{i} p'$ *implies* $\exists q'. q \dashrightarrow^{i}=^{\epsilon}{\dashrightarrow} q'$ *and* $\langle p', q' \rangle \in \mathcal{R}$,

R5. $p \dashrightarrow^{\omega} p'$ *implies* $\exists q'. q =^{\omega}{\Rightarrow} q'$ *and* $\langle p', q' \rangle \in \mathcal{R}$.

We write $p \sqsubseteq_{EA} q$ *if there is an EA-refinement* $\mathcal{R}$ *with* $\langle p, q \rangle \in \mathcal{R}$, *and* $P \sqsubseteq_{EA} Q$ *if, for each* $p \in S_P^0$, *there is a* $q \in S_Q^0$ *with* $p \sqsubseteq_{EA} q$. *If* $p \sqsubseteq_{EA} q$ *and* $q \sqsubseteq_{EA} p$, *we employ the symbol* $p \sqsupseteq\sqsubseteq_{EA} q$, *and similar for EMIAs* P, Q.

The refinement relation $\sqsubseteq_{EA}$ is reflexive and transitive and, hence, a preorder. Moreover, we have $p \in D_P$ iff $q \in D_Q$ for all $\langle p, q \rangle \in \mathcal{R}$ due to R1. Optional input-transitions, which may be refined to required or forbidden behaviour, are expressed as a disjunctive must-transition containing a fatal error state in its set of target states. For example, optional $a?$-transitions from a state p_0 to states p_1 and p_2 are modelled as $p_0 \xrightarrow{a?} \{p_1, p_2, p_3\}$ for some fatal error state $p_3 \in D_P$.

IA's parallel composition operator synchronises input and output transitions to τ-transitions. In contrast, we define a multicast parallel composition, where an output can synchronise with multiple input transitions, as in MI [21] and MIA [6]. We leave out MIA's separate hiding due to space constraints.

Definition 4 (Parallel Composition). *Let* P *and* Q *be EMIAs. We call* P *and* Q *composable if* $O_P \cap O_Q = \emptyset$. *If* P *and* Q *are composable, the multicast parallel composition* $P \parallel Q$ *is defined by* $S_{P \parallel Q} := S_P \times S_Q$, $I_{P \parallel Q} := (I_P \cup I_Q) \setminus O_{P \parallel Q}$, $O_{P \parallel Q} := O_P \cup O_Q$, $S_{P \parallel Q}^0 := S_P^0 \times S_Q^0$, $D_{P \parallel Q} := (D_P \times S_Q) \cup (S_P \times D_Q)$, *and the transition relations are given by the following rules:*

P1. $\langle p, q \rangle \xrightarrow{\alpha} P' \times \{q\}$ *if* $p \xrightarrow{\alpha} P'$ *and* $\alpha \notin A_Q$,

P2. $\langle p, q \rangle \xrightarrow{\alpha} \{p\} \times Q'$ *if* $\alpha \notin A_P$ *and* $q \xrightarrow{\alpha} Q'$,

P3. $\langle p, q \rangle \xrightarrow{\alpha} P' \times Q'$ *if* $p \xrightarrow{a} P'$ *and* $q \xrightarrow{a} Q'$ *for some* $a \in A_P \cap A_Q$.

P4. $\langle p, q \rangle \dashrightarrow^{\alpha} \langle p', q \rangle$ *if* $p \dashrightarrow^{\alpha} p'$ *and* $\alpha \notin A_Q$,

P5. $\langle p, q \rangle \dashrightarrow^{\alpha} \langle p, q' \rangle$ *if* $\alpha \notin A_P$ *and* $q \dashrightarrow^{\alpha} q'$,

P6. $\langle p, q \rangle \dashrightarrow^{\alpha} \langle p', q' \rangle$ *if* $p \dashrightarrow^{a} p'$ *and* $q \dashrightarrow^{a} q'$ *for some* $a \in A_P \cap A_Q$.

We also write $p \parallel q$ for $\langle p, q \rangle$. IA-based interface theories usually define a communication mismatch for p at q as a situation where an action $a \in O_P \cap I_Q$ is permitted at p and not required at q. In EMIA, such a situation is modelled with the help of an $a?$-must-transition from q to a target set Q' that includes some fatal error state $q' \in D_Q$, as explained above. Parallel composition is associative and commutative. Further, $\sqsubseteq_{EA}$ is a precongruence wrt. $\parallel$:

Proposition 5 (Compositionality). *If* P_1, P_2, Q *are EMIAs s.t.* $P_1 \sqsubseteq_{EA} P_2$ *and* P_2, Q *are composable, then* P_1 *and* Q *are composable and* $P_1 \parallel Q \sqsubseteq_{EA} P_2 \parallel Q$.

Perspective-based specification is concerned with specifying a system component from separate perspectives s.t. the component satisfies each of these perspective specifications; for example, each requirement for a component might describe a perspective. The component's overall specification is the most general specification refining all perspective specifications, i.e., it is the greatest lower bound wrt. the refinement preorder. This conjunction operator is defined in two stages:

Definition 6 (Conjunctive Product). *Let P, Q be EMIAs with equal alphabets. The conjunctive product of P and Q is $P \& Q := (S_{P \& Q}, I, O, \longrightarrow_{P \& Q},$*

$- \rightarrow_{P \& Q}, S^0_{P \& Q}, D_{P \& Q})$ *with* $S_{P \& Q} := S_P \times S_Q$, $S^0_{P \& Q} := S^0_P \times S^0_Q$, $D_{P \& Q} := D_P \times D_Q$, *and the transition relations are given by the following rules:*

C1. $\langle p, q \rangle \xrightarrow{i} \{ \langle p', q' \rangle \mid p' \in P', \ q - \xrightarrow{i} = \xrightarrow{\epsilon} q' \}$ *if* $p \xrightarrow{i} P'$ *and* $q - \xrightarrow{i} = \xrightarrow{\epsilon}$,

C2. $\langle p, q \rangle \xrightarrow{i} \{ \langle p', q' \rangle \mid p - \xrightarrow{i} = \xrightarrow{\epsilon} p', \ q' \in Q' \}$ *if* $p - \xrightarrow{i} = \xrightarrow{\epsilon}$ *and* $q \xrightarrow{i} Q'$,

C3. $\langle p, q \rangle \xrightarrow{\omega} \{ \langle p', q' \rangle \mid p' \in P', \ q = \xrightarrow{\omega} q' \}$ *if* $p \xrightarrow{\omega} P'$ *and* $q = \xrightarrow{\omega}$,

C4. $\langle p, q \rangle \xrightarrow{\omega} \{ \langle p', q' \rangle \mid p = \xrightarrow{\omega} p', \ q' \in Q' \}$ *if* $p = \xrightarrow{\omega}$ *and* $q \xrightarrow{\omega} Q'$,

C5. $\langle p, q \rangle - \xrightarrow{i} \langle p', q' \rangle$ *if* $p - \xrightarrow{i} = \xrightarrow{\epsilon} p'$ *and* $q - \xrightarrow{i} = \xrightarrow{\epsilon} q'$,

C6. $\langle p, q \rangle - \xrightarrow{\omega} \langle p', q' \rangle$ *if* $p = \xrightarrow{\omega} p'$ *and* $p = \xrightarrow{\omega} q'$,

C7. $\langle p, q \rangle - \xrightarrow{\tau} \langle p', q \rangle$ *if* $p = \xrightarrow{\tau} p'$,

C8. $\langle p, q \rangle - \xrightarrow{\tau} \langle p, q' \rangle$ *if* $q = \xrightarrow{\tau} q'$.

A state $\langle p, q \rangle$ of $P \& Q$ is a candidate for refining both p and q. Because $\langle p, q \rangle$ cannot require and forbid the same action a or be at once fatal and non-fatal, some states p and q do not have a common refinement. In such cases, $\langle p, q \rangle$ is called *inconsistent* and has to be removed from the candidates, including the removal of all states that require transitions leading to inconsistent states.

Definition 7 (Conjunction). *The set $F \subseteq S_{P \& Q}$ of logically inconsistent states is defined as the smallest set satisfying the following rules:*

F1. $\langle p, q \rangle \in (D_P \times (S_Q \setminus D_Q)) \cup ((S_P \setminus D_P) \times D_Q)$ *implies* $\langle p, q \rangle \in F$,

F2. $\langle p, q \rangle \notin D_{P \& Q}, p \xrightarrow{i}$ *and* $q - \xrightarrow{i}$ *implies* $\langle p, q \rangle \in F$,

F3. $\langle p, q \rangle \notin D_{P \& Q}, p - \xrightarrow{i}$ *and* $q \xrightarrow{i}$ *implies* $\langle p, q \rangle \in F$,

F4. $\langle p, q \rangle \notin D_{P \& Q}, p \xrightarrow{\omega}$ *and* $q = \xrightarrow{\omega}_{\not\tau}$ *implies* $\langle p, q \rangle \in F$,

F5. $\langle p, q \rangle \notin D_{P \& Q}, p = \xrightarrow{\omega}_{\not\tau}$ *and* $q \xrightarrow{\omega}$ *implies* $\langle p, q \rangle \in F$,

F6. $\langle p, q \rangle \xrightarrow{\alpha} R$ *and* $R \subseteq F$ *implies* $\langle p, q \rangle \in F$.

The conjunction $P \wedge Q$ is obtained from $P \& Q$ by deleting all states in F. This deletes all transitions exiting deleted states and removes all deleted states from targets of must-transitions. If $S^0_{P \wedge Q} = \emptyset$, then P and Q are called inconsistent.

Fatal states are excluded in Rules F2 through F5 because we do not care about consistency for fatal error states. Note that the states in D and F are different in nature: D-states represent states with possible but unwanted behaviour. F-states represent contradictory specifications that are impossible to implement. Conjunction is the greatest lower bound wrt. the refinement preorder $\sqsubseteq_{EA}$:

Proposition 8 (∧ is And). *If P and Q are EMIAs with equal alphabets, then (i) $\exists R.\ R \sqsubseteq_{EA} P$ and $R \sqsubseteq_{EA} Q$ iff P and Q are consistent. Further, if P and Q are consistent, then, for any R, (ii) $R \sqsubseteq_{EA} P$ and $R \sqsubseteq_{EA} Q$ iff $R \sqsubseteq_{EA} P \wedge Q$.*

As a standard category theoretic result, Proposition 8 implies that $\wedge$ is associative:

Corollary 9 (Associativity of ∧). *Conjunction is strongly associative, i.e., for all EMIAs P, Q, and R, if one of $P \wedge (Q \wedge R)$ and $(P \wedge Q) \wedge R$ is defined, then both are defined and $P \wedge (Q \wedge R) \sqsupseteq\sqsubseteq_{EA} (P \wedge Q) \wedge R$.*

We close this section with a remark on alphabet extension. Conjunction, disjunction and refinement are defined for EMIAs with equal alphabets. For perspective-based specification, it is of interest to consider EMIAs with different alphabets [6]. Following the lines of MI and MIA, the operations on EMIAs can be lifted to different alphabets by extending the alphabets of the operands by their mutually foreign actions. When a specification's alphabet is extended, the least possible assumptions should be made on a new action a, while the same specification wrt. known actions should hold before and after a. This can be achieved by adding an optional a-loop to each state. For output actions this is straightforward, but the exact meaning of optional input transitions depends on the desired composition concept (cf. Sect. 1, Issue (D)). Therefore, a separate alphabet extension operator has to be defined for unanimous, broadcast and error-sensitive parallel composition. Besides this, there is nothing surprising to expect from alphabet extension, and we leave out the formal definition here for brevity.

4   Relation to Other Interface Theories

The majority of IA-based interface theories prune errors. Therefore, it is important to investigate the relation between such error-pruning interface theories and our non-pruning EMIA theory. We do this for MIA [6] because it is the most general IA-based interface theory to date in that it is nondeterministic rather than deterministic and optimistic rather than pessimistic, thus subsuming MI [21] and MIO [4] (wrt. strong compatibility), resp. We establish here a Galois insertion between MIA and EMIA, i.e., a Galois connection $\langle \gamma, \alpha \rangle$ for which $\alpha \circ \gamma = \mathrm{id}_{\mathsf{MIA}}$ [10] (up to $\sqsupseteq\sqsubseteq_{\mathsf{MIA}}$). Recall that states from which a communication mismatch is reachable via output- or τ-transitions are called illegal. Intuitively, α abstracts from EMIAs by considering all illegal states to be equivalent, and γ concretises MIAs as EMIAs without any loss of information. Note that γ is different from the error-completion presented in [22] that is motivated by algorithmic considerations only. Error-completion preserves an interface's semantics when replacing missing inputs by transitions to an error state. In contrast, EMIA refines the semantics of MIA by retaining error states.

Definition 10 (MIA [6]). Modal Interface Automata *(MIA) are defined like EMIAs (cf. Definition 1), except that, instead of D_P, there is a universal state u_P that is only permitted as target of input may-transitions.*

An important difference between fatal error states and u_P is revealed in the different notion of refinement. While EMIA employs a variant of modal refinement [18] that preserves and reflects fatal error states, MIA adopts (ordinary) modal refinement in general but provides the possibility to employ IA-refinement where necessary. This is achieved by state u_P, which may be refined arbitrarily.

Definition 11 (MIA-Refinement [6]). *Let P, Q be MIAs with equal alphabets. $\mathcal{R} \subseteq S_P \times S_Q$ is a MIA-refinement relation if, for all $\langle p, q \rangle \in \mathcal{R} \setminus (S_P \times \{u_Q\})$, the rules of Definition 3 hold when replacing R1 by: $p \neq u_P$.*

Parallel composition of MIAs is defined through reachability of illegal states:

Definition 12 (Backward Closure). *Let P be a MIA or EMIA and $S \subseteq S_P$. The Ω-backward closure of S in P is the smallest set $\mathrm{bcl}_P^\Omega(S) \subseteq S_P$ s.t. $S \subseteq \mathrm{bcl}_P^\Omega(S)$ and, for all $\omega \in \Omega_P$ and $p' \in \mathrm{bcl}_P^\Omega(S)$, if $p \overset{\omega}{-\!\!-\!\!\rightarrow} p'$, then $p \in \mathrm{bcl}_P^\Omega(S)$.*

Definition 13 (MIA-Parallel Composition [6]). *For composable MIAs P, Q, the parallel product $P \otimes Q$ is defined by ignoring fatal error states in Definition 4. We say that there is a* communication mismatch *for p at q, in symbols* $\mathrm{mis}(p, q)$, *if there is an $a \in O_P \cap I_Q$ with $p \overset{a}{-\!\!-\!\!\rightarrow}$ and $q \overset{a}{-\!\!\not\rightarrow}$. The set of* illegal states *is defined as $E_{P \otimes Q} := \mathrm{bcl}_{P \otimes Q}^\Omega(\{\langle p, q \rangle \mid \mathrm{mis}(p, q) \text{ or } \mathrm{mis}(q, p)\} \cup (S_P \times \{u_Q\}) \cup (\{u_P\} \times S_Q))$. The parallel composition $P \parallel Q$ is the MIA given by the state set $S_{P \parallel Q} := (S_{P \otimes Q} \setminus E_{P \otimes Q}) \cup \{u_{P \parallel Q}\}$, the alphabets $I_{P \parallel Q} := I_{P \otimes Q}$ and $O_{P \parallel Q} := O_{P \otimes Q}$, and the transition relations obtained from $P \otimes Q$ by replacing all $i?$-transitions of states $\langle p, q \rangle$ having an $i?$-transition to $E_{P \otimes Q}$ by a transition $\langle p, q \rangle \overset{i}{-\!\!-\!\!\rightarrow} u_{P \parallel Q}$. If $S_{P \otimes Q}^0 \subseteq E_{P \otimes Q}$, then $S_{P \parallel Q}^0 := \{u_{P \parallel Q}\}$, else $S_{P \parallel Q}^0 := S_{P \otimes Q}^0 \setminus E_{P \otimes Q}$.*

The set $\mathrm{bcl}_P^\Omega(D_P) \setminus D_P$ of an EMIA P corresponds roughly to the set of illegal states in IA, EIO, MI and MIA. In contrast to these theories, EMIA requires one to match transitions of such states during refinement. The resulting refinement relation is comparable to other refinement preorders for error-free interfaces, but is more detailed for erroneous ones. Indeed, MIA can be seen as an abstraction of EMIA, where all states in $\mathrm{bcl}_P^\Omega(D_P) \setminus D_P$ are deemed equivalent (cf. Theorem 19).

Definition 14 (MIA-Conjunction [6]). *Let P and Q be MIAs with equal alphabets. The* MIA-conjunctive product *is defined by ignoring fatal error states in Definition 6 and adding the following rules for u:*

$$
\begin{aligned}
&CE1. \ \langle p, u_Q \rangle \overset{\alpha}{\longrightarrow} P' \times \{u_Q\} &&\text{if } p \overset{\alpha}{\longrightarrow} P', \\
&CE2. \ \langle u_P, q \rangle \overset{\alpha}{\longrightarrow} \{u_P\} \times Q' &&\text{if } q \overset{\alpha}{\longrightarrow} Q', \\
&CE3. \ \langle p, u_Q \rangle \overset{\alpha}{-\!\!-\!\!\rightarrow} \langle p', u_Q \rangle &&\text{if } p \overset{\alpha}{-\!\!-\!\!\rightarrow} p', \\
&CE4. \ \langle u_P, q \rangle \overset{\alpha}{-\!\!-\!\!\rightarrow} \langle u_P, q' \rangle &&\text{if } q \overset{\alpha}{-\!\!-\!\!\rightarrow} q'.
\end{aligned}
$$

The MIA-conjunction *is obtained from the MIA-conjunctive product by pruning logically inconsistent states according to Rules F2 through F6 of Definition 7.*

An input i forbidden at state p is modelled as a missing transition in MIA and, equivalently, as an i-must-transition from p to a fatal error state in EMIA. Hence, a MIA's behaviour can be modelled by an EMIA where non-fatal states are input-enabled. We write EMIA' for the collection of such EMIAs.

The Galois insertion between MIA and EMIA consists of a concretisation $\gamma : \text{MIA} \rightarrow \text{EMIA}'$ and an abstraction $\alpha : \text{EMIA}' \rightarrow \text{MIA}$ s.t. $\langle \gamma, \alpha \rangle$ is a Galois connection and $(\alpha \circ \gamma)(Q) \sqsupseteq \sqsubseteq_{\text{MIA}} Q$. The main idea behind α is to consider the states $\text{bcl}_P^\Omega(D_P) \setminus D_P$ as equivalent, yielding equivalence classes of EMIAs; α assigns a MIA to each of these equivalence classes. Vice versa, γ assigns to each MIA the disjunction of an equivalence class of EMIAs.

Definition 15 (Abstraction Function from EMIA' to MIA). *Let* $P \in$ *EMIA' and* $C_P := \text{bcl}_P^\Omega(D_P) \setminus D_P$. *The MIA-abstraction of* P *is the MIA* $\alpha(P) := (S_{\alpha(P)}, I_P, O_P, \longrightarrow_{\alpha(P)}, \dashrightarrow_{\alpha(P)}, S_{\alpha(P)}^0, u_{\alpha(P)})$ *with the state sets* $S_{\alpha(P)} := (S_P \setminus (C_P \cup D_P)) \dot{\cup} \{u_{\alpha(P)}\}$ *and* $S_{\alpha(P)}^0 := S_P^0 \cap S_{\alpha(P)}$. *The transitions of* $\alpha(P)$ *are obtained from* P *by replacing all* $i?$-*transitions leading from a state* p *to states in* C_P *by* $p \xdashrightarrow{i?} u_{\alpha(P)}$. *The kernel equivalence* $\equiv_\alpha \subseteq \text{EMIA}' \times \text{EMIA}'$, *which is defined by* $P \equiv_\alpha Q$ *iff* $\alpha(P) \sqsupseteq \sqsubseteq_{\text{MIA}} \alpha(Q)$ *and has equivalence classes* $[P]_\alpha$, *yields a canonical bijection* $\bar{\alpha} : \text{EMIA}'/\equiv_\alpha \rightarrow \text{MIA}$.

To define the concretisation function γ we need a disjunction operator:

Definition 16 (Disjunction). *For a family of EMIAs* $\mathcal{P} := (P_j)_{j \in J}$ *with equal alphabets, we define the* disjunction *of* $\mathcal{P}$ *as the EMIA:*

$$\bigvee_{j \in J} P_j := (\dot{\bigcup}_{j \in J} S_{P_j}, I, O, \dot{\bigcup}_{j \in J} \longrightarrow_{P_j}, \dot{\bigcup}_{j \in J} \dashrightarrow_{P_j}, \dot{\bigcup}_{j \in J} S_{P_j}^0, \dot{\bigcup}_{j \in J} D_{P_j}).$$

Proposition 17 ($\vee$ is Or). *If* P_j, *for* $j \in J$, *and* R *are EMIAs with equal alphabets, then* $\bigvee_{j \in J} P_j \sqsubseteq_{\text{EA}} R$ *iff* $P_j \sqsubseteq_{\text{EA}} R$ *for all* $j \in J$.

Disjunction on MIAs is defined analogously by ignoring fatal error states and replacing u_P and u_Q by $u_{P \vee Q}$. Obviously, α is homomorphic wrt. disjunction.

Definition 18 (Concretisation Function from MIA to EMIA'). *The concretisation function* $\gamma : \text{MIA} \rightarrow \text{EMIA}'$ *is defined as* $\gamma(P) := \bigvee \bar{\alpha}^{-1}(P)$.

The mappings α and γ defined in Definitions 15 and 18 are monotonic, which is key to the proof of our main result that α and γ form a Galois insertion:

Theorem 19 (Galois Insertion). *The maps* $\alpha : \text{EMIA}' \rightarrow \text{MIA}$ *and* $\gamma : \text{MIA} \rightarrow$ *EMIA' defined in Definitions 15 and 18 form a Galois insertion between MIA and EMIA' up to* $\sqsupseteq \sqsubseteq_{\text{MIA}}$, *i.e.,* $P \sqsubseteq_{\text{EA}} \gamma(Q)$ *iff* $\alpha(P) \sqsubseteq_{\text{MIA}} Q$ *and* $(\alpha \circ \gamma)(Q) \sqsupseteq \sqsubseteq_{\text{MIA}} Q$.

Proof (sketch). $\alpha \circ \gamma = \text{id}_{\text{MIA}}$ by homomorphicity of α wrt. $\vee$; standard monotonicity and extensivity arguments establish $\langle \gamma, \alpha \rangle$ as a Galois connection. $\square$

α is homomorphic wrt. parallel composition but not wrt. conjunction: although $\alpha(P \wedge Q) \sqsubseteq_{\mathrm{MIA}} \alpha(P) \wedge \alpha(Q)$ holds for $P, Q \in \mathsf{EMIA}'$ because α is monotonic, the converse direction "$\sqsupseteq_{\mathrm{MIA}}$" does not hold in general, because MIA's replacement of illegal states by u—which must be reproduced by α—is a non-continuous operation. For the same reason, γ is not homomorphic wrt. parallel composition; however, γ satisfies the inequality $\gamma(P \parallel Q) \sqsupseteq_{\mathrm{EA}} \gamma(P) \parallel \gamma(Q)$ for MIAs P, Q.

5 Discussion

In this section we illustrate how the fatal error states employed in EMIA solve Issues (A)–(D) criticised in Sect. 1. In particular, we establish that EMIA treats unwanted behaviour more intuitively (Issue (A)), that EMIA, in contrast to MIA, is an assembly theory (Issue (B)), that EMIA provides better support for specifying product families (Issue (C)), and that EMIA unifies the composition concepts of MTS and interface theories (Issue (D)). We do this mostly along the example of Sect. 2 and also use this example to demonstrate the Galois abstraction from EMIA to MIA.

Issue (A): In EMIA, the garage's constraint that a car shall not drive in or out in state g_1 would be specified by a drive?-transition to a fatal error state $*$, which represents an unresolvable error as is illustrated in specification G' in Fig. 3. In the resulting parallel composition $G' \parallel C$, also shown in Fig. 3, driving in or out too early in state $\langle g_1, c_2 \rangle$, when the door is still closed, leads to the fatal error state $*$, where the car crashes into the door. This information is not removed and

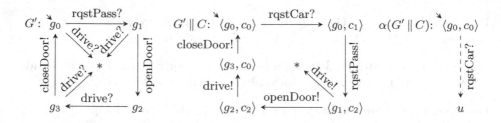

Fig. 3. Driving assistant system in EMIA and its Galois abstraction.

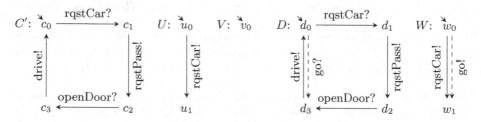

Fig. 4. Corrected car C', user interfaces U and V, and product families D and W.

cannot be redefined to not being an accident by refining $G' \parallel C$. Keeping this information is essential for pinning down the location and the cause of the error within the specification. Because G' forbids action drive? between rqstPass? and openDoor! but allows drive? after openDoor!, we can infer that specification C must be aware of action openDoor! in order to be compatible with G'. This way, a software design tool based on EMIA can propose possible specification changes to the designer. For example, the tool may propose to add action openDoor? to the car's alphabet and to insert an openDoor?-transition between rqstPass! and drive!, so as to avoid the fatal error state $*$ that is reachable from $\langle g_1, c_2 \rangle$. The resulting specification is shown as C' in Fig. 4.

Galois abstraction: Figure 3 (right) illustrates the abstraction function α of the Galois insertion between MIA and EMIA. We have $C_{G' \parallel C} := \mathrm{bcl}_{G' \parallel C}^{\Omega}(D_{G' \parallel C}) \setminus D_{G' \parallel C} = \{\langle g_1, c_2 \rangle, \langle g_0, c_1 \rangle\}$ (cf. Sect. 4). The rqstCar?-must-transition at $\langle g_0, c_0 \rangle$ leading to $C_{G' \parallel C}$ is replaced by a rqstCar?-may-transition to $u_{\alpha(G' \parallel C)}$. Due to α being a homomorphism wrt. $\parallel$, this result corresponds exactly to the MIA shown in Fig. 2 (right).

Issue (B): When adding the specification of a simple user interface, shown as U in Fig. 4, as a third component to the specifications G and C of Fig. 1, the three components G, C and U are pairwise optimistically compatible. However, the composed system $G \parallel C \parallel U$ is incompatible, because the mismatch for action drive! is reachable from the initial state $\langle g_0, c_0, u_0 \rangle$. In other words, MIA is not by itself an assembly theory. A different but related problem arises in pessimistic theories: the user interface specification V in Fig. 4 promises to never request a car. The components G and C are pessimistically incompatible and $(G \parallel C) \parallel V$ is undefined. However, $G \parallel (C \parallel V)$ is a perfectly valid composition.

To lift their interface theory MIO to an assembly theory, Hennicker and Knapp propose an enrichment EMIO of MIO by error states similar to our fatal errors [14]. However, they do not develop EMIO into a full interface theory: EMIOs are only employed to describe the result of a multi-component parallel composition and to check the communication safety of such an assembly. In addition, refinement is lifted to assemblies by providing an error-preserving refinement relation for EMIOs, which is similar to EA-refinement. However, no further operations like parallel composition or conjunction are defined for assemblies; instead, EMIO forms a second layer on top of MIO, and an EMIO is re-interpreted as MIO via an encapsulation function that removes all error-information. In contrast to this loose integration, EMIA provides a uniform and tight integration of interfaces and assemblies by directly including its canonical assembly theory in the sense of [14]. In particular, EMIA does not need two separate refinement relations for interfaces and assemblies.

Theorem 20 (Assembly Theory). *EMIA induces a* canonical *assembly theory (i.e., where encapsulation is equivalent to parallel composition).*

The proof is straightforward by checking the conditions of the definitions in [14] (cf. [12]). Because encapsulation corresponds to $\parallel$ and the assembly refinement preorder to $\sqsubseteq_{\mathrm{EA}}$, EMIA directly includes its canonical assembly theory.

Translating the above examples of assemblies with U and V into EMIA, the composition $G' \parallel C \parallel U$ resembles $G' \parallel C$ (Fig. 3), except that action rqstCar is an output instead of an input. Further, $(G' \parallel C) \parallel V$ and $G' \parallel (C \parallel V)$ are equivalent in EMIA. In both examples, compatibility is checked via reachability of fatal error states. However, it is up to the system designer to decide which error behaviour yields an incompatibility, i.e., compatibility is not necessarily a global concept as is the case for optimistic and pessimistic compatibility.

Issue (C): Consider specifications D and W of a car and a user interface product family, resp., both of which are shown in Fig. 4. These specifications allow product variations of a car and a user interface, which enable drivers to initiate the automatic driving assistance manually (go!), e.g., when parking in a different garage that is not equipped with an automatic door opener. Obviously, a user interface that provides this feature is incompatible with a car that does not, i.e., although some product combinations of D and W are compatible, some of them are not. Hence, D and W are incompatible, and no information that might help finding compatible product combinations is provided in current interface theories (see also the discussion about actual and potential errors in Sect. 2). In EMIA, the optional go?-transition at state d_0 would be modelled as a disjunctive go?-must-transition from d_0 to $\{d_3, *\}$, for a fatal error state $*$. We refer to this specification as D'. The specified error information is still present in the parallel composition of D' and W, so that one may derive additional conditions on the go-transitions. These conditions result in compatible refinements of D' and W, which describe compatible sub-families of the original product families. For example, refining the optional go?-transition into a mandatory one in D', or removing the optional go!-transition in W; both result in appropriate restrictions to sub-families. The necessary error information is present in the EMIA parallel composition of D' and W (cf. Fig. 5).

Issue (D): MTS and interface theories combining IA with MTS share many aspects of the modality semantics wrt. refinement. However, the meaning of may- and must-modalities differs wrt. parallel composition. Required and forbidden actions never cause an error in a parallel composition in MTS: either all components *unanimously* agree on implementing an action, or the action is forbidden in the composed system. The possibility to disagree on transitions enables an environment to control all transitions of an MTS, such that they

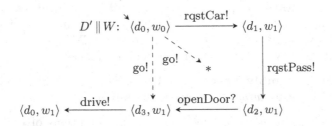

Fig. 5. Composition of product lines D' and W in EMIA.

may be interpreted as input-transitions from an interface theoretic view. However, the MTS parallel composition does not directly scale to output actions, because these cannot be controlled by the environment. Consequently, previous interface theories have adopted an IA-like *error-aware* parallel composition that is tightly bound to a global compatibility concept. In contrast, EMIA's explicit error representation allows for a *local* description of compatibility that is independent of composition. Thus, EMIA unifies unanimous and error-aware parallel composition, i.e., it permits the mixing of these composition concepts within a specification. As an aside, note that EMIA collapses to MTS when considering input actions only.

6 Conclusions

Our interface theory EMIA is a uniformly integrated specification framework that is applicable at different levels of abstraction, e.g., component-based design, product line specification and programming with behavioural types. EMIA bridges the gaps between MTS [18], interface theories [1,2,4,6,7,9,17,20,21] and assembly theories [14]. It is based on a concept of *error-awareness*, whereby EMIA's refinement preorder reflects *and* preserves fatal error states. While recent interface theories [6,21] considered the problem of how to enforce required behaviour, our finer-grained error semantics also solves the dual and previously open problem of how to forbid unwanted behaviour.

We proved that EMIA is related to the IA-based interface theory MIA [6] via a Galois insertion, rendering MIA into an abstraction of EMIA. In the abstract theory, errors may be considered as models of unknown behaviour for which no guarantees can be made, while in EMIA errors model unwanted behaviour for which we know that it must not be implemented. This difference between EMIA and related interface theories can be captured in a more concise way when considering error states axiomatically. In related theories [6,21], an error state e satisfies the laws $e \parallel q = e$, meaning that a composed system is in an erroneous state if a component is, and $e \sqsubseteq p \Rightarrow p = e$, meaning that an error cannot be introduced when refining an ordinary state. In EMIA, the additional law $p \sqsubseteq e \Rightarrow p = e$ is satisfied, i.e., refining cannot redefine an erroneous situation to be non-erroneous.

Regarding future work we intend to add alphabet extension and quotienting, and wish to capture differences and commonalities of different interface theories via axiomatisations. We also plan to implement EMIA in a formal methods tool, e.g., Mica [8], the MIO-Workbench [4] or MoTraS [15], and to adapt EMIA as a behavioural type theory for the Go Programming Language [13]. Such tools would enable us to evaluate EMIA on larger, more realistic examples, e.g., the docking system studied in the context of IA in [11].

Acknowledgements. We are grateful to Ferenc Bujtor, Walter Vogler and the anonymous reviewers for their helpful suggestions.

References

1. de Alfaro, L., Henzinger, T.A.: Interface automata. In: Foundations of Software Engineering (FSE), pp. 109–120. ACM (2001)
2. de Alfaro, L., Henzinger, T.A.: Interface-based design. In: Broy, M., Grünbauer, J., Harel, D., Hoare, T. (eds.) NATO Advanced Study. NATOS, vol. 195, pp. 83–104. Springer, Heidelberg (2005)
3. Bauer, S.S., David, A., Hennicker, R., Larsen, K.G., Legay, A., Nyman, U., Wąsowski, A.: Moving from specifications to contracts in component-based design. In: de Lara, J., Zisman, A. (eds.) FASE 2012 and ETAPS 2012. LNCS, vol. 7212, pp. 43–58. Springer, Heidelberg (2012)
4. Bauer, S.S., Mayer, P., Schroeder, A., Hennicker, R.: On weak modal compatibility, refinement, and the MIO workbench. In: Esparza, J., Majumdar, R. (eds.) TACAS 2010. LNCS, vol. 6015, pp. 175–189. Springer, Heidelberg (2010)
5. Beyer, D., Chakrabarti, A., Henzinger, T.A., Seshia, S.A.: An application of web-service interfaces. In: International Conference on Web Services (ICWS), pp. 831–838. IEEE (2007)
6. Bujtor, F., Fendrich, S., Lüttgen, G., Vogler, W.: Nondeterministic modal interfaces. In: Italiano, G.F., Margaria-Steffen, T., Pokorný, J., Quisquater, J.-J., Wattenhofer, R. (eds.) SOFSEM 2015. LNCS, vol. 8939, pp. 152–163. Springer, Heidelberg (2015)
7. Bujtor, F., Vogler, W.: Error-pruning in interface automata. In: Geffert, V., Preneel, B., Rovan, B., Štuller, J., Tjoa, A.M. (eds.) SOFSEM 2014. LNCS, vol. 8327, pp. 162–173. Springer, Heidelberg (2014)
8. Caillaud, B.: Mica: a modal interface compositional analysis library (2011). http://www.irisa.fr/s4/tools/mica/. Accessed 2 Dec 2015
9. Chen, T., Chilton, C., Jonsson, B., Kwiatkowska, M.: A compositional specification theory for component behaviours. In: Seidl, H. (ed.) ESOP 2012 and ETAPS 2012. LNCS, vol. 7211, pp. 148–168. Springer, Heidelberg (2012)
10. Cousot, P., Cousot, R.: Abstract interpretation: a unified lattice model for static analysis of programs by construction or approximation of fixpoints. In: Principles of Programming Languages (POPL), pp. 238–252. ACM (1977)
11. Emmi, M., Giannakopoulou, D., Păsăreanu, C.S.: Assume-guarantee verification for interface automata. In: Cuellar, J., Sere, K. (eds.) FM 2008. LNCS, vol. 5014, pp. 116–131. Springer, Heidelberg (2008)
12. Fendrich, S., Lüttgen, G.: A generalised theory of interface automata, component compatibility and error. Technical report, Bamberger Beiträge zur Wirtschaftsinformatik und angewandten Informatik 98, Bamberg University (2016)
13. Gareis, J.: Prototypical integration of the modal interface automata theory in Google Go. Master's thesis, Bamberg University, Germany (2015)
14. Hennicker, R., Knapp, A.: Moving from interface theories to assembly theories. Acta Informatica 52(2–3), 235–268 (2015)
15. Křetínský, J., Sickert, S.: MoTraS: a tool for modal transition systems and their extensions. In: Van Hung, D., Ogawa, M. (eds.) ATVA 2013. LNCS, vol. 8172, pp. 487–491. Springer, Heidelberg (2013)
16. Larsen, K.G.: Modal specifications. In: Sifakis, J. (ed.) AVMFSS 1989. LNCS, vol. 407, pp. 232–246. Springer, Heidelberg (1989)
17. Larsen, K.G., Nyman, U., Wąsowski, A.: Modal I/O automata for interface and product line theories. In: De Nicola, R. (ed.) ESOP 2007 and ETAPS 2007. LNCS, vol. 4421, pp. 64–79. Springer, Heidelberg (2007)

18. Larsen, K.G., Xinxin, L.: Equation solving using modal transition systems. In: Logic in Computer Science (LICS), pp. 108–117. IEEE (1990)
19. Lohstroh, M., Lee, E.A.: An interface theory for the internet of things. In: Calinescu, R., Rumpe, B. (eds.) SEFM 2015. LNCS, vol. 9276, pp. 20–34. Springer, Heidelberg (2015)
20. Lüttgen, G., Vogler, W., Fendrich, S.: Richer interface automata with optimistic and pessimistic compatibility. Acta Informatica **52**(4–5), 305–336 (2015)
21. Raclet, J.B., Badouel, E., Benveniste, A., Caillaud, B., Legay, A., Passerone, R.: A modal interface theory for component-based design. Fund. Inform. **108**(1–2), 119–149 (2011)
22. Tripakis, S., Stergiou, C., Broy, M., Lee, E.A.: Error-completion in interface theories. In: Bartocci, E., Ramakrishnan, C.R. (eds.) SPIN 2013. LNCS, vol. 7976, pp. 358–375. Springer, Heidelberg (2013)

On Implementing a Monitor-Oriented Programming Framework for Actor Systems

Ian Cassar and Adrian Francalanza[✉]

CS, ICT, University of Malta, Msida, Malta
{icas0005,afra1}@um.edu.mt

Abstract. We examine the challenges of implementing a framework for automating Monitor-Oriented Programming in the context of actor-based systems. The inherent modularity resulting from delineations induced by actors makes such systems well suited to this style of programming because monitors can surgically target parts of the system without affecting the computation in other parts. At the same time, actor systems pose new challenges for the instrumentation of the *resp.* monitoring observations and actions, due to the intrinsic asynchrony and encapsulation that characterise the actor model. We discuss a prototype implementation that tackles these challenges for the case of Erlang OTP, an industry-strength platform for building actor-based concurrent systems. We also demonstrate the effectiveness of our Monitor-Oriented Programming framework by using it to augment the functionality of a third-party software written in Erlang.

1 Introduction

Monitor-Oriented Programming (MOP) [9,10] (also termed *monitoring* [23,40]), is a code design principle advocating for the separation of concerns between the core functionality of a system and ancillary functionality that deals with aspects such as safety, security, reliability and robustness. MOP organises code in a layered onion-style architecture where the innermost core consists of the plain-vanilla system, and the outer layers are made up of *monitors* — software entities that observe the execution of the inner layers and react to these observations. Monitor actions typically include basic notifications of detected behaviour (to outer layers), the suppression of inner-layer observable behaviour, the filtering of stimuli coming from outer layers, and adaptation actions that affect the structure and future behaviour of the inner layers.

Software development and maintenance can benefit from MOP in various ways. For instance, MOP facilitates an *incremental deployment* strategy where outer layers may be added at a later stage, which may improve the time-to-market of a development process (*e.g.*, in the Simplex Architecture [42], monitoring was proposed as an automated method for upgrade-control systems). Arguably, this also fits better with real-world development processes, where requirements often become apparent at later stages of development. Monitoring may also be used as a means of software *customisation*, where every deployed system instance comes

E. Ábrahám and M. Huisman (Eds.): IFM 2016, LNCS 9681, pp. 176–192, 2016.
DOI: 10.1007/978-3-319-33693-0_12

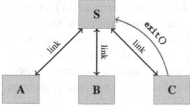
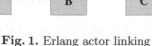
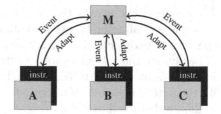

Fig. 1. Erlang actor linking   **Fig. 2.** Proposed monitoring extension

with its own auxiliary requirements in terms of security practices, privacy policies and robustness requirements that are handled by dedicated monitors [16,40]. MOP is also used as a discipline for augmenting systems with a *last line of defense*, so as to improve execution correctness and robustness. For instance, they can shield the inner layers by filtering harmful external stimuli [6], or steer the execution of the inner system to remain within its *"stability envelope"*, from where a system can be controlled using safe and well-understood procedures [9]. In fact, monitors are the main mechanism used in formal techniques such as Runtime Verification (RV) [10,33] and Security/Edit Automata [34,40].

A restricted flavour of MOP is already used extensively in a number of actor-based technologies for building reactive systems, such as the Erlang [8] and Scala [27] programming languages, and the AKKA concurrency framework for Java [1]. In particular, these actor systems — collections of self-contained, asynchronously-executing, interacting processes called actors — are typically organised in hierarchical fashion, where *supervisor* actors monitor other actors at a lower layer through a mechanism called *process linking*. In the example of Fig. 1 (left) the supervisor actor S is linked to three actors A, B and C; when either child actor fails, a special exit() notification is sent to S who is set to *trap* these *exit* messages[1] and react to them [8,35]. Common coding practices for such technologies then advocate for the *fail-fast* design pattern, whereby inner-layer actors should focus on the core functionality of the system and not engage in defensive programming that attempts to anticipate and handle errors locally [8]; instead, actors should fail as soon as such errors are encountered, so as to allow their abnormal termination to be detected and handled by the *resp.* supervisor monitors. Once a (process) failure is detected, a supervisor may react in a number of ways: in the case of the Erlang language, a supervisor may reinstate the failed actor or replace it by a *"limp-home"* surrogate actor, terminate other actors at the same layer that are potentially *"infected"* by the error, or even fail themselves so as to allow the abnormal termination notification to percolate to monitors in outer layers that are better equipped to handle the error.

In [7], the authors propose an abstract formal model for extending this mechanism (based on supervision trees and process linking) to a more comprehensive MOP model:

---

[1] Setting the trap_exit flag to false causes linked actors to fail upon receiving an exit message.

1. They extend the events that are monitored for, from mere (actor) failures to sequences of actor events that include message communication and actor spawning. As depicted in Fig. 2, this allows monitors to react to a wider range of behaviour and take preemptive action *before* actors fail. As is often the case in MOP frameworks [10, 37], the authors use a formal logic to rigorously specify the actor behaviour of interest to the monitor, namely the logic presented in [26] and studied in [24].
2. They propose a range of adaptation actions that a monitor may take in response to some observed behaviour, but also argue that for such adaptations to be effective, fine-tuned synchronisations between the monitor and a subset of the actors are required. Thus, they define language extensions to the logic of [24, 26] that permit the specification of *synchronisation strategies* and develop (sound) type-based analysis techniques to identity erroneous synchronisation procedures.

In this paper, we follow up on this work and study *implementability* aspects of the formal model proposed in [7]. In particular, we focus on one representative actor-based technology — the Erlang platform [8, 35] — and identify concrete instances of monitorable events and adaptation actions that are useful to MOP in such a setting. We then study the feasibility of such adaptation actions, together with the implementability of the synchronisation mechanisms designed in [7] wrt. the constraints of the runtime environment of the platform. In fact, we show that we can build a tool that *fully automates* the synthesis of monitors observing and reacting to the actor behaviour specified in the extended logic of [7]. Finally, we demonstrate the effectiveness and utility of the implemented framework by augmenting ancillary robustness functionality of a third-party software through our MOP framework.

To our knowledge, this is the first prototype implementation of a MOP framework for actor systems that allows programmers to add functionality in an incremental and disciplined manner through layers of monitors (implemented as actors themselves). Although the modular nature of actor-based systems facilitates the delineation of monitoring analysis and actions to a target subset of the system, the model poses new challenges to MOP. In particular, the encapsulated nature of actor state (as defined by formal models such as [2,3] and attested by the Erlang implementation [35]) makes it hard for the monitor to access and change it. In addition, the asynchronous nature of actor executions complicates the task of synchronising observed behaviour with timely administration of monitor actions. In fact, our work appears to be one of the first to introduce synchronous monitoring atop an inherently asynchronous computing platform.

The rest of the paper is structured as follows. Section 2 reviews the logic used for specifying the monitor behaviour for our MOP framework. Subsequently, in Sects. 3 and 4 we discuss the implementation challenges for building an actor-centric MOP framework for this logic. Section 5 validates this framework by using it to administer MOP extensions to a third-party actor-based system. Sect. 6 discusses related work and concludes.

2 Monitor Specification Language

We adopt the specification language of [7] to describe monitor behaviour in our study, restated here as the abstract syntax of Fig. 3. There are mild cosmetic changes reflecting the syntax used in the implementation presented in this paper: *e.g.*, the guard constructs $[p]$ rel $\vec{v}$. c and $^*[p]$ rel $\vec{v}$. c in Fig. 3 correspond to the *resp.* necessity formulas $[p]_{\vec{v}}^{a} c$ and $[p]_{\vec{v}}^{b} c$ of the formal logic (in [7], the qualifiers a and b differentiate between asynchronous (a) and blocking (b) pattern matching), and the termination constructs flag and end correspond to the *resp.* logic formulas ff and tt. In spite of these syntactic changes, the construct semantics is identical to that in [7].

$c, d \in$ SPEC ::= flag	(detect)	| end	(terminate)
| $c \& d$	(conjunction)	| if b then c else d	(branch)
| rec $X.c$	(recursion)	| X	(recursive call)
| $[p]$ rel $\vec{v}$. c	(guard)	| $^*[p]$ rel $\vec{v}$. c	(blocking guard)
| $A(x)$ rel $\vec{v}$. c	(asyn. adaptation)	| $S(x)$ rel $\vec{v}$. c	(sync. adaptation)

Fig. 3. Monitor specification syntax

The logic is defined over streams of visible events, α, generated by the monitored system made up of *actors* — independently-executing processes that are uniquely-identifiable by a process identifier, have their own local memory, and can either spawn other actors or interact with other actors in the system through asynchronous messaging; we use $i, j, h \in$ PID to denote the unique identifiers. For the Erlang implementation we discuss in this paper, events monitored include the sending of messages, $i > j \, ! \, v$, (containing the value v from actor with identifier i to actor j), the receipt of messages, $i \, ? \, v$, (containing the value v received by actor i), function calls, call$(i, \{m, f, l\})$, (at actor i for function f in module m with argument list l) and function returns, ret$(i, \{m, f, a, v\})$ (at actor i for function f in module m with argument arity a and return value v). Event patterns, $p, q \in$ PAT, follow a similar structure to that of events, but may contain term variables $x, y, z \in$ VAR (in place of values) that are bound to values $v, u \in$ VAL (where PID $\subseteq$ VAL), at runtime through pattern matching (we use $\vec{v}$ to denote lists of values).

Example 1. The pattern $x > j \, ! \, \{y, \text{true}\}$ describes an output event from an *arbitrary* actor x to a *specific* actor j, carrying a tuple value where the first item y is unspecified but the second item must be the value true. It can match with the event $i > j \, ! \, \{5, \text{true}\}$ returning the substitution $\{i, 5/x, y\}$. However, the same pattern does *not* match with either $i \, ? \, \{5, \text{true}\}$ (different type of event) or $i > h \, ! \, \{5, \text{false}\}$ (same event type but the event argument j conflicts with h, as does true with false).   ∎

In addition to term variables, the abstract syntax in Fig. 3 also assumes a distinct denumerable set of *formula variables* $X, Y, \ldots \in$ LVAR, used to define recursive specifications. It is also parameterised by a set of *decidable* boolean expressions, $b, c \in \text{BOOL}$, and the aforementioned set of event patterns. Monitor specifications include commands for flagging violations, flag, and terminating (silently), end, conjunctions, $c_1 \& c_2$, recursion, rec $X . c$, and conditionals to reason about data, if b then c_1 else c_2. The specification syntax in Fig. 3 includes *two* guarding constructs, $[p]$ rel $\vec{i}$. c and *$[p]$ rel $\vec{i}$. c, instructing the *resp.* monitor to observe system events that match pattern p, and progressing as c if the match is successful. Following [7], these constructs encompass directives for *blocking* and *releasing* actor executions, depending on the events observed. The guarding construct *$[p]$ rel $\vec{i}$. c is *blocking*, meaning that it *suspends* the execution the actor whose identifier is the *subject* of the event matched by the pattern (*e.g.*, actor i is the subject in the events $i > j \,!\, v$, $i < j \,?\, v$, call$(i, \{m, f, l\})$ and ret$(i, \{m, f, a, r\})$). By contrast, the guarding construct $[p]$ rel $\vec{i}$. c does not block any actor when its pattern is matched. However, for both constructs $[p]$ rel $\vec{i}$. c and *$[p]$ rel $\vec{i}$. c, pattern *mismatch* terminates monitoring, but *also* releases all the blocked actors in the list of identifiers $\vec{i}$. The syntax in Fig. 3 also specifies two adaptation constructs, $A(j)$ rel $\vec{i}$. c and $S(j)$ rel $\vec{i}$. c. Both constructs instruct the monitor to administer an adaptation action (A and S) on actor j, releasing the (blocked) actors in $\vec{i}$ afterwards, then progressing as c. The only difference between these two constructs is that the adaptation in $S(j)$ rel $\vec{i}$. c, namely S, expects the target actor j to be *blocked* (*i.e.*, synchronised with the monitor) when the adaptation is administered, and must therefore be blocked by some preceding guarding construct.

Example 2. Consider the monitor script below. It instructs the monitor to analyse two output events, first from actor i and then from actor j, sent to the same destination x (which is pattern-matched and determined at runtime). If the outputted values sent are equivalent, $y == z$, monitoring terminates. Otherwise, the monitor terminates the execution of the recipient actor x, restarts the two sender actors i and j, and recurses.

$$\text{rec } X . *[i > x \,!\, y] \text{ rel } [] . *[j > x \,!\, z] \text{ rel } [i] . \text{ if } y == z \text{ then end else}$$
$$kill(x) \text{ rel } [] . \, restart(i) \text{ rel } [] . \, restart(j) \text{ rel } [i, j] . \, X$$

The *restart* adaptation action is synchronous, requiring the actors i and j to be blocked (the *kill* adaptation is not). Therefore, the script specifies an *incremental strategy* for synchronising with actors i and j before the *resp.* adaptations are administered: matching with pattern $i > x \,!\, y$ blocks actor i, whereas pattern-matching with $j > h \,!\, z$ (for some actor h instantiated for x in $j > x \,!\, z$ by the previous match) blocks actor j. However, mismatching with pattern $j > h \,!\, z$ *releases* the previously blocked actor i, thereby allowing it to continue executing as normal because the monitor would terminate and the adaptation would not be administered. Importantly, if we assume that actor j's behaviour does not depend on communications from actor i, the temporary pause of actor i does not visibly affect computation since actors execute asynchronously *wrt.* to one another. See [7] for a complete formal description of the synchronisation mechanism. ■

3 Instrumenting Actors

In Erlang, actors limit the sharing of data by explicitly sending copies of this data to the destination actor; identifiers act as unique actor addresses. These *asynchronous* messages are received at the destination actor's *mailbox* (a message queue buffer) and can be exclusively read by this actor using pattern-matching, which retrieves the first message in the mailbox matching a specified pattern; this two-step communication mechanism allows the recipient actor to prioritize certain messages over others by potentially reading them out-of-order of arrival. Asynchronous actor execution is one of the tenets of the actor model and, in the case of Erlang, has lead to systems that are more scalable, maintainable and resilient — asynchronous actor computation is inherently modular, easier to understand in isolation, and its failure can be readily quarantined [8,35].

By contrast, monitors (expressed as actors) require tighter synchronisations *wrt.* the execution of actors they observe. Adequate MOP would occasionally need to momentarily pause the execution of an actor — typically after observing an event generated by it — while continuing to observe behaviour generated by other (independently executing) actors; in the event that an aggregate behaviour is detected, the monitor could then either issue notifications involving the paused actor (thereby attaining timelier detections) or else administer adaptations on the paused actor. Complex adaptations consisting of multiple operations often require adaptee actors to be inactive for their correct administration. In our case, the specifications of Fig. 3 necessitate an incremental synchronisation mechanism whereby actors are cumulatively synchronised to (and desynchronised from) a monitor during their execution, based on the observed behaviour.

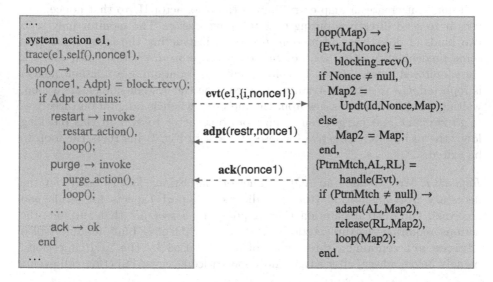

Fig. 4. The runtime adaptation protocol between a system actor (left) and the monitor (right)(Color figure online).

The implementability of this synchronisation mechanism hinges on the capability of externally interrupting the execution of an actor. In order to encapsulate the execution of an actor, the Erlang OTP libraries [35] (the layer of abstraction provided by the Erlang Virtual Machine) specifically limit external actor interventions to either actor killing[2] or asynchronous messaging. Neither method provides the desired functionality: (actor) killing is too coarse of an intervention, whereas sending an interrupt message to an actor does not guarantee that it will be picked up or handled adequately by the receiving actor.

Our solution was to engineer an implementation that uses an Aspect-Oriented Programming (AOP) framework to instrument injections at specific points of interest in the the monitored actors' code, and then use messaging (from the monitor) to trigger synchronisation procedures at specific stages of the monitored actor's computation; see Fig. 4, where the red code constitutes the code injected on the instrumented actors. The points of interest required by our aspect-based instrumentation are derived automatically from the patterns of the guarding constructs used in the specification scripts of Fig. 3. In particular, these patterns provide the necessary information to generate advices for AOP injections that match events at specific parts in the monitored system's source code and report back these events to the monitor for processing (first line of the injected code in Fig. 4). In the case of a blocking guard, further code is injected implementing the synchronisation protocol (injected code in Fig. 4, second line onwards).

In the actor code shown in Fig. 4 (left), specification script non-blocking guards (Fig. 3) translate into reported events with `null` nonces whereas blocking guards generate a fresh nonce uniquely identifying a blocking session (an actor may be blocked multiple times during the course of a monitored execution). Once the monitor — the code in Fig. 4 (right) — receives an event with a non-null nonce, it creates a map entry linking the *resp.* actor ID to that nonce, and uses it to send directives during that blocking session. The monitor may send two kinds of directives: *adaptation directives*, instructing the actor to execute some predefined function (*cf.* Sect. 4), or *resumption directives* which unblock the monitored actor. After a blocking event (*i.e.*, containing a non-null nonce) is reported, the injected instrumentation code on the system-side enters a loop, waiting for directive messages from the monitor: whereas adaptation directives (*e.g.*, `restart` and `purge`) cause the monitored actor to stay in this blocking loop, the resumption directive (denoted by `ack` in Fig. 4) instructs the loop to be exited.

Remark 1. We extended an AOP Framework for Erlang [32] to carry out the necessary instrumentation (the tool did not support aspects for sends and receives). Our instrumentation thus requires an *aspect file* that specifies the actions requiring instrumentation, along with a purpose built module called `advices.erl` containing three types of advices used by the AOP injections, namely before_advice, after_advice and upon_advice advices. Function call events

---

[2] This may be either explicit using the BIF `exit/2` or implicit through process linking [8].

specified in the aspect file generate before_advice advices woven *before* the function invocation, whereas for outputs and function returns, the AOP weaves after_advice advices (after_advice are necessary for function returns, since return values are only known *after* the return of the call). For mailbox reading, the *resp.* Erlang `receive` construct may contain multiple pattern-guarded clauses *i.e.*,

$$\texttt{recieve } g_1\text{->}exp_1; \quad g_2\text{->}exp_2; \quad g_3\text{->}exp_3; \ldots; g_n\text{->}exp_n \text{ end.}$$

The AOP thus weaves upon_advice advice for every guarded expression matching the message pattern defined by the receive aspects, as specified in the aspect file. *E.g.*,

$$\texttt{recieve } g_1\text{->upon\_advice}(..), exp_1; \quad g_2\text{->}exp_2; \quad g_3\text{->upon\_advice}(..), exp_3; \ldots \text{ end.}$$

4 Implementing Adaptations

The instrumentation setup outlined in Sect. 3 enables the implementation of a wide range of adaptation actions that can be administered on individual actors using their unique actor ID. We here discuss a number of these that were successfully implemented as pre-defined adaptations by our prototype implementation. Following [7], these adaptations fall under two main categories, namely *asynchronous* and *synchronous* adaptations.

Asynchronous adaptations may be applied to actors whose execution need not necessarily be synchronised to that of the *resp.* effectuating monitor at the time of the adaptation. This is permissible because the *resp.* administration can execute correctly independently of the status of the adaptee's execution, typically because the execution environment provides the necessary interface for the adaptation to be effectuated *externally* from the monitor. Erlang OTP prioritises actor encapsulation and provides a *limited interface* for external interference. Accordingly, our prototype implementation offers the following predefined asynchronous adaptations: actor *killing*, using the OTP `exit()` library function, actor registering and deregistering with a global name, using `register()` and `deregister()` OTP functions, actor memory optimisation using the OTP `garbage_collect()` function, exit message un/trapping setting using the OTP `process_flag()` function, and a composite adaptation that terminates the execution of all the actor linked to an actor (apart from itself), defined in terms of the `process_info()` and `exit()` OTP functions. These adaptations are generic in nature and agnostic to the instrumentation infrastructure discussed in Sect. 3 — in fact, they can also be used in asynchronous monitoring setups such as that of [26]. There are however scenarios where asynchronous adaptations would need to be applied to synchronised actors (*e.g.*, suspending the execution of an actor before killing it may guarantee a more timely monitor intervention); our prototype implementation allows this as well.

By contrast, synchronous adaptations require the adaptee's execution to be synchronised to that of the effectuating monitor (*i.e.*, temporarily suspended), as outlined in Sect. 3. In the case of the Erlang, one major reason for this requirement is the limited set of handles offered to externally affect the adaptee's execution — apart from the OTP functions mentioned above, messaging is the only other way of influencing an actor's execution. However, for a MOP framework to be effective, some adaptations would ideally have access an actor's internal state, even though the OTP restricts this to the owning actor exclusively. In our particular context (*i.e.*, Erlang), the only plausible method of carrying out such adaptations is that of sending a message instructing the recipient actor to carry out the adaptation itself. Note, however, that sending such a message to an actor that is not synchronised may either (*i*) be ignored by an adaptee that does not block to perform a mailbox read, or be not picked up since messages may be read out-of-order (*ii*) interfere abnormally with an actor's execution, either because the recipient actor does not know how to interpret the message directive, or because the directive-message reaches the actor at an execution point where it was expecting another type of message. The instrumentation in Sect. 3 avoids these pitfalls by forcing the actor to (autonomously) relinquish control (at specific execution points) to the observing monitor, which then sends it a message with the appropriate directive. Synchronisations are required for other reasons apart from those relating to Erlang OTP constraints. For instance, an adaptation may consist of a number of smaller actions that need to appear as one atomic action. Again, the instrumentation of Sect. 3 yields a straightforward implementation for this by suspending the adaptee's execution at the beginning and releasing it once the full list of sub-actions is completed. As a proof-of-concept, our implementation offers the pre-defined synchronous actions below:

- `purge(x)`: This adaptation requires access to (part of) the internal state of an actor (*i.e.*, its mailbox). It is implemented as a loop of non-blocking receives (using the `receive after 0` construct) consuming all the messages in the mailbox.
- `silent_kill(x)`: This composite adaptation terminates the execution of the argument actor x *without* informing the sibling actors to which it is linked. It is implemented by first obtaining the list of actor IDs to which it is currently linked (using `process_info(self(), links)`) and then unlinking it from this list of actors (using `unlink()`) and finally killing the adaptee once it is completely severed.
- `restart(x)`: The main complication when implementing this adaptation is that of preserving the identifier of the restarted adaptee, since other actors may be using it; a naive implementation using killing and spawning would yield a fresh identifier for the restarted actor. Our implementation keeps the adaptee alive, empties its mailbox and process dictionary [8,35] can then calls the original function with which it was spawned initially. This requires modifying spawn functions through AOP instrumentation) so as to record the actor spawn information (*i.e.*, the function spawned and its arguments) in its process

dictionary; this information is then retrieved when the restart adaptation is invoked.

– untrace(x): This action makes events from actor x unmonitorable. It extends the instrumented code of Fig. 4 with a flag indicating whether an actor should report events or not. By default, the flag is set to true whereas the action inverts it.

Remark 2. Other pre-defined adaptations can be added to the existing suite. For instance, one can define a runtime-enforcement *deletion* operation in the form of *synchronous* adaptations that intercept specific messages, using the message consumption mechanism of the purge() adaptation discussed above but refined for specific message patterns. One can also have an application-specific *asynchronous* adaptation that sends messages as *insertion* operations in a runtime-enforcement setup [34]. Since Erlang is higher-order and treats functions as first-class citizens, the framework can also be easily extended to handle dynamic adaptations that are not part of the predefined suite.   ∎

5   Augmenting Functionality Through MOP

As a representative system for our evaluation we consider Yaws [30,43], a third-party, (open source) HTTP webserver that uses actors to handle multiple client connections. For every client connection, the server assigns a dedicated (concurrent) handler that services HTTP client requests, thereby parallelising processing for multiple clients.

Figure 5 depicts the Yaws protocol for establishing client connections. Upon creation, an *acceptor* component spawns a *connection handler* to be assigned to the next client connection. The acceptor component waits for client connection requests while the unassigned handler waits for the next TCP connection request. Clients send connection requests through standard TCP ports (1), which are received as messages in the *handler's* mailbox. The current handler accepts these requests by reading the *resp.* message from its mailbox and (2) sending a message containing its own *Id* and the *port* of the connected client to the *acceptor*; this acts as a notification that it is now engaged in handling the connection of a specific client. Upon receiving the connection request message, the *acceptor* records the information sent by the handler and (3) spawns a *new* handler listening for future connection requests. Once it is assigned a handler, the connected

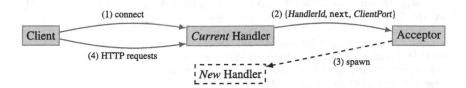

Fig. 5. Yaws client connection protocol

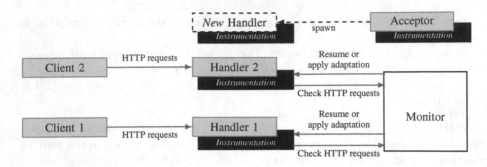

Fig. 6. Reinforced Yaws client connection protocol

client interacts *directly* with it using (4) standard HTTP requests; these normally consist of six (or more) HTTP headers containing the information such as the client's User Agent, Accept-Encoding and the Keep-Alive flag status. In Yaws, HTTP request information is *not* sent in one go but follows a protocol of messages: it starts by sending the http_req, followed by six http_header messages containing client information, terminated by a final http_eoh message. The dedicated connection handler inspects the client information received in the headers, and services the HTTP request accordingly.

To asses the effectiveness of our framework, we used our MOP tool to define Yaws extensions that augment its functionality. We here showcase one such extension, strengthening Yaws against *dot-dot-slash* attacks that exploit a directory traversal vulnerability [29]. Through additional monitor layers, the extended Yaws can detect malicious client requests (by comparing the requested URLs against a *white-list*) and take the necessary remedial actions. For our exposition, we define the monitoring script below assuming the following simplifications: (i) we consider a simple white-list with two files (*i.e.*, pic.png and site.html) and (ii) we only vet the first request of every new client. Intuitively, the script specifies that every time a client connects, and the handler actor assigned by the server receives an HTTP GET request for a file stored on the server, followed by 6 HTTP headers ($h1$ to $h6$) and the end-of-headers notification, then the requested file can only refer to either for pic.png or site.html. If not the *handler* is *killed*, and the *mailbox* contents of the server's *acceptor* actor is *purged*.

```
1   rec X.(
2     *[acc?{hId,next,_}] rel [].
3     [ret(hId,{yaws,do_recv,3,{ok,{http_req,'GET',{abs_path,path},_}}})] rel [acc].
4     [ret(hId,{yaws,do_recv,3,{ok,h1}})] rel [acc].
5     ...
6     [ret(hId,{yaws,do_recv,3,{ok,h6}})] rel [acc].
7     *[ret(hId,{yaws,do_recv,3,{ok,http_eoh}})] rel [acc].
8     if (path == ''/pic.png'' orelse path == ''/site.html'')
9       then untrace(hId) rel [acc, hId]. X
10      else silent_kill(hId) rel []. purge(acc) rel [acc,hId]. X
11  )
```

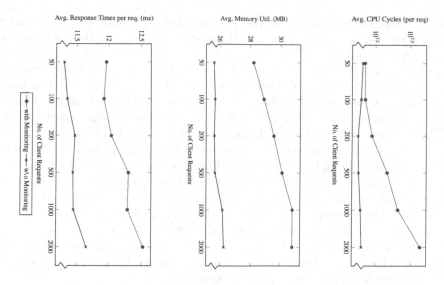

Fig. 7. MOP performance overheads (Color figure online)

Through pattern-matching, the script binds the assigned handler with variable
hId (line 2), which is then used for pattern-matching with the HTTP `GET` request,
the 6 HTTP headers, and the ending header `http_eoh` (lines 3 to 7)[3]. On line 3,
the file requested is bound to the variable *path* and checked against the white-
list (line 8). The guard commands on lines 2 and 7 block `acc` and *hId* resp.
(whereas `acc` may be known prior deployment, the Id bound to *hId* can only be
determined at runtime). If the white-list check is successful, the script removes
hId from the list of traceable actors, releases it together with `acc`, and recurs
on the script variable X (line 9). Otherwise, a synchronous kill action is applied
on *hId*, the mailbox contents of the `acc` actor are purged, and the two adaptees
are released before recursing (line 10). If the HTTP message sequence is not
matched at any point, the blocked actor `acc` is also released (lines 3 to 7).

From this script, our prototype implementation generates the augmented
system depicted in Fig. 6. Our tool automates the necessary instrumentation
required for the acceptor actor and every dynamically created handler actor.
This instrumentation reports events to a monitor actor, also synthesised from
the above script, which processes events and reacts by administering adaptation
actions accordingly.

We also examined the overheads introduced by our MOP framework in terms
of our Yaws case study. We considered a number of monitor scripts (similar to the
one discussed earlier) and calculated the relative overheads when subjecting the
resulting (augmented) webserver to varying client loads (measured as number

---

[3] These input operations are encapsulated by OTP library functions that are part
of the Erlang VM. To keep the VM standard, we instead instrumented on the call
returns of these functions.

of server requests) in terms of (*i*) the average CPU utilization; (*ii*) the memory required per client request; and (*iii*) the average time taken for the server to respond to batches of simultaneous client request. The experiments were carried out on an Intel Core 2 Duo T6600 processor with 4 GB of RAM, running Microsoft Windows 7 and EVM version R16B03. For each script and client load, we average out three sets of readings; since the variation between different monitor scripts was not substantial we again averaged the results and reported them in Fig. 7. The overheads obtained are at an acceptable level, especially since that monitoring is not merely observing the system but adding functionality (*e.g.*, at the worst level, the Memory overhead averaged at 17.4 %. Figure 7 does show a sharp increase in CPU overheads (46.7 % at 2000 requests). This is in part attributed to the code serialisations introduced by the monitor synchronisations, which create inevitable bottlenecks and wasted CPU cycles when processing multiple requests (*e.g.*, in the previous script, blocking the acceptor process prohibits it from servicing other client requests in waiting). However, such steep overheads where not reflected in the average response times per client request (*e.g.*, we recorded 7.4 % overheads at 2000 requests).

6 Conclusion

We present implementability results for a MOP framework targeting actor-based systems of a representative, industry-strength platform. The concrete contributions are:

1. A prototype[4] implementation that can *fully automate* the synthesis and instrumentation of monitors from formal descriptions specifying the system behaviour to be observed and the monitor actions to take in response. The implementation gives fine-grained control for non-trivial monitor actions to be carried out while imposing few system-monitor synchronisations (in accordance with the actor computational model), affecting only the sub-system targeted by the monitor actions.
2. A validation of the generality and effectiveness of the approach. We show that the functionality of third-party software can indeed be extended (with relative ease) by our framework, thereby attaining the MOP separation of concerns described in Sect. 1. Moreover, we give evidence that this can also be done feasibly, maintaining reasonable overheads when the extended system is subjected to varying stress loads.

The implementation is backed up by a formal model describing the monitor behaviour and a type system guaranteeing that synchronous monitor actions are only applied to blocked actors, as previous presented in [7]. For future work, we plan to incorporate techniques for lowering the monitor overheads (*e.g.*, code inlining [22]), and to extend our incremental synchronisation mechanisms to other monitor specification logics.

---

[4] The implementation can be downloaded from
   https://bitbucket.org/casian/adapter.

Related Work. Monitoring can be either inlined [11,22,41] or consolidated a separate code unit; we opted for the latter option. In multithreaded settings, inlining of inter-thread monitoring requires a *choreographed* setup [25,41] whereas we could afford an *orchestrated* solution whereby a *centralised* monitor analyses events and issues remedial actions. Monitor inlining tends to yield lower overheads and is generally more expressive because it has full access of the system code [22]. By contrast, having monitoring as a separate unit minimally alters the code of the monitored system (all the decision branching is performed inside the monitor), is less error-prone (orchestration tends to be easier to program than monitor choreographies), allows monitor computation to be offloaded to other machines [14], and facilitates compositional analysis whereby monitors are treated in isolation [23,24].

As opposed to *offline* monitoring, which assumes complete execution traces (logs) and executes *after* the system terminates its computation (*e.g.*, [4,17,18]), *online* monitoring executes alongside the system and has the ability to influence its computation. The prevalently used online monitoring frameworks typically employ synchronous instrumentation [5,11,14,19,31]. However, there are a few tools relying exclusively on asynchronous monitoring [12,13,26], which is easier to instrument since system components can be treated as black-boxes. In fact, if the monitor adaptations of Sect. 4 are limited to the asynchronous ones, then the less intrusive instrumentation setup of [26] (based on the tracing mechanism offered by the Erlang VM [35]) would suffice.

There are also frameworks offering *both* synchronous and asynchronous monitoring, such as MOP [10,11], JPAX [28,39] and DB-Rover [20,21]; in these tools, the specifier can choose whether to monitor synchronously or asynchronously for a property. By contrast, we offer finer-grained control that allows a monitor to *switch* between synchronous and asynchronous modes (and vice-versa) within the same property. We are aware of one other work that studies these fine-grained monitor controls [15], proposing a model where decoupling between system and monitor executions can be inserted, together with *explicit* mechanisms for pausing the system while the lagging (asynchronous) monitor execution catches up. There are nevertheless key differences between our work and that of [15]: (*i*) they treat the monitored system as one monolithic entity whereas we have the facility of introducing synchronisations with parts of the system; (*ii*) they assume a synchronous monitoring setup and introduce asynchrony at certain points of the computation whereas, contrarily, our setting starts off with a completely decoupled system-monitor setup and introduces synchronisations when needed. Also, we study adaptations in this setting whereas [15] limit themselves to detections.

MOP frameworks that support monitor adaptations typically lean more towards giving full flexibility [36,37] by allowing the specifier to define recovery procedures in the host language of the monitored system (*e.g.*, Java code in the case of JavaMOP [10]). Our current framework takes a different approach, offering only a finite subset of pre-defined adaptations that are classified into two groups (synchronous and asynchronous). Although less expressive, our approach allows for a cleaner separation between the monitor specification logic and the implementation of the system (our adaptations are implementation-agnostic abstract actions as opposed to actual Erlang code) which, in turn, facilitates the analysis of monitor scripts (*e.g.*, the type system presented in [7]).

EnforceMOP [36] is a JavaMOP extension for monitoring multithreaded computation, where they also use a centralised monitor for analyses across threads. However, as opposed to our setting, this centralised monitor does not have its own thread of control and is implemented as a static Java object that is invoked by inlined code in the *resp.* threads. Event reporting is thus necessarily synchronous, whereas our non-blocking event reporting is asynchronous and free of deadlock errors (the two-way handshake protocol of our blocking events amount to synchronous monitoring). Since they give full expressive power when defining remedial monitor actions, EnforceMOP employs additional runtime checks to avert errors introduced by the monitor itself; by contrast we offer predefined monitor actions and check for errors prior to deployment.

The implementation solutions discussed in this paper can be potentially applied to other MOP frameworks targeting asynchronous component-based systems, such as Enterprise Service Bus (ESB) architectures [12,38]. BusMOP [38] is an instance of the MOP suite of tools [37] where monitoring is used for component-based systems (COTS - Components Off The Shelf) made up of uniquely-identifiable devices connected to a bus. The tool treats components as black-boxes which limits monitor actions that can be taken. On the contrary, our framework adopts more of a grey-box approach for actors which allows for more powerful instrumentation mechanism and a wider range of adaptation actions. The monitoring in [38] is also completely synchronous and at a lower level of abstraction than ours (*e.g.*, they can monitor for low-level events such as memory reads and writes on the bus). The work in [12] is another example of a black-box monitor treatment of components; they study RV instrumentation alternatives on an ESB; the instrumentations considered are exclusively asynchronous and monitoring is limited to detections (*i.e.*, they do not support monitor adaptations).

References

1. Akka website. http://www.akka.io
2. Agha, G.: Actors: A Model of Concurrent Computation in Distributed Systems. MIT Press, Cambridge (1986)
3. Agha, G., Mason, I.A., Smith, S.F., Talcott, C.L.: A foundation for actor computation. J. Funct. Program. **7**, 1–72 (1997)
4. Andrews, J.H., Zhang, Y.: General test result checking with log file analysis. IEEE Trans. Softw. Eng. **29**, 634–648 (2003)
5. Barringer, H., Falcone, Y., Havelund, K., Reger, G., Rydeheard, D.: Quantified event automata: towards expressive and efficient runtime monitors. In: Giannakopoulou, D., Méry, D. (eds.) FM 2012. LNCS, vol. 7436, pp. 68–84. Springer, Heidelberg (2012)
6. Bielova, N., Massacci, F.: Do you really mean what you actually enforced? Edited automata revisited. Int. J. Inf. Secur. **10**(4), 239–254 (2011)

7. Cassar, I., Francalanza, A.: Runtime adaptation for actor systems. In: Bartocci, E., et al. (eds.) RV 2015. LNCS, vol. 9333, pp. 38–54. Springer, Heidelberg (2015). doi:10.1007/978-3-319-23820-3_3

8. Cesarini, F., Thompson, S.: ERLANG Programming, 1st edn. O'Reilly, Sebastopol (2009)

9. Chen, F., Roşu, G.: Towards monitoring-oriented programming: a paradigm combining specification and implementation. ENTCS **89**, 106–125 (2003). Elsevier

10. Chen, F., Roşu, G.: Java-MOP: a monitoring oriented programming environment for Java. In: Halbwachs, N., Zuck, L.D. (eds.) TACAS 2005. LNCS, vol. 3440, pp. 546–550. Springer, Heidelberg (2005)

11. Chen, F., Roşu, G.: MOP: an efficient and generic runtime verification framework. In: OOPSLA, pp. 569–588. ACM Press (2007)

12. Colombo, C., Dimech, G., Francalanza, A.: Investigating instrumentation techniques for ESB runtime verification. In: Calinescu, R., Rumpe, B. (eds.) SEFM 2015. LNCS, vol. 9276, pp. 99–107. Springer, Heidelberg (2015)

13. Colombo, C., Francalanza, A., Gatt, R.: Elarva: a monitoring tool for Erlang. In: Khurshid, S., Sen, K. (eds.) RV 2011. LNCS, vol. 7186, pp. 370–374. Springer, Heidelberg (2012)

14. Colombo, C., Francalanza, A., Mizzi, R., Pace, G.J.: PolyLARVA: runtime verification with configurable resource-aware monitoring boundaries. In: Eleftherakis, G., Hinchey, M., Holcombe, M. (eds.) SEFM 2012. LNCS, vol. 7504, pp. 218–232. Springer, Heidelberg (2012)

15. Colombo, C., Pace, G.J.: Fast-forward runtime monitoring — an industrial case study. In: Qadeer, S., Tasiran, S. (eds.) RV 2012. LNCS, vol. 7687, pp. 214–228. Springer, Heidelberg (2013)

16. Coppo, M., Dezani-Ciancaglini, M., Venneri, B.: Self-adaptive monitors for multiparty sessions. In: PDP, pp. 688–696. IEEE Computer Society (2014)

17. d'Amorim, M., Havelund, K.: Event-based runtime verification of Java programs. SIGSOFT Softw. Eng. Notes **30**(4), 1–7 (2005)

18. D'Angelo, B., Sankaranarayanan, S., Sánchez, C., Robinson, W., Finkbeiner, B., Sipma, H.B., Mehrotra, S., Manna, Z.: LOLA: runtime monitoring of synchronous systems. In: TIME, pp. 166–174. IEEE (2005)

19. Decker, N., Leucker, M., Thoma, D.: jUnitRV–adding runtime verification to jUnit. In: Brat, G., Rungta, N., Venet, A. (eds.) NFM 2013. LNCS, vol. 7871, pp. 459–464. Springer, Heidelberg (2013)

20. Delgado, N., Gates, A.Q., Roach, S.: A taxonomy and catalog of runtime software-fault monitoring tools. IEEE Trans. Softw. Eng. **30**(12), 859–872 (2004)

21. Drusinsky, D.: Monitoring temporal rules combined with time series. In: Hunt Jr., W.A., Somenzi, F. (eds.) CAV 2003. LNCS, vol. 2725, pp. 114–117. Springer, Heidelberg (2003)

22. Erlingsson, U.: The inlined reference monitor approach to security policy enforcement. Ph.D. thesis, Cornell University (2004)

23. Francalanza, A.: A theory of monitors (extended abstract). In: FoSSaCS (2016, to appear)

24. Francalanza, A., Aceto, L., Ingolfsdottir, A.: On verifying Hennessy-Milner logic with recursion at runtime. In: Bartocci, E., et al. (eds.) RV 2015. LNCS, vol. 9333, pp. 71–86. Springer, Heidelberg (2015). doi:10.1007/978-3-319-23820-3_5

25. Francalanza, A., Gauci, A., Pace, G.J.: Distributed system contract monitoring. JLAP **82**(5–7), 186–215 (2013)

26. Francalanza, A., Seychell, A.: Synthesising correct concurrent runtime monitors. FMSD **46**(3), 226–261 (2015)

27. Haller, P., Sommers, F.: Actors in Scala. Artima Inc., Mountain View (2012)
28. Havelund, K., Roşu, G., Programs, M.J.: Monitoring Java programs with Java PathExplorer. ENTCS **55**(2), 200–217 (2001)
29. Hernandez, A., Yaws 1.89: directory traversal vulnerability. http://www.exploit-db.com/exploits/15371/. Accessed 1 Dec 2015
30. Kessin, Z.: Building Web Applications with Erlang: Working with REST and Web Sockets on Yaws. O'Reilly Media, Sebastopol (2012)
31. Kim, M., Viswanathan, M., Kannan, S., Lee, I., Sokolsky, O.: Java-MaC: a run-time assurance approach for Java programs. FMSD **24**(2), 129–155 (2004)
32. Krasnopolski, A.: AOP for Erlang. http://erlaop.sourceforge.net/
33. Leucker, M., Schallhart, C.: A brief account of runtime verification. JLAP **78**(5), 293–303 (2009)
34. Ligatti, J., Bauer, L., Walker, D.: Edit automata: enforcement mechanisms for run-time security policies. IJIS **4**(1–2), 2–16 (2005)
35. Logan, M., Merritt, E., Carlsson, R.: Erlang and OTP in Action. Manning, Greenwich (2011)
36. Luo, Q., Roşu, G.: EnforceMOP: a runtime property enforcement system for multithreaded programs. In: ISSTA, New York, NY, USA, pp. 156–166. ACM (2013)
37. Meredith, P.O., Jin, D., Griffith, D., Chen, F., Roşu, G.: An overview of the MOP runtime verification framework. STTT **14**(3), 249–289 (2012)
38. Pellizzoni, R., Meredith, P.O., Caccamo, M., Rosu, G.: Hardware runtime monitoring for dependable COTS-based real-time embedded systems. In: RTSS, pp. 481–491. IEEE (2008)
39. Roşu, G., Havelund, K.: Rewriting-based techniques for runtime verification. Autom. Softw. Eng. **12**(2), 151–197 (2005)
40. Schneider, F.B.: Enforceable security policies. ACM Trans. Inf. Syst. Secur. **3**(1), 30–50 (2000)
41. Sen, K., Vardhan, A., Agha, G., Roşu, G.: Efficient decentralized monitoring of safety in distributed systems. In: ICSE, pp. 418–427 (2004)
42. Sha, L., Rajkumar, R., Gagliardi, M.: A software architecture for dependable and renewable industrial computing systems. In: International Conference on Process Control. IEEE (1995)
43. Vinoski, S.: Yaws: yet another web server. IEEE Internet Comput. **15**(4), 90–94 (2011)

Towards a Thread-Local Proof Technique for Starvation Freedom

Gerhard Schellhorn[1]([✉]), Oleg Travkin[2], and Heike Wehrheim[2]

[1] Institut für Informatik, Universität Augsburg, 86135 Augsburg, Germany
schellhorn@informatik.uni-augsburg.de
[2] Institut für Informatik, Universität Paderborn, 33098 Paderborn, Germany
{oleg82,wehrheim}@uni-paderborn.de

Abstract. Today, numerous elaborate algorithms for the effective synchronization of concurrent processes operating on shared memory exist. Of particular importance for the verification of such concurrent algorithms are thread-local proof techniques, which allow to reason about the sequential program of one process individually. While thread-local verification of safety properties has received a lot of attention in recent years, this is less so for liveness properties, in particular for liveness under the assumption of fairness.

In this paper, we propose a new *thread-local* proof technique for *starvation freedom*. Starvation freedom states that under a weakly fair schedule every process will eventually make progress. We contrast our new proof technique with existing global proof techniques based on ranking functions, and employ it exemplarily for the proof of starvation freedom of ticket locks, the standard locking algorithm of the Linux kernel.

1 Introduction

With the advent of multi-core systems, numerous new parallel algorithms operating on shared memory are being developed and come into use every year. Verifying correctness of parallel algorithms is challenging due to the intricate behavior caused by the various interleavings of processes. Moreover, such algorithms are typically designed for use by an arbitrary number of processes (e.g., concurrent data structures), and the verification task is thus to show correctness for any number of clients, i.e., we need to verify a *parameterized system*. More specifically, we are given a parallel system

$$Par(N) = Seq_1 \parallel \ldots \parallel Seq_N$$

(where Seq_1 to Seq_N are sequential programs), and the verification task is to prove a property φ for all $N \geq 1$. In general, verification of parameterized systems is undecidable [3]. Nevertheless, a number of approaches (being more or less automatic) have been developed to show properties of parameterized systems (see overview in [24]).

Our specific interest here is in liveness properties, specifically *starvation freedom*. The property of starvation freedom (see [9] for a definition and comparison

E. Ábrahám and M. Huisman (Eds.): IFM 2016, LNCS 9681, pp. 193–209, 2016.
DOI: 10.1007/978-3-319-33693-0_13

of progress properties) states that in a concurrent system every process will eventually make progress. Starvation freedom assumes some *fairness* [17] constraint (weak or strong): the scheduling of processes should not delay certain processes infinitely long. The prevailing proof principle for liveness properties of parallel (parameterized) systems is *global reasoning*: Early approaches for proving termination of parallel programs enhance local termination proofs of processes with cross-checks of interference freedom wrt. all other processes [2,18] while later approaches use global well-founded ranking functions estimating the distance to a target state [7,15].

In this paper, we present a new *local* proof principle for liveness properties of parameterized systems. More specifically, the method is tailored towards showing *starvation freedom under weak fairness*. It is based on the principle of rely-guarantee reasoning (RG) [10]: properties are shown locally for one process while relying on certain assumptions for other processes. While rely-guarantee reasoning is a well-established technique for proving safety, this is less so for liveness. The reason for this is that rely-guarantee reasoning for liveness properties needs to be *non-circular* in order to be sound [1]. We build our new proof technique on top of the existing framework RGITL [21,22], a program logic for reasoning about interleaved programs. The technique uses standard rely-guarantee reasoning to establish (safety) relies and guarantees of processes (including system invariants), and then uses these to establish an *admissible waits-for relation* on processes. The waits-for relation describes on which other processes a blocked process needs to wait in order to make progress. Admissibility requires (among other properties) that the waits-for relation is acyclic, thereby eventually guaranteeing progress. Admissibility can be *locally* checked for single processes using the already established relies and guarantees. We thus obtain a local proof technique for starvation freedom which is proven sound using the interactive prover KIV [6].

We exemplify our new reasoning principle on the example of the ticket lock of [16], the standard locking algorithm of the Linux kernel. To see how the local proof principle compares to global techniques, we furthermore develop a global proof of starvation freedom of the ticket lock using a proof rule of [15] employing ranking functions. On this, we see that the local technique can more naturally capture the principal reason for the ticket lock being starvation free in its proof obligations.

Related Work. Most closely related to us is the forthcoming paper [13] which presents a (quite complex) program logic for proving liveness properties (starvation and deadlock freedom) of concurrent objects. The proofs for concrete algorithms are done manually in [13] while ours are mechanized by a theorem prover (as is the general theory). Their proof of the ticket lock example is significantly more complex, e.g. we do not need to reason about lists of tickets. Like us, [13] builds on a rely-guarantee reasoning principle using a combination of separation logic and RG [23]. Slightly less related (because they treat different properties) are the compositional termination proofs for multi-threaded programs in [20] (which have no direct support of fairness), the RG-proofs of [8] for wait, obstruction and lock freedom (also no fairness support) and the deadlock-freedom proofs of [4].

2   Background

We start by describing the ticket lock algorithm used to illustrate our proof technique. We will then go on with defining basic notations.

Ticket Lock. The *ticket lock* [16] is a synchronization mechanism employed to achieve mutual exclusion of critical sections among parallel processes, and can be viewed as an optimization of Lamport's bakery algorithm [12]. In ticket locks, processes take tickets in the order of their arrival before entering the critical section. The process with the lowest ticket number not yet served is being served next. Ticket locks guarantee starvation freedom: under weak fairness assumptions every process will eventually reach its critical section.

The ticket lock involves two global variables: *served*, the ticket of the process currently being served, and *next*, the number of the next ticket to be taken. Initially, *served* and *next* are 1. Furthermore, every process has a local variable *lnext* in which to store its own ticket. The variable *lnext* is initially 0 for all processes. We use the notation *p.lnext* to refer to the local variable *lnext* of a process p. We assume an arbitrary but finite number N of processes with identifiers from a set *PId* to concurrently execute the ticket lock. One execution of the ticket lock algorithm involves executing the following piece of code (line 0 and 5 can be ignored for the moment):

```
0:    act:=true;
1:    ⟨lnext := next; next := next + 1⟩;
2:    while (lnext != served)
2a:        skip;
3:    skip;      // critical section;
4:    served:=served + 1;
5:    act:=false
6:
```

The brackets ⟨...⟩ embrace an atomic block: the ticket is taken and the *next* counter increased atomically. The algorithm thus starts with atomically setting *lnext* to *next* and incrementing *next* by 1. A process then spins until its local next number equals *served*. Afterwards it will enter its critical section. Upon exit of the critical section it increments *served*, thereby allowing the next process to enter.

More generally, we are interested in algorithms of the following shape. We have a finite number N of processes with process identifiers $p \in PId$. Each process executes a given algorithm Op_p operating on variables $\underline{x}$ ($\underline{x}$ being a sequence of variables) an arbitrary number of times. We equip every such algorithm with an additional auxiliary local variable *act* indicating the activity of a process (lines 0 and 5 above). This lets us state our liveness property in a uniform way. Thus the code for a process p looks as follows:

$$Seq_p(\underline{x}, act) := \left((act := true;\ Op_p(\underline{x});\ act := false)\ \textbf{or}\ \textbf{skip} \right)^* \qquad (1)$$

Here, the star operator is used to denote finite or infinite iteration, including no execution at all. The non-deterministic choice with **skip** indicates other irrelevant steps of the process in between calls of the algorithm. A parallel composition of N processes is a *program* and is written as $Seq_1 \ || \ ... \ || \ Seq_N$. In general, we thus consider *parameterized systems* here and are interested in verifying properties of parameterized systems. Our parameter is the number N of processes, and a property is true for a parameterized system if it holds for every N.

Starvation freedom in a program means that all processes currently running (having set act to true) will eventually return to an idle state, i.e., a state in which act is false. Starvation freedom stated in temporal logic (LTL) is thus

$$\forall p \in PId : \Box(p.act \rightarrow \Diamond \neg p.act)$$

Semantics. We define the semantics of programs as a set of *traces* (sequences of states). Since one of our proof techniques uses rely-guarantee reasoning, we assume any program to run in an environment, i.e., in a trace program alternate with environment steps.

Definition 1. *A state $s : Var \rightarrow Val$ from the set of states Σ is a (type-consistent) mapping from variables to values. A trace $tr = (s_0, s_0', s_1, s_1', ...)$ is a sequence of states. In this, transitions from s_i to s_i' represent program steps and transitions from s_i' to s_{i+1} environment steps. The length $\#tr \in \mathbb{N} \cup \{\infty\}$ of a trace tr may be finite or infinite, and it counts the number of program steps. A finite trace with $\#tr = n$ consists of $n + 1$ unprimed and n primed states, with the last state (last(tr)) being s_n.*

The first step is always a program step. Program and environment steps are alternating. Later on, we also refer to variables after an environment step as double primed variables, i.e., $\underline{x}$ refers to current variables, $\underline{x}'$ to variables after the program, and $\underline{x}''$ to variables after the environment step. The first state of any trace tr, $first(tr)$, is s_0. An empty trace consists of just the state $first(tr)$ and has $\#tr = 0$. We denote the suffix of tr starting in state s_i as $tr[i..]$ where $0 \le i \le \#tr$. For the semantics of programs we assume that the program variables $\underline{x}$ are a subset of Var.

The semantics of a program P is defined as a set $runs(P)$ of traces (we write $tr \in runs(P)$ or $tr \models P$) where the program steps are determined by the program, while the environment steps are arbitrary and will later on be constrained by logic formulas. Finite runs correspond to terminating executions of the program. For our second approach (Sect. 4) using rely-guarantee reasoning, a direct definition of $tr \models P$ (recursive over program structure) is possible, see [21]. However, our first approach needs an encoding of P into a transition system. This provides a temporal formula φ_P, and $tr \models P$ is then defined as $tr \models \varphi_P$. We use temporal logic formulas (inspired by LTL) to specify properties of runs (and thus of programs), and to constrain environment steps.

Definition 2. *The syntax of formulas φ and their validity on a trace tr is inductively defined. A formula can be one of the following:*

- *A predicate logic formula: Then $tr \models \varphi$ iff $first(tr) \models \varphi$, where the latter is defined as usual in predicate logic.*
- *A predicate logic formula using primed and double primed variables: The semantics is as before, but x' is evaluated as $s_0'(x)$ and x'' is evaluated as $s_1(x)$ whenever $\#tr \neq 0$. By convention, both x' and x'' are evaluated as $s_0(x)$ for an empty trace.*
- *A next formula: $tr \models \bigcirc\varphi$ iff $\#tr \neq 0$ and $tr[1..] \models \varphi$.*
- *An until formula: $tr \models \varphi_1$ until φ_2 iff there exists some $m \leq \#tr$ such that $tr[m..] \models \varphi_2$ and for all $k < m$: $tr[k..] \models \varphi_1$.*
- *A formula last characterizing empty traces: $tr \models$ last iff $\#tr = 0$.*
- *Propositional compositions of formulas with the usual semantics.*

As usual in LTL, we use $\Diamond \varphi$ to stand for *true* **until** φ and $\Box \varphi$ to be $\neg \Diamond \neg\varphi$. We also use **if** φ **then** φ_1 **else** φ_2 as an abbreviation of $(\varphi \rightarrow \varphi_1) \wedge (\neg\varphi \rightarrow \varphi_2)$.

Using primed and double primed variables allows for characterization of program and environment steps. A predicate logic formula $guar(\underline{x}, \underline{x}')$ using a sequence of unprimed and primed variables (a *guarantee*) constrains program steps. Semantically it can be viewed as a relation $guar \subseteq \Sigma \times \Sigma$ between two states s and s'. As an example $x = x'$ constrains the first program step not to change x, while temporal formula $\Box\, x' = x''$ constrains the environment never to change x (a rely condition for all environment steps). Formula $\Diamond$ **last** is used to characterize finite (terminating) runs.

To define the semantics of programs $Par(N) = Seq_1 \parallel \ldots \parallel Seq_N$, we encode each process $p \in PId$ into a set of *transitions* $\tau_i[p] \subseteq \Sigma \times \Sigma$. To this end, we add a new variable pc symbolizing the program counter to the set of variables. The transitions are then defined as formulas $\tau_i[p](\underline{x}, \underline{x}')$ over unprimed and primed versions of the program variables. Essentially we get a transition for i ranging over every line of the algorithm, e.g. for line 1 of the ticket lock we get

$$\tau_1[p] := p.pc = 1 \wedge p.pc' = 2 \wedge p.lnext' = next \wedge next' = next + 1\,.$$

To shorten notation, we implicitly assume that all program variables not mentioned (here: *served*, $q.pc$ and $q.lnext$ for $q \neq p$) are unchanged[1]. A transition is *enabled* for some variables $\underline{x}$, written $En(\tau_i[p](\underline{x}))$ if there exists some succeeding state for which the transition formula is satisfied.

The full transition relation $\tau[p]$ of one process $p \in PId$ is the union of all relations $\tau_k[p]$ (i.e., the disjunction of all formulas). The behavior of one process p in an arbitrary environment therefore can be characterized by the formula

$$\varphi_p = init_p(\underline{x}) \wedge \Box\big(\textbf{if } \neg\,\textbf{last then } \tau[p](\underline{x}, \underline{x}') \textbf{ else } \neg\,En(\tau[p](\underline{x}))\big)$$

where $init_p$ describes the initial states of process p (here: $p.lnext = 0$). Note that the formula characterizes runs, for which the transition relation is not enabled in the last state, i.e., not only prefixes of runs. Note furthermore, that this formula imposes no restrictions on the steps of the environment in a trace. The transition

---

[1] The encoding in the theorem prover KIV does this explicitly.

relation τ of the full program *Par* is the union of all $\tau[p]$ for $p \in PId$. Finally, the semantics of the full program is given as

$$\varphi_{Par} := init \wedge \square \left(\textbf{if } \neg \textbf{last then } \tau(\underline{x}, \underline{x}') \textbf{ else } \neg En(\tau(\underline{x}))\right)$$

$$\wedge \forall p. \square \left(\square En(\tau[p](\underline{x})) \rightarrow \Diamond \tau[p](\underline{x}, \underline{x}')\right)$$

Again *init* is a constraint on the initial states (here: the conjunction of all $init_p$ together with $served = next = 1$). The second line gives the usual constraint for weak fairness of scheduling between processes: if a process becomes continuously enabled, it will eventually do a step (the direct semantics of the (fair) interleaving operator in [21] also enforces this constraint). In our first approach (not using rely-guarantee reasoning) we constrain the environment of the top-level program to do nothing (formally $\square(\underline{x}' = \underline{x}'')$), i.e., to prove a property ψ for the program *Par* we prove

$$\varphi_{Par} \wedge \square(\underline{x}' = \underline{x}'') \rightarrow \psi$$

The second approach uses a rely condition $\square \, rely(\underline{x}', \underline{x}'')$ for the top-level environment that may even tolerate some nontrivial behavior of the environment.

3 Global Proofs of Starvation Freedom

In the following, we present two ways of proving starvation freedom of parameterized systems. The first approach given in this section is a standard *global* proof technique employing ranking functions following [14,15]. The next section will then introduce a new *local* proof technique.

Proof Principle. For proving the above property of starvation freedom, i.e., $\forall p \in PId. \square(p.act \rightarrow \Diamond \neg p.act)$, we can use a variant of a proof rule from [15] called WELL-JP ("parameterized well-founded response under justice"). The proof rule considers response properties of the form $\square(\varphi \rightarrow \Diamond \psi)$ for parameterized systems. The following version is an adaption of WELL-JP to a setting where we assume weak fairness for *processes*, not for specific transitions as usually assumed by Manna and Pnueli.

The general idea of the proof rule is to define *ranking functions* $\delta_i : \Sigma \rightarrow A$, $i = 0..max$, mapping states in Σ onto a well-founded ordering $(A, <)$. The proof rule involves a number of premises stating that the ranking functions constantly decreases thereby guaranteeing the target state satisfying ψ to be reached. Additionally, the proof rule involves a number of *intermediate assertions* for processes $\varphi_0[q], \varphi_1[q], \ldots, \varphi_m[q]$ (q being a process) which describe sets of states reached while moving from a source state satisfying φ to the target state ψ. Associated to every intermediate assertion $\varphi_i[q]$, we have a ranking function δ_i and a *helpful process* $proc_i[q]$. The helpful process is the process helping us with the progress: when this process executes its next transition, the ranking is decreased.

The proof rule WELL-JP is given in Fig. 1 (a formula φ' standing for φ with a prime added to all variables). As an explanation, the four premises of the proof rule have the following meaning:

$J1 : \varphi \rightarrow \psi \vee \bigvee_{j=0}^{max} \exists\, q \in Pld.\ \varphi_j[q]$

$J2 : \forall\, i = 0..max, p \in Pld.$

$\qquad \varphi_i[p] \wedge \tau \rightarrow \psi' \vee (\varphi_i'[p] \wedge \delta_i' = \delta_i) \vee \bigvee_{j=0}^{max} \exists\, q \in Pld.\ \varphi_j'[q] \wedge \delta_j' < \delta_i$

$J3 : \forall\, i = 0..max, p \in Pld.\ \varphi_i[p] \wedge \tau[proc_i[p]] \rightarrow \psi' \vee \bigvee_{j=0}^{max} \exists\, q \in Pld.\ \varphi_j'[q] \wedge \delta_j' < \delta_i$

$J4 : \forall\, i = 0..max, p \in Pld.\ \varphi_i[p] \rightarrow En(\tau[proc_i[p]])$

$$\overline{\qquad\qquad \Box(\varphi \rightarrow \Diamond\psi) \qquad\qquad}$$

Fig. 1. Proof rule WELL-JP

[**J1**] a φ-state (the source state) is either already a ψ-state (the target) or satisfies one of the intermediate assertions for one of the processes;

[**J2**] executing the transition of the program in an intermediate assertion state brings us to the state ψ, or we stay in the intermediate assertion and keep the ranking function, or we go to another intermediate assertion and decrease the ranking function;

[**J3**] when we are in an intermediate assertion i (belonging to process p) and execute the transition of the helpful process $proc_i$, we either reach ψ or definitely decrease rank; and

[**J4**] helpful processes $proc_i[q]$ are always enabled in states where the corresponding intermediate assertion $\varphi_i[q]$ holds.

Together, this guarantees that we eventually reach the target state.

Application to Ticket Lock. Now to the ticket lock and the property $\Box(p.act \rightarrow \Diamond \neg p.act)$ which we want to prove for all processes p. This property itself refers to a process. In the following, we thus slightly rephrase the property to $\Box(self.act \rightarrow \Diamond \neg self.act)$ as to distinguish the process in the property from those in the proof rule. Again, we use the notation $\tau_i[q]$ to refer to the transition of process q associated to line number i in the program (given in Sect. 2).

For verifying starvation freedom with rule WELL-JP, we first of all need to find ranking functions, intermediate assertions and helpful processes. The ranking function has to somehow *count* the distance between the current state and our target state which is one where $\neg self.act$ holds. For this, we need to distinguish four situations: (1) Process $self$ has set its local variable act to true, but not yet taken a ticket (then $self.pc = 1$ holds), and (2) process $self$ has taken a ticket but needs to wait because someone else is being served (i.e., $\exists\, q.q.lnext = served \wedge q \neq self$), (3) $self$ is currently being served ($self.lnext = served$) and finally (4) $self$ has been served but has not set the local variable act to false ($self.pc = 5$). We put (2) and (3) together by simply stating that there exists a q (including possibly $self$) such that $q.lnext = served$ and $hasTicket(self)$, i.e., $self$ is at location 2, 2a, 3 or 4. This range, in which some process is currently being served (possibly $self$), needs to be further split into the four possible program lines.

These 6 different situations are captured in the intermediate assertions (i.e., max used in WELL-JP is 5). As stated by the proof rule, the intermediate assertions are parameterized by process identifiers q (although not all of them have q occurring in the formula). Below we give all $\varphi_i[q]$'s together with their associated helpful processes $proc_i[q]$. In this, we let $hasTicket(p) \stackrel{\wedge}{=} p.pc = 2 \vee p.pc = 2a \vee p.pc = 3 \vee p.pc = 4$.

$$\varphi_5[q] = self.pc = 1 \qquad\qquad\qquad\qquad\qquad proc_5[q] = self$$
$$\varphi_4[q] = q.lnext = served \wedge q.pc = 2a \wedge hasTicket(self) \quad proc_4[q] = q$$
$$\varphi_3[q] = q.lnext = served \wedge q.pc = 2 \wedge hasTicket(self) \quad proc_3[q] = q$$
$$\varphi_2[q] = q.lnext = served \wedge q.pc = 3 \wedge hasTicket(self) \quad proc_2[q] = q$$
$$\varphi_1[q] = q.lnext = served \wedge q.pc = 4 \wedge hasTicket(self) \quad proc_1[q] = q$$
$$\varphi_0[q] = self.pc = 5 \qquad\qquad\qquad\qquad\qquad proc_0[q] = self$$

For these six intermediate assertions, we next need six ranking functions. The well-founded ordering we use here is the set $A = (\mathbb{N}\cup\infty) \times \{5, 4, 3, 2, 1, 0\}$ together with the ordering $(n_1, c_1) < (n_2, c_2)$ if $n_1 < n_2$ or $n_1 = n_2$ and $c_1 < c_2$. The basic idea behind the ranking functions for the intermediate assertions $\varphi_4, \varphi_3, \varphi_2$ and φ_1 is to count the number of processes queuing before $self$ to get served (first component in the pair) plus to record how far the process currently being served is from increasing $served$ at the end. In the last ranking function δ_0, the value of $served$ is already increased and thus the distance is 0. The ranking functions are thus

$$\delta_5 = (\infty, 5) \qquad \delta_i = (self.lnext - served, i) \quad \text{for} \quad i = 1..4 \qquad \delta_0 = (0, 0)$$

The first ranking function $\delta_5 = (\infty, 5)$ is the maximum distance. In intermediate assertion φ_5, process $self$ has not even taken a ticket and thus has the maximal distance to the target. The helpful process in this case is process $self$ itself, which needs to take the ticket. The other helpful processes are either the process q currently served, or – in case of 0 – process $self$ again which finally has to set act to false again.

Having fixed helpful processes, intermediate assertions and ranking functions, we next need to prove all the implications in the premises of the proof rule. To this end, we need further invariants about the algorithm which we then use for proving J1 to J4. We define $noTicket(p) \stackrel{\wedge}{=} \neg hasTicket(p)$, and then use the invariants of Fig. 2 where $preds(p) \stackrel{\wedge}{=} |\{q \mid hasTicket(q) \wedge q.lnext < p.lnext\}|$ is the number

$$INV_0 \stackrel{\wedge}{=} served \leq next \wedge served \neq 0 \neq next$$
$$INV_1 \stackrel{\wedge}{=} (\forall p.\, noTicket(p)) \vee (\exists p.\, p.lnext = served \wedge hasTicket(p))$$
$$INV_2 \stackrel{\wedge}{=} \forall n.\, served \leq n < next \rightarrow (\exists p.\, p.lnext = n \wedge hasTicket(p))$$
$$INV_3 \stackrel{\wedge}{=} \forall p, p0.\, p \neq p0 \wedge hasTicket(p) \wedge hasTicket(p0) \rightarrow p.lnext \neq p0.lnext$$
$$INV_4 \stackrel{\wedge}{=} \forall p.\, p.lnext < next$$
$$INV_5 \stackrel{\wedge}{=} next = served + |\{p \mid hasTicket(p)\}|$$
$$INV_6 \stackrel{\wedge}{=} \forall p.\, LINV(p)$$
$$INV_7 \stackrel{\wedge}{=} \forall p.\, hasTicket(p) \rightarrow p.lnext = served + preds(p)$$
$$INV_8 \stackrel{\wedge}{=} \forall p.\, served \leq p.lnext < next \rightarrow hasTicket(p)$$
$$INV_9 \stackrel{\wedge}{=} \forall p.\, noTicket(p) \rightarrow |\{p \mid hasTicket(p)\}| = 0$$

Fig. 2. Invariants of ticket lock algorithm

of predecessor processes of p, i.e., processes being served before p, and $LINV$ is some local invariant on the processes (which we elide due to lack of space).

With the help of these invariants we can prove all premises J1 to J4 within the interactive theorem prover KIV [6]. The proof effort was approximately two days to get an initial formalization of the algorithm and the proof obligations, and another two to three days to get all proofs done (including revisions of our initial formalization). See [11] for the mechanized proofs.

4   Local Proofs of Starvation Freedom

Our thread-local proof method is based on proving properties φ_p of the sequential program Seq_p of one individual thread p, which can be written in RGITL [21] (the rely-guarantee+temporal framework which we use) as $Seq_p \rightarrow \varphi_p$. Generic theorems guarantee that the proof technique is *compositional*, i.e., the local properties imply a global property φ of the whole system (under some predicate logic side conditions), i.e., $Par \rightarrow \varphi$. Our proofs always consist of two parts: first, a classical rely-guarantee (RG) assertion is proved (see next paragraph) that ensures that certain rely conditions hold for the environment steps of Seq_p. Building on the RG proof, we next develop local proof obligations for Seq_p which imply starvation freedom. We demonstrate the new technique on the ticket lock algorithm. Furthermore, we have verified two other, more difficult case studies, to demonstrate the generality of the method. Information on these case studies can be found at the end of the section.

Rely-Guarantee Proofs. We use a variant of rely-guarantee calculus [10] similar to the one in [5] as our basis, which establishes partial correctness assertions of Par by decomposing them into assertions about each Seq_p. For uniformity of the approach we assume that the whole system Par is alternating its steps with *global environment steps*, characterized by a predicate $rely(\underline{x}', \underline{x}'')$ over the program variables $\underline{x}$. Proof obligations are formulated from the local view of one process p. In this view, steps of Seq_p alternate with steps of a *local environment*. One local environment step collapses a finite sequence of steps of other processes alternated with global environment steps into one local environment step, and the rely predicate $rely_p(\underline{x}', \underline{x}'')$ describes its effect. Obviously, $rely_p$ therefore has to be reflexive and transitive (denoted *reflx* and *trans*).

A rely-guarantee assertion is a partial correctness assertions for a program P with program variables $\underline{x}$. It uses a precondition $pre(\underline{x})$ and a postcondition $post(\underline{x})$ for the initial and final state. Dually to the rely predicate $rely$, a guarantee predicate $guar(\underline{x}, \underline{x}')$ characterizes steps of the program P. For readability we drop the program variables $\underline{x}$ in the following, whenever they are clear from the context. For a predicate $pr(\underline{x})$, we also shorten $pr(\underline{x}')$ and $pr(\underline{x}'')$ to pr' and pr''. We write a rely-guarantee assertion[2] as

$$\langle R, I, G \rangle : \{pre\} \, P \, \{post\} \tag{2}$$

---

[2] The notation in KIV proofs is $pre \rightarrow [: \underline{x} \mid R, G, I, P]post$.

Since in applications a significant part of the rely as well as of the guarantee condition often is to preserve an invariant $I(\underline{x})$ (i.e. $guar := G \wedge (I \to I')$ and $rely := R \wedge (I' \to I''))$, we write $\langle R, I, G \rangle$ instead of $\langle rely, guar \rangle$ as in [5].

Intuitively, assertion (2) means the following: when program P is started in a state satisfying pre and all environment transitions up to some position j fulfill $rely$, then the next program step, if it exists, will satisfy $guar$. If the step does not exist (i.e., position j is the final one), then $post$ holds. The program can only invalidate its guarantee if the environment has invalidated the rely prior to this. Since our logic is able to distinguish program and environment steps, and has programs as formulas, (2) abbreviates

$$P \wedge pre \to \neg \left(rely \ \textbf{until} \ \neg (\textbf{if last then } post \ \textbf{else } guar) \right) \qquad (3)$$

and the rules we state for RG assertions can be derived from the more basic laws about LTL formulas. In particular, for a program Par (parallel composition of sequential programs) we can prove the following soundness theorem for RG reasoning in the interactive prover KIV. This theorem allows to compose local properties of components Seq_p into a global property of Par.

Theorem 1 (Rely-Guarantee Rule for Parallel Composition). *If a rely-guarantee condition*

$$\langle R_p, I_p, G_p \rangle : \{pre_p\} Seq_p \{post_p\}$$

together with the six side conditions

(RG1) $\forall q \in Pid. \ q \neq p \wedge guar_p \to rely_q$, *(RG2)* $trans(R_p)$, *(RG3)* $reflx(G_p)$,
(RG4) $stable(pre_p, R_p)$, *(RG5)* $stable(post_p, R_p)$, *(RG6)* $pre_p \to I_p$

holds for all $p \in PId$, then

$$\langle \bigwedge_{p \in PId} R_p, \bigwedge_{p \in PId} I_p, \bigvee_{p \in PId} G_p \rangle : \{\bigwedge_{p \in PId} pre_p\} \ Par \ \{\bigwedge_{p \in PId} post_p\}$$

is true for $Par = [Seq_1 \ || \ \dots \ || \ Seq_N]$.

Proof: See [21], Sect. 7. □

Side condition $stable(pre_p, R_p)$ (and similar for $post_p$) enforces, that any step satisfying the rely must preserve pre_p, i.e. $pre'_p \wedge R_p \to pre''_p$.

When Seq_p is defined as in (1) of Sect. 2, then using a predicate $idle_p$ that is valid in states where Seq_p does not run Op_p (in particular $idle_p$ will imply $\neg p.act$), the condition on the sequential processes can be simplified to

$$\langle R_p, I_p, G_p \rangle : \{idle_p\} Op_p \{idle_p\} \qquad (4)$$

(i.e., we omit the assignments to act) by setting $pre_p = post_p := idle_p$ and applying standard RG rules for sequential programs (see e.g. [5]). Thus, the rely-guarantee calculus requires to prove (4) and all six side conditions to establish that the whole system is partially correct. For our proof of starvation freedom it is important that a successful RG proof also establishes that all runs of Op_p in the context of Par satisfy

$$idle_p \land \Box(G_p \land R_p \land I_p \land I'_p \land (\text{last} \to idle_p))$$

States, where process p does not execute Op_p satisfy $idle_p$, all steps of p satisfy G_p, all environment steps satisfy R_p, and all states the process passes through satisfy the invariant I_p. We will make use of this knowledge in the next section when defining proof obligations for starvation freedom.

Local Proof Principle. The new local proof principle for starvation freedom we define here is based on the following observation: For a system not to be starvation free, there must be a process p that has started an operation but is not able to finish. Because of fair scheduling, this process is scheduled repeatedly, which implies that there is a non-terminating run of Op_p (which can assume $rely_p$ for its environment steps). Now an infinite run of an algorithm trivially implies that the algorithm must repeat one of its loops infinitely often[3]. Typically such critical loops are "spin" loops as in the example, where we cannot reason *locally* that the loop decreases some well-founded measure and must therefore terminate. Such a loop therefore *waits* for other processes to do suitable steps, that enable process p to leave the loop. The essence of a proof for starvation freedom is therefore, to show that p does not have to wait forever for some other process.

We therefore define a predicate $waitsFor(p, q)(\underline{x})$ such that $s \models waitsFor(p, q)$, if process p is waiting for process q in state s to provide some help before it can leave one of its critical loops. From this predicate, the *wait set* $W(p)$ of process p is defined as $W(p) = \{q \mid waitsFor(p, q)\}$.

For a starvation free algorithm a definition of waiting that matches the intuition above should have the following properties.

Definition 3. *A predicate waitsFor is admissible for an algorithm Op if it has the following properties for all processes $p \in PId$:*

(W1) No waiting for and by idle processes:
$idle_p \to \forall\, q \in PId. \; \neg\; waitsFor(p, q) \land \neg\; waitsFor(q, p)$

(W2) No waits-for cycles:
$waitsFor$ is acyclic

(W3) While already waiting no further increase of wait set by local process steps:
$W(p) \ne \varnothing \land G_p \land I_p \land I'_p \;\to\; W(p) \supseteq W'(p)$

(W4) Empty wait sets guarantee progress:
$idle_p \land \Box(R_p \land I_p \land I'_p) \land Op_p \land \Box\Diamond\, W(p) = \varnothing \;\to\; \Diamond\, \text{last}$

(W5) Transitivity of waits-for predicate:
$trans(waitsFor)$

(W6) No increase of wait sets by environment steps:
$R_p \land I'_p \land I''_p \;\to\; W'(p) \supseteq W''(p)$

---

[3] For simplicity, we assume the algorithm is not recursive. However, the argument of getting stuck in a recursion is not really different.

Property (W3) captures the fact that entering e.g. a critical loop should determine the wait set. While the process waits, its own steps should not add new processes q to it. Otherwise such a process q should have been included right at the start. The progress property (W4) is the only temporal property needed. It captures the intuition that not waiting is sufficient for termination of the currently running operation. If at any point in time the environment of p ensures that $W(p)$ is emptied again in finite time, then p will be able to leave any critical loop and the running operation will terminate ($\Diamond$ **last**).

Together, properties (W3) and (W6) imply that every time a process starts waiting by entering a critical loop, further steps will either keep its wait set unchanged, or remove elements from the set. The latter case is not enforced, so it still seems possible that the wait set could stay non-empty forever. However, we will prove that this is not the case: the conditions already enforce that the wait set becomes empty after finite time, such that any critical loop is left, and starvation freedom is implied. This proves soundness of our new local reasoning technique.

Theorem 2. *Let R_p, G_p be the rely and guarantee predicates and I_p the invariant of a successful rely-guarantee proof (as formalized in Theorem 1) with $pre_p := idle_p$ and $post_p := idle_p$, $p \in PId$. Then the following holds:*

If an admissible waitsFor predicate exists, then the system Par is starvation free, i.e.

$$Par \wedge idle \;\rightarrow\; \forall\, p \in PId. \; \Box(p.act \rightarrow \Diamond \neg p.act)$$

holds, where $idle = (\forall\, p \in PId. \; idle_p)$.

Proof: We prove the theorem indirectly. Assume there is a process p that is active, but does not go back to an idle state in some global run. Then by fairness this process is infinitely often scheduled, so we can find a local infinite run of Op_p, say $(s_0, s_0', \ldots)$. By condition (W4) the wait set in this run does not become repeatedly empty. It will be non-empty from some point in time n on. If W_m denotes the wait set of p in state s_m, then $W_m \neq \varnothing$ for all $m \geq n$. Conditions (W3) and (W6) imply that $W_n \supseteq W_{n+1} \supseteq W_{n+2} \supseteq \ldots$. Since none of the sets is empty, and the initial set W_n is finite, the sequence will eventually (at some time n_0) become a constant, non-empty set S, i.e., $W_m = S$ for all $m \geq n_0$. Process p has to wait for the processes in S indefinitely.

Since *waitsFor* is acyclic, and every W_m is finite and non-empty we can find for each $m \geq n_0$ one process $q_m \in W_m$ that does not have to wait in state s_m, i.e. $W(q_m) = \varnothing$. This process may be a different one for each state s_m (and is of course never p). However, since the sequence of states is infinite and the choice is among the finitely many processes in S there is at least one process q that is always in S and infinitely often has $W(q) = \varnothing$. We derive a contradiction for this process q.

Since the local states of the run of p are part of the states of the global run, the infinitely many states where q has an empty wait set also appear in the global run. They also appear in the local run of q since steps other than the steps of q satisfy $rely_q$ and therefore will leave the set empty by condition (W6). Since q repeatedly has an empty wait set, it must finish its currently running operation by condition (W4), and thereby enter a state s with $idle_q$. Since $idle_q$ is stable over $rely_q$, a state with $idle_q$ will also appear in the local run of p. However, this is a contradiction as q cannot be in the wait set of p when q is idle by condition (W1). $\qquad\square$

The proof relies on the fact, that the global runs of Par are interleavings of local runs of the processes, and that for a fair interleaving each global run can be decomposed into full runs of each process p (note, that for unfair scheduling the decomposition gives an execution, but not a run for any process that is no longer scheduled after some time).

We note that weakening the conditions (W3) and (W6) to the cardinality of $W(p)$ not increasing (thus getting closer to a rank function) is not possible. While the cardinality of the sets still gets stable, it is no longer guaranteed that there is a process q which is in *every* W_m for $m \geq n_0$. Instead two processes q_1 and q_2 could then flip back and forth between one being idle and the other forming $W(p)$, thus starving p, while neither q_1 nor q_2 starves itself.

We have formalized the proof in RGITL, where the set of runs (i.e. the semantics) of an interleaved program is directly defined as the interleaving of individual runs of the components. Unfortunately, space limits prevent us from detailing the mechanized proof documented on the Web [11] here. The proof strategy follows the one we have used for deriving Theorem 1 and the proof rule for lock-freedom (see Sect. 10 of [21]).

Application to the Ticket Lock. We define the *waitsFor* predicate as

$$waitsFor(p, q) := served \leq q.lnext < p.lnext$$

Process p waits for process q, if q is served before p. This predicate is trivially acyclic and transitive. Since processes q in idle state have $q.lnext < served$, condition (W1) is trivially satisfied. The proof thus reduces to the RG proof (4) together with its side conditions, and the main (temporal) admissibility condition of progress. We prove the RG conditions first, and to this end need to find rely, guarantee and invariant predicates.

For the ticket lock, I_p is a subset of the invariants used for the global version, namely $I_p = INV_0 \wedge INV_2 \wedge INV_3$. It simply states $served \leq next$ and that each ticket k with $served \leq k < next$ has a unique owner with $p.lnext = k$ (which implies mutual exclusion already). Note that since the thread local proof is directly conducted over the program, it does (and can) not mention a program counter like $hasTicket$ does in the global approach. The rely condition is

$$R_p := served' \leq served'' \wedge next' \leq next'' \wedge p.lnext' = p.lnext''$$
$$\wedge\ W''(p) \supseteq W'(p) \wedge (served' \leq p.lnext' \rightarrow served'' \leq p.lnext'')$$

The properties of the first line should be obvious. The second line trivializes condition (W6) and ensures that the other processes cannot do steps that skip process p from being served by moving $served$ from a value below $p.lnext$ to one

$$\frac{Pre_x^{x_0} \wedge I_x^{x_0} \wedge x_1 = t_x^{x_0} \to G(x_0, x_1) \wedge I_x^{x_1} \qquad \langle R, G, I \rangle \{ Pre_x^{x_0} \wedge x_1 = t_x^{x_0} \wedge R(x_1, x) \wedge I \}\ P\ \{Post\}}{\langle R, I, G \rangle \{ Pre \wedge I \}\ x := t;\ P\ \{Post\}}$$

$$\frac{Pre_x^{x_0} \wedge x_1 = t_x^{x_0} \wedge R(x_1, x) \wedge (\square R) \wedge (\square \lozenge W = \varnothing) \wedge P \to \lozenge \mathbf{last}}{Pre \wedge (\square R) \wedge (\square \lozenge W = \varnothing) \wedge x := t;\ P \to \lozenge \mathbf{last}}$$

Fig. 3. Symbolic execution rules for RG and (W4)

above it. The guarantee is defined as

$$
\begin{aligned}
G_p := (\ & next' = next \wedge p.lnext' = p.lnext \\
\vee\ & next' = next + 1 \wedge p.lnext' = next \wedge served = served') \\
\wedge\ & (served \neq served' \to p.lnext = served \wedge served' = served + 1) \\
\wedge\ & (served < p.lnext \to W(p) \supseteq W'(p)) \wedge (\forall\, q \neq p.\ q.lnext' = q.lnext)
\end{aligned}
$$

The first three lines give the obvious guarantees about acquiring and releasing a lock. Again, the third line makes proving (W3) trivial (and it adds the standard frame assumption for other processes). The predicate logic proof that $guar_p$ implies $rely_q$ is simple. It finally remains to do the local RG proof (i.e., $\langle R_p, I_p, G_p \rangle : \{idle_p\} Op_p \{idle_p\}$) with these instances and to prove the main condition (W4) of admissibility. Both proofs step through the algorithm using symbolic execution (that computes strongest postconditions for each statement, and uses invariants similar to Hoare-calculus). The rules for assignment used in both proofs are exemplarily shown in Fig. 3. Note that KIV does *not* directly implement these rules, instead they are derived from the general principle

$$(s_0, s_0', s_1, \ldots) \models \tau(x, x', x'') \wedge \circ \psi \quad \Leftrightarrow \quad (s_1, \ldots) \models \exists\, x_0, x_1. \tau(x_0, x_1, x) \wedge \psi$$

which removes the first step of a run, and is valid for predicate logic assertions τ for the first step, fresh variables x_0, x_1 and temporal ψ. Unwinding rules like

$$\varphi\ \mathbf{until}\ \psi \leftrightarrow \psi \vee (\neg\, \mathbf{last} \wedge \varphi \wedge \circ(\varphi\ \mathbf{until}\ \psi)) \qquad x := t;\ P \leftrightarrow x' = t \wedge \circ P$$

are used to bring formulas into this form. This works for all LTL formulas and programs (see [21] for a proof). For the (W4) goal both the assumption $\square \lozenge W(p) = \varnothing$ as well as the termination goal $\lozenge\, \mathbf{last}$ are preserved by program steps. The proof[4] of (W4) is slightly easier than the RG proof, since it does not have to prove the guarantee as a side goal (first premise of the RG rule of Fig. 3). It is however a bit longer, since each time a spin loop is reached, an induction over the number of steps is needed, until $W - \varnothing$ holds. The RG proof has 83

---

[4] Both proofs are done for a slight extension of the theory we do not discuss in this paper. This extension establishes linearizability (simply due to mutual exclusion) for an arbitrary operation in the critical section by using slightly enhanced versions of R_p, I_p and G_p.

steps and 43 interactions, the proof of (W4) has 163 steps and 61 interactions. The proof effort is mainly in finding suitable relies and guarantees. With these fixed, the proofs can be done in a day of work. For comparison, the mechanized proofs for deriving Theorem 2 are much more complex (ca. 1100 steps with 700 interactions for ca. 40 theorems and lemmata).

Other Algorithms Verified. To ensure that our approach is not specific to one example, we have verified two other more complex algorithms (see again [11] for the mechanized proofs). The first is the so-called MCS lock [16], which uses a pointer based queue, so the small-model theorem of [7] that allows to reduce a proof to model checking finite instances (that is applicable for the ticket lock) cannot be applied. The algorithm uses two spin loops: One for acquiring the lock, and one for releasing the lock. Therefore $W(p)$ is non-empty twice for two different reasons: First when waiting for the processes in queue which get the lock before p. This part is similar to the ticket lock. Second, when the lock is released. Then p must wait for the next process q that still has to set the tail pointer before p can transfer the lock to q.

The second algorithm is the Filter Lock of [19]. This algorithm uses an array of as many elements ("levels") as there are processes. Each level can store a process id (the so-called "victim" of this level). The victim p must wait (in a loop) on the level, until another process q overwrites the entry with q, thereby declaring itself as victim. The wait set of p for this example is therefore non-empty on each level while the process is a victim (and contains those process q it still checks for in the loop). The algorithm is interesting, since it shows that the method is not restricted to queue based algorithms, here every process can be overtaken by all others on each level once. It also shows a limitation of the approach presented here. We could only verify a slightly simplified version, which increases the level and sets itself as victim in a single atomic step, while the original algorithm uses two steps. The full version can be verified, but needs an extension of the proof method that is beyond the scope of this paper.

5   Conclusion

In this paper, we have presented a novel technique for proving starvation free-dom of processes in parameterized systems. The key difference between our and other techniques[5] is the ability to *locally* reason about a process (plus the full mechanization of starvation freedom proofs of specific algorithms as well as the proof of soundness of the new theory). This makes our proof technique more natural since we reason about the code of a single process just assuming some relies of other processes. Many thread-local progress arguments that would have to be encoded using a global rank function are given locally in this approach (e.g. termination of the loop of Filter Lock, that iterates over levels from 1..N). Furthermore, we think that the idea of a *waitsFor* relation naturally formal-izes a basic principle behind a large number of concurrent algorithms and their

---

[5] With the exception of [13] discussed in the introduction.

progress properties, and thus setting up a *waitsFor* relation for a concrete algorithm is relatively easy. The definition of ranking functions, on the other hand, involves giving a very precise upper bound on the distance to the target. As our two proofs for the ticket lock show, the local proof also needs less invariants on the algorithm.

So far, our new local technique still has one *temporal* proof obligation (condition (W4) of admissibility). This is the one point where the global technique improves over the local one. As future work, we want to study variations of the current approach. We aim to make the proof technique applicable to other forms of progress properties. Furthermore, we would like to identify the limitations of our approach more accurately.

References

1. Abadi, M., Lamport, L.: Conjoining specifications. ACM Trans. Program. Lang. Syst. **17**(3), 507–534 (1995)
2. Apt, K.R., de Boer, F.S., Olderog, E.-R.: Proving termination of parallel programs. In: Feijen, W.H.J., van Gasteren, A.J.M., Gries, D., Misra, J. (eds.) Beauty is Our Business - A Birthday Salute to Edsger W. Dijkstra. Springer, New York (1990)
3. Apt, K.R., Kozen, D.: Limits for automatic verification of finite-state concurrent systems. Inf. Process. Lett. **22**(6), 307–309 (1986)
4. Boström, P., Müller, P.: Modular verification of finite blocking in non-terminating programs. In: ECOOP, LIPIcs, vol. 37, pp. 639–663 (2015)
5. de Roever, W.-P., de Boer, F., Hannemann, U., Hooman, J., Lakhnech, Y., Poel, M., Zwiers, J.: Concurrency Verification: Introduction to Compositional and Noncompositional Methods. Cambridge Tracts in Theoretical Computer Science, vol. 54. Cambridge University Press, Cambridge (2001)
6. Ernst, G., Pfähler, J., Schellhorn, G., Haneberg, D., Reif, W.: KIV - overview and VerifyThis competition. Softw. Tools Technol. Transf. **17**, 1–18 (2014)
7. Fang, Y., Piterman, N., Pnueli, A., Zuck, L.D.: Liveness with invisible ranking. STTT **8**(3), 261–279 (2006)
8. Gotsman, A., Cook, B., Parkinson, M.J., Vafeiadis, V.: Proving that non-blocking algorithms don't block. In: POPL, pp. 16–28. ACM (2009)
9. Herlihy, M., Shavit, N.: On the nature of progress. In: Fernàndez Anta, A., Lipari, G., Roy, M. (eds.) OPODIS 2011. LNCS, vol. 7109, pp. 313–328. Springer, Heidelberg (2011)
10. Jones, C.B.: Specification and design of (parallel) programs. In: IFIP Congress, pp. 321–332 (1983)
11. Proofs of starvation freedom in KIV (2015). http://www.informatik.uni-augsburg.de/swt/projects/Starvation-Free.html
12. Lamport, L.: A new solution of Dijkstra's concurrent programming problem. Commun. ACM **17**(8), 453–455 (1974)
13. Liang, H., Feng, X.: A program logic for concurrent objects under fair scheduling. In: POPL (2016, to appear)
14. Manna, Z., Pnueli, A.: Temporal Verification of Reactive Systems - Safety. Springer, Berlin (1995)
15. Manna, Z., Pnueli, A.: Temporal Verification of Reactive Systems: Progress. Published online, Draft (1996)

16. Mellor-Crummey, J.M., Scott, M.L.: Algorithms for scalable synchronization on shared-memory multiprocessors. ACM Trans. Comput. Syst. **9**(1), 21–65 (1991)
17. Olderog, E.-R., Apt, K.R.: Fairness in parallel programs: the transformational approach. ACM Trans. Program. Lang. Syst. **10**(3), 420–455 (1988)
18. Owicki, S.S., Gries, D.: An axiomatic proof technique for parallel programs I. Acta Inf. **6**, 319–340 (1976)
19. Peterson, G.L.: Myths about the mutual exclusion problem. Inf. Process. Lett. **12**(3), 115–116 (1981)
20. Popeea, C., Rybalchenko, A.: Compositional termination proofs for multi-threaded programs. In: Flanagan, C., König, B. (eds.) TACAS 2012. LNCS, vol. 7214, pp. 237–251. Springer, Heidelberg (2012)
21. Schellhorn, G., Tofan, B., Ernst, G., Pfähler, J., Reif, W.: RGITL: a temporal logic framework for compositional reasoning about interleaved programs. Ann. Math. Artif. Intell. (AMAI) **71**, 131–174 (2014)
22. Tofan, B., Schellhorn, G., Reif, W.: A compositional proof method for linearizability applied to a wait-free multiset. In: Albert, E., Sekerinski, E. (eds.) IFM 2014. LNCS, vol. 8739, pp. 357–372. Springer, Heidelberg (2014)
23. Vafeiadis, V., Parkinson, M.: A marriage of rely/guarantee and separation logic. In: Caires, L., Vasconcelos, V.T. (eds.) CONCUR 2007. LNCS, vol. 4703, pp. 256–271. Springer, Heidelberg (2007)
24. Zuck, L.D., Pnueli, A.: Model checking and abstraction to the aid of parameterized systems (a survey). Comput. Lang. Syst. Struct. **30**(3–4), 139–169 (2004)

Reasoning About Inheritance and Unrestricted Reuse in Object-Oriented Concurrent Systems

Olaf Owe$^{(\boxtimes)}$

Department of Informatics, University of Oslo, Oslo, Norway
olaf@ifi.uio.no

Abstract. Code reuse is a fundamental aspect of object-oriented programs, and in particular, the mechanisms of inheritance and late binding provide great flexibility in code reuse, without semantical limitations other than type-correctness. However, modular reasoning about late binding and inheritance is challenging, and formal reasoning approaches place semantical restrictions on code reuse in order to preserve properties from superclasses. The overall aim of this paper is to develop a formal framework for modular reasoning about classes and inheritance, supporting unrestricted reuse of code, as well as of specifications. The main contribution is a Hoare-style logic supporting free reuse, worked out for a high-level concurrent object-oriented language. We also show results on verification reuse, based on a combination of Hoare-style logic and static checking. An example illustrates the difference to comparable reasoning formalisms.

1 Introduction

In the setting of object-oriented programs, it is desirable to support modular reasoning, allowing separate reasoning of each class and allowing open programs in the sense that the class hierarchy may be extended downwards. Code reuse is a fundamental property of object-orientation, and flexible reuse implies that a class should not put semantic restrictions on reuse in subclasses. However, modular reasoning with flexible code reuse, late binding, and inheritance is an unsolved challenge. Behavioral subtyping [15] is the most common reasoning approach, restricting subclasses to obey the super-class specifications.

Behavioral subtyping is based on the *substitution principle*, i.e., an object variable declared of class C may at run-time refer to an object of class C or a subclass of C. By exploiting the notion of interfaces, this may be replaced by the *interface substitution principle:* an object variable declared of interface F may at run-time refer to an object supporting F or a subinterface of F. This property can be guaranteed by type checking, but requires that all object variables are declared of an interface, and that interface specifications are respected by a subinterface [12,19]. Then reasoning about remote calls $o.m(..)$ can be done using the declared interface of o; however, it does not reduce the restrictions

---

This work was supported by the project *IoTSec* of the Norwegian Research Council.

E. Ábrahám and M. Huisman (Eds.): IFM 2016, LNCS 9681, pp. 210–225, 2016.
DOI: 10.1007/978-3-319-33693-0_14

on self calls (or local calls) imposed by behavioral subtyping. Lazy behavioral subtyping [10] relaxes this condition; only behavior that is needed to verify self calls in a superclass must be respected by a subclass redefining the method. This gives added flexibility, allowing a larger class of changes without violating reasoning modularity, but reasoning about free code reuse is still not possible without modifying superclass code or specifications.

Consider two classes A and B such that A is above B (i.e., B inherits A). It may happen that B is not a behavioral subclass of A. Then an object variable x declared of class A may at run-time point to a B object. This would be problematic wrt. reasoning, and unexpected behavior may occur. Such cases are non-trivial to detect [24] – and to solve: If all classes are code-wise as desired, one can either weaken the specification of A or split the class hierarchy, for instance redefining B without inheriting A. In the former case, reasoning made about other classes depending on A must be redone, possibly weakening the specifications of these classes. In the latter case, one is giving up on reuse. Each case has severe draw-backs. In the setting suggested in this paper we use separate hierarchies for reuse and for behavior [2,6]. Classes A and B must be seen through interfaces. Then the specifications of the classes A and B can be strong (give a strong characterization), and A may implement several interfaces, say I_i, while B may implement some of these. An object variable x of interface I_i can point to a B object if and only if B implements I_i, which is checked by static typing. Thus class reuse is possible even if B does not implement all behavior of A, and the behavior of B can be decided independently of A. Reasoning control is established by verifying each class and its implements clauses.

The contribution of this paper is the development of a reasoning framework allowing reasoning about free code reuse. More specifically, we present a Hoare-style logic for modular reasoning about inheritance, late binding, and free reuse of code and specifications. We build on the general approach of *behavioral interface subtyping* [18]. Each class is only required to satisfy its invariant and interface specifications, as well as any other local specifications given in, or inherited by, the class. This means that a method redefined in a subclass may break the requirements of the superclass, even the minimal requirements imposed in the case of lazy behavioral subtyping; and a subclass need not support the interface(s) of the base class. As opposed to lazy behavioral subtyping, no superclass requirements are imposed on a subclass. The consistency of a class is determined by looking at the class itself, its interfaces, and reused code from superclasses. The main idea of behavioral interface subtyping is that in order to reason about self calls we need to be aware of the class of this object. For each class C we reason about the requirements of that class under the assumption that the class of this is exactly C. Thus if at run-time the class of an executing object is C, we may rely on the reasoning about self calls done in the verification C, and for remote calls we rely on the interface substitution principle. This gives rise to sound reasoning, however, the soundness proof in [18] is presented at an abstract level, without considering a specific calculus presenting the details of self calls and late binding. We present here such a logic. In order to achieve reuse of verification results, we combine the logic and static checking.

Pr	$::=$	$[In^*\ Cl]^+$	program
In	$::=$	**interface** $F([T\ p]^*)$	
		$[\textbf{extends}\ [F(\bar{e})]^+]^?\{S^*\ I\}$	interface declaration
Cl	$::=$	**class** $C([T\ cp]^*)[\textbf{implements}\ [F(\bar{e})]^+]^?$	
		$[\textbf{inherits}\ [C(\bar{e})]^+]^?$	
		$\{[T\ w\ [:=e]^?]^*\ [s]^?\ M^*\ S^*\ I\}$	class definition
M	$::=$	$T\ m([T\ x]^*)\ B\ P$	method definition
S	$::=$	$T\ m([T\ x]^*)\ P$	method signature
B	$::=$	$\{[[T\ x\ [:=e]^?]^+;]^?\ [s;]^?\ \textbf{return}\ e\}$	method body
T	$::=$	$F\mid \text{Any}\mid \text{Void}\mid \text{Bool}\mid \text{String}\mid \text{Int}\mid \text{Nat}\mid \ldots$	types
v	$::=$	$x\mid w$	variables (local/field)
e	$::=$	$\text{null}\mid \text{void}\mid \text{this}\mid \text{caller}\mid v\mid cp\mid f(\bar{e})\mid (e)$	pure expressions
s	$::=$	$\textbf{skip}\mid v:=e\mid v:=\textbf{new}\ C(\bar{e})\mid s;s$	basic statements
		$\mid v:=e.m(\bar{e})\mid v:=C:m(\bar{e})$	remote/static call
		$\mid \textbf{await}\ v:=e.m(\bar{e})\mid \textbf{await}\ e$	releasing statements
		$\mid \textbf{if}\ e\ \textbf{then}\ s\ [\textbf{else}\ s]^?\ \textbf{fi}$	if statement
P	$::=$	$[\textbf{[}\ [A,]^?A\ \textbf{]}\ ]^*$	pre-/postcondition
I	$::=$	$[\textbf{inv}\ A]^?\ [\textbf{where}\ A^+]^?$	invariant specification

Fig. 1. Core language syntax. F denotes an interface name, C a class name, m a method name, p a formal interface parameter, cp a formal class parameter, w a field, x a method parameter or local variable. We let $[\ ]^*$, $[\ ]^+$ and $[\ ]^?$ denote repeated, repeated at least once, and optional parts, respectively; and $\bar{e}$ is a (possibly empty) expression list. Expressions e are side-effect free. Assertions A are Boolean expressions (possibly quantified) and may refer to the local history **h**. The specification $[\,A\,]$ abbreviates $[\,true,A\,]$.

We consider the setting of asynchronously communicating concurrent objects. In this setting, verification of systems of concurrent objects can be done compositionally. We build on results for inheritance-fee reasoning [8,9], avoiding here the complications of futures and recursion. The presented logic is oriented towards automatic verification in the sense that for given class and interface specifications, the generation of verification conditions can be mechanized.

2   A Core Language

For the purpose of this paper, we consider a strongly typed, high-level core language inspired by Creol [12]. The syntax is given in Fig. 1. Several tools including interpreters and compilers exist for versions of this language (http://tools.hats-project.eu/). A program consists of interfaces and classes. A class C may implement a number of interfaces. Class instances represent concurrent and active objects, while local data structure is defined by data types (syntax not given here). An interface may extend other (super)interfaces, adding declarations of methods, requirements, and invariants. A class may extend a (super)class while adding method definitions/redefinitions, requirements, and invariants.

For simplicity we assume read-only access to method and class parameters, as well as this for referring to the current object, and inside a method, caller for referring to the calling object.

When an interface **extends** another (super)interface, all declarations and specifications are inherited. When a class **inherits** another (super)class, all code and specifications are inherited unless redefined, i.e., a pre/post pair is inherited unless another is stated, and an invariant is inherited unless another is stated, and a method body is inherited unless the method is redefined. Likewise, the implementation clause of a superclass is inherited unless a new implementation clause is provided. Thus a subclass need not support all the interfaces supported by the superclass, nor respect the superclass invariant. Note that this is different from other specification/reasoning frameworks such as Eiffel, *Spec#* [3], JML [4], and Boogie [14].

The language obeys the interface substitution principle, guaranteed through type checking [12,19]. Object variables must be typed by interfaces (as opposed to classes). A remote call $v := o.m(\bar{e})$ is type correct if the interface of o supports a method m such that the types of the actual parameters $\bar{e}$ are subtypes of (or equal to) those of the formal parameters of m, and the result type of m is a subtype of v. The self call $v := \text{this}.m(\bar{e})$ is allowed when the class of this supports a method m. For simplicity we assume type correctness, and assume that a class does not offer multiple method declarations with the same name. (Otherwise, we could index the method name by the input and output types.) We assume late binding of methods called by dot-notation, i.e., for an object o of run-time class C the execution of a remote call $o.m(...)$ binds to the definition of m in C, if any, or else that of the closest superclass with a definition of m. Similarly, the self call $\text{this}.m(\bar{e})$ binds to the closest superclass B with a definition of m, starting with the the run-time class of this. This definition of m is denoted $B : m$. The notation $B : m$ may also be used in program code, resulting in static binding to a superclass B (or above). We distinguish between *exported methods*, those exported through an interface of the class, and *private methods*, those not exported through any interface of the class. Private methods must be called by the notations $\text{this}.m$ (dynamic) or $B : m$ (static).

Each object o has its own virtual processor and executes methods calls with o as callee, and has a process queue with method instantiations caused by incoming calls along with suspended method executions. An await statement puts the current method execution on the object's process queue, allowing an enabled process to continue. A *conditional await statement*, **await** c, is enabled when the condition c is enabled, and an *await call statement*, **await** $v := o.m(\bar{e})$, is enabled when the result of the remote call has arrived. In contrast, the current method must wait while a *blocking call*, $v := o.m(\bar{e})$, is executed, unless $o = \text{this}$, in which case the call is executed as a normal stack-based local call.

Specifications are given by means of invariants, pre/post specifications of methods, and implementation clauses. The class invariant must hold in all states exposed through an interface, i.e., it must hold at suspension points and end of public methods. Methods may be specified by pre/post specifications. This is needed for reasoning about self calls, in particular blocking self calls, when the class invariant may be temporary violated. Multiple pre/post specifications of a method are allowed, specifying complementary properties (see Sect. 3), and a class may implement multiple interfaces. A class not stating nor inheriting an **implements** clause, implements the empty interface Any, which is the super-interface of all interfaces (and with no requirements).

Inheritance. To describe inheritance more precisely, we look at which items are defined in a class and which items are inherited by a class, and from which super-class. Let B be the direct superclass of C. Inheritance of methods, specifications, and interfaces are explained by the semantic functions

- $bind(C, m) = C$, if C defines a body for m, otherwise $bind(B, m)$.
- $spec(C, m) = C$, if C has a pre/post specification of m, otherwise $spec(B, m)$.
- $inv(C) = C$, if C defines an invariant, otherwise $inv(B)$.
- $face(C) = C$, if C includes an implements clause, otherwise $face(B)$.

These functions are partial, being undefined if no superclass has the required item. Inheritance corresponds to point-wise updates of the semantic functions. For instance, $spec(B, m)$ may be overridden by $spec(C, m)$ even if $bind(B, m)$ is not, and $spec(C, m)$ may even violate $spec(B, m)$. In addition all fields are inherited (if names clash, we use the class name to qualify).

History-Based Specification. The local history h of a class/interface is the time sequence of communication events observed by this object, including

- method calls made by this object, denoted $this \rightarrow o.m(\bar{e})$
- method calls received by this object, denoted $o \rightarrow\!\!\!\!\rightarrow this.m(\bar{e})$
- method returns made by this object, denoted $o \leftarrow this.m(\bar{e}; e)$
- method returns received by this object, denoted $this \leftarrow o.m(\bar{e}; e)$, and
- creation events made by this object, denoted $this \rightarrow o.\textbf{new}\, C(\bar{e})$

where o represents the other part in the communication. Note that these events are not visible to o, when $o \neq this$. Thus the local histories of different objects are by definition disjoint. In the example of this paper histories will only be concerned about method completions, i.e., $\leftarrow$ and $\leftarrow\!\!\leftarrow$ events.

Sequence Notation. A sequence h is either *empty* or of the form $h; x$ where x is the last element. The notation h/s denotes the projection of h restricted to elements in the set s, $\#$ denotes sequence length, and x **before** x' **in** h denotes that x appears before x' in h, i.e., $\#(h'/\{x\}) \leq \#(h'/\{x'\})$ for any sequence prefix h' of h. For a local history h we let h/F denote the projection to the *alphabet* of F, given by events of the form $this \rightarrow o.\textbf{new}\, C(\bar{e})$, $this \rightarrow o.m(\bar{e})$, and $this \leftarrow o.m(\bar{e}; e)$, as well as events of the form $o \rightarrow\!\!\!\!\rightarrow this.m(\bar{e})$ and $o \leftarrow this.m(\bar{e}; e)$ for m offered by F. Similar notation applies to classes C, thus $\rightarrow\!\!\!\!\rightarrow this.m$ and $\leftarrow this.m$ events are restricted to methods defined or inherited in the class.

For a global history H we have that

$$(o \rightarrow o'.m(\bar{e}))\quad \textbf{before}\ (o \rightarrow\!\!\!\!\rightarrow o'.m(\bar{e}))\quad \textbf{in}\, H$$
$$(o \rightarrow o'.m(\bar{e}))\quad \textbf{before}\ (o \leftarrow o'.m(\bar{e}; e))\quad \textbf{in}\, H$$
$$(o \leftarrow o'.m(\bar{e}; e))\quad \textbf{before}\ (o \leftarrow o'.m(\bar{e}; e))\quad \textbf{in}\, H$$

which is formalized by the wellformedness predicate used in the compositional rule for global reasoning [26], which expresses that the global invariant is the conjunction of the wellformedness predicate and all object interface invariants. Since the alphabets of the objects are by definition disjoint, the wellformedness predicate is needed to connect the different object invariants.

The invariant of a class C may refer to fields, $\mathbf{h}$, and constants, including this. The invariant must be maintained by each non-private method of the class (possibly inherited), and a class must satisfy each implemented interface. A method specification may in addition refer to the formal parameters (including the caller) and the result (return). When seen from another class with a larger alphabet, a C invariant must hold on the original alphabet of C.

The invariant of an interface F may refer to the local history $\mathbf{h}$ (and the constant this) but not fields since these are not visible at the interface level. An invariant $I(\mathbf{h})$ of an interface F is understood as $I(\mathbf{h}/F)$ in a subinterface or class. Thus we define $I_F(\mathbf{h})$ as $I(\mathbf{h}/F)$, and similarly for classes. Abstract variables can be expressed by abstraction functions (say F) over the history, typically by inductive definitions with left hand sides of the form $F(empty)$ and $F(\mathbf{h}; e)$ for each kind of event e, as demonstrated in the example below.

A Small Example

Figure 2 defines a class BANK, a subclass BANKPLUS, and related interfaces, illustrating typical code reuse, adding complexity to a simple base class. The purpose of the (somewhat contrived) private method upd is to demonstrate the difference between non-lazy and lazy behavioral subtyping. The subclass does not respect the base class specification. Similar complications arise when adding transaction fees or interest calculations, while other extensions, such as adding a transaction history, would respect the base class specification. Code reuse is clearly useful both when base class specifications are respected and not.

Interface $Bank$ states that the balance (as returned by bal) is the sum of amounts deposited (by add) or withdrawn (by sub) from the bank account, ignoring unsuccessful add and sub calls, and that add calls always succeed. Interface $PerfectBank$ extends $Bank$ by stating that all sub calls succeed, while interface $BankPlus$ extends $Bank$ by stating that balance is always non-negative.

Interface and type names are capitalized while class names are in upper case letters. The specification of interface Bank illustrates history-based specification. The abstraction function sum calculates the balance from the local history. Note that only method return events are used in the specification. In the inductive definition of sum, **others** is used to match other cases, and underscore (_) is used to match any expression. The keyword **inv** identifies invariants and **where** identifies auxiliary function definitions. In assertions, **inv** refers to the current invariant, while $C:$ **inv** refers to the invariant of class C.

The class BANK uses a private method upd called by both add and sub. The upd method is specified by two complementary pre/post pairs, each specifying a property of the method. The invariant says that the value of the field bal is the sum calculated over the local history. The subclass BANKPLUS inherits the pre/post specifications of bal and add from BANK, but not the ones for upd and

216   O. Owe

```
interface Bank { Bool sub(Nat x)
 Bool add(Nat x) [return = true]
 Int bal() [return = sum(h)]
 where sum(empty) = 0, -- sum calculates the balance
  sum(h; (_←this.add(x;true))) = sum(h)+x,
  sum(h; (_←this.sub(x;true))) = sum(h)−x,
  sum(h;others) = sum(h) }

interface PerfectBank extends Bank { Bool sub(Nat x) [return = true]}

interface BankPlus extends Bank { inv sum(h)>=0 }

class BANK implements PerfectBank { Int bal:=0;
 Bool upd(Int x){bal:=bal+x; return true} [return = true]
                 [inv, bal=sum(h)+x and return = true]
 Bool add(Nat x){Bool ok; ok:=this.upd(x); return ok} [return = true]
 Bool sub(Nat x){Bool ok; ok:=this.upd(−x); return ok} [return = true]
 Int bal(){return bal} [return = bal]
 inv bal = sum(h) }

class BANKPLUS implements BankPlus inherits BANK{
 Bool upd(Int x){Bool ok:=(bal+x>=0);
  if ok then ok:=BANK:upd(x)fi; return ok}
           [inv, bal>=0 and bal = sum(h)+if return then x else 0]
           [bal' = bal, return = (bal'+x>= 0)]
 Bool sub(Nat x) [bal' = bal, return = (bal'>= x)] -- renewed specification
 inv BANK:inv and bal >=0 }

class CLIENT { Seq[String] paid; Bank acc; acc:= new BANK;
 Bool salary(Nat x){Bool ok; ok:=acc.add(x); return ok}
 Bool bill(String kid, Nat x, Bank y){ Bool ok:=false;
  if not kid in paid then await ok:=acc.sub(x);
   if ok then y.add(x); paid:=(paid;kid) fi fi; return ok }
 inv paid = p(h) -- p gives the sequence of successful bill payments
 where p(empty) = empty,
  p(h; (_←this.bill(k,x,y;true))) = (p(h); k),
  p(h; others) = p(h) }
```

Fig. 2. A bank example, violating behavioral and lazy behavioral subtyping.

sub, which are redefined and therefore not inherited. In fact the subclass violates the pre/post specifications for *upd* and *sub* in BANK. Likewise the **implements** clause is redefined and therefore not inherited. In this example, the subclass does not obey the requirements imposed by behavioral subtyping, since BANKPLUS violates the BANK interface *PerfectBank*, nor by lazy behavioral subtyping since BANKPLUS violates the BANK postcondition of *upd*, which is needed for the local *upd* calls in the verification of BANK.

For the sake of completeness a client class is included, showing also blocking and non-blocking calls. The CLIENT invariant expresses that paid corresponds to successful bill payments, calculated over the history by $p(\mathbf{h})$, defined inductively.

3   Hoare-Style Reasoning

The considered core language is chosen with respect to simplicity of semantics, avoiding the complexity of shared variables and low-level synchronization primitives. We consider partial correctness, expressed by Hoare triples of the form $[P] \, S \, [Q]$, meaning that the condition Q holds in any post-state of the statement s provided the condition P holds in the pre-state [11]. The language satisfies the classical Hoare axiom for assignment

$$\vdash [Q_e^x] \, x := e \, [Q]$$

since there are no side-effects of expressions, remote access to fields, nor shared variables (even though object variables give rise to aliasing). Here Q_e^x denotes Q with all (free) occurrences of x replaced by e. Rules for skip and if-statements are standard, and so is the rule for sequential composition (see Fig. 3), because there is no interference between objects since their local conditions are on disjoint variables. In particular the histories of two objects do not share events.

Late binding implies that a method call may behave differently depending on the class of the executing object. Also calls binding to the same body may behave differently since self calls in the body may depend on the class of the executing object. For instance in the *Bank* example a call to *sub* binds to BANK:*sub* (regardless of the class of the executing object), but the *upd* call in the body of BANK:*sub* binds to either BANK:*upd* or BANKPLUS:*upd* depending on the class of the executing object, BANK or BANKPLUS, respectively. For B above C, we use the notation $body_{C::B:m}$ to refer to the execution of the body of m in class B (or above) when this object is of class C. A late bound self call this.$m(..)$ binds to $body_{C::C:m}$, and the static call $B : m(..)$ binds to $body_{C::B:m}$, and both are executed as a stack-based local call. Given that class $bind(B, m)$ contains a method definition $m(\overline{x})\{s; \mathbf{return}\, e\}$, we define $body_{C::B:m}$ by

$$\mathbf{h} := (\mathbf{h}; \mathsf{caller} \rightarrow\!\!\!\!\rightarrow \mathsf{this}.m(\overline{x})); \, s; \mathsf{return} := e; \mathbf{h} := (\mathbf{h}; \mathsf{caller} \leftarrow \mathsf{this}.m(\overline{x}; \mathsf{return})) \quad (1)$$

which incorporates the appropriate effects on the local history. It follows that

$$body_{C::B:m} = body_{C::bind(B,m):m}$$

And we have $body_{C::B:m} = body_{B::B:m}$ if the execution of the former body does not lead to suspension nor self calls below B. Such equivalences can be detected (underestimated) by static checking following each execution path of the body of m, following static calls and remote calls where the callee might be this. Such equivalences can be exploited for verification reuse, as shown in the example.

Type checking ensures that binding succeeds, i.e., for all method calls in a type correct program each call binds to a body, apart from remote calls on object variables that are null. Note that calls to null may appear in the history, allowing specifications about the absence of such calls. We let $body_{C::C:init}$ denote the initialization code of C.

Verification of a Class. According to the idea of behavioral interface subtyping, each class C is verified separately under the assumption that the class of this object is exactly C. A major complication is that reasoning about reused code from a superclass is in general different than the reasoning made in the superclass. Hoare-style reasoning must be done relative to the class C of this object. We use the notation $\vdash_C [P] s [Q]$, where C represent the class of this object. And $\vdash_C Q$ means that the assertion Q can be proved in the context of the specification functions available in C. We write $\vdash [P] s [Q]$ rather than $\vdash_C [P] s [Q]$ when the class context of s is irrelevant for the reasoning.

The notation $\vdash_C B : m(\overline{x})[P, Q]$ abbreviates $\vdash_C [P] body_{C::B:m} [Q]$, and $\vdash_C m(\overline{x})[P, Q]$ abbreviates $\vdash_C C : m(\overline{x})[P, Q]$. This notation is convenient when considering class specifications given by pre/postconditions. For a condition Q we let the notation Q/F denote $Q^h_{h/F}$ where F is a class or interface.

Let I_C denote the given invariant of class C. In order to *verify a class* C the following verification conditions must be proved:

1. $\vdash_C I_C \Rightarrow (I_F/F)$, for each invariant I_F of an interface F of class $face(C)$
2. $\vdash_C init()[true, I_C]$ (i.e., the class initialization establishes I_C)
3. $\vdash_C m(\overline{x})[I_C, I_C]$, for each public method m of C (i.e., maintenance of I_C)
4. $\vdash_C m(\overline{x})[I_C \wedge (P/F), Q/F]$, if an interface F of $face(C)$ contains $m(\overline{x})[P, Q]$
5. $\vdash_C m(\overline{x})[P, Q]$, if C contains or inherits $m(\overline{x})[P, Q]$ ($bind(C, m)$ is defined).

Here 1 and 4 ensure that each interface of C is satisfied, 2 and 3 that the class invariant is satisfied, and 5 ensures any additional pre/post specifications of C, including inherited ones. Note that in 4 we assume the class invariant in the precondition of a public method, since calls from other objects are started in an invariant state. Only blocking self calls may start in non-invariant states.

Each class is verified separately in this way (considering inherited superclass code). Together with correct typing of object variables, this ensures that each object variable will satisfy its declared interfaces, and each object of (run-time) class C will satisfy the interfaces of C. This implies that the compositional rule for reasoning about concurrent object systems is sound, see [18]. Furthermore, the reasoning about inherited code ensures that each late bound self call made at run-time will satisfy the pre/post specifications given in C.

Reasoning Rules
Figure 3 presents all rules related to self calls and histories. For a class C we use $\vdash_C$ to express provability in the context of C as explained. For code in class C this corresponds to normal class-based reasoning. For code inherited by C, reasoning about suspension and self calls depends on C, as reflected in Rule static call, keeping the C context when moving to a superclass B. The importance of the context C is evident in the rule for **await** where it is essential that we use I_C, and in the

assign
$$\vdash [Q_e^x]\, x := e\, [Q]$$

await guard
$$\vdash_C [I_C \wedge L \wedge h' = \mathbf{h}]\ \mathbf{await}\ b\, [b \wedge I_C \wedge L \wedge h' \leq \mathbf{h}]$$

new
$$\vdash [\forall v'.\ \mathit{fresh}(v', \mathbf{h}) \Rightarrow Q_{v',\mathbf{h};(\mathrm{this}\to v'.\,\mathbf{new}\,C(\bar{e}))}^{v,\mathbf{h}}]\, v := \mathbf{new}\ C(\bar{e})\, [Q]$$

blocking call
$$\vdash [\forall v'.\ o \neq \mathrm{this} \wedge Q_{v',\mathbf{h};(\mathrm{this}\to o.m(\bar{e}));(\mathrm{this}\leftarrow o.m(\bar{e};v'))}^{v,\mathbf{h}}]\, v := o.m(\bar{e})\, [Q]$$

call on this
$$\frac{\vdash_C [P]\, v := C : m(\bar{e})\, [Q]}{\vdash_C [P]\, v := \mathrm{this}.m(\bar{e})\, [Q]}$$

self call
$$\frac{\vdash_C [P]\, v := \mathrm{this}.m(\bar{e})\, [Q]}{\vdash_C [o = \mathrm{this} \wedge P]\, v := o.m(\bar{e})\, [Q]}$$

static call
$$\frac{\vdash_C [P]\, body_{C::B:m}\, [Q_{\mathbf{h};(\mathrm{this}\leftarrow \mathrm{this}.m(\bar{e};v))}^{\mathbf{h}}]}{\vdash_C [P_{\bar{e},\mathrm{this},\mathbf{h};(\mathrm{this}\to \mathrm{this}.m(\bar{e}))}^{\bar{x},\mathrm{caller},\mathbf{h}} \wedge L]\, v := B : m(\bar{e})\, [Q_{\bar{e},\mathrm{this},v}^{\bar{x},\mathrm{caller},\mathrm{return}} \wedge L]}$$

entailment
$$\frac{\vdash_C [P_j]\, s\, [Q_j], \text{all } j \in J \qquad \vdash_C (\wedge_{j\in J}[[P_j, Q_j]]) \Rightarrow [[P, Q]]}{\vdash_C [P]\, s\, [Q]}$$

if
$$\frac{\vdash_C [P \wedge b]\, s\, [Q] \qquad \vdash_C [P \wedge \neg b]\, s'\, [Q]}{\vdash_C [P]\ \mathbf{if}\ b\ \mathbf{then}\ s\ \mathbf{else}\ s'\ \mathbf{fi}\ [Q]}$$

Fig. 3. Hoare style rules and axioms. Primed variables represent fresh logical variables, $\mathit{fresh}(v', \mathbf{h})$ expresses that v' does not occur in $\mathbf{h}$, L denotes a local assertion, i.e., without occurrences of fields, and $L_{C::B:m}$ denotes an assertion without fields (potentially) modified by body $body_{C::B:m}$ (statically checked). In rule static call we assume for simplicity that v does not occur in e.

call rules, where both C and B are used to get the relevant pre/postconditions. In general the pre/postconditions of a method m vary both with respect to the enclosing class B and the context class C.

Since we allow multiple pre/postconditions of a given method, we need the entailment rule in order to derive implications of multiple pre/postconditions, using the *relational meaning* of a pre/postcondition $[P, Q]$ given by

$$[[P, Q]] \triangleq \forall \bar{z}.\ P_{\overline{w}_{in}, \mathbf{h}_{in}}^{\overline{w},\mathbf{h}} \Rightarrow Q_{\overline{w}_{out}, \mathbf{h}_{out}}^{\overline{w},\mathbf{h}}$$

where $\bar{z}$ is the list of logical variables in $[P, Q]$, x_{in} denotes the pre-state ("*in*") value of a variable x, and x_{out} denotes the post-state ("*out*") value of x. (Constants including parameters, this, and return are not quantified nor substituted.) For instance, from the two pre/postconditions $[bal \geq x, \mathrm{return} = \mathit{true}]$ and $[bal < x, \mathrm{return} = \mathit{false}]$ we may derive $[bal' = bal, \mathrm{return} = bal' \geq x]$. And the standard consequence rule can be derived from the entailment rule.

The effects on $\mathbf{h}$ from the side of a caller are reflected in the call rules, whereas the effects on $\mathbf{h}$ from the side of the callee are reflected in the definition of *body*, see (1). Self calls give rise to both effects. Rule new is similar, with the additional requirement that the generated object is locally fresh. (Global uniqueness follows by including the parent object in the identity.) According to Rule call on this, the call $v := \text{this}.m(\overline{x})$ is equivalent to the static call $v := C : m(\overline{x})$ where C is the class of this object. The rules self call and blocking call treat blocking calls according to whether the callee equals this. For a call such that the premise of rule self call would not be type correct, we may conclude that $o \neq \text{this}$. This can be formalized by letting the type analysis rewrite a call $v := o.m(\overline{e})$ to $v := o..m(\overline{e})$ whenever the call $v := \text{this}.m(\overline{e})$ is not type correct, and adding the Hoare axiom

$$\vdash [\forall v' \cdot Q^{v,\,\mathbf{h}}_{v',\mathbf{h};(\text{this}\rightarrow o.m(\overline{e}));(\text{this}\leftarrow o.m(\overline{e};v'))}]\ v := o..m(\overline{e})\ [Q]$$

for such "external calls" (syntactically indicated by ".."), to improve reasoning. This static analysis of object disjointness may be strengthened, for instance by considering static parent-child connections or ownership.

Reasoning about a suspending call **await** $v := o.m(\overline{e})$ is equivalent to reasoning about the pseudo-code

$$\mathbf{h} := (\mathbf{h}; \text{this}\rightarrow o.m(\overline{e}));\ \mathbf{await}\ \mathit{true};\ v' := \text{some};\ \mathbf{h} := (\mathbf{h}; \text{this}\leftarrow o.m(\overline{e};v'));\ v := v'$$

where "some" represents a non-deterministic value, i.e., $[\forall x \cdot Q]\ x := \text{some}\ [Q]$. When o is this and m is non-public, one must add the premise $\vdash_C m(\overline{x})[I_C, I_C]$ in order to ensure that the self call preserves the invariant of C.

New properties of a method $B:m$ can be derived from old properties using the entailment rule or by analysis of $body_{C::B:m}$. Entailment is useful at the level of method specifications since it is natural to keep track of verified properties at this level. The proof of a pre/post specification of m in C will be based on the invariant of C, which may differ from that of B. Thus a pre/post specification of m in B cannot in general be guaranteed in a subclass C. The static call rule reflects this by referring to both B and C.

Since each class is analyzed separately, typically in the order defined, we obtain an open world and modular verification system. In the analysis of a class C we may need to consider superclasses of C, but not subclasses. We may reuse superclass verification results as follows: For code inherited from a superclass B, we may derive $\vdash_C B : m(\overline{x})[P,Q]$ from $\vdash_B B : m(\overline{x})[P,Q]$ when the body does not lead to suspension nor self calls of methods redefined below B. Otherwise, new pre/post conditions for a method body can be established by new analysis of the body. Thus $\vdash_C B : m(\overline{x})[P,Q]$ follows from $\vdash_B B : m(\overline{x})[P,Q]$ and $body_{C::B:m} = body_{B::B:m}$. The latter condition can be guaranteed by static analysis considering all possible self calls, which gives an integration of Hoare logic and static checking.

Verification of the Example

Let B denote bank and let I_B denote the invariant of B. From our definition of class verification we get the following verification conditions for class bank

1. $\vdash_B I_B \Rightarrow I_{PerfectBank}(\mathbf{h}/PerfectBank)$ (entailment of interface invariant)
2. $\vdash_B I_B \, {}^{\mathbf{h},bal}_{empty,0}$ (class initialization establishes I_B)
3. $\vdash_B bal(x)[I_B, I_B]$ (implementation of bal maintains I_B)
4. $\vdash_B add(x)[I_B, I_B]$ (implementation of add maintains I_B)
5. $\vdash_B sub(x)[I_B, I_B]$ (implementation of sub maintains I_B)
6. $\vdash_B bal(x)[I_B, \text{return} = sum(\mathbf{h}/Bank)]$ (pre/post spec. from $Bank$)
7. $\vdash_B bal(x)[true, \text{return} = bal]$ (pre/post spec. from B)
8. $\vdash_B add(x)[true, \text{return} = true]$ (pre/post spec. from B)
9. $\vdash_B sub(x)[true, \text{return} = true]$ (pre/post spec. from B)
10. $\vdash_B upd(x)[true, \text{return} = true]$ (pre/post spec. from B)
11. $\vdash_B upd(x)[I_B, bal = sum(\mathbf{h}) + x \wedge \text{return} = true]$ (pre/post spec. from B)

Here (1) is trivial since there is no *PerfectBank* invariant. Verification conditions (2–5) state that I_B is an invariant of B, and (6–11) ensure the stated pre/post specifications. Note that (8) ensures the pre/post specification for *add* from *Bank*, and (9) ensures the one for *sub* from *PerfectBank*. The verification of the conditions is straight forward as it does not involve any superclass code. For (6) the class invariant in the precondition is needed. History projections may be ignored in this example due to the others clause in the definition of *sum*. Note that the private method *upd* does not maintain the invariant.

According to the definition of class correctness, verification of class BANKPLUS amounts to the following conditions (letting BP denote BANKPLUS)

1. $\vdash_{BP} I_{BP} \Rightarrow sum(\mathbf{h}/BankPlus) \geq 0$ (implication of invariants)
2. $\vdash_{BP} I_{BP} \, {}^{\mathbf{h},bal}_{empty,0}$ (establishment of BP inv.)
3. $\vdash_{BP} B : bal(x)[I_{BP}, I_{BP}]$ (maintenance of BP inv.)
4. $\vdash_{BP} B : add(x)[I_{BP}, I_{BP}]$ (maintenance of BP inv.)
5. $\vdash_{BP} B : sub(x)[I_{BP}, I_{BP}]$ (maintenance of BP inv.)
6. $\vdash_{BP} B : bal(x)[I_{BP}, \text{return} = sum(\mathbf{h})]$ (pre/post given in $Bank$)
7. $\vdash_{BP} B : bal(x)[true, \text{return} = bal]$ (pre/post given in B)
8. $\vdash_{BP} B : add(x)[true, \text{return} = true]$ (pre/post given in B)
9. $\vdash_{BP} B : sub(x)[b' = bal, \text{return} = b' \geq x]$ (pre/post given in B)
10. $\vdash_{BP} upd(x)[b' = bal, \text{return} = b' + x \geq 0]$ (pre/post given in BP)
11. $\vdash_{BP} upd(x)[I_{BP}, bal \geq 0 \wedge bal = sum(\mathbf{h}) + \mathbf{if} \ \text{return} \ \mathbf{then} \ x \ \mathbf{else} \ 0]$ (BP)

Verification of these conditions can be summarized as follows: (1,2,3) are trivial, (4,5) follow from (11), (6) follows from (3,7) by entailment, (8,9) follow from (10), (7) follows from verification of BANK by observing that $body_{BP::B:bal}$ equals $body_{B::B:bal}$ since the body has no self calls nor suspension, and (10,11) are straight forward, using $body_{BP::B:upd} = body_{B::B:upd}$.

Again we notice that the private method *upd* does not maintain the invariant (and is not required to), that the invariant is needed in the proof of (6), and that significant reuse of proofs from the verification of BANK was possible (7–11).

4   Related Work

Class inheritance is a central feature of object orientation which allows subclasses to be designed by reusing and redefining the code of superclasses with a flexibility that goes beyond behavioral subtyping [4,25]. However, proof systems usually restrict code reuse to behavioral subtyping [2,15]. For example, a recent survey of challenges and results for the verification of sequential object-oriented programs [13] relies on behavioral subtyping when reasoning about late binding and inheritance. In contrast, proof systems studying late bound methods without relying on behavioral subtyping have been shown to be sound and complete by Pierik and de Boer [21], but assume a closed world (i.e., all classes must be known).

Specification inheritance is used to enforce behavioral subtyping in [7], where subtypes inherit specifications from their supertypes. Virtual methods [22] similarly allow incremental reasoning by committing to certain abstract properties about a method, which must hold for all its implementations. In particular, the verification platforms for *Spec#*[3] and JML [4] rely on versions of behavioral subtyping. Wehrheim [28] investigates behavioral subtyping for active, concurrent objects, classifying different notions of behavioral sybtyping.

The fragile base class problem emerges when seemingly harmless superclass updates lead to unexpected behavior of subclass instances [17]. Many variations of the problem relate to imprecise specifications and assumptions made in super- or subclasses. By supporting static method calls one can refer to and reuse original versions of methods, making method requirements and assumptions explicit, which reduces the fragile base class problem.

Recently incremental reasoning, both for single and multiple inheritance, has been considered in the context of *separation logic* [5,20]. These approaches distinguish "static" specifications, given for each method implementation, from "dynamic" specifications used to verify late-bound calls, somewhat similar to the approach of lazy behavioral subtyping [10], discussed earlier.

In order to obtain a more flexible specification language, it has been suggested to allow clauses like: this **is** $C \Rightarrow I$, which expresses that the clause only needs to hold when the current object is exactly a C object (and not a subclass object) [13]. This allows more complete invariant (or pre/post) specification of a particular class without imposing such clauses on subclasses, since this **is** C is false in a (proper) subclass of C. However, for reasoning about remote calls with behavioral subtyping, the restrictions of behavioral subtyping remain.

Problems related to object patters have been studied recently. Designs with collaborating objects pose problems with respect to modular reasoning about common (non-local) invariants. [16,27] discuss reasoning when such invariants may be temporarily broken. [27] controls reasoning about invariants that are broken at certain points in the program. [16] provides specific constructs controlling the invariants. A notion of global invariants for collaborating objects is suggested in [23] considering sequential OO programs and patterns. For instance in the observer/subject pattern, the invariant for the pattern is placed in the observer class and its verification involves both classes. In our system, the invariant would partly be in the subject class (say expressing that all subscribers have been notified about the current "value") and partly in the observer class (expressing that the local copy of the "value" has been updated according to the notifications). Interfaces are not used, but the paper mentions reverification of inherited code as a way to achieve better flexibility in inheritance. Another typical example of non-local invariants is the handling of doubly-linked lists. In our setting doubly-linked lists can be treated by ensuring that when a "previous" pointer is set, the "next" pointer of the previous object is correct. This can be expressed as a local property by means of an invariant saying that the *setnext* call has ended before the matching *setprevious* call has ended.

When reasoning with class invariants, the framework should determine in which states the invariant should hold (so-called *invariant states*). Clearly the set of invariant states should be as small as possible without compromising soundness, since this allows stronger invariants. Callbacks should only appear in invariant states. Then any external call may assume the invariant. In our approach the class invariant I_C must hold in any state where suspension occurs or where an externally called method is completed. This allows us to assume the invariant after suspension. Therefore public methods must maintain the class invariant. Blocking self calls to private or public methods need not be done in invariant states; however, such calls may lead to suspension, in which case one would need to prove $\vdash_C [P] s [I_C]$ where s is the path to the suspension point and P is the condition at the point of the self call. And if the suspension is a suspending call to a private method, one needs to verify that the method maintains the invariant. The current analysis is able to detect this, as well as the relevant class context, due to the $\vdash_C$ notation. Thus in our system, class verification guarantees that callbacks happen in invariant states. And there is no need for pack/unpack operation to control class invariants [14].

5   Conclusions

We have presented a verification logic for modular reasoning of concurrent object-oriented programs supporting free reuse of code and specifications. In contrast to earlier approaches, the reasoning of a class does not impose restrictions on subclasses. Object variables are typed by interfaces and remote field access is not supported. Each class C is verified separately, and reused super-class code is re-analyzed under the assumption that this object is of class C. We use history-based specifications, which allow compositional reasoning. The main complication of our logic concerns reasoning about self calls and reused superclass code, something which was not worked out in [18]. Our solution uses a notion of proof context and a notation for static method binding. Our framework considers all main aspects of object-orientation, and represents a general solution that may be used for other object-oriented languages with late binding and inheritance, including sequential languages, but assumes typing with interfaces and no remote field access.

The mechanism of static calls proved helpful for reuse of pre/postconditions for superclass methods. It is also helpful in controlling the fragile base class problem [17]. The considered language involves some additional challenges caused by concurrency with suspension mechanisms and non-blocking calls. Nonetheless, our reasoning system gives rise to quite simple Hoare-style reasoning, similar to reasoning about sequential programs, with the addition of sequential effects on the local history. Our notion of inheritance is flexible with respect to reuse of both code and specifications (more flexible than [18]). The distinction of public and private methods was essential in practice, as demonstrated in the example.

Apart from the (non-trivial) formulation of specifications, our system gives rise to automatic generation of verification conditions, where left-constructive Hoare analysis gives a verification condition at each suspension point and method start. For verification of a method pre/post pair one may first check if it follows from earlier results by the entailment rule, and if not, analyze the body. In future work, we would like to build an automated verification system based on our approach, for instance using the KeY system, which already has support for a version of our language without inheritance [1].

The integration aspect of this work lies in the combination of a Hoare logic and an equivalence over inherited and non-inherited code, which allows reuse of verification results in subclasses. The example illustrates the value of verification reuse, showing that all cases of reuse of a method together with its specification, resulted in verification reuse. The equivalence of code (i.e., of method bodies) is detected by static analysis and exploited in verification. In addition, the static detection of $o \neq$ this gives simplification at the reasoning level.

In the reasoning system we have not considered loops and recursion, which can be handled as usual. Extension to multiple inheritance is possible (for instance solving the diamond problem as in [10]). A discussion of soundness is beyond the scope of this paper. A main part of the soundness proof would be to establish that the class context reflects the run-time class of the executing object. Soundness for the language without inheritance can be done as in [9].

Acknowledgment. The anonymous referees have provided valuable feedback.

References

1. Ahrendt, W., Dylla, M.: A system for compositional verification of asynchronous objects. Sci. Comput. Program. **77**(12), 1289–1309 (2012)
2. America, P.: A behavioural approach to subtyping in object-oriented programming languages. 443, Phillips Research Laboratories, January/April (1989)
3. Barnett, M., Leino, K.R.M., Schulte, W.: The Spec# programming system: an overview. In: Barthe, G., Burdy, L., Huisman, M., Lanet, J.-L., Muntean, T. (eds.) CASSIS 2004. LNCS, vol. 3362, pp. 49–69. Springer, Heidelberg (2005)
4. Burdy, L., Cheon, Y., Cok, D.R., Ernst, M., Kiniry, J., Leavens, G.T., Leino, K.R.M., Poll, E.: An overview of JML tools and applications. In: FMICS 2003, Electron. Notes Theor. Comput. Sci. **80**, 73–89 (2003). Elsevier
5. Chin, W.-N., David, H., Nguyen, H.-H., Qin, S.: Enhancing modular OO verification with separation logic. In: POPL 2008, pp. 87–99. ACM (2008)
6. Dahl, O.-J.: Verifiable Programming, vol. Prentice Hall. International Series in Computer Science, New York (1992)

7. Dhara, K.K., Leavens, G.T.: Forcing behavioural subtyping through specification inheritance. In: 18th International Conference on Software Engineering, pp. 258–267. IEEE (1996)
8. Din, C.C., Owe, O.: Compositional reasoning about active objects with shared futures. Formal Aspects Comput. **27**, 1–22 (2014)
9. Din, C.C., Owe, O.: A sound and complete reasoning system for asynchronous communication with shared futures. JLAP **83**(5–6), 360–383 (2014)
10. Dovland, J., Johnsen, E.B., Owe, O., Steffen, M.: Lazy behavioral subtyping. J. Logic Algebraic Program. **79**(7), 578–607 (2010)
11. Hoare, C.A.R.: An axiomatic basis of computer programming. Commun. ACM **12**, 576–580 (1969)
12. Johnsen, E.B., Owe, O., Creol, I.C.Y.: A type-safe object-oriented model for distributed concurrent systems. Theor. Comp. Sci. **365**(1–2), 23–66 (2006)
13. Leavens, G.T., Naumann, D.A.: Behavioral subtyping, specification inheritance, and modular reasoning. ACM Trans. Program. Lang. Syst. **37**(4), 13 (2015)
14. Leino, K.R.M., Wallenburg, A.: Class-local Object Invariants. In: 1st India Software Engineering Conference (ISEC 2008), pp. 57–66. ACM (2008)
15. Liskov, B.H., Wing, J.M.: A behavioral notion of subtyping. ACM Trans. Program. Lang. Syst. **6**(16), 1811–1841 (1994)
16. Middelkoop, R., Huizing, C., Kuiper, R., Luit, E.J.: Invariants for non-hierarchical object structures. Electron. Notes Theor. Comput. Sci. **195**, 211–229 (2008)
17. Mikhajlov, L., Sekerinski, E.: A study of the fragile base class problem. In: Jul, E. (ed.) ECOOP '98 – Object-Oriented Programming. LNCS, vol. 1445, pp. 355–382. Springer, Heidelberg (1998)
18. Owe, O.: Verifiable programming of object-oriented and distributed systems. In: From Action System to Distributed Systems, pp. 61–80. Taylor & Francis (2016)
19. Owe, O., Ryl, I.: On combining object orientation, openness and reliability. In: Norwegian Informatics Conference (NIK 1999), Tapir (1999)
20. Parkinson, M.J., Biermann, G.M.: Separation logic, abstraction, and inheritance. In: POPL 2008, ACM (2008)
21. Pierik, C., de Boer, F.S.: A proof outline logic for object-oriented programming. Theor. Comput. Sci. **343**(3), 413–442 (2005)
22. Poetzsch-Heffter, A., Müller, P.O.: A programming logic for sequential Java. In: Swierstra, S.D. (ed.) ESOP 1999. LNCS, vol. 1576, pp. 162–176. Springer, Heidelberg (1999)
23. Polikarpova, N., Tschannen, J., Furia, C.A., Meyer, B.: Flexible invariants through semantic collaboration. CoRR, abs/1311.6329 (2013)
24. Pradel, M., Gross, T.R.: Automatic testing of sequential and concurrent substitutability. In: International Conference on Software Engineering (ICSE) (2013)
25. Soundarajan, N., Fridella, S.: Inheritance: From code reuse to reasoning reuse. In: Fifth International Conference on Software Reuse (ICSR5), pp. 206–215. IEEE (1998)
26. Soundararajan, N.: A proof technique for parallel programs. Theor. Comput. Sci. **31**(1–2), 13–29 (1984)
27. Summers, A.J., Drossopoulou, S.: Considerate reasoning and the composite design pattern. In: Barthe, G., Hermenegildo, M. (eds.) VMCAI 2010. LNCS, vol. 5944, pp. 328–344. Springer, Heidelberg (2010)
28. Wehrheim, H.: Behavioral subtyping relations for active objects. Formal Methods Syst. Des. **23**(2), 143–170 (2003)

A Formal Model of the Safety-Critical Java Level 2 Paradigm

Matt Luckcuck$^{(\boxtimes)}$, Ana Cavalcanti, and Andy Wellings

Department of Computer Science, University of York, York YO10 5GH, UK
ml881@york.ac.uk

Abstract. Safety-Critical Java (SCJ) introduces a new programming paradigm for applications that must be certified. The SCJ specification (JSR 302) is an Open Group Standard, but it does not include verification techniques. Previous work has addressed verification for SCJ Level 1 programs. We support the much more complex SCJ Level 2 programs, which allows the programming of highly concurrent multi-processor applications with Java threads, and wait and notify mechanisms. We present a formal model of SCJ Level 2 that captures the state and behaviour of both SCJ programs and the SCJ API. This is the first formal semantics of the SCJ Level 2 paradigm and is an essential ingredient in the development of refinement-based reasoning techniques for SCJ Level 2 programs. We show how our models can be used to prove properties of the SCJ API and applications.

1 Introduction

Safety-Critical Java (SCJ) [20] is a version of Java that embeds a new programming paradigm for applications that must be certified for example, using the highest level of the avionics standard ED-12/DO-178 [4]. To aid certification, SCJ is organised into three compliance levels. Level 0 applications are simple single-processor programs executed by a cyclic executive. Level 1 applications introduce concurrency and less-restricted release patterns. By contrast, Level 2 applications are highly concurrent, potentially multi-processor, and make use of suspension and a variety of release patterns.

The verification of SCJ programs requires specific techniques, but these are not covered by the SCJ specification. Verification has been addressed for Level 1, but not Level 2. SCJ, and its Level 2 profile in particular, present several challenges for verification. The new programming paradigm of SCJ restricts the program structure and provides a predictable memory model. The unique features of Level 2 allow programming applications that may contain multiple modes of operation or independently developed subsystems, and computations that require non-standard release patterns or suspension [23].

In this paper, we provide support for verification of SCJ Level 2 programs by modelling its programming paradigm using the state-rich process algebra *Circus* [24]. This is a combination of Z [18] for modelling state, CSP [8] for modelling behaviour, and Morgan's refinement calculus [14]. A *Circus* program is

© Springer International Publishing Switzerland 2016
E. Ábrahám and M. Huisman (Eds.): IFM 2016, LNCS 9681, pp. 226–241, 2016.
DOI: 10.1007/978-3-319-33693-0_15

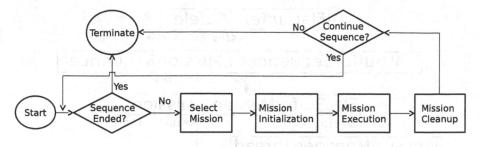

Fig. 1. Mission phases

organised around processes, which contain variables and actions, to describe a data model and reactive behaviours. Each process has a main action that defines its behaviour, possibly using a combination of other actions in the process. Communication between processes is achieved via channels. In our work we use the *Circus* extensions *OhCircus* [2], which introduces object orientation and inheritance, and *Circus* Time [16] to specify timers and deadlines.

Circus has already been used to model SCJ Level 1 [25]. *Circus* has also been used to produce a refinement strategy [3] to derive SCJ programs that are correct by construction. Our models provide the the possibility of extending the refinement strategy to target SCJ Level 2 programs.

What we present in this paper is the first formalisation of SCJ Level 2. The SCJ API covers approximatively 112 pages of the specification [20] as a collection of approximately 36 classes and interfaces. Our work characterises a semantics for SCJ Level 2 programs. To support its use, we have developed a tool that generates *Circus* models from SCJ programs. We have used the models to prove, via model checking, properties of both the SCJ API and of specific programs.

In Sect. 2 we describe the unique features of the SCJ Level 2 paradigm. Section 3 describes our modelling approach, model structure, and how we model Java synchronisation and suspension behaviour. Section 4 describes the direct applications of our models for verification, including a brief account of our tool. Section 5 presents related work. Finally, Sect. 6 concludes this paper with a summary of our contribution and a discussion of future work.

2   Safety-Critical Java Level 2 Paradigm

Safety-Critical Java (SCJ) is a version of Java that adopts a new programming paradigm. SCJ programs have a specific concurrent design and use region-based memory management (instead of garbage collection); specialised virtual machines [15,17] are available to execute SCJ programs. SCJ also uses the real-time constructs introduced in the Real-Time Specification for Java [21], but enforces a more structured programming paradigm.

An SCJ program is controlled by a *safelet* object, which manages the top-level *mission sequencer*. This is used to activate an application-defined sequence

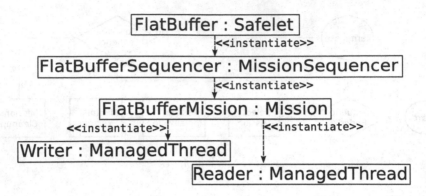

Fig. 2. Object diagram of the Flatbuffer

of *missions*. A mission encapsulates a particular function or phase of operation as a set of *schedulable objects* to perform a particular task. An SCJ API supports the programming of these components.

Each mission progresses through an initialisation, execution, and cleanup phase, as shown in Fig. 1. During initialisation, a mission's schedulable objects are created and registered. These schedulables are activated simultaneously at the start of the execution phase. A mission's schedulables execute until one of them requests termination, or they all terminate, when a cleanup phase is performed. At the end of the cleanup phase, the mission may indicate that no further missions should execute, in which case the sequence will terminate. If not, and there are more missions to run, the next mission is prepared.

At Level 2, schedulable objects may adopt one of four release patterns. Periodic event handlers execute once in a given time period, aperiodic event handlers execute when triggered by a method call, one-shot event handlers execute once after a time offset, and managed threads simply run to completion. Level 2 supports the execution of concurrent missions by allowing missions to manage schedulable mission sequencers. Level 2 can also use Java suspension methods, wait() and notify(), but they may only be called on this.

To illustrate some of the features of SCJ Level 2 programs we introduce FlatBuffer, which is a simple solution to the Producer-Consumer Problem, using a one-place buffer. FlatBuffer is structurally simple, only containing one mission and two schedulables, but uses two of Level 2's unique features: managed threads and suspension. Larger examples of applications that use the unique features of Level 2 can be found in [23].

Figure 2 shows an object diagram of the FlatBuffer program at the end of its mission's initialise phase. It is controlled by the safelet FlatBuffer, which starts the top-level mission sequencer FlatBufferMissionSequencer. This mission sequencer starts the mission, FlatBufferMission, which starts the two managed threads. The Writer is the producer and the Reader is the consumer.

The FlatBufferMission holds the buffer and controls access to it. The mission has a bufferEmpty() method to indicate if the buffer if empty or full, a

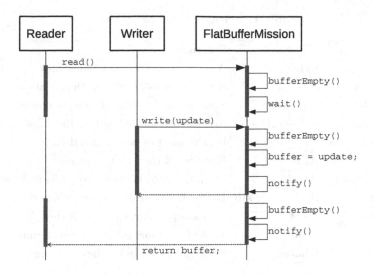

Fig. 3. Sequence diagram of an example execution of FlatBuffer

read() method to control reading from and resetting the buffer, and a write() method to control updating the buffer. The read() and write() methods both use synchronisation to control access to the buffer.

In an example execution of FlatBuffer, illustrated in Fig. 3, the Reader runs first, and calls the mission's read() method. The method calls bufferEmpty() on the mission, which returns a boolean indicating that the buffer is empty. Because there is nothing to read, the method calls wait() to suspend the Reader.

Next, the Writer runs, calling the mission's write() method. This method calls bufferEmpty() on the mission, which still indicates that the buffer is empty, prompting the Writer to update the buffer. Then, the method calls notify() on the mission – which resumes the Reader. When the Reader resumes, it is still inside the read() method. The method calls bufferEmpty(), which indicates that the buffer is full, so the value is read and the buffer is reset. Since this is a simple test program, the Writer terminates the mission after 5 writes.

Despite SCJ's restricted infrastructure, the unique features of Level 2 mean that its programs can become very complex. Providing the first semantics for this paradigm and devising a model for Level 2 programs is, therefore, a challenging task. We need to deal with a variety of schedulable objects, a preemptive scheduler that guarantees absence of priority inversion, a complex protocol for termination of missions, and suspension in the context of all of these features. We discuss our approach to modelling SCJ Level 2 in the next section.

3 Modelling Approach

We view the programming paradigm of SCJ separately from its realisation in Java. We capture this paradigm, abstracting away from most of the details of its Java implementation. Our modelling approach is agnostic of Java.

Table 1. Summary of *Circus* operators

Action	Syntax	Description
Skip	**Skip**	A simple operator that terminates
Simple prefix	$c \longrightarrow A$	Simple synchronisation with no data
Input prefix	$c?x \longrightarrow A$	Synchronisation with a value bound to x
Output prefix	$c!x \longrightarrow A$	Synchronisation outputting the value of x
Parameter prefix	$c.x \longrightarrow A$	Synchronisation with some data x
Sequence	$A;\ B$	Executes A then B in sequence
External choice	$A \square B$	Offers a choice between two actions A and B
Interrupt	$A \triangle c \longrightarrow$ **Skip**	Executes A unless c occurs, which terminates A
Recursion	$\mu X \bullet A;\ X$	A process X that executes A then X
Wait	**wait** t	Waits for t time units and then terminates
Chaos	**Chaos**	The action that immediately diverges

We model the state and behaviour of application objects in the program and the use of suspension. We also capture exceptions, but not the Java exception handling mechanism. We only capture exceptions where they indicate a misuse of the paradigm. Specifically we capture exceptions when: a thread is interrupted, a thread attempts to use suspension without holding the lock, a thread attempts to lock an object with a priority lower than the thread's, a method receives an inappropriate argument, or a mission attempts to register a schedulable that is already registered to another or the same mission.

Our models consist of two parallel components, following the approach in [25]. The framework component captures the behaviour of the library supporting the SCJ API and is reused for all programs. The application component captures the specific behaviour of a particular program. Each framework process has a counterpart application process. The complete specification of the framework model [12] comprises approximately 3700 lines of *Circus* over 11 processes.

Table 1 summarises the *Circus* action operators that we use in this paper. Most of them are familiar to users of CSP. We describe them to support the discussion of our model; a comprehensive account of *Circus* is in [24]. We note that *Circus* processes can also be combined using most CSP operators.

We describe our models in Sect. 3.1 and present our approach in more detail in Sect. 3.2 using the mission models as an example. Finally, in Sect. 3.3, we discuss how we model synchronisation and suspension.

3.1   Model Overview

Each SCJ library class and application object is represented by a *Circus* process. Each process retains the name of the class it models, suffixed with '*FW*' for framework processes or '*App*' for application processes. Methods are represented

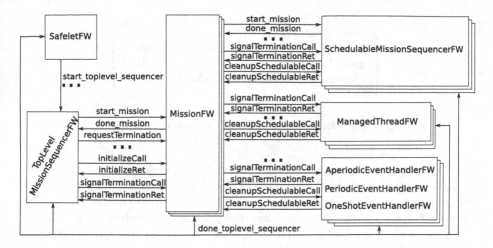

Fig. 4. Level 2 model structure

by an action in the relevant process. Method calls and returns are represented by (usually pairs of) events; this allows method calls between processes.

Figure 4 shows the framework processes in our model and the channels that they use to communicate. The channels with underscores in their names are control signals (for example, *start_mission*) and those in camel case represent method calls (for example, *initializeCall* and *initializeRet*). Some of the channels have been omitted for brevity, indicated by three dots. The layering indicates potentially multiple instances in one model. Each of these framework processes communicate with an application process; these are not shown in Fig. 4.

When a framework process encounters application-specific behaviour, it signals its application counterpart to take control and perform the behaviour. Control is returned to the framework with another signal. These signals are call-return event pairs that retain the method name, suffixed with '*Call*', for the event modelling the method call, or '*Ret*', for the event modelling its return.

Each application process is assigned a unique identifier, allowing framework processes to communicate with their application counterparts. An exception is the *SafeletFW* process, which only has one instance because there is only one safelet in an SCJ program. If a program class has multiple instances in the program, then each instance has its own *Circus* process identifier.

Our model uses *OhCircus* classes to capture non-reactive behaviour, such as methods that are purely data operations. *OhCircus* classes are similar to Java classes: they may hold variables, specify constructors, make use of inheritance, and must be instantiated before use. Specifically, data operations are captured in methods, which may be called from processes. In contrast to *Circus* processes, *OhCircus* classes can be related by inheritance.

Instead of simply adding Level 2 features to the Level 1 model [25], we also capture Level 1 features not found in the previous model. Namely, we consider that a period or deadline may be overrun and capture exceptions and synchronisation.

$$InitializePhase \ \widehat{=}$$
$$\left(\begin{array}{l} initializeCall \ . \ FlatBufferMissionMID \longrightarrow \\ register \ ! \ ReaderSID \ ! \ FlatBufferMissionMID \longrightarrow \\ register \ ! \ WriterSID \ ! \ FlatBufferMissionMID \longrightarrow \\ initializeRet \ . \ FlatBufferMissionMID \longrightarrow \\ \textbf{Skip} \end{array} \right)$$

Fig. 5. The *FlatBufferMissionApp*'s *InitializePhase* action

While Level 1 programs may not use suspension, they are allowed to use synchronisation. In addition, in contrast to the Level 1 model, we provide separate framework processes for each of the three kinds of event handlers, each encapsulating their particular release pattern. This simplifies the application models considerably and lessens the burden on translation. Further, as already mentioned, our model raises an exception if a schedulable is registered twice.

Safelet. The framework process *SafeletFW* handles the operations of the safelet. *SafeletFW* gets the identifier of the top-level mission sequencer from its application counterpart and starts it. Additionally it raises an exception if the program attempts to register a schedulable that is already registered. This is the process that defines the main execution flow of the program.

Mission Sequencers. Two framework processes model mission sequencers. The *TopLevelMissionSequencerFW* process models the top-level mission sequencer and the *SchedulableMissionSequencerFW* models a mission sequencer used as a schedulable. This simplifies both processes because they each only have to be involved in events relevant to their context.

Both flavours of mission sequencer fetch the identifier of the next mission from their application counterpart and start that mission. However, *SafeletFW* starts *TopLevelMissionSequencerFW*, which signals to the entire model when it is terminating, to indicate that the program is done.

SchedulableMissionSequencerFW is started by a mission and signals to that mission once terminated. Since it is a schedulable, it must respond to termination requests from either its controlling mission or the mission it is executing.

Mission. The *MissionFW* process is started by a mission sequencer process. It then allows its application counterpart to register schedulables. It starts each schedulable and deals with their termination and cleanup. If requested, it terminates itself and its active schedulables, and signals to its controlling mission sequencer that it has done. In Sect. 3.2 we describe the *MissionFW* process in more detail and present the model of one of its actions.

Schedulables. Schedulables are modelled by *PeriodicEventHandlerFW*, for periodic event handlers; *AperiodicEventHandlerFW*, for aperiodic event handlers;

OneShotEventHandlerFW, for one-shot event handlers; *ManagedThreadFW*, for managed threads; and *SchedulableMissionSequencerFW*, for mission sequencers used as schedulables. Each is started by a mission, performs its behaviour, accepts termination requests from its mission, and cleans up after it terminates.

Each event handler has actions that control its specific release pattern. Event handlers may have deadlines associated with them, and periodic event handlers have an associated period. Our models consider that periods may be overrun and deadlines may be missed, and captures the response if this happens. This allows our models to be used to check if, for example, an event handler may overrun its deadline. Managed threads are simpler and begin their release as soon as they are started. Mission sequencers used as schedulables are described above.

3.2 Mission Example

The *Circus* model of a mission is ideal to illustrate our modelling approach. The FlatBuffer application in Sect. 2 contains one mission, `FlatBufferMission`, which we model using three components described next.

As previously indicated, like every mission, an instance of *MissionFW* represents the behaviour of the mission prescribed by the SCJ paradigm. It is outlined above. The non-reactive application-specific behaviour is captured in the *OhCircus* class *FlatBufferMissionClass*. It contains the *buffer* variable, corresponding to the buffer field of the `FlatBufferMission`, and the `bufferEmpty()` method, because it is purely a data operation without any reactive behaviour.

The *FlatBufferMissionApp* process captures the reactive application-specific behaviour of the mission. It has actions modelling the behaviour of the API methods `initialize()` and `cleanup()` and actions modelling the application-defined methods: *writeSyncMeth*, *readSyncMeth*, and *bufferEmptyMeth*. It stores a reference to an instance of *FlatBufferMissionClass*, which contains the method `bufferEmpty()`. The *bufferEmptyMeth* action wraps this method, so that it can be called by other processes.

Channels on which the instance of *MissionFW* and *FlatBufferMissionApp* communicate are parametrised by the mission identifier *FlatBufferMission*; this ensures that the *FlatBufferMissionApp* communicates with the right framework process. The *FlatBufferMissionApp* instantiates and communicates with the *FlatBufferMissionClass* to call its `bufferEmpty()` method.

$$
\begin{aligned}
&\textit{Register} \mathrel{\widehat{=}} \\
&\quad \textit{register ? s ! mission} \longrightarrow \\
&\qquad \left(\begin{array}{l}
\left(\begin{array}{l}
\textit{checkSchedulable . mission ? check} : (\textit{check} = \textbf{True}) \longrightarrow \\
\textit{AddSchedulable}
\end{array} \right) \\
\Box \\
\left(\begin{array}{l}
\textit{checkSchedulable . mission ? check} : (\textit{check} = \textbf{False}) \longrightarrow \\
\textit{throw . illegalStateException} \longrightarrow \\
\textbf{Chaos}
\end{array} \right)
\end{array} \right)
\end{aligned}
$$

Fig. 6. The *MissionFW*'s *Register* action

In an SCJ program, the Mission's initialize() method is overridden to register the schedulables that this particular mission manages. In Fig. 5 we show the *InitializePhase* action of the *FlatBufferMissionApp* process, which models the initialize() method in FlatBufferMission. The events *initializeCall* and *initializeRet* model the call to and return from initialize().

The registration of a schedulable is modelled by the event *register.s.m*, where m is the identifier of the mission registering the schedulable and s is the identifier of the schedulable being registered. The order of registration shown in Fig. 5 corresponds to the order in the program. After registration, all registered schedulables are started simultaneously.

In *MissionFW*, *initializeCall* triggers the *Register* action (Fig. 6), which accepts a *register* event, with any schedulable identifier as long as the mission identifier is the same as this mission's. The *checkSchedulable* event indicates, via the variable *check*, if the schedulable may be registered.

If *check* is **True**, then *Register* can add the schedulable. If *check* is **False**, then the schedulable is already registered and we use the *throw* channel to model an exception being thrown and then diverge (**Chaos**). This allows the detection of an attempt to register a schedulable more than once.

3.3 Synchronisation and Suspension

The synchronisation model of SCJ constrains that of Java. First, SCJ programs cannot use synchronized blocks, only synchronized methods. Second, threads queue for a lock in order of eligibility. In SCJ, the most eligible thread is the thread at the highest priority level that has been waiting for the longest time. We model this using the type *PriorityQueue*, which is a total function from *PriorityLevel* to injective sequences of *ThreadID*. *PriorityLevel* is a free type containing the priorities available to the system and *ThreadID* is the set of thread identifiers.

Our models use extra processes to control synchronisation and suspension. In SCJ, each schedulable is executed by a thread. In our model, schedulables that call a synchronised method are associated with an instance of the *ThreadFW* process. *ThreadFW* holds the thread identifier and keeps track of its priority and interrupted status. Overall, the framework model of a schedulable that calls a synchronised method is the parallel composition of its associated *ThreadFW* process with the appropriate framework process, which depends on the type of schedulable (event handler, managed thread, and so on).

Additionally, each object used as a lock is associated with an instance of the *ObjectFW* process, which stores the threads waiting on this object and controls the threads trying to lock this object. In the FlatBuffer, the mission is used as a lock, so it has an associated instance of *ObjectFW*. Again, the overall framework model of each object that represents a paradigm component and is used as a lock is its framework process in parallel with an instance of *ObjectFW*. Non-paradigm objects used as locks are modelled in the framework by just an instance of *ObjectFW*.

$$
readSyncMeth \cong \mathbf{var}\ ret : \mathbb{Z} \bullet
$$

$$
\left(
\begin{array}{l}
readCall\ .\ FlatBufferMissionMID\ ?\ caller\ ?\ thread \longrightarrow \\
\left(
\begin{array}{l}
startSyncMeth\ .\ FlatBufferMissionOID\ .\ thread \longrightarrow \\
lockAcquired\ .\ FlatBufferMissionOID\ .\ thread \longrightarrow \\
\left(
\left(
\mu X \bullet
\left(
\begin{array}{l}
\mathbf{var}\ loopVar : \mathbb{B} \bullet loopVar := bufferEmpty(); \\
\mathbf{if}\ (loopVar = \mathbf{True}) \longrightarrow \\
\quad
\left(
\begin{array}{l}
waitCall\ .\ FlatBufferMissionOID\ .\ thread \longrightarrow \\
waitRet\ .\ FlatBufferMissionOID\ .\ thread \longrightarrow \\
\mathbf{Skip}
\end{array}
\right)\ ;\ X \\
[]\ (loopVar = \mathbf{False}) \longrightarrow \mathbf{Skip} \\
\mathbf{fi}
\end{array}
\right)
\right)\ ; \\
\mathbf{var}\ out : \mathbb{Z} \bullet out := this\ .\ buffer; \\
this\ .\ buffer := 0; \\
notify\ .\ FlatBufferMissionOID\ !\ thread \longrightarrow \\
ret := out \\
endSyncMeth\ .\ FlatBufferMissionOID\ .\ thread \longrightarrow \\
readRet\ .\ FlatBufferMissionMID\ .\ caller\ .\ thread\ !\ ret \longrightarrow \mathbf{Skip}
\end{array}
\right) ;
\end{array}
\right)
$$

Fig. 7. The *FlatBufferMission* process's *readSyncMeth* action

The FlatBuffer program uses synchronisation and suspension to control access to the buffer in its mission. The synchronised `read()` method suspends the calling thread (by calling `wait()`) if the buffer is empty. This is wrapped in a loop that checks if the buffer is empty, to deal with spurious wake ups.

The `FlatBufferMission`'s `read()` method is modelled by the *readSyncMeth* action in the *FlatBufferMissionApp* process (Fig. 7), which shows the pattern we use for modelling all synchronised methods. The action begins and ends with the familiar call-return event pair, *readCall* and *readRet*, which correspond to the call to and return from the method. In this case, however, because this is a synchronised method, these events take an extra parameter *thread*, which is the identifier of the thread that is calling the method.

The *ObjectFW* process associated with the *FlatBufferMissionApp* process controls the synchronisation and suspension behaviour using the *startSyncMeth*, *lockAcquired*, and *endSyncMeth* events. The *startSyncMeth* event models the beginning of a synchronized method and triggers the *ObjectFW* process to request a lock on this object by the thread calling this action.

Because the lock may already be held by another thread, the *readSyncMeth* action waits for the *lockAcquired* event (from the *ObjectFW* process) to signal that it has the lock and can proceed. After the body of the method, the *endSync* event signals that the synchronised method is complete, to trigger *ObjectFW* to release the lock on the mission currently held by the calling thread. We note that SCJ does not support Java's `ReentrantLock`, however, SCJ does support reentrant locking by allowing synchronised methods to call other synchronised methods in the same object. The *ObjectFW* process provides this behaviour; to unlock the object, after the first *lockAquired* event, each subsequent *startSyncMeth* event (which must be from the same thread) must be matched by a *endSyncMeth* event from the locking thread.

We model the call to `wait()` using the call-return event pair *waitCall* and *waitRet*. These events take the identifier of the associated *ObjectFW* instance (*FlatBufferMissionOID*, in Fig. 7) and the identifier of the *thread* calling this action. The instance of *ObjectFW* associated with the mission adds *thread* to its queue of waiting threads. The process calling *waitCall* waits for *waitRet* to communicate its identifier.

We model the call to `notify()` using the event *notify*. Like *waitCall* and *waitRet*, this event also takes the identifier of the associated *ObjectFW* process and the identifier of the *thread* calling this action. The *notify* event triggers the *ObjectFW* process to resume the most eligible thread. If there are no waiting threads, then *ObjectFW* allows the call to *notify*, but does nothing. To resume a thread, *ObjectFW* calls *waitRet* with the identifier of the thread to be resumed. SCJ Level 2 can also use `notifyAll()`, which resumes all the waiting threads. We model a call to `notifyAll()` with the event *notifyAll*. It triggers the *ObjectFW* to call *waitRet* with the identifier of each waiting thread in eligibility order.

The complete *Circus* models of the framework processes can be found in [12], and the application processes of the FlatBuffer in [11]. In the next section, we discuss the validation and application of our models.

4   Initial Evaluation

Our *Circus* model is written to closely correspond with the SCJ API. We have frozen development of our model at version 0.100 of the SCJ language specification. One of the authors is a member of the SCJ Expert Group, which helped in clarifying ambiguities in the language specification.

Our model of Level 2 is based on the *Circus* model of Level 1 presented in [25], which has been validated against the SCJ language specification. Our model adds the features of Level 2 and updates the model to reflect recent changes in the language specification.

Our modelling effort has influenced the development of SCJ. In [13], which is under review, we present a model of the SCJ termination protocol and a proposed simplified termination protocol. The comparison of these models shows that our proposed protocol reduces the number of states in the system. This simplified protocol is useful for improving programmer understanding and further modelling efforts. Our simplified termination protocol was adopted by the SCJ expert group from version 0.96.

We have, by hand, translated 10 SCJ programs to *Circus* using our approach; the examples are summarised in Table 2. The programs are constructed to cover the features of SCJ. They range from simple tests of SCJ's features, such as different release patterns or synchronisation and suspension, to more complex programs that use nested mission sequencers to provide concurrent missions.

Table 2. Summary of SCJ programs translated by hand

Name	Description	№ classes
Mission1	A single mission with periodic event handler that releases an aperiodic event handler	5
Mission2	A single mission with a managed thread and a one-shot event handler	5
ThreeOneShots	A single mission with three one-shot event handlers	6
ThreeThreads	A single mission with three managed threads	6
SequentialMissions	Two sequential missions, each with two managed threads	8
NestedSequencer1	A single mission with a single nested mission sequencer	7
NestedSequencer2	A mission, with three nested mission sequencers. Each has one mission controlling a periodic event handler	14
NestedSequencer3	A mission, with a nested mission sequencer that has two sequential nested missions, each with a managed thread.	8
NestedSequencer4	A complicated example using two levels of nesting. It contains 4 missions and 3 managed threads	12
NestedSequencer5	Extends NestedSequencer4, combines complex nesting, all schedulable types, and sequential missions	12

Further, we have developed a prototype tool[1] to automatically generate the *Circus* application models of a given SCJ application, called $T^{ight}R^{ope}$. We have used this prototype to produce the application models of the FlatBuffer application presented in this paper and a more complex example, both summarised in Table 3. The 10 hand-translated examples, and more realistic programs, will be considered for automatic translation as $T^{ight}R^{ope}$ matures.

$T^{ight}R^{ope}$ is a small Java program that compiles an SCJ application and explores the resulting abstract syntax trees to extract the information required for the translation. $T^{ight}R^{ope}$ generates the *Circus* processes, *OhCircus* classes, and *Circus* channels required to model the application-specific behaviour of the input program. These are combined with the existing fixed models of the framework previously described, to form a specification of the whole program.

To facilitate model checking and animation using FDR3 [5], we have translated our models of the framework and of full programs into CSPm. This translation has been optimised so that FDR3 can check specifications of even complex programs in an acceptable amount of time. We have proved that the CSPm version of the

---

[1] $T^{ight}R^{ope}$ can be found at www.cs.york.ac.uk/circus/hijac/tools.html.

Table 3. Summary of SCJ programs translated by $\mathrm{T^{ight}R^{ope}}$

Name	Description	№ classes	Translation time (in seconds)
FlatBuffer	Small program using managed threads and synchronisation	6	1.2
Aircraft	Program using a schedulable mission sequencer to represent phases of aircraft flight	25	2.3

framework model is deadlock- and divergence-free, which lends extra validation to the framework. We have also proved that the models of the full programs that we translated do not deadlock or diverge.

Using the version of the CSP animator ProBE that is included in FDR3, we have animated the CSPm versions of the framework model and compared their behaviour with that prescribed in the SCJ language specification. This gives us confidence that the models capture the behaviour of the SCJ API. We have also used ProBE to examine the behaviour of these full models, to compare them to the running programs. We have compared the execution of our example SCJ Level 2 programs, using the IceLab [9] implementation, to animations of our models of these programs. These comparisons examined the behaviour and output from the executing programs with the corresponding events in the animated model to ensure that they have the same behaviour.

Future work in the analysis of our models includes extending the checks we make to cover more SCJ-specific criteria. We intend to check that the program does not attempt to register its top-level mission sequencer or throw any of the exceptions that we model. Because we model exceptions using an event followed by divergence, they are flagged by a divergence-freedom check. However, the counter examples provided by a specific check would be more useful during SCJ development. These SCJ-specific checks will be standardised for easy reuse.

In summary, because our framework model captures the behaviour of the SCJ paradigm separately from the program-specific behaviour, we can reason about it in isolation. We have used FDR3 to prove that the framework model does not deadlock or diverge. Models of full SCJ Level 2 programs can be model checked and animated in FDR3. Our formal semantics of the Level 2 paradigm enables further areas of study for SCJ Level 2, such as theorem proving.

5 Related Work

This is the first work supporting verification for SCJ Level 2 programs. K-Java [1] models a subset of SE Java 1.4 and produces executable specifications for model checking. However, SCJ programs have features not included in SE Java. The authors of [22] present a technique for translating SCJ programs into timed automata models. However, their technique appears to only be aimed at Levels 0 and 1. Further, neither of these techniques provide support for top-down refinement of SCJ Level 2 programs or refinement-based reasoning.

RSJ [10] is a adaptation of the Java PathFinder [7] that explores all possible schedulings of the threads within an SCJ program to check for scheduling-dependent errors. It, however, does not cater for SCJ Level 2 programs.

Older versions of the SCJ specification define annotations for specifying compliance level, behavioural, or memory restrictions. Previous approaches to ensuring the safety of SCJ programs have used these annotations to provide run-time checks [19] or to specify checkable program constraints [6]. However, the memory annotations have been moved to an appendix of the standard as they were judged not ready for standardisation.

Our modelling approach is similar to that of [25] in capturing the paradigm of SCJ Level 1. The underlying structure of programs written in Level 2 and Level 1 is the same, however, Level 2 allows much more complicated program hierarchies and provides more complicated features (such as suspension).

6   Conclusion

We have presented the first formal semantics of SCJ Level 2, using the *Circus* family of specification languages. It is an essential ingredient to enable customised top-down development of SCJ Level 2 programs that are correct by construction. Our models provide this development process with a target for SCJ Level 2.

The features *Circus* provides make it a good fit for modelling object-orientated languages, such as SCJ. A *Circus* process provides similar encapsulation to classes and the language can capture variables and methods. This means that our models correspond very closely to the programs they model.

We have validated our model of the SCJ API and Level 2 programs by translating them into CSPm and model checking it using FDR3 to show that it does not deadlock or diverge. Our prototype tool, called T^{ight}R^{ope}, has produced *Circus* models of SCJ applications. Work is ongoing to update the tool, so that it can generate the models for all of our example applications.

In addition to the further areas of study that our work enables, future work includes the formalisation of the translation strategy that we use to derive the application models from the SCJ programs. The translation strategy also needs to be evaluated on more applications to further test our modelling approach.

Acknowledgements. This research reported in this paper is funded by the UK EPSRC under grant EP/H017461/1. No new primary data was produced during this work. One of the authors is a member of the SCJ Expert Group; we would like to thank the other members of the Expert Group. We would also like to thank Frank Zeyda, Alan Burns, and Thomas Gibson-Robinson for their very helpful suggestions.

References

1. Bogdanas, D., Roşu, G.: K-Java: a complete semantics of Java. SIGPLAN Not. **50**(1), 445–456 (2015)
2. Cavalcanti, A., Sampaio, A., Woodcock, J.: Unifying classes and processes. Softw. Syst. Model. **4**(3), 277–296 (2005). http://dx.doi.org/10.1007/s10270-005-0085-2
3. Cavalcanti, A., Wellings, A., Woodcock, J., Wei, K., Zeyda, F.: Safety-critical Java in circus. In: Proceedings of the 9th International Workshop on Java Technologies for Real-Time and Embedded Systems, JTRES 2011, pp. 20–29. ACM, New York, NY, USA (2011). http://doi.acm.org/10.1145/2043910.2043915
4. EUROCAE and RTCA: Software Considerations in Airborne Systems and Equipment Certification. Norm ED-12C, EUROCAE (2012)
5. Gibson-Robinson, T., Armstrong, P., Boulgakov, A., Roscoe, A.: Failures Divergences Refinement (FDR) Version 3 (2013). www.cs.ox.ac.uk/projects/fdr/
6. Haddad, G., Hussain, F., Leavens, G.T.: The design of SafeJML, a specification language for SCJ with support for WCET specification. In: Proceedings of the 8th International Workshop on Java Technologies for Real-Time and Embedded Systems, JTRES 2010, pp. 155–163. ACM, New York, NY, USA (2010). http://doi.acm.org/10.1145/1850771.1850793
7. Havelund, K., Pressburger, T.: Model checking JAVA programs using JAVA PathFinder. Int. J. Softw. Tools Technol. Transf. **2**(4), 366–381 (2000). http://dx.doi.org/10.1007/s100090050043
8. Hoare, C.A.R.: Communicating sequential processes (2004). www.usingcsp.com/cspbook.pdf
9. IceLab. www.icelab.dk/index.html
10. Kalibera, T., Parizek, P., Malohlava, M., Schoeberl, M.: Exhaustive testing of safety-critical Java. In: Proceedings of the 8th International Workshop on Java Technologies for Real-Time and Embedded Systems, JTRES 2010, pp. 164–174. ACM, New York, NY, USA (2010). http://doi.acm.org/10.1145/1850771.1850794
11. Luckcuck, M.: hiJaC Case Studies (2016). www.cs.york.ac.uk/circus/hijac/case.html. Accessed 14 Jan 2016
12. Luckcuck, M.: Safety-Critical Java Level 2 Framework Model (2016). www.cs.york.ac.uk/circus/publications/techreports/reports/SCJLevel2Framework.pdf
13. Luckcuck, M., Wellings, A., Cavalcanti, A.: Safety-Critical Java: Level 2 in Practice (submitted)
14. Morgan, C.: Programming from Specifications. Prentice-Hall, Inc., USA (1990)
15. Schoeberl, M.: A Java processor architecture for embedded real-time systems. J. Syst. Architect. **54**(1–2), 265–286 (2008). http://www.sciencedirect.com/science/article/pii/S1383762107000963
16. Sherif, A., Cavalcanti, A., Jifeng, H., Sampaio, A.: A process algebraic framework for specification and validation of real-time systems. Formal Aspects Comput. **22**(2), 153–191 (2009)
17. Søndergaard, H., Korsholm, S.E., Ravn, A.P.: Safety-critical Java for low-end embedded platforms. In: Proceedings of the 10th International Workshop on Java Technologies for Real-Time and Embedded Systems, JTRES 2012, pp. 44–53. ACM, New York, NY, USA (2012)
18. Spivey, J.M.: The Z Notation: A Reference Manual. International Series in Computer Science. Prentice-Hall, Inc. Upper Saddle River (1992)
19. Tang, D., Plsek, A., Vitek, J.: Static checking of safety critical Java annotations. In: Proceedings of the 8th International Workshop on Java Technologies for Real-Time and Embedded Systems, pp. 148–154. ACM, Prague, Czech Republic (2010)

20. The Open Group: Safety-critical Java technology specification V0.100. Technical report, The Open Group, 27 December 2014. http://jcp.org/en/jsr/detail?id=302
21. The Real-Time for Java Expert Group: Real-Time Specification for Java Language Specification (2005). www.timesys.com/java/
22. Thomsen, B., Luckow, K.S., Leth, L., Bøgholm, T.: From safety critical java programs to timed process models. In: Burrows, M., et al. (eds.) Degano Festschrift. LNCS, vol. 9465, pp. 319–338. Springer, Heidelberg (2015). doi:10.1007/978-3-319-25527-9_21
23. Wellings, A., Luckcuck, M., Cavalcanti, A.: Safety-critical Java level 2: motivations, example applications and issues. In: Proceedings of the 11th International Workshop on Java Technologies for Real-time and Embedded Systems, JTRES 2013, pp. 48–57. ACM, New York, NY, USA (2013). http://doi.acm.org/10.1145/2512989.2512991
24. Woodcock, J., Cavalcanti, A.: The semantics of *Circus*. In: Bert, D., Bowen, J.P., C. Henson, M., Robinson, K. (eds.) B 2002 and ZB 2002. LNCS, vol. 2272, pp. 184–203. Springer, Heidelberg (2002)
25. Zeyda, F., Lalkhumsanga, L., Cavalcanti, A., Wellings, A.: Circus models for safety-critical Java programs. Comput. J. **57**, 1046–1091 (2013). http://comjnl.oxfordjournals.org/content/early/2013/07/02/comjnl.bxt060.abstract

Safety and Liveness

Deciding Monadic Second Order Logic over ω-Words by Specialized Finite Automata

Stephan Barth$^{(\boxtimes)}$

Ludwig-Maximilians-Universität München, Munich, Germany
stephan.barth@ifi.lmu.de

Abstract. Several automata models are each capable of describing all
ω-regular languages. The most well-known such models are Büchi, parity, Rabin, Streett, and Muller automata. We present deeper insights and
further enhancements to a lesser-known model. This model was chosen
and the enhancements developed with a specific goal: Decide monadic
second order logic (MSO) over infinite words more efficiently.

MSO over various structures is of interest in different applications,
mostly in formal verification. Due to its inherent high complexity, most
solvers are designed to work only for subsets of MSO. The most notable
full implementation of the decision procedure is MONA, which decides
MSO formulae over finite words and trees.

To obtain a suitable automaton model, we further studied a representation of ω-regular languages by regular languages, which we call
loop automata. We developed an efficient algorithm for homomorphisms
in this representation, which is essential for deciding MSO. Aside from
the algorithm for homomorphism, all algorithms for deciding MSO with
loop automata are simple. Minimization of loop automata is basically
the same as minimization of deterministic finite automata. Efficient minimization is an important feature for an efficient decision procedure for
MSO. Together this should theoretically make loop automata a well-
suited model for efficiently deciding MSO over ω-words.

Our experimental evaluation suggests that loop automata are indeed
well suited for deciding MSO over ω-words efficiently.

1 Introduction

Decidability of monadic second order logic (MSO) over ω-words, (alternative
names are: full MSO, S1S; MSO alone is also used sometimes for MSO over
ω-words) was shown in 1962 [3], using nondeterministic Büchi automata (NBA).
MSO has a central position in model checking as it subsumes some important
relevant specification languages, e.g. linear temporal logic (LTL) and Presburger
arithmetic. Nevertheless MSO is rather used for its rich theory than practically
as efficient implementations are missing for most variants of MSO; a gap this
paper helps to close.

This research was funded by the DFG (German Research Foundation), within the
Research Training Group 1480: Programm- und Modell-Analyse (PUMA).

© The Author(s) 2016
E. Ábrahám and M. Huisman (Eds.): IFM 2016, LNCS 9681, pp. 245–259, 2016.
DOI: 10.1007/978-3-319-33693-0_16

The most mature implementation of any variant of MSO is MONA [8], an implementation of the decision procedure for weak MSO over words and trees (wMSO, also WS1S and WS2S), a variant of MSO deciable by the use of finite automata. In MONA, minimization in every step is crucial for the efficiency [10], We use this insight to handle MSO over ω-words efficiently. Beside technical insights, the success of MONA also supports the relevance of decision procedures for MSO.

1.1   State of the Art in Minimizing Automata

Within reasonable time, modern computers with state of the art minimization procedures can handle automata of very different sizes. In case of deterministic finite automata (DFA), automata with millions of states can be minimized, due to its $n \log n$-TIME minimization procedure [9]. Widespread models for ω-regular languages have no well scaling complete minimization procedures. Hence, the existing minimization procedures cannot handle more than 20 states.

We studied minimization of NBA in our own work. We failed to minimize automata whose minimal automaton needs more than 10 states in reasonable time [1].

Minimization of Deterministic Büchi automata (DBA) does not work well over 20 states [5].

No minimization procedure is published for deterministic parity automata (DPA). As DPA subsume DBA, it is unlikely, that a minimization procedure based on the same principles will succed for automata with more than 20 states.

Even incomplete heuristics are used, that fail to minimize bigger automata, for example [6], which fails to compute when used for automata with more than 30 states.

These comparable small numbers are not least due to the complexity of these problems, PSPACE-complete for minimizing NBA (corollary from [11], Lemma 3.2.3), NP-complete for DBA and DPA [12].

With more computational power only DFA would allow for minimization of notably bigger automata. The other algorithms do not scale well.

Thus, mostly incomplete heuristics that miss much of opportunities for minimization are used in applications. This situation is comparable to finite automata, where minimization for nondeterministic finite automata (NFA) also lacks efficiency, which is why MONA relies on DFA. Full minimization is not necessary in the decision procedure, but some normalization of automata or other procedures for preventing an unbounded amount of extra states are. There are normalization procedures for Büchi automata [7], but they are not helpful for deciding MSO as normalization is also PSPACE-complete; the normalization in [7] is not successful for automata with more than 20 states.

1.2   Our Approach

In order to obtain a model well suited for deciding MSO, we have chosen a lesser-known automata model for ω-regular languages only by the criterion how good it can be minimized. Then we developed the missing procedures that are necessary for deciding MSO. The main ingredients of this model are an already known method for representing ω-regular languages by regular ones [4]. Thus, only an efficient minimization procedure for regular languages is needed.

To represent ω-regular languages by regular ones, we take the representation introduced in [4]: for given ω-regular languages L, $L_\$:= \{u\$v \mid uv^\omega \in L\}$ is regular. We call $L_\$$ the loop language of L, an automaton for $L_\$$ loop automaton, and L-X the loop automaton model that results from using the automaton model X for loop languages. Algorithms for converting between NBA and loop deterministic finite automata (L-DFA) were presented in 1994 [4]. For deciding MSO, we investigate further to construct an algorithm to perform various operations directly on loop automata. Most notably, an algorithm for performing homomorphisms is presented here.

First experimental results hint that the decision procedure with loop automata is often considerably more efficient than a more classical NBA/DPA approach, which can be considered state of the art. Though on few formulae the NBA/DPA approach is a bit more efficient than L-DFA, our research hints that they are the most appropriate model for deciding MSO among the known models. This result was to be expected considering the already-mentioned research from the MONA team that minimization in every step is crucial in deciding wMSO [10].

The main advantage of L-DFA is, that the minimization procedure of DFA can be directly be applied, hence automata with millions of states can be minimized, in contrast to the under 20 states for conventional ω-automata.

1.3 Related Work

[3] showed the decidability of MSO over ω-words. NBA were introduced to do so. This procedure was very inefficient. Beside enhancements in complementation of Büchi automata, this is still to consider state of the art, nevertheless.

[13] summarizes the current state of NBA complementation. Using the best known complementation algorithm for NBA greatly enhances the efficiency of the method from [3]. This is used as comparison in the experimental evaluation in Sect. 4.

The MONA tool [8] is a successful implementation of wMSO. An analysis by the MONA team is used as hint for what might contribute to efficiency [10]. For this paper, we focus on their result that minimization after every step is the most important optimization in the decision procedure.

[4] introduces loop automata (albeit not given a name) and transformations between them and NBA. However, they authors did not provide an algorithm for performing homomorphisms, which are essential for deciding MSO.

[7] also uses loop automata, but only as intermediate device for normalizing NBA. No algorithms for working directly on loop automata are presented.

[2] study ω-languages, which only consist of ultimate periodic words. In there, the representation as loop automaton is used and some algorithms are workes out, but only for the special case of these restricted languages.

1.4 Main Contribution

The main contribution of this paper is a more efficient decision procedure for MSO over ω-words. This consists of identifying loop languages as suitable automata model and the homomorphism algorithm for loop languages in Theorem 4. The more detailed characterization of loop languages in Theorem 2, may further help to improve the handling of loop languages. Furthermore, the experimental evaluation in Sect. 4 indicates, that this method is indeed more efficient than existing ones.

2   Notion and Prerequisites

Definition 1 (Alphabet, Word). *An alphabet is a finite set. A word w is a finite or infinite series of elements of the alphabet. w_i denotes the i-th element of the series, also called the i-th letter of the word w.*

Definition 2 (Büchi and Finite Automata, Path). *The first letter in the abbreviation determines whether deterministic (D) or nondeterministic (N) automata are refered to. Büchi (DBA/NBA) and finite automata (DFA/NFA) are tuples $\mathfrak{A} = (Q, \Sigma, \delta, q_0, F)$, where*

- *$Q = \{q_0, \ldots, q_{n-1}\}$ is a finite set of states;*
- *Σ is a finite set, the alphabet;*
- *δ is a function, in case of deterministic automata, $\delta : Q \times \Sigma \to Q$, in case of nondeterministic automata $\delta : Q \times \Sigma \to \mathbb{P}(Q)$;*
- *q_0 is the initial state and the first state of the canonical enumeration;*
- *$F \subseteq Q$ is the set of final states.*

To treat deterministic automata as nondeterministic, $\delta(q, a)$ with $\{\delta(q, a)\}$.

In an automaton $\mathfrak{A}$, there is a path from $q \in Q$ to $q' \in Q$ labeled with word w, written as $q \xrightarrow{w} q'$, when $q = q' \wedge w = \varepsilon$ or w starts with the letter a the remainder of the word is v and there is a state q'' with $q'' \in \delta(q, a)$ and $q'' \xrightarrow{v} q'$.

A finite word $w \in \Sigma^*$ is considered to be accepted by a finite automaton, if there is a state $q \in F$ such that $q_0 \xrightarrow{w} q$. An infinite word $w \in \Sigma^\omega$ is considered to be accepted by a Büchi automaton, if there is a state $q \in F$ such that w can be split in subwords, each of finite length greater than zero $w = u v_0 v_1 v_2 \ldots$, such that $q_0 \xrightarrow{u} q$ and for all $i \in \mathbb{N}_0$ it holds that $q \xrightarrow{v_i} q$.

Definition 3 (Monadic Second Order Logic). *Monadic Second Order Logic (MSO) formulae are of the form: $\varphi, \psi := x < y \mid x \in X \mid \exists x.\varphi \mid \exists X.\varphi \mid \neg\varphi \mid \varphi \vee \psi$*

MSO exists in several variants. The specific type of the first order (x, y) and second order variables (X) in this definition depends on the variant of MSO considered. MSO over ω-words means $x, y \in \mathbb{N}$, $X \subseteq \mathbb{N}$; this can be decided with Büchi automata [3]; any other model for ω-regular languages can be used as well, as long as algorithms for conjunction, complementation and homomorphisms are known.

Theorem 1 (MSO over ω-Words is Decidable, Büchi 1962 [3]). *For a MSO formula with no free variables it is decidable, whether it holds. For a formula with free variables it is decidable whether the formula is satisfiable and whether it is falsifiable.*

Proof (sketch).

The values of the variable of the formula ψ are stored in an infinite word. Herein the i-th letter encodes the relation between the number i and each variable. That is, for each variable X we store, whether $i \in X$. First order variables are encoded as second order variables that contain precisely one number. To encode the values of the variables use an alphabet of $2^{\text{number of variables}}$ letters, each letter for one combination of variable values.

An automaton can be constructed by structural induction over the formula. Most notable existential quantification corresponds to homomorphisms, which are examined in Theorem 4. □

3 Representation of ω-Regular Languages by Regular Languages

Definition 4 (Loop Language). *For a given ω-regular language L, $L_\$:= \{u\$v \mid uv^\omega \in L\}$.*

We call $L_\$$ the loop language of L, an automaton for $L_\$$ loop automaton, and L-X the loop automaton model that results from using the automaton model X for loop languages. By M_ω, we denote an ω-regular language for the regular language M with the property that $M_{\omega\$} = M$. Note that not for every regular language M a language M_ω exists.

Transformations between nondeterministic Büchi automata (NBA) accepting L and deterministic finite automata (DFA) accepting $L_\$$ were presented in 1994 [4].

Note that $L_\$$ and thus the minimal DFA are uniquely determined, hence the known efficient minimization procedures for DFA work for L-DFA as well.

It is thus natural to base a decision procedure for MSO on loop automata. However, in doing so, one faces the obstacle that homomorphism has to be implemented on the level of loop automata.

It might be this obstacle has prevented other authors from following this path. This is precisely the gap we are closing in this paper.

We present two example languages in the usual ω-style, as well as in loop style in Table 1.

3.1 Properties of Loop Languages

Definition 5 (Representative). *Given a finite alphabet Σ, a new letter $\$ \notin \Sigma$, and an ultimately periodic ω-word $w \in \Sigma^\omega$, a finite word $u\$v$, with $uv^\omega = w$, is called representative of w.*

250   S. Barth

Table 1. Two examples of languages for comparing the ω-regular language and its corresponding loop language

ω-regular expression	$(a\vert b)^*b^\omega$	$(a\vert b)^*(ab)^\omega$
Büchi automaton		
Loop regular expression	$(a\vert b)^*\$b^+$	$(a\vert b)^*\$((ab)^+\vert(ba)^+)$
Loop DFA		

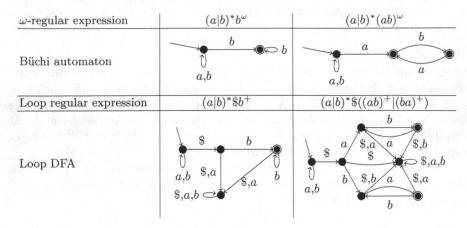

Definition 6 (Duplication and Rotation). *For regular languages $L \subseteq (\Sigma \cup \{\$\})^*$, the following are defined*

- *up-duplication holds for $L :\Leftrightarrow \forall u, v \in \Sigma^*.(u\$v \in L \Rightarrow \forall i \in \mathbb{N}_1.u\$v^i \in L)$*
- *down-duplication holds for $L :\Leftrightarrow \forall u, v \in \Sigma^*.(u\$v \in L \Leftarrow \exists i \in \mathbb{N}_1.u\$v^i \in L)$*
- *up-rotation holds for $L :\Leftrightarrow \forall u, v \in \Sigma^*, a \in \Sigma.(u\$av \in L \Rightarrow ua\$va \in L)$*
- *down-rotation holds for $L :\Leftrightarrow \forall u, v \in \Sigma^*, a \in \Sigma.(u\$av \in L \Leftarrow ua\$va \in L)$*

Theorem 2 (Characterization of Loop Languages). *A language is loop if and only if the following holds*

- *regular: L is regular*
- *wellformed: $L \subseteq \Sigma^*\$\Sigma^+$*
- *representative independence: for all words u, v, x, and y it holds that if $uv^\omega = xy^\omega$, then $u\$v \in L \iff x\$y \in L$*
  Representative independence is further equivalent to the conjunction of up-duplication, down-duplication, up-rotation, down-rotation.

Proof. Regularity of loop languages has already been proven [4].

Wellformedness has to hold as only wellformed words represent ω-words. Representative independence has to hold because $L_\$$ represents L and membership cannot depend on the chosen representative. Furthermore, given representative independence all four (up/down)-(rotation/duplication) properties have to hold, as $\forall i \in \mathbb{N}_1, a \in \Sigma.(uv^\omega = u(v^i)^\omega \wedge u(av)^\omega = ua(va)^\omega)$.

On the other hand, given these properties and any word in L, the representative of minimal length for the same ω-word has to be in the language as well (by down-) and every representative of this word has to be in the language (by up-).

These properties are sufficient for loopness, as there exists an algorithm to construct an ω-regular language L_ω out of every language $L_\$$ with the stated properties. That transformation algorithm was given in [4]. □

A minor remark here is that, except for the empty language, every loop automaton has at least 4 states, resulting from wellformedness:

- q_0: The starting state; must not be final;
- $q_1 = \delta(q_0, \$)$: Different from q_0, as no $ may ever occur in a word afterwards; may not be final;
- $\delta(q_1, \$)$: Rejection sink; different from all states before; may not be final;
- at least one final state.

3.2   Homomorphism Closure of Loop Automata

Definition 7 (Homomorphism). *Let L be a formal language over the finite alphabet Σ, Γ another finite alphabet and $f : \Sigma \to \Gamma$.*
$f(L) := \{w \mid \exists v \in L.(|v| = |w| \wedge \forall i \in \mathbb{N}_0.w_i = f(v_i))\}$ *is called the homomorphism defined by f.*

Applying homomorphisms on NBA is simple: replace all letters a by $f(a)$.

The problem with loop automata is that given an homomorphism f it is possible that $f(L_\$) \neq (f(L))_\$$. Hence applying the homomorphisms directly on the regular language does not yield the correct result.

Example 1. Given $L = a(ab)^\omega$, $f = \{a \mapsto a, b \mapsto a\}$ it holds that $L_\$ = a(ab)^*\$(ab)^+|aa(ba)^*\$(ba)^+$, $f(L_\$) = a(aa)^*\$(aa)^+|aa(aa)^*\$(aa)^+ = a^+\$(aa)^+$, $f(L) = a^\omega$, $(f(L))_\$ = a^*\$a^+$.
This results in $f(L_\$) \neq (f(L))_\$$.

Therefore, up till now the only known way to do so far was to convert the L-DFA to an NBA (resulting in $O(n^5)$ states for an n state L-DFA), to perform the homomorphism n the NBA and to convert it back to an L-DFA (resulting in $2^{O(n^2)}$ states for an n state NBA). This leads to a total state blowup of $2^{O(n^{10})}$ states. Our new construction does not need Büchi automata and results in a smaller state blowup of $2^{O(n^2)}$ states.

It is not surprising that this operation is costly, as homomorphism on DFA already results in up to 2^n states for an n state automaton.

Lemma 1. *Given a homomorphism f, it holds, that*
$(f(L))_\$ = \{u\$v \mid \exists i, j \in \mathbb{N}_1.uv^i\$v^j \in f(L_\$)\}$

Proof. Note that $\$ \mapsto \$$ and no other letter maps to $\$$, as $\$$ is not part of the ω-language.
$f(L_\$)$

- is regular: $L_\$$ is regular and homomorphisms map regular languages to regular ones;
- is wellformed, as letters are mapped to letters by f and $\$$ is kept unmodified;
- is not representative independent, but admits up-(duplication/rotation), as

- up-duplication: $u\$v \in f(L_\$) \Rightarrow \exists u'\$v' \in L_\$.(u\$v = f(u'\$v'))$
  $\overset{\text{up-duplication of } L_\$}{\Longrightarrow} \exists u'\$v' \in L_\$.(u\$v = f(u'\$v') \wedge \forall i \in \mathbb{N}_1.u'\$v'^i \in L_\$) \Rightarrow$
  $\forall i \in \mathbb{N}_1.u\$v^i \in f(L_\$)$
- up-rotation: $u\$av \in f(L_\$) \Rightarrow \exists u'\$a'v' \in L_\$.(u\$av = f(u'\$a'v'))$
  $\overset{\text{up-rotation of } L_\$}{\Longrightarrow} \exists u'\$a'v' \in L_\$.(u\$av = f(u'\$a'v') \wedge u'a'\$v'a' \in L_\$) \Rightarrow$
  $ua\$va \in f(L_\$)$

– contains at least one representative for every ultimate periodic word in $f(L)$:
  Given $uv^\omega \in f(L)$, there is some $u'v'^\omega \in L$ with $f(u'v'^\omega) = uv^\omega$. Note that
  neither necessarily $f(u') = u$, nor $f(v') = v$. With $u'v'^\omega \in L$ it also holds, that
  $u'\$v' \in L_\$$, as well as $f(u'\$v') \in f(L_\$)$. Consider that $f(u')(f(v'))^\omega = uv^\omega$.
  $f(u'\$v') \in f(L_\$)$ is hence a representative of uv^ω;
– contains no representatives for words not in $f(L)$, as for every $u\$v \in f(L_\$)$,
  there exists $u'\$v' \in L_\$$ with $f(u'\$v') = u\$v$. As $u'\$v' \in L_\$$, $u'v'^\omega \in L$ and
  $f(u'v'^\omega) \in f(L)$. Hence, $u\$v$ is a representative for a word in $f(L)$.

Hence, if all words, which are down-(rotated/duplicated) variants of words
in $f(L_\$)$ are added to the language, we obtain $(f(L))_\$$. It is sufficient to ensure
down-rotation of the form $uv\$v \in L \Rightarrow u\$v \in L$, as up-rotation holds. Therefore,
$(f(L))_\$ = \{u\$v \mid \exists i, j \in \mathbb{N}_1.uv^i\$v^j \in f(L_\$)\}$.

□

Theorem 3. *Given an NFA $\mathfrak{A}$ with n states, $\{u\$v \mid \exists i, j \in \mathbb{N}_1.uv^i\$v^j \in L(\mathfrak{A})\}$
can be accepted by a DFA with $2^n \cdot (2^{n^2} + 1) = 2^{n^2+n} + 2^n = 2^{O(n^2)}$ states.*

Proof. Given an NFA $\mathfrak{A} = (Q = \{q_0, \ldots, q_{n-1}\}, \Sigma, \Delta, q_0, F)$, construct a DFA
$\mathfrak{B} = (Q', \Sigma, \delta, q'_0, F')$ with
  let $\vartheta(M, a) = \{q \mid \exists p \in M.(p, a, q) \in \Delta\}$

– $Q' = \mathbb{P}(Q) \times (\mathbb{P}(Q)^n \cup \{()\})$
– $\delta((M, ()), a) = \begin{cases} (\vartheta(M, a), ()) & \text{if } a \neq \$ \\ (M, (\{q_0\}, \ldots, \{q_{n-1}\})) & \text{if } a = \$ \end{cases}$
  $\delta((M, (M_0, \ldots, M_{n-1})), a) = \begin{cases} (M, (\vartheta(M_0, a), \ldots, \vartheta(M_{n-1}, a))) & \text{if } a \neq \$ \\ (\{\}, ()) & \text{if } a = \$ \end{cases}$
– $q'_0 = (\{q_0\}, ())$
– $F' = \{(M, (M_0, \ldots, M_{n-1})) \mid$ Let (P, O) be the least fixpoint of the function
  $f(P, O) = (P \cup M \cup \{q \mid \exists i.q \in M_i \wedge q_i \in P\}, O \cup \vartheta(P, \$) \cup \{q \mid \exists i.q \in M_i \wedge q_i \in O\}), F \cap O \neq \varnothing\}$

Let $w = uv^i\$v^j \in L(\mathfrak{A})$. There are $p_0, \ldots, p_i, o_0, \ldots, o_j \in Q$ such that
$q_0 \overset{u}{\longrightarrow} p_0, \forall 0 \leq k < i.p_k \overset{v}{\longrightarrow} p_{k+1}, p_i \overset{\$}{\longrightarrow} o_0, \forall 0 \leq k < j.o_k \overset{v}{\longrightarrow} o_{k+1}$ and
$o_j \in F$, as w is accepted by $\mathfrak{A}$. The run of $\mathfrak{B}$ on $u\$v$ includes one $\$$-transition,
hence the state reached is of the form $(M, (M_0, \ldots, M_{n-1}))$. For every k, M_k con-
tains precisely the states that can be reached from q_k with word v. Let (P, O) be
the least fixpoints as in the definition of F'. $p_0 \in P$, as $p_0 \in M$. If $p_k \in P$ then
$p_{k+1} \in P$, hence $p_i \in P$. This then leads to $o_0 \in O$. If $o_k \in O$ then $o_{k+1} \in O$,
hence $o_j \in O$. As $o_j \in F$, $F \cap O \neq \varnothing$.

Conversely, if $u\$v$ if accepted by $\mathfrak{B}$, let $(M, (M_0, \ldots, M_{n-1})) \in F'$ be the state reached at the end of the run of $\mathfrak{B}$. Let (P, O) be the least fixpoints as in the definition of F'. There is a final state $r \in O$. There is an $l \in \mathbb{N}$ and a $r' \in \vartheta(P, \$)$ such that $r' \xrightarrow{v^l} r$. Furthermore, there is $m \in \mathbb{N}$ and $r'' \in M$ such that $r'' \xrightarrow{v^m\$} r'$. As $q_0 \xrightarrow{u} r''$, $uv^m\$v^l$ is accepted by $\mathfrak{A}$.

$\square$

Theorem 4. *The homomorphism of an L-DFA $\mathfrak{A}$ with language $L_\$$ can be constructed with at most $2^{O(n^2)}$ states.*

Proof. For doing so, perform the following steps

1. compute a nondeterministic finite automaton (NFA) $\mathfrak{B}$ for $f(L_\$)$ (keeps the number of states)
2. transform the NFA into a DFA for the modified language as in Theorem 3. That is the required L-DFA (this transformation needs $2^{O(n^2)}$ states)

By Lemma 1, the language of this DFA is $(f(L))_\$$. All together, homomorphisms on loop automata can be computed in at most $2^{O(n^2)}$ states.

$\square$

Remark 1 (Proposed Decision Procedure for MSO over ω-Words with L-DFA). Concluding we propose as decision procedure to encode the formulae quite like it was done Büchi.

For $x < y$ and $x \in X$ two concrete automata have to be chosen.

Complementation, intersection, union, and minimization of L-DFA is rather trivial given the algorithms for DFA: It is the same, but for the complement, there the result has to be intersected with $\Sigma^*\$\Sigma^+$. This is used to handle $\neg\varphi$ and $\varphi \vee \psi$.

The homomorphism from Theorem 4 is used to compute $\exists x.\varphi$ and $\exists X.\varphi$.

With that, loop automata can be used for deciding MSO.

4   Experimental Evaluation

The base of this experimental evaluation is a set of hand crafted formulae, given in Appendix A, and some random formulae. These are recursively computed by $\text{form}(1, \{x, y\}, \{X\})$, where form is defined by the following expressions:

$\text{form}(n, f, s) :=$ randomly select line with probability proportional to its weight

formula	weight
$x < y$	1
$x \in X$	1
$z := \text{freshname}; \exists z.\text{form}(n+1, f \cup \{z\}, s)$	1
$Z := \text{freshname}; \exists Z.\text{form}(n+1, f, s \cup \{Z\})$	1
$\neg\text{form}(n+1, f, s)$	1
$\text{form}(n+1, f, s) \vee \text{form}(n+1, f, s)$	$\frac{5}{n}$
$\text{form}(n+1, f, s) \wedge \text{form}(n+1, f, s)$	$\frac{5}{n}$

The line used for the construction of the formula is randomly selected taking the weight into account. For a call with the weights $p_i, i = 0, \ldots, 6$, each line k is chosen with probability $\frac{p_k}{\sum_{i=0}^{6} p_i}$. Variable names are randomly chosen with equal probability out of the set f for first order and s for second order variables; for $x < y$, x and y are different.

This formula generation was chosen such that it can generate every MSO-formula, the generation terminates with probability 1, and generates reasonable large formulae for experiments.

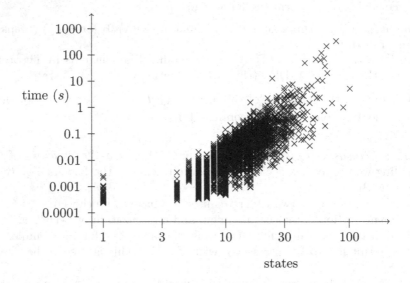

Fig. 1. Runtime and maximal state count of the decision procedures for random formulae

A scatterplot with maximal state count in the decision procedure and runtime (Intel i5-2540M, 2.60 GHz) of our implementation with 5000 of these formulae is given in Fig. 1. No formula lead to timeout or out of memory.

For comparing with state of the art, we use a more classical procedure using NBA and DPA. Just the maximal state count in the run of the decision procedure is compared, as it is more significant than the runtime, as the runtime depends more on the quality of implementation than the count of states and both implementations are not optimized in regards to runtime. While in practice the runtime is more important then the statecount, this comparison aims for comparing how well suited the different automata models are for deciding MSO and not on how well speed optimized the current implementations are; in fact both are more optimized for simplicity and debugging the automata themselves than for runtime. Especially the time efficiency of our NBA/DPA implementation is suboptimal so using our implementation would not result in a meaningful comparison.

A further advantage is that comparison can be done with a particularly strong minimization heuristic in the NBA/DPA approach, which increases the confidence in L-DFA to be better suited for deciding MSO as further advantages might be able to reduce the state count for the NBA/DPA approach, while L-DFA are already at their global minimum.

Complementation of NBA is done via transformation to DPA, as advised by [13]. There are some widely used minimization heuristics for NBA and DPA. The two heuristic in this experiment are: (1) In the DPA, for every pair of states is checked whether merging these keeps the language the same. This heuristic subsumes quite some widely used heuristics, but it is not frequently used as such, as it is too slow for most applications.

(2) Additionally, on the NBA it is checked whether the automaton gets smaller after complemented two times. Given the high complexity of the complementation procedure, this sounds quite time intensive. Nevertheless, it even speeds up the decision process in many cases.

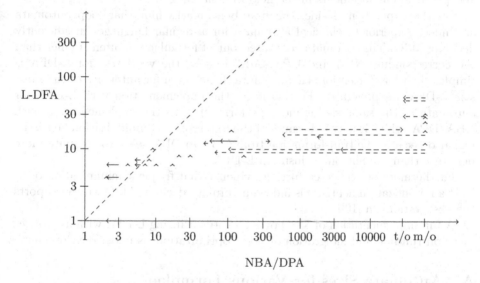

Fig. 2. Comparison of maximal state count in the run of the decision procedures for random formulae; arrowheads compare L-DFA against NBA/DPA with strong minimization heuristic; arrowtails compare L-DFA against NBA/DPA with weak minimization heuristic

On the other hand, there are formulae, for which the advantage from the heuristical minimization (1) is not that big. In fact, there are even very few counterintuitive examples, for which the state count is smaller when the state merging heuristic is not used; Appendix A, second table entry gives an example of such a formula.

The L-DFA approach indeed turns out to be a lot more efficient than the NBA/DPA-approach for many formulae.

Figure 2 contains the maximal automata sizes in the course of the decision procedure of 40 random formulae. Each formula is given as arrow. The size of the L-DFA is given in y-direction. The size of the NBA/DPA with only minimization heuristic (1) is given as arrow tail, the size with both heuristics is given as arrowhead. If the sizes coincide, this is denoted as arrow of length zero, directing upwards. Dashed arrows denote that at least one end is timeout (t/o) or memoryout (m/o). All these sizes are the maximal state count in the run. L-DFA have a strong advantage here. It becomes even bigger, the larger the resulting automata are.

5   Conclusion

We now have all necessary algorithms to decide MSO with loop automata. Hence, we now have an automaton model for ω-regular languages that is suitable for deciding MSO and allows for efficient minimization at the same time. Along with its applicability for MSO, these deeper insights might offer further theoretical and practical enhancements in the field of ω-languages.

On the experimental side, the first benchmarks hint that loop automata are indeed superior to classical automata for ω-regular languages in efficiently deciding MSO. The automata computed out of formulae are often smaller than the corresponding NBA and DPA. Additionally, the word test for L-DFA is simpler than for conventional ω-automata, hence even for automata of the same size L-DFA are preferable. Furthermore, the implementation with L-DFA for automata of the same size is more performant than the implementation with NBA/DPA, which is mostly because of the more complex minimization heuristic, but also because the transformation from NBA to DPA needs to compute more per state than the homomorphism on L-DFA.

Furthermore, we collected further evidence that frequent minimization or at least a minimization heuristic is indeed helpful for deciding MSO which supports the observations in [10].

A full implementation of MSO over ω-words utilizing L-DFA with a stronger focus on runtime and integration of other optimizations is under development.

A   Automata Sizes for Various Formulae

In Table 2 formulae are enlisted together with the efficiency with the classical NBA/DPA approach as well as with L-DFA.

The formulae are on the one hand formulae that appear often in model checking, such as fairness. The formulae are collected in a random like manner, with the goal to cover a broad part of the behaviour of the MSO solvers.

Efficiency is measured mainly in state count of the automata here. The resulting state count and the maximum state count for any subformula in the course of the decision procedure are recorded. The two lines in each cell denote these.

Timeout (t/o) after more than at least an hour, and memory out (m/o) when using more than 1 GB of RAM are stated in these cases. In some cases fine tuning in the solving procedure allowed for a partial handguided solving. Some

Table 2. State count of automata from MSO formulae for biggest intermediate result and end result

Formula	NBA/DPA Strong min	NBA/DPA Weak min	L-DFA
$(x \in X \wedge \neg x \in Y) \vee (x \in Y \wedge \neg x \in X)$	14/11	17/16	9
	14/11	17/16	9
$\neg \exists x.((x \in X \wedge \neg x \in Y) \vee$	33/4	30/79	9
$(x \in Y \wedge \neg x \in X))$	5/4	5/79	4
$\text{after}(X, Y) := \forall x.(x \in X \Rightarrow$	18/5	33/11	9
$\exists y.(y > x \wedge y \in Y))$	6/3	27/11	7
$\text{fair}(X, Y) := \text{after}(X, Y) \wedge \text{after}(Y, X)$	42/27	288/313	9
	42/27	288/313	9
$\forall X.(\text{fair}(X, Y) \Rightarrow \text{fair}(Y, Z))$	(14377)/	m/o	14
	$(6131)^{\text{a}}$		12
$\text{suc}(x, y) := x < y \wedge$	20/32	26/41	10
$\forall z.(\neg x < z \vee \neg z < y)$	6/5	14/17	6
$\text{suc2}(x, y) := \exists z.(\text{suc}(x, z) \wedge \text{suc}(z, y))$	780/32	783/41	10
	8/6	19/15	7
$\text{suc4}(x, y) := \exists z.(\text{suc2}(x, z) \wedge \text{suc2}(z, y))$	780/32	783/41	10
	12/8	29/20	9
$\text{suc8}(x, y) := \exists z.(\text{suc4}(x, z) \wedge \text{suc4}(z, y))$	780/32	783/41	13
	20/12	43/27	13
$\text{inf}(X) := \forall u \exists v.(u < v \wedge v \in X)$	8/5	17/11	9
	5/3	13/6	4
$\text{inf}(X) \vee \text{inf}(Y)$	9/5	25/290	9
	7/5	25/290	4
$(\text{inf}(U) \vee \text{inf}(V)) \Rightarrow (\text{inf}(X) \vee \text{inf}(Y))$	15/6	m/o	9
	14/6		6
$\exists U.((\text{inf}(U) \vee \text{inf}(V)) \Rightarrow$	15/8	m/o	9
$(\text{inf}(X) \vee \text{inf}(Y)))$	15/8		6
$\text{infsuc}(X, Y) := \forall u \exists x, y.(u < x \wedge$	394/31	397/41	18
$\text{suc}(x, y) \wedge x \in X \wedge y \in Y)$	6/3	19/10	8
$\exists Y.(\text{infsuc}(X, Y) \wedge \text{infsuc}(Z, Y))$	394/508	m/o	20
	73/508		6
$\text{zeroin}(X) := \exists u.(u \in X \wedge \neg \exists v.(v < u))$	19/5	27/9	6
	9/8	9/9	6
$\text{alter}(X) := \text{zeroin}(X) \wedge \forall x, y.$	53/90	61/719	12
$(\text{suc}(x, y) \Rightarrow x \in X \iff \neg y \in X)$	4/3	11/11	9
$\text{offset}(X, Y) := \forall i \forall j.(\text{suc}(i, j) \wedge$	28/31	31/169	11
$i \in X \Rightarrow j \in Y)$	4/3	9/163	9

Table 2. (*Continued*)

Formula	NBA/DPA Strong min	NBA/DPA Weak min	L-DFA
$\text{offset}(X,Y) \wedge \text{offset}(Y,Z) \wedge \text{offset}(Z,X)$	49/40	81/163	107
	49/40	81/163	107
$\text{offset}(V,W) \wedge \text{offset}(W,X)\wedge$	97/(444)[b]	161/444	2331
$\text{offset}(X,Y) \wedge \text{offset}(Y,Z) \wedge \text{offset}(Z,V)$		161/444	2331
$\exists Y.(\text{offset}(X,Y) \wedge \text{offset}(Y,Z))$	28/31	41/163	29
	21/14	29/26	29
$\text{insm}(i,j,U,V,W) := (j \in U \Rightarrow$	7/13	8/23	15
$i \in V \vee i \in W)$	7/13	8/23	15
$\forall i \forall j.(\text{suc}(i,j) \Rightarrow \text{insm}(i,j,U,V,Z)\wedge$	t/o[c]	m/o	198
$\text{insm}(i,j,V,X,V) \wedge \text{insm}(i,j,X,Y,V)\wedge$			16
$\text{insm}(i,j,Y,Z,X) \wedge \text{insm}(i,j,Z,U,Y)$			
$\forall x \exists y.(x < y \wedge y \in X \wedge y \in Y)$	12/5	21/13	9
	5/3	16/7	4
$\forall x \exists y.(x < y \wedge y \in X \wedge y \in Y)\wedge$	40/6	165/118	9
$\forall x \exists y.(x < y \wedge y \in X \wedge y \notin Y)$	6/3	153/118	6
$\forall x \exists y.(x < y \wedge y \in X \wedge y \in Y)\wedge$	641/44	m/o	18
$\forall x \exists y.(x < y \wedge y \in X \wedge y \notin Y)\wedge$	85/44		18
$\forall x \exists y.(x < y \wedge y \notin X \wedge y \in Y)\wedge$			
$\forall x \exists y.(x < y \wedge y \notin X \wedge y \notin Y)$			

[a]Timeout in minimization of DPA. With weaker minimization, it ended up in this result.

[b]Minimization of parity automaton did not finish in a day.

[c]Computation did not finish in over a day. When it was stopped, it was in the process of computing a DPA out of an NBA and had already over 190000 states.

formulae needed too long the minimizing heuristics but got far more states with general weaker minimization. In that case, the states are given in braces.

References

1. Barth, S., Hofmann, M.: Learn with SAT to minimize Büchi automata. In: Faella, M., Murano, A. (eds.) GandALF. EPTCS, vol. 96, pp. 71–84 (2012)
2. Bresolin, D., Montanari, A., Puppis, G.: A theory of ultimately periodic languages and automata with an application to time granularity. Acta Informatica **46**(5), 331–360 (2009)
3. Büchi, J.R.: On a decision method in restricted second order arithmetic. In: Nagel, E., Suppes, P., Tarski, A. (eds.) Proceedings of the 1960 International Congress on Logic, Methodology and Philosophy of Science (LMPS 1960), pp. 1–11. Stanford University Press, June 1962
4. Calbrix, H., Nivat, M., Podelski, A.: Ultimately periodic words of rational omega-languages. In: Brookes, S., Main, M., Melton, A., Mislove, M., Schmidt, D. (eds.) MFPS 1993. LNCS, vol. 802, pp. 554–566. Springer, Heidelberg (1994). doi:10.1007/3-540-58027-1_27
5. Ehlers, R.: Minimising deterministic Büchi automata precisely using SAT solving. In: Strichman, O., Szeider, S. (eds.) SAT 2010. LNCS, vol. 6175, pp. 326–332. Springer, Heidelberg (2010)
6. Ehlers, R., Finkbeiner, B.: On the virtue of patience: minimizing Büchi automata. In: Pol, J., Weber, M. (eds.) SPIN 2010. LNCS, vol. 6349, pp. 129–145. Springer, Heidelberg (2010)
7. Farzan, A., Chen, Y.-F., Clarke, E.M., Tsay, Y.-K., Wang, B.-Y.: Extending automated compositional verification to the full class of omega-regular languages. In: Ramakrishnan, C.R., Rehof, J. (eds.) TACAS 2008. LNCS, vol. 4963, pp. 2–17. Springer, Heidelberg (2008)
8. Henriksen, J.G., Jensen, J., Jørgensen, M., Klarlund, N., Paige, B., Rauhe, T., Sandholm, A.: Mona: monadic second-order logic in practice. In: Brinksma, E., Cleaveland, W.R., Larsen, K.G., Margaria, T., Steffen, B. (eds.) TACAS 1995. LNCS, vol. 1019, pp. 89–110. Springer, Heidelberg (1995)
9. Hopcroft, J.E.: An $n \log n$ algorithm for minimizing states in a finite automaton. Technical report CS-TR-71-190, Stanford University (1971)
10. Klarlund, N., Møller, A.: MONA implementation secrets. In: Yu, S., Păun, A. (eds.) CIAA 2000. LNCS, vol. 2088, pp. 571–586. Springer, Heidelberg (2001)
11. Kozen, D.: Lower bounds for natural proof systems. In: FOCS, pp. 254–266. IEEE Computer Society (1977)
12. Schewe, S.: Minimisation of deterministic parity and buchi automata and relative minimisation of deterministic finite automata. CoRR, abs/1007.1333 (2010)
13. Tsai, M.-H., Fogarty, S., Vardi, M.Y., Tsay, Y.-K.: State of Büchi complementation. In: Domaratzki, M., Salomaa, K. (eds.) CIAA 2010. LNCS, vol. 6482, pp. 261–271. Springer, Heidelberg (2011)

Property Preservation for Extension Patterns of State Transition Diagrams

Christian Prehofer[(⊠)]

Fortiss GmbH, Munich, Germany
prehofer@fortiss.org

Abstract. In this paper, we consider extensions of state machines with additional functionality. We analyze how typical safety or liveness properties are affected when extending or refining the model. We identify several classes of extensions where properties are preserved. The extensions include adding new transitions at a state, refining transitions, as well as adding failure cases and adding additional, new functionality. We propose new concepts for refinements based on elimination of added behavior with context to capture property-preserving extensions in a precise and (mostly) syntactic way.

1 Introduction

State transition diagrams (in short: SD) are used in various forms to design software components, e.g., modeling a software component which interacts with the environment based on events. In this paper, we consider property preservation when extending state transition diagrams by adding new functionality or by adding implementation detail. The idea is to start with a high-level model which is extended incrementally towards an actual implementation by refining and adding appropriate features. Each extension step extends an SD by adding new states and transitions. On a conceptual level, the approach is similar to work on aspect- and feature-based programming languages, where generic results for specific patterns exist (see [1]).

As an example consider the extension in Fig. 1, which adds a snooze feature to an alarm clock. In the state machine, transitions are of the form i/o, where i is an input event, and o is a sequence of output events. By convention, we show the added elements of the new feature in bold text and thicker lines. In this example, a typical property is that the alarm rings when it is set and that it stops eventually. It is easy to see that the behavior of the original base SD is preserved if no *Snooze* event occurs. Also, if the snooze feature is used, it will eventually return to *AlarmOff*, unless the snooze feature is used infinitely often.

We start with a base model of a system, where the key properties of the system can be captured formally, as in the example above. We use a behavioral semantics based on the observable traces of input and output events, respectively. Behavior preservation means that the resulting output trace is unchanged for all input streams, possibly under some abstraction.

© Springer International Publishing Switzerland 2016
E. Ábrahám and M. Huisman (Eds.): IFM 2016, LNCS 9681, pp. 260–274, 2016.
DOI: 10.1007/978-3-319-33693-0_17

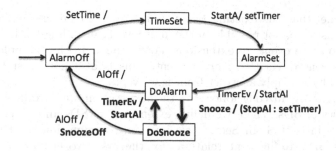

Fig. 1. Alarm extended by a snooze feature

The focus here is on extensions which add behavior, but do not change the existing behavior. This means that the output behavior, which is defined explicitly in a SD, does not change under an extension. We do however permit additional behavior, both for the input and the output. This means that after some period with new, added behavior, the system returns to the old behavior. For this, we consider abstractions to eliminate such added behavior and identify several new cases for this.

We identify here four classes of extensions where new behavior is added but still some properties are preserved. The first class consists of extensions which add behavior by new transitions at a state, as e.g. shown in Fig. 1. The second pattern refines transitions, i.e. details the behavior of some event. The third one is adding failure cases and the fourth one is adding other additional and new functionality. The last one preserves the fewest properties but has broader applicability.

Prior works on SD refinement has covered basic cases like adding states or adding/removing transitions, e.g. [2–5]. Recent work on patterns for state machine refinement considers simpler state machines without output events [6], which considerably simplifies refinement compared to our setting. The work in [7] has developed the case of the first pattern, yet in a simplified form where the abstractions are easily recognized by specific events. Here, we generalize this and also consider more patterns.

The main goal in this paper is to capture semantics-preserving extensions in a syntactic way. To relate the extended SD and the base SD, we devise a new abstraction mechanism to abstract from the behavior added by an extension. While many existing approaches simply abstract from new events (e.g. [4,8,9]), we need to carefully consider the context when an execution enters and leaves an extension.

In particular, we cover extensions which modify or refine transitions and consider the context of transitions to ensure refinement. For instance, in Fig. 1, there is a transition from the new state *DoSnooze* to *AlarmOff* with event *AlOff*. This is a refinement as there is a similar, corresponding transition from the state *DoAlarm*. In this case, we can map the behavior of the extended SD to the original. For this, we use context-based elimination on the trace level to ensure refinement, i.e. that the existing behavior is preserved under the abstraction. This is, for instance, not possible in the above work, including [7]. Furthermore, we permit to reuse events in extensions. For instance, in the example in Fig. 1, the timer is reused via the *StartAl* event. This is also not possible in other approaches which simply abstract from new events.

The paper is organized as follows. In the next section, we introduce the syntax and semantics of SDs. Then, we define extensions on SDs and different classes of extensions in Sect. 3. In Sect. 4, we introduce assumptions and refinement relations for SDs. Refinement relations for the first two classes of extensions are discussed in Sect. 4.1. In Sect. 5, we discuss what kinds of properties are preserved by these classes of extensions.

2   State Transition Diagrams and Extensions

We model software systems by SDs, which are deterministic w.r.t. the input, as defined below.

Definition 1. *An SD is a tuple (St, s_0, I, O, T) consisting off*

(i) a set of states St, with an initial state $s_0 \in St$,
(ii) a set of input events I, which is disjoint from a set of output events O,
(iii) A partial transition function $T : St \times I \mapsto St \times O^*$.

For convenience, we often omit the initial state and just write (St, I, O, T). We denote transitions as i/o, where o is a sequence of output events.

Our semantic model employs an external black-box view of the system. It is based on the events from the outside that trigger transitions. In other words, only the observed input and output events are considered, not the internal states. A possible execution can be specified by a trace, consisting of the sequence of input events and the resulting output of the SD, as detailed below.

The set of all input sequences is denoted as the set of input streams $I^\omega = I^* \cup I^\infty$, including finite I^* and infinite streams I^∞. As each output of a transition yields a sequence of events, we have (possibly infinite) sequences over finite event sequences as output traces, which is defined as $(O^*)^\omega$. **Traces** of the form (i_s, o_s) describe the behavior of an SD for an input sequence $i_s \in I^\omega$ and the corresponding output with $o_s \in (O^*)^\omega$.

We denote the empty stream as _ and write $i_s : i'_s$ to concatenate two streams, where i_s is assumed to be finite. Similarly, $a : i_s$ creates a stream from an element a by appending the stream i_s. When clear from the context, we often write just a instead of $a : \_$. We denote by $I \backslash In$ the elimination of elements of In from I and by $O + I$ the union of disjoint sets.

Assuming a stream $i_s = i_1 : i_2 : i_3, \ldots$, we write $i_s[n] = i_n$ for the nth-element, and $i_s[n \ldots] = i_n : i_{n+1}, \ldots$ for the suffix at position n. We extend this notation to traces accordingly, i.e. $t[n]$ is defined as $(i_s[n], o_s[n])$. Thus, $o_s[n]$ is the corresponding sequence of output events for the input $i_s[n]$.

For an SD S and a finite or infinite input stream i_s, we say S is **defined** for i_s, if there is always a defined transition (specified by T) for each input event in

i_s when executing S with input i_s. This is written as $Def(S, i_s)$. Note that we use input-enabled semantics of SDs, which means any input is possible at any time. Thus we use the notion of definedness and later use assumptions to limit the input.

We write $S(i_s)$ to denote the output of S for i_S if S is defined for i_s. Two SDs are considered equivalent if they behave equivalently for all inputs, i.e. produce the same output.

In addition to the functional view, we also use the notation

$$t' = (i_1/o_1) :: (i_2/o_2) :: \ldots$$

to denote traces of elements with inputs i_k and output sequences o_k. We can easily extract the corresponding input stream via $In(t') = i_1 : i_2 : \ldots$ and $Out(t') = o_1 : o_2 : \ldots$. Then, application of such a trace to a SD S is defined as $S(t')$ iff $S(In(t')) = Out(t')$.

For instance in Fig. 1, a possible trace t_{ex}, with input events above the corresponding output events, is shown in the table below.

Input	SetTime	StartA	TimerEv	Snooze	TimerEv	AlOff
Output		setTimer	StartAl	StopAl : setTimer	StartAl	

2.1 Extensions of State Transition Diagrams

When adding new features to an SD, we use the following notion of syntactic extensions of SDs. An **extension** is an SD over (St, I, O, T), but without initial states as extensions are not to be executed (before adding them to another SD). While we permit any syntactically valid extensions in the definition below, this will be restricted further below to analyze property preservation on the behavioral level.

An SD $S = (St, I, O, T)$ is extended by a **pure extension** $E = (St + St', I + I', O + O', T')$ resulting in $S' = (St + St', I + I', O + O', T + T')$, assuming T and T' are disjoint and S' is a valid SD.

Thus extensions result from adding new states, transitions, events of E to S. For convenience we treat T as a set of transitions, hence $T + T'$ is the union of transition sets. The transitions in E can use events in S, but they cannot redefine or overwrite existing transitions in S, as for each state only one transition with a specific input event i is permitted.

Examples of extensions are shown via the bold states and transitions, e.g. in Fig. 1. An extension can be seen as a "partial SD" with states and transitions, but no initial states. For instance, if an extension includes a transition from state s to s', these two states may be added by E or may be in S.

For transition refinement, we need to extend the above definition, as we also need to change transitions. A **transition extension** is defined as a modification of a transition which changes destination state and adds output events. Formally, an SD $S = (St, I, O, T)$ with a transition i/o from state s is extended by a (transition) extension E, if E is of the form $E = (St + St', I + I', O + O', T' + \{(i/(o : e))\})$ and E is an extension of $S = (St, I, O, T \setminus \{(i/o)\})$.

As above, we show in our graphical notation only the added events in bold and only show the new destination state. An example of a transition refinement is shown in Fig. 2, where the transition triggered by *SetTime* is extended (wrt the base SD in Fig. 1).

3   Extension Patterns of State Transition Diagrams

In the following, we introduce several patterns for extending SDs. The goal is to identify classes of extensions for which we can determine that certain properties are preserved, as discussed below.

We first define a property on extensions to identify an extension on the trace level by trigger events. The simplest case is that an extension adds completely new transitions, which are marked by entry and exit events (as in [7]). In addition to the entry and exit events, we will also use a "context" of events, which is shared by the original SD and the extension. This means that the extension only modifies some transitions, e.g. via a transition refinement, for the entry event. For exit events, we will also permit such a "shared transition". In this case, we need to ensure that the original and the extended SD end up in the same state. This is needed to ensure the behavior after the traversal of the extension is identical to the case of an execution in the base SD.

Definition 2. *Assume an SD $S = (St, I, O, T)$ as well as an extension E with events (I', O'). Assume further there is a set of disjoint **entry end exit events** $E_{en}, E_{ex}, \subseteq (I' \setminus I) + (O' \setminus O)$. We say that the extension E is **entry-exit triggered**, if for each transition in E from a state s to state t with input event i and output sequence o the following conditions hold:*

- *If $s \in St$, then i or o include an element from E_{en} (entry transition).*
- *If $t \in St$, then i or o include an element from E_{ex} (exit transition).*

This definition essentially says that an extension is always entered with an entry event and, correspondingly, returning to the old SD with exit events.

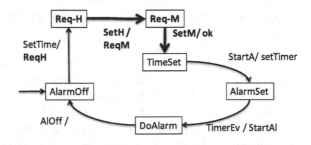

Fig. 2. Alarm with a refinement of transition *SetTime*

E.g. *Snooze* is an entry trigger in the example of Fig. 1. In this way, we will be able to recognize extensions on the trace level. We also call a transition **entry transition**, if it is triggered by an (entry) event. Similarly, an **exit transition** must have an element of E_{ex} as trigger event.

We introduce in the following four patterns of SD extensions of an SD S. For these, we later consider refinement concepts and property preservation. The first pattern, extension at state, adds transitions at one state s, which lead back to s (within some context as detailed later). Thus, the behavior proceeds as before, after the extension is traversed. There are cases where we can permit that the extension leads to other states. A typical case is a transition extension, which is the second pattern.

If an extension E of S does not lead back to the expected state s, but to a different one, say s', we can permit this in some case. This is the case if both S and E have transitions to s' with the same events, plus some exit trigger in E. As an example consider the snooze example Fig. 1. Here, the event *AlOff* leads to the *AlarmOff* state, both from the extension as well as in the original state. Thus, we can achieve behavior preservation for this case, as both cases lead to the same state. For this we define the following:

For a transition i/o_n from s to s' in an SD S, we say that a transition $i/(o_n : e)$ is an **exit transition with context from** s with trigger e in E, if it leads to state s' as well.

Definition 3. *Assume an SD $S = (St, I, O, V, T)$ and an entry-exit triggered, pure extension E with events (I', O'). Then E is an **extensions at a state** s if all entry transitions start at s and all exit transition must return to s, or have a context in S from state s.*

Extensions at a state s add new behavior local to some state s in St. This means adding new transitions from s triggered by an entry event e, as well as new states. For such extensions, behavior is local to the state as the control flow in the extension may return only to s and does not change the control flow beyond this. Such an extension typically adds optional behavior at some state, which may however loop or terminate. Hence it may not return to the base SD. For instance, in Fig. 1, the state *DoAlarm* is extended by the snooze feature.

A transition refinement, defined next, details the behavior of a transition from state s to s'. Note that we will use the term refinement on SDs below in terms of behavior preservation, which is different from the syntactic refinement presented here. The idea is to refine a transition into several transitions. This is initiated by an output event from the SD S itself, here e, in contrast to other cases which are externally triggered. Based on this trigger, the external environment may adapt to the new behavior. As an example for a transition refinement consider the base SD in Figs. 1 and 2, where the transition triggered by *SetTime* is refined to enter hours (state *Req-H*) and minutes (state *Req-M*).

Definition 4. *Assume an SD $S = (St, I, O, T)$ and an entry-exit triggered extension E with an update of a transition $tr \in T$. Assume $tr = i/o$ is a transition from state s to s' in S. Then S' is a **(syntactic) transition refinement** of S by E if*

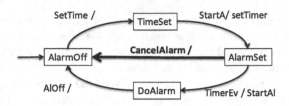

Fig. 3. Alarm with added cancel transition

– the extension E includes a transition refinement for tr, concatenating a new entry event e to the output o, and
– all exit transitions lead to the state s' or they have a context in S from s'.

The next pattern adds failure cases.

Definition 5. *Assume an SD S = (St, I, O, T) and a pure extension E with events (I', O'). Then E is **adding failure cases** if it adds one new transition, triggered by a new event not in I. This transition must lead back to the initial state s_0.*

For instance, in Fig. 3, a cancel transition is introduced. The other remaining pattern of extensions adds other functionality, which must however be triggered by new entry events. We only assume that this new behavior is initiated by new events, after which the behavior may change. This means to add behavior which is different from the original behavior.

Definition 6. *Assume an SD S = (St, I, O, V, tr) and a pure extension E with events (I', O'). Then E adds **additional functionality**, if all new transitions which start at states of St are triggered with new events (not in I).*

It is easy to see that the above three patterns are instances of this case. This pattern has broader applicability, but will also preserve fewer properties. As an example for an added functionality consider Fig. 4, where a new countdown (CD) feature is added, which works alternatively to the alarm clock.

4   Assumptions on SDs and Refinement

Generally speaking, the goal of refinement is to extend an SD while preserving behavior and compatibility. An important aspect of refinement is to consider the permitted inputs. For instance, assume-guarantee specifications [10] can be used to specify which "guarantees" hold for the permitted inputs (under the assumptions).

Here, we use assumptions to specify the permitted input. In general, assumptions can be used for two different reasons. We can either exclude unwanted cases or handle unspecified cases. Unspecified cases are cases which shall be defined in a later phase by incremental refinement, while unwanted cases must be avoided by the environment and are not allowed. The main purpose of assumptions in our treatment of extensions is to specify which inputs are allowed in what phase of a SD execution. For instance, when traversing an extension, we may only permit specific events.

We will use predicates over finite and infinite streams. We denote assumptions as a predicate A where $A(i)$ is a Boolean value over a stream i. Assuming an SD S and an assumption A, we write

$$A/S$$

or $A/Def(S)$, which then denotes that S is defined for inputs i, i.e. $Def(i_s)$, whenever $A(i_s)$ holds.

Regarding refinement, we consider in the following a notion with equality of the output traces: Assuming a specification A/S, then A'/S' is a **refinement** of A/S, if $A(i_s) \implies A'(i_s)$ for all i_s, and $A(i_s)$ implies $S(i_s) = S'(i_s)$.

This means that S and S' must behave identically for the input permitted by A for S', i.e. when A holds. In other words, when S' is restricted to the input for A for S, they behave the same. Internally, the two SDs may differ in states and transitions.

A typical, basic case of refinement is what we call (backwards) compatibility: Assume A/S and S' is an extension of S, then A/S' is called **(backwards) compatibility**, assuming that A only permits inputs over I. Backwards compatibility means that a system behaves identical to the original system, as long as no new events occur in the input. In other words, the system behaves as before for the "old" input specified by A.

4.1   Elimination-Based Refinement with Context

In the following, we detail our approach to refinement based on behavior elimination. The idea is to eliminate the behavior of the newly added features on the trace level, in order to compare the extended SD with the original one. Many typical notions of abstraction or refinement only abstract from newly added events (e.g. [4,8,9]), which is very easy to define. Here, we eliminate larger trace segments which correspond to the behavior of extensions.

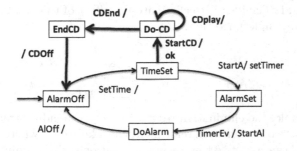

Fig. 4. Alarm with added countdown functionality

As discussed above, the point is that extensions can be recognized either by new input events, or by adding additional output. This holds for both start and end of a trace segment corresponding to a trace in an extension. These trace segments may also share some "context" with the original system. We have two cases here. The simple case is that the start and end of the trace segment are identified by a new entry event. The other case is adding new output events. For entry events, this corresponds to a transition refinement. For the exit case, this may be the case of an exit transition with context.

To formalize the notion of extensions, we use *partial traces* with an empty input event of the form $(\_, o)$. Note that these are not suitable for execution. To merge streams with overlaps, we define $+$ to merge two stream elements: $(i/o) + (i'/o') = (i/(o : o'))$ if $i' = \_$, and $(i/o) :: (i'/o')$ otherwise. Thus we merge transitions with empty input with the subsequent transition. This merge operations extends canonically to longer traces.

We assume in the following an SD S with events (I, O) is extended by E to S' with events (I', O').

Definition 7 (Trace extension step). *Assume a set of trigger events T_i from $I'\backslash I$ and T_o from $O'\backslash O$. Let $t = s :: c :: c' :: s'$ be a trace of S. Then a* **trace extension** *of t over S' is a trace*

$$t' = s :: (c + tr) :: e :: (c' + tr') :: s',$$

with contexts c and c', where $(c + tr) :: e :: (c' + tr')$ is a traversal in E, s and e are finite traces, and c, c' are finite, partial traces. We assume e has no trigger events, and tr, tr' are single transitions with a trigger event. If there is an infinite traversal $(c + tr) :: e$ in E, then also $t' = s :: (c + tr) :: e$ is a trace extension.

We call c and c' contexts, as these are the parts which are shared in both S and the extension E. Note that in a trace t, trace extensions do not overlap as e has no trigger events. Hence, we define an **elimination**, denoted as

$$elim(t)$$

as the removal of all trace extensions. Similarly, the set $ext(t)$ is defined as all traversals of E in t, as defined above. Note that this set may be infinite.

As an example, we continue with the above trace t_{ex} from Sect. 2 for the alarm SD in Fig. 1. The idea is to eliminate the effect of the new snooze feature, which we show by underlined text:

Input:	SetTime	StartA	TimerEv	Snooze	TimerEv	AlOff
Output:	_	setTimer	StartAl	(stopAl :setTimer	StartAl	SnozzeOff

In this example, the elimination results in a corresponding trace of the base SD. As an example of a transition refinement consider Fig. 2, where the transition with input *SetTime* is refined by several transitions. The elimination removes the effect of the new transition, which we show by underlined text in the following trace:

Input:	SetTime	SetH	SetM	StartA	TimerEv	AlOff
Output:	ReqH	ReqM	ok	setTimer	StartAl	

Note that the elimination here removes only the event $ReqM$, which is the trigger event, from the output sequence corresponding to the input $SetTime$ (and the empty sequence _ remains). If an extension terminates under specific assumptions, then we can establish a stronger property.

Definition 8 (Elimination-based Refinement). *Assume S, S' and an entry-exit triggered extension E as above. The extended system A'/S' is a **weak elimination-based refinement** of A/S, if $A(i_s) \implies A'(i_s)$ for all i_s, and if for all traces t' in A'/S', $elim(t')$ is a trace in A/S. Furthermore, A'/S' is a **(strong) elimination-based refinement of** A/S, if any traversal in an extension terminates in A'/S'.*

The notion of elimination-based refinement states that elimination of traces in S' yields traces in S. We say property $A_{A,AE}$ **preserves** A and AE, if A implies $A_{A,AE}$ and $A_{A,AE}(t)$ implies $A(elim(t))$ and AE holds for all elements of $ext(t)$.

For an extension E of S to S', we say AE/E **terminates** if there is no infinite traversal through E which is permitted by AE. For a property A over streams, we say A is **input-consistent**, if $A(i_s)$ implies $A(i'_s)$ for all prefixes i'_s of i_s. This assumption is needed for weak refinements, as an extension may not terminate. Consider an input i which is permitted for the base SD. Then, in an extension an entry event may occur at i', which is a prefix of i. The elimination on the trace of the extended SD will cut off the trace after i' in case of divergence. For the refinement to hold, i' must then also be permitted in the assumptions for the base SD. Based on this, we can now show the main refinement result:

Theorem 1 (Refinement). *Assume S is extended to S' with an extension at state or transition refinement E, and A is an input-consistent property. If A/S, AE/E and $A_{A,AE}$ is a property that preserves A and AE, then $A_{A,AE}/S'$ is a weak refinement of A/S. Furthermore, if there are no infinite sequences of extension traversals in $A_{A,AE}/S'$ with empty entry and exit contexts, then $A_{A,AE}/S'$ is a strong refinement of S.*

We should note that assumptions are needed to ensure termination (for strong refinement), and to ensure that the executions are defined. For weak refinement, it is often possible to take all input streams where S' is defined and which preserve A. For strong refinement, termination must be ensured by assumptions, if there are cases where extensions may loop.

5   SD Extensions and Property Preservation

In the last section, we have presented refinement results for the four classes of SD extensions. These results are now used to show what kinds of properties are

Table 1. Identified cases of property preservation under SD extensions

	Simple response (liveness)	Simple reachability (liveness)	Invariants on events (safety)	Compatibility
Extension at states	In case of strong refinement with Theorem 2		If holds for extension	+
Transition refinement	In case of strong refinement with Theorem 2		If holds for extension	o
Adding failures	o	+	+	+
Additional functionality	o	o	If holds for extension	+

preserved under such extensions. First, we discuss how to formalize properties and then present a classification of properties. As we consider the externally visible system behavior, we specify properties over the observed traces. For this purpose, we use basic linear temporal operators, following [11].

We assume in the following traces of the form $t = (i, o)$ over an SD S with assumptions A over I and O and with A/S as above. Assume P, Q are predicates over transitions or the form i/o, where we write $P(i, o)$. Based on properties on individual transitions or positions in a trace, we can introduce the usual temporal operators. First, $\Box P$, or "always P" holds for a trace t at position n, if P holds for $t[n + m]$ for all $m = 0, 1, 2, \ldots$. For an infinite trace t, $\Diamond P$, or "eventually P", holds at some position n, if $P(t[m])$ holds for some valid $m \geq n$. For a finite trace t, $\Diamond P$ holds for a valid position n in t, if there is an execution of A/S with a trace t', such that t is a prefix of t' (or identical) for which the property holds.

These temporal formulae express properties over traces, and easily extend to sets of traces. We only use basic property patterns. For a full definition of linear temporal logic we refer to related work [11]. For instance, $\Box(P \implies \Diamond Q)$ means that in any position of a traces, if P holds, Q will hold eventually.

In examples, we may just write the name of an event to denote the property that this event occurs (at some position). As an example, we may write $\Box(setTimer \implies \Diamond AlOff)$, which means that the event $setTimer$ is always followed by $AlOff$.

For properties, there is a very useful classification in [12], which also evaluates how often these properties are used in practical applications. We focus on basic "leads to" or response properties, as well as invariants, which cover a large class of properties used in typical specifications as shown in [12]. As discussed in [12], the property may occur in combination with different scopes, which define events which limit the scope of the property. For simplicity and lack of space, we focus on such basic properties without scopes. This is also why we do not introduce full temporal logic in this section.

We show in the top line of Table 1 four typical classes of properties and identify when all properties of a specific class are preserved. We first explain the column entries. In the first column, **simple response** refers to properties of the form $\Box(P \implies \Diamond Q)$, where some event specified by P is always followed by some events specified by Q. This is also called "leads to" property. In the second column, **simple reachability** refers to events which are reached from the initial state. Formally, we have $\Diamond Q$. This is called existence in [12]. More generally, universal reachability means that a property can be reached from any position. This is formalized as $\Box\Diamond Q$ and is a typical liveness property. For instance, in our alarm example $\Box\Diamond setTime$ expresses that it is always possible to set the time again, which means that the system does not stop.

In the following, we explain the entries in the table. Note that "+" means property preservation and "o" means no generic results (individual case needs to be considered). In the other cases, additional conditions for property preservation are stated.

For simple response and reachability, the table expresses that strong refinement based on Theorem 1 can be used for basic response and reachability properties, assuming that the extension terminates. This is shown in the following theorem. The main point is that strong refinement can add new segments to a trace t, but eventually the trace is completely executed (which does not hold for weak refinement).

Theorem 2 (Property Preservation). *Assume $S = (St, I, O, T)$ is extended to S' with extension at state or transition refinement E, A/S, AE/E and $A_{A,AE}/S'$ is a strong refinement of A/S. Further, assume P and Q are properties over I and O. Then simple response ($\Box(P \implies \Diamond Q)$) and simple reachability ($\Box\Diamond Q$) properties hold for $A_{A,AE}/S'$, if they hold for A/S and AE/E.*

For instance, for the alarm plus snooze example in Fig. 1, we have strong refinement if we assume the termination of the added snooze feature. This avoids the cases that the (terminating) feature is triggered infinitely often in the state *DoAlarm*. Formally, consider an assumption predicate P_a for which the basic alarm SD is defined. Furthermore, assume a predicate P_s for which the extension snooze is defined and no infinite repetition of $(Snooze : TimerEv)$ is permitted. Under P_s and P_a, we can show that alarm extended by snooze is a strong refinement of the alarm SD. The intuition is that only traces are possible where there is no infinite loop in state *DoAlarm*. Then,

$$\Box(setTime \implies \Diamond AlOff)$$

is preserved by this extension. Thus it holds for alarm plus snooze, if it holds for the basic alarm SD. Note that the assumptions may not permit the *stopalarm* event, and thus it may not hold for the base SD.

Furthermore, reachability is also preserved by our notion of adding failures, as these extensions return to the initial state. For the basic alarm plus Cancel Alarm example, this means that the following property is preserved:

$$\Box\Diamond AlOff$$

This means that it is always possible that the alarm is stopped, and this is preserved by the extension.

By invariants on events we refer to safety properties which hold for all executions, but can be identified on a local basis (not using implication as above) This is typically of the form $\square P$. An invariant on events can express that some specific output event does not happen. In [12], this corresponds to universality or absence patterns. Such invariants can be checked syntactically for extensions, just by checking which events may occur. Thus, they are modular with respect to conservative SD extensions. This also holds by construction for failure cases, as these reset the variables and return to the initial state. Note that we assume here that the invariant does not refer to the newly added error event. In that case, an invariant could simply say that some error event (e.g. $CancelAl$) does not occur, which is not preserved.

In the last column, (backwards) compatibility, as defined above, means that the behavior is not changed if the extension is not used, i.e. there is no input which triggers it. If the extension is triggered by an input event, it is easy to see that properties are preserved. On the other hand transition refinements are triggered internally by new outputs, thus properties may not be preserved.

For more complex properties, more detailed analysis may be needed. For instance, in case a property says that a eventually happens, but always before b, this may not be preserved by an extension of one of the first two kinds, as the extension may add an output b. Also, assumptions can restrict inputs and can hence ensure that certain properties hold; it is open if such generic results are possible.

6   Related Work

There is recent work on refinement on algebraic state machine models, which follows a similar approach by identifying some classes of refinements [6]. This approach considers state machines (and traces) with input events only, i.e. no output events. This clearly simplifies refinement and does not cover the cases of extending or modifying transitions with new output events. Also, [6] does not discuss what kind of properties may be preserved.

The contribution of this paper is a set of refinement patterns in a new formal framework for elimination-based refinement, plus an analysis of property preservation. Regarding the refinement patterns, this paper is more general as the work in [7], which only covers refinement on states in a more limited form. The work in [13] has considered transition refinement for non-deterministic SDs using chaos-based semantics. In particular, this semantics makes it difficult to reason about definedness and termination, as done here. In addition, we consider here also failure cases, which were absent in [13]. Also, for both, no detailed analysis of property preservation is presented.

There exists considerable work on refinement on various kinds of state-based models. Most of these works performs abstraction by simple elimination of new events, e.g. [4,8,9]. This concept is used in many other works on refinement, not limited only to state machines, and is often generalized to refinement mappings of events or data structures. This permits refinement or simulation relations based on abstraction from new events. Other such refinement and simulation techniques for SD-like models can e.g. be found in [14,15]. For a more comprehensive handling of new events, we also refer to recent work in [16]. This work is based on Event-B and discusses different ways of handling new events. It does however not discuss refinement patterns on state machines nor preservation of properties for such. Similarly, [17] provides general refinement concepts, but no patterns and property preservation.

Earlier works on calculi for statechart refinement [2–4] have developed several rules for refinement, which correspond to our case of adding additional functionality and thus do not address the other patterns.

7 Conclusions

The goal of this paper was to identify practical cases of SD extensions which do not modify the behavior of the original SD, under some reasonable assumptions. We have identified four patterns of typical SD extensions where we can capture the impact of the extensions on the behavior of the SD for certain classes of properties. A main point is that these patterns can be identified syntactically.

To establish property preservation, we have defined new refinement relations for extensions at a state, transition refinement and failure cases. Furthermore, we have formalized refinement in a common framework. The framework is based on elimination-based refinement with contexts, which generalizes existing refinement relations. In particular, we use context, i.e. overlaps of the base SD and the extension on the trace level, for the abstraction relation. This is needed for transition refinements and also in case the extension returns to other states.

While the examples and refinement cases may appear simple, existing patterns in the literature do not cover the cases considered here. Existing, simpler forms of abstraction and refinement do not easily cover the notion of refinement here for several reasons. One reason is that extensions can reuse existing events, which is useful for practical application but not permitted in many formalisms. Secondly, we allow modification and refinement of transitions, which can be captured by elimination with context to relate the old and new, refined behavior. Furthermore, we use assumptions to formalize under what conditions an extension may diverge, thus permitting extensions to diverge or abort.

For these extensions, we have discussed property preservation for typical patterns of properties in a systematic way. In many cases, specific kinds of properties are preserved by an extension. In this way, behavior preserving refinements can be created automatically based on simple, mostly syntactic criteria, which is important for practical application in tools. If extensions may loop or diverge, we may need assumptions to ensure that the traversals return to the base SD in order to establish strong refinement. The idea is that a user can simply add an extension, following the above classes, without the need to explicitly formalize some abstraction or simulation relation.

References

1. Djoko, S.D., Douence, R., Fradet, P.: Aspects preserving properties. In: Proceedings of the ACM SIGPLAN Symposium on Partial Evaluation and Semantics-Based Program Manipulation, PEPM 2008, pp. 135–145. ACM, New York, NY, USA (2008)
2. Klein, C., Prehofer, C., Rumpe, B.: Feature specification and refinement with state transition diagrams. In: Fourth IEEE Workshop on Feature Interactions in Telecommunications Networks and Distributed, pp. 284–297. IOS Press (1997)
3. Rumpe, B., Klein, C.: Automata describing object behavior. In: Specification of Behavioral Semantics in Object-Oriented Information Modeling, pp. 265–286. Kluwer Academic Publishers, Berlin (1996)
4. Scholz, P.: Incremental design of statechart specifications. Sci. Comput. Program. **40**(1), 119–145 (2001). doi:10.1016/S0167-6423(00)00026-5
5. Schönborn, J., Kyas, M.: Refinement patterns for hierarchical UML state machines. In: Arbab, F., Sirjani, M. (eds.) FSEN 2009. LNCS, vol. 5961, pp. 371–386. Springer, Heidelberg (2010)
6. Frappier, M., Gervais, F., Laleau, R., Milhau, J.: Refinement patterns for ASTDs. In: Formal Aspects of Computing, pp. 1–23 (2013)
7. Prehofer, C.: Assume-guarantee specifications of state transition diagrams for behavioral refinement. In: Johnsen, E.B., Petre, L. (eds.) IFM 2013. LNCS, vol. 7940, pp. 31–45. Springer, Heidelberg (2013)
8. Reeve, G., Reeves, S.: Logic and refinement for charts. In: Proceedings of the 29th Australasian Computer Science Conference, ACSC 2006, vol. 48, pp. 13–23. Australian Computer Society Inc., Darlinghurst, Australia (2006)
9. Broy, M.: Multifunctional software systems: structured modeling and specification of functional requirements. Sci. Comput. Program. **75**(12), 1193–1214 (2010)
10. Alfaro, L., Henzinger, T.: Interface-based design. In: Broy, M., Grünbauer, J., Harel, D., Hoare, T. (eds.) Engineering Theories of Software Intensive Systems. NATO Science Series, vol. 195, pp. 83–104. Springer, Heidelberg (2005)
11. Baier, C., Katoen, J.-P., et al.: Principles of Model Checking, vol. 26202649. MIT Press, Cambridge (2008)
12. Dwyer, M., Avrunin, G., Corbett, J.: Patterns in property specifications for finite-state verification. In: Proceedings of the 1999 International Conference on Software Engineering, pp. 411–420 (1999)
13. Prehofer, C., Scholz, P.: Behavioral refinement of non-deterministic state transition diagrams based on behavior elimination. In: Proceedings of the 17th International Software Product Line Conference Co-located Workshops, pp. 26–33. ACM, New York (2013)
14. Schrefl, M., Stumptner, M.: Behavior-consistent specialization of object life cycles. ACM Trans. Softw. Eng. Methodol. **11**(1), 92–148 (2002)
15. Simons, A.J.H., Stannett, M.P., Bogdanov, K.E., Holcombe, W.M.L.: Plug and play safely: rules for behavioural compatibility. In: IProceedings of 6th IASTED International Conference on Software Engineering and Applications, pp. 263–268 (2002)
16. Schneider, S., Treharne, H., Wehrheim, H.: The behavioural semantics of event-b refinement. Formal Aspects Comput. **26**(2), 1–30 (2012)
17. Harbird, L., Galloway, A., Paige, R.F.: Towards a model-based refinement process for contractual state machines. In: 13th IEEE International Symposium on Object/Component/Service-Oriented Real-Time Distributed Computing Workshops (ISORCW), pp. 108–115. IEEE (2010)

Symbolic Reachability Analysis of B Through ProB and LTSmin

Jens Bendisposto[1], Philipp Körner[1], Michael Leuschel[1], Jeroen Meijer[2]([✉]),
Jaco van de Pol[2], Helen Treharne[3], and Jorden Whitefield[3]

[1] Institut für Informatik, Heinrich Heine University Düsseldorf, Düsseldorf, Germany
{bendisposto,leuschel}@cs.uni-duesseldorf.de,
p.koerner@uni-duesseldorf.de
[2] Formal Methods and Tools, University of Twente, Enschede, The Netherlands
{j.j.g.meijer,j.c.vandepol}@utwente.nl
[3] Department of Computer Science, University of Surrey, Guildford, UK
{h.treharne,j.whitefield}@surrey.ac.uk

Abstract. We present a symbolic reachability analysis approach for
B that can provide a significant speedup over traditional explicit state
model checking. The symbolic analysis is implemented by linking ProB
to LTSmin, a high-performance language independent model checker.
The link is achieved via LTSmin's Pins interface, allowing ProB to benefit from LTSmin's analysis algorithms, while only writing a few hundred
lines of glue-code, along with a bridge between ProB and C using ØMQ.
ProB supports model checking of several formal specification languages
such as B, Event-B, Z and Tla$^+$. Our experiments are based on a wide
variety of B-Method and Event-B models to demonstrate the efficiency of
the new link. Among the tested categories are state space generation and
deadlock detection; but action detection and invariant checking are also
feasible in principle. In many cases we observe speedups of several orders
of magnitude. We also compare the results with other approaches for
improving model checking, such as partial order reduction or symmetry
reduction. We thus provide a new scalable, symbolic analysis algorithm
for the B-Method and Event-B, along with a platform to integrate other
model checking improvements via LTSmin in the future.

Keywords: B-Method · Event-B · ProB · LTSmin · Symbolic
reachability

1 Introduction

In this paper we describe the process, technique and design decisions we made for
integrating the two tooling sets: LTSmin and ProB. Bicarregui et al. suggested,
in a review of projects which applied formal methods [6], that providing useable

---

J. Meijer—Supported by STW SUMBAT grant: 13859.
J. van de Pol—Supported by the 3TU.BSR project.
J. Whitefield—Partly supported by EPSRC grant: EP/M506655/1.

E. Ábrahám and M. Huisman (Eds.): IFM 2016, LNCS 9681, pp. 275–291, 2016.
DOI: 10.1007/978-3-319-33693-0_18

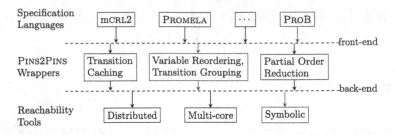

Fig. 1. Modular PINS architecture of LTSMIN [17]

tools remained a challenge. Recent use of the PROB tool in a rail system case study [16], where model checking large industrial sized complex specifications was performed, illustrated that there continues to be limitations with the tooling. Model checking CSP‖B [28] specifications in PROB was the original motivator for this research, and based on a promising initial exploration [30], this paper defines a systematic integration of the two tooling sets.

LTSMIN is a high-performance language-independent model checker that allows numerous modelling language front-ends to be connected to various analysis algorithms, through a common interface, as shown in Fig. 1. It offers a wide spectrum of parallel and symbolic algorithms to deal with the state space explosion of different verification problems. This connecting interface is called the PARTITIONED INTERFACE to the Next-State function (PINS), the basis of which consists of a state-vector definition, an initial state, a partitioned successor function (NEXTSTATE), and labelling functions [17]. It is through PINS that we have been able to leverage the PROB tool, therefore allowing us to take advantage of LTSMIN's algorithmic back-ends. In this paper we focus on the new PROB language front-end, the grouping of transitions, and the symbolic back-end. In Sect. 5 we also briefly discuss state variable orders.

PROB [19] is an animator and model checker for many different formal languages [26], including the classical B-Method [2], Event-B [1], CSP, CSP‖B, Z and TLA+. PROB can perform automatic or step by step animation of B machines, and can be used to systematically verify the behaviour of machines. The verification can identify states which do not meet the invariants, do not satisfy assertions or that deadlock. At the heart of PROB is a constraint solver, which enables the tool to animate and model check high-level specifications. The built-in model checker is a straightforward, explicit state model checker (albeit augmented with various features such as symmetry reduction [20] or partial order reduction [11]). The explicit state model checker TLC can also be used as a backend [12].

The purpose of this paper is to make use of the advanced features of the LTSMIN model checker, such as symbolic reachability analysis, by linking the PROB state exploration engine with LTSMIN. This is achieved through a C programming interface [4] within the PROB tool, allowing the representation of a state to be compatible for LTSMIN's consumption. In this paper the integration focuses on what is required in order to perform symbolic reachability analysis of B-Method and Event-B specifications. The contribution of this research is a new tool integration, which can be used as a platform for further extensions.

The paper is structured as follows: Sect. 2 presents an overview of the B-Method, a running example and an illustration of definitions of transition systems used by LTSMIN. Section 3 details the symbolic reachability analysis and Sect. 4 outlines the implementation details. Section 5 provides empirical results from performing reachability analysis benchmarking examples in PROB alone and using the new integration of the two tools. The paper concludes in Sect. 6 with reflections and future work.

2   Preliminaries: B-Method and Transition Systems

In this section we provide an overview of the B-Method and the foundations used within LTSMIN.

A B machine consists of a collection of clauses and a collection of operations. The **MACHINE** clause declares the abstract machine and gives it its name. The **VARIABLES** clause declares the variables that are used to carry the state information within the machine. The **INVARIANT** clause gives the type of the variables, and more generally it also contains any other constraints on the allowable machine states. The **INITIALISATION** clause determines the initial state(s) of the machine. Operations in a machine are events that change the state of a machine and can have input parameters. Operations can be of the form **SELECT** P **THEN** S **END** where P is a guard and S is the action part of the operation. The predicate P must include the type of any input variables and also give conditions on when the operation can be performed. When the guard of an operation is true then the operation is enabled and can be performed. If the guard is the simple predicate *true* then the operation form is simplified to **BEGIN** S **END**. An operation can also be of the form **PRE** P **THEN** S **END** so that the predicate is a precondition and if the operation is invoked outside its precondition then this results in a divergence (we do not illustrate this in our running example). Finally, the action part of an operation is a *generalised substitution*, which can consist of one or more assignment statements (in parallel) to update the state or assign to the output variables of an operation. Conditional statements and nondeterministic choice statements are also permitted in the body of the operation. The example in Fig. 2 illustrates the *MutexSimple* machine with three variables and five operations. Its initial state is deterministic and *wait* is set to MAXINT. For MAXINT=1 we get 4 states; the state space constructed by ProB can be found in Fig. 3. From the initial state only the guards for Enter and Leave are true. Following an Enter operation the value of the cs variable is true which means that the guard of the CS_Active operation is true and the system can indicate that it is in the critical section by performing the CS_Active operation.

The example presented could also be considered as an **Event-B** example since it is a simple guarded system. We do not elaborate further on the notation

```
1  MACHINE MutexSimple
2  VARIABLES cs, wait, finished
3  INVARIANT
4      cs: BOOL & wait: NATURAL & finished: NATURAL
5  INITIALISATION cs := FALSE || wait := MAXINT || finished := 0
6  OPERATIONS
7      Enter     = SELECT cs = FALSE & wait > 0 THEN
                    cs := TRUE || wait := wait − 1 END;
8      Exit      = SELECT cs = TRUE THEN
                    cs := FALSE || finished := finished + 1 END;
9      Leave     = BEGIN cs := FALSE END;
10     CS_Active = SELECT cs = TRUE THEN skip END;
11     Restart   = SELECT finished > 0 THEN
                    wait := wait + 1 || finished := finished − 1 END
12 END
```

Fig. 2. *MutexSimple* B-Method machine example

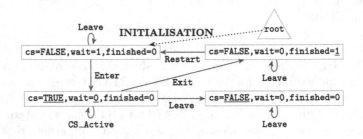

Fig. 3. *MutexSimple* statespace for MAXINT=1

of Event-B in this paper but note that the results in the subsequent sections are also applicable to Event-B.

As far as symbolic reachability analysis is concerned, a formal model is seen to denote a transition system. LTSMIN adopts the following definition:

Definition 1 (Transition System). *A Transition System (TS) is a structure $(S, \rightarrow, I)$, where S is a set of states, $\rightarrow \subseteq S \times S$ is a transition relation and $I \subseteq S$ is a set of initial states. Furthermore, let $\rightarrow^*$ be the reflexive and transitive closure of $\rightarrow$, then the set of reachable states is $R = \{s \in S \mid \exists s' \in I . s' \rightarrow^* s\}$.*

A B-Method and Event-B model induces such a transition system: initial states are defined by the initialisation clause and the individual operations together define the transition relation $\rightarrow$. Figure 3 shows the transition system[1] for the machine in Fig. 2. As can be seen in Fig. 3, the transition relation is annotated with operation names. For symbolic reachability analysis it is actually very important that we divide the transition relation into groups, leading to the concept of a partitioned transition system:

---

[1] One subtle issue is that LTSMIN actually only supports a single initial state; this is solved by introducing the artificial *root* state linked to the initial states proper. We ignore this technical issue in the paper.

Definition 2 (Partitioned Transition System). *A Partitioned Transition System (PTS) is a structure* $\mathcal{P} = (S^N, G, \rightarrow^M, I^N)$, *where*

- $S^N = S_1 \times \ldots \times S_N$ *is the set of states, which are vectors of* N *values,*
- $G = (\rightarrow_1, \ldots, \rightarrow_M)$ *is a vector of* M *transition groups* $\rightarrow_i \subseteq S^N \times S^N$ *(*$\forall 1 \leq i \leq$ M*)*
- $\rightarrow^M = \bigcup_{i=1}^{M} \rightarrow_i$ *is the overall transition relation induced by* G, *i.e., the union of the* M *transition groups, and*
- $I^N \subseteq S^N$ *is the set of initial states.*

We write $s \rightarrow_i t$ *when* $(s, t) \in \rightarrow_i$ *for* $1 \leq i \leq$ M, *and* $s \rightarrow^M t$ *when* $(s, t) \in \rightarrow^M$.

For example $I^N = \{(FALSE, MAXINT, 0)\}$ in the running example. Note that G in Definition 2 does not necessarily form a partition of $\rightarrow^M$, overlap is allowed between the individual groups.

3 Symbolic Reachability Analysis for B

Computing the set of reachable states (R) of a transition system can be done efficiently with symbolic algorithms if many transition groups $\rightarrow_i$ touch only a few variables. This concept is known as event locality [9]. Many models of transition systems in the B-Method employ event locality. In the B-Method event locality occurs in operations, where only a few variables are read from, or written to. For example in Fig. 2 operation CS_Active only reads from cs and Leave only writes to cs. This event locality benefits the symbolic reachability analysis, so that the algorithm is capable of coping with the well known state space explosion problem. Since the B-Method employs event locality we build on the foundations of earlier work on LTSMIN [7,23] and extend it to PROB. To perform symbolic reachability analysis of the B-Method, PROB should provide LTSMIN with read matrices and write matrices. These matrices inform LTSMIN about the locality of events in the B-Method.

Read independence is an important concept, it allows one to reuse the successor states computed in one state s for all states s' which differ just by read-independent variables from s, and vice versa.

Definition 3 (Read Independence). *Two state vectors s, s' are equivalent except on index j, denoted by* $s \approx_j s'$, *iff* $\forall k \neq j : s_k = s'_k$.

Transition group i is read-overwrite independent *from state variable j, iff* $\forall s, s', t \in S^N$ *such that* $s \approx_j s'$ *and* $s \rightarrow_i t$, *we have that* $s' \rightarrow_i t$.

Transition group i is read-copy independent *from state variable j, iff* $\forall s, s', t \in S^N$ *such that* $s \approx_j s'$ *and* $s \rightarrow_i t$, *we have that* $s' \rightarrow_i (t_1, \ldots, t_{j-1}, s'_j, t_{j+1}, \ldots, t_N)$.

A transition group is read independent *iff it is either read-overwrite or read-copy independent.*

If an event never reads but may write to a variable j it generally does not satisfy the above definition. For example, the operation MayReset = IF $cs = $ **true**

THEN *wait* := 0 END would neither be read-copy nor read-overwrite independent (for state vectors with *cs* = **false** it satisfies the definition of the former and for *cs* = **true** the latter, but neither for all state vectors). LTSMIN can also deal with more liberal independence notions, but we have not yet implemented this in the present paper.

Definition 4 (Write Independence). *Transition group i is write-independent from state variable j, if* $\forall\, s, t \in S^N$: $(s_1, \ldots, s_j, \ldots, s_N) \rightarrow_i (t_1, \ldots, t_j, \ldots, t_N) \Longrightarrow (s_j = t_j)$, *i.e. state variable j is never modified by transition group i.*

We illustrate the above definitions below.

Definition 5 (Dependency Matrices). *For a PTS* $\mathcal{P} = (S^N, G, \rightarrow^M, I^N)$, *the write matrix is an* M × N *matrix* $WM(\mathcal{P}) = WM^{\mathcal{P}}_{M \times N} \in \{0,1\}^{M \times N}$, *such that* $(WM_{i,j} = 0) \Longrightarrow$ *transition group i is* write independent *from state variable j. Furthermore, the read matrix is an* M × N *matrix* $RM(\mathcal{P}) = RM^{\mathcal{P}}_{M \times N} \in \{0,1\}^{M \times N}$, *such that* $(RM_{i,j} = 0) \Longrightarrow$ *transition group i is* read independent *from state variable j.*

In this paper we will use sufficient syntactic conditions to ensure Definitions 3 and 4 and obtain the read and write matrix from Definition 5. Indeed, we compute for every operation syntactically which variables are read from and which variables are written to.

- If an operation does not write to a variable, its transition group is write independent according to Definition 4 and the corresponding entry in *WM* is 0.
- If an operation does not read a variable, its transition group is read independent according to Definition 3, unless it maybe written to (e.g., because the assignment is in the branch of an if-then-else). In this case, we will mark the variable as both write and read independent. Also, note that when the assignment within an operation is of the form f(X) := E then the operation should have a read dependency on the function f (in addition to the write dependency).

For our example in Fig. 2 the syntactic read-write information is as follows:

From the matrices we can infer if a variable is read-copy or read-overwrite independent: a variable that is read independent and not written to (i.e., write independent) is read-copy independent, otherwise it is read-overwrite independent.

We can thus infer that:

- the transition group of Enter is read-copy and write independent on finished.
- Exit is read-copy and write independent on wait.
- Leave is read-copy and write independent on wait and finished and read-overwrite independent on cs.
- CS_Active is read-copy and write independent on wait and finished and write independent on cs (but not read-independent on cs).
- Leave is read-copy and write independent on cs.

	cs	wait	finished
Enter	1	1	0
Exit	1	0	1
Leave	0	0	0
CS_Active	1	0	0
Restart	0	1	1

(a) Read matrix (RM)

	cs	wait	finished
Enter	1	1	0
Exit	1	0	1
Leave	1	0	0
CS_Active	0	0	0
Restart	0	1	1

(b) Write matrix (WM)

Fig. 4. Dependency matrices

3.1 Exploration Algorithm

We now present the core of the symbolic reachbility analysis algorithm of LTSMIN. Algorithm 1 computes the set of reachable states R (represented as a decision diagram) and it uses the independence information to minimise the number of next state computations that have to be carried out, i.e., re-using the next states $\{t \mid s \rightarrow_i t\}$ computed for a single state s for many other states s' according to Definitions 3 and 4. Algorithm 1 will, while it keeps finding new states, expand the partial transition relation with potential successor states, and apply the expanded relation to the set of new states.

Four key functions that make Algorithm 1 highly performant are the following. [2] The (1) *read projection* $\pi_i^r = \pi_i^{RM}$ and (2) *write projection* $\pi_i^w = \pi_i^{WM}$ take as argument a state vector and produce a state vector restricted to the read and write dependent variables of group i, respectively. Furthermore these function are extended to apply to sets directly, e.g., given the examples in Figs. 2 and 4, a read projection for Leave is $\pi_3^r(\{(\underline{FALSE}, 0, 0), (\underline{FALSE}, 0, 1), (\underline{FALSE}, 1, 0)\}) = \{(\underline{FALSE})\}$. This is illustrated in Fig. 6 and used at Line 2 in Algorithm 2. The read projection prevents LTSMIN from doing two unnecessary next state calls to PROB, since Leave is *read-copy* independent on wait and finished.

The function (3) NEXTSTATE$_i$ takes a read projected state and projects (with π_i^w) all successor states of transition group i. The partial transition relation $\rightarrow_i^P$ is learned on the fly, and NEXTSTATE$_i$ is used to expand $\rightarrow_i^P$. An example next state call for Enter is NEXTSTATE$_1((\underline{FALSE}, 1)) = \{(\underline{TRUE}, 0)\}$.

Lastly, (4) NEXT takes a set of states, a partial transition relation, a row of the read and write matrix and outputs a set of successor states.

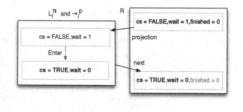

Fig. 5. One iteration with Enter

For example, applying the partial relation of Enter to the initial state yields NEXT($\{(\underline{FALSE}, \underline{1}, 0)\}, \{((\underline{FALSE}, 1), (\underline{TRUE}, 0))\}, (1, 1, 0), (1, 1, 0)) =$

---

[2] We refrain from giving their formal definitions; they can be found in [23].

$\{(\underline{TRUE}, \underline{0}, 0)\}$. Note that in this example **Enter** is *read-copy* independent on **finished** and thus NEXT will copy its value from the initial state.

The usage of these four key functions is also illustrated in Fig. 5. The figure shows that first the projection is done for **Enter**, then $\hookrightarrow_i^{\mathrm{P}}$ is expanded with a NEXTSTATE$_i$ call, lastly relation $\hookrightarrow_i^{\mathrm{P}}$ is applied to the initial state, producing the first successor state.

Figure 6 shows for each operation the transition relation $\hookrightarrow_i^{\mathrm{P}}$ and the projected states on which they are computed. Definition 3 ensures that the projected state space shown in Fig. 6 can be used to compute the effect of each of these operations for the *entire* state space (using **next**).

Algorithm 1. REACHBREADTH-FIRST

> **Input** : $I^{\mathrm{N}} \subseteq S^{\mathrm{N}}, \mathrm{M} \in \mathbb{N}, RM, WM$
> **Output:** The set of reachable states $\mathcal{R}$
> 1 $\mathcal{R} \leftarrow I^{\mathrm{N}}; \mathcal{L} \leftarrow \mathcal{R};$
> 2 **for** $1 \leq i \leq \mathrm{M}$ **do** $\mathcal{R}_i^{\mathrm{P}} \leftarrow \varnothing; \hookrightarrow_i^{\mathrm{P}} \leftarrow \varnothing;$
> 3 **while** $\mathcal{L} \neq \varnothing$ **do**
> 4 $\quad$ LEARNTRANS$(); \mathcal{N} \leftarrow \varnothing;$
> 5 $\quad$ **for** $1 \leq i \leq \mathrm{M}$ **do**
> 6 $\quad\quad$ $\mathcal{N} \leftarrow \mathcal{N} \cup \mathrm{NEXT}(\mathcal{L}, \hookrightarrow_i^{\mathrm{P}}, RM_i, WM_i);$
> 7 $\quad$ $\mathcal{L} \leftarrow \mathcal{N} - \mathcal{R}; \mathcal{R} \leftarrow \mathcal{R} \cup \mathcal{N};$
> 8 **return** $\mathcal{R}$

Algorithm 2. LEARNTRANS

> **Description:** Extends $\hookrightarrow_i^{\mathrm{P}}$
> 1 **for** $1 \leq i \leq \mathrm{M}$ **do**
> 2 $\quad$ $\mathcal{L}^{\mathrm{P}} \leftarrow \pi_i^r(\mathcal{L});$
> 3 $\quad$ **for** $s^{\mathrm{P}} \in \mathcal{L}^{\mathrm{P}} - \mathcal{R}_i^{\mathrm{P}}$ **do**
> 4 $\quad\quad$ $\hookrightarrow_i^{\mathrm{P}} \leftarrow \hookrightarrow_i^{\mathrm{P}} \cup \{(s^{\mathrm{P}}, d^{\mathrm{P}}) \mid$
> 5 $\quad\quad\quad$ $d^{\mathrm{P}} \in \mathrm{NEXTSTATE}_i(s^{\mathrm{P}})\};$
> 6 $\quad$ $\mathcal{R}_i^{\mathrm{P}} \leftarrow \mathcal{R}_i^{\mathrm{P}} \cup \mathcal{L}^{\mathrm{P}};$

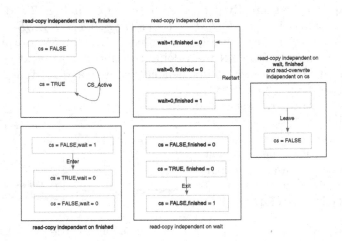

Fig. 6. MutexSimple, operations computed on their projected state space

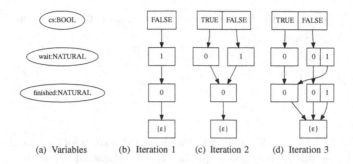

(a) Variables   (b) Iteration 1   (c) Iteration 2   (d) Iteration 3

Fig. 7. LDDs of the reachable states

3.2 List Decision Diagrams

The symbolic reachability algorithm in Sect. 3.1 uses List Decision Diagrams (LDDs) to store the reachable states and transition relations. Similar to a Binary Decision Diagram, an LDD [7] represents a set of vectors. Due to the sharing of state vectors within an LDD, the memory usage can be very low, even for very large state spaces. Three example LDDs for the running example are given in Fig. 7. The LDDs represent the set of reachable states $\mathcal{R}$ in Algorithm 1 at each iteration of Line 3. In an LDD every path from the top left node to $\{\epsilon\}$ is a state, e.g., the initial state $(FALSE, 1, 0)$ in Fig. 7b. A node in an LDD represents a unique set of (sub) vectors, e.g., $\{\epsilon\}$ represents the set of zero-length vectors and the right-most 0 of variable `wait` in Fig. 7d encodes the set $\{(0,0), (0,1), (1,0)\}$. Figure 7c shows that firing `Enter` will add $(TRUE, 0, 0)$ to $\mathcal{R}$. In Fig. 7d $(FALSE, 0, 0)$ and $(FALSE, 0, 1)$ are added to R, by firing `Leave` and `Exit` respectively. The benefit of using LDDs for state storage is due to the sharing of state vectors. For example, the subvector $(FALSE)$ of the states $\{(FALSE, 0, 0), (FALSE, 0, 1), (FALSE, 1, 0), (FALSE, 1, 1)\}$ in iteration 3 is encoded in the LDD with a single node. For bigger state spaces the sharing can be huge; resulting in a low memory footprint for the reachability algorithm.

3.3 Performance: NextState Function

There are two big differences of Algorithm 1 with classical explicit state model checking as used by PROB [19]. First, the state space is represented using an LDD datastructure, which enables sharing amongst states. Second, independence is used to apply the NEXTSTATE function not state by state, but for entire sets of states in one go. For each of the 4 states in Fig. 3, the explicit model checking algorithm of PROB would check whether each of the 5 operations is enabled; resulting in 20 next-state calls. With LTSMIN's symbolic reachability Algorithm 1, only 12 NEXTSTATE calls are made. This is shown in the following table, where + means enabled, − means disabled, and C means that LTSMIN has reused the results of a previous call to PROB.

If we initialise `wait` with MAXINT $= 500$, the state space has 251,002 states. The runtime with PROB is 70 s, with LTSMIN+PROB 48 s and LTSMIN performs

State#	cs	wait	finished	Enter	Exit	Leave	CS_Active	Restart
1	FALSE	1	0	+	C	C	C	−
2	TRUE	0	0	−	+	+	+	−
3	FALSE	0	0	−	−	C	−	C
4	FALSE	0	1	C	−	C	C	+

only 6012 NEXTSTATE calls. The example does not have a lot of concurrency and uses only simple data structures (and thus the overhead of the LTSMIN's PROB front-end is more of a factor compared to the runtime of ProB for computing successor states); other examples will show greater speedups (see Sect. 5). But the purpose of this example is to illustrate the principles.

4   Technical Aspects and Implementation

We used a distributed approach to integrate PROB and LTSMIN. Both tools are stand-alone applications, so a direct integration, i.e., turning one of the tools into a shared library would require considerable effort. We therefore added extensions to both tools that convert the data formats and use sockets to communicate with each other. A high level view of the integration is shown in Fig. 8. We use the ØMQ [14] library for communication. ØMQ is oriented around message queues and can be used as both, a networking library with very high throughput and as a concurrency framework. We have chosen ØMQ because it worked very well in previous work [4]. Although we do not (yet) have to care about concurrency in this work, the reactor abstraction provided by ØMQ was very handy in the PROB extension. It allows to implement a server that receives and processes messages without much effort.

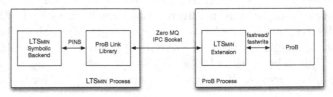

Fig. 8. High level design showing the integration

The communication is always initiated by LTSMIN; it sends a message and blocks until it receives the answer from PROB. We usually run both tools on a single computer using interprocess (IPC) sockets, but it is only a matter of configuration to run the tools on different machines using TCP sockets. We currently only support Linux and Mac OS. The communication protocol is straightforward. Reachability analysis is initiated from LTSMIN by sending an initialisation packet. PROB answers with a message containing the relevant static information about a model, such as the dependency matrices that LTSMIN requires (see Sect. 3). Each matrix is encoded as a 2-dimensional array, which is not optimal for a sparse matrix but is not an issue because we only send the matrices once. The packet also contains the list of variables, their types, the list of transition groups, and the initial state.

States are represented as a list of so called **chunks**. A chunk is one of the elements in the state vector according to Definition 2. In the case of B, each chunk is a value of one of the state variables. Because LTSMIN will not look inside the chunks, we simply use the binary representation of PROB's Prolog term that represents the value of a variable. This has the advantage, that PROB does not have to keep information about the state space. It can always recover a state from the chunks that are sent by LTSMIN. The transition groups correspond to B operations as explained in Sect. 2. Like chunks the transition groups are only used as names in LTSMIN.

Once the initial setup is done, LTSMIN will start to ask PROB for successor states for **specific** transition groups. It will send a next-state message containing a state and a transition group. The state, that LTSMIN sends is a list of chunks and PROB's LTSMIN extension can directly consume them and construct a Prolog term that internally represents a state. Using this constructed state and the transition group, the extension will then ask PROB for all successor states. The result is a list of Prolog terms, each representing a successor state. The extension transforms the list of states into a list of lists of chunks and sends them back to LTSMIN. This is repeated until LTSMIN has explored all necessary states and sends a termination signal.

The next-state messaging is similar to Fig. 5, the projection is achieved by replacing all read independent variables by a dummy value.

5   Experiments

To demonstrate that the combination of PROB and LTSMIN improves the performance of the reachability analysis and deadlock detection compared with the standalone version of PROB, we use a wide range of B and Event-B models. Our benchmark suite contains puzzles (e.g., towers of Hanoi) as well as specifications of protocols (e.g., Needham-Schroeder), algorithms (e.g., Simpson's four slot algorithm) and industrial specifications (e.g., a choreography model by SAP, a cruise control system by Volvo and a fault tolerant automatic train protection system by Siemens).[3]

The experiments were run on Ubuntu 15.10 64-bit, with 8 GB RAM, 120 GB SSD and an Intel Sandybridge Mobile i5 2520M 2.50 GHz Dual core. The version of PROB used in this paper is 1.5.1-beta3, and LTSMIN tag LTSminProB-iFM2016.[4]

Figure 9 summarises a selection of the experiments that we ran. The last two models are Event-B models. In these experiments we used Breadth-First Search (BFS) and looked for deadlocks. A deadlock was found only for the Philosophers model (this is also why there are no next state call statistics for this model). The table also contains the number of next state calls for PROB reachability

---

[3] More detailed descriptions can be found in [5].

[4] Reproduction notes at https://github.com/utwente-fmt/ProB-LTSmin-iFM16.

Benchmark	Events	States	ProB Nxt St Calls	LTSmin NxtSt Calls	ProB Wall (ms)	LTSmin CPU (ms)	LTSmin Wall (ms)	Speedup
CAN_BUS	21	132600	2784560	3534	122850	660	1590	77.264
ConcurrentCounters	4	110813	443249	113032	21820	2760	13820	1.579
Cruise_finite1	26	1361	35361	1667	2900	100	1020	2.843
file_system	8	698	5577	1198	1900	180	4660	0.41
MutexSimple	5	10	46	26	10	10	190	0.053
Philosophers	5				480	40	590	0.814
SiemensMiniPilot_Abrial0	9	181	1621	182	100	20	260	0.385
Simpson_Four_Slot	9	46658	419906	2089	17310	200	860	20.128
Train1_Lukas_POR	8	24637	197082	101441	33660	6480	50260	0.670
nota	11	80719	887899	588	287970	130	660	436.318
pkeyprot2	10	4412	44111	2004	22190	210	1710	12.977
Ref5_Switch_mch	38	29861	1134681	1281	160600	490	1260	127.460
obsw_M001	21	589279	12374779	23406	2051320	1620	12420	165.163

Fig. 9. B and Event-B Machines, with BFS and deadlock detection

analysis on its own and when called from LTSmin's symbolic reachability analysis algorithm (i.e., our new integration see Sect. 3.3) without deadlock checking. One can clearly see that we obtain a considerable reduction in wallclock time. The ProB time is the walltime of the ProB reachability analysis and initial state computation and does not include parsing and loading. The LTSmin CPU time column shows how much time is spent in the LTSmin side of the symbolic reachability analysis algorithm. The LTSmin wall time shows the total walltime, and this also contains the time spent in the communication layer and waiting for the ProB process to compute the next states. To compare the benefit of our new algorithm we compute the speedup of the walltime in the last column by dividing the ProB walltime from column 5 with the LTSmin walltime in column 7.

We can see that for some of the smaller models the overhead of setting up LTSmin does not pay off. However, for all larger models, except for the Train1_Lukas_POR model considerable speedups were obtained.

A major result we achieved with non default settings for LTSmin, is for elevator12.eventb. This model is not listed in Fig. 9, because ProB runs out of memory on the hardware configuration used for this experiment. LTSmin computed in 34 s, with 96,523 NextState calls, that the model has 1,852,655,841 states. As reachability algorithm we chose chaining [27], and to compute a better variable order, we ran Sloan's bandwidth reduction algorithm [29] on the dependency matrix.

As far as memory consumption is concerned; when performing reachability analysis on CAN_BUS, the ProB process consumes 370 MB real memory, while the LTSmin process consumes 633 MB, with the default settings. With the default settings LTSmin will allocate 2^{22} elements (≈ 100 MB) for the node table and 2^{24} elements (≈ 500 MB) for the operations cache. If we choose a smaller node table and operations cache for the LDD package (both 2^{18} elements),

LTSMIN consumes only 22 MB. The default settings for LTSMIN are geared towards larger symbolic state spaces than that of CAN_BUS. The default node table and cache are too big for CAN_BUS, and thus not completely filled during reachability.

We have also run our new symbolic reachability analysis on Z and TLA$^+$ models. For example, we successfully validated the video rental Z model from [10]. For 2 persons and 2 titles and maximum stock level of 4, LTSMIN generates the 23009 states in 1.75 s compared to 52.4 s with PROB alone. The model contained useless constants; after removing them PROB runs in 1.6 s; the runtime of LTSMIN stays unchanged. We were unable to use the output of z2sal [10] using SAL [25] and its symbolic model checker for comparison.

In summary, Fig. 9 shows that for several non-trivial B and Event-B models, considerable improvements can be obtained using the symbolic reachability analysis technique described in this paper.

Alternate Approaches. Other techniques for improving model checking for B-Method and Event-B models have been developed and evaluated in the recent years. We have run a further set of experiments using a selection of those methods; the complete results can be found in [5] For technical reasons, the experiments were run on different hardware than above, a MacBook Air with 2.2 GHz i7 processor and 8 GB of RAM. We summarise the findings here and compare the results with our new symbolic model checking algorithm.

Benchmark	PROB POR		PROB Hash		TLC		PROB no opt
	ms	Speedup	ms	Speedup	sec	Speedup	ms
CAN_BUS	138720	0.80	98390	1.12	3	37	110400
ConcurrentCounters	50	345.8	18400	1.06	1	17	17290
file_system	2380	0.37	210	4.24	29	0.03	890
Simpson_Four_Slot	20860	0.70	9550	1.52	1	15	14530
Train1_Lukas_POR	34030	0.75	28930	0.88	4	6	25740
nota	490	509.22	14780	16.88	10	25	249520
Ref5_Switch_mch	215160	0.59	124500	1.01	6	21	126170
obsw_M001	2150520	0.80	76190	22.53	55	31	1716770

The authors in [12] presented a translation from the B-Method to TLA$^+$, with the goal of using the **Tlc** model checker [32] as backend. TLC has no constraints solving capabilities, and as such that it can only deal with lower level models. On the other hand, its execution can be considerably faster than PROB, and its explicit state model checking engine (which stores fingerprints) is very efficient. On the downside, there is a small probability that fingerprint collisions can occur. The experiments show that TLC does not deal well with benchmark programs which require constraint solving (graph isomorphism, JobsPuzzle, ...), running up to three orders of magnitude slower than PROB or LTSMIN with PROB.

288 J. Bendisposto et al.

However, it does deal very well with lower level models, e.g., it is faster than LTSMIN for ConcurrentCounters. For many benchmark models, even those not requiring constraint solving, our symbolic reachability analysis is faster.

For example, for the nota example, TLC runs in about 10 s—faster than PROB without any optimisation—but slower than LTSMIN by less than a second.

Symmetry reduction [20] can be very useful; but exponential improvements usually occur only on academic examples. Here we have experimented with the hash marker symmetry reduction, which is PROB's fastest symmetry method, but is generally not guaranteed to explore all states. The method gives the best results for certain models (e.g., file_system). But for several of the larger, industrial examples shown above, its benefit is not of the same scale as LTSMIN. In future, we will investigate combining PROB's symmetry reduction with the new LTSMIN algorithm.

We have also experimented with **partial order reduction**. [11] uses a semantic preprocessing phase to determine independence (different from our purely syntactic determination; see Sect. 3). As such, it can induce a slow down for some examples where this does not pay off (e.g., file_system). PROB's partial order reduction obtains the best times for certain models with a large degree of concurrency (ConcurrentCounters, SiemensMiniPilot_Abrial, and nota). However, once we start doing invariant checking, [11] does not scale nearly as well (e.g., it takes 134 s instead of 0.5 s for LTSMIN checking the nota model). But even without invariant checking, there are plenty examples where the symbolic reachability analysis approach is better (e.g., Cruise_finite1, Philosophers, Simpson_Four_Slot and almost two orders of magnitude for CAN_BUS). In summary:

- TLC is good for models not requiring constraint solving. It is a very efficient, explicit state model checker. However, models often have to be rewritten (such as CAN_BUS), and there is a small chance of having fingerprint collisions.
- Symmetry reduction excels when models make use of deferred sets. However, the hash marker method is not guaranteed to explore all states.
- Partial order reduction is very good for models with a large degree of concurrency. However, it can cause slow downs and is less suited for invariant checking.
- The new symbolic reachability analysis algorithm deals well with concurrency and is by far the fastest method for certain larger, industrial models, such as CAN_BUS, obsw_M001, elevator12, the ABZ landing gear model or Abrial's mechanical press. LTSMIN is currently the only tool set that uses a symbolic representation of the state space that is connected to PROB.

6 More Related Work, Future Work and Conclusion

We have already evaluated the use of TLC [32] for model checking B. Another explicit state model checker for B has been presented in [21], which uses lazy enumeration. Symbolic model checking [8] has been used for railway applications in [31]. The best known symbolic model checker is probably SMV [22], which uses a low-level input language. Some comparisons between using SMV and PROB have been conducted in [15], where models were translated by hand. For abstract state machines there is the AsmetaSMV [3] tool, which automatically translates ASM specifications to SMV. It is our impression that the translation often leads to a considerable blowup of the model, encoded in SMV's low-level language, also affecting performance. We did one experiment on a Tic-Tac-Toe model provided for AsmetaSMV: NuSMV 2.6 took over 13 s to find a configuration where the cross player wins; PROB (without LTSMIN) took 0.2 s model checking time for the same property on a similar B model. Another experiment involved puzzle 3 of the RushHour game: PROB solves this in 5 s, while NuSMV still had not found a solution after 120 min.

Other symbolic model checkers that perform comparable well to LTSMIN include MARCIE [13] and PETRIDOTNET[24].

The paper provides a stable architectural link between PROB and LTSMIN that can be extended. First, we plan to provide LTSMIN with more fine-grained information about the models, both statically and dynamically. Dynamically, PROB will transmit to LTSMIN which variables have actually been written by an operation, enabling a more extensive independence notion to be used. Statically, PROB will transmit the individual guards of operations and provide variable read matrices for the guards. We will also transmit the individual invariants in the same manner, to enable analysis of the invariants. (It is actually already possible to check invariants using the present integration, simply by encoding invariants as operations. We have done so with success for some of the examples, e.g., the nota from Sect. 5.) When PROB transmits individual guards, we also hope to use the guard-based partial order optimisations of LTSMIN [18] and enable LTL model checking with LTSMIN.

These future directions will strengthen the capability of the verification tools and hence further encourage the application of formal methods within industry as identified in [6], for example to support complex railway systems verification in CSP∥B. This will require both more fine-grained static and dynamic information.

In summary, we have presented a new scalable, symbolic analysis algorithm for the B-Method and Event-B, along with a platform to integrate other model checking improvements via LTSMIN in the future.

References

1. Abrial, J.R.: Modeling in Event-B: System and Software Engineering. Cambridge University Press, Cambridge (2010)
2. Abrial, J.: The B-Book - Assigning Programs to Meanings. Cambridge University Press, Cambridge (2005)
3. Arcaini, P., Gargantini, A., Riccobene, E.: AsmetaSMV: a way to link high-level ASM models to low-level NuSMV specifications. In: Frappier, M., Glässer, U., Khurshid, S., Laleau, R., Reeves, S. (eds.) ABZ 2010. LNCS, vol. 5977, pp. 61–74. Springer, Heidelberg (2010)
4. Bendisposto, J.: Directed and Distributed Model Checking of B Specifications. Ph.D. thesis, University of Düsseldorf (2015). http://docserv.uni-duesseldorf.de/servlets/DocumentServlet?id=34472

5. Bendisposto, J., Körner, P., Leuschel, M., Meijer, J., van de Pol, J., Treharne, H., Whitefield, J.: Symbolic Reachability Analysis of B through ProB and LTSmin. CoRR abs/1603.04401 (2016)
6. Bicarregui, J.C., Fitzgerald, J.S., Larsen, P.G., Woodcock, J.C.P.: Industrial practice in formal methods: a review. In: Cavalcanti, A., Dams, D.R. (eds.) FM 2009. LNCS, vol. 5850, pp. 810–813. Springer, Heidelberg (2009)
7. Blom, S., van de Pol, J.: Symbolic reachability for process algebras with recursive data types. In: Fitzgerald, J.S., Haxthausen, A.E., Yenigun, H. (eds.) ICTAC 2008. LNCS, vol. 5160, pp. 81–95. Springer, Heidelberg (2008)
8. Burch, J.R., Clarke, E.M., McMillan, K.L., Dill, D.L., Hwang, L.J.: Symbolic model checking: 10^{20} states and beyond. IC **98**(2), 142–170 (1992)
9. Ciardo, G., Marmorstein, R.M., Siminiceanu, R.: The saturation algorithm for symbolic state-space exploration. STTT **8**(1), 4–25 (2006)
10. Derrick, J., North, S., Simons, A.J.H.: Z2SAL - building a model checker for Z. In: Börger, E., Butler, M., Bowen, J.P., Boca, P. (eds.) ABZ 2008. LNCS, vol. 5238, pp. 280–293. Springer, Heidelberg (2008)
11. Dobrikov, I., Leuschel, M.: Optimising the ProB model checker for B using partial order reduction. In: Giannakopoulou, D., Salaün, G. (eds.) SEFM 2014. LNCS, vol. 8702, pp. 220–234. Springer, Heidelberg (2014)
12. Hansen, D., Leuschel, M.: Translating B to TLA^{+} for validation with TLC. In: Ait Ameur, Y., Schewe, K.-D. (eds.) ABZ 2014. LNCS, vol. 8477, pp. 40–55. Springer, Heidelberg (2014)
13. Heiner, M., Rohr, C., Schwarick, M.: MARCIE – model checking and reachability analysis done efficiently. In: Colom, J.-M., Desel, J. (eds.) PETRI NETS 2013. LNCS, vol. 7927, pp. 389–399. Springer, Heidelberg (2013)
14. Hintjens, P.: ZeroMQ: Messaging for Many Applications. O'Reilly Media Inc, Sebastopol (2013)
15. Hörne, T., van der Poll, J.A.: Planning as model checking: the performance of ProB vs NuSMV. In: SAICSIT Conference ACM ICPS, vol. 338, pp. 114–123. ACM (2008)
16. James, P., Moller, F., Nguyen, H.N., Roggenbach, M., Schneider, S., Treharne, H., Trumble, M., Williams, D.: Verification of scheme plans using CSP||B. In: Counsell, S., Núñez, M. (eds.) SEFM 2013. LNCS, vol. 8368, pp. 189–204. Springer, Heidelberg (2014)
17. Kant, G., Laarman, A., Meijer, J., van de Pol, J., Blom, S., van Dijk, T.: LTSmin: high-performance language-independent model checking. In: Baier, C., Tinelli, C. (eds.) TACAS 2015. LNCS, vol. 9035, pp. 692–707. Springer, Heidelberg (2015)
18. Laarman, A., Pater, E., Pol, J., Hansen, H.: Guard-based partial-order reduction. Int. J. Softw. Tools Technol. Transfer, 1–22 (2014). doi:10.1007/s10009-014-0363-9
19. Leuschel, M., Butler, M.J.: ProB: an automated analysis toolset for the B method. STTT **10**(2), 185–203 (2008)
20. Leuschel, M., Massart, T.: Efficient approximate verification of B via symmetry markers. Ann. Math. Artif. Intell. **59**(1), 81–106 (2010)
21. Matos, P.J., Fischer, B., Marques-Silva, J.: A lazy unbounded model checker for EVENT-B. In: Breitman, K., Cavalcanti, A. (eds.) ICFEM 2009. LNCS, vol. 5885, pp. 485–503. Springer, Heidelberg (2009)
22. McMillan, K.L.: Symbolic Model Checking. Ph.D. thesis, Boston (1993)
23. Meijer, J., Kant, G., Blom, S., van de Pol, J.: Read, write and copy dependencies for symbolic model checking. In: Yahav, E. (ed.) HVC 2014. LNCS, vol. 8855, pp. 204–219. Springer, Heidelberg (2014)

24. Molnár, V., Darvas, D., Vörös, A., Bartha, T.: Saturation-based incremental LTL model checking with inductive proofs. In: Baier, C., Tinelli, C. (eds.) TACAS 2015. LNCS, vol. 9035, pp. 643–657. Springer, Heidelberg (2015)
25. de Moura, L., Owre, S., Shankar, N.: The SAL language manual. Technical report, SRI International, technical Report SRI-CSL-01-02 (Rev. 2) (2003)
26. Plagge, D., Leuschel, M.: Seven at a stroke: LTL model checking for high-level specifications in B, Z, CSP, and more. STTT **11**, 9–21 (2010)
27. Roig, O., Cortadella, J., Pastor, E.: Verification of asynchronous circuits by BDD-based model checking of petri nets. In: Proceedings ATPN, pp. 374–391 (1995)
28. Schneider, S., Treharne, H.: CSP theorems for communicating B machines. Formal Asp. Comput. **17**(4), 390–422 (2005)
29. Sloan, S.W.: A FORTRAN program for profile and wavefront reduction. Int. J. Numer. Meth. Eng. **28**(11), 2651–2679 (1989)
30. Whitefield, J.: Linking PROB and LTSMIN (2015), Final Year Dissertation, University of Surrey
31. Winter, K.: Optimising ordering strategies for symbolic model checking of railway interlockings. In: Margaria, T., Steffen, B. (eds.) ISoLA 2012, Part II. LNCS, vol. 7610, pp. 246–260. Springer, Heidelberg (2012)
32. Yu, Y., Manolios, P., Lamport, L.: Model checking TLA$^+$ specifications. In: Pierre, L., Kropf, T. (eds.) CHARME 1999. LNCS, vol. 1703, pp. 54–66. Springer, Heidelberg (1999)

Model Learning

Enhancing Automata Learning
by Log-Based Metrics

Petra van den Bos[(✉)], Rick Smetsers, and Frits Vaandrager

Institute for Computing and Information Sciences, Radboud University,
Nijmegen, The Netherlands
petra@cs.ru.nl

Abstract. We study a general class of distance metrics for deterministic
Mealy machines. The metrics are induced by weight functions that specify the relative importance of input sequences. By choosing an appropriate weight function we may fine-tune a metric so that it captures some
intuitive notion of quality. In particular, we present a metric that is
based on the minimal number of inputs that must be provided to obtain
a counterexample, starting from states that can be reached by a given
set of logs. For any weight function, we may boost the performance of
existing model learning algorithms by introducing an extra component,
which we call the *Comparator*. Preliminary experiments show that use
of the Comparator yields a significant reduction of the number of inputs
required to learn correct models, compared to current state-of-the-art
algorithms. In existing automata learning algorithms, the quality of subsequent hypotheses may decrease. Generalising a result of Smetsers et al.,
we show that the quality of hypotheses that are generated by the Comparator never decreases.

1 Introduction

In the platonic boolean world view of classical computer science, which goes
back to McCarthy, Hoare, Dijkstra and others, programs can only be correct
or incorrect. Henzinger [14] argues that this boolean classification falls short of
the practical need to assess the behaviour of software in a more nuanced fashion
against multiple criteria. He proposes to introduce quantitative fitness measures
for programs, in order to measure properties such as functional correctness, performance and robustness. This paper introduces such quantitative fitness measures in the context of black-box testing, an area in which, as famously observed
by Dijkstra [10], it is impossible to establish correctness of implementations.

The scenario that we consider in this paper starts from some legacy software
component. Being able to retrieve models of such a component is potentially very
useful. For instance, if the software is changed or enriched with new functionality,

P. van den Bos—Supported by STW project 13859 (SUMBAT).
R. Smetsers—Supported by NWO project 628.001.009 (LEMMA).
F. Vaandrager—Supported by STW project 11763 (ITALIA).

© Springer International Publishing Switzerland 2016
E. Ábrahám and M. Huisman (Eds.): IFM 2016, LNCS 9681, pp. 295–310, 2016.
DOI: 10.1007/978-3-319-33693-0_19

one may use a learned model for regression testing. Also, if the source code is hard to read and poorly documented, one may use a model of the software for model-based testing of a new implementation, or even for generating an implementation on a new platform automatically.

The construction of models from observations of component behaviour can be performed using model learning (e.g. regular inference) techniques [8]. One such technique is *active learning* [2,25]. In active learning, a so-called Learner interacts with a System Under Learning (SUL), which is a black-box reactive system the Learner can provide inputs to and observe outputs from. By interacting with the SUL, the Learner infers a *hypothesis*, a state machine model that intends to describe the behaviour of the SUL. In order to find out whether a hypothesis is correct, we will typically use some conformance testing method. If the SUL passes the test, then the model is deemed correct. If the outputs of the SUL and the model differ, the test constitutes a counterexample, which may then be used by the Learner to construct an improved hypothesis.

Active learning has been successfully applied to learn models of (and find mistakes in) implementations of major protocols such as TCP [12] and TLS [9]. We have also used the approach to learn models of embedded control software at Océ [21] and to support refactoring of software at Philips HealthTech [19]. A key issue in black-box model learning, however, is assessing the correctness of the learned models. Since testing may fail to find a counterexample for a model, we can never be sure that a learned model is correct. Hence there is an urgent need for appropriate quantitative fitness measures.

Given a correct model S of the behaviour of the SUL, and a hypothesis model H, we are interested in distance metrics d that satisfy the following three criteria:

1. $d(H, S) = 0$ iff H and S have the same behaviour.
2. For any $\varepsilon > 0$, there exists a finite test suite T such that if H and S behave the same for all tests in T, it follows that $d(H, S) < \varepsilon$.
3. Metric d captures some intuitive notion of quality: the smaller $d(H, S)$, the better the quality of hypothesis H.

The first criterion is an obvious sanity property that any metric should satisfy. The second criterion says that, even though we can never exclude that H and S behave differently, we may, for any $\varepsilon > 0$, come up with a finite test suite T to check whether $d(H, S) < \varepsilon$. By running all the tests in T we either establish that H is a ε-approximation of S, or we find a counterexample that we can use to further improve our hypothesis model H. The third criterion is somewhat vague, but nevertheless extremely important. In practice, engineers will only be willing to invest further in testing if this leads to a quantifiable increase of demonstrated quality. They usually find it difficult to formalise their intuitive concept of quality, but typically require that a refactored implementation of a legacy component behaves the same for a set of common input sequences that have been recorded in log files, or specified as part of a regression test suite.

In this paper, we introduce a new, general class of metrics for deterministic Mealy machines that satisfy criteria (1) and (2). Our metrics are induced by weight functions that specify the relative importance of input sequences.

By choosing an appropriate weight function we may fine-tune our metric so that it also meets criterion (3). In particular, we present metrics that are based on the minimal number of inputs that must be provided to obtain a counterexample starting from states that can be reached by a given set of logs. We also show that, given any weight function, we may boost the performance of existing learning algorithms by introducing an extra component, which we call the *Comparator*. Preliminary experiments show that use of the Comparator yields a significant reduction of the number of inputs required to learn a correct model for the SUL, compared to a current state-of-the-art algorithm. Existing learning algorithms do not ensure that the quality of subsequent hypotheses increases [23]. In fact, we may have $d(H', S) < d(H, S)$, even when hypothesis H is a refinement of hypothesis H'. Generalising a result of Smetsers et al. [23], we show that the quality of hypotheses never decreases when using the Comparator.

Related Work. Our research is most closely related to work of Smetsers et al. [23], which studies a simple distance metric, known from concurrency theory [3], in the setting of active learning. This metric is based on the minimal number of inputs required to obtain a counterexample: the longer this counterexample is, the closer a hypothesis is to the target model. Our work generalises the results of [23] to a much larger class of metrics, including log-based metrics that more accurately capture intuitive notions of quality.

The area of *software metrics* [24] aims to measure alternative implementations against different criteria. While software metrics mostly measure the quality of the software development process and static properties of code, our work is more ambitious since it considers the dynamic behaviour of software.

Henzinger [14] presents a general overview of work on behaviour-based metrics. Most research in this area thus far has been concerned with *directed metrics*, that is, metrics that are not required to be symmetrical. The idea is that for a given system X and requirement r, the distance function d describes the degree to which system X satisfies requirement r. Černý et al. [6], for instance, define a metric that is applied to an implementation and a specification. It is based on simulation relations between states of the two systems. If the specification simulates the implementation, then the distance is 0. However, if there is a state pair (q, q'), such that q does not simulate q', then a 'simulation failure game' is played. At a point where the specification has no transition with the same label as a transition of the implementation, the specification is allowed to choose some transition, at the cost of one penalty point. The distance between the two systems is then defined as the total number of penalty points reached when the implementation maximises, and the specification minimises the average number of penalty points. In our work we use metrics to compare hypotheses. Since we compare hypotheses in both directions, we use undirected (symmetric) metrics in our work. Thrane et al. [26] study directed metrics between weighted automata [11]. In contrast, our work shows how weighted automata can be used to define undirected metrics between unweighted automata.

De Alfaro et al. [1] study directed and undirected metrics in both a linear time and a branching time setting. Most related to our work are the results on undirected linear distances. The starting point for the linear distances is the distance $\|\sigma - \rho\|_\infty$ between two traces σ and ρ, which measures the supremum of the differences in propositional valuations at corresponding positions of σ and ρ. The distance between two systems is then defined as the Hausdorff distance of their sets of traces. De Alfaro et al. [1] provide a logical characterization of these distances in terms of a quantitative version of LTL, and present algorithms for computing distances over metric transition systems, in particular an $\mathcal{O}(n^4)$ algorithm for computing distances between states of a deterministic metric transition system, where n is the size of the structure. The undirected linear distance metric of De Alfaro et al. [1] does not meet our second criterion for distance metrics (existence of finite test suites). However, the authors extend their results to a discounted context in which distances occurring after i steps are multiplied by α^i, where α is a discount factor in $[0, 1]$. We expect that finite test suites do exist for the discounted metrics of De Alfaro et al. [1], but it is not evident that the $\mathcal{O}(n^4)$ algorithm for computing distances generalizes to the metric setting.

There are intriguing relations between our results and the work of Brandán Briones et al. [5] on a semantic framework for test coverage. In [5] also a general class of weight functions is introduced, which are called *weighted fault models*, which includes a finiteness condition in order to enable test coverage. However, weighted fault models do not induce a metric (since they may assign weight 0 to certain sequences) and hence the resulting theory is quite different.

2   Preliminaries

Sequences. Let I be any set. The set of finite sequences over I is denoted I^*. Concatenation of finite sequences is denoted by juxtaposition. We use ϵ to denote the empty sequence. The sequence containing a single element $e \in I$ is denoted as e. The length of a sequence $\sigma \in I^*$, i.e. the number of concatenated elements of σ, is denoted with $|\sigma|$. We write $\sigma \leq \rho$ to denote that σ is a prefix of ρ.

Mealy Machines. We use Mealy machines as models for reactive systems.

Definition 1. *A Mealy machine is a tuple $M = (\Sigma, \Gamma, Q, q^0, \delta, \lambda)$, where Σ is a nonempty, finite set of inputs, Γ is a nonempty, finite set of outputs, Q is a finite set of states, $q^0 \in Q$ is the initial state, $\delta : Q \times \Sigma \to Q$ is a transition function, and $\lambda : Q \times \Sigma \to \Gamma$ is a transition output function. Functions δ and λ are extended to $Q \times \Sigma^*$ by defining, for all $q \in Q$, $i \in \Sigma$ and $\sigma \in \Sigma^*$,*

$$\delta(q, \epsilon) = q\,, \quad \delta(q, i\sigma) = \delta(\delta(q, i), \sigma),$$
$$\lambda(q, \epsilon) = \epsilon\,, \quad \lambda(q, i\sigma) = \lambda(q, i)\lambda(\delta(q, i), \sigma).$$

Observe that for each state and input pair exactly one transition is defined. The semantics of a Mealy machine are defined in terms of output functions:

Definition 2. *An output function over Σ and Γ is a function $A : \Sigma^* \to \Gamma^*$ that maps each sequence of inputs to a corresponding sequence of outputs such that, for all $\sigma, \rho \in \Sigma^*$, $|\sigma| = |A(\sigma)|$, and $\sigma \leq \rho \Rightarrow A(\sigma) \leq A(\rho)$.*

Definition 3. *The semantics of a Mealy machine M are defined by the output function A_M given by $A_M(\sigma) = \lambda(q^0, \sigma)$, for all $\sigma \in \Sigma^*$.*

Let $M_1 = (\Sigma, \Gamma, Q_1, q_1^0, \delta_1, \lambda_1)$ and $M_2 = (\Sigma, \Gamma, Q_2, q_2^0, \delta_2, \lambda_2)$ be two Mealy machines that share common sets of input and output symbols. We say M_1 and M_2 are *equivalent*, denoted $M_1 \approx M_2$, iff $A_{M_1} = A_{M_2}$. An input sequence $\sigma \in \Sigma^*$ *distinguishes* states $q_1 \in Q_1$ and $q_2 \in Q_2$ iff $\lambda_1(q_1, \sigma) \neq \lambda_2(q_2, \sigma)$. Similarly, σ distinguishes M_1 and M_2 iff $A_{M_1}(\sigma) \neq A_{M_2}(\sigma)$.

3   Weight Functions and Metrics

The metrics that we consider in this paper are parametrized by weight functions. Intuitively, a weight function specifies the importance of input sequences: the more weight an input sequence has, the more important it is that the output it generates is correct.

Definition 4. *A weight function for a nonempty, finite set of inputs Σ is a function $w : \Sigma^* \to \mathbb{R}^{>0}$ such that, for all $t > 0$, $\{\sigma \in \Sigma^* \mid w(\sigma) > t\}$ is finite.*

The finiteness condition in the above definition asserts that, even though the domain Σ^* is infinite, a weight function may only assign a value larger than t to a finite number of sequences, for any $t > 0$. Therefore, weight functions must involve some form of *discounting* by which long input sequences get smaller weights. This idea is based on the intuition that "a potential bug in the far-away future is less troubling than a potential bug today" [7].

Example 5. Let us define a weight function w by $w(\sigma) = 2^{-|\sigma|}$, for each $\sigma \in \Sigma^*$. Let $t \in \mathbb{R}^{>0}$. In order to see that w is a weight function, observe that

$$w(\sigma) > t \Leftrightarrow 2^{-|\sigma|} > t \Leftrightarrow |\sigma| < -\log_2 t.$$

Since Σ is finite, this implies that the set $\{\sigma \in \Sigma^* \mid w(\sigma) > t\}$ is finite, as required.

Below we define how a weight function induces a distance metric on output functions. Intuitively, the most important input sequence two output functions disagree on, i.e. the sequence with maximal weight, determines the distance.

Definition 6. *Let A, B be output functions over Σ and Γ, and let w be a weight function over Σ. Then the distance metric $d(A, B)$ induced by w is defined as:*

$$d(A, B) = \max\{w(\sigma) \mid \sigma \in \Sigma^* \wedge A(\sigma) \neq B(\sigma)\},$$

with the convention that $\max \emptyset = 0$. Sequence $\sigma \in \Sigma^*$ is a w-maximal distinguishing sequence for A and B if $A(\sigma) \neq B(\sigma)$ and $w(\sigma) = d(A, B)$.

Note that $d(A, B)$ is well-defined: the set $\{w(\sigma) \mid \sigma \in \Sigma^* \wedge A(\sigma) \neq B(\sigma)\}$ is either empty or contains, by the finiteness restriction for weight functions, a maximal element. Observe that for all output functions A and B with $A \neq B$ there exists a w-maximal distinguishing sequence.

Theorem 7. *Let Σ and Γ be nonempty, finite sets of inputs and outputs, and let $\mathcal{A}$ be the set of all output functions over Σ and Γ. Then the function d of Definition 6 is an ultrametric in the space $\mathcal{A}$ since, for any $A, B, C \in \mathcal{A}$,*

1. $d(A, B) = 0 \Leftrightarrow A = B$ *(identity of indiscernibles)*
2. $d(A, B) = d(B, A)$ *(symmetry)*
3. $d(A, B) \leq \max(d(A, C), d(C, B))$ *(strong triangle inequality)*

Proof

1. If $A = B$ then $d(A, B) = 0$ by definition of d and the convention $\max \emptyset = 0$. We prove the converse implication by contraposition. Assume $A \neq B$. Then there exists a $\sigma \in \Sigma^*$ such that $A(\sigma) \neq B(\sigma)$. Since, by definition of w, $w(\sigma) > 0$ it follows, by definition of d, that $d(A, B) \neq 0$.
2. Follows directly from the symmetry in the definition of d.
3. We consider four cases:
   (a) If $d(A, B) = 0$ then $d(A, B) \leq \max(d(A, C), d(C, B))$ holds trivially.
   (b) If $d(A, C) = 0$ then $A = C$ by identity of indiscernibles and $d(A, B) \leq \max(d(A, C), d(C, B))$ holds trivially.
   (c) If $d(C, B) = 0$ then $C = B$ by identity of indiscernibles and $d(A, B) \leq \max(d(A, C), d(C, B))$ holds trivially.
   (d) Assume $d(A, B) \neq 0$, $d(A, C) \neq 0$ and $d(C, B) \neq 0$. Let σ_1 be a w-maximal distinguishing sequence for A and B, let σ_2 be a w-maximal distinguishing sequence for A and C, and let σ_3 be a w-maximal distinguishing sequence for C and B. Let $t_1 = w(\sigma_1)$, $t_2 = w(\sigma_2)$, and $t_3 = w(\sigma_3)$. We prove $t_1 \leq \max(t_2, t_3)$ by contradiction. Suppose $t_1 > \max(t_2, t_3)$. By definition of d, we know that for all σ with $w(\sigma) > t_2$, $A(\sigma) = C(\sigma)$. Similarly, we know that for all σ with $w(\sigma) > t_3$, $C(\sigma) = B(\sigma)$. Thus, for all σ with $w(\sigma) \geq t_1$, $A(\sigma) = C(\sigma) = B(\sigma)$. This contradicts the fact that $w(\sigma_1) = t_1$ and $A(\sigma_1) \neq B(\sigma_1)$.

For any weight function w, we lift the induced distance metric from output functions to Mealy machines by defining, for Mealy machines M and M', $d(M, M') = d(A_M, A_{M'})$. Observe that $d(M, M') = 0$ iff $M \approx M'$. Also, for each $\varepsilon > 0$, the set $\{\sigma \in \Sigma^* \mid w(\sigma) \geq \varepsilon\}$ is finite. Thus there exists a finite test suite that we may apply to either find a counterexample that proves $M \not\approx M'$ or to establish that $d(M, M') < \varepsilon$.

4   Log-Based Metrics

A *log* $\tau \in \Sigma^*$ is an input sequence that has been observed during execution of the SUL. We assume a finite set $L \subset \Sigma^*$ of logs that have been collected from the SUL. For technical reasons, we require that ϵ is included in L.

Let S be an unknown model of an SUL, and let H be a learned hypothesis for S. Since S and H are Mealy Machines, we may associate to each log $\tau \in L$ unique states $q \in Q_S$ and $q' \in Q_H$, that are reached by taking the transitions for the input symbols of τ, starting from q_S^0 and q_H^0 respectively. In this case, we say that τ *visits the state pair* (q, q'). Next, we can search for a sequence ρ that distinguishes q and q'. Now, $\tau\rho$ distinguishes q_S^0 and q_H^0, and hence $S \not\approx H$. We may define the distance of S and H in terms of the minimal number of inputs required to distinguish any pair of states (q, q') that is visited by some log $\tau \in L$.

We will now formalize the above intuition by defining a weight function and a distance metric. For this we need an auxiliary definition that describes how to decompose any trace σ into a maximal prefix that is contained in L, and a subsequent suffix.

Definition 8. *Let $\sigma \in \Sigma^*$ be an input sequence. An L-decomposition of σ is a pair (τ, ρ) such that $\tau \in L$ and $\tau\rho = \sigma$. We say that (τ, ρ) is a maximal L-decomposition if $|\tau|$ is maximal, i.e. for all L-decompositions (τ', ρ') of σ we have $|\tau'| \leq |\tau|$.*

Observe that, since $\epsilon \in L$, each sequence σ has a unique maximal L-decomposition (τ, ρ). We can now define the weight function w_L as a variant of the weight function of Example 5 in which the weight is not determined by the length of σ but rather by the length of the suffix ρ of the maximal L-decomposition.

Definition 9. *Let A be an output function over Σ and Γ, and let $\sigma \in \Sigma^*$. Then the weight function w_L is defined as $w_L(\sigma) = 2^{-|\rho|}$, where (τ, ρ) is the maximal L-decomposition of σ. We write d_L for the distance metric induced by w_L.*

In order to see that w_L is indeed a proper weight function in the sense of Definition 4, fix a $t > 0$ and derive:

$$\{\sigma \in \Sigma^* \mid w_L(\sigma) > t\} =$$
$$\{\sigma \in \Sigma^* \mid \exists \tau, \rho : 2^{-|\rho|} > t \wedge (\tau, \rho) \text{ is a maximal } L\text{-decomposition of } \sigma\} \subseteq$$
$$\{\tau\rho \in \Sigma^* \mid 2^{-|\rho|} > t \wedge \tau \in L\} =$$
$$\{\tau\rho \in \Sigma^* \mid |\rho| < -\log_2 t \wedge \tau \in L\}$$

Since both Σ and L are finite the last set is finite, and therefore the first set is finite as well.

Observe that the metric d_L coincides with the metric of [3,23] if we take as set L of logs the singleton set $\{\epsilon\}$, as we then only take into account w-maximal distinguishing sequences starting in the initial state.

Example 10. Let us illustrate our log-based metric with a simple coffee machine. The machine is always used as follows. First, a coffee pod is placed, then the machine is provided with water, then the button is pressed to obtain coffee, and finally the machine is cleaned. The logs for the coffee machine consist

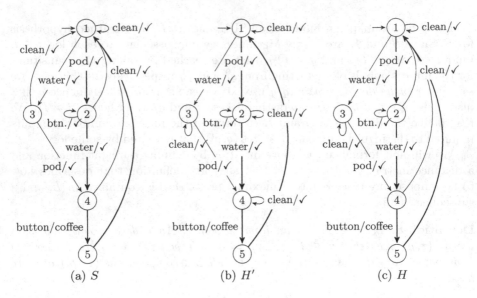

Fig. 1. Models of a coffee machine. The machine has one button (abbreviated as btn. in state 2), can be provided with a pod and water, and can be cleaned. It can produce coffee, or remain quiescent (✓) after an input. The logged trace is displayed with bold arrows. Some insignificant self-loops are not displayed.

of the sequence *pod water button clean* and all of its proper prefixes (i.e., *pod water button*, *pod water*, *pod*, and the empty sequence ϵ).

Figure 1 presents three models for the coffee machine. The model shown in Fig. 1a is the correct model S, and the models shown in Fig. 1b and c, respectively, are hypotheses H' and H for S. Observe that both hypotheses produce correct output for all logs, but that they nevertheless have some incorrect transitions. In H', the *clean* transitions are incorrect in states 2, 3 and 4. In H only the erroneous *clean* transition in state 3 remains.

Let us compute the distances of H' and H to S. A w_L-maximal distinguishing sequence to discover inequivalence of H' and S is *pod water clean button*. At the end of this sequence, H' outputs *coffee*, while S remains quiescent, i.e., output ✓. Despite that the sequence is of length four, it only takes two inputs to discover the error starting from a state that can be reached via a log, since state 4 is reached by *pod water*. Therefore, the distance between H' and S according to our metric is 2^{-2}.

A w_L-maximal distinguishing sequence to discover the remaining error in H is *water clean pod button*: H outputs *coffee* at the end of this sequence, where it should remain quiescent. Since the prefix *water* has never been observed in logs, it takes four inputs to discover this error starting from a state that has been visited by a log: state 1 is known because it is reached by the empty sequence ϵ. As a result, the distance between H and S according to our metric is 2^{-4}.

Observe that these distances capture the subtle improvement in H compared to H' (as $2^{-4} < 2^{-2}$), despite that four inputs are required in both hypotheses to discover an error. Both H' and H are wrong, but the problem with H' is more serious, as the error is visible after two transitions starting from a state that is reached during normal use of the system, instead of four transitions in H. In the metric of [3,23], both hypotheses would be considered equally distant to S for this reason.

Algorithm. Van den Bos [4] presents an algorithm for finding w_L-maximal distinguishing sequences for two given models. As we will see, such an algorithm is extremely useful as a component in model learning. The input of the algorithm of Van den Bos [4] consists of two Mealy machines H and H' that agree on all inputs from L, that is, $A_H(\sigma) = A_{H'}(\sigma)$, for all $\sigma \in L$. (This can be realized, for instance, by first checking for each hypothesis model whether it is consistent with all the logs in L.) The key idea of the algorithm is that minimal length distinguishing sequences (for pairs of states) are gathered by constructing a partition of indistinguishable states. By processing the partition, a distinguishing sequence of minimal length is found for each pair of states in $Q_H \times Q_{H'}$, or it is established that the states are equivalent. After that, a w_L-maximal distinguishing sequence can be found by picking a minimal length distinguishing sequence that is visited by some log in L. Intuitively, the time complexity of the search for these sequences can be deferred from the fact that a table has to be filled for all state pairs. Indeed, it follows that the algorithm is quadratic, i.e. of $\mathcal{O}(pn^2)$, where n is the sum of the number of states of H and H', and p is the number of inputs. In [22] it is shown that minimal length distinguishing sequences for all pairs of states can even be found in $\mathcal{O}(pn \log n)$.

Weighted Automata. There are many possible variations of our log-based metrics. We may for instance consider variations in which the weight of a log is partially determined by its frequency. We may also assign a higher weight to logs in which certain "important" inputs occur. All such variations can be easily defined using the concept of a *weighted automaton* [11], i.e., an automaton in which states and transition carry a certain weight. Below we define a slightly restricted type of weighted automaton, called *weighted Mealy machine*, which only assigns weights to transitions.

Definition 11. *A weighted Mealy machine is a tuple $M = (\Sigma, \Gamma, Q, q^0, \delta, \lambda, c)$, where $(\Sigma, \Gamma, Q, q^0, \delta, \lambda)$ is a Mealy machine and $c : Q \times \Sigma \to \mathbb{R}^{>0}$ is a cost function. Cost function c is extended to $Q \times \Sigma^*$ by defining, for all $q \in Q$, $i \in \Sigma$ and $\sigma \in \Sigma^*$, $c(q, \epsilon) = 1$ and $c(q, i\sigma) = c(q, i) \cdot c(\delta(q, i), \sigma)$. The cost function $c_M : \Sigma^* \to \mathbb{R}^{>0}$ induced by M is defined as $c_M(\sigma) = c(q^0, \sigma)$.*

A cost function c_M is not always a weight function in the sense of Definition 4, since it may assign an unbounded weight to infinitely many sequences. However, if the weight of any *cycle* in M is less than 1 then c_M is a weight function.

Definition 12. *Let $M = (\Sigma, \Gamma, Q, q^0, \delta, \lambda, c)$ be a weighted Mealy machine. A path of M is an alternating sequence $\pi = q_0 i_0 q_1 \cdots q_{n-1} i_{n-1} q_n$ of states in Q and inputs in Σ, beginning and ending with a state, such that, for all $0 \leq j < n$, $\delta(q_j, i_j) = q_{j+1}$. Path π is a cycle if $q_0 = q_n$ and $n > 0$. The weight of path π is defined as the product of the weights of the contained transitions: $\prod_{j=0}^{n-1} c(q_j, i_j)$.*

Theorem 13. *Let M be a weighted Mealy machine, then c_M is a weight function iff all cycles have weight (strictly) less than 1.*

Let L be a prefix closed set of logs (i.e. all prefixes of a log in L are also included in L). Then the weight function w_L of Definition 9 can alternatively be defined as the weight function c_M induced by a weighted automaton M with states taken from $L \cup \{\bot\}$, that is, the set of logs extended with an extra sink state $\bot$, initial state ϵ, and transition function δ and cost function c defined as:

$$\delta(q, i) = \begin{cases} qi & \text{if } q \in L \wedge qi \in L \\ \bot & \text{otherwise} \end{cases} \qquad c(q, i) = \begin{cases} 1 & \text{if } q \in L \wedge qi \in L \\ \frac{1}{2} & \text{otherwise} \end{cases}$$

Note that, by Theorem 13, c_M is indeed a weight function.

5   An Adapted Learning Algorithm

In this section, we will explain how weight functions and their induced metrics can be used to improve model learning.

Active learning is a learning framework in which a Learner can ask questions (*queries*) to a Teacher, as visualized in Fig. 2a. We assume that the Teacher is capable of answering queries correctly according to the Minimally Adequate Teacher (MAT) model of Angluin [2]. The Teacher knows a Mealy machine S which is unknown to the Learner. Initially, the Learner only knows the input and output symbols of S. The task of the Learner is to learn S by asking two types of queries:

- With a *membership query* (MQ), the Learner asks what the response is to an input sequence $\sigma \in \Sigma^*$. The Teacher answers with the output sequence $A_S(\sigma)$.
- With an *equivalence query* (EQ), the Learner asks whether a hypothesized Mealy machine H is correct, that is, whether $H \approx S$. The Teacher answers *yes* if this is the case. Otherwise it answers *no* and supplies a *counterexample*, which is a sequence $\sigma \in \Sigma^*$ that produces a different output sequence for both Mealy machines, that is, $A_H(\sigma) \neq A_S(\sigma)$.

Starting from Angluin's seminal L^* algorithm [2], many algorithms have been proposed for learning a Mealy machine H that is equivalent to S via a finite number of queries. We refer to [15] for an excellent recent overview. In applications in which one wants to learn a model of a black-box reactive system, the Teacher typically consists of a System Under Learning (SUL) that answers the membership queries, and a conformance testing (CT) tool [16] that approximates the equivalence queries using a set of *test queries* (TQs). A test query consists

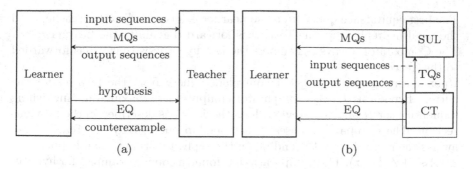

Fig. 2. Active learning framework (a) and implementation for black-box learning (b).

of asking the SUL what the response is to an input sequence $\sigma \in \Sigma^*$, similar to a membership query. A schematic overview of such an implementation of active learning is shown in Fig. 2b.

We will now explain how weight functions and the metrics they induce can be used to enhance active learning. Our idea is to place a new "Comparator" component in between the Learner and the Teacher, as displayed in Fig. 3. The Comparator ensures that the distance of subsequent hypotheses to the target model S never increases. Moreover, the Comparator may replace an equivalence query by a single membership query. This speeds up the learning process, since a Teacher typically answers an equivalence query by running a large number of test queries generated by a conformance testing algorithm. In the printer controller case study of [21], for instance, on average more than 270.000 test queries were used to implement a single equivalence query.

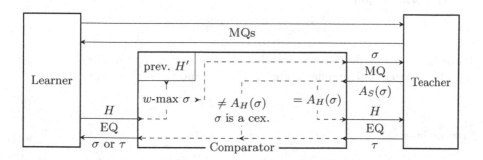

Fig. 3. Active learning framework with the Comparator in the middle.

Assume we have a weight function w and an oracle which, for given models H and H' with $H \not\approx H'$, produces a w-maximal distinguishing sequence, that is, a sequence $\sigma \in \Sigma^*$ with $d(H, H') = w(\sigma)$ and $A_H(\sigma) \neq A_{H'}(\sigma)$. The behavior of the Comparator component can now be described as follows:

- The first equivalence query from the Learner is forwarded to the Teacher, and the resulting reply from the Teacher is forwarded again to the Learner.
- The Comparator always remembers the last hypothesis that it has forwarded to the Teacher.
- Upon receiving any subsequent equivalence query from the Learner for the current hypothesis H, the Comparator computes a w-maximal distinguishing sequence σ for H and the previous hypothesis H', as described in the previous section. The Comparator poses a membership query σ to the Teacher and awaits the reply $A_S(\sigma)$. Depending on the reply, two things may happen:
    1. $A_S(\sigma) \neq A_H(\sigma)$. The Comparator has found a counterexamples for hypothesis H, and returns *no* together with σ to the Learner in response to the equivalence query.
    2. $A_S(\sigma) = A_H(\sigma)$. The Comparator forwards the equivalence query to the Teacher, waits for the reply, and forwards this to the Learner.

From the perspective of the Learner, the combination of a Comparator and a Teacher behave like a regular Teacher, since all membership and equivalence queries are answered appropriately and correctly. Hence the Learner will succeed to learn a correct hypothesis H after posing a finite number of queries.

Conversely, from the perspective of the Teacher, the Comparator and the Learner together behave just like a regular Learner that poses membership and equivalence queries. A key property of the Comparator/Learner combination, however, is that the quality of hypotheses never decreases. We claim that, whenever the Comparator first poses an equivalence query for H' and then for H, we always have $d(S, H) \leq d(S, H')$. In order to see why this is true, observe that when the Comparator poses the equivalence query for H it has found a w-maximal distinguishing sequence σ for H and H'. Therefore we know that $A_H(\sigma) \neq A_{H'}(\sigma)$ and

$$w(\sigma) = d(H', H) \tag{1}$$

Through a membership query σ the Comparator has also discovered that $A_S(\sigma) = A_H(\sigma)$. This implies $A_S(\sigma) \neq A_{H'}(\sigma)$ and thus

$$w(\sigma) \leq d(S, H') \tag{2}$$

Now we infer

$$d(S, H) \leq \text{(by the strong triangle inequality, Theorem 7)}$$
$$\max(d(S, H'), d(H', H)) = \text{(by equation (1))}$$
$$\max(d(S, H'), w(\sigma)) = \text{(by inequality (2))}$$
$$d(S, H').$$

Hence, the distance between subsequent hypotheses and S never increases.

6   Case Studies

In this section, we present two case studies in which we measure the effect of a Comparator for the log-based metrics from Sect. 4. In the first case study, we learn a model for the Engine Status Manager (ESM), a piece of industrial software that controls the transition from one status to another in Océ printers. In the second case study we learn a model for the Windows 8 TCP server.

Engine Status Manager. In [20], a first attempt was made to learn a model for the ESM using the algorithm of Rivest and Schapire [18] as implemented in LEARNLIB [17]. A manually constructed reference model was used to determine the success of the learning algorithm. The author did not succeed in learning the complete model, as it took the Teacher too long to find a counterexample at some point. A second attempt was made in [21]. In this work, an adaptation of a finite state machine testing algorithm by Lee and Yannakakis [16] was used by the Teacher to find counterexamples. The authors succeeded in learning a complete, correct model with 3410 states for the ESM through a sequence of more than 100 hypotheses. Particularly because of the large number of hypotheses, this case study appeared to be a suitable case to test the impact of a Comparator.

Using the same setup for the Learner and the Teacher as in [21], we have conducted twenty independent runs for each of the following three experiments.

(a) The classical setting without a Comparator.
(b) A setting with a Comparator and the trivial log set $L = \{\epsilon\}$. This setup resembles the algorithm presented by Smetsers et al. [23].
(c) A setting with a Comparator, using the aforementioned algorithm for finding w-maximal distinguishing sequences on a nontrivial set of logs.

No real logs were available to us for setup (c), because no appropriate logging method was in place to obtain real user logs from, and setting up such logging would be tedious. Instead, we developed a method to generate logs that resemble real logs. In [20], a couple of 'paths', directly inferred from the ESM, are given. Such a path is a sequence of subsets of the input alphabet. An input sequence for the ESM can be obtained by concatenating inputs from the subsequent subsets of the path. More specifically, the algorithm for doing this keeps track of the sequence σ it has constructed, the current state q, the set of already visited states V, and the index k of the current subset of the path. Initially, $\sigma = \epsilon$, $q = q^0$, $V = \{q^0\}$, and $k = 0$. The algorithm extends σ with an input i from subset k if $\delta(q, i) \notin V$. In that case, q and V are updated accordingly. Else, we search for an input in subset $k + 1$. Only sequences with their last input in the last subset of a path are included in the logs. In total, we have generated 9800 logs for each run.

Experimental results are shown in Table 1. On average over 20 runs, setup (c) (with Comparator) requires 25.8 % fewer inputs than setup (a) (no Comparator), and 16.8 % fewer inputs than setup (b) (the algorithm of [23]) to learn a correct

Table 1. Number of inputs used to learn a model for the ESM ($n = 20$).

Setup	Mean	Std. dev.	Median	Min	Max
(a)	416 519 487	119 015 166	404 307 465	109 781 273	686 385 316
(b)	371 248 375	57 005 155	377 724 597	290 072 340	545 535 231
(c)	308 928 853	50 719 369	295 863 646	243 197 179	430 523 416

Table 2. Number of inputs used to learn a model for a TCP server ($n = 500$).

Setup	Mean	Std. dev.	Median	Min	Max
(a)	163 463	154 353	106 750	35 694	1 076 538
(b)	162 948	191 222	105 487	40 927	2 380 343
(c)	159 409	141 255	110 545	41 471	1 168 348

model for the ESM. A non-parametrical, distribution independent statistical test was used to determine that this result is significant ($p < 0.05$, $z = -4.15$).

TCP. In [13], active learning was used to obtain a model for the Windows 8 TCP server. Using the aforementioned Learner and Teacher algorithms, the authors succeeded in learning a model of 38 states through a series of 13 hypotheses. We have conducted 500 runs for each of the experimental setups described above, using the model of [13] as an SUL. Experimental results are shown in Table 2. Unfortunately, we found no significant reduction in inputs when using the Comparator. We conjecture that this is due to the inherent simplicity of the model.

7   Conclusions and Future Work

We have presented a general class of distance metrics on Mealy machines that may be used to formalize intuitive notions of quality. Preliminary experiments show that our metrics can be used to obtain a significant reduction of the number of inputs required to learn large black-box models. For smaller models, no reduction was found. Therefore, we conjecture that the utility of our metrics increases as models become more complex. In future work, we plan to perform more experiments to verify these results. In addition, we wish to do experiments with real logs, instead of generated ones. Another topic for future research is to develop efficient algorithms for computing w-maximal distinguishing sequences for the weight functions induced by weighted Mealy machines. Bounding the distance between a hypothesis and the unknown target model during learning remains a challenging problem. Our experiments have produced discouraging results in this sense, since the quality of a hypothesis is hard to predict because of the high variance for different experimental runs.

References

1. De Alfaro, L., Faella, M., Stoelinga, M.: Linear and branching system metrics. IEEE Trans. Software Eng. **35**(2), 258–273 (2009)
2. Angluin, D.: Learning regular sets from queries and counterexamples. Inf. Comput. **75**(2), 87–106 (1987)
3. De Bakker, J.W., Zucker, J.I.: Processes and the denotational semantics of concurrency. Inf. Control **54**(12), 70–120 (1982)
4. Van den Bos, P.: Enhancing active automata learning by a user log based metric. Master's thesis, Radboud University Nijmegen (2015)
5. Briones, L.B., Brinksma, E., Stoelinga, M.: A semantic framework for test coverage. In: Graf, S., Zhang, W. (eds.) ATVA 2006. LNCS, vol. 4218, pp. 399–414. Springer, Heidelberg (2006)
6. Černý, P., Henzinger, T.A., Radhakrishna, A.: Simulation distances. In: Gastin, P., Laroussinie, F. (eds.) CONCUR 2010. LNCS, vol. 6269, pp. 253–268. Springer, Heidelberg (2010)
7. de Alfaro, L., Henzinger, T.A., Majumdar, R.: Discounting the future in systems theory. In: Baeten, J.C.M., Lenstra, J.K., Parrow, J., Woeginger, G.J. (eds.) ICALP 2003. LNCS, vol. 2719, pp. 1022–1037. Springer, Heidelberg (2003)
8. de la Higuera, C.: Grammatical Inference. Cambridge University Press, Cambridge (2010)
9. de Ruiter, J., Poll, E.: Protocol state fuzzing of TLS implementations. In: USENIX Security 2015, pp. 193–206. USENIX Association, Washington, D.C., August 2015
10. Dijkstra, E.W.: The humble programmer. CACM **15**(10), 859–866 (1972)
11. Droste, M., Kuich, W., Vogler, H.: Handbook of Weighted Automata, 1st edn. Springer, Heidelberg (2009)
12. Fiterău-Broştean, P., Janssen, R., Vaandrager, F.: Learning fragments of the TCP network protocol. In: Lang, F., Flammini, F. (eds.) FMICS 2014. LNCS, vol. 8718, pp. 78–93. Springer, Heidelberg (2014)
13. Fiterău-Broştean, P., Janssen, R., Vaandrager, F.: Combining model learning and model checking to analyze TCP implementations. Submitted to CAV (2016). http://www.sws.cs.ru.nl/publications/papers/fvaan/FJV16/
14. Henzinger, T.: Quantitative reactive modeling and verification. Comput. Sci. Res. Dev. **28**(4), 331–344 (2013)
15. Isberner, M.: Foundations of Active Automata Learning: An Algorithmic Perspective. Ph.D. thesis, Technical University of Dortmund (2015)
16. Lee, D., Yannakakis, M.: Principles and methods of testing finite state machines-a survey. Proc. IEEE **84**(8), 1090–1123 (1996)
17. Raffelt, H., Steffen, B., Berg, T., Margaria, T.: LearnLib: a framework for extrapolating behavioral models. STTT **11**(5), 393–407 (2009)
18. Rivest, R.L., Schapire, R.E.: Inference of finite automata using homing sequences. Inf. Comput. **103**(2), 299–347 (1993)
19. Schuts, M., Hooman, J., Vaandrager, F.: Refactoring of legacy software using model learning and equivalence checking: an industrial experience report. In: Proceedings of iFM (2016)
20. Smeenk, W.: Applying automata learning to complex industrial software. Master's thesis, Radboud University Nijmegen, September 2012
21. Smeenk, W., Moerman, J., Vaandrage, F., Jansen, D.N.: Applying Automata Learning to Embedded Control Software. In: Butler, M., Conchon, S., Zaïdi, F. (eds.) ICFEM 2015. LNCS, vol. 9407, pp. 67–83. Springer, Heidelberg (2015). doi:10.1007/978-3-319-25423-4_5

22. Smetsers, R., Moerman, J., Jansen, D.N.: Minimal separating sequences for all Pairs of states. In: Dediu, A.-H., Janoušek, J., Martín-Vide, C., Truthe, B. (eds.) LATA 2016. LNCS, vol. 9618, pp. 181–193. Springer, Heidelberg (2016). doi:10.1007/978-3-319-30000-9_14

23. Smetsers, R., Volpato, M., Vaandrager, F., Verwer, S.: Bigger is not always better: on the quality of hypotheses in active automata learning. In: Proceedings of ICGI, JMLR: W&CP, vol. 34, pp. 167–181 (2014)

24. Sommerville, I.: Software Engineering. Addison-Wesley Publishing Company, Boston (2001)

25. Steffen, B., Howar, F., Merten, M.: Introduction to Active automata learning from a practical perspective. In: Bernardo, M., Issarny, V. (eds.) SFM 2011. LNCS, vol. 6659, pp. 256–296. Springer, Heidelberg (2011)

26. Thrane, C., Fahrenberg, U., Larsen, K.G.: Quantitative analysis of weighted transition systems. J. Logic Algebraic Program. 79(7), 689–703 (2010)

Refactoring of Legacy Software Using Model Learning and Equivalence Checking: An Industrial Experience Report

Mathijs Schuts[1]([⊠]), Jozef Hooman[2,3], and Frits Vaandrager[3]

[1] Philips, Best, The Netherlands
mathijs.schuts@philips.com
[2] Embedded Systems Innovation (ESI) by TNO, Eindhoven, The Netherlands
jozef.hooman@tno.nl
[3] Department of Software Science, Radboud University, Nijmegen, The Netherlands
f.vaandrager@cs.ru.nl

Abstract. Many companies struggle with large amounts of legacy software that is difficult to maintain and to extend. Refactoring legacy code typically requires large efforts and introduces serious risks because often crucial business assets are hidden in legacy components. We investigate the support of formal techniques for the rejuvenation of legacy embedded software, concentrating on control components. Model learning and equivalence checking are used to improve a new implementation of a legacy control component. Model learning is applied to both the old and the new implementation. The resulting models are compared using an equivalence check of a model checker. We report about our experiences with this approach at Philips. By gradually increasing the set of input stimuli, we obtained implementations of a power control service for which the learned behaviour is equivalent.

1 Introduction

The high-tech industry creates complex cyber physical systems. The architectures for these systems evolved over many decades through a constant stream of product innovations. This usually leads to so-called *legacy* components that are hard to maintain and to extend [24,25]. Typically, these components are based on obsolete technologies, frameworks, and tools. Documentation might not be available or outdated and the original developers are often no longer available. In addition, the existing regression test set for validating the component will be very limited in most cases.

Given these characteristics, innovations that require changes of legacy components are risky. Many legacy components implicitly incorporate important business knowledge, hence failures will lead to substantial losses. To avoid a risky greenfield approach, starting from scratch, several techniques are being developed to extract the crucial business information hidden in legacy components in a (semi-)automated way and to use this information to develop a refactored version of the component.

© Springer International Publishing Switzerland 2016
E. Ábrahám and M. Huisman (Eds.): IFM 2016, LNCS 9681, pp. 311–325, 2016.
DOI: 10.1007/978-3-319-33693-0_20

There are several approaches to extract this hidden information. Static analysis methods concentrate on the analysis and transformation of source code. For instance, the commercial Design Maintenance System (DMS)[1] has been used in several industrial projects to re-engineer code. DMS is based on abstract syntax tree (AST) representations of programs [3].

Whereas static analysis techniques focus on the internal structure of components, learning techniques aim at capturing the externally visible behaviour of a component. Process mining extracts business logic based on event logs [23]. In [17], a combination of static analysis and process mining has been applied to a financial management system, identifying tasks, actors, and their roles. Process mining can be seen as a passive way of learning which requires an instrumentation of the code to obtain event logs.

Active learning techniques [4,22] do not require code instrumentation, but need an adapter to interact with a running system. In this approach, a learning algorithm interacts with a software component by sending inputs and observing the resulting output, and uses this information to construct a state machine model. Active learning has, for instance, been successfully applied to learn models of (and to find mistakes in) implementations of protocols such as TCP [12] and TLS [8], to establish correctness of protocol implementations relative to a given reference implementation [2], and to generate models of a telephone switch [18] and a printer controller [21]. Learning-based testing [11] combines active learning and model checking. In this approach, which requires the presence of a formal specification of the system, model checking is used to guide the learning process. In [11] three industrial applications of learning-based testing are described from the web, automotive and finance domains.

In this paper, we report about a novel industrial application of active learning to gain confidence in a refactored legacy component using formal techniques. In the absence of any formal specification of the legacy system, the use of model checking and learning-based testing was not possible. Instead we decided to use a different combination of tools, similar to the approach of [2,13]. The model learning tool LearnLib [15] was used to learn Mealy machine models of the legacy and the refactored implementation. These models were then compared to check if the two implementations are equivalent. Since the manual comparison of large models is not feasible, we used an equivalence checker from the mCRL2 toolset [7] for this task. In brief, our approach can be described as follows (see also Fig. 1):

1. Implementation A (the legacy component) is explored by a model learner. The output of the model learner is converted to an input format for the equivalence checker, model MA.
2. Implementation B (the refactored component) is explored by a model learner. The output of the model learner is converted to an input format for the equivalence checker, model MB.
3. The two models are checked by the equivalence checker. The result of the equivalence checker can be:

---

[1] www.semanticdesigns.com.

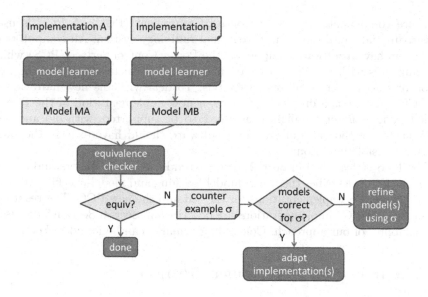

Fig. 1. Approach to compare legacy component and refactored version

- The two models are equivalent. In this case we are done.
- The two models are not equivalent and a counterexample is provided: a sequence of inputs σ for which the outputs produced by the two models are different. In this case we proceed to step 4.
4. Because models A and B have been obtained through a finite number of tests, we can never be sure that they correctly describe implementations A and B, respectively. Therefore, if we find a counterexample σ for the equivalence of models MA and MB, we first check whether implementation A and model MA behave the same for σ, and whether implementation B and model MB behave the same for σ. If there is a discrepancy between a model and the corresponding implementation, this means that the model is incorrect and we ask the model learner to construct a new model based on counterexample σ, that is, we go back to step 1 or 2. Otherwise, counterexample σ exhibits a difference between the two implementations. In this case we need to change at least one of the implementations, depending on which output triggered in response to input σ is considered unsatisfactory behaviour. Note that also the legacy component A might be changed, because the counterexample might indicate an unsatisfactory behaviour of A. After the change, a corrected implementation needs to be learned again, i.e., we go back to step 1 or 2.

Since the learning of an implementation can take a substantial amount of time, we start with a limited subset of input stimuli for the model-learner and increase the number of stimuli once the implementations are equivalent for a smaller number of stimuli. Hence, the approach needs to be executed iteratively.

We report about our experiences with the described approach on a real development project at Philips. The project concerns the introduction of a new hardware component, the Power Control Component (PCC). A PCC is used to start-up and shutdown an interventional radiology system. All computers in the system have a software component, the Power Control Service (PCS) which communicates with the PCC over an internal control network during the execution of start-up and shutdown scenarios. To deal with the new hardware of the PCC, which has a different interface, a new implementation of the PCS is needed. Since different configurations have to be supported, with old and new PCC hardware, the old and new PCS software should have exactly the same externally visible behaviour.

The PCS is described in Sect. 2 to the extend needed for understanding this paper. Section 3 describes the use of model-learning and model-checking to compare the two PCS implementations for the old and the new PCC. The results of testing the two PCS implementations are described in Sect. 4. Section 5 discusses the scalability of our approach. Concluding remarks can be found in Sect. 6.

2   The Industrial Development Project

2.1   Power Control Service

For starting up and shutting down an interventional radiology system multiple components are involved. The Power Control Component (PCC) is a hardware component that gets the mains power input from the hospital. It conditions the mains power, switches the power taps that are connected to system's internal components and acts as the master of the system when executing start-up and shutdown scenarios. All computers in the system are powered by the PCC and are controlled by the PCC via a Power Control Service (PCS) that connects to the PCC via the system's internal control network.

Figure 2 depicts the PCS in its context. The PCS is a software component that is used to start and stop subsystems via their Session Managers (SMs). In addition to the start-up and shutdown scenarios executed by the PCC, the PCS is also involved during service scenarios such as upgrading the subsystem's software.

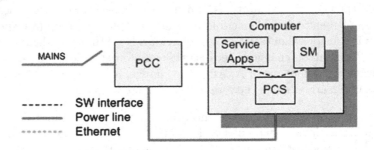

Fig. 2. Context power control service

In a typical shutdown scenario, the user presses the off button and the shutdown scenario is initiated by the PCC. The PCC sends an event to all PCSs. The PCS stops the SMs. Once the SMs are stopped, the PCS triggers the Operating System (OS) to shutdown. In the end, the OS will stop the PCS.

Another scenario is to switch from closed profile to open profile when the system is in the operational state. In closed profile only the clinical application can be executed by the user of the system. Open profile is used during development for testing purposes. In this scenario, the service application triggers the PCS to switch to open profile. The PCS will then stop the SMs. When the PCS is ready, the service application reboots the PC. After the reboot, the OS starts up the PCS and the PCS starts a subset of the SMs based on the SM's capabilities. In open profile, the service application can also start the clinical application by providing the PCS with the OpenProfileStartApplication trigger.

2.2   Refactoring

The PCS implementation for the old PCC is event-based. An event is handled differently based on the value of global flags in the source code. Hence, all state behaviour is implicitly coded by these flags, which makes the implementation unmaintainable. The development of a new implementation for supporting the new PCC is an opportunity to create a maintainable implementation. The new implementation makes the state behaviour explicit by a manually crafted state machine.

To be able to support both the old and the new PCC, the PCS software has been refactored such that the common behaviour for both PCCs is extracted. Figure 3(a) depicts the PCS before refactoring. The Host implements the IHost interface that is used by the service application. The implementation of the PCS after refactoring is show in Fig. 3(b).

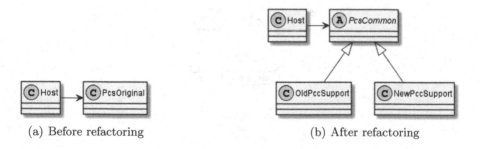

(a) Before refactoring   (b) After refactoring

Fig. 3. Class diagrams of PCS design

The PcsCommon class implements the ISessionManager interface to control the SMs. The OldPccSupport class contains the legacy implementation for the old PCC whereas a NewPccSupport class deals with the new PCC. Both classes inherit from the PcsCommon class to achieve the same internal interface for the Host.

Depending on the configuration, the Host creates an instance of either the Old-PccSupport or the NewPccSupport class.

The PCS as depicted in Fig. 3(b) is written in C++ and consists of a total of 3365 Lines Of Code (LOC): Host has 741 LOC, PcsCommon has 376 LOC, OldPccSupport has 911 LOC, and NewPccSupport has 1337 LOC.

The unit test cases were adapted to include tests for the new implementation. It was known that the unit test set is far from complete. Hence, we investigated the possibility to use model-learning to get more confidence in the equivalence of the old and new implementations.

3   Application of the Learning Approach

To learn models of our implementations, we used the LearnLib tool [19], see http://learnlib.de/. For a detailed introduction into LearnLib we refer to [22]. In our application we used the development 1.0-SNAPSHOT of LearnLib and its MealyLearner which is connected to the System Under Learning (SUL) by means of an adapter and a TCP/IP connection.

3.1   Design of the Learning Environment

Figure 4 depicts the design used for learning the PCS component. Creating an initial version of the adapter took about 8 h, because the test primitives of the existing unit test environment could be re-used.

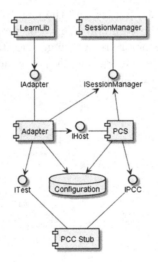

Fig. 4. Design learning environment

With this design, the PCS can be learned for both the old and the new PCC. The adapter automatically changes the configuration of the PCS such that the PCS knows if it needs to instantiate the old or the new implementation. Depending on the old or new PCC, the adapter instantiates a different PCC stub.

3.2 Learned Output

The Mealy machine that is the result of a LearnLib session is represented as a "dot" file, which can be visualized using Graphviz[2]. A fragment of a model is shown in Table 1.

Table 1. Fragment of a learned dot-file

```
digraph g {
start0 [label="" shape="none"];

s0 [shape="circle" label="0"];
s1 [shape="circle" label="1"];
s2 [shape="circle" label="2"];
s3 [shape="circle" label="3"];
s4 [shape="circle" label="4"];
s5 [shape="circle" label="5"];
s6 [shape="circle" label="6"];
s7 [shape="circle" label="7"];
s8 [shape="circle" label="8"];
s0 -> s1 [label="|PCC(StateSystemOn)| / |PCS(Running);SM1(Running);SM2(Running)|"];
s0 -> s2 [label="|PCC(StateSystemOff)| / |PCS(Running);SM1(Stopped);SM2(Stopped);Dev(Shutdown)|"];
s1 -> s2 [label="|PCC(ButtonSystemOff)| / |PCS(Running);SM1(Stopped);SM2(Stopped);Dev(Shutdown)|"];
s1 -> s3 [label="|Host(goToOpenProfile)| / |PCS(Stopped);SM1(Stopped);SM2(Stopped);Dev(OpenProfile)|"];
...
start0 -> s0;
}
```

3.3 Checking Equivalence

For models with more than five states it is difficult to compare the graphical output of LearnLib for different implementations. Therefore, an equivalence checker is used to perform the comparison. In our case, we used the tool support for mCRL2 (micro Common Representation Language 2) which is a specification language that can be used for specifying system behaviour. The mCRL2 language comes with a rich set of supporting programs for analysing the behaviour of a modelled system [7].

Once the implementation is learned, a small script is used to convert the output from LearnLib to a mCRL2 model. Basically, the learned Mealy machine is represented as an mCRL2 process `Spec(s:States)`. As an example, the two transitions of state s0 in the dot-file

```
s0 -> s1 [label="|PCC(StateSystemOn)| / |PCS(Running);SM1(Running);SM2(Running)|"];
s0 -> s2 [label="|PCC(StateSystemOff)| / |PCS(Running);SM1(Stopped);SM2(Stopped);Dev(Shutdown)|"];
```

are translated into the following process algebra construction:

```
(s==s0) -> (
  (PCC(StateSystemOn) . PCS(Running) . SM1(Running) . SM2(Running) . Spec(s1)) +
  (PCC(StateSystemOff) . PCS(Running) . SM1(Stopped) . SM2(Stopped) . Dev(Shutdown) . Spec(s2))
)
```

A part of the result of translating the model of Table 1 to mCRL2 is shown in Table 2.

---

[2] www.graphviz.org/.

Table 2. Fragment of mCRL2 model

```
sort States = struct s0 | s1 | s2 | s3 | s4 | s5 | s6 | s7 | s8;
OsStim = struct StartPcs | StopPcs;
PCCStim = struct StateSystemOn | StateSystemOff | ...;
HostStim = struct stopForInstallation | startAfterInstallation | ...;
ServiceStates = struct Running | Stopped;
DevStates = struct OpenProfile | Shutdown;

act OS:OsStim;
act PCC:PCCStim;
act Host:HostStim;
act PCS:ServiceStates;
act SM1:ServiceStates;
act SM2:ServiceStates;
act Dev:DevStates;

proc Spec(s:States)=
 (s==s0) -> (
  (PCC(StateSystemOn) . PCS(Running) . SM1(Running) . SM2(Running) . Spec(s1)) +
  (PCC(StateSystemOff) . PCS(Running) . SM1(Stopped) . SM2(Stopped) . Dev(Shutdown) . Spec(s2))
 ) +
 (s==s1) -> (
  (PCC(ButtonSystemOff) . PCS(Running) . SM1(Stopped) . SM2(Stopped) . Dev(Shutdown) . Spec(s2)) +
  (Host(goToOpenProfile) . PCS(Stopped) . SM1(Stopped) . SM2(Stopped) . Dev(OpenProfile) . Spec(s3)) +
  (Host(goToClosedProfile) . PCS(Stopped) . SM1(Stopped) . SM2(Stopped) . Spec(s4)) +
  (Host(openProfileStartApplication) . PCS(Running) . SM1(Running) . SM2(Running) . Spec(s1)) +
  (Host(openProfileStopApplication) . PCS(Running) . SM1(Running) . SM2(Running) . Spec(s1)) +
  (OS(StartPcs) . PCS(Running) . SM1(Running) . SM2(Running) . Spec(s1)) +
  (OS(StopPcs) . PCS(Stopped) . SM1(Stopped) . SM2(Stopped) . Spec(s4))
 ) +
 (s==s2) -> (
  ...
 );

init Spec(s0);
```

Given two (deterministic) Mealy machines, the labelled transition systems for the associated mCRL2 processes are also deterministic. Since the labelled transition systems also do not contain any τ-transitions, trace equivalence and bisimulation equivalence coincide, and there is no difference between weak and strong equivalences [10]. Thus, two Mealy machines are equivalent iff the associated mCRL2 processes are (strong) trace equivalent, and the mCRL2 processes are (strong) trace equivalent iff they are (strong) bisimulation equivalent.

3.4   Investigating Counterexamples

When the equivalence check indicates that the two models are not equivalent, the mCRL2 tool provides a counterexample. To investigate counterexamples, we created a program that reads a produced counterexample and executes this on the implementations. In the design depicted in Fig. 4, the LearnLib component has been replaced by the counterexample program. As before, switching between the two implementations can be done by instructing the adapter. In this way, the standard logging facilities of program execution are exploited to study the counterexample.

4   Results of Learning the Implementations of the PCS

In this section we describe the results of applying the approach of Sect. 1 to the implementations of the PCS component.

4.1   Iteration 1

The first iteration was used to realize the learning environment as is described in Sect. 3.1. An adapter was created to interface between the PCS and LearnLib. Because the communication between the PCS and the adapter is asynchronous, the adapter has to wait some time before the state of the PCS can be examined. In this iteration we performed a few try runs to tweak the wait time needed before taking a sample. In addition, the first iteration was used to get an impression on how long learning the PCS takes with different numbers of stimuli. The necessary waiting time of 10 second after a stimulus for learning the PCS is quite long, and this greatly influenced the time needed for learning models.

4.2   Iteration 2

After a first analysis of the time needed for model learning in iteration 1, we decided to start learning with 9 stimuli. These 9 stimuli were all related to basic start-up/shutdown and service scenarios. We learned the PCS implementation for the old PCC and the PCS implementation for the new PCC. The results are presented in Table 3. The table has a column for the number of stimuli, for the number of states and transitions found, and for the time it took for LearnLib to learn the implementations.

Table 3. Results learning PCS with 9 stimuli

	Stimuli	States	Transitions	Time (in seconds)
PCS implementation for old PCC	9	8	43	32531
PCS implementation for new PCC	9	3	8	1231

Note that learning a model for the old implementation took 9 h. (This excludes the time used to test the correctness of the final model.) As described in Sect. 3.3, the learned models were converted to mCRL2 processes. Next, the mCRL2 tools found a counterexample starting with:

PCC(StateSystemOn), PCS(Running), SM1(Running), SM2(Running), ...

We investigated this counterexample and found an issue in the PCS implementation for the new PCC. The new implementation did not make a distinction between the SystemOff event, and the ServiceStop and ServiceShutdown events.

Note that before performing the learning experiment the new and old implementations were checked using the existing regression test cases. This issue was not found by the existing unit test cases.

4.3 Iteration 3

In the third iteration, the PCS implementation for the new PCC was re-learned after solving the fix. Table 4 describes the results.

Table 4. Results learning PCS with 9 stimuli

	Stimuli	States	Transitions	Time (in seconds)
PCS implementation for old PCC	9	8	43	32531
PCS implementation for new PCC	9	7	36	8187

An equivalence check with the mCRL2 tools resulted in a new counterexample of 23 commands:
PCC(StateSystemOn), PCS(Running), SM1(Running), SM2(Running),
Host(goToOpenProfile), PCS(Stopped), SM1(Stopped), SM2(Stopped),
Dev(OpenProfile), OS(StartPcs), PCS(Running), SM1(Stopped),
SM2(Running), Dev(OpenProfile), Host(openProfileStopApplication),
PCS(Running), SM1(Stopped), SM2(Running), Dev(OpenProfile),
PCC(ButtonSystemOff), PCS(Running), SM1(Stopped), SM2(Running).

When we executed this counterexample on the PCS implementation for the old PCC, we found the following statement in the logging of the PCS: "Off button not handled because of PCS state (Stopping)". A quick search in the source code revealed that the stopSessionManagers method prints this statement when the Stopping flag is active. This is clearly wrong, because this flag is set by the previous stimulus, i.e., the openProfileStopApplication stimulus. The PCS implementation for the old PCC was adapted to reset the Stopping flag after handling the openProfileStopApplication stimulus.

4.4 Iteration 4

In the fourth iteration, the PCS implementation for the old PCC was re-learned after solving the fix. Table 5 describes the results after re-learning. Note that, after correcting the error, learning the model for the old implementation only takes slightly more than one hour. When checking the equivalence, the mCRL2 tool reports that the two implementation are (strong) trace equivalent for these 9 stimuli.

Table 5. Results learning PCS with 9 stimuli

	Stimuli	States	Transitions	Time (in seconds)
PCS implementation for old PCC	9	7	36	4141
PCS implementation for new PCC	9	7	36	8187

4.5   Iteration 5

As a next step we re-learned the implementations for the complete set of 12 stimuli; the results are shown in Table 6. Note that learning the new implementation takes approximately 3.5 h. The mCRL2 tools report that the two obtained models with 12 stimuli are trace equivalence and bisimulation equivalent.

Table 6. Results learning PCS with 12 stimuli

	Stimuli	States	Transitions	Time (in seconds)
PCS implementation for old PCC	12	9	65	10059
PCS implementation for new PCC	12	9	65	12615

5   Scalability of the Learning Approach

Using model learning we found issues in both a legacy software component and in a refactored implementation. After fixing these issues, model learning helped to increase confidence that the old and the new implementations behave the same. Although this is a genuine industrial case study, the learned Mealy machine models are very small. Nevertheless, learning these tiny models already took up to 9 h. For applying these techniques in industry there is an obvious need to make model learning more efficient in terms of the time needed to explore a system under learning. Clearly, our approach has been highly effective for the PCC case study. But will it scale?

Below we present an overview of some recent results that make us optimistic that indeed our approach can be scaled to a large class of more complex legacy systems.

5.1   Faster Implementations

The main reason why model learning takes so long for the PCC case study is the long waiting time in between input events. As a result, running a single test sequence (a.k.a. membership query) took on average about 10 s. One of the authors was involved in another industrial case study in which a model for a printer controller was learned with 3410 states and 77 stimuli [21]. Even though more than 60 million test sequences were needed to learn it, the task could be completed within 9 h because on average running a single test sequence took only 0.0005 s. For most software components the waiting times can be much smaller than for the PCS component studied in this paper. In addition, if the waiting times are too long then sometimes it may be possible to modify the components (just for the purpose of the model learning) and reduce the response times. For our PCC case study such an approach is difficult. The PCS controls the Session Managers (SMs), which are Windows services. After an input event we want to observe the resulting state change of the SMs, but due to the unreliable timing of the OS we need to wait quite long. In order to reduce waiting times we would need to speed up Windows.

5.2 Faster Learning and Testing Algorithms

There has been much progress recently in developing new algorithms for automata learning. In particular, the new TTT learning algorithm that has been introduced by Isberner [16] is much faster than the variant of Angluin's L^* algorithm [4] that we used in our experiments. Since the models for the PCS components are so simple, the L^* algorithm does not need any intermediate hypothesis: the first model that L^* learns is always correct (that is, extensive testing did not reveal any counterexample). The TTT algorithm typically generates many more intermediate hypotheses than L^*. This means that it becomes more important which testing algorithm is being used. But also in the area of conformance testing there has been much progress recently [9,21]. Figure 5 displays the results of some experiments that we did using an implementation of the TTT algorithm that has become available very recently in LearnLib, in combination with a range of testing algorithms from [9,21]. As one can see, irrespective of the test method that is used, the TTT algorithm reduces the total number of input events needed to learn the final PCS model with a factor of about 3.

5.3 Using Parallelization and Checkpointing

Learning and testing can be easily parallelized by running multiple instances of the system under learning (in our case the PCS implementation) at the same time. Henrix [14] reports on experiments in which doubling the number of parallel instances nearly doubles the execution speed (on average with a factor 1.83). Another technique that may speed-up learning is to save and restore software states of the system under learning (checkpointing). The benefit is that if the learner wants to explore different outgoing transitions from a saved state q it only needs to restore q, which usually is much faster than resetting the system and bringing it back to q by an appropriate sequence of inputs. Henrix [14] reports on experiments in which checkpointing with DMTCP [5] speeds up the learning process with a factor of about 1.7.

5.4 Using Abstraction and Restriction

The number of test/membership queries of most learning algorithms grows linearly with the number of inputs. However, these algorithms usually assume an oracle that provides counterexamples for incorrect hypothesis models. Such an oracle is typically implemented using a conformance testing algorithm. In practice, conformance testing often becomes a bottleneck when the number of inputs gets larger. Thus we seek methods that help us to reduce the number of inputs.

To get confidence that two implementations with a large number of stimuli exhibit the same behaviour, a simple but practical approach is to apply model learning for multiple smaller subsets of stimuli. This will significantly reduce the learning complexity, also because the set of reachable states will typically be smaller for a restricted number of stimuli. Models learned for a subset of the inputs may then be used to generate counterexamples while learning models for

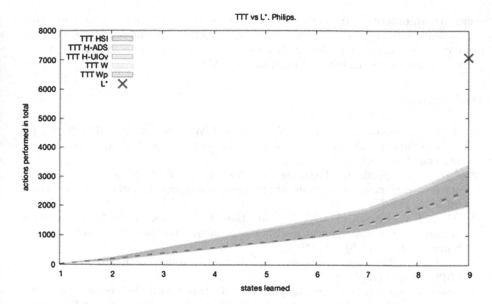

Fig. 5. Experiments with TTT algorithm for final PCS implementation for new PCC. The used test methods (W, Wp, hybrid adaptive distinguishing sequences, hybrid UIOv) were all randomised. For each test method 100 runs were performed. In each case 95 % of the runs were in the shaded area. The dotted lines give the median run for a given test method.

larger subsets on inputs. Smeenk [20] reports on some successful experiments in which this heuristic was used.

A different approach, which has been applied successfully in many case studies, is to apply abstraction techniques that replace multiple concrete inputs by a single abstract input. One may, for instance, forget certain parameters of an input event, or only record the sign of an integer parameter. We refer to [1,6] for recent overviews of these techniques.

6   Concluding Remarks

We presented an approach to get confidence that a refactored software component has equivalent external control behaviour as its non-refactored legacy software implementation. From both the refactored implementation and its legacy implementation, a model is obtained by using model learning. Both learned models are then compared using an equivalence checker. The implementations are learned and checked iteratively with increasing sets of stimuli to handle scalability. By using this approach we found issues in both the refactored and the legacy implementation in an early stage of the development, before the component was integrated. In this way, we avoided costly rework in a later phase of the development. As future work, we intend to apply our approach to other software components that will be refactored, including a substantially larger component.

Acknowledgements. We are most grateful to Joshua Moerman for helping with the experiments with the TTT algorithm. We also thank Petra van den Bos for careful proofreading of an earlier version. This research was supported by STW project 11763 (ITALIA) and the Dutch national program COMMIT.

References

1. Aarts, F., Jonsson, B., Uijen, J., Vaandrager, F.W.: Generating models of infinite-state communication protocols using regular inference with abstraction. Formal Methods Syst. Des. **46**(1), 1–41 (2015)
2. Aarts, F., Kuppens, H., Tretmans, G.J., Vaandrager, F.W., Verwer, S.: Improving active Mealy machine learning for protocol conformance testing. Mach. Learn. **96**(1–2), 189–224 (2014)
3. Akers, R.L., Baxter, I.D., Mehlich, M., Ellis, B.J., Luecke, K.R.: Case study: re-engineering C++ component models via automatic program transformation. Inf. Softw. Technol. **49**(3), 275–291 (2007)
4. Angluin, D.: Learning regular sets from queries and counterexamples. Inf. Comput. **75**(2), 87–106 (1987)
5. Ansel, J., Arya, K., Cooperman, G.: DMTCP: transparent checkpointing for cluster computations and the desktop. In: IEEE Parallel and Distributed Processing Symposium (2009)
6. Cassel, S.: Learning component behavior from tests: theory and algorithms for automata with data. Ph.D. thesis, University of Uppsala (2015)
7. Cranen, S., Groote, J.F., Keiren, J.J.A., Stappers, F.P.M., de Vink, E.P., Wesselink, W., Willemse, T.A.C.: An overview of the mCRL2 toolset and its recent advances. In: Piterman, N., Smolka, S.A. (eds.) TACAS 2013 (ETAPS 2013). LNCS, vol. 7795, pp. 199–213. Springer, Heidelberg (2013)
8. de Ruiter, J., Poll, E.: Protocol state fuzzing of tls implementations. In: 24th USENIX Security Symposium (USENIX Security 2015), pp. 193–206. USENIX Association (2015)
9. Dorofeeva, R., El-Fakih, K., Maag, S., Cavalli, A.R., Yevtushenko, N.: FSM-based conformance testing methods: a survey annotated with experimental evaluation. Inf. Softw. Technol. **52**(12), 1286–1297 (2010)
10. Engelfriet, J.: Determinacy - (observation equivalence = trace equivalence). Theor. Comput. Sci. **36**, 21–25 (1985)
11. Feng, L., Lundmark, S., Meinke, K., Niu, F., Sindhu, M.A., Wong, P.Y.H.: Case studies in learning-based testing. In: Yenigün, H., Yilmaz, C., Ulrich, A. (eds.) ICTSS 2013. LNCS, vol. 8254, pp. 164–179. Springer, Heidelberg (2013)
12. Fiterău-Broştean, P., Janssen, R., Vaandrager, F.: Learning fragments of the TCP network protocol. In: Lang, F., Flammini, F. (eds.) FMICS 2014. LNCS, vol. 8718, pp. 78–93. Springer, Heidelberg (2014)
13. Groce, A., Peled, D., Yannakakis, M.: Adaptive model checking. Logic J. IGPL **14**(5), 729–744 (2006)
14. Henrix, M.: Performance improvement in automata learning. Master thesis, Radboud University, Nijmegen (2015)
15. Howar, F., Isberner, M., Merten, M., Steffen, B.: LearnLib tutorial: from finite automata to register interface programs. In: Margaria, T., Steffen, B. (eds.) ISoLA 2012, Part I. LNCS, vol. 7609, pp. 587–590. Springer, Heidelberg (2012)
16. Isberner, M.: Foundations of active automata learning: an algorithmic perspective. Ph.D. thesis, Technical University of Dortmund (2015)

17. Kalsing, A.C., do Nascimento, G.S., Iochpe, C., Thom, L.H.: An incremental process mining approach to extract knowledge from legacy systems. In: Enterprise Distributed Object Computing Conference (EDOC), pp. 79–88 (2010)
18. Margaria, T., Niese, O., Raffelt, H., Steffen, B.: Efficient test-based model generation for legacy reactive systems. In: 9th IEEE International High-Level Design Validation and Test Workshop, pp. 95–100 (2004)
19. Raffelt, H., Steffen, B., Berg, T., Margaria, T.: LearnLib: a framework for extrapolating behavioral models. STTT **11**(5), 393–407 (2009)
20. Smeenk, W.: Applying automata learning to complex industrial software. Master thesis, Radboud University, Nijmegen, September 2012
21. Smeenk, W., Moerman, J., Vaandrager, F., Jansen, D.N.: Applying automata learning to embedded control software. In: Butler, M., et al. (eds.) ICFEM 2015. LNCS, vol. 9407, pp. 67–83. Springer, Heidelberg (2015). doi:10.1007/978-3-319-25423-4_5
22. Steffen, B., Howar, F., Merten, M.: Introduction to active automata learning from a practical perspective. In: Bernardo, M., Issarny, V. (eds.) SFM 2011. LNCS, vol. 6659, pp. 256–296. Springer, Heidelberg (2011)
23. van der Aalst, W.: Process Mining - Discovery Conformance and Enhancement of Business Processes. Springer, Heidelberg (2011)
24. Wagner, C.: Model-Driven Software Migration: A Methodology. Springer Vieweg, Heidelberg (2014)
25. Warren, I.: The Renaissance of Legacy Systems - Method Support for Software System Evolution. Springer, London (1999)

On Robust Malware Classifiers by Verifying Unwanted Behaviours

Wei Chen[1]([⊠]), David Aspinall[1], Andrew D. Gordon[1,2],
Charles Sutton[1], and Igor Muttik[3]

[1] University of Edinburgh, Edinburgh, UK
{wchen2,csutton}@inf.ed.ac.uk, {David.Aspinall,Andy.Gordon}@ed.ac.uk
[2] Microsoft Research Cambridge, Cambridge, UK
[3] Intel Security, Alesbury, UK
igor.muttik@intel.com

Abstract. Machine-learning-based Android malware classifiers perform badly on the detection of new malware, in particular, when they take API calls and permissions as input features, which are the best performing features known so far. This is mainly because signature-based features are very sensitive to the training data and cannot capture general behaviours of identified malware. To improve the robustness of classifiers, we study the problem of learning and verifying *unwanted behaviours* abstracted as automata. They are common patterns shared by malware instances but rarely seen in benign applications, e.g., intercepting and forwarding incoming SMS messages. We show that by taking the verification results against unwanted behaviours as input features, the classification performance of detecting new malware is improved dramatically. In particular, the precision and recall are respectively 8 and 51 points better than those using API calls and permissions, measured against industrial datasets collected across several years. Our approach integrates several methods: formal methods, machine learning and text mining techniques. It is the first to automatically generate unwanted behaviours for Android malware detection. We also demonstrate unwanted behaviours constructed for well-known malware families. They compare well to those described in human-authored descriptions of these families.

Keywords: Mobile security · Static analysis · Software verification · Machine learning · Malware detection

1 Introduction

Android malware, including trojans, spyware and other kinds of unwanted software, has been increasingly seen in the wild and even on official app stores [17,37]. To automatically detect Android malware, machine learning methods have been applied to train malware classifiers [5,8,21,22,36]. Among them, the tool Drebin [8] extracts a broad range of features, such as permissions, components, API calls and intents, then trains an SVM classifier. DroidAPIMiner [5]

© Springer International Publishing Switzerland 2016
E. Ábrahám and M. Huisman (Eds.): IFM 2016, LNCS 9681, pp. 326–341, 2016.
DOI: 10.1007/978-3-319-33693-0_21

uses refined API calls and relies on the KNN (k-nearest neighbours) algorithm. Another interesting tool is CHABADA [22] which detects outliers (abnormal API usage) within clusters of applications by exploiting OC-SVM (one-class SVM). All of these classifiers were trying to obtain good fits to the training data by using different methods and variant kinds of features. However, the robustness of malware classifiers has received much less consideration. As we will show in Table 2, the classification performance of detecting new malware is poor, in particular, when API calls and permissions are used as input features, which are the most popular and the best performing features known so far.

On the other hand, researchers and malware analysts have organised malware instances into hundreds of families [30, 37], e.g., Basebridge, Geinimi, Ginmaster, Spitmo, Zitmo, etc. These malware instances share certain unwanted behaviours, for example, sending premium messages constantly, collecting personal information, loading classes from hidden payloads then executing commands from remote servers, and so on. Except for some inaccurate online analysis reports [1–4, 24] of identified malware families, however, people have no idea of what exactly happens in these malware instances.

We want to learn unwanted behaviours exhibited in hundreds and thousands of malware instances and verify the application in question, e.g., an application submitted to an app store, to deny them. We will show that verifying these unwanted behaviours can improve the robustness of Android malware classifiers. Our approach integrates formal methods, machine learning, and text mining techniques, and proceeds as follows.

- **Formalisation.** We approximate an Android application's behaviours by a finite-state automaton, that is, a set of finite control-sequences of events, actions, and annotated API calls. Since different API calls might indicate the same behaviour, we abstract the automaton by aggregating API calls into permission-like phrases. We call it a *behaviour automaton*.
- **Learning.** An *unwanted behaviour* is a common behaviour which is shared by malware instances and has been rarely seen in benign applications. We develop a machine-learning-centred method to infer unwanted behaviours, by efficiently constructing and selecting sub-automata from behaviour automata of malware instances. This process is guided by the behavioural difference between malware and benign applications.
- **Refinement.** To purify unwanted behaviours, we exploit the family names of malware instances to help figure out the most informative unwanted behaviours. We compare unwanted behaviours with the human-authored descriptions for malware families, to confirm that they match well with patterns described in these descriptions.
- **Verification.** We check whether the application in question has any security fault by verifying whether the intersection between its behaviour automaton and an unwanted behaviour is not empty.

We take malware instances released in different years respectively as training, validation and testing sets. They were collected from several industrial datasets.

- **Training and Validation.** We collected 3,000 malware instances, which have
  been discovered between 2011 and 2013, and 3,000 benign applications. They
  include some famous benign applications, such as Google Talk, Amazon Kin-
  dle, and Youtube, and so on; and all malware instances from Malware Genome
  Project [37] and most malware instances from Mobile-Sandbox [30]. These
  malware instances have been manually investigated and organised into around
  200 families by third-party researchers and malware analysts. By reading their
  online malware analysis reports [1–4,24], we learned what bad things would
  happen in these malware instances. We divided them into a training set and
  a validation set. Each of them consists of 1,500 malware instances across all
  families and 1,500 benign applications.
- **Testing.** We test using a collection of 1,500 malware instances, which were
  released in 2014, and 1,500 benign applications. These malware instances were
  from Intel Security and have been investigated by malware analysts. But, there
  is no family information or online analysis report for them. We have no idea of
  their unwanted behaviours. The collection of benign applications, which was
  collected in 2014, is disjoint from the collection of benign applications used
  for training and validation, which was collected between 2011 and 2013. These
  two collections were all supplied by Intel Security.

We use API calls, permissions, and the verification results against unwanted
behaviours as input features; then apply L1-Regularized Linear Regression [32]
to train classifiers. The evaluation on the testing set shows that the precision and
recall of using unwanted behaviours are respectively 8 and 51 points better than
those of using API calls and permissions. As shown in Table 2, using API calls
and permissions as input features, can achieve very good precision and recall
on the validation set, however, its classification performance on the testing set
is poor. That is, unwanted behaviours are more general than API calls and
permissions. This is needed in practice: to mitigate over-fitting and improve the
robustness of malware classifiers.

Our approach is the first to learn unwanted behaviours from Android malware
instances. The main contributions of this paper are to:

- demonstrate that it is hard to detect new malware for classifiers trained on
  identified Android malware instances, by using signature-based features;
- show that using semantics-based features like unwanted behaviours dramatically improves the classification performance of new malware detection;
- supply a static analysis tool to construct behaviour automata from the bytecode, considering a broad range of features of the Android framework;
- apply a novel machine-learning-centred algorithm to efficiently choose salient
  sub-automata to characterise unwanted behaviours;
- apply a refinement approach to look up the most informative unwanted behaviours, by making use of the family names of malware instances.

Related Work. The idea to abstract applications' behaviours as automata is
similar with the behaviour abstraction in [11,34]. The behaviour automata are
close to permission-event graphs [16], and more compact than embedded call

graphs [21] and behaviour graphs [35]. None of them has been exploited to automatically generate verifiable properties.

The idea to learn unwanted behaviours is close to the methodology proposed by Fredrikson et al. to synthesize malware specification [19]. In their work, a data dependence graph with logic constraints on nodes and edges was used to characterise an application's behaviours. From the graphs of malware instances and benign applications they constructed so-called significant subgraphs that maximise the information gain. Then, the optimal collections of subgraphs were selected using the formal concept analysis. The main drawback of this method is its scalability. Also, the training and testing sets were very unbalanced, i.e., the number of benign applications is much less than that of malware instances. We overcome these limitations by using behaviour automata as the abstract model, training and testing on large and balanced datasets.

The unwanted behaviours can be considered as instances of security automata [28]. Our verification approach is the same as the automata-theoretic model checking [33]. In total, 19 malicious properties for Android applications were manually constructed and specified as first-order LTL formulae in [23]. Some benign and malicious properties specified in LTL were verified against hundreds of Android applications in [16]. But, none of these properties was automatically constructed.

Among others, Angluin's [7] and Biermann's [12] algorithms were developed to learn regular expressions from sample finite strings. To apply similar ideas in unwanted behaviour construction, we have to extract enough finite strings from applications to approximate their behaviours. Compared with our construction of behaviour automata, this would be more complex and expensive.

2   An Example Unwanted Behaviour

Let us consider a malware family called Ggtracker. A brief human-authored description of this family which was produced by Symantec [4] is as follows.

It sends SMS messages to a premium-rate number. It monitors received SMS messages and intercepts SMS messages. It may also steal information from the device.

One of the unwanted behaviours we have learned from malware instances in this family can be expressed as the regular expression: SMS_RECEIVED.SEND_SMS. The approach to learn these unwanted behaviours will be elaborated in Sect. 4. It denotes the behaviour of sending an SMS message out *immediately* after an incoming SMS message is received without the interaction from the user. Some behaviours of the application in question are not the same as the unwanted behaviours, but, they often have the unwanted behaviours as sub-sequences. For example, the behaviour SMS_RECEIVED.READ_PHONE_STATE.SEND_SMS contains SMS_RECEIVED.SEND_SMS as a subsequence. To capture behaviours sharing the same patterns with the unwanted behaviours, if a behaviour contains an unwanted behaviour as a sub-sequence, we consider this behaviour as unwanted as well. We call them *extended* unwanted behaviours. So, we generalise from the above unwanted behaviour and construct the following automaton ψ:

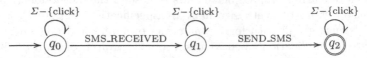

Here, we use the symbol Σ to denote the collection of events, actions, and permission-like phrases and the word "click" to denote that there is no interaction from the user. In Sect. 4.2 we will show a method to refine unwanted behaviours by making use of the family names of malware instances. To distinguish and compare these unwanted behaviours, we use respectively *unwanted*, *ext. unwanted*, and *ext. unwanted for families* to denote them.

We now want to verify whether a target application has the above unwanted behaviour. Let us consider the following behaviour automaton $\mathcal{A}$:

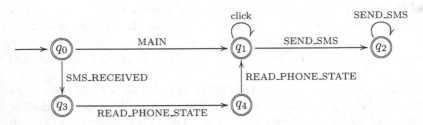

It is constructed from the bytecode of an Android application using static analysis. Its source code and the method to construct behaviour automata will be given in Sect. 3. It tells us: this application has two entries which are respectively specified by actions MAIN and SMS_RECEIVED; it will collect information like the phone state, then send SMS messages out; the behaviour of sending SMS messages can also be triggered by an interaction from the user, e.g., click a button, touch the screen, long-press a picture, etc., which is denoted by the word "click". A string accepted by this automaton characterises a behaviour of this application. All states in this automaton are accepting states since any prefix of an application's behaviours is one of its behaviours as well.

Because the intersection between $\mathcal{A}$ and ψ is not empty, we consider this application is unsafe with respect to the unwanted behaviour ψ. In Sect. 5, we will show that this verification against unwanted behaviours can improve the classification performance of new malware detecting.

3   Behaviour Automata

We use a simplified synthetic application to illustrate the construction of behaviour automata.

3.1   An Example Android Application

This application will constantly send out the device ID and the phone number by SMS messages in the background when an incoming SMS message is received. Its source code and part of its manifest file follow.

```
public class Main extends                              /* Main.java */
  Activity implements View.OnClickListener {
  private static String info = "";
  protected void onCreate(Bundle savedInstanceState) {
    Intent intent = getIntent();
    info = intent.getStringExtra("DEVICE_ID");
    info += intent.getStringExtra("TEL_NUM");
    SendSMSTask task = new SendSMSTask();
    task.execute(); }
  public void onClick (View v) {
    SendSMSTask task = new SendSMSTask();
    task.execute(); }
  private class SendSMSTask extends AsyncTask<Void, Void, Void> {
    protected Void doInBackground(Void... params) {
      while (true) {
        SmsManager sms = SmsManager.getDefault();
        sms.sendTextMessage("1234", null, info, null, null); }
      return null; }}}

public class Receiver extends BroadcastReceiver {        /* Receiver.java */
  public void onReceive(Context context, Intent intent) {
    Intent intent = new Intent();
    intent.setAction("com.main.intent");
    TelephonyManager tm = (TelephonyManager)
    getBaseContext().getSystemService(Context.TELEPHONY_SERVICE);
    intent.putExtra("DEVICE_ID", tm.getDeviceId());
    intent.putExtra("TEL_NUM", tm.getLine1Number());
    sendBroadcast(intent); }}

                                                    /* AndroidManifest.xml */
<activity android:name="com.example.Main" >
  <intent-filter>
    <action android:name="android.intent.action.MAIN" />
    <action android:name="com.main.intent" />
  </intent-filter>
</activity>
<receiver android:name="com.example.Receiver" >
  <intent-filter>
    <action android:name="android.provider.Telephony.SMS_RECEIVED" />
  </intent-filter>
</receiver>
```

As specified in AndroidManifest.xml, the Main activity can handle a specific Intent called "com.main.intent" and the Receiver will be triggered by an incoming SMS message (SMS_RECEIVED). After the Receiver collects the device ID and the phone number, it will send them out by a broadcast with the intent "com.main.intent". This broadcast is then handled by the Main activity in the method onCreate. Afterwards, SMS messages containing the device ID and the phone number are sent out in the background in an AsyncTask.

3.2   An Example Behaviour Automaton

From the bytecode of this application, we construct the following automaton.

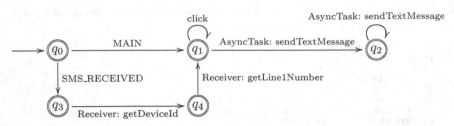

This automaton is constructed from finite traces of actions, events, and annotated API calls using static analysis. Actions reflect what happens in the environment and what kind of service an application requests for, e.g., an incoming
message is received, the device finishes booting, the application wants to send
an email by using the service supplied by an email-client, etc. Events denote the
interaction from the user, e.g., clicking a picture, pressing a button, scrolling
down the screen, etc. Annotated API calls tell us whether the application does
anything we are interested in. For instance, getDeviceID, getLine1Number, and
sendTextMessage are annotated API calls in the above example.

For a single behaviour there are often several related API methods. For example, getDeviceId, getLine1Number, and getSimSerialNumber are all related to
the behaviour of reading phone state. We categorise API methods into a set
of permission-like phrases, which describe behaviours of applications, so as to
remove redundancy caused by API calls which indicate the same behaviour. This
results in an abstract automaton, so-called a *behaviour automaton*. It has several
advantages, including: more resilient to variants of behaviours, such as swapping
two API calls related to the same behaviour; more compact automata, which
are good for human-understanding and further analysis, by reducing the number of labels on the edges. For instance, the behaviour automaton for the above
example is the automaton $\mathcal{A}$ depicted in Sect. 2.

3.3   The Implementaion

In our implementation, we use an extension of permission-governed API methods generated by PScout [9] as annotations. The Android platform tools aapt
and dexdump are respectively used to extract the manifest information and to
decompile the bytecode into the assembly code, from which we construct the
automaton. It took around two weeks to generate automata for 10,000 applications using a multi-core desktop computer. More technical details are as follows.

– *Multiple Entries.* A class becomes an entry if a system action, e.g., MAIN and
  SMS_RECEIVED, has been declared as one of its intent-filters in the manifest file. For developer-defined actions, e.g., "com.main.intent" in the earlier
  example, their corresponding classes become entries only when an instance
  of a class is explicitly created at some control-reachable point from a system
  entry.

- *Class Exploration.* Starting from an entry class, from the callbacks of each visited class, we collect new classes by exploring the new-instance and start-component relations.
- *Component life-cycle.* We organise the callbacks in each Android component according to its life-cycle, e.g., the life-cycle of AsyncTask is modelled as:

- *Inter-Procedural Calls.* We build an inter-procedural call graph for each callback in each reachable class.
- *New-Instances and Start-Components.* For each new-instance and each start-component relation, we add an ϵ-transition from the entry-point of new-instance or start-component statement to the entry-point of the call graph for the target class. The original transitions for these statements in the caller's call graphs are replaced by ϵ-transitions. Intuitively, this models the asynchronisation by non-deterministic choices. For example, for the statement sendBroadcast in onReceive method, we have:

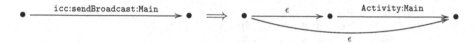

- *Callbacks.* We collect the following functions as callbacks: overridden methods of Android component classes, implementations of abstract functions declared in listener interfaces, and callbacks defined in layout files.
- *Inter-Component Communications.* We search through all methods for start-component API calls, e.g., startService, startActivity, sendBroadcast, etc. We decide whether there is a data-flow from a register containing a constant to the entry-point of a start-component statement, and if so, we decide whether this constant is a system action, a developer-defined action, or a developer-defined class name. For the first two, we search the manifest file for possible matched components. The last one has been dealt as a start-component relation in the class exploration.

We don't model registers, fields, assignments, operators, pointer-aliases, arrays or exceptions. The choice of which features to model is a trade-off between efficiency and precision.

4   Learning and Refining Unwanted Behaviours

Once a behaviour automaton has been constructed for each malware instance, we want to capture the common behaviour shared by malware, which is rarely seen in benign applications, so-called an *unwanted behaviour*.

4.1 Salient Sub-Automata

The space of candidate behaviours, which consists of the intersection and difference between behaviour automata, in theory, is exponential in the number of sample applications. To combat this, we approximate this space by searching for a "salient" subspace. The searching process is guided by the behavioural difference between malware and benign applications. We formalise this process as the algorithm in Fig. 1.

The main process construct_features takes a collection G of behaviour automata as input and outputs a set F of salient sub-automata with their weights W. Here, a sub-automaton is *salient* if it is actually used in a linear classifier, i.e., its weight is not zero.

Function: construct_features (G, α)
Input: G – a group of behaviour automata
 $\qquad \alpha$ – the lower bound on the classification accuracy
Output: salient sub-automata and their weights
1:    $G_{i \in [0..N-1]} \leftarrow$ divide the set G into N groups
2:    for $i \in [0..N-1]$
3:      $F_i \leftarrow$ merge_features $(G_i, \emptyset)$
4:    for $(s \leftarrow 2; s \leq N; s \leftarrow s \times 2)$
5:      for $i \in [s-1..N-1]$
6:        $j \leftarrow i - (s/2)$
7:        $(F_i, \_), (F_j, \_) \leftarrow$ diff_features (F_i, α), diff_features (F_j, α)
8:        if $(i+1)\%s = 0$ then
9:          $F_i \leftarrow$ merge_features (F_i, F_j)
10:       elif $(i+1) > (N/s) \times s$ and $(i+1)\%(s/2) = 0$ then
11:         $F_j \leftarrow$ merge_features (F_i, F_j)
12:   return diff_features $(F_{s/2-1}, \alpha)$
Function: merge_features (E, F)
1:    for $e \in E$
2:      for $f \in F$
3:        if $f - e \neq \emptyset$ then $F \leftarrow F \cup \{f - e\}$
4:        if $f \cap e \neq \emptyset$ then $F \leftarrow F \cup \{f \cap e\}$
5:        if $f - e \neq f$ and $f \cap e \neq f$ then $F \leftarrow F - \{f\}$
6:        $e \leftarrow e - f$
7:      if $e \neq \emptyset$ then $F \leftarrow F \cup \{e\}$
8:    return F
Function: diff_features (F, α)
1:    $D \leftarrow$ add an equal number of randomly-chosen benign applications
2:        into the set of malware instances from which F was collected
3:    $W, acc \leftarrow$ train (D, F)
4:    if $acc > \alpha$ then $F \leftarrow \{f \in F \mid W_f \neq 0\}$
5:    return F, W

Fig. 1. The algorithm for the construction of salient sub-automata.

We divide G into N groups: $G_0, \ldots, G_i, \ldots, G_{N-1}$. For each group, we construct sub-automata by computing the intersection and difference between automata within this group, i.e., merge_features $(G_i, \emptyset)$. This results in N feature sets $F_0, \ldots, F_i, \ldots, F_{N-1}$. The sub-automata in each set are disjoint. Then, we merge sub-automata from different groups, i.e., merge_features (G_i, G_j). This process stops when all groups have been merged into a single group.

Before merging sub-automata from two different groups, for each group, we train a linear classifier, i.e., train (D, F), using a training set D and a feature set F. This training set consists of behaviour automata of malware instances in the group and an equal number of behaviour automata of randomly-chosen benign applications. The input feature set F consists of disjoint sub-automata, which are constructed from behaviour automata of malware instances in the group. Then, if the classification accuracy acc on the training set is above a lower bound α, we return sub-automata with non-zero weights. Otherwise, we return all features in F. This process differentiates salient features by adding benign applications. It is formalised as the function diff_features.

In our implementation, we adopt L1-Regularized Logistic Regression [32] as the training method. This is because this method is specially designed to use fewer features. The lower bound α on the classification accuracy is set to 90 %. We put malware instances from the same malware family into one group so that the searching process is more directed. We have also designed and implemented a multi-process program to accelerate the construction, i.e., construct sub-automata for each group simultaneously. It took around one week to process $4,000$ malware instances using a multi-core desktop computer. At the end of the computation, we produced around $1,000$ salient sub-automata.

4.2 Refinement

We will use these salient sub-automata to characterise unwanted behaviours. A straightforward way is to choose automata by their weights, for example, those with negative weights, i.e., $\{f \in F \mid W_f < 0\}$. To purify unwanted behaviours, we want to exploit the family names of malware instances to figure out the most informative ones, that is, to choose a small set of salient sub-automata to characterise unwanted behaviours for each family. Here are several candidate methods.

- *Top-n-negative.* For a linear classifier, intuitively, a feature with a negative weight more likely indicates an unwanted behaviour, and a feature with a positive weight more likely indicates a normal behaviour. This observation leads us to refine unwanted behaviours by using sub-automata with negative weights, i.e., choose the top-n features from the set $\{f \in F \mid W_f < 0\}$ by ranking the absolute values of their weights.
- *Subset-search.* For each malware family, we choose a subset X of salient sub-automata, such that it largely covers and is strongly associated with malware instances in this family. Formally, we use $Pr(f|X)$ to denote the probability that a malware instance belonging to a family f if all automata in X are sub-automata of the behaviour automaton of this instance, and $Pr(X|f)$ to denote

the probability that all automata in X are sub-automata of the behaviour automaton of a malware instance if this instance belongs to f. We use their F_1-measure as the evaluation function to look up subsets. i.e., $\frac{2Pr(f|X)Pr(X|f)}{Pr(f|X)+Pr(X|f)}$. Since exhaustively searching a power-set space is expensive, we adopt Beam Search [25, Chap. 6] to approximate the best K-subsets.

- *TF-IDF.* Another method is to consider features as terms, features from malware instances in a family as a document, and the multi-set of features as the corpus. We rank features by their TF-IDF (term frequency and inverse document frequency) and choose a maximum of m features to characterise unwanted behaviours of each family.

We use the salient sub-automata produced in previous subsection and construct unwanted behaviours for each family by combining all methods discussed earlier. We list human-authored descriptions and learned unwanted behaviours of 10 prevalent families in Table 1. These descriptions for families were collected from their online analysis reports [1–4,24].

A subjective comparison shows that these learned unwanted behaviours compare well to their human-authored descriptions. Also, they reveal trigger conditions of some behaviours, which were often lacking in human-authored descriptions. For example, the expression BOOT_COMPLETED.SEND_SMS denotes that after the device finishes booting, this application will send a message out; the expression UMS_CONNECTED.LOAD_CLASS means that when a USB mass storage is connected to the device, this application will load some code from a library or a hidden payload; and the unwanted behaviour for Droiddream shows that if the phone state changes (PHONE_STATE), this application will collect information then access the Internet. Within the human-authored descriptions displayed in Table 1, only two behaviours are not captured by learned unwanted behaviours: "gain root access" for Droiddream and the behaviour of Spitmo.

5   Evaluation: Detecting New Malware

We are concerned with whether unwanted behaviours can help improve the robustness of malware classification. As we will show in Table 2, a linear classifier using API calls and permissions as input features, which are the most popular and the best performing input features for Android malware detectors [5,8,10,14,22,36], performs badly on new malware instances (the testing set), although it has a very good classification performance on the validation set. In this section, we will show that unwanted behaviours improve the classification performance of new malware detection.

The training, validation, and testing sets are the same as those described in Sect. 1. Permissions and lists of API calls appearing in the code are extracted from these applications as input features to train classifiers as baselines. We construct behaviour automata for all applications, then apply methods discussed in Sect. 4.1 to learn unwanted behaviours from malware instances in the training set. We check whether the intersection between the behaviour automaton of the

Table 1. Learned unwanted behaviours versus human-authored descriptions.

Human-authored description	Learned unwanted behaviours in regular expressions
Arspam. *Sends spam SMS messages to contacts on the compromised device* [4]	1. BOOT_COMPLETED.SEND_SMS
Anserverbot. *Downloads, installs, and executes payloads* [1].	1. UMS_CONNECTED.LOAD_CLASS*. (ACCESS_NETWORK_STATE | READ_PHONE_STATE | INTERNET). (ACCESS_NETWORK_STATE | READ_PHONE_STATE | INTERNET | LOAD_CLASS)*
Basebridge. *Forwards confidential details (SMS, IMSI, IMEI) to a remote server* [2]. *Downloads and installs payloads* [1,4]	1. UMS_CONNECTED.(INTERNET | LOAD_CLASS | READ_PHONE_STATE | ACCESS_NETWORK_STATE)+
Cosha. *Monitors and sends certain information to a remote location* [4]	1. MAIN.click.(click | ACCESS_FINE_LOCATION | DIAL)*.DIAL.(click | ACCESS_FINE_LOCATION | DIAL)*. (INTERNET | ϵ)
	2. SMS_RECEIVED.(INTERNET | ACCESS_FINE_LOCATION)+
Droiddream. *Gains root access, gathers information (device ID, IMEI, IMSI) from an infected mobile phone and connects to several URLs in order to upload this data* [1,2]	1. PHONE_STATE.(ACCESS_NETWORK_STATE | READ_PHONE_STATE+. INTERNET).(ACCESS_NETWORK_STATE | INTERNET)*
Geinimi. *Monitors and sends certain information to a remote location* [4]. *Introduces botnet capabilities with clear indications that command and control (C&C) functionality could be a part of the Geinimi code base* [3]	1. ϵ | MAIN.click+.VIBRATE.(click | VIBRATE)*.RESTART_PACKAGES. (MAIN.(click | VIBRATE)*.RESTART_PACKAGES)*
	2. BOOT_COMPLETED.(ACCESS_NETWORK_STATE | click | INTERNET | RESTART_PACKAGES | ACCESS_FINE_LOCATION)+
Ggtracker. *Monitors received SMS messages and intercepts SMS messages* [2]	1. MAIN.READ_PHONE_STATE
	2. SMS_RECEIVED.SEND_SMS
Ginmaster. *Sends received SMS messages to a remote server* [24]. *Downloads and installs applications without user concern* [24]	1. BOOT_COMPLETED.LOAD_CLASS
	2. MAIN.SEND_SMS
Spitmo. *Filters SMS messages to steal banking confirmation codes* [4]	1. NEW_OUTGOING_CALL.READ_PHONE_STATE.INTERNET.(INTERNET | ϵ)
Zitmo. *Opens a backdoor that allows a remote attacker to steal information from SMS messages received on the compromised device* [4]	1. SMS_RECEIVED.SEND_SMS
	2. MAIN.READ_PHONE_STATE
	3. MAIN.SEND_SMS

application in question and an (extended) unwanted behaviour is not empty. We collect these verification results as input features to train the target classifiers. For both baselines and target classifiers, we use L1-Regularized Logistic Regression [32] as the training method. The classification performance is reported in Table 2. The precision and recall are calculated as follows:

$$\text{precision} = \frac{tp}{tp + fp} \quad \text{and} \quad \text{recall} = \frac{tp}{tp + fn},$$

where tp, fp, and fn respectively denote the true positives, false positives, and false negatives. This table confirms that:

- The unwanted behaviours dramatically improve the classification performance on new malware instances. The classification performance using API calls and permissions as input features is very good on the validation set, i.e., the precision and recall are respectively 93% and 98%. However, this is just over-fitting to the training set, since its performance on the testing set is bad, in particular, the precision is 65% and recall is 15%. This means that a lot of new behaviours cannot be captured by API calls and permissions. By using the verification results against unwanted behaviours as input features, we improve the precision to 73% and the recall to 66%, as shown in the row of "ext. unwanted for families".
- The generalisation from the unwanted behaviours to the extended unwanted behaviours helps improve the classification performance as well. We increase the precision from 53% (in the row of "unwanted") to 69% (in the row of "ext. unwanted"). Although we lose several percent of recall, we get a better F_1-measure between precision and recall.
- Refining unwanted behaviours using the family names helps improve the classification performance of detecting new malware. The precision is increased from 69% (in the row of "ext. unwanted") to 73% (in the row of "ext. unwanted

Table 2. The classification performance using different features.

Feature training (2011–13)	Validation (2011–13)		Testing (2014)		#Salient/#feature
	Precision	Recall	Precision	Recall	
Signature-based features (baselines)					
Permissions	89%	99%	53%	21%	59/175
Apis	91%	98%	61%	15%	1443/52432
Apis & permissions	93%	98%	**65%**	**15%**	735/52607
Semantics-based features (targets)					
Unwanted	66%	91%	53%	74%	634/886
Ext. unwanted	75%	87%	69%	66%	581/886
Ext. unwanted for families	72%	72%	**73%**	**66%**	**131/131**
Mixed features					
All	**95%**	**99.5%**	65%	7.5%	870/61149

for families"), while maintaining the same recall. This refinement also helps reduce the number of features which are actually used in a linear classifier, i.e., totally 131 features were used, rather than 581 features.
- Combining syntax-based and semantics-based features results in over-fitting to the training dataset. By doing this, although the trained classifier can achieve the best classification performance on the validation dataset, its classification performance on the testing dataset is poor, in particular, the recall is as low as 7.5 % (in the row of "all").

6 Conclusion and Further Work

To learn compact and verifiable unwanted behaviours from Android malware instances is challenging and has not yet been considered. Compared with manually-composed properties, unwanted behaviours, which are automatically constructed from malware instances, will be much easier to be updated on the changes of behaviours exhibited in new malware instances. To the best of our knowledge, our approach is the first to automatically construct temporal properties from Android malware instances. We show that unwanted behaviours help improve the robustness of malware classifiers, in particular, they dramatically increase the precision and recall of detecting new malware. These unwanted behaviours can not only be used to eliminate potentially new instances of known malware families, but also help people's understanding of unwanted behaviours exhibited in these families.

Some unwanted behaviours cannot be captured by our formalisation, e.g., gaining root access, in which specific commands are executed, and some are not captured precisely enough, e.g., botnet controls, in which the communication between the app and the remote server has to be modelled. In further work, we want to extend the current formalisation to capture more sophisticated behaviours precisely. We will also try to combine the output of dynamic analysis, e.g., traces produced by CopperDroid [27] or MonitorMe [23], with that of static analysis to approximate applications' behaviours. It would be interesting to explore whether properties expressed in LTL are needed in the practice of Android malware detection and whether it is possible to learn them from malware.

The verification method adopted in this paper is straightforward and simple. More efficient and complex methods, e.g., the method discussed in [29] and model checking pushdown systems [18], will be considered in future.

The applications in current datasets were released between 2011 and 2014. More interesting comparison and study will be done when we get applications released in 2015 as another testing set.

Except for the unwanted behaviours, it is worth investigating whether other machine learning methods can help improve the robustness of malware classifiers, e.g., semi-supervised learning [15], the ensemble learning [13], the adaptive boosting [20], etc. We will also compare the robustness of popular machine methods, e.g., decision trees [26], SVM [31], naive Bayes, KNN [6], etc.

It is also interesting to study whether unwanted behaviours can convince people of the automatic malware detection.

References

1. Malware Genome Project (2012). http://www.malgenomeproject.org/
2. Forensic Blog (2014). http://forensics.spreitzenbarth.de/android-malware/
3. Juniper Networks (2015). https://www.juniper.net/security/auto/includes/ mobile_signature_descriptions.html
4. Symantec security response (2015). http://www.symantec.com/security_response/
5. Aafer, Y., Du, W., Yin, H.: DroidAPIMiner: mining API-level features for robust malware detection in Android. In: Zia, T., Zomaya, A., Varadharajan, V., Mao, M. (eds.) SecureComm 2013. LNICST, vol. 127, pp. 86–103. Springer, Heidelberg (2013)
6. Altman, N.S.: An introduction to kernel and nearest-neighbor nonparametric regression. Am. Stat. **46**(3), 175–185 (1992)
7. Angluin, D.: Learning regular sets from queries and counterexamples. Inf. Comput. **75**(2), 87–106 (1987)
8. Arp, D., et al.: Drebin: efficient and explainable detection of Android malware in your pocket. In: NDSS, pp. 23–26 (2014)
9. Au, K.W.Y., et al.: PScout: analyzing the Android permission specification. In: CCS, pp. 217–228 (2012)
10. Barrera, D., Kayacik, H.G., van Oorschot, P.C., Somayaji, A.: A methodology for empirical analysis of permission-based security models and its application to Android. In: CCS, pp. 73–84 (2010)
11. Beaucamps, P., Gnaedig, I., Marion, J.-Y.: Behavior abstraction in malware analysis. In: Barringer, H., et al. (eds.) RV 2010. LNCS, vol. 6418, pp. 168–182. Springer, Heidelberg (2010)
12. Biermann, A.W., Feldman, J.A.: On the synthesis of finite-state machines from samples of their behavior. IEEE Trans. Comput. **21**(6), 592–597 (1972)
13. Breiman, L.: Random forests. Mach. Learn. **45**, 5–32 (2001)
14. Chakradeo, S., Reaves, B., Traynor, P., Enck, W.: MAST: triage for market-scale mobile malware analysis. In: WiSec, pp. 13–24 (2013)
15. Chapelle, O., Schlkopf, B., Zien, A.: Semi-Supervised Learning. The MIT Press, Cambridge (2010)
16. Chen, K.Z., et al.: Contextual policy enforcement in Android applications with permission event graphs. In: NDSS (2013)
17. Enck, W., Octeau, D., McDaniel, P., Chaudhuri, S.: A study of Android application security. In: USENIX Security Symposium (2011)
18. Esparza, J., Hansel, D., Rossmanith, P., Schwoon, S.: Efficient algorithms for model checking pushdown systems. In: Emerson, E.A., Sistla, A.P. (eds.) CAV 2000. LNCS, vol. 1855, pp. 232–247. Springer, Heidelberg (2000)
19. Fredrikson, M., et al.: Synthesizing near-optimal malware specifications from suspicious behaviors. In: Proceedings of the IEEE Symposium on Security and Privacy, SP 2010, pp. 45–60 (2010)
20. Freund, Y., Schapire, R.E.: A decision-theoretic generalization of on-line learning and an application to boosting. J. Comput. Syst. Sci. **55**(1), 119–139 (1997)
21. Gascon, H., Yamaguchi, F., Arp, D., Rieck, K.: Structural detection of Android malware using embedded call graphs. In: AISec, pp. 45–54 (2013)
22. Gorla, A., et al.: Checking app behavior against app descriptions. In: ICSE, pp. 1025–1035 (2014)
23. Küster, J.-C., Bauer, A.: Monitoring real Android malware. In: Bartocci, E., et al. (eds.) RV 2015. LNCS, vol. 9333, pp. 136–152. Springer, Heidelberg (2015). doi:10. 1007/978-3-319-23820-3_9

24. McAfee Threat Center (2015). http://www.mcafee.com/uk/threat-center.aspx
25. Norvig, P.: Paradigms of Artificial Intelligence Programming: Case Studies in Common Lisp, 1st edn. Morgan Kaufmann Publishers Inc., San Francisco (1992)
26. Quinlan, J.R.: C4.5 Programs for Machine Learning. Morgan Kaufmann Publishers Inc., San Francisco (1993)
27. Reina, A., Fattori, A., Cavallaro, L.: A system call-centric analysis and stimulation technique to automatically reconstruct Android malware behaviors. In: European Workshop on System Security (EUROSEC) (2013)
28. Schneider, F.B.: Enforceable security policies. ACM Trans. Inf. Syst. Secur. **3**(1), 30–50 (2000)
29. Song, F., Touili, T.: LTL model-checking for malware detection. In: Piterman, N., Smolka, S.A. (eds.) TACAS 2013 (ETAPS 2013). LNCS, vol. 7795, pp. 416–431. Springer, Heidelberg (2013)
30. Spreitzenbarth, M., et al.: Mobile-sandbox: combining static and dynamic analysis with machine-learning techniques. Int. J. Inf. Secur. **14**(2), 141–153 (2015)
31. Steinwart, I., Christmann, A.: Support Vector Machines. Springer, New York (2008)
32. Tibshirani, R.: Regression shrinkage and selection via the lasso. J. Roy. Stat. Soc. Ser. B **58**, 267–288 (1994)
33. Vardi, M.Y., Wolper, P.: Automata-theoretic techniques for modal logics of programs. J. Comput. Syst. Sci. **32**(2), 183–221 (1986)
34. Whaley, J., Martin, M.C., Lam, M.S.: Automatic extraction of object-oriented component interfaces. SIGSOFT Softw. Eng. Notes **27**(4), 218–228 (2002)
35. Yang, C., et al.: Droidminer: automated mining and characterization of fine-grained malicious behaviors in Android applications. In: ESORICS, pp. 163–182 (2014)
36. Yerima, S.Y., Sezer, S., McWilliams, G., Muttik, I.: A new Android malware detection approach using bayesian classification. In: AINA, pp. 121–128 (2013)
37. Zhou, Y., Jiang, X.: Dissecting Android malware: characterization and evolution. In: IEEE Symposium on Security and Privacy, pp. 95–109 (2012)

SAT and SMT Solving

Efficient Deadlock-Freedom Checking Using Local Analysis and SAT Solving

Pedro Antonino[✉], Thomas Gibson-Robinson, and A.W. Roscoe

Department of Computer Science, University of Oxford, Oxford, UK
{pedro.antonino,thomas.gibson-robinson,bill.roscoe}@cs.ox.ac.uk

Abstract. We build upon established techniques of deadlock analysis by formulating a new sound but incomplete framework for deadlock freedom analysis that tackles some sources of imprecision of current incomplete techniques. Our new deadlock candidate criterion is based on constraints derived from the analysis of the state space of pairs of components. This new characterisation represents an improvement in the accuracy of current incomplete techniques; in particular, the so-called non-hereditary deadlock-free systems (i.e. deadlock-free systems that have a deadlocking subsystem), which are neglected by most incomplete techniques, are tackled by our framework. Furthermore, we demonstrate how SAT checkers can be used to efficiently implement our framework in a way that, typically, scales better than current techniques for deadlock analysis. This is demonstrated by a series of practical experiments.

1 Introduction

Deadlock freedom is usually an important goal when developing and verifying a concurrent system. A system is deadlock free if and only if it cannot reach a state in which it can perform no further actions. Moreover, many safety properties can be reduced to verifying deadlock freedom of modified systems [12]. Unsurprisingly, even when restricted to deadlock analysis, existing automated verification techniques still suffer from the state explosion problem.

Incomplete techniques for deadlock analysis [6,14,15] have been proposed in attempts to circumvent the state explosion problem. These frequently scale far better than the full state analysis required by model checking, and are sound in proving deadlock freedom, but (i) tend not to provide examples of deadlocks when they fail and (ii) can fail even for some deadlock-free systems; the latter is what is meant by "incomplete". One can see this incompleteness as the price to pay for achieving scalability.

Current incomplete techniques are typically built around the principle that a deadlock state, under reasonable assumptions, always presents a cycle of *ungranted requests* between components of the system[1]. An ungranted request

---

[1] Depending on the properties of the underlying communicating system, one might be able to restrict such cycles to *proper cycles* which have at least three nodes, and where all the nodes are distinct.

© Springer International Publishing Switzerland 2016
E. Ábrahám and M. Huisman (Eds.): IFM 2016, LNCS 9681, pp. 345–360, 2016.
DOI: 10.1007/978-3-319-33693-0_22

arises from a component to another if and only if the former is trying to communicate with the latter, but they cannot agree on any event. To prove the absence of such a cycle, these methods rely on local properties of the system, derived from the analysis of individual components or pairs of them, to construct (either explicitly or implicitly) and analyse a dependency graph. These approaches have two important sources of imprecision. Firstly, under our assumptions, a cycle is a necessary condition for a deadlock state but not a sufficient one. So, despite being deadlock free, some deadlock-free systems present these cycles and, as such, they cannot be handled by these methods. For instance, *non-hereditary* deadlock-free systems, namely, deadlock-free systems that have a subsystem that can deadlock, cannot be tackled by current techniques using local analysis. Secondly, to keep the analysis of these dependency graphs efficient, some local properties, which could be used to improve accuracy, are ignored because they focus on proposing polynomially checkable conditions in terms of the local information collected.

In this paper, we present a new incomplete method for establishing deadlock freedom that alleviates these sorts of imprecision. Instead of looking for cycles, we look for *complete snapshots* of the system that are fully consistent with derived local properties. A complete snapshot is an assignment of component states to components that depicts a possible state of the concurrent system. Unlike others, our method uses a condition that is not known to be polynomially checkable. While unsurprising in itself, this new criterion has proved to be efficiently determinable using the power of SAT checking. Our work has been inspired by Martin's definition of the State Dependency Digraph [15] (see Sect. 3), and by the successful use of SAT checkers for livelock analysis reported in [17].

Outline. Section 2 briefly introduces CSP's operational semantics, which is the formalism upon which our strategy is based. However, this paper can be understood purely in terms of communicating systems of LTSs, and knowledge of CSP is not a prerequisite. Section 3 presents some current incomplete techniques for deadlock analysis. In Sect. 4, we introduce our technique. Section 5 outlines the accuracy of our method. In the following section, we give an encoding of our deadlock-freedom analysis as a SAT problem. Section 7 presents some experiments conducted to assess the accuracy and efficiency of our framework. Finally, in Sect. 8, we present our concluding remarks.

2   Background

Communicating Sequential Processes (CSP) [13,20] is a notation used to model concurrent systems where processes interact, exchanging messages. Here we describe some structures used by the refinement checker FDR3 [10] in implementing CSP's operational semantics. As this paper does not depend on the details of CSP, we do not describe the details of the language or its semantics. These can be found in [20].

CSP's operational semantics interpret language terms in a *labelled transition system* (LTS)[2].

Definition 1. *A labelled transition system is a 4-tuple* $(S, \Sigma, \Delta, \hat{s})$ *where:*

- S *is a set of states;*
- Σ *is the alphabet (i.e. a set of events);*
- $\Delta \subseteq S \times \Sigma \times S$ *is a transition relation;*
- $\hat{s} \in S$ *is the starting state.*

For the purposes of this paper, the events τ (the silent event) and $\checkmark$ (the termination signal) are considered members of Σ, since there is no difference between them and regular events in the context of deadlock analysis, and their behaviour can be accommodated in the supercombinator framework we use.

As a convention, $\Sigma^- \mathrel{\hat{=}} \Sigma \cup \{-\}$, where $- \notin \Sigma$. We write $s \xrightarrow{e} s'$ if $(s, e, s') \in \Delta$. There is a path from s to s' with the sequence of events $\langle e_1, \ldots, e_n \rangle$, represented by $s \xrightarrow{\langle e_1, \ldots, e_n \rangle} s'$, if there exist $s_1, \ldots, s_{n-1}$ such that $s \xrightarrow{e_1} s_1 \ldots s_{n-1} \xrightarrow{e_n} s'$. A *trace* of a transition system is a path such that the initial state is $\hat{s}$.

While CSP, in common with many other languages, can have its operational semantics given in SOS (Structural Operational Semantics) style, FDR3 represents them as combinators, a notation which is itself compositional and allows complex CSP constructs, including communicating systems, to be represented as *supercombinator machines*. A supercombinator machine consists of a set of component LTSs along with a set of rules that describe how the transitions should be combined. A rule combines transitions of (a subset of) the components and determines the event the machine performs. We also use these machines to analyse the behaviour of communicating systems. For simplicity in our analysis, we restrict FDR3's normal definition of supercombinator machines in a way that corresponds to there being a static communicating system with all communication between components being pairwise:

Definition 2. *A triple-disjoint supercombinator machine is a pair* $(\mathcal{L}, \mathcal{R})$ *where:*

- $\mathcal{L} = \langle L_1, \ldots, L_n \rangle$ *is a sequence of component LTSs;*
- $\mathcal{R}$ *is a set of rules of the form* (e, a) *where:*
  - $e \in (\Sigma^-)^n$ *specifies the event that each component must perform, where* $-$ *indicates that the component performs no event. e must also be triple-disjoint, that is, at most two components must be involved in a rule.*
    - $\ast$ *triple_disjoint*$(e) \mathrel{\hat{=}} \forall i, j, k : \{1 \ldots n\} \mid i \neq j \wedge j \neq k \wedge i \neq k \bullet$
    $$e_i = - \vee e_j = - \vee e_k = -$$
  - $a \in \Sigma$ *is the event the supercombinator performs.*

---

[2] FDR3 uses a more general representation of a process called a *generalised labelled transition system* (GLTS). Nevertheless, this extension can be simply converted into a traditional LTS and working with LTS makes our definitions considerably simpler.

This restriction is similar to ones adopted in related work to ours [6,15]. Henceforth, we omit the mention of triple-disjoint.

Given a supercombinator machine, a corresponding LTS can be constructed.

Definition 3. *Let* $S = (\langle L_1, \ldots, L_n \rangle, \mathcal{R})$ *be a supercombinator machine where* $L_i = (S_i, \Sigma_i, \Delta_i, \hat{s}_i)$. *The LTS induced by* S *is the tuple* $(S, \Sigma, \Delta, \hat{s})$ *such that:*

- $S = S_1 \times \ldots \times S_n$;
- $\Sigma = \bigcup_{i=1}^{n} \Sigma_i$;
- $\Delta = \{((s_1, \ldots, s_n), a, (s_1', \ldots, s_n')) \mid \exists ((e_1, \ldots, e_n), a) : \mathcal{R} \bullet \forall i : \{1 \ldots n\} \bullet;$
    $(e_i = - \wedge s_i = s_i') \vee (e_i \neq - \wedge (s_i, e_i, s_i') \in \Delta_i)\}$
- $\hat{s} = (\hat{s}_1, \ldots, \hat{s}_n)$.

From now on, we use *system state* (*component state*) to designate a state in the system's (component's) LTS.

Definition 4. *A LTS* $(S, \Sigma, \Delta, \hat{s})$ *deadlocks in a state* s *if and only if* *deadlocked*(s) *holds, where:*

- *deadlocked*(s) $\hat{=}$ *reachable*(s) $\wedge$ *blocked*(s)
- *reachable*(s) $\hat{=}$ $\exists tr : \Sigma^* \bullet \hat{s} \xrightarrow{tr} s$
- *blocked*(s) $\hat{=}$ $\neg \exists s' : S \,; e : \Sigma \bullet s \xrightarrow{e} s'$

When considering the deadlock detection problem, for the sake of decidability, we only analyse supercombinator machines with a finite number of components, which are themselves represented by finite LTSs with finite alphabets.

3   Related Work

Two of the authors of this paper have previously investigated the role played by local analysis in establishing deadlock freedom in [1,4,8,18]. These works introduce a formalisation of design patterns that can be used for designing deadlock-free systems. Despite being efficient, as these techniques analyse components in isolation, they can be restrictive since only a handful of behavioural patterns are available.

In [5,6,14,15], fully-automated but incomplete techniques for deadlock freedom are introduced. These techniques are proposed for different contexts and types of concurrency: [6] proposes a method for analysing syntactically-restricted shared-variable concurrent programs, [5] adapts [6] to a more general setting meant to describe component-based message-passing systems, [14] proposes a method for architecturally-restricted component-based systems interacting via message passing, and [15] proposes a method for syntactically-restricted message-passing concurrent systems. All these methods were designed, to some extent, around the principle that under reasonable assumptions about the system, any deadlock state would contain a proper cycle of ungranted requests. So, to prove deadlock freedom, they would use local properties of the system, derived from analysing individual components and communicating pairs of components, to construct an ungranted-requests graph and show that such a cycle cannot arise in any conceivable state of the system.

To discuss in more detail how such approaches work, we present the *SDD framework*[3] developed by Martin in [15]. We regard our framework as a development on the SDD. Martin's analysis of SDDs is one of the most general prior approaches to local deadlock analysis.

In that work [15], the local properties used to prove deadlock freedom are derived from the analysis of pairs of components, or rather a projection of the system over a pair of its components.

Definition 5. *Let* $\mathcal{S} = (\langle L_1, \ldots, L_n \rangle, \mathcal{R})$ *be a supercombinator machine. The pairwise projection* $\mathcal{S}_{i,j}$ *of the machine* $\mathcal{S}$ *on components* i *and* j *is given by:*

$$\mathcal{S}_{i,j} = (\langle L_i, L_j \rangle, \{((e_i, e_j), a) | (e, a) \in \mathcal{R} \wedge (e_i \neq - \vee e_j \neq -)\})$$

In Martin's approach, a dependency digraph is constructed and then analysed for absence of cycles. The dependency digraph constructed has a node for each state of each component, and an edge from a state s of component i to a state s' of component j if and only if $reachable_{i,j}((s, s'))$ and $ungranted\_request_{i,j}(s, s')$ hold where: $reachable_{i,j}$ denotes the *reachable* predicate for the LTS induced by $\mathcal{S}_{i,j}$; $ungranted\_request_{i,j}(s, s')$ holds when, in their respective states (i in s and j in s'), component i is willing to synchronise with j (according to $\mathcal{S}_{i,j}$), but they cannot agree on any event.

Under the assumption that components neither terminate nor deadlock, a cycle of ungranted requests is a necessary condition for a system deadlock. Hence, the absence of cycles in the dependency digraph is a proof of deadlock freedom, whereas a cycle represents a potential deadlock which we call a *SDD candidate*.

Definition 6. *Let* $\mathcal{S} = (\langle L_1, \ldots, L_n \rangle, \mathcal{R})$ *be a supercombinator machine, where* $L_i = (S_i, \Sigma_i, \Delta_i, \hat{s}_i)$. *Let* $\mathcal{U}$ *be the disjoint union of all* S_i *and* $s_{i,j}$ *denotes state* j *of the component* i. *A sequence of component states* $c \in \mathcal{U}^*$ *is a SDD candidate if and only if for all* $i \in \{1 \ldots |c|\}$, *given that* $c_i = s_{j,k}$ *and* $c_{i \oplus 1} = s_{l,m}$, $reachable_{j,l}((s_{j,k}, s_{l,m}))$ *and* $ungranted\_request_{j,l}(s_{j,k}, s_{l,m})$ *hold, where* $\oplus$ *denotes addition modulo the length of* c.

This method can carry out deadlock-freedom verification very efficiently: a digraph can be shown to have no cycles in linear time using a modified *depth-first-search*. This efficiency, however, comes with a price as the use of a cycle as a candidate makes this method imprecise in several ways. Firstly, a cycle might not be consistent with basic sanity conditions such as it must have a single node per component (after all no component can be in two different states in a single deadlock). Secondly, a cycle is only partially consistent with the local reachability and local blocking properties derived from the analysis of pairs of components. Note that only adjacent elements in the cycle are guaranteed to be pairwise reachable and pairwise blocked. So, there may be local properties of

---

[3] SDD stands for State Dependency Digraph.

non-adjacent component states not tested for that might eliminate some SDD candidate. Finally, a cycle, as a necessary condition, is bound to arise in some deadlock-free systems. Thus, in such cases, this framework is ineffective. The reason why these sources of imprecision are not addressed is that these methods look for polynomially checkable conditions for guaranteeing deadlock freedom and tackling any of these sources of imprecision is likely to make the problem of finding a candidate in the dependency digraph NP-complete.

4   A New Framework for Deadlock-Freedom Verification Using Local Analysis

In this section, we propose a new way of detecting potential deadlocks. Instead of looking for cycles, we look for complete snapshots of the system that are fully consistent with the local reachability and blocking information. A complete snapshot is a tuple containing a component state per component in the system. So, a deadlock candidate for this framework, which we call a *pair candidate*, is given as follows.

Definition 7. *Let* $S = (\langle L_1, \ldots, L_n \rangle, \mathcal{R})$ *be a supercombinator machine, and* $(S, \Sigma, \Delta, \hat{s})$ *its induced LTS. A state* $s = (s_1, \ldots, s_n) \in S$ *is a* pair candidate *if and only if* $pair\_candidate(s)$ *holds, where:*

- $pair\_candidate(s) \triangleq pairwise\_reachable(s) \wedge blocked(s)$
- $pairwise\_reachable(s) \triangleq \forall i, j : \{1 \ldots n\} \mid i \neq j \bullet reachable_{i,j}((s_i, s_j))$

This new characterisation creates a framework that uses more information to disprove potential deadlock candidates if compared to prior techniques using pairwise analysis of components. By analysing complete snapshots, only complete states of the system are examined, and as a consequence, our framework is able to prove that systems possessing ungranted-requests cycles are deadlock free.

Two remarks about the *blocked* condition deserve mention. Firstly, the blocking condition seems to be global, but in fact, it can be validated using individual and pairwise component analyses. As systems are triple disjoint, a state is blocked if and only if all components can neither perform an individual event nor communicate with another component. Secondly, this blocking condition is exact, so in our framework, false negatives can only arise from the fact that the derived local reachability properties may not prove the unreachability of a candidate.

Our framework is sound, as absence of pair candidates implies deadlock freedom. The following theorem follows from the fact that reachability implies pair-reachability. Its proof can be found in [3].

Theorem 1. *Let* $S = (\langle L_1, \ldots, L_n \rangle, \mathcal{R})$ *be a supercombinator machine and* $(S, \Sigma, \Delta, \hat{s})$ *its induced LTS. For any* $s \in S$,

$$\neg pair\_candidate(s) \implies \neg deadlocked(s)$$

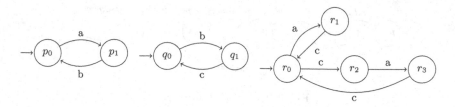

Fig. 1. LTSs of components L_1, L_2 and L_3, respectively.

This criterion will be shown to be more accurate than the SDD one, but it remains incomplete because it relies on local analysis to approximate reachability: there may well be pair candidates that are not actually reachable.

Example 1. Let $\mathcal{S} = (\langle L_1, L_2, L_3 \rangle, \mathcal{R})$ be the supercombinator machine such that the components are described graphically in Fig. 1 and they must synchronise on shared events. That is, $\mathcal{R} = \{((a, -, a), a), ((b, b, -), b), ((-, c, c), c)\}$.

For this system, the state (p_0, q_0, r_3) is pairwise-reachable and blocked, but not reachable. Thus, it constitutes a pair candidate but not a deadlock.   □

What we have done here is to use a characterisation of what a deadlock state looks like in conjunction with an approximation to the reachability criterion for states. What it searches for are not *reachable* deadlocks, but rather *pair-consistent* deadlocks. Therefore, we call it *Pair*. One could easily imagine using different local groups of components to determining consistency, or applying similar approaches to analyse communicating systems for individual states that have properties other than being deadlocked.

5   Accuracy of the Pair Framework

In this section, we shed light on the class of systems that can be successfully proved deadlock free by Pair by comparing it to the SDD framework. In this comparison, we first outline the class of systems tackled by SDD and then we show that our approach tackles a strictly larger class of systems.

The SDD framework has been able to successfully prove deadlock freedom for some relevant classes of system. Martin has shown that his framework can prove deadlock freedom for systems designed using two well-known design rules: the *resource-allocation* and *client-server* rules. The resource allocation rule has been proposed initially as a mechanism for avoiding deadlocks when allocating the resources of an operating system to programs [9], whereas client-server protocols constitute a very common paradigm for the interaction of distributed system. Both rules prevent cycles of ungranted requests from arising.

5.1   Pair Is at Least as Good as SDD

A deadlocked state is only guaranteed to exhibit a cycle of ungranted requests if a system (or supercombinator machine) is *live*, namely all its components are

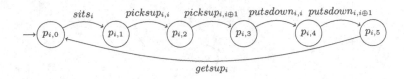

Fig. 2. LTS of philosopher i.

deadlock-free and termination-free. So, in this section, to compare Pair with SDD, we limit ourselves to live systems.

In this restricted setting, we show that our approach can prove deadlock freedom for a system whenever SDD can. This follows from the claim that for a live system, a blocked state must exhibit a cycle of ungranted requests.

Lemma 1 (Theorem 1 in [15]). *Let S be a live supercombinator machine, $(S, \Sigma, \Delta, \hat{s})$ its induced LTS, and $\mathcal{U}$ the disjoint union of all the component states of each component.*

$$\exists\, s : S \bullet blocked(s) \implies \exists\, c : \mathcal{U}^* \bullet sdd\_candidate(c)$$

Theorem 2. *Let S be a live supercombinator machine, $(S, \Sigma, \Delta, \hat{s})$ its induced LTS, and $\mathcal{U}$ the disjoint union of all the component states of each component.*

$$\neg\, \exists\, c : \mathcal{U}^* \bullet sdd\_candidate(c) \implies \neg\, \exists\, s : S \bullet pair\_candidate(s)$$

5.2 Pair Is More Accurate Than SDD

Even though SDD is accurate for a reasonably large and relevant class of systems, it is unable to prove deadlock freedom for non-hereditary deadlock-free systems. This is shown by Lemma 1: if a subsystem deadlocks then there must exist a cycle of ungranted requests between the states of components in this subsystem that constitutes a SDD candidate. Roughly speaking, SDD can be seen as a method that tries to prove *hereditary* deadlock freedom (i.e. that no subsystem can deadlock) using local analysis. On the other hand, our method can prove deadlock freedom for both hereditary and non-hereditary deadlock-free systems, such as the following example.

Example 2. This well-known example system is composed of three different components: forks, philosophers and a butler. We parametrise our system with N, which denotes the number of philosophers in the system.

A philosopher has access to a table at which it can pick up two forks to eat: one at its left-hand side and the other at its right-hand side. A fork is placed, and shared, between philosophers sitting adjacently in the table. The behaviour of philosopher (fork) i is depicted in Fig. 2 (3). $\oplus$ stands for addition modulo N.

Given that these components synchronise on their shared events, the philosophers and forks can reach a deadlock state in which all philosophers have acquired their left-hand side forks and, as a consequence, no right-hand side fork is left

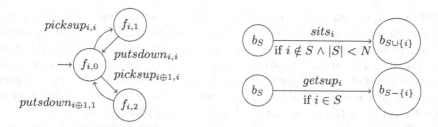

Fig. 3. LTS of fork i and transitions of the butler process.

to be acquired. The butler is introduced to prevent all the philosophers from sitting at the table at the same time, thereby precluding this deadlock state. We use b_S to depict the state in which the butler has allowed the philosophers in S to the table. So, the butler states space is given by the set of all b_S where $S \in \mathbb{P}(\{1 \ldots N\}) - \{\{1 \ldots N\}\}$. Its transitions are created as depicted in Fig. 3, and its initial state is given by $b_\emptyset$.

The complete system has N philosophers, N forks and a butler, and these components synchronise on their shared events. Despite being deadlock free, this system has a cycle of component states that forms a SDD candidate, namely, where all the philosophers have acquired their left-hand fork:

$$\langle p_{0,2}, f_{1,1}, p_{1,2}, f_{2,1}, \ldots, p_{N-2,2}, f_{N-1,1}, p_{N-1,2}, f_{0,1} \rangle$$

However, this SDD candidate cannot be extended to a pair candidate, because the latter would have to include a butler state, and no butler state is consistent with this combination of philosopher states.   □

This example shows that the Pair method is strictly more accurate than SDD. Going a step further, this can be seen as representative of the class of non-hereditary deadlock-free systems where one or more components prevent some subsystem's deadlock from being reached. Note that many concurrent systems use components implementing mutual exclusion algorithms or semaphores to prevent other components reaching undesired states such as a deadlock.

Moreover, our method has better accuracy than SDD even for hereditary deadlock-free systems, thanks to the fact that we use local reachability and blocking information to its full extent. This increase in accuracy, however, comes with a price. The explicit exploration of, only, localised state spaces helps to tame the complexity of checking our deadlock-freedom condition. Nevertheless, by strengthening the candidate's definition in relation to prior techniques, we end up with an NP-complete problem [3].

6   Pair Candidate Detection Using a SAT Solver

In this section, we propose a procedure that encodes the pair-candidate detection problem in terms of propositional satisfiability, which can later be checked by a SAT solver. Given a supercombinator machine as an input, our procedure creates a propositional formula in conjunctive normal form (CNF). A satisfying assignment for this formula gives a pair candidate: the variables assigned to true correspond to a combination of component states that forms a pair candidate, whereas a proof of unsatisfiability entails deadlock freedom for the input system. The use of intermediate structures in our encoding procedure and the application of a SAT solver in the process of deadlock checking was inspired by the success of the SLAP tool [17], which uses SAT solvers for the verification of livelocks[4].

We consider for the sake of presentation that we are translating the supercombinator machine $\mathcal{S} = (\langle L_1, \ldots, L_n \rangle, \mathcal{R})$, where $L_i = (S_i, \Sigma_i, \Delta_i, \hat{s}_i)$. Additionally, we assume component states are unique across the system and that $s_{i,j}$ denotes the state j of the component i. Our encoding procedure can be divided into two parts: an initial one where intermediate structures are calculated from the supercombinator machine, and a final one where the boolean formula is generated based on these intermediate structures.

The intermediate structures can be seen as storing information that is later used to filter out combinations of component states that do not belong to a valid pair candidate. The first intermediate structure created, $RequireSync_i$, stores for each component the states in which cooperation is required. So, it provides information to filter out component states that can act independently and are, therefore, trivially not blocked.

Definition 8. $RequireSync_i = \{s | s \in S_i \land \neg independent_i(s)\}$

- $independent_i(s) \triangleq \exists (e, a) : \mathcal{R} \bullet (e_i \neq - \land \forall k : \{1 \ldots n\} \mid k \neq i \bullet e_k = -)$
$$\land (\exists s' : S_i \bullet (s, e_i, s') \in \Delta_i)$$

The structure $CanSync$ stores blocking information about pairs of components. It provides information to filter out pairs of component states in which components can interact. The triple disjointness assumption means that this pairwise information is enough to determine whether a system state is blocked.

Definition 9

$$CanSync = \bigcup_{i,j \in \{1 \ldots n\} \land i \neq j} \left\{ (s, s') \,\middle|\, \begin{array}{l} s \in RequireSync_i \land s' \in RequireSync_j \land \\ reachable_{i,j}((s, s')) \land sync_{i,j}(s, s') \end{array} \right\}$$

- $sync_{i,j}(s, s') = \exists (e, a) : \mathcal{R} \,; t : S_i \,; t' : S_j \bullet (s, e_i, t) \in \Delta_i \land (s', e_j, t') \in \Delta_j$

The last structure NPR (Not Pairwise Reachable) collects local reachability information and is used to filter out pairs of components that are not mutually reachable.

---

[4] There are some significant differences with SLAP: here the propositional formula is satisfied by a possible deadlock, whereas in SLAP the propositional formula is satisfied by a *proof of livelock freedom*. We might also note that livelock arises from a sequence of states, whereas deadlock arises in a single one.

Definition 10

$$NPR = \bigcup_{i,j \in \{1...n\} \wedge i \neq j} \left\{ (s, s') \middle| \begin{array}{l} s \in RequireSync_i \wedge s' \in RequireSync_j \wedge \\ \neg reachable_{i,j}((s, s')) \end{array} \right\}$$

In the second phase of our encoding procedure, we construct a boolean formula based on these derived structures. The formula generated is a conjunction of three constraints; each of them uses the information encompassed in a derived structure to filter out invalid combinations of component states. For the construction of our formula, we use our state representation $s_{i,j}$ to denote the boolean variable representing this state. So, the assignment $s_{i,j} = true$ might be seen as claiming that this state belongs to a pair candidate, whereas $s_{i,j} = false$ means it does not.

The first constraint, *State*, restricts the space of valid combinations of component states to complete snapshots. As discussed, only states in *RequireSync* structure are relevant.

Definition 11

$$State \triangleq \bigwedge_{i \in \{1...n\}} (\bigvee_{s \in RequireSync_i} s) \wedge \bigwedge_{i \in \{1...n\}} (\bigwedge_{s,s' \in RequireSync_i \wedge s \neq s'} (\neg s \vee \neg s'))$$

The second constraint restricts the space of valid combinations of component states to the ones respecting local reachability properties.

Definition 12. $Reachable \triangleq \bigwedge_{(s,s') \in NPR} (\neg s \vee \neg s')$

Finally, the last constraint ensures that the space of valid combinations of component states are the ones respecting our blocking requirement.

Definition 13. $Blocked \triangleq \bigwedge_{(s,s') \in CanSync} (\neg s \vee \neg s')$

7 Practical Evaluation

In this section, we evaluate our framework in practice; we modified FDR3 to generate our SAT encoding which is then checked by the Glucose 4.0 solver [7]. Our prototype and the models used in this section are available at [2]. We describe two experiments in this section: the first one evaluates deadlock freedom for randomly generated systems, the second one evaluates deadlock freedom for some deadlock-free benchmark problems. The experiments were conducted on a dedicated machine with a quad-core Intel Core i5-4300U CPU @ 1.90 GHz, 8 GB of RAM, and the Fedora 20 operating system. In these experiments, we compare our prototype with the Deadlock Checker [16] and FDR3's deadlock freedom assertion [10]. Deadlock Checker implements the *SDD* framework, whereas FDR3 is a complete method that performs explicit space exploration. When appropriate, we combine FDR3's explicit state exploration with partial order reduction (FDRp) [11] or compression techniques (FDRc) [19].

In the first experiment, we verify models of randomly-generated live systems, but with fixed communication topologies. Our goal with this experiment is to test our tool against scripts made by non-experts. We verify systems whose communication topologies are grid-like, fully connected, or a pair of rings. The parameter N is related to the size of these systems. The choice of these communication topologies was based on the fact that many CSP benchmark problems use one of these or a variation. For each of topology and N, we generate 900 random systems.

In Table 1, we summarise the accuracy results obtained. For the accuracy comparison, we take FDR3's deadlock assertion out, as it is a complete method. Also, the reason why we sometimes present the absolute number of deadlock-free systems is that we use FDR3 to get the exact number of deadlock-free systems, but when FDR3 times out, this number is unavailable. In Table 2, for FDR3, we present the figures for the method that worked best. So, for the pair of rings, applying partial order reduction made FDR3 scale better, whereas for the other two cases, explicit state exploration was the best option.

Based on the data gathered in this first experiment, we can conclude that our prototype provides a far better compromise between accuracy and speed than the Deadlock Checker for the systems checked. The fact that hereditary deadlock freedom is more difficult to achieve than deadlock freedom seems to be the reason why our approach is substantially more accurate. In terms of efficiency, we see that our method scales fairly well for the generated systems. It fared better than FDR3 even when combined with sophisticated techniques to combat the state space explosion problem. For most of the cases, our method also fared better than the Deadlock Checker. For the cases in which the Deadlock Checker scales better, we can see a considerable difference in the accuracy of the two methods that justifies the difference in their speed.

Table 1. Accuracy comparison; the numbers not in parentheses depict the percentages of deadlock free systems proved as so. The numbers in parentheses represent the total number of deadlock free systems proved as so.

N	Rings		Grid		Fully	
	Pair	SDD	Pair	SDD	Pair	SDD
3	99.13	64.34	100	34.44	93.98	18.67
4	99.67	68.19	(599)	(106)	98.76	6.4
5	99.71	73.57	(635)	(96)	98.11	1.8
6	98.98	77.41	(644)	(92)	99.25	1.1
7	100	76.14	(771)	(30)	99.28	0.1
8	(469)	(385)	(773)	(57)	99.65	0
9	(500)	(422)	(779)	(28)	99.83	0
10	(517)	(444)	(774)	(8)	99.52	0
15	(590)	(491)	(900)	(0)	(692)	(0)
20	(645)	(547)	(900)	(0)	(703)	(0)
25	(680)	(566)	(887)	(0)	(742)	(0)

Our second experiment consists of applying deadlock verification methods to some benchmark problems that are carefully designed to be deadlock free. We chose four benchmark problems that are proved deadlock free by Pair. These problems are the sliding window protocol (SWP), a binary telephone switch (Telephone), the mad postman routing algorithm (Routing), and the butler solution to the dining philosophers (Butler). These problems are discussed in

Table 2. Efficiency comparison; we measure in seconds the time taken to check deadlock freedom for the 900-systems batch, and * means that the methods has timed out. We establish a time out of 2000 s for checking each batch.

	Rings			Grid			Fully		
N	Pair	SDD	FDR3p	Pair	SDD	FDR3	Pair	SDD	FDR3
3	37.38	66.04	40.91	40.47	71.01	70.27	37.39	65.64	42.74
4	37.88	67.65	42.89	44.89	76.57	*	39.04	70.02	43.36
5	39.00	68.30	51.60	52.67	90.50	*	39.74	74.19	43.97
6	39.67	69.97	103.83	60.85	104.07	*	42.46	83.18	48.96
7	41.07	71.69	788.03	70.39	113.95	*	45.50	92.91	61.47
8	41.12	73.11	*	84.67	128.41	*	49.24	103.08	118.78
9	41.90	73.71	*	101.18	142.65	*	53.91	115.87	415.87
10	42.67	75.31	*	124.80	157.76	*	60.32	125.60	1897.71
15	46.75	80.52	*	326.56	249.27	*	108.99	210.65	*
20	52.09	89.03	*	797.25	385.99	*	208.37	372.44	*
25	57.48	95.74	*	1745.72	566.27	*	382.89	645.74	*

detail in [20]. For each of these benchmarks, we vary a parameter N which relates to the size of these systems. Table 3 presents the results of this second experiment, which suggests that our method scales similarly to the combination

Table 3. Benchmark efficiency comparison. We measure in seconds the time taken to check deadlock freedom for each system. * means that the methods has timed out; we establish a time out of 40 s for checking each system. - means that the method is unable to prove deadlock freedom for the system.

	SWP				
N	FDR3	SDD	Pair	FDR3c	FDR3p
3	0.29	0.88	0.14	0.24	0.21
4	2.83	40.83	0.58	1.13	3.57
5	42.79	*	3.23	4.62	*
6	*	*	18.38	25.25	*
7	*	*	*	*	*

	Telephone				
N	FDR3	SDD	Pair	FDR3c	FDR3p
3	*	-	0.06	0.17	*
4	*	-	0.11	2.93	*
5	*	-	0.32	*	*
6	*	-	1.34	*	*
7	*	-	6.27	*	*
8	*	-	31.68	*	*

	Butler				
N	FDR3	SDD	Pair	FDR3c	FDR3p
3	0.06	-	0.06	0.09	0.06
4	0.07	-	0.6	0.10	0.07
5	0.26	-	0.6	0.10	0.43
6	0.11	-	0.7	0.12	0.08
7	0.32	-	0.9	0.14	0.13
8	1.91	-	0.12	0.17	0.22
9	16.80	-	0.19	0.22	0.52

	Routing				
N	FDR3	SDD	Pair	FDR3c	FDR3p
3	*	0.10	0.06	0.10	*
4	*	0.11	0.09	0.14	*
5	*	0.13	0.13	0.18	*
10	*	0.30	0.99	0.71	*
20	*	1.11	13.27	4.45	*
30	*	3.30	*	16.72	*

of FDR3's assertion techniques with compression techniques. We point out that the effective use of compression techniques requires a careful and skilful application of those, whereas our method is fully automatic. In fact, our strategy seems to be the most efficient option for all but the Routing problem in which both the Deadlock Checker and FDR3's assertion with compression techniques outperform us.

Unsurprisingly, for some other benchmark problems our method is not able to prove deadlock freedom. The reason is that, for these cases, deadlock freedom depends on some global invariant preserved by the system (or perhaps by larger subsets of the system than the pairs used here), and as argued, this type of reasoning is beyond the capabilities of our method. For instance, proving deadlock freedom for the Milner's scheduler problem, which is a fairly simple benchmark problem, is out of our method's reach. The issue with Milner's scheduler is that it is essentially a token ring which depends on the fact that there is always precisely one token present; this latter property cannot be proved by local analysis of the sort we employ.

8   Conclusion

We have introduced a new test for deadlock freedom that extends the capabilities of current state-of-the-art incomplete approaches. To do so, we introduced a stronger deadlock candidate definition and we brought the power of SAT checking to bear on a style of local analysis of systems that reaches back decades. Like other incomplete methods, we sacrifice completeness to achieve scalability. This incomplete nature makes, for instance, our technique (and any other one that uses local analysis) unable to prove deadlock freedom for systems in which this property is guaranteed by some invariant on the global behaviour of systems.

Our method rivals the speed of current incomplete approaches but gives a considerable increase in accuracy. For the systems tested, it appears to perform strongly in terms of speed when compared to SDD, compression and partial order techniques. As for accuracy, our method is strictly more accurate than SDD, and in particular, it is able to tackle non-hereditary deadlock-free systems, a class of systems neglected by most incomplete techniques. Our ambition is to have a deadlock checker which can be used on systems developed by non-experts who do not necessarily have any knowledge of established design patterns for deadlock freedom, such as those previously proposed by two of the authors.

As a future work, we plan to improve accuracy, without excessively damaging speed, by proposing methods to efficiently calculate some global invariants. This should not make our method complete, but it should enable the handling of systems which are deadlock free by some global property of the system. Additionally, we intend to extend our framework to produce counter-examples and/or other useful debugging information.

Acknowledgments. We are grateful to Jöel Ouaknine and James Worrell for many fruitful discussions concerning this work. The first author is a CAPES Foundation scholarship holder (Process no: 13201/13-1). The second and third authors are partially sponsored by DARPA under agreement number FA8750-12-2-0247.

References

1. Antonino, P.R.G., Oliveira, M.M., Sampaio, A.C.A., Kristensen, K.E., Bryans, J.W.: Leadership election: an industrial SoS application of compositional deadlock verification. In: Badger, J.M., Rozier, K.Y. (eds.) NFM 2014. LNCS, vol. 8430, pp. 31–45. Springer, Heidelberg (2014)
2. Antonino, P., Roscoe, A.W., Gibson-Robinson, T.: Experiment package (2015). http://www.cs.ox.ac.uk/people/pedro.antonino/exp.zip
3. Antonino, P., Roscoe, A.W., Gibson-Robinson, T.: Efficient deadlock analysis using local analysis and SAT solving. Technical report, University of Oxford (2015). http://www.cs.ox.ac.uk/people/pedro.antonino/techreport.pdf
4. Antonino, P., Sampaio, A., Woodcock, J.: A refinement based strategy for local deadlock analysis of networks of CSP processes. In: Jones, C., Pihlajasaari, P., Sun, J. (eds.) FM 2014. LNCS, vol. 8442, pp. 62–77. Springer, Switzerland (2014)
5. Attie, P.C., Bensalem, S., Bozga, M., Jaber, M., Sifakis, J., Zaraket, F.A.: An abstract framework for deadlock prevention in BIP. In: Beyer, D., Boreale, M. (eds.) FMOODS/FORTE 2013. LNCS, vol. 7892, pp. 161–177. Springer, Heidelberg (2013)
6. Attie, P.C., Chockler, H.: Efficiently verifiable conditions for deadlock-freedom of large concurrent programs. In: Cousot, R. (ed.) VMCAI 2005. LNCS, vol. 3385, pp. 465–481. Springer, Heidelberg (2005)
7. Audemard, G., Simon, L.: Predicting learnt clauses quality in modern SAT solvers. In: IJCAI 2009, San Francisco, CA, USA, pp. 399–404 (2009)
8. Brookes, S.D., Roscoe, A.W.: Deadlock analysis in networks of communicating processes. Distrib. Comput. 4, 209–230 (1991)
9. Coffman, E.G., Elphick, M., Shoshani, A.: System deadlocks. ACM Comput. Surv. (CSUR) 3(2), 67–78 (1971)
10. Gibson-Robinson, T., Armstrong, P., Boulgakov, A., Roscoe, A.W.: FDR3 — a modern refinement checker for CSP. In: Ábrahám, E., Havelund, K. (eds.) TACAS 2014. LNCS, vol. 8413, pp. 187–201. Springer, Heidelberg (2014)
11. Gibson-Robinson, T., Hansen, H., Roscoe, A.W., Wang, X.: Practical partial order reduction for CSP. In: Havelund, K., Holzmann, G., Joshi, R. (eds.) NFM 2015. LNCS, vol. 9058, pp. 188–203. Springer, Switzerland (2015)
12. Godefroid, P., Wolper, P.: Using partial orders for the efficient verification of deadlock freedom and safety properties. FMSD 2(2), 149–164 (1993)
13. Hoare, C.A.R.: Communicating Sequential Processes. Prentice-Hall, Upper Saddle River (1985)
14. Lambertz, C., Majster-Cederbaum, M.: Analyzing component-based systems on the basis of architectural constraints. In: Arbab, F., Sirjani, M. (eds.) FSEN 2011. LNCS, vol. 7141, pp. 64–79. Springer, Heidelberg (2012)
15. Martin, J.M.R.: The design and construction of deadlock-free concurrent systems. Ph.D. thesis, University of Buckingham (1996)
16. Martin, J.M.R., Jassim, S.A.: An efficient technique for deadlock analysis of large scale process networks. In: Fitzgerald, J., Jones, C.B., Lucas, P. (eds.) FME 1997. LNCS, vol. 1313, pp. 418–441. Springer, Heidelberg (1997)
17. Ouaknine, J., Palikareva, H., Roscoe, A.W., Worrell, J.: A static analysis framework for livelock freedom in CSP. LMCS 9(3), 1–53 (2013)
18. Roscoe, A.W., Dathi, N.: The pursuit of deadlock freedom. Inf. Comput. 75(3), 289–327 (1987)

19. Roscoe, A.W., Gardiner, P.H.B., Goldsmith, M.H., Hulance, J.R., Jackson, D.M., Scattergood, J.B.: Hierarchical compression for model-checking CSP or how to check 10^{20} dining philosophers for deadlock. In: Brinksma, E., Cleaveland, W.R., Larsen, K.G., Margaria, T., Steffen, B. (eds.) TACAS 1995. LNCS, vol. 1019, pp. 133–152. Springer, Heidelberg (1995)
20. Roscoe, A.W.: Understanding Concurrent Systems. Springer, London (2010)

SMT Solvers for Validation
of B and Event-B Models

Sebastian Krings$^{(\boxtimes)}$ and Michael Leuschel

Institut für Informatik, Universität Düsseldorf,
Universitätsstr. 1, 40225 Düsseldorf, Germany
{krings,leuschel}@cs.uni-duesseldorf.de

Abstract. We present an integration of the constraint solving kernel of
the PROB model checker with the SMT solver Z3. We apply the combined
solver to B and Event-B predicates, featuring higher-order datatypes and
constructs like set comprehensions. To do so we rely on the finite set logic
of Z3 and provide a new translation from B to Z3, better suited for constraint solving. Predicates can then be solved by the two solvers working hand in hand: constraints are set up in both solvers simultaneously
and (intermediate) results are transferred. We thus combine a constraint
logic programming based solver with a DPLL(T) based solver into a single
procedure. The improved constraint solver finds application in many validation tasks, from animation of implicit specifications, to test case generation, bounded and symbolic model checking on to disproving of proof
obligations. We conclude with an empirical evaluation of our approach
focusing on two dimensions: comparing low and high-level encodings of
B as well as comparing pure PROB to PROB combined with Z3.

Keywords: B-Method · Event-B · SMT · Animation

1 Introduction and Motivation

B [1] and its successor Event-B [2] are two specification languages for the formal development of software and systems following the correct-by-construction
approach. Both languages are rooted in set-theory and support different higher
order data types like relations, functions and sequences. PROB [19,20] is a model
checker for both languages featuring explicit state model checking as well as different constraint based techniques [13,18] for the analysis of specifications.

Originally, the PROB kernel has been tailored towards satisfiable formulas,
acting primarily as a model finder [19,20]. Recent additions to PROB have
extended the kernel in a different direction. With the introduction of PROB-
based (dis-)proving of Event-B proof obligations, detecting the unsatisfiability
of predicates shifted into focus [15].

PROB's kernel is developed in SICStus Prolog [8]. The integer part of the
solver is mostly based on the CLP(FD) library. Custom extensions and solvers
are implemented for sets, relations and records. Furthermore, support for quantifiers has been added on top of CLP(FD). The different solvers are integrated

© The Author(s) 2016
E. Ábrahám and M. Huisman (Eds.): IFM 2016, LNCS 9681, pp. 361–375, 2016.
DOI: 10.1007/978-3-319-33693-0_23

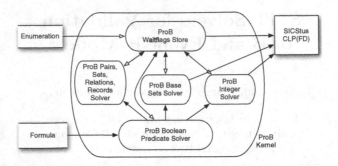

Fig. 1. PROB kernel overview

using "waitflags" to control which constraints should be tackled. Truth values between solvers are communicated using reification variables. Figure 1 gives an overview.

This approach is fundamentally different from the DPLL(T) [12] approach employed by modern SMT solvers like Z3 [9]. In [15] we already compared both approaches for Event-B proof obligations and outlined that neither is able to outperform the other: there are a considerable number of proof obligations that can only be solved by one of them. Hence, our idea is to combine the particular strengths into a single solving procedure. In Sect. 1.1 we will show some examples for strengths and weaknesses and argue towards our integrated approach.

Our new translation from B to Z3 and its integration is included in the latest nightly release of PROB. Information regarding installation and usage is available at:

http://stups.hhu.de/ProB/Using_ProB_with_Z3.

1.1   Small Experiments

To outline some of the weaknesses of the CLP(FD) based solving kernel, have a look at the following predicate: $X > 3 \land X < 7 \land X < Y \land Y < X$. Classic CLP(FD) style domain propagation first sets up the domains $4..6$ for X and $-\infty .. \infty$ for Y. In a second step, all values that cannot be part of a solution are removed from the domains. Both domains end up being empty. Hence, the predicate is detected as unsatisfiable. As soon as we drop one of the constraints on X, CLP(FD) is unable to do so and has to resort to enumeration. For example, the predicate $X < Y \land Y < X$ can not be proven unsatisfiable by PROB's CLP(FD) kernel alone, as both domains for X and Y are infinite $(-\infty .. \infty)$. Similarly, $X < 7 \land X < Y \land Y < X$ leads to an infinite sequence of narrowed down domains, never reaching inconsistency. Z3 on the other hand easily detects the unsatisfiability.

The CLP(FD) based solver in PROB however can handle certain higher-order constructs like set comprehensions better than the SMT solvers: look for example at the predicate $(2 \mapsto 4) \in \{y | \exists (x).(y = (x \mapsto x + 2))\}$. It states that the pair $(2 \mapsto 4)$ is a member of the set of all pairs y that are of the form $(x, x + 2)$. The predicate is identified as true by PROB. Of course the performance of Z3 highly depends on the translation. Choosing a low-level translation, the predicate can be broken down to $4 = 2 + 2$ and be solved by Z3. If we stay on the high-level of set logics, the set comprehension has to be described using universal quantification. If translated this way, Z3 runs into a timeout.

Additionally, the CLP(FD) based solver performs better for model finding tasks that involve non-linear integer constraints. As an example take the verbal arithmetic puzzle to find (non-equal) digits K, I, S, P, A, O, N such that $KISS * KISS = PASSION$. In B this can be written as $(1000 * K + 100 * I + 10 * S + S) * (1000 * K + 100 * I + 10 * S + S) = 1000000 * P + 100000 * A + 10000 * S + 1000 * S + 100 * I + 10 * O + N$. As each letter should represent a single digit, constraints like $0 \leq K \leq 9$ are added for all the variables. Finally, we add pairwise disequalities for all variables. The resulting predicate is solved by PROB in milliseconds, while Z3 answers unknown.

In the following sections we suggest a possible integration between the CLP(FD) and SMT approaches, trying to gain the advantages of both.

2   New High-Level Translation of B to Z3

The following section will explain both our new translation from B to Z3 and how we integrated Z3 into PROB in order to solve constraints given in B or Event-B. First, in Sect. 2.1 we outline a normal form for B that avoids certain constructs that are hard to translate. Primarily, this is achieved by replacing several expressions by equivalent ones using different operators. Following, in Sect. 2.2 we translate constraints given in normalized B into the (set-)logic of Z3. Lastly, Sect. 3 explains how PROB's kernel and the SMT solver are integrated in order to combine both solvers.

2.1   Normalizing B / Event-B

B and Event-B feature many constructs that are not directly available in Z3's input language. In preparation of the translation from B to SMT in Sect. 2.2, we use rewrite rules to transform a B predicate into a normal form that is easier to translate. All these transformation rules are meant to be applied repeatedly until a fixpoint is reached.

In a first step, we replace certain negated operators available in B by the negation of the regular operator. For instance, we replace $x \notin y$ by $\neg(x \in y)$. In addition, we have to rewrite set operations involving strict subsets to subsets and (dis-)equalities. See Table 1 for the operators and their translations.

Currently, the set logics of SMT solvers have no direct support for intervals or the bounded B integer sets NAT, NAT1, INT. We thus rewrite constraints featuring membership in one of these to a conjunction of disequalities, e.g.,

$$x \in 1..5 \Leftrightarrow 1 \leq x \wedge x \leq 5.$$

Table 1. Normalization of operators

B	Normalized B
$E \neq S$	$\neg(E = S)$
$E \notin S$	$\neg(E \in S)$
$E \not\subset S$	$\neg(E \subset S)$
$E \not\subseteq S$	$\neg(E \subseteq S)$
$E \subset S$	$\neg(E = S) \wedge (E \subseteq S)$

Membership in unions, intersections or set differences of these are handled by decomposing into multiple conjuncts or disjuncts respectively, e.g.,

$$x \in -2..5 \cap \text{NAT} \Leftrightarrow (-2 \leq x \wedge x \leq 5) \wedge (0 \leq x \wedge x \leq \text{MAXINT}).$$

PROB represents relations and functions as sets of tuples. Usually, the set is computed exhaustively. For certain relations or functions, e.g., infinite ones, PROB tries to keep the set symbolic. Furthermore, B allows set theoretic operators to be applied to functions as well. For these two reasons, we cannot simply express B functions as uninterpreted functions in SMT-LIB. We represent functions in SMT-LIB the same way we do in PROB. This makes it necessary to rewrite some B expressions on functions. For instance, we rewrite the function application using a temporary variable:

$$f = \{(1 \mapsto 4), (2 \mapsto 2)\} \wedge x = f(1)$$

becomes

$$f = \{(1 \mapsto 4), (2 \mapsto 2)\} \wedge \exists t.x = t \wedge (1 \mapsto t) : f.$$

During normalization, we have to keep in mind that well-definedness conditions of a predicate might change. In the given examples, if we request the function value of f at 3, the predicate is not well-defined:

$$f = \{(1 \mapsto 4), (2 \mapsto 2)\} \wedge x = f(3)$$

We have applied the function f outside of its domain. In contrast,

$$f = \{(1 \mapsto 4), (2 \mapsto 2)\} \wedge \exists t.x = t \wedge (3 \mapsto t) : f.$$

is well-defined and evaluates to false. In several cases, we add well-defined conditions later on. We show an example, division, in Sect. 2.2. Note that Rodin creates a separate proof obligation for well-definedness. Hence, one can assume well-definedness to be handled by those proof obligations.

Several other operators like domain(restriction) or range(restriction) can be rewritten to set comprehensions. For example, the following equality holds for the domain of a function f:

$$\text{dom}(f) = \{y | \exists x.(x \mapsto y) \in f\}.$$

More definitions of (Event-)B operators in terms of set comprehension can be found in the "reference" books on B [1,2,25].

B features record datatypes comparable to those supported by Z3. However, using Z3 record types have to be introduced and typed before constraints can be applied to the fields. In normalized B, the declaration of a constrained record is hence split in the declaration of a general record conjoined with a predicate constraining the fields. A record membership expression like

$$r : struct(f1 : 11..20, f2 : 12..30)$$

becomes

$$\text{type of r} \wedge r'f1 \geq 11 \wedge 20 \geq r'f1 \wedge r'f2 \geq 12 \wedge 30 \geq r'f2.$$

Some functions included in B, like the two arithmetic functions min and max or the cardinality of a set, are not directly available in SMT-LIB. We hence add temporary variables and supply certain axioms as we did to encode function application. For instance, the expression $\min(S)$ is replaced by variable t and the following additional constraints are added:

- $\forall m.m \in S \Rightarrow t \leq m$, i.e., the temporary variable is less or equal to all members of the set.
- $\exists m.m \in S \wedge t = s$, i.e., t is equal to one of the members of S.

We encode max using the same pattern. For the cardinality, we add a constraint stating that c is the cardinality of S if there exists a bijection between the interval $1..c$ and S. For the empty set, this holds for any $c \leq 0$. Hence, we add $c \geq 0$ to Z3, resulting in $\text{card}(\varnothing) = 0$.

The choice of axioms supplied to Z3 in order to define the B functions influences the performance. We could provide more properties of max, e.g.,

$$\max(S1) > \max(S2) \Rightarrow \forall c.c \in S2 \wedge \exists s.s \in S1 \wedge s > c.$$

Additional axioms might aid Z3 in detecting unsatisfiable predicates. However, they might also decrease performance as they have to be considered during reasoning.

The rules above transform a B predicate into an equivalent B predicate. However, we could go even further, depending on how we employ Z3: For animation and (explicit state) model checking, we have to use an equivalent formula, as we rely on the models. In contrast, for certain symbolic model checking algorithms or proof attempts, we could use rewriting rules that transform a B predicate into an equisatisfiable predicate. The added freedom could be used to tailor the formula towards the solvers' strengths. We will address this in future work.

While nearly all complicated B constructs can be rewritten to set comprehensions, not all of the resulting predicates can be solved by Z3. So far, we did not have any success with the following operators:

- The *general union, general intersection, general sum* and *general product*. For instance, the general union of $U \in \mathbb{P}(\mathbb{P}(S))$ could be rewritten as $union(U) = \{x | x \in S \land (\exists s.s \in U \land x \in s)\}$. However, the existential quantification inside the set comprehension leads to highly involved constraints later on.
- The construction of (non-empty) powersets. Again we could translate $\mathbb{P}(X) = \{s | s \subseteq X\}$.
- The iteration and closure operators of classical B.

2.2   Translation Rules

We feed the normalized constraints generated in the previous section into the C / C++ APIs of Z3. In particular we use logics including support for sets. Z3 realizes those using the techniques described in [23].

Any logic including integer arithmetic, sets and quantifiers already covers most of the expressions occurring in our normalized constraints. Thus, we can pass most of the constraints unmodified. There are however some exceptions:

- Some common operators have different semantics in B and SMT-LIB.
- SMT-LIB as well as Z3 do not support set comprehensions natively. We will translate those by using a universal quantification constraining all members of a set variable.
- User-given sets have to be mapped to SMT-LIB sorts.

For an approach that is based on translation to be both sound and complete we have to ensure that semantical differences are taken into account. In particular, B features a distinct concept of well-definedness, i.e., operators may only be applied under certain conditions. This contrasts with SMT-LIB treating operators as total functions that always return a result. Additionally, the results of applying certain operators differ as well.

Integer division is a prominent example: B uses a division that rounds towards zero. In contrast, SMT-LIB semantics define a division rounding towards $-\infty$. Furthermore, B does not allow division by zero while for SMT solvers division is a total function, e.g., for the predicate $x = 1/0$ Z3 returns the solution $x = 0$. In order to overcome these differences, we set up $x = a/b$ using SMT-LIB's if-then-else as

$$\text{ite}(a > 0, a/b, \text{ite}(b > 0, (a/b) + 1, (a/b) - 1)) \land b \neq 0.$$

For the sake of brevity we can not fully discuss the semantical differences between B and SMT-LIB in this article.

Now, let us have a look at the translation of set comprehensions. A B expression like

$$\neg(r \in \{x | x \mod 2 = 1\})$$

is submitted to Z3 using a temporary variable and axiomatizing the set comprehension. The resulting constraint is

$$\neg(\exists tmp.(r \in tmp \land \forall v.v \in tmp \Leftrightarrow v \mod 2 = 1)).$$

So far we do not provide any additional hints like instantiation triggers to Z3.

In addition to given types likes INTEGER, the B method features user defined types represented as deferred or enumerated sets. We translate those to custom SMT-LIB sorts. For enumerated sets we additionally introduce the identifiers and enforce their disequality using an additional constraint. Z3 natively supports sorts with given cardinality. Hence, if the cardinality of a user-given type can be computed statically by PROB we can submit said cardinality to Z3.

3   Integration of Solvers

We investigated different modes of using Z3 together with the PROB kernel:

- Use it alone without relying on PROB. This approach was quickly abandoned due to the (currently) untranslatable predicates outlined in Sects. 2.1 and 2.2. Additionally, some translations have to resort to quantification that hinders proof efforts and model finding.
- Use Z3 solely for falsification of B predicates. If we only rely on the SMT solvers for the detection of unsatisfiability, we can safely skip untranslatable parts of the predicate without risking unsound results (as those parts will be checked by PROB's solver). However, many predicates cannot be disproven once important parts are missing.
- We could employ a cooperative approach where parts of a predicate are given to one or both of the SMT solvers, while other parts are handled by the PROB kernel. In this case, we would translate partial assignments back and forth between the two solvers in order to communicate intermediate results.
- Lastly, we could use a fully integrated approach where the whole predicate is given to the PROB kernel and as much as is translatable is given to the SMT solvers. In addition to partial assignments we could transport information about inferred or learned clauses or unsatisfiable cores back and forth.

The first approach was quickly discarded, because the SMT solvers alone are often too weak to solve interesting predicates. This is mostly due to cumbersome translations of higher-order B expressions like set cardinality. The same holds true for the second approach. Even though the SMT solvers are able to falsify several predicates that PROB cannot falsify (see Sect. 1.1), much is left to be desired. Hence, we investigated the integrated approaches more thoroughly.

The third approach is comparable to the one taken in [24], translating B to SAT. The key problem to this approach is to decide which predicate to translate and submit to Z3 and which ones to keep in PROB. In [24] the authors used a greedy approach: every predicate that can be translate will be translated.

However, we integrated the two solvers further and set up constraints in both simultaneously. We delay the call to Z3 until after the deterministic propagation phase of PROB and also submit the information inferred so far. Additionally, we use the unsat core found by Z3 to control backtracking on the PROB Prolog side and to lift PROB from backtracking to backjumping. Details on both techniques are given below.

```
Data: Predicate P, (partial) State S
Result: fails iff P is unsat, succeeds with model iff P is sat; might time out
procedure boolean solve(P, S)
    set_up_clpfd_variables(S)
    set_up_smt_variables(S)
    while exists conjunct C in P that has not been set up do
        D = to_clpfd_solver(C)          // domains D from clpfd propagation
        smt_result = to_smt_solver(C,D)          // transfer C and domains
        if smt_result = unsat then
            backjump using unsat core
        end
    end
    while exists unbound variable V in S do
        clpfd_labeling(V)                          // binds V to value
        smt_result = to_smt_solver(V)  // V now bound: transfer new value
        if smt_result = unsat then
            backjump using unsat core
        end
    end
    return S with all variables labeled
```

Algorithm 1. Integrated Constraint Solver

Transferring CLP(FD) Domains to the SMT Solvers. As can be seen in Algorithm 1 communication with the SMT solver starts after the deterministic propagation phase. During this phase, PROB tries to deterministically infer knowledge about the values of the variables in a predicate. For instance, from $X > 3 \land Y > X$ PROB infers $Y > 4$. The underlying propagation rules are not limited to arithmetic but support further B constructs like set theory. Before a predicate is submitted to Z3, all the statically inferred information is added to it.

Controlled Backjumping Using the Unsat Core. In case Z3 detects unsatisfiability, we can use Z3's unsat core computation in order to perform backjumping inside PROB's kernel. The unsat core contains a subset of the conjuncts C taken from P as outline in Algorithm 1. Note that this subset does not necessarily contain the conjunct submitted last. Inside PROB's kernel we can now backjump until at least one of the conjuncts inside the unsat core has been removed from both the SMT solver and the CLP(FD) solver. After the backjump, PROB can choose a different path inside case distinctions or decide on different heuristics. Thus, the backjump has cut of parts of the search space PROB would have explored otherwise.

4 Limitations

One key limitation of our approach is related to the type system of B. There is no strict differentiation between functions, sets and sequences. For instance, one

Table 2. Results of running provers

Model	# POs	SMT	HL-SMT		PROB		PROB/SMT	
			prove	disprove	prove	disprove	prove	disprove
Landing Gear System 1, Su, et al.	2328	1478	2196	0	2311	0	2303	0
Landing Gear System 2, Su, et al.	1188	548	741	0	1176	0	1152	0
Landing Gear System 3, Su, et al.	341	171	77	0	290	0	262	0
CAN Bus, Colley	534	296	316	0	276	0	340	1
Graph Coloring, Andriamiarina, et al.	254	119	51	0	0	0	51	0
Landing Gear System, Hansen, et al.	74	59	55	0	74	0	74	0
Landing Gear System, Mammar, et al.	433	265	212	0	400	0	413	0
Landing Gear System, André, et al.	619	263	77	0	567	5	533	4
Pacemaker, Neeraj Kumar Singh	370	198	369	0	354	0	370	0
Stuttgart 21 interlocking, Wiegard	202	46	18	0	125	2	123	0

can apply the set union operator to two functions leading to a result that might not be a function.

For the same to be allowed in the SMT-LIB translation, we had to use a common representation: we express relations and functions as sets of pairs connecting input and output values; sequences are encoded as sets of pairs consisting of the sequence index and the value.

Using this common base representation, all B and Event-B operators can be encoded. However, we cannot use more sophisticated SMT-LIB representations anymore. In particular, sequences could have been mapped to SMT-LIB arrays, resulting in improved performance due to the usage of specialized decision procedures.

Another limitation is the missing support for set cardinality in Z3's set logic. Although it was part of the initial proposal for the SMT-LIB finite set theory [16] it has not yet been implemented in Z3. We thus encode $c = \text{card}(S)$ as

$$\exists t. t \in S \rightarrowtail [1, c]$$

i.e., we search for a total bijection from S to the interval $[1, c]$. This encoding is quite cumbersome and often leads to Z3 answering "unknown". Cardinality constraints however have to be used in the translation of some B operators, e.g., to compute the next index of a sequence upon concatenation. Hence, those can often not be solved as well.

5 Empirical Results

In this section we will evaluate two different aspects. First, we want to know how our new high-level translation of set theory in Z3 compares to the more low-level approach of the SMT translation outlined in [10,11]. Second, we want to evaluate if it is it worthwhile to integrate Z3 into PROB and to communicate back and forth. In order to find out, we compare the integrated solution to Z3 and PROB on their own.

We benchmarked the following configurations:

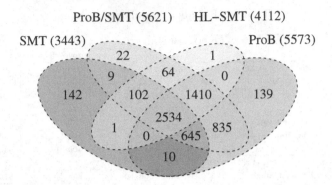

Fig. 2. Performance on proof obligations

- **SMT**, the SMT solvers plugin for Rodin as presented in [10,11],
- **HL-SMT**, our high-level translation from Event-B to SMT featuring Z3's set theory, alone without PROB's solver,
- **ProB**, a plain version of PROB's constraint solving kernel, and
- **ProB/SMT**, PROB's constraint solving kernel integrated with Z3.

For better comparability, we used the same set of benchmarks already employed in [15]:

- Answers to the ABZ-2014 landing gear case study [6]. Beside our own version [14], we also used the three models by Su and Abrial [26], a model by André, Attiogbé and Lanoix [4], as well as a model by Mammar and Laleau [21].
- A model of the Stuttgart 21 Railway station interlocking by Wiegard, derived from Chap. 17 of [2] with added timing and performance modeling.
- A model of a controller area network (CAN) bus developed by Colley.
- A formal development of a graph coloring algorithm by Andriamiarina and Méry. The graphs to be colored are finite, but unbounded and not fixed in the model.
- A model of a pacemaker by Méry and Singh [22].

For the benchmarks, we have used Rodin 3.2, version 2.1.0 of the Atelier B provers plugin and version 1.2.1 of the SMT plugin. For better comparability, we did not use the bundled SMT solvers CVC3 and veriT. Instead, we relied on Z3 version 4.4.1 as used in the PROB integration as well. PROB was used in version 1.5.1-beta3, connected through the disprover plugin version 3.0.8. We used a global timeout of 25 s for a single proof attempt.

All benchmarks were run on a MacBook Pro featuring a 2.6 GHz i7 CPU and 8 GB of RAM. We did not parallelize the benchmarks in order to avoid issues due to hyper-threading or scheduling. Benchmarks were run using a dedicated evaluation plugin[1] for the Rodin platform. The data is presented as follows:

---

[1] See https://github.com/wysiib/ProverEvaluationPlugin for sources and instructions.

- Figure 2 shows a Venn diagram comparing the number of discharged proof obligations by each of the configurations mentioned above.
- Table 2 shows how the individual configurations perform on the different models. In particular it distinguishes between proof and disprove.
- Table 3 shows how the individual configurations perform on different kinds of proof obligations.

Regarding the different performance of the high-level vs. the low-level SMT translation we have mixed results. Judging by the total numbers, the high-level approach is superior: as can be seen in Fig. 2 it is able to discharge 4112 proof obligations, while the low-level approach only discharges 3443. However, there is also a considerable amount of proof obligations that can be discharged with the low-level approach but not with the high-level one. Since the original SMT plugin does not support disprove of POs, we cannot say anything about the performance. The high-level approach is unable to disprove a single of the defective obligations.

Comparing PROB solo and together with Z3 paints a similar picture. The integrated solution is superior but the margin is small. Again, 149 proof obligations cannot be discharged anymore once the SMT integration is enabled. Virtually all of these result in a timeout afterwards. Since a global timeout is used and Z3 takes up to much time PROB misses the solution. We could indeed use a local timeout for the integrated SMT solver. However, we did not find a sensible heuristic to decide when to give time to Z3 vs. giving it to the PROB kernel.

Regarding disproving, integrating Z3 into PROB lead to the discovery of a new counter-example. Despite our usage of the CAN Bus model in [15] the error went unnoticed till now. Yet again, some counter-examples previously found cannot be discovered by the integrated solver in the given timeframe.

Table 2 outlines for which models we see better or worse performance for the high-level SMT translation. In particular the landing gear systems and the Stuttgart 21 interlocking models show a decline in successfully discharged POs when compared with the low-level SMT translation. This models feature a considerable amount of concrete data that can easily be translated using the low-level approach. We assume that some of these POs can be discharged on the boolean level, without any higher-order reasoning. Table 2 also shows that these are the models where PROB alone works well.

The high-level SMT approach, both with and without PROB integration performs better for more abstract models like the CAN Bus, the graph coloring algorithm and the pacemaker model. This stresses our assumption that integration the high-level SMT translation into PROB is worthwhile as they represent orthogonal technologies that could benefit from one another.

6 Related Work

As mentioned above, in [10, 11] the authors present an integration of SMT solvers into Rodin [3], an IDE for Event-B development. In this scenario, the SMT solvers are used as provers in order to discharge Event-B proof obligations. The authors investigate two different ways of translating Event-B to SMT-LIB.

Table 3. Performance of provers on different kinds of proof obligations

Kind of PO	# POs	SMT	HL-SMT	PROB	PROB/SMT
Feasibility of non-det. action	59	40 (67.8 %)	52 (88.1 %)	44 (74.6 %)	57 (96.6 %)
Guard strengthening	300	13 (4.3 %)	139 (46.3 %)	258 (86.0 %)	254 (84.7 %)
Invariant preservation	4938	3106 (62.9 %)	3741 (75.8 %)	4488 (90.9 %)	4552 (92.2 %)
Natural number for a numeric variant	6	5 (83.3 %)	6 (100.0 %)	4 (66.7 %)	6 (100.0 %)
Action simulation	153	104 (68.0 %)	86 (56.2 %)	134 (87.6 %)	142 (92.8 %)
Theorem	97	29 (29.9 %)	26 (26.8 %)	66 (68.0 %)	62 (63.9 %)
Decreasing of variant	6	6 (100.0 %)	6 (100.0 %)	6 (100.0 %)	6 (100.0 %)
Well definedness	779	140 (18.0 %)	56 (7.2 %)	570 (73.2 %)	539 (69.2 %)
Feasibility of a witness	1	0 (0.0 %)	0 (0.0 %)	1 (100.0 %)	1 (100.0 %)
Well definedness of a witness	4	0 (0.0 %)	0 (0.0 %)	2 (50.0 %)	2 (50.0 %)
	6343	3443 (54.3 %)	4112 (64.8 %)	5573 (87.9 %)	5621 (88.6 %)

For SMT solvers in general they suggest the *ppTrans* approach. Here, set theory and arithmetic are broken down into first-order formulas using uninterpreted functions for membership, etc. On the one hand, this approach is more flexible than the one presented in this paper: it does not rely on the API of a specific SMT solver. On the other hand, the resulting formulas only approximate the Event-B semantics, as operators are replaced by uninterpreted functions. The authors thus add certain set theoretic axioms to the SMT problem in order to recover from this.

A second approach, called λ-*based* relies on an extension to SMT-LIB provided by the veriT solver [7]. Set theoretic constructs are then translated into λ-expressions. The major shortcoming of this approach is that sets of sets cannot be handled.

Many of the rewrite rules presented here are similar to those in [10,11]. The key difference is that we rely on the given set theory of Z3 instead of translating further into first-order logic.

In addition to other SMT-based approaches, there are different ways of solving B and Event-B predicates. PROB itself mainly relies on constraint logic programming. There is also the formerly mentioned backend [24] translating B to Kodkod [27]. Kodkod then uses a SAT solver to find solutions to the given formulas.

7 Future Work

For the future, we have different directions in mind. First of all, we would like to investigate whether using an equisatisfiable translation instead of an equivalent one is of use. In particular for approaches like proving or disproving as discussed in [15] we expect improved performance.

We also want to tighten the integration of the SMT solvers and PROB. Currently we are transporting partial assignments and we use the unsat core to control backjumping on the Prolog side. In future, we want to investigate, whether we can access and use clauses learned on the SMT side in order to set up further constraints on the Prolog side. For instance, we want to investigate whether we can use interpolants or conflict clauses in case of unsatisfiable predicates.

Regarding our translation to SMT-LIB, the benchmarks show that in particular the usage of quantifiers can be improved. One possibility to do so is to further investigate how to set instantiation triggers for comprehensions typically occurring in our scenarios. In [17] the authors already outlined a general approach that can serve as a starting point. Another option is to try to reduce the amount of quantifiers we use. This could be achieved by providing a custom theory to the SMT solvers, i.e., including inference rules for min and max that avoid the quantifiers introduced in Sect. 2.2. Changing the set of axioms we supply to Z3 in order to define min and max is certainly another direction that should be evaluated.

Another technique we want to implement should help us to overcome some of the limitations discussed in Sect. 4. As mentioned, the B type system allows to use set operators on sequences. Hence, we had to encode sequence using the a representation as sets of pairs. A static check could investigate, how operators are applied in a B machine. It could determine, if sequences are only used with sequence operators. In this case, we could employ a more efficient translation to SMT-LIB, e.g., encode them as arrays.

Regarding benchmarks and applications, we would like to move from solving predicates to explicit state model checking and later to symbolic model checking and constrained based validation techniques.

8   Discussion and Conclusion

One motivation for the integration of SMT solvers into PROB was to overcome the weaknesses we spotted in our previous work [15]: PROB should be enabled to handle infinite domains and detection of unsatisfiability should be improved.

With the suggested high-level translation of B to SMT-LIB both goals could be achieved. The integrated solution is able to discharge more proof obligations than PROB alone. In many cases, translation into the high-level (set) logics of Z3 seems advantageous over a low-level translation to predicate logic. Indeed, in our experimental evaluation on Event-B proof obligations, our new high-level translation discharges 4112 proof obligations in total, out of which 1475 cannot be discharged by the previous SMT translation [10,11].

Our evaluation also showed, that there is not only a gain in the number of proof obligations: the low-level translation discharges 806 proof obligations that are not discharged by our new translation. Yet, it is not clear when to employ a high-level and when to employ a low-level approach. A practical solution is to use both in a solver portfolio.

It remains yet to be seen, how SMT solvers like Z3 will evolve regarding high-level theories. The current version of the SMT-LIB standard only features a "possible declaration for a theory of sets and relations" [5]. How and if different possibilities are realized will certainly influence the impact SMT solvers have in the formal methods community.

Summarizing, we provided new ways to tackle the complexity of constraints in B and Event-B. We provided a new high-level translation of B to Z3's input language, which can be used on its own or integrated into PROB's solver. This high-level SMT based solver appears to be an orthogonal addition to the other solvers, solving many constraints that could not be solved by the previous low-level translation and is better suited at finding models. Our evaluation also confirms that the integration of the ProB solver with Z3 provides the best overall result, discharging 5621 proof obligations. We hope that these new capabilities open up new applications, from synthesis to improved symbolic validation techniques such as bounded model checking.

Acknowledgements. We would like to thank the reviewers of iFM'2016 for their useful feedback. In addition, we thank Christoph Schmidt for implementing parts of the translation.

References

1. Abrial, J.-R.: The B-Book: Assigning Programs to Meanings. Cambridge University Press, Cambridge (1996)
2. Abrial, J.-R.: Modeling in Event-B: System and Software Engineering. Cambridge University Press, Cambridge (2010)
3. Abrial, J.-R., Butler, M., Hallerstede, S., Voisin, L.: An open extensible tool environment for Event-B. In: Liu, Z., Kleinberg, R.D. (eds.) ICFEM 2006. LNCS, vol. 4260, pp. 588–605. Springer, Heidelberg (2006)
4. Attiogbé, C., Lanoix, A.: Modelling and analysing the landing gear system: a solution with Event-B/Rodin. Solution to ABZ 2014 case study (2014)
5. Barrett, C., Fontaine, P., Tinelli, C.: The SMT-LIB Standard: Version 2.5. Technical report, Department of Computer Science, The University of Iowa (2015). www.SMT-LIB.org
6. Boniol, F., Wiels, V.: The landing gear system case study. In: Boniol, F., Wiels, V., Ait Ameur, Y., Schewe, K.-D. (eds.) ABZ 2014. CCIS, vol. 433, pp. 1–18. Springer, Heidelberg (2014)
7. Bouton, T., de Oliveira, D.C.B., Déharbe, D., Fontaine, P.: veriT: an open, trustable and efficient SMT-solver. In: Schmidt, R.A. (ed.) CADE 2009. LNCS, vol. 5663, pp. 151–156. Springer, Heidelberg (2009)
8. Carlsson, M., Mildner, P.: Sicstus prolog — the first 25 years. Theor. Pract. Logic Program. **12**(1–2), 35–66 (2012)
9. de Moura, L., Bjørner, N.S.: Z3: an efficient SMT solver. In: Ramakrishnan, C.R., Rehof, J. (eds.) TACAS 2008. LNCS, vol. 4963, pp. 337–340. Springer, Heidelberg (2008)

10. Déharbe, D., Fontaine, P., Guyot, Y., Voisin, L.: SMT solvers for rodin. In: Derrick, J., Fitzgerald, J., Gnesi, S., Khurshid, S., Leuschel, M., Reeves, S., Riccobene, E. (eds.) ABZ 2012. LNCS, vol. 7316, pp. 194–207. Springer, Heidelberg (2012)

11. Déharbe, D., Fontaine, P., Guyot, Y., Voisin, L.: Integrating SMT solvers in Rodin. Sci. Comput. Program. **94**(Part 2), 130–143 (2014)

12. Ganzinger, H., Hagen, G., Nieuwenhuis, R., Oliveras, A., Tinelli, C.: DPLL(T): fast decision procedures. In: Alur, R., Peled, D.A. (eds.) CAV 2004. LNCS, vol. 3114, pp. 175–188. Springer, Heidelberg (2004)

13. Hallerstede, S., Leuschel, M.: Constraint-based deadlock checking of high-level specifications. Theor. Pract. Logic Program. **11**(4–5), 767–782 (2011)

14. Hansen, D., Ladenberger, L., Wiegard, H., Bendisposto, J., Leuschel, M.: Validation of the ABZ landing gear system using ProB. In: Boniol, F., Wiels, V., Ait Ameur, Y., Schewe, K.-D. (eds.) ABZ 2014. CCIS, vol. 433, pp. 66–79. Springer, Heidelberg (2014)

15. Krings, S., Bendisposto, J., Leuschel, M.: From failure to proof: the ProB disprover for B and Event-B. In: Calinescu, R., Rumpe, B. (eds.) SEFM 2015. LNCS, vol. 9276, pp. 199–214. Springer, Heidelberg (2015)

16. Kröning, D., Rümmer, P., Weissenbacher, G.: A proposal for a theory of finite sets, lists, and maps for the SMT-LIB standard. In: Informal Proceedings SMT Workshop (2009)

17. Leino, K.R.M., Monahan, R.: Reasoning about comprehensions with first-order SMT solvers. In: Proceedings ACM SAC, pp. 615–622 (2009)

18. Leuschel, M., Bendisposto, J., Dobrikov, I., Krings, S., Plagge D.: From animation to data validation: the prob constraint solver 10 years on. In: Boulanger, J.-L. (ed.) Formal Methods Applied to Complex Systems: Implementation of the B Method, Chap. 14, pp. 427–446. Wiley ISTE, Hoboken (2014)

19. Leuschel, M., Butler, M.: ProB: a model checker for B. In: Araki, K., Gnesi, S., Mandrioli, D. (eds.) FME 2003. LNCS, vol. 2805, pp. 855–874. Springer, Heidelberg (2003)

20. Leuschel, M., Butler, M.: ProB: an automated analysis toolset for the B method. Int. J. Softw. Tools Technol. Transf. **10**(2), 185–203 (2008)

21. Mammar, A., Laleau, R.: Modeling a landing gear system in Event-B. In: Boniol, F., Wiels, V., Ait Ameur, Y., Schewe, K.-D. (eds.) ABZ 2014. CCIS, vol. 433, pp. 80–94. Springer, Heidelberg (2014)

22. Méry, D., Singh, N.K.: Formal specification of medical systems by proof-based refinement. ACM Trans. Embed. Comput. Syst. **12**(1), 15:1–15:25 (2013)

23. Moura, L.M.D., Bøjrner. N.: Generalized, efficient array decision procedures. In: Formal Methods in Computer-Aided Design, pp. 45–52 (2009)

24. Plagge, D., Leuschel, M.: Validating B, Z and TLA+ using ProB and Kodkod. In: Giannakopoulou, D., Méry, D. (eds.) FM 2012. LNCS, vol. 7436, pp. 372–376. Springer, Heidelberg (2012)

25. Schneider, S.: The B-Method: An Introduction. Cornerstones of Computing. Palgrave, London (2001)

26. Su, W., Abrial, J.-R.: Aircraft landing gear system: approaches with Event-B to the modeling of an industrial system. In: Boniol, F., Wiels, V., Ait Ameur, Y., Schewe, K.-D. (eds.) ABZ 2014. CCIS, vol. 433, pp. 19–35. Springer, Heidelberg (2014)

27. Torlak, E., Jackson, D.: Kodkod: a relational model finder. In: Grumberg, O., Huth, M. (eds.) TACAS 2007. LNCS, vol. 4424, pp. 632–647. Springer, Heidelberg (2007)

Avoiding Medication Conflicts for Patients with Multimorbidities

Andrii Kovalov[1] and Juliana Küster Filipe Bowles[2(✉)]

[1] German Aerospace Center (DLR), Simulation and Software Technology,
Braunschweig, Germany
andrii.kovalov@dlr.de
[2] School of Computer Science, University of St Andrews,
St Andrews KY16 9SX, Scotland
jkfb@st-andrews.ac.uk

Abstract. Clinical pathways are care plans which detail essential steps in the care of patients with a specific clinical problem, usually a chronic disease. A pathway includes recommendations of medications prescribed at different stages of the care plan. For patients with three or more chronic diseases (known as *multimorbidities*) the multiple pathways have to be applied together. One common problem for such patients is the adverse interaction between medications given for different diseases. This paper proposes a solution for avoiding medication conflicts for patients with multimorbidities through the use of formal methods. We introduce the notion of a pharmaceutical graph to capture the medications associated to different stages of a pathway. We then explore the use of an optimising SMT solver (Z3) to quickly find the set of medications with the minimal number and severity of conflicts which is assumed to be the safest. We evaluate the approach on a well known case of an elderly patient with five multimorbidities.

1 Introduction

There is an increasing number of people in Europe and in the UK with three or more long term conditions, also known as *multimorbidities*. In Europe, the current number of people with multimorbidities is estimated at around 50 million [7], and in the UK it is currently around 1.9 million [8]. Chronic diseases often develop simultaneously in response to common risk factors such as smoking, diet, ageing, and inactivity [3,18]. The four most common chronic diseases are cancer, chronic obstructive pulmonary disease (COPD), coronary heart disease, and diabetes.

Despite the growing prevalence of chronic disease, strategies for improving the management of patients with co-morbidities remain under-explored. In clinical settings processes are complex and necessarily rely on a range of interacting social agents including physicians, administrators and patients who in turn are

---

This work is partially supported by EPSRC grant EP/M014290/1.

E. Ábrahám and M. Huisman (Eds.): IFM 2016, LNCS 9681, pp. 376–390, 2016.
DOI: 10.1007/978-3-319-33693-0_24

influenced by a number of social, technical and organisational factors. This complexity can result in variation in how physicians practice, appropriate care is documented, and healthcare costs are managed [19]. To reduce inconsistencies clinical guidelines have emerged which are based on the best existing evidence and which aim to support clinical staff and improve the quality of healthcare. There are currently around 180 clinical guidelines published by the National Institute for Clinical Excellence (NICE)[1]. However, current guidelines almost entirely focus on single conditions. As a result, applying multiple guidelines to a patient may potentially result in conflicting recommendations for care. In the UK and Europe there have been calls for improved integration of existing guidelines for patients with multimorbidities [7,12], but this is still very much an open problem.

To encourage the translation of national guidelines into local protocols, and subsequently clinical practice, *clinical pathways* have been developed. Clinical pathways are care plans which detail essential steps in the care of patients with a specific clinical problem, usually a chronic disease [6]. These pathways frequently use graphical descriptions of evidence and options, and are typically represented in a single or a series of flow charts [9,16]. A pathway includes recommendations of medications prescribed at different stages of the care plan. One common problem for patients with multiple long term conditions is the adverse interaction between medications given for different diseases. We concentrate on such medication interactions in this paper, and introduce a notion of a *pharmaceutical graph* for a chronic disease as a formal representation of the medications and medication groups underlying a clinical pathway. These pharmaceutical graphs and the information on known adverse medication conflicts are used to answer the fundamental question of *what is the best care plan and what are the most effective medications in the treatment of patients with multimorbidities?*

The main contribution of our paper is a solution for avoiding medication conflicts for patients with multimorbidities through the use of formal methods. We explore the use of an optimising SMT solver (Z3) to quickly find the set of medications with the minimal number and severity of conflicts which is assumed to be the safest. We evaluate our approach with a very well known case in the medical domain taken from [5] of a hypothetical 79-year-old woman with five long term conditions: hypertension, diabetes mellitus (type 2), osteoarthritis, osteoporosis and chronic obstructive pulmonary disease (COPD).

This paper is structured as follows. We start by setting the context of our work and describing some of the most relevant existing related work in Sect. 2. Section 3 introduces our notion of *pharmaceutical graph* which is extracted for each disease from the corresponding documented clinical pathways. Since our approach makes use of SMT solvers, in Sect. 4 we describe how to derive logical formulae from the pharmaceutical graphs and medication conflicts. Our approach is evaluated in Sect. 5, and its performance is compared with other possible solutions. We conclude our paper in Sect. 6 with a discussion of current limitations and ideas for future work.

---

[1] NICE www.nice.org.uk.

2   Related Work

The National Institute for Clinical Excellence (NICE) has a considerable number of documented pathways for care and treatment of diseases including the most common chronic conditions such as cancer, chronic obstructive pulmonary disease, coronary heart disease, diabetes, hypertension, osteoarthritis, chronic heart failure, chronic kidney disease, depression and so on. The pathways are nonetheless essentially single-disease descriptions, and there is little advice on how to combine or consider two or more of them when addressing the needs of patients with multimorbidities. Better approaches for integrated care are lacking and urgently needed.

In clinical practice, the main suggestion is to enrich pathways with additional information. This includes recommendations regarding certain comorbidities, discussion of benefits and risks of treatment, and advice on treating elderly patients [5,10,15].

More recently, the possibility of developing automated techniques for integrated care has drawn attention from the computer science community. Several approaches were introduced with the aim of formalising and merging existing single-disease pathways to produce a treatment advice for patients with multiple diseases. A few different approaches are described next.

One approach is to model pathways using ontologies [1,2,11]. The authors focus on eliminating duplicated tasks across different pathways (e.g. blood tests), reusing the results of common activities and avoiding medication conflicts. Although ontologies are an expressive modelling instrument, the automatic merging of multiple ontologies seems problematic.

Another approach also making use of ontologies is carried out under the project GLARE [17] which instead of automatically merging guidelines provides an interactive interface for clinicians to analyse multiple guidelines at different levels of detail.

A different approach is shown in [13] where the authors use rewriting rules to eliminate conflicts in merged guidelines.

A research somewhat similar to ours is presented in [20]. The authors encode individual pathways as sets of formulas in first-order logic and use an automated theorem prover to find a combined treatment plan. The medication conflicts are also represented as logical expressions, and if a conflict is detected then special 'Revision Operators' are invoked that rewrite fragments of logical expressions so that the conflict may disappear. These operators correspond to some medical actions that are performed to resolve a conflict (such as the co-prescription of an additional medication). If the Revision Operators cannot resolve the conflict then the algorithm fails to produce any treatment suggestion.

Our approach is similar in that we also transform medical knowledge into logical expressions and use a tool (an SMT solver rather than a theorem prover) to automatically produce treatment advice. However, unlike [20], we take into account the medical utility of the produced advice, and try to generate not just any possible advice, but the *best and safest* possible recommendation with

respect to given knowledge on medication conflicts. The advantage of our approach is that we will be able to provide a solution even if certain conflicts cannot
be avoided. In the case of patients with 5 or more multimorbidities, it is likely
that some conflicts are indeed unavoidable and the aim in such cases is to reduce
it to a more favourable alternative.

3   Pharmaceutical Graphs

The goal of our research is to help clinicians make more informed decisions, and
more concretely medication prescriptions that result in the minimal amount and
severity of medication conflicts. In other words, we would like to find the safest
set of medications for a patient with multiple diseases. We take into account
three types of conflicts:

- Drug-drug conflicts (when two medicines taken together have some negative
  effect or decrease effectiveness of each other),
- Drug-disease conflicts (e.g. any medication that increases blood pressure conflicts with hypertension),
- Drug-patient conflicts (personal medication intolerances and allergies).

To detect and avoid these conflicts we need to know which medications can
be prescribed according to the clinical pathway. As the pathways are written
informally in natural language, we first need to create a formal representation
of a pathway. We developed a representation which we call a *pharmaceutical
graph* which is a directed acyclic graph with one initial node where the nodes
represent medication prescriptions. Normally a clinical pathway suggests several
alternative medications for the doctor to choose from. Likewise, in our pharmaceutical graph a node can contain multiple medications one of which should be
prescribed.

Examples of pharmaceutical graphs for Diabetes Melitus and Hypertension
are shown in Fig. 1. For clarity we included a dummy initial node with the disease
name that does not contain any medications. For Diabetes this dummy node is
also necessary for branching.

Often the pathways recommend not a single medication, but a medication
group such as *Sulfonylurea*. In this case we include all individual Sulfonylureas
into the node. In Fig. 1 for the medication groups the number of individual
medications is shown in brackets. It is important to list all the medications in a
group because they might have different conflicts.

Pharmaceutical graphs capture two features of the original pathways: the
structure (ordering and branching) and the advised medications. A maximal
path in a pharmaceutical graph (from the initial node to a leaf node) represents
a choice of medications in a treatment plan. For example, one maximal path
(prescription) in the Diabetes graph could be Metformin, Sitagliptin, Insulin.

Having such maximal paths for multiple pharmaceutical graphs, we can
detect the above mentioned three types of drug-related conflicts in them.

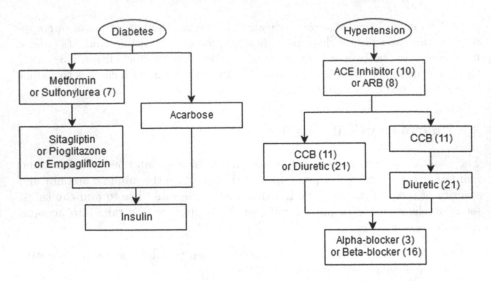

Fig. 1. Pharmaceutical graphs for Diabetes and Hypertension based on NICE pathways. ACE - angiotensin-converting-enzyme, ARB - angiotensin receptor blocker, CCB - calcium channel blocker. The numbers in brackets represent the number of individual medications in a group.

Additionally, we consider the severity of medication conflicts and how suitable given medications are known to be for the treatment of certain conditions. To distinguish between major and minor conflicts we assign negative integer scores to them. Similarly, we assign positive scores to the medications depending on their efficacy. Our aim is to obtain a treatment plan with the highest score considered to be the safest and most effective for a particular patient. In this way we can produce a reasonable treatment advice even when certain conflicts cannot be avoided. Note that it is outside the scope of our work to assign scores to drugs. The safety and effectiveness of drugs is subject to evaluations carried out in clinical pharmacology and biopharmaceutics data research. Pharmaceutical companies assign scores to drugs based on evidence-based safety and effectiveness.

Our question is, therefore, formulated as follows: *Having a set of pharmaceutical graphs and a set of conflicts, what are the prescriptions (maximal paths) for all the graphs that result in the highest total score?* The total score here is the sum of the positive scores of all the chosen medications and the negative scores of the triggered conflicts. Thus, we have transformed a medical problem into a computation problem. In the next section we show how we tackle it using an optimising SMT (satisfiability modulo theories) solver.

4   Transformation into an SMT Problem

SMT solvers extend the boolean satisfiability problem (SAT) with additional theories for integers, arrays, etc. Given a predicate over boolean and integer variables, an SMT solver can check if there exists an assignment for the variables that turns the predicate into true. If such assignments exist, an SMT solver produces one of these assignments.

We are using an SMT solver Z3 developed at Microsoft research [14] which has a built-in optimisation functionality. In other words, Z3 can produce not just any satisfying assignment but an optimal assignment with respect to some objective function [4].

The core idea of our work is to translate the pharmaceutical graphs and the medication conflicts into logical and arithmetic expressions and use Z3 to generate maximal paths for the pharmaceutical graphs with the highest possible total score.

There are two parts of this translation that we would like to discuss in the following subsections - the representation of the graph structure and the representation of the medications and conflicts along with their scores.

4.1   Translating the Graph Structure

We need to translate the structure of the pharmaceutical graphs into logical expressions and make Z3 produce a maximal path.

First, we shrink the original pharmaceutical graph in order to reduce the number of variables we need to represent its structure (see Fig. 2).

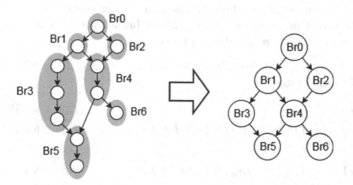

Fig. 2. Original pharmaceutical graph with branches shown in grey (left) and the shrinked branch graph (right).

To do this, we divide the nodes of the pharmaceutical graph into different *branches*. A branch here is the longest possible sequence of nodes where there is a path between the first and the last node, and along this path all the nodes except the last one have exactly one outgoing edge, and all the nodes except the first one have exactly one incoming edge. The branches are graphically shown in Fig. 2 with grey regions.

An important property of such a branch is that for any maximal path in the pharmaceutical graph either the whole branch is on the path or the whole branch is not on the path. Therefore, we can treat a maximal path as a sequence of branches. If we substitute each branch with a single node, we will get a shrinked branch graph (see Fig. 2, right) that will have the same maximal paths as the original pharmaceutical graph (in terms of branch sequences).

Our idea is to create a boolean variable for each branch and use Z3 to assign these branch variables to true or false so that there will be one maximal path consisting of 'true' branches and all the rest will be 'false'. To do this, we specify logical assertions that would filter out all the invalid assignments of the branch variables (that do not make one maximal path). We tried and compared two different approaches to produce these logical assertions.

The first and a more naive approach, which is taken in [20], is to explicitly enumerate all the maximal paths. Illustrating this for the graph in Fig. 2, we obtain the following logical statement:

$$(Br0 \land Br1 \land Br3 \land Br5 \land \neg Br2 \land \neg Br4 \land \neg Br6) \lor$$
$$(Br0 \land Br1 \land Br4 \land Br5 \land \neg Br2 \land \neg Br3 \land \neg Br6) \lor \ldots$$

For the second approach, we designed a set of *branching rules* that are applied to every node in the graph and produce some logical statements. The rules are as follows:

1. The initial branch is always true
2. If the current branch is true then one of its direct successors is true and the other direct successors are false (if there are direct successors)
3. If all the direct predecessors of the current branch are false then the current branch is false (if there are direct predecessors)

For example, for branches $Br0$, $Br1$ and $Br4$ in Fig. 2 the following statements will be generated.

$Br0$	(rule 1 for Br0)
$Br0 \implies (Br1 \land \neg Br2) \lor (\neg Br1 \land Br2)$	(rule 2 for Br0)
$Br1 \implies (Br3 \land \neg Br4) \lor (\neg Br3 \land Br4)$	(rule 2 for Br1)
$\neg Br0 \implies \neg Br1$	(rule 3 for Br1)
$Br4 \implies (Br5 \land \neg Br6) \lor (\neg Br5 \land Br6)$	(rule 2 for Br4)
$\neg Br1 \land \neg Br2 \implies \neg Br4$	(rule 3 for Br4)

We are interested in the variable assignments that turn these statements true for all the nodes of a branch graph, so we pass these statements as assertions to Z3, and get an assignment representing a maximal path.

Proposition 1. *The three branching rules ensure that exactly one maximal path in a branch graph will consist of true nodes, and all the other nodes will be false.*

Proof. First we will show that there will be a maximal path consisting of true nodes. The initial node in the branch graph will be true (rule 1). This means one of its direct successors will also be true (rule 2), one of the direct successors of this true successor will be true as well (rule 2) and so on until a leaf node for which rule 2 will not produce any statements. Therefore, there will be a path starting in the initial node and finishing in a leaf node (i.e. a maximal path) consisting of true branches.

We will now prove by contradiction that no other node can be true. Let us assume there is a node A which is true and does not belong to this maximal path. A is not the initial node (because otherwise it would belong to a maximal path by definition). Therefore, A has some direct predecessor B. This predecessor may or may not belong to the maximal path. If it belongs to the maximal path it should have another direct successor C apart from A which is true and lies on the path. Consequently, A cannot be true because according to rule 2 all the other direct successors of B apart from C should be false.

If no direct predecessor of A belongs to the maximal path, at least one of them should be true (otherwise A would be false according to rule 3). This true predecessor should also have a true predecessor (rule 3) and so on, so there will be a chain of true predecessors. Our graph is acyclic and has only one initial node, so if we follow the edges backwards from any node we will always come to the initial node which lies on the maximal path. Therefore, in this chain of true predecessors there will be some node D which has a direct predecessor that belongs to the chosen maximal path. As we already showed above, this node D cannot be true. We have come to a contradiction, so a true node A that does not belong to the maximal path cannot exist. $\square$

It is hard to tell whether the naive approach or the approach with the branching rules is more suitable for our task because it depends on how Z3 processes the statements internally. We compare both approaches in Sect. 5.

4.2 Translating Medications, Conflicts and Scores

Aside from having a maximal path in the pharmaceutical graph we also need to choose the individual medications in every node along this path. Therefore, if a node belongs to a 'true' branch we want to pick one medication. Additionally, as we already mentioned, every medication has an integer score which we also need to pass to Z3.

For example, in the Diabetes graph shown in Fig. 1 there is a node 'Metformin or Sulfonylurea'. Let us assume this node has the identifier $N1$ and belongs to a branch $Br1$, the score of Metformin is 100 and the score of Sulfonylurea is 70. Sulfonylureas are a medication group rather than a single medication, but we ignore this for the moment.

The assertions we generate for this node are shown below.

$Br1 \implies (Metformin \land \neg Sulfonylurea) \lor (\neg Metformin \land Sulfonylurea)$

$\neg Br1 \implies \neg Metformin \land \neg Sulfonylurea$

$N1\_Score =$ if($Metformin$)then 100 else if($Sulfonylurea$)then 70 else 0

For every medication we create a boolean variable that denotes whether it is prescribed or not. If the node lies on the chosen maximal path ($Br1$ is true) then one medication out of two will be set to true, otherwise both will be false.

We also introduce an integer variable $N1\_Score$ which will get different value depending on which medication is picked (Z3 supports integers and if-then-else expressions). We create score variables for every node of the pharmaceutical graph and then sum them to get the total medication score.

As for the conflicts, we represent them as integer variables in the following way.

$Conflict1\_Score =$ if ($Nadolol \land Diabetes$) then -5000 else 0

$Conflict2\_Score =$ if ($Sitagliptin$) then -1000 else 0

$Conflict3\_Score =$ if ($Metformin \land Acarbose$) then -100 else 0

Here $Conflict1$ is a major drug-disease conflict, $Conflict2$ is a moderate allergy and $Conflict3$ is a minor drug-drug conflict.

The total score is then the sum of the medication scores (which are non-negative) and the conflict scores which are negative when a conflict is triggered.

To put it all together, we start with a set of pharmaceutical graphs corresponding to the diseases of a particular patient and a set of conflicts which may arise. Then we generate Z3 code as explained above and run Z3 with the total score as the objective function. The output of Z3 are the assignments of the branch and medication variables that correspond to a treatment plan with the highest score.

In the next section, we show an example of using this system and discuss the results.

5   Evaluation

To evaluate our approach, we model a medically well known case from [5] of a hypothetical 79-year-old woman with five diseases: hypertension, diabetes mellitus (type 2), osteoarthritis, osteoporosis, and chronic obstructive pulmonary disease (COPD).

5.1   Medical Data Collection

We used two sources of medical information. We use the clinical pathways for the diseases as documented by NICE and an online portal Drugs.com[2] to get the data on the medication groups and conflicts.

---

[2] http://www.drugs.com.

NICE pathways are available in the form of flowcharts with supporting text. A fragment of the diabetes pathway is shown in Fig. 3. On the left side it shows the graphical representation of the current aspect of the pathway (in the example the therapy for lowering blood-glucose for patients with type 2 diabetes). Details for the current node being highlighted (Metformin) are shown in the text on the right side.

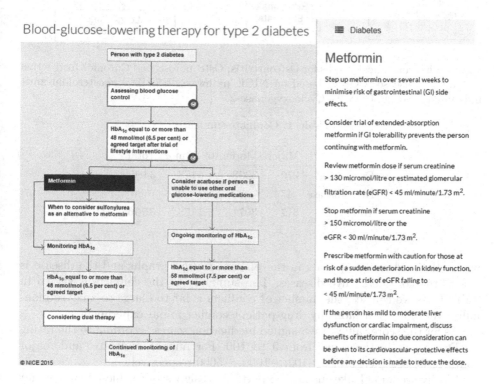

Fig. 3. Fragment of a NICE clinical pathway for type 2 diabetes.

Given such a documented pathway for a long term condition, the first step is to extract the information about the medications and transform it into our pharmaceutical graph. We did this manually for all five long term conditions considered. The resulting pharmaceutical graphs are shown in Figs. 1 and 4.

When pathways recommended a medication group, we expanded it based on the data from Drugs.com. In total for all five diseases, our pharmaceutical graphs contain 127 medications.

To get all the possible drug-drug conflicts, we used an interaction checker of Drugs.com[3]. To get the drug-disease conflicts, we examined the medication profiles on Drugs.com. We only considered drug-drug conflicts where both conflicting medications appear in our pharmaceutical graphs and drug-disease conflicts

---
[3] http://www.drugs.com/drug_interactions.html.

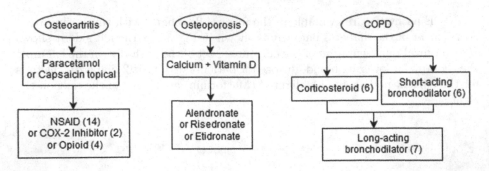

Fig. 4. Pharmaceutical graphs for Osteoartritis, Osteoporosis and Chronic Obstructive Pulmonary Disease (COPD) based on NICE pathways. NSAID - nonsteroidal anti-inflammatory drug, COX-2 - Cyclooxygenase-2.

Table 1. Conflicts summary

	Major	Moderate	Minor	Total
Drug-drug	270	3038	178	3486
Drug-disease	47	33	0	80
Total	317	3071	178	**3566**

where the medication appears in the pharmaceutical graphs and the disease is one of the considered five diseases. The summary of the conflicts is shown in Table 1. As we can see, the number of conflicts is far too large to analyse manually. We did not include any drug-patient conflict in our experiment.

As for the score values, we assigned medication scores according to the rating on Drugs.com in the range from 0 to 100. For minor, moderate, and major conflicts we assigned values -100, -1000, -5000 respectively.

Ideally we would like medical experts to assign score values, however, for our experiment we just assigned values that seemed reasonable to us and in accordance to the pharmaceutical ratings mentioned above.

5.2 Experiment Results

To run this experiment, we created a simple application which takes the pharmaceutical graphs and the conflicts as an input, generates the corresponding Z3 code, runs it, parses Z3 output and renders the resulting optimal set of maximal paths using Graphviz.

The output of our application for this experiment (with 5 diseases, 127 medications, and 3566 conflicts) is shown in Fig. 5. As we can see, the best recommendation still causes four moderate conflicts, and the total score is dominated by the score of these conflicts. In this case the doctor might decide to exclude some medications from the treatment, because the negative effect caused by the conflicts may outweigh the benefits.

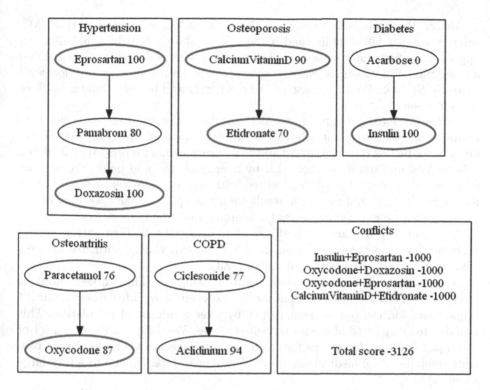

Fig. 5. Optimal medication prescriptions for a hypotetical patient with five diseases generated by Z3.

To evaluate the performance of the system, we ran the experiment on an off the shelf laptop with 16 GB RAM and a quad-core 2.6 GHz processor. We tried both approaches to produce logical assertions discussed in Subsect. 4.1. The average run time with the explicit enumeration of maximal paths is 7.6 s, while with the branching rules it is 8.1 s, so the explicit enumeration works marginally faster for this case.

In our opinion, the system runs fast enough to be used in a clinical environment as a decision support tool.

The real run time is likely to be less because doctors might exclude medications that are not certified or that are known to have many negative interactions. Additionally, doctors might pick a particular medication or branch manually and therefore reduce the amount of computations required. Moreover, it is only a minority of patients that will have five or more concomitant conditions.

5.3 Other Approaches

In addition to using optimising Z3, we evaluated several other approaches that turned out to be less efficient.

Before the optimising version of Z3 was released, we tried iterative SMT solving using a hill-climbing and a dichotomy approaches. In a hill-climbing approach we first obtained some initial solution with score S_0, and then added an assertion $FinalScore > S_0$. The solver would return another solution with score $S_1, S_1 > S_0$. We then continued to get better and better solutions until we hit 'unsatisfiable'.

In the dichotomy approach we used the fact that the best score lies in a bounded interval. It cannot be greater than the sum of all the medication scores and cannot be less then the sum of all the negative conflict scores. We calculated this interval and iteratively halved it by examining the mid-point. We used an SMT solver to check if a solution existed with the score greater or equal to this mid-point, and depending on the result took the upper or the lower half of the interval until we reached an interval containing only the highest score.

These approaches are much slower than using the built-in optimising Z3 functionality (run time is over an hour for the experiment with five diseases compared to under 10 s for the optimising Z3).

We also tried to find the optimal solution using A*. This worked comparatively well on smaller problems, but for the experiment with five diseases our A* implementation ran out of memory (1 Gb) after a minute of calculation. This was due to the growth of the set of visited states. We defined a state as a set of incomplete or complete paths for the input pharmaceutical graphs. Every possible combination of medications resulted in a new state, leading to a very large search space.

We conclude from this evaluation that the approach based on SMT solving is more appropriate than A* for heavily constrained problems (in our case the constraints are the numerous medication conflicts). For such problems it is hard to define a good cost under-approximation function for A* which makes the algorithm explore wrong directions.

6   Conclusions

Our work shows that a treatment advice for a patient with multimorbidities can be produced automatically using an SMT solver. This approach can be used in a clinical decision support tool as it works reasonably fast. Our work acts as a proof of concept for a tool which is being developed for clinicians.

Additionally, the approach allows us to choose a certain medication or a pathway branch manually. We believe that this kind of interactive analysis can be useful to get some insight into the different treatment options and their consequences.

Our current way of modelling the clinical pathways and underlying medication conflicts also has some limitations.

First of all, the dosages and the timing information for conflicts should be taken into account. Some interactions may arise only when the medications are taken simultaneously or if the dose is large enough.

Secondly, it is not clear how to assign numerical scores to medications in general, and especially in the case of branching. The branches may contain different number of medications, and a longer branch will likely get a higher score. Therefore, the scores should be somehow balanced.

Finally, our current approach aims at avoiding, but not resolving conflicts. For instance, sometimes it is necessary to co-prescribe additional medications in order to mitigate a certain adverse interaction, and we currently do not consider this issue.

In future work we aim to address these limitations, and eventually create a tool that will help clinicians deliver better care for an increasing number of patients suffering from multimorbidities.

References

1. Abidi, S.R.: Ontology-based knowledge modeling to provide decision support for comorbid diseases. In: Riaño, D., ten Teije, A., Miksch, S., Peleg, M. (eds.) KR4HC 2010. LNCS, vol. 6512, pp. 27–39. Springer, Heidelberg (2011)
2. Abidi, S.R., Abidi, S.S.R.: Towards the merging of multiple clinical protocols and guidelines via ontology-driven modeling. In: Combi, C., Shahar, Y., Abu-Hanna, A. (eds.) AIME 2009. LNCS, vol. 5651, pp. 81–85. Springer, Heidelberg (2009)
3. Barnett, K., Mercer, S., Norbury, M., Watt, G., Wyke, S., Guthrie, B.: Epidemiology of multimorbidity and implications for health care, research, and medical education: a cross-sectional study. Lancet 380(9836), 37–43 (2012)
4. Bjørner, N., Phan, A.-D., Fleckenstein, L.: νZ - an optimizing SMT solver. In: Baier, C., Tinelli, C. (eds.) TACAS 2015. LNCS, vol. 9035, pp. 194–199. Springer, Heidelberg (2015)
5. Boyd, C.M., Darer, J., Boult, C., Fried, L.P., Boult, L., Wu, A.W.: Clinical practice guidelines and quality of care for older patients with multiple comorbid diseases: implications for pay for performance. JAMA 294(6), 716–724 (2005)
6. Campbell, H., Hotchkiss, R., Bradshaw, N., Porteous, M.: Integrated care pathways. BMJ 316(7125), 133–137 (1998)
7. Directorate-General for Health, Food Safety, European Commission: Conference "Which priorities for a European policy on multimorbidity?", Final report, Brussels, 27 October 2015
8. Long term conditions compendium of information, 3rd edn., Department of Health (2012)
9. Hawley, S., Zikmund-Fisher, B., Ubel, P., Jancovic, A., Lucas, T., Fagerlin, A.: The impact of the format of graphical presentation on health-related knowledge and treatment choices. Patient Educ. Couns. 73(3), 448–455 (2008)
10. Hughes, L.D., McMurdo, M.E.T., Guthrie, B.: Guidelines for people not for diseases: the challenges of applying UK clinical guidelines to people with multimorbidity. Age Ageing 42(1), 62–69 (2013)
11. Jafarpour, B., Abidi, S.S.R.: Merging disease-specific clinical guidelines to handle comorbidities in a clinical decision support setting. In: Peek, N., Marín Morales, R., Peleg, M. (eds.) AIME 2013. LNCS, vol. 7885, pp. 28–32. Springer, Heidelberg (2013)
12. Kenning, C., Fisher, L., Bee, P., Bower, P., Coventry, P.: Primary care practitioner and patient understanding of the concepts of multimorbidity and self-management: a qualitative study. SAGE Open Med. 1, 1–11 (2013)

13. López-Vallverdú, J.A., Riaño, D., Collado, A.: Rule-based combination of comorbid treatments for chronic diseases applied to hypertension, diabetes mellitus and heart failure. In: Lenz, R., Miksch, S., Peleg, M., Reichert, M., Riaño, D., ten Teije, A. (eds.) ProHealth 2012 and KR4HC 2012. LNCS, vol. 7738, pp. 30–41. Springer, Heidelberg (2013)
14. de Moura, L., Bjørner, N.S.: Z3: an efficient SMT solver. In: Ramakrishnan, C.R., Rehof, J. (eds.) TACAS 2008. LNCS, vol. 4963, pp. 337–340. Springer, Heidelberg (2008)
15. Mutasingwa, D.R., Ge, H., Upshur, R.E.: How applicable are clinical practice guidelines to elderly patients with comorbidities? Can. Fam. Physician 57(7), e253–e262 (2011)
16. Negrini, S., Giovannoni, S., Minozzi, S., Barneschi, G., Bonaiuti, D., Bussotti, A., D'Arienzo, M., Lorenzo, N.D., Mannoni, A., Mattioli, S., Modena, V., Padua, L., Serafini, F., Violante, F.: Diagnostic therapeutic flow-charts for low back pain patients: the Italian clinical guidelines. Europa Medicophysica 42(2), 151–70 (2006)
17. Piovesan, L., Molino, G., Terenziani, P.: An ontological knowledge and multiple abstraction level decision support system in healthcare. Decis. Analytics 1(1), 8 (2014)
18. Salive, M.E.: Multimorbidity in older adults. Epidemiol. Rev. 35(1), 75–83 (2013)
19. Shaneyfelt, T., Mayo-Smith, M., Rothwangl, J.: Are guidelines following guidelines? the methodological quality of clinical practice guidelines in the peer-reviewed medical literature. JAMA 281(20), 1900–1905 (1999)
20. Wilk, S., Michalowski, M., Tan, X., Michalowski, W.: Using first-order logic to represent clinical practice guidelines and to mitigate adverse interactions. In: Miksch, S., Riano, D., Teije, A. (eds.) KR4HC 2014. LNCS, vol. 8903, pp. 45–61. Springer, Heidelberg (2014)

Testing

Temporal Random Testing for Spark Streaming

Adrián Riesco(✉) and Juan Rodríguez-Hortalá

Universidad Complutense de Madrid, Madrid, Spain
{ariesco,juanrh}@fdi.ucm.es

Abstract. With the rise of Big Data technologies, distributed stream processing systems (SPS) have gained popularity in the last years. Among them, Spark Streaming stands out as a particularly attractive option with a growing adoption in the industry. In this work we explore the combination of temporal logic and property-based testing for testing Spark Streaming programs, by adding temporal logic operators to ScalaCheck generators and properties. This allows us to deal with the time component that complicates the testing of Spark Streaming programs and SPS in general. In particular we propose a discrete time linear temporal logic for finite words, that allows to associate a timeout to each temporal operator in order to increase the expressiveness of generators and properties. Finally, our prototype is presented with some examples.

Keywords: Stream processing systems · Spark streaming · Property-based testing · Random testing · Linear temporal logic · Scala · Big data

1 Introduction

With the rise of Big Data technologies [14], distributed stream processing systems (SPS) [1,14,25] have gained popularity in the last years. These systems are used to continuously process high volume streams of data, with applications ranging from anomaly detection [1], low latency social media data aggregation [14], or the emergent IoT market. Although the first precedents of stream processing systems come back as far as the early synchronous data-flow programming languages like Lutin [18] or Lustre [10], with the boom of SPS a plethora of new systems have arisen [12,20,25], characterized by a distributed architecture designed for horizontal scaling. Among them Spark Streaming [25] stands out as a particularly attractive option, with a growing adoption in the industry. In this work we focus on Spark Streaming. Spark [24] is a distributed processing engine that is quickly consolidating as an alternative to Hadoop MapReduce [14], due to an extended memory hierarchy that allows for an increased performance in

This research has been partially supported by MINECO Spanish projects *Strong-Soft* (TIN2012-39391-C04-04), CAVI-ART (TIN2013-44742-C4-3-R), and *TRACES* (TIN2015-67522-C3-3-R), and by the Comunidad de Madrid project N-Greens Software-CM (S2013/ICE-2731).

© Springer International Publishing Switzerland 2016
E. Ábrahám and M. Huisman (Eds.): IFM 2016, LNCS 9681, pp. 393–408, 2016.
DOI: 10.1007/978-3-319-33693-0_25

```
scala> val cs : RDD[Char] = sc.parallelize("let's count some letters", numSlices=3)
scala> cs.map{(_, 1)}.reduceByKey{_+_}.collect()
res4: Array[(Char, Int)] = Array((t,4), ( ,3), (l,2), (e,4), (u,1), (m,1), (n,1), (r,1),
                                  (',1), (s,3), (o,2), (c,1))
```

Fig. 1. Letter count in spark

many situations, and a collection-based higher level API inspired in functional programming that together with a "batteries included" philosophy accelerates the development of Big Data processing applications. These "batteries" include libraries for scalable machine learning, graph processing, a SQL engine, and Spark Streaming. The core of Spark is a batch computing framework [24], that is based on manipulating so called Resilient Distributed Datasets (RDDs), which provide a fault tolerant implementation of distributed multisets. Computations are defined as transformations on RDDs, that should be deterministic and side-effect free, as the fault tolerance mechanism of Spark is based on its ability to recompute any fragment (partition) of an RDD when needed. Hence Spark programmers are encouraged to define RDD transformations that are pure functions from RDD to RDD, and the set of predefined RDD transformations includes typical higher-order functions like map, filter, etc., as well as aggregations by key and joins for RDDs of key-value pairs. We can also use Spark actions, which allow us to collect results into the program driver or store them into an external data store. Spark actions are impure, but idempotent actions are recommended in order to ensure a deterministic behavior even in the presence of recomputations triggered by the fault tolerance or speculative task execution mechanisms.[1] Spark is written in Scala and offers APIs for Scala, Java, Python, and R; in this work we focus on the Scala API. The example in Fig. 1 uses the Scala Spark shell to implement a variant of the famous word count example that in this case computes the number of occurrences of each character in a sentence. For that we use parallelize, a feature of Spark that allows us to create an RDD from a local collection, which is useful for testing. We start with a set of chars distributed among 3 partitions, we pair each char with a 1 by using map, and then group by first component in the pair and sum by the second by using reduceByKey and the addition function (_+_), thus obtaining a set of (char, frequency) pairs. We collect this set into an Array in the driver with collect.

These notions of transformations and actions are extended in Spark Streaming from RDDs to DStreams (Discretized Streams), which are series of RDDs corresponding to micro batches. These batches are generated at a fixed rate according to the configured *batch interval*. Spark Streaming is synchronous in the sense that given a collection of input and transformed DStreams, all the batches for each DStream are generated at the same time as the batch interval is met. Actions on DStreams are also periodic and are executed synchronously for each micro batch. The code in Fig. 2 is the streaming version of the code in Fig. 1. Here we want to process a DStream of characters, where batches are obtained by

---

[1] See https://spark.apache.org/docs/latest/programming-guide.html for more details.

```
object HelloSparkStreaming extends App {
  val conf = new SparkConf().setAppName("HelloSparkStreaming")
                            .setMaster("local[5]")
  val sc = new SparkContext(conf)
  val batchInterval = Duration(100)
  val ssc = new StreamingContext(sc, batchInterval)
  val batches = "let's count some letters, again and again"
                .grouped(4)
  val queue = new Queue[RDD[Char]]
  queue ++= batches.map(sc.parallelize(_, numSlices = 3))
  val css : DStream[Char] = ssc.queueStream(queue,
                                 oneAtATime = true)
  css.map{(_, 1)}.reduceByKey{_+_}.print()
  ssc.start()
  ssc.awaitTerminationOrTimeout(5000)
  ssc.stop(stopSparkContext = true)
}
```

```
-------------------------
Time: 1449638784400 ms
-------------------------
(e,1)
(t,1)
(l,1)
(',1)
...
-------------------------
Time: 1449638785300 ms
-------------------------
(i,1)
(a,2)
(g,1)
-------------------------
Time: 1449638785400 ms
-------------------------
(n,1)
```

Fig. 2. Letter count in spark streaming

splitting a String into pieces by making groups (RDDs) of 4 consecutive characters, using **grouped**. We use the testing utility class `QueueInputDStream`, which generates batches by picking RDDs from a queue, to generate the input DStream by parallelizing each substring into an RDD with 3 partitions. The program is executed using the local master mode of Spark, which replaces slave nodes in a distributed cluster by threads, which is useful for developing and testing.

The Problem of Testing. As the field has grown mature, several standard architectures for streaming processing like the Lambda Architecture [14] or reactive streams [12] have been proposed for implementing a cost effective, always up-to-date view of the data that allows the system to react on time to events. These architectures deal in different ways with trade-offs between latency, performance, and system complexity. The bar is also raised by the sophistication of the algorithms involved. To keep up with the speed on the input data stream, approximate algorithms with sublinear performance are used, even for otherwise simple aggregations [8]. Similarly, specialized machine learning and data stream mining algorithms are adapted to the stream processing context [15].

Moreover, dealing with time and events makes SPS-based programs intrinsically hard to test. There are several proposals in the literature that deal with the problem of testing and modeling systems that deal with time. In this work, we focus on Pnueli's approach [17] based on the use of temporal logic for testing reactive systems. Our final goal is facilitating the adoption of temporal logic as an every day tool for testing SPS-based programs. But, how could we present temporal logic in a way accessible to the average programmer? We propose exploring how property-based testing (PBT) [7], as realized in ScalaCheck [16], can be the answer, using it as a bridge between formal logic and software development practices like test-driven development (TDD) [5]. The point is that PBT is a testing technique with a growing adoption in the industry, that already exposes first order logic to the programmer. In PBT a test is expressed as a property, which is a formula in a restricted version of first order logic that relates program input and output. The testing framework checks the property by evaluating it against a bunch of randomly generated inputs. If a counterexample for the property is found then the test fails, otherwise it passes. The following is a "hello world" ScalaCheck property that checks the commutativity of addition:[2]

```
class HelloPBT extends Specification with ScalaCheck {
  def is = s2"""Hello world PBT spec, where int addition is commutative $intAdditionCommutative"""
  def intAdditionCommutative =
    Prop.forAll("x" |: arbitrary[Int], "y" |: arbitrary[Int]) { (x, y) => x + y === y + x
  }.set(minTestsOk = 100) }
```

PBT is based on *generators* (the functions in charge of computing the inputs) and *assertions* (the formula to be checked), that together with a *quantifier* form a *property*. In the example above the universal quantifier `Prop.forAll` is used to define a property that checks the assertion `x + y === y + x` for 100 values for x and y randomly generated by two instances of the generator `arbitrary[Int]`. Each of those pairs of values generated for x and y is called a *test case*, and a test case that refutes the assertions of a property is called a *counterexample*. Here `arbitrary` is a higher order generator that is able to generate random values for predefined and custom types. Besides universal quantifiers, ScalaCheck supports existential quantifiers — although these are not much used in practice [16,22]—, and logical operators to compose properties. PBT is a sound procedure to check the validity of the formulas implied by the properties, because if a counterexample is found it gives a definitive proof that the property is false. However, it is not complete, as there is no guarantee that the whole space of test cases is explored exhaustively, so if no counterexample is found then we cannot conclude that the property holds for all possible test cases that could had been generated. PBT is a lightweight approach that does not attempt to perform sophisticated automatic deductions, but it provides a very fast test execution that is suitable for the TDD cycle, and empirical studies [7,21] have shown that in practice random PBT obtains good results, with a quality comparable to more sophisticated techniques. This goes in the line of assuming that in general testing of non trivial systems is often incomplete, as the effort of completely modeling all the possible behaviors of the system under test with test cases is not cost effective in most software development projects, except for critical systems.

We already have programmers using first order logic to write the properties for the test cases. So to realize our proposal, all that is left is extending ScalaCheck to be able to use temporal logic operators from some variant of propositional LTL [6]. We will give the details for our temporal logic in the next section; for the time being consider that we have temporal operators with bounded time such as *always* φ *in* t, which indicates that φ must hold for the next t instants, or φ *until* ψ *in* t, which indicates that φ currently holds and, before t instants of time elapse, ψ must hold. That way we would obtain a propositional LTL formula extended with an outer universal quantifier over the test cases produced by the generators. This temporal logic should use discrete time, as DStreams are discrete. Also, the logic should fit the simple property checking

---

[2] Here we use the integration of ScalaCheck with the Specs2 [21] testing library.

mechanism of PBT, that requires fast evaluation of each test case. For this reason we use a temporal logic for finite words, like those used in the field of runtime verification [13], instead of using infinite ω-words as usual in model checking. Although any Spark DStream is supposed to run indefinitely, so it might well be modeled by an infinite word, in our setting we only model a finite prefix of the DStream. This allows us to implement a simple and fast sound procedure for evaluating test cases, because if a prefix of a DStream refutes a property then the whole infinite DStream also refutes the property. On the other hand the procedure is not complete because only a prefix of the DStream is evaluated, but anyway PBT was not complete in the first place. Hence our *test cases* will be *finite prefixes* of DStreams, that correspond to *finite words* in this logic. In Sect. 2 there is a precise formulation of our logic LTL_{ss}, for now let's consider a concrete example in order to get a quick grasp of our proposal.

Example 1. We would like to test a Spark Streaming program that takes a stream of user activity data and returns a stream of banned users. To keep the example simple, we assume that the input records are pairs containing a Long user id, and a Boolean value indicating whether the user has been honest at that instant. The output stream should include the ids of all the users that have been malicious now or in a previous instant. So, the test subject that implement this has type testSubject : DStream[(Long, Boolean)] => DStream[Long]). Note that a trivial, stateless implementation of this behavior that just keeps the first element of the pair fails to achieve this goal, as it is not able to remember which users had been malicious in the past.

```
def statelessListBannedUsers(ds : DStream[(Long, Boolean)]) :
    DStream[Long] = ds.map(_._1)
```

To define a property that captures this behavior, we start by defining a *generator* for (finite prefixes of) the input stream. As we want this input to change with time, we use a temporal logic formula to specify the generator. We start by defining the atomic non-temporal propositions, which are generators of micro batches with type Gen[Batch[(Long, Boolean)]], where Batch is a class extending Seq that represents a micro batch. We can generate good batches, where all the users are honest, and bad batches, where a user has been malicious. We generate batches of 20 elements, and use 15L as the id for the malicious id:

```
val batchSize = 20
val (badId, ids) = (15L, Gen.choose(1L, 50L))
val goodBatch = BatchGen.ofN(batchSize, ids.map((_, true)))
val badBatch = goodBatch + BatchGen.ofN(1, (badId, false))
```

So far generators are oblivious to the passage of time. But in order to exercise the test subject thoroughly, we want to ensure that a bad batch is indeed generated, and that several arbitrary batches are generated after it, so we can check that once a user is detected as malicious, it is also consider malicious in subsequent instants. And we want all this to happen within the confines of the generated finite DStream prefix. This is where *timeouts* come into play. In our

temporal logic we associate a timeout to each temporal operator, that constrains
the time it takes for the operator to resolve. For example in a use of *until* with a
timeout of t, the second formula most hold before t instants have passed. Translated to generators this means that in each generated DStream prefix a batch for
the second generator is generated before t batches have passed, i.e. between the
first and the t-th batch. This way we facilitate that the interesting events had
enough time to happen during the limited fraction of time considered during the
evaluation of the property.

```
val (headTimeout, tailTimeout, nestedTimeout) = (10, 10, 5)
val gen = BatchGen.until(goodBatch, badBatch, headTimeout) ++
          BatchGen.always(Gen.oneOf(goodBatch, badBatch), tailTimeout)
```

The resulting generator `gen` has type `Gen[PDStream[(Long, Boolean)]]`,
where `PDStream` is a class that represents sequences of micro batches corresponding to a DStream prefix. Here `headTimeout` limits the number of batches
before the bad batch occurs, while `tailTimeout` limits the number of arbitrary
batches generated after that. The output stream is simply the result of applying
the test subject to the input stream. Now we define the *assertion* that completes
the property, as a *temporal logic formula*.

```
type U = (RDD[(Long, Boolean)], RDD[Long])
val (inBatch, outBatch) = ((_ : U)._1, (_ : U)._2)
val formula : Formula[U] = {
  val allGoodInputs = at(inBatch)(_ should foreachRecord(_._2 == true))
  val badInput = at(inBatch)(_ should existsRecord(_ == (badId, false)))
  val noIdBanned = at(outBatch)(_.isEmpty)
  val badIdBanned = at(outBatch)(_ should existsRecord(_ == badId))

  ((allGoodInputs and noIdBanned) until badIdBanned on headTimeout) and
  (always { badInput ==> (always(badIdBanned) during nestedTimeout) }
           during tailTimeout)  }
```

Atomic non-temporal propositions correspond to assertions on the micro-
batches for the input and output DStreams. That is expressed by the type alias
`U` for the universe of atomic propositions. The functions `inBatch` and `outBatch`
can be combined with `at` and a Specs2 assertion to define non-temporal atomic
propositions like `allGoodInputs`, that states that all the records in the input
DStream correspond to honest users. But we know that this will not be hap-
pening forever, because `gen` eventually creates a bad batch, so we combine the
atomic propositions using temporal operators to state things like "we have good
inputs and no id banned until we ban the bad id" and "each time we get a bad
input we ban the bad id for some time." Here we use the same timeouts we used
for the generators, to enforce the formula within the time interval where the
interesting events are generated. Also, we use an additional `nestedTimeout` for
the nested *always*. Timeouts for operators that apply an universal quantification
on time, like *always*, limit the number of instants that the quantified formula
needs to be true for the whole formula to hold. In this case we only have to check

badIdBanned for nestedTimeout batches for the nested always to be evaluated to true. Following ideas from the field of runtime verification [3,4], we consider a 3-valued logic where the third value corresponds to an inconclusive result used as the last resort when the input finite word is consumed before completely solving the temporal formula. Timeouts for universal time quantifiers help relaxing the formula so its evaluation is conclusive more often, while timeouts for existential time quantifiers like *until* make the formula more strict. We consider that it is important to facilitate expressing properties with a definite result, as quantifiers like *exists*, that often lead properties to an inconclusive evaluation, have been abandoned in practice by the PBT user community [16,22].

Finally, we use our temporal universal quantifier forAllDStream to put together the temporal generator and formula, getting a property that checks the formula for all the finite DStreams prefixes produced by the generator:

```
forAllDStream(gen)(testSubject)(formula).set(minTestsOk = 20)
```

The property fails as expected for the faulty trivial implementation above, and succeeds for a correct stateful implementation [19].

The rest of the paper is organized as follows: Sect. 2 describes our logic for testing stream processing systems, while Sect. 3 presents its implementation for Spark. Section 4 discusses some related work. Finally, Sect. 5 concludes and presents some subjects of future work. An extended version of this paper can be found in [19].

2 A Temporal Logic for Testing Spark Streaming Programs

We present in this section a linear temporal logic for defining properties on stream processing systems. We first define the basics of the logic and then show some interesting properties to prove formulas in an efficient way.

2.1 A Linear Temporal Logic with Timeouts for Practical Specification of Stream Processing Systems

We present in this section LTL_{ss}, a linear temporal logic that specializes LTL_3 [3] by allowing timeouts in temporal connectives. LTL_3 is an extension of LTL for runtime verification that takes into account that only *finite* executions can be checked, and hence a new value ? (inconclusive) can be returned if a property cannot be evaluated to either *true* ($\top$) or *false* ($\bot$). These values form a lattice with $\bot \leq ? \leq \top$.

LTL_{ss} pays closer attention than LTL_3 to finite executions by limiting the scope of temporal connectives. This allows users (i) to obtain either $\top$ or $\bot$ for any execution given it has a given length, which can be computed beforehand, and (ii) to define more precise formulas, since it is possible to indicate in an easy way the period when it is expected to hold. Moreover, as we will see in Sect. 2.2, we have devised an efficient algorithm for evaluating these formulas.

Formulae Syntax. In line with [3], assume a finite set of atomic propositions AP. We consider the alphabet $\Sigma = \mathcal{P}(AP)$. A finite word over Σ is any $u \in \Sigma^*$, i.e. any finite sequence of sets of atomic propositions. We use the notation $u = a_1 \ldots a_n$ to denote that u has length n and a_i is the letter at position or time i in u. Each letter a_i corresponds to a set of propositions from AP that hold at time i. LTL_{ss} is a variant of propositional lineal temporal logic where formulas $\varphi \in LTL_{ss}$ are defined as:

$$\varphi ::= \bot \mid \top \mid p \mid \neg\varphi \mid \varphi \vee \varphi \mid \varphi \wedge \varphi \mid \varphi \rightarrow \varphi \mid X\varphi \mid \Diamond_t\varphi \mid \Box_t\varphi \mid \varphi \, U_t \, \varphi \mid \varphi \, R_t \, \varphi$$

for $p \in AP$, and $t \in \mathbb{N}^+$ a timeout. We will use the notation $X^n\varphi, n \in \mathbb{N}^+$, as a shortcut for n applications of the operator X to φ. The intuition underlying these formulas, that are formally defined below, is:[3]

- $X\varphi$, read "next φ," indicates that φ holds in the next state.
- $\Diamond_t\varphi$, read "eventually φ in t," indicates that φ holds in any of the next t states (including the current one).
- $\Box_t\varphi$, read "always φ in t," indicates that φ holds in all of the next t states (including the current one).
- $\varphi_1 \, U_t \, \varphi_2$, read "$\varphi_1$ holds until φ_2 in t," indicates that φ_1 holds until φ_2 holds in the next t states, including the current one. It is enough for φ_1 to hold until the state previous to the one where φ_2 holds.

Note that if $t = \infty$ then LTL_{ss} would correspond to LTL_3. However, since our programs can only process finite words, we only work with $t \in \mathbb{N}^+$. In this case it is possible to discard the inconclusive value and obtain only definite values if some constraints hold between the word and the formula being tested.

Logic for Finite Words. The logic for finite words proves judgements $u, i \vDash \varphi : v$ for $u \in \Sigma^*$, $i \in \mathbb{N}^+$, and $v \in \{\top, \bot, ?\}$.

$$u, i \vDash \Diamond_t\varphi : \begin{cases} \top & \text{if } \exists k \in [i, min(i + (t-1), len(u))].\ u, k \vDash \varphi : \bot \\ \bot & \text{if } i + (t-1) \leq len(u) \wedge \forall k \in [i, i + (t-1)].\ u, k \vDash \varphi_1 : \bot \\ ? & \text{otherwise} \end{cases}$$

$$u, i \vDash \Box_t\varphi : \begin{cases} \top & \text{if } i + (t-1) \leq len(u) \wedge \forall k \in [i, i + (t-1)].\ u, k \vDash \varphi : \top \\ \bot & \text{if } \exists k \in [i, min(i + (t-1), len(u))].\ u, k \vDash \varphi : \bot \\ ? & \text{otherwise} \end{cases}$$

$$u, i \vDash \varphi_1 \, U_t \, \varphi_2 : \begin{cases} \top & \text{if } \exists k \in [i, min(i + (t-1), len(u))].\ u, k \vDash \varphi_2 : \top \wedge \\ & \quad \forall j \in [i, k).\ u, j \vDash \varphi_1 : \top \\ \bot & \text{if } \exists k \in [i, min(i + (t-1), len(u))].\ u, k \vDash \varphi_1 : \bot \wedge \\ & \quad \forall j \in [i, k].\ u, j \vDash \varphi_2 : \bot \\ \bot & \text{if } i + (t-1) \leq len(u) \wedge \forall k \in [i, i + (t-1)].\ u, k \vDash \varphi_1 : \top \wedge \\ & \quad \forall l \in [i, min(i + (t-1), len(u))].\ u, l \vDash \varphi_2 : \bot \\ ? & \text{otherwise} \end{cases}$$

---

[3] Due to space limitations, the results for *release* are available in [19].

$$u, i \vDash X\varphi : \begin{cases} ? & \text{if } i = len(u) \\ v & \text{if } i < len(u) \wedge u, i+1 \vDash \varphi : v \end{cases}$$

The intuition underlying this definition is that, if the word is too short to check all the steps indicated by a temporal operator and neither $\top$ or $\bot$ can be obtained before finishing the word, then ? is obtained. Otherwise, the formula is evaluated to either $\top$ or $\bot$ just by checking the appropriate sub-word. In the following we say $u \vDash \varphi$ iff $u, 1 \vDash \varphi : \top$. Note that these formulas, when used as generators, produce finite words that fulfill the formula. In our tool these words are minimal in the sense that it stops as soon as the word fulfills the formula. By using temporal logic not only for the formulas but also for the data generators, we obtain a simple setting that is easy to grasp for average programmers.

Example 2. Assume the set of atomic propositions $AP \equiv \{a, b, c\}$ and the word $u \equiv \boxed{\{b\}}\ \boxed{\{b\}}\ \boxed{\{a,b\}}\ \boxed{\{a\}}$. Then we have the following results:

- $u \vDash (\Diamond_4 c) : \bot$, since c does not hold in the first four states.
- $u \vDash (\Diamond_5 c) : ?$, since we have consumed the whole word, c did not hold in those states, and the timeout has not expired.
- $u \vDash \Box_4 (a \vee b) : \top$, since either a or b is found in the first four states.
- $u \vDash \Box_5 (a \vee b) : ?$, since the property holds until the word is consumed, but the user required more steps.
- $u \vDash \Box_5 c : \bot$, since the proposition does not hold in the first state.
- $u \vDash (b \, U_2 \, a) : \bot$, since a holds in the third state, but the user wanted to check just the first two states.
- $u \vDash (b \, U_5 \, a) : \top$, since a holds in the third state and, before that, b held in all the states.
- $u \vDash \Box_4 (a \rightarrow Xa) : ?$, since we do not know what happens in the fifth state, which is required to check the formula in the fourth state (because of next).
- $u \vDash \Box_2 (b \rightarrow \Diamond_2 a) : \bot$, since in the first state we have b but we do not have a until the third state.
- $u \vDash b \, U_2 \, X(a \wedge Xa) : \top$, since $X(a \wedge Xa)$ holds in the second state (that is, $a \wedge Xa$ holds in the third state, which can also be understood as a holds in the third and fourth states).

Example 3. The generator defined by the formula $\Box_2 (b \rightarrow \Diamond_2 a)$ above would randomly generate words such as $\boxed{\{b\}}\ \boxed{\{a,b\}}\ \boxed{\{a\}}$, $\boxed{\{a\}}\ \boxed{\{a\}}\ \boxed{\{a\}}$, or $\boxed{\{a\}}\ \boxed{\{b\}}\ \boxed{\{a\}}$, among others.

We need now a decision procedure for evaluating formulas. Although we can use the formal definitions above to define it, we would obtain a procedure that requires the whole stream to be traversed before taking the next step, greatly worsening the performance of the tool. We propose in the next section a transformation that allows us to implement a stepwise algorithm. Details on the naïve procedure can be found in [19].

2.2   A Transformation for Stepwise Evaluation

In order to define this stepwise evaluation, it is worth noting that all the properties are finite (that is, all of them can be proved or disproved after a finite number of steps). It is hence possible to express any formula only using the temporal operator X, which leads us to the following definition.

Definition 1 (Next Form). *We say that a formula $\psi \in LTL_{ss}$ is in next form iff. it is built by using the following grammar:*

$$\psi ::= \bot \mid \top \mid p \mid \neg\psi \mid \psi \vee \psi \mid \psi \wedge \psi \mid \psi \rightarrow \psi \mid X\psi$$

It is possible to obtain the next form of any formula $\varphi \in LTL_{ss}$ as:

Definition 2 (Next Transformation). *Given an alphabet Σ and a formula $\varphi \in LTL_{ss}$, the function $nt(\varphi)$ computes another formula $\varphi' \in LTL_{ss}$, such that φ' is in next form and $\forall u \in \Sigma^*.u \vDash \varphi \iff u \vDash \varphi'$.*

$$
\begin{aligned}
nt(a) &= a, \quad a \in \{\top, \bot, p\}\\
nt(\neg\varphi) &= \neg nt(\varphi)\\
nt(\varphi_1 \; op \; \varphi_2) &= nt(\varphi_1) \; op \; nt(\varphi_2), \text{ with } op \text{ either } \vee, \wedge, \text{ or } \rightarrow .\\
nt(X\varphi) &= X nt(\varphi)\\
nt(\Diamond_t\varphi) &= nt(\varphi) \vee X nt(\varphi) \vee \ldots \vee X^{t-1} nt(\varphi)\\
nt(\Box_t\varphi) &= nt(\varphi) \wedge X nt(\varphi) \wedge \ldots \wedge X^{t-1} nt(\varphi)\\
nt(\varphi_1 \; U_t \; \varphi_2) &= nt(\varphi_2) \vee (nt(\varphi_1) \wedge X nt(\varphi_2)) \vee\\
&\quad (nt(\varphi_1) \wedge X nt(\varphi_1) \wedge X^2 nt(\varphi_2)) \vee \ldots \vee\\
&\quad (nt(\varphi_1) \wedge X nt(\varphi_1) \wedge \ldots \wedge X^{t-2} nt(\varphi_1) \wedge X^{t-1} nt(\varphi_2))
\end{aligned}
$$

for $p \in AP$ and $\varphi, \varphi_1, \varphi_2 \in LTL_{ss}$.

It is easy to see that the formula obtained by this transformation is in *next form*, since it only introduces formulas using the X operator. The equivalence between formulas is stated in Theorem 1 (the proof is available in [19]):

Theorem 1. *Given an alphabet Σ and formulas $\varphi, \varphi' \in LTL_{ss}$, such that $\varphi' \equiv nt(\varphi)$, we have $\forall u \in \Sigma^*.u \vDash \varphi \iff u \vDash \varphi'$.*

Example 4. We show how to transform some of the formulas from Example 2:

- $nt(\Diamond_4 c) = c \vee Xc \vee X^2 c \vee X^3 c$
- $nt(b \; U_2 \; a) = a \vee (b \wedge Xa)$
- $nt(\Box_2(b \rightarrow \Diamond_2 a)) = (b \rightarrow (a \vee Xa)) \wedge X(b \rightarrow (a \vee Xa))$
- $nt(b \; U_2 \; X(a \wedge Xa)) = X(a \wedge Xa) \vee (b \wedge X^2(a \wedge Xa))$

Once the next form of a formula has been computed, it is possible to evaluate it for a given word just by traversing its letters. We just evaluate the atomic formulas in the present moment (that is, those properties that does not contain the next operator) and remove the next operator otherwise, so these properties will be evaluated for the next letter. This method is detailed as follows:

Definition 3 (Letter Simplification). *Given a formula ψ in next form and a letter $s \in \Sigma$, the function $ls(\psi, s)$ simplifies ψ with s as follows:*

- $ls(\top, s) = \top$.
- $ls(\bot, s) = \bot$.
- $ls(p, s) = p \in s$.
- $ls(\neg\psi, s) = \neg ls(\psi)$.

- $ls(\psi_1 \vee \psi_2, s) = ls(\psi_1) \vee ls(\psi_2)$.
- $ls(\psi_1 \wedge \psi_2, s) = ls(\psi_1) \wedge ls(\psi_2)$.
- $ls(\psi_1 \rightarrow \psi_2, s) = ls(\psi_1) \rightarrow ls(\psi_2)$.
- $ls(X\psi, s) = \psi$.

Using this function and applying propositional logic when definite values are found it is possible to evaluate formulas in a step-by-step fashion.[4] This transformation gives also the intuition that inconclusive values can be avoided if we use a word as long as the number of next operators nested in the transformation plus 1. A formal definition for this property can be found in [19].

3 Temporal Logic for Property-Based Testing

Our prototype extends ScalaCheck to support LTL_{ss} formulas for testing Spark Streaming programs. We use Spark's local mode to execute the test locally, so it is limited by the computing power of a single machine, but can be easily integrated in a continuous integration pipeline (e.g. the one for this same project https://travis-ci.org/juanrh/sscheck). Besides, our system is able to test programs without any modification. The system is available at https://github.com/juanrh/sscheck/releases.

Mapping Spark Streaming Programs into LTL_{ss}. Instead of using wall-clock time, like e.g. in Specs2's future matchers [21], we consider the logical time as discretized by the batch interval. At each instant, for each DStream we can see an RDD for the current batch as it was computed instantaneously. In practice the synchronization performed by Spark Streaming makes it appear like that, when enough computing resources are available. We define our atomic propositions as assertions over those RDDs. We have implemented an algebraic data type as a Scala trait `Formula`, that is parameterized on a universe type for the alphabet. The universe is a tuple of RDDs with one component for each DStream: e.g. in the example at the end of Sect. 1 the universe was defined by the alias `type U = (RDD[Double], RDD[Long])`, where the first component is the current batch for the input DStream and the second the current batch for the output DStream. `Formula` has a child case class for each of the constructions in LTL_{ss}, with a couple of exceptions. $\bot$, $\top$, and atomic propositions are all represented by the case class `Now`, which is basically a wrapper for a function from the universe into a ScalaCheck `Prop.Status` value, that represents a truth value. We need a function because we have to repeatedly apply it to each of the batches that are generated for each DStream. We provide suitable Scala implicit conversions for defining these functions more easily, using specs2 matchers: for example, at the end of Sect. 1, the argument of the `always` used to define the value `formula` is implicitly converted into a `Now` object. The other exception is `Solved`, that

---

[4] Note that the value? is only reached when the word is consumed and this simplification cannot be applied.

is used to represented formulas that have been evaluated completely. Although LTL_{ss} is a propositional temporal logic, in our prototype we add an additional outer universal quantifier on the test cases, as usual in PBT, so the test passes iff none of the generated test cases is able to refute the formula. Currently we do not support nesting of first order ScalaCheck quantifiers inside LTL_{ss} formulas.

We have also implemented higher-order ScalaCheck generators corresponding to temporal operators, where each generated test case represents a finite prefix of a DStream. For that we use the classes `Batch[A]` and `PDStream[A]`— that stands for prefix DStream—extending `Seq[A]` and `Seq[Batch[A]]` with additional operations like batch-wise union of PDStream.

Evaluating Temporal Properties. We provide a trait `DStreamTLProperty` with a method `forAllDStream`, as described in Sect. 1, for specifying properties on functions that transform DStreams, using the logic LTL_{ss}. The class `Formula` has methods for computing the next form, and for performing a step in the letter simplification process from Definition 3 by consuming a value of the type of the universe. On property evaluation we use `TestInputStream` from [11] to transform each `PDStream[A]` into a `DStream[A]`, and apply the test subject to create a derived DStream. Then we register a `foreachRDD` action on the input DStream that updates a `Formula` object for each new generated batch. For each test case we create a fresh streaming context, which is important for test case isolation in stateful transformations. We then start the Spark streaming context to start the computation, and then run a standard ScalaCheck `forall` property to generate the test cases. As soon as a `Solved` formula with failing status is reached, we stop the streaming context and return a failing property, and so ScalaCheck reports the current test case as a counterexample for the formula.

The resulting system has a reasonable performance. On a more realistic example based on official Spark training (computing the most popular hastag in a stream of tweets[5]), our system evaluates 50 test cases in 2 min and 4 s running in an Intel i7-4810MQ CPU with 16 GB RAM. The `batchDuration` parameter can be tuned according to the power of the machine: smaller values for faster machines, to complete the test earlier, and bigger values for slower machines, so the machine has more time to compute each of the batches.

4   Related Work

We can consider the system presented in this paper an evolution of the data-flow approaches devised for reactive systems in the past decades; we focus here in Lustre [10] and Lutin [18], since we consider they present a number of features that are representative of this kind of systems. In fact, the idea underlying both stream processing systems and data-flow reactive systems is very similar:

---

[5] See   https://github.com/juanrh/sscheck-examples/blob/master/src/test/scala/es/ucm/fdi/sscheck/spark/demo/twitter/TwitterAmpcampDemo.scala   and   https://github.com/juanrh/sscheck-examples/wiki/TwitterAmpcampDemo-execution   for the execution logs.

precessing a potentially infinite input stream while generating an output stream. Moreover, they usually work with formulas considering both the current state and the previous ones, which are similar to the "forward" ones presented here. There are, however, some differences between these two approaches, being an important one that sscheck is executed in a parallel way using Spark.

Lustre is a programming language for reactive systems that is able to verify safety properties by generating random input streams. The random generation provided by sscheck is more refined, since it is possible to define some patterns in the stream in order to verify some behaviors that can be omitted by purely random generators. Moreover, Lustre specializes in the verification of critical systems and hence it has features for dealing with this kind of systems, but lacks other general features as complex data-structures, although new extensions are included in every new release. On the other hand, it is not possible to formally verify systems in sscheck; we focus in a lighter approach for day-to-day programs and, since it supports all Scala features, its expressive power is greater. Lutin is a specification language for reactive systems that combines constraints with temporal operators. Moreover, it is also possible to generate test cases that depend on the previous values that the system has generated. First, these constraints provide more expressive power than the atomic formulas presented here, and thus the properties stated in Lutin are more expressive than the ones in sscheck. Although more expressive formulas are an interesting subject of future work, we have focused in this work in providing a framework where the properties are "natural" even for engineers who are not trained in formal methods; once we have examined the success of this approach we will try to move into more complex properties. Second, our framework completely separates the input from the output, and hence it is not possible to share information between these streams. Although sharing this information is indeed very important for control systems, we consider that stream processing systems usually deal with external data and hence this relation is not so relevant for the present tool. Finally, note that an advantage of sscheck consists in using the same language for both programming and defining the properties.

In a similar note, we can consider runtime monitoring of synchronous systems like LOLA [9], a specification language that allows the user to define properties in both past and future LTL. LOLA guarantees bounded memory for monitoring and allows the user to collect statistics at runtime. On the other hand, and indicated above, sscheck allows to implement both the programs and the test in the same language and provides PBT, which simplifies the testing phase, although actual programs cannot be traced. TraceContract [2] is a Scala library that uses a shallow internal DSL for implementing a logic for trace analysis. That logic is a hybrid between state machines and temporal logic, that is able to express both past time and future time temporal logic formulas, and that allows a form of first order quantification over the events that constitute the traces. On the other hand TraceContract is not able to generate test cases, and it is not integrated with any standard testing library like Specs2.

Regarding testing tools for Spark, the most clear precedent is the unit test framework Spark Test Base [11], which also integrates ScalaCheck for Spark but only for Spark core. To the best of out knowledge, there is no previous library supporting property-based testing for Spark Streaming.

5   Conclusions and Ongoing Work

In this paper we have explored the idea of extending property-based testing with temporal logic and its application to testing programs developed with a stream processing system. Instead of developing an abstract model of stream processing systems that could be applied to any particular implementation and performing testing against a translation of actual programs into that model, we have decided to work with a concrete system, Spark Streaming, in our prototype. In this way the tests are executed against the actual test subject and in a context closer to the production environment where programs will be executed. We think this could help with the adoption of the system by professional programmers, as it integrates more naturally with the tool set employed in disciplines like test driven development. For this same reason we have used Specs2, a mature tool for behavior driven development, for dealing with the difficulties integrating of our logic with Spark and ScalaCheck. Along the way we have devised the novel finite-word discrete-time linear temporal logic LTL_{ss}, in the line of other temporal logics used in runtime verification. We think it allows to easily write expressive and strict properties about temporal aspects of programs.

Our next movement will be showing the system to programmers and draw conclusions from their opinions and impressions. There are many open lines of future work. On the practical side our prototype still needs some work to get a robust system. Also, adding support for arbitrary nesting of ScalaCheck `forall` and `exists` quantifiers inside LTL_{ss} formula would be an interesting extension. We also consider developing versions for other languages with Spark API, in particular Python, or supporting other SPS, like Apache Flink. Besides, we plan to explore whether the execution of several test cases in parallel minimize the test suite execution time. In the theoretical side, we should give a formal characterization of the language generated by our generators. Finally, we intend to explore other formalisms for expressing temporal and cyclic behaviors [23].

References

1. Akidau, T., Balikov, A., Bekiroğlu, K., Chernyak, S., Haberman, J., Lax, R., McVeety, S., Mills, D., Nordstrom, P., Whittle, S.: MillWheel: fault-tolerant stream processing at internet scale. Proc. VLDB Endowment **6**(11), 1033–1044 (2013)
2. Barringer, H., Havelund, K.: TraceContract: A scala DSL for trace analysis. In: Butler, M., Schulte, W. (eds.) FM 2011. LNCS, vol. 6664, pp. 57–72. Springer, Heidelberg (2011)
3. Bauer, A., Leucker, M., Schallhart, C.: Monitoring of real-time properties. In: Arun-Kumar, S., Garg, N. (eds.) FSTTCS 2006. LNCS, vol. 4337, pp. 260–272. Springer, Heidelberg (2006)

4. Bauer, A., Leucker, M., Schallhart, C.: The good, the bad, and the ugly, but how ugly is ugly? In: Sokolsky, O., Taşıran, S. (eds.) RV 2007. LNCS, vol. 4839, pp. 126–138. Springer, Heidelberg (2007)
5. Beck, K.: Test Driven Development: By Example. Addison-Wesley Professional, Boston (2003)
6. Blackburn, P., van Benthem, J., Wolter, F. (eds.): Handbook of Modal Logic. Elsevier, Philadelphia (2006)
7. Claessen, K., Hughes, J.: QuickCheck: A lightweight tool for random testing of Haskell programs. ACM Sigplan Not. **46**(4), 53–64 (2011)
8. Cormode, G., Muthukrishnan, S.: An improved data stream summary: The count-min sketch and its applications. J. Algorithms **55**(1), 58–75 (2005)
9. D'Angelo, B., Sankaranarayanan, S., Sánchez, C., Robinson, W., Finkbeiner, B., Sipma, H.B., Mehrotra, S., Manna, Z.: LOLA: runtime monitoring of synchronous systems. In: Proceedings of the 12th International Symposium on Temporal Representation and Reasoning, TIME, pp. 166–174. IEEE Computer Society (2005)
10. Halbwachs, N.: Synchronous programming of reactive systems. Springer International Series in Engineering and Computer Science, vol. 215. Kluwer Academic Publishers, Dordrecht (1992)
11. Karau, H.: Spark-testing-base (2015). http://blog.cloudera.com/blog/2015/09/making-apache-spark-testing-easy-with-spark-testing-base/
12. Kuhn, R., Allen, J.: Reactive Design Patterns. Manning Publications, Greenwich (2014)
13. Leucker, M., Schallhart, C.: A brief account of runtime verification. J. Logic Algebraic Program. **78**(5), 293–303 (2009)
14. Marz, N., Warren, J.: Big Data: Principles and Best Practices of Scalable Realtime Data Systems. Manning Publications Co., Stamford (2015)
15. Morales, G.D.F., Bifet, A.: SAMOA: Scalable advanced massive online analysis. J. Mach. Learn. Res. **16**, 149–153 (2015)
16. Nilsson, R.: ScalaCheck: The Definitive Guide. IT Pro, Artima Incorporated, Upper Saddle River (2014)
17. Pnueli, A.: Applications of temporal logic to the specification and verification of reactive systems: a survey of current trends. In: de Bakker, J.W., de Roever, W.-P., Rozenberg, G. (eds.) Current Trends in Concurrency. LNCS, vol. 224, pp. 510–584. Springer, Heidelberg (1986)
18. Raymond, P., Roux, Y., Jahier, E.: Lutin: a language for specifying and executing reactive scenarios. EURASIP J. Emb. Syst. **2008**, 1–11 (2008). Article ID: 753821
19. Riesco, A., Rodríguez-Hortalá, J.: A lightweight tool for random testing of stream processing systems (extended version). Technical Report SIC 02/15, Departamento de Sistemas Informáticos y Computación de la Universidad Complutense de Madrid, September 2015. http://maude.sip.ucm.es/~adrian/pubs.html
20. Schelter, S., Ewen, S., Tzoumas, K., Markl, V.: All roads lead to Rome: optimistic recovery for distributed iterative data processing. In: Proceedings of the 22nd ACM international conference on Conference on information & knowledge management, pp. 1919–1928. ACM (2013)
21. Shamshiri, S., Rojas, J.M., Fraser, G., McMinn P.: Random or genetic algorithm search for object-oriented test suite generation? In: Proceedings of the on Genetic and Evolutionary Computation Conference, pp. 1367–1374. ACM (2015)
22. Venners, B.: Re: Prop.exists and scalatest matchers (2015). https://groups.google.com/forum/#!msg/scalacheck/Ped7joQLhnY/gNH0SSWkKUgJ
23. Wolper, P.: Temporal logic can be more expressive. Inf. Control **56**(1/2), 72–99 (1983)

24. Zaharia, M., Chowdhury, M., Das, T., Dave, A., Ma, J., McCauley, M., Franklin, M.J., Shenker, S., Stoica, I.: Resilient distributed datasets: A fault-tolerant abstraction for in-memory cluster computing. In: Proceedings of the 9th USENIX conference on Networked Systems Design and Implementation, p. 2. USENIX Assoc (2012)
25. Zaharia, M., Das, T., Li, H., Hunter, T., Shenker, S., Stoica, I.: Discretized streams: fault-tolerant streaming computation at scale. In: Proceedings of the 24th ACM Symposium on Operating Systems Principles, pp. 423–438. ACM (2013)

Combining Static Analysis and Testing
for Deadlock Detection

Elvira Albert, Miguel Gómez-Zamalloa, and Miguel Isabel$^{(\boxtimes)}$

Complutense University of Madrid (UCM), Madrid, Spain
miguelis@ucm.es

Abstract. Static deadlock analyzers might be able to verify the absence of deadlock. However, they are usually not able to detect its presence. Also, when they detect a potential deadlock cycle, they provide little (or even no) information on their output. Due to the complex flow of concurrent programs, the user might not be able to find the source of the anomalous behaviour from the abstract information computed by static analysis. This paper proposes the combined use of static analysis and testing for effective deadlock detection in asynchronous programs. When the program features a deadlock, our combined use of analysis and testing provides an effective technique to catch deadlock traces. While if the program does not have deadlock, but the analyzer inaccurately spotted it, we might prove deadlock freedom.

1 Introduction

In concurrent programs, *deadlocks* are one of the most common programming errors and, thus, a main goal of verification and testing tools is, respectively, proving deadlock freedom and *deadlock detection*. We consider an *asynchronous* language which allows spawning asynchronous tasks at distributed locations, with no shared memory among them, and which has two operations for blocking and non-blocking synchronization with the termination of asynchronous tasks. In this setting, in order to detect deadlocks, all possible *interleavings* among tasks executing at the distributed locations must be considered. Basically, each time that the processor can be released, any of the available tasks can start its execution, and all combinations among the tasks must be tried, as any of them might lead to deadlock.

Static analysis and testing are two different ways of detecting deadlocks. As static analysis examines all possible execution paths and variable values, it can reveal deadlocks that could not manifest until weeks or months after releasing the application. This aspect of static analysis is especially important in security assurance – security attacks try to exercise an application in unpredictable and

This work was funded partially by the EU project FP7-ICT-610582 ENVISAGE: Engineering Virtualized Services (http://www.envisage-project.eu), by the Spanish MINECO projects TIN2012-38137 and TIN2015-69175-C4-2-R, and by the CM project S2013/ICE-3006.

© Springer International Publishing Switzerland 2016
E. Ábrahám and M. Huisman (Eds.): IFM 2016, LNCS 9681, pp. 409–424, 2016.
DOI: 10.1007/978-3-319-33693-0_26

untested ways. However, due to the use of approximations, most static analyses can only verify the absence of deadlock but not its presence, i.e., they can produce false positives. Moreover, when a deadlock is found, state-of-the-art analysis tools [6,7,12] provide little (and often no) information on the source of the deadlock. In particular, for deadlocks that are complex (involve many tasks and locations), it is essential to know the task interleavings that have occurred and the locations involved in the deadlock, i.e., provide a concrete *deadlock trace* that allows the programmer to identify and fix the problem.

In contrast, testing consists of executing the application for concrete input values. Since a deadlock can manifest only on specific sequences of task interleavings, in order to apply testing for deadlock detection, the testing process must systematically explore all task interleavings. The primary advantage of *systematic testing* [4,14] for deadlock detection is that it can provide the detailed deadlock trace. There are two shortcomings though: (1) Although recent research tries to avoid redundant exploration as much as possible [1,3–5], the search space of systematic testing (even without redundancies) can be huge. This is a threat to the application of testing in concurrent programming. (2) There is only guarantee of deadlock freedom for finite-state terminating programs (terminating executions with concrete inputs).

This paper proposes a seamless combination of static analysis and testing for effective deadlock detection as follows: an existing static deadlock analysis [6] is first used to obtain *abstract* descriptions of potential deadlock cycles which are then used to guide a testing tool in order to find associated deadlock traces (or discard them). In summary, the main contributions of this paper are:

1. We extend a standard semantics for asynchronous programs with information about the task interleavings made and the status of tasks.
2. We provide a formal characterization of *deadlock state* which can be checked along the execution and allows us to early detect deadlocks.
3. We present a new methodology to detect deadlocks which combines testing and static analysis as follows: the deadlock cycles inferred by static analysis are used to guide the testing process towards paths that might lead to a deadlock cycle while discarding deadlock-free paths.
4. We have implemented our methodology in the SYCO system (see Sect. 6) and performed a thorough experimental evaluation on some classical examples.

2   Asynchronous Programs: Syntax and Semantics

We consider a distributed programming model with explicit locations. Each location represents a processor with a procedure stack and an unordered buffer of pending tasks. Initially all processors are idle. When an idle processor's task buffer is non-empty, some task is selected for execution. Besides accessing its own processor's global storage, each task can post tasks to the buffers of any processor, including its own, and synchronize with the termination of tasks. The language uses *future variables* to check if the execution of an asynchronous

$$(\text{MSTEP})\ \ selectLoc(S) = loc(\ell, \bot, h, \mathcal{Q}),\ \mathcal{Q} \neq \emptyset,\ selectTask(\ell) = tsk(tk, m, l, s),$$

$$\frac{S \diamond \rho_0 \overset{\ell \cdot tk}{\leadsto}{}^{*} S' \diamond \rho}{S \overset{\ell \cdot tk}{\longrightarrow} S'}$$

$$(\text{NEWLOC})\ \ \frac{tk = tsk(tk, m, l, pp{:}x = \text{new } D; s),\ fresh(\ell'),\ h' = newheap(D),\ l' = l[x \to \ell']}{loc(\ell, tk, h, \mathcal{Q} \cup \{tk\}) \diamond \rho_0 \leadsto loc(\ell, tk, h, \mathcal{Q} \cup \{tsk(tk, m, l', s)\}) \cdot loc(\ell', \bot, h', \{\}) \diamond \rho_0}$$

$$(\text{ASYNC})\ \ \frac{tk = tsk(tk, m, l, pp{:}y{=}x!m_1(\bar{z}); s),\ l(x){=}\ell_1,\ fresh(tk_1),\ l_1{=}buildLocals(\bar{z}, m_1, l)}{\begin{array}{c} loc(\ell, tk, h, \mathcal{Q} \cup \{tk\}) \cdot loc(\ell_1, \_, \_, \mathcal{Q}') \diamond \rho_0 \leadsto loc(\ell, tk, h, \mathcal{Q} \cup \{tsk(tk, m, l, s)\}) \cdot \\ loc(\ell_1, \_, \_, \mathcal{Q}' \cup \{tsk(tk_1, m_1, l_1, body(m_1))\}) \cdot fut(y, o_1, tk_1, ini(m_1)) \diamond \rho_0 \end{array}}$$

$$(\text{RETURN})\ \ \frac{tk = tsk(tk, m, l, pp{:}\text{return}; s),\ \rho_1 = \text{return}}{loc(\ell, tk, h, \mathcal{Q} \cup \{tk\}) \diamond \rho_0 \leadsto loc(\ell, \bot, h, \mathcal{Q} \cup \{tsk(tk, m, l, \epsilon)\}) \diamond \rho_1}$$

$$(\text{AWAIT1})\ \ \frac{tk = tsk(tk, m, l, pp{:}y.\text{await}; s),\ tsk(tk_1, \_, \_, s_1) \in \mathsf{Loc},\ s_1 = \epsilon}{\begin{array}{c} loc(\ell, tk, h, \mathcal{Q} \cup \{tk\}) \cdot fut(y, \_, tk_1, \_) \diamond \rho_0 \leadsto \\ loc(\ell, tk, h, \mathcal{Q} \cup \{tsk(tk, m, l, s)\}) \cdot fut(y, \_, tk_1, \_) \diamond \rho_0 \end{array}}$$

$$(\text{AWAIT2})\ \ \frac{tk = tsk(tk, m, l, pp{:}y.\text{await}; s),\ tsk(tk_1, \_, \_, s_1) \in \mathsf{Loc},\ s_1 \neq \epsilon,\ \rho_1 = pp{:}y.\text{await}}{\begin{array}{c} loc(\ell, tk, h, \mathcal{Q} \cup \{tk\}) \cdot fut(y, \_, tk_1, \_) \diamond \rho_0 \leadsto \\ loc(\ell, \bot, h, \mathcal{Q} \cup \{tk\}) \cdot fut(y, \_, tk_1, \_) \diamond \rho_1 \end{array}}$$

$$(\text{BLOCK1})\ \ \frac{tk = tsk(tk, m, l, pp{:}y.\text{block}; s),\ tsk(tk_1, \_, \_, s_1) \in \mathsf{Loc},\ s_1 = \epsilon}{\begin{array}{c} loc(\ell, tk, h, \mathcal{Q} \cup \{tk\}) \cdot fut(y, \_, tk_1, \_) \diamond \rho_0 \leadsto \\ loc(\ell, tk, h, \mathcal{Q} \cup \{tsk(tk, m, l, s)\}) \cdot fut(y, \_, tk_1, \_) \diamond \rho_0 \end{array}}$$

$$(\text{BLOCK2})\ \ \frac{tk{=}tsk(tk, m, l, pp{:}y.\text{block}; s),\ tsk(tk_1, \_, \_, s_1) \in \mathsf{Loc},\ s_1 \neq \epsilon,\ \rho_1 = pp{:}y.\text{block}}{loc(\ell, tk, h, \mathcal{Q} \cup \{tk\}) \cdot fut(y, \_, tk_1, \_) \diamond \rho_0 \leadsto loc(\ell, tk, h, \mathcal{Q} \cup \{tk\}) \cdot fut(y, \_, tk_1, \_) \diamond \rho_1}$$

Fig. 1. Macro-step semantics of asynchronous programs

task has finished. An asynchronous call $m(\bar{z})$ spawned at location x is associated with a future variable f as follows $f = x\ !\ m(\bar{z})$. Instructions $f.\text{block}$ and $f.\text{await}$ allow, respectively, blocking and non-blocking synchronization with the termination of m. When a task completes, or when it is awaiting with a non-blocking await for a task that has not finished yet, its processor becomes idle again, chooses the next pending task, and so on. The number of distributed locations need not be known a priori (e.g., locations may be virtual). Syntactically, a location will therefore be similar to a *concurrent object* and can be dynamically created using the instruction **new**. The program consists of a set of methods of the form $M{::=}T\ m(\bar{T}\ \bar{x})\{s\}$, where statements s take the form $s{::=}s; s \mid x{=}e \mid \textbf{if } e \textbf{ then } s \textbf{ else } s \mid \textbf{while } e \textbf{ do } s \mid \textbf{return} \mid b = \textbf{new} \mid f = x\ !\ m(\bar{z}) \mid f.\text{await} \mid f.\text{block}$. For the sake of generality, the syntax of expressions e and types T is left open.

Figure 1 presents the semantics of the language. The information about ρ in bold font is part of the extensions for testing in Sect. 4 and should be ignored for now. A *state* or *configuration* is a set of locations and future variables $loc_0 \cdots loc_n \cdot fut_0 \cdots fut_m$. A *location* is a term $loc(\ell, tk, h, \mathcal{Q})$ where ℓ is the location identifier, tk is the identifier of the *active task* that holds the location's lock or $\bot$ if the location's lock is free, h is its local heap, and $\mathcal{Q}$ is the set of tasks in the location. A *future variable* is a term $fut(id, \ell, tk, m)$ where id is a unique future variable identifier, ℓ is the location identifier that executes the task tk awaiting for the future, and m is the initial program point of tk. A *task* is a term $tsk(tk, m, l, s)$ where tk is a unique task identifier, m is the method name executing in the task, l is a mapping from local variables to their values, and s is the sequence of instructions to be executed or ϵ if the task has terminated. We assume that the execution starts from a `main` method without parameters. The initial state is $St = \{loc(0, 0, \bot, \{tsk(0, main, l, body(main))\}$ with an initial location with identifier 0 executing task 0. Here, l maps local variables to their initial values (**null** in case of reference variables) and $\bot$ is the empty heap. $body(m)$ is the sequence of instructions in method m, and we can know the program point pp where an instruction s is in the program as follows $pp{:}s$.

As locations do not share their states, the semantics can be presented as a macro-step semantics [14] (defined by means of the transition "$\longrightarrow$") in which the evaluation of all statements of a task takes place serially (without interleaving with any other task) until it gets to an `await` or `return` instruction. In this case, we apply rule MSTEP to select an available task from a location, namely we apply the function $selectLoc(S)$ to select non-deterministically one *active* location in the state (i.e., a location with a non-empty queue) and $selectTask(\ell)$ to select non-deterministically one task of ℓ's queue. The transition $\rightsquigarrow$ defines the evaluation within a given location. NEWLOC creates a new location without tasks, with a fresh identifier and heap. ASYNC spawns a new task (the initial state is created by $buildLocals$) with a fresh task identifier tk_1, and it adds a new future to the state. $ini(m)$ refers to the first program point of method m. We assume $\ell \neq \ell_1$, but the case $\ell = \ell_1$ is analogous, the new task tk_1 is added to Q of ℓ. The rules for sequential execution are standard and are thus omitted. AWAIT1: If the future variable we are awaiting for points to a finished task, the await can be completed. The finished task t_1 is only looked up but it does not disappear from the state as its status may be needed later on. AWAIT2: Otherwise, the task yields the lock so that any other task of the same location can take it. RETURN: When **return** is executed, the lock is released and will never be taken again by that task. Consequently, that task is *finished* (marked by adding the instruction ϵ). BLOCK2: A y.`block` instruction waits for the future variable but without yielding the lock. Then, when the future is ready, BLOCK1 allows continuing the execution.

In what follows, a *derivation* or *execution* $E \equiv St_0 \longrightarrow \cdots \longrightarrow St_n$ is a sequence of macro-steps (applications of rule MSTEP). The derivation is *complete* if St_0 is the initial state and $\nexists St_{n+1} \neq St_n$ such that $St_n \longrightarrow St_{n+1}$. Since the execution is non-deterministic, multiple derivations are possible from a state. Given a state St, $exec(St)$ denotes the set of all possible derivations starting at St. We sometimes label transitions with $\ell \cdot tk$, the name of the location ℓ and task tk selected (in rule MSTEP) or evaluated in the step (in the transition $\rightsquigarrow$). The systematic exploration of $exec(St)$ thus corresponds to the standard systematic testing setting with no reduction of any kind.

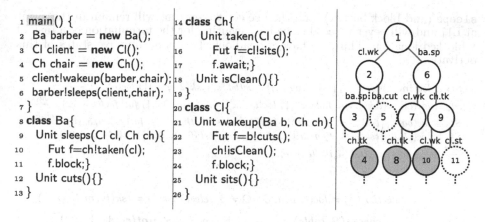

```
1  main() {
2    Ba barber = new Ba();
3    Cl client = new Cl();
4    Ch chair = new Ch();
5    client!wakeup(barber,chair);
6    barber!sleeps(client,chair);
7  }
8  class Ba{
9    Unit sleeps(Cl cl, Ch ch){
10     Fut f=ch!taken(cl);
11     f.block;}
12   Unit cuts(){}
13 }
```

```
14 class Ch{
15   Unit taken(Cl cl){
16     Fut f=cl!sits();
17     f.await;}
18   Unit isClean(){}
19 }
20 class Cl{
21   Unit wakeup(Ba b, Ch ch){
22     Fut f=b!cuts();
23     ch!isClean();
24     f.block;}
25   Unit sits(){}
26 }
```

Fig. 2. Classical sleeping barber problem (left) and execution tree (right)

3 Motivating Example

Our running example is a simple version of the classical sleeping barber problem where a barber sleeps until a client arrives and takes a chair, and the client wakes up the barber to get a haircut. Our implementation in Fig. 2 has a main method shown on the left and three classes Ba, Ch and Cl implementing the barber, chair and client, respectively. The main creates three locations barber, client and chair and spawns two asynchronous tasks to start the wakeup task in the client and sleeps in the barber, both tasks can run in parallel. The execution of sleeps spawns an asynchronous task on the chair to represent the fact that the client takes the chair, and then blocks at line 11 (L11 for short) until the chair is taken. The task taken first adds the task sits on the client, and then awaits on its termination at L17 without blocking, so that another task on the location chair can execute. On the other hand, the execution of wakeup in the client spawns an asynchronous task cuts on the barber and one on the chair, isClean, to check if the chair is clean. The execution of the client blocks until cuts has finished. We assume that all methods have an implicit return at the end.

Figure 2 summarizes the systematic testing tree of the main method by showing some of the macro-steps taken. Derivations that contain a dotted node are not deadlock, while those with a gray node are deadlock. A main motivation of our work is to detect as early as possible that the dotted derivations will not lead us to deadlock and prune them. Let us see two selected derivations in detail. In the derivation ending at node 5, the first macro-step executes cl.wakeup and then ba.cuts. Now, it is clear that the location cl will not deadlock, since the block at L24 will succeed and the other two locations will be also able to complete their tasks, namely the await at L17 of location ch can finish because the client is certainly not blocked, and also the block at L11 will succeed because the task in taken will eventually finish as its location is not blocked. However, in the branch of node 4, we first select wakeup (and block client), then we select

sleeps (and block barber), and then select **taken** that will remain in the await at L17 and will never succeed since it is awaiting for the termination of a task of a blocked location. Thus, we have a deadlock. Let us outline five states of this derivation:

$$St_1 \equiv loc(ini, ..) \cdot loc(cl, .., \{tsk(1, wk, ..)\}) \cdot loc(ba, .., \{tsk(2, sp, ..)\}) \cdot loc(ch, ..) \xrightarrow{cl,1}$$

$$St_2 \equiv loc(cl, .., \{tsk(1, wk, f_0.block)\}) \cdot loc(ba, .., \{tsk(3, cut, ..), ..\}) \cdot fut(f_0, ba, 3, 12) \cdots \xrightarrow{ba,2}$$

$$St_3 \equiv loc(ba, .., \{tsk(2, sp, f_1.block)\}) \cdot loc(ch, .., \{tsk(5, tk, ..), ..\}) \cdot fut(f_1, ch, 5, 15) \cdots \xrightarrow{ch,5}$$

$$St_4 \equiv loc(ch, .., \{tsk(5, tk, f_2.await), ..\}) \cdot loc(cl, .., \{tsk(6, st, ..), ..\}) \cdot fut(f_2, cl, 6, 25) \cdots$$

$$\xrightarrow{ch,4} St_4' \equiv loc(ch, ..\{tsk(4, isClean, \epsilon), ..\}) \cdots$$

$$(\text{MSTEP2}) \quad \frac{\begin{array}{c} selectLoc(S) = loc(\ell, \bot, h, \mathcal{Q}), \mathcal{Q} \neq \emptyset, selectTask(\ell) = tsk(tk, m, l, pp : s), \\ \textbf{check}_\mathcal{C}(S, table), S \diamond \rho_0 \overset{\ell \cdot tk}{\leadsto^*} S' \diamond \rho, S \neq S', \textbf{not}(deadlock(S')) \\ clock(n), table' = table \cup t_{\ell,tk,pp} \mapsto \langle n, \rho \rangle \end{array}}{(S, table) \xrightarrow{\ell \cdot tk} (S', table')}$$

Fig. 3. MSTEP2 rule for combined testing and analysis

The first state is obtained after executing the **main** where we have the initial location *ini*, three locations created at L2, L3 and L4, and two tasks at L5 and L6 added to the queues. Note that each location and task is assigned a unique identifier (we use numbers as identifiers for tasks and short names as identifiers for locations). In the next state, the task **wakeup** has been selected and fully executed (we have shortened the name of the methods, e.g., **wk** for **wakeup**). Observe at St_2 the addition of the future variable created at L22. In St_3 we have executed task **sleeps** in the barber and added a new future term. In St_4 we execute task **taken** in the chair (this state is already deadlock as we will see in Sect. 4.2), however location chair can keep on executing an available task **isClean** generating St_4'. From now on, we use the location and task names instead of numeric identifiers for clarity.

4   Testing for Deadlock Detection

The goal of this section is to present a framework for early detection of deadlocks during systematic testing. This is done by enhancing our standard semantics with information which allows us to easily detect *dependencies* among tasks, i.e., when a task is awaiting for the termination of another one. These dependencies are necessary to detect in a second step *deadlock states*.

4.1   An Enhanced Semantics for Deadlock Detection

In the following we define the *interleavings table* whose role is twofold: (1) It stores all decisions about task interleavings made during the execution. This way, at the end of a concrete execution, the exact ordering of the performed macro-steps can be observed. (2) It will be used to detect deadlocks as early as possible, and, also to detect states from which a deadlock cannot occur, therefore allowing to prune the execution tree when we are looking for deadlocks. The interleavings table is a mapping with entries of the form $t_{\ell,tk,pp} \mapsto \langle n, \rho \rangle$, where:

- $t_{\ell,tk,pp}$ is a *macro-step identifier*, or *time identifier*, that includes: the identifiers of the location ℓ and task tk that have been selected in the macro-step, and the program point pp of the first instruction that will be executed;
- n is an integer representing the time when the macro-step starts executing;
- ρ is the status of the task after the macro-step and it can take three values as it can be seen in Fig. 1: block or await when executing these instructions on a future variable that is not ready (we also annotate in ρ the information on the associated future); return that allows us to know that the task finished.

We use a function $clock(n)$ to represent a clock that starts at 0, is increased by one in every execution of $clock$, and returns the current value $\mathbf{n}$. The initial entry is $t_{0,0,1} \mapsto \langle 0, \rho_0 \rangle$, 0 being the identifier for the initial location and task, and 1 the first program point of *main*. The clock also assigns the value 0 as the first element in the tuple and a fresh variable in the second element ρ_0. The next macro-step will be assigned clock value 1, next 2, and so on. As notation, we define the relation $t \in table$ if there exists an entry $t \mapsto \langle n, \rho \rangle \in table$, and the function $status(t, table)$ which returns the status ρ_t such that $t \mapsto \langle n, \rho_t \rangle \in table$. The semantics is extended by changing rule MSTEP as in Fig. 3. The function deadlock will be defined in Theorem 1 to stop derivations as soon as deadlock is detected. Function check$_{\mathcal{C}}$ should be ignored for now, it will be defined in Sect. 5.2. Essentially, there are two new aspects: (1) The state is extended with the status ρ, namely all rules include a status ρ attached to the state using the symbol $\diamond$. The status is showed in bold font in Fig. 1 and can get a value in rules block2, await2 and return. The initial value ρ_0 is a fresh variable. (2) The state for the macrostep is extended with the interleavings table *table*, and a new entry $t_{\ell,tk,pp} \mapsto \langle n, \rho \rangle$ is added to *table* in every macrostep if there has been progress in the execution, i.e., $S' \neq S$, n being the current clock time.

Example 1. The interleavings table below (left) is computed for the derivation in Sect. 3. It has as many entries as macro-steps in the derivation. We can observe that subsequent time values are assigned to each time identifier so that we can then know the order of execution. The right column shows the future variables in the state that store the location and task they are bound to.

St_1	$t_{ini,main,1} \mapsto \langle 0, return \rangle$	$\emptyset$
St_2	$t_{cl,wakeup,21} \mapsto \langle 1, 24{:}f_0.block \rangle$	$fut(f_0, ba, cuts, 12)$
St_3	$t_{ba,sleeps,9} \mapsto \langle 2, 11{:}f_1.block \rangle$	$fut(f_1, ch, taken, 15)$
St_4	$t_{ch,taken,15} \mapsto \langle 3, 17{:}f_2.await \rangle$	$fut(f_2, cl, sits, 25)$

4.2   Formal Characterization of Deadlock State

Our semantics can easily be extended to detect deadlock just by redefining function *selectLoc* so that only locations that can proceed are selected. If, at a given state, no location is selected but there is at least a location with a non-empty queue then there is a deadlock. However, deadlocks can be detected earlier. We present the notion of *deadlock state* which characterizes states that contain a *deadlock chain* in which one or more tasks are waiting for each other's termination and none of them can make any progress. Note that, from a deadlock state, there might be tasks that keep on progressing until the deadlock is finally made explicit. Even more, if one of those tasks runs into an infinite loop, the deadlock will not be captured using this naive extension. The early detection of deadlocks is crucial to reduce state exploration as our experiments show in Sect. 6.

We first introduce the auxiliary notion of *waiting interval* which captures the period in which a task is waiting for another one to terminate. In particular, it is defined as a tuple $(t_{stop}, t_{async}, t_{resume})$ where t_{stop} is the macro-step at which the location stops executing a task due to some block/await instruction, t_{async} is the macro-step at which the task that is being awaited is selected for execution, and, t_{resume} is the macro-step at which the task will resume its execution. t_{stop}, t_{async} and t_{resume} are time identifiers as defined in Sect. 4.1. t_{resume} will also be written as $next(t_{stop})$. When the task stops at t_{stop} due to a block instruction, we call it *blocking interval*, as the location remains blocked between t_{stop} and $next(t_{stop})$ until the awaited task, selected in t_{async}, has already finished. The execution of a task can have several points at which macro-steps are performed (e.g., if it contains several await or block the processor may be lost several times). For this reason, we define the set of successor macro-steps of the same task from a macro-step: $suc(t_{\ell, tk, pp_0}, table) = \{t_{\ell, tk, pp_i} : t_{\ell, tk, pp_i} \in table, t_{\ell, tk, pp_i} \geq t_{\ell, tk, pp_0}\}$.

Definition 1 (Waiting/Blocking Intervals). *Let $St = (S, table)$ be a state, $I = (t_{stop}, t_{async}, t_{resume})$ is a waiting interval of St, written as $I \in St$, iff:*

1. $\exists\ t_{stop} = t_{\ell, tk_0, pp_0} \in table,\ \rho_{stop} = status(t_{stop}) \in \{pp_1 : x.\texttt{await}, pp_1 : x.\texttt{block}\}$,
2. $t_{resume} \equiv t_{\ell, tk_0, pp_1},\ fut(x, \ell_x, tk_x, pp(M)) \in S$,
3. $t_{async} \equiv t_{\ell_x, tk_x, pp(M)}, \nexists\ t \in suc(t_{async}, table)$ *with* $status(t) = return$.

If $\rho_{stop} = x.\texttt{block}$, then I is blocking.

In condition 3, we can see that if the task starting at t_{async} has finished, then it is not a waiting interval. This is known by checking that this task has not reached return, i.e., $\nexists\ t \in suc(t_{async}, table)$ such that $status(t) = return$. In condition 1, we see that in ρ_{stop} we have the name of the future we are awaiting (whose corresponding information is stored in fut, condition 2). In order to define t_{resume} in condition 2, we search for the same task tk_0 and same location ℓ that executes the task starting at program point pp_1 of the await/block, since this is the point that the macro-step rule uses to define the macro-step identifier t_{ℓ, tk_0, pp_1} associated to the resumption of the waiting task.

Example 2. Let us consider again the derivation in Sect. 3. We have the following blocking interval $(t_{cl,wakeup,21}, t_{ba,cuts,12}, t_{cl,wakeup,24}) \in St_2$ with $St_2 \equiv (S_2, table_2)$, since $t_{cl,wakeup,21} \in table_2$, $status(t_{cl,wakeup,21}, table_2) = [24{:}f.\texttt{block}]$, $(f, ba, cuts, 12) \in St_2$ and $t_{ba,cuts,12} \notin table_2$. This blocking interval captures the fact that the task at $t_{cl,wakeup,21}$ is blocked waiting for task *cuts* to terminate. Similarly, we have the following two intervals in St_4: $(t_{ba,sleeps,9}, t_{ch,taken,15}, t_{ba,sleeps,11})$ and $(t_{ch,taken,15}, t_{cl,sits,25}, t_{ch,taken,17})$.

The following notion of *deadlock chain* relies on the waiting/blocking intervals of Definition 1 in order to characterize chains of calls in which intuitively each task is waiting for the next one to terminate until the last one which is waiting on the termination of a task executing on the initial location (that is blocked). Given a time identifier t, we use $loc(t)$ to obtain its associated location identifier.

Definition 2 (Deadlock Chain). *Let $St = (S, table)$ be a state. A chain of time identifiers $t_0, ..., t_n$ is a* deadlock chain *in St, written as $dc(t_0, ..., t_n)$ iff $\forall t_i \in \{t_0, ..., t_{n-1}\}$ s.t. $(t_i, t'_{i+1}, next(t_i)) \in St$ one of the following conditions holds:*

1. $t_{i+1} \in suc(t'_{i+1}, table)$, or
2. $loc(t'_{i+1}) = loc(t_{i+1})$ and $(t_{i+1}, \_, next(t_{i+1}))$ is blocking.
and for t_n, we have that $t_{n+1} \equiv t_0$, and condition 2 holds.

Let us explain the two conditions in the above definition: In condition (1), we check that when a task t_i is waiting for another task to terminate, the waiting interval contains the initial time t'_{i+1} in which the task will be selected. However, we look for any waiting interval for this task t_{i+1} (thus we check that t_{i+1} is a successor of time t'_{i+1}). As in Definition 2, this is because such task may have started its execution and then suspended due to a subsequent await/block instruction. Abusing terminology, we use the time identifier to refer to the task executing. In condition (2), we capture deadlock chains which occur when a task t_i is waiting on the termination of another task t'_{i+1} which executes on a location $loc(t'_{i+1})$ which is blocked. The fact that is blocked is captured by checking that there is a blocking interval from a task t_{i+1} executing on this location. Finally, note the circularity of the chain, since we require that $t_{n+1} \equiv t_0$.

Theorem 1 (Deadlock state). *A state St is deadlock, written* **deadlock**(S), *if and only if there is a deadlock chain in St.*

Derivations ending in a deadlock state are considered complete derivations. We prove that our definition of deadlock is equivalent to the standard definition of deadlock in [6] (proof can be found in [16]).

Example 3. Following Example 1, St_4 is a deadlock state since there exists a *deadlock chain* $dc(t_{cl,wakeup,21}, t_{ba,sleeps,9}, t_{ch,taken,15})$. For the second element in the chain $t_{ba,sleeps,9}$, condition 1 holds as $(t_{ba,sleeps,9}, t_{ch,taken,15}, t_{ba,sleeps,11}) \in St_4$ and $t_{ch,taken,15} \in suc(t_{ch,taken,15}, table_4)$. For the first element

$t_{cl,wakeup,21}$, condition 2 holds since $(t_{cl,wakeup,21}, t_{ba,cuts,12}, t_{cl,wakeup,24}) \in St_4$ and $(t_{ba,sleeps,9}, t_{ch,taken,15},\ t_{ba,sleeps,11})$ is blocking. Condition 2 holds analogously for $t_{ch,taken,15}$.

5 Combining Static Deadlock Analysis and Testing

This section proposes a deadlock detection methodology that combines static analysis and systematic testing as follows. First, a state-of-the-art deadlock analysis is run, in particular that of [6], which provides a set of abstractions of potential *deadlock cycles*. If the set is empty, then the program is deadlock-free. Otherwise, using the inferred set of deadlock cycles, we systematically test the program using a novel technique to guide the exploration towards paths that might lead to deadlock cycles. The goals of this process are: (1) finding concrete deadlock traces associated to the feasible cycles, and, (2) discarding unfeasible deadlock cycles, and in case all cycles are discarded, ensure deadlock freedom for the considered input or, in our case, for the `main` method under test. As our experiments show in Sect. 6, our technique allows reducing significantly the search space compared to the full systematic exploration.

5.1 Deadlock Analysis and Abstract Deadlock Cycles

The deadlock analysis of [6] returns a set of abstract deadlock cycles of the form $e_1 \xrightarrow{p_1:tk_1} e_2 \xrightarrow{p_2:tk_2} ... \xrightarrow{p_n:tk_n} e_1$, where $p_1,...,p_n$ are program points, $tk_1,...,tk_n$ are *task abstractions*, and nodes $e_1,...,e_n$ are either *location abstractions* or task abstractions. Three kinds of arrows can be distinguished, namely, *task-task* (a task is awaiting for the termination of another one), *task-location* (a task is awaiting for a location to be idle) and *location-task* (the location is blocked due the task). *Location-location* arrows cannot happen. The abstractions for tasks and locations can be performed at different levels of accuracy during the analysis: the simple abstraction that we will use for our formalization abstracts each concrete location ℓ by the program point at which it is created ℓ_{pp}, and each task by the method name executing. They are abstractions since there could be many locations created at the same program point and many tasks executing the same method. Both the analysis and the semantics can be made *object-sensitive* by keeping the k ancestor abstract locations (where k is a parameter of the analysis). For the sake of simplicity of the presentation, we assume $k = 0$ in the formalization (our implementation uses $k = 1$).

Example 4. In our working example there are three abstract locations, ℓ_2, ℓ_3 and ℓ_4, corresponding to locations barber, client and chair, created at lines 2, 3 and 4; and six abstract tasks, *sleeps*, *cuts*, *wakeup*, *sits*, *taken* and *isClean*. The following cycle is inferred by the deadlock analysis: $\ell_2 \xrightarrow{11:sleeps} taken \xrightarrow{17:taken} sits \xrightarrow{25:sits} \ell_3 \xrightarrow{24:wakeup} cuts \xrightarrow{12:cuts} \ell_2$. The first arrow captures that the location created at L2 is blocked waiting for the termination of task `taken` because of the synchronization at L11 of task `sleeps`. Observe that cycles contain dependencies also between tasks, like the second arrow, where we capture that `taken` is waiting for `sits`. Also, a dependency between a task (e.g., `sits`) and a location (e.g., ℓ_3) captures that the task is trying to execute on that (possibly) blocked location. Abstract deadlock cycles can be provided by the analyzer to the user. But, as it can observed, it is complex to figure out from them why these dependencies arise, and in particular the interleavings scheduled to lead to this situation.

5.2   Guiding Testing Towards Deadlock Cycles

Given an abstract deadlock cycle, we now present a novel technique to guide the systematic execution towards paths that might contain a representative of that abstract deadlock cycle, by discarding paths that are guaranteed not to contain such a representative. The main idea is as follows: (1) From the abstract dead-lock cycle, we generate *deadlock-cycle constraints*, which must hold in all states of derivations leading to the given deadlock cycle. (2) We extend the execution semantics to support deadlock-cycle constraints, with the aim of stopping derivations as soon as cycle-constraints are not satisfied. Uppercase letters in constraints denote variables to allow representing incomplete information.

Definition 3 (Deadlock-cycle constraints). *Given a state $St = (S, table)$, a deadlock-cycle constraint takes one of the following three forms:*

1. *$\exists t_{L,T,PP} \mapsto \langle N, \rho \rangle$, which means that there exists or will exist an entry of this form in table (*time constraint*)*
2. *$\exists fut(F, L, Tk, p)$, which means that there exists or will exist a future variable of this form in S (*fut constraint*)*
3. *$\mathsf{pending}(Tk)$, which means that task Tk has not finished (*pending constraint*)*

The following function ϕ computes the set of deadlock-cycle constraints associated to a given abstract deadlock cycle.

Definition 4 (Generation of deadlock-cycle constraints). *Given an abstract deadlock cycle $e_1 \xrightarrow{p_1:tk_1} e_2 \xrightarrow{p_2:tk_2} \ldots \xrightarrow{p_n:tk_n} e_1$, and two fresh variables L_i, Tk_i, ϕ is defined as $\phi(e_i \xrightarrow{p_i:tk_i} e_j \xrightarrow{p_j:tk_j} \ldots, L_i, Tk_i) =$*

$$
\begin{cases}
\{\exists t_{L_i, Tk_i, \_} \mapsto \langle \_, \mathsf{sync}(p_i, F_i) \rangle, \exists fut(F_i, L_j, Tk_j, p_j)\} \cup \phi(e_j \xrightarrow{p_j:tk_j} \ldots, L_j, Tk_j) & \text{if } e_j = tk_j \\
\{\mathsf{pending}(Tk_i)\} \cup \phi(e_j \xrightarrow{p_j:tk_j} \ldots, L_i, Tk_j) & \text{if } e_j = \ell
\end{cases}
$$

Notation $\mathsf{sync}(p_i, F_i)$ is a shortcut for $p_i:F_i.\mathtt{block}$ or $p_i:F_i.\mathtt{await}$. Uppercase letters appearing for the first time in the constraints are fresh variables. The first case handles location-task and task-task arrows (since e_j is a task abstraction), whereas the second case handles task-location arrows (e_j is an abstract location). Let us observe the following: (1) The abstract location and task identifiers of the abstract cycle are not used to produce the constraints. This is because constraints refer to concrete identifiers. Even if the cycle contains the same identifier on two different nodes or arrows, the corresponding variables in the constraints cannot be bound (i.e., we cannot use the same variables) since they could refer to different concrete identifiers. (2) The program points of the cycle (p_i and p_j) are used in time and fut constraints. (3) Location and task identifier variables of fut constraints and subsequent time or pending constraints are bound (i.e., the same variables are used). This is done using the 2nd and 3rd parameters of function ϕ. (4) In the second case, Tk_j is a fresh variable since the location executing Tk_i can be blocked due to a (possibly) different task. Intuitively, deadlock-cycle constraints characterize all possible deadlock chains representing the given cycle.

Example 5. The following deadlock-cycle constraints are computed for the cycle in Example 4: $\{\exists t_{L_1,Tk_1,\_} \mapsto \langle\_, 11{:}F_1.block\rangle, \exists fut(F_1, L_2, Tk_2, 15), \exists t_{L_2,Tk_2,\_} \mapsto \langle\_,$ $17{:}F_2.await\rangle, \exists fut(F_2, L_3, Tk_3, 25), \mathsf{pending}(Tk_3), \exists t_{L_3,Tk_4,\_} \mapsto \langle\_, 24{:}F_3.block\rangle, \exists$ $fut(F_3, L_4, Tk_5, 12), \mathsf{pending}(Tk_5)\}$. They are shown in the order in which they are computed by ϕ. The first four constraints require *table* to contain a concrete time in which *some* barber sleeps waiting at L11 for a *certain* chair to be taken at L15 and, during another concrete time, this one waits at L17 for a *certain* client to sit at L25. The client is not allowed to sit by the 5th constraint. Furthermore, the last three constraints require a concrete time in which *this* client waits at L24 to get a haircut by *some* barber at L12 and that haircut is never performed. Note that, in order to preserve completeness, we are not binding the first and the second barber. If the example is generalized with several clients and barbers, there could be a deadlock in which a barber waits for a client which waits for another barber and client, so that the last one waits to get a haircut by the first one. This deadlock would not be found if the two barbers are bound in the constraints (i.e., if we use the same variable name). In other words, we have to account for deadlocks which traverse the abstract cycle more than once.

The idea now is to monitor the execution using the inferred deadlock-cycle constraints for the given cycle, with the aim of stopping derivations at states that do not satisfy the constraints. The following boolean function $\mathsf{check}_{\mathfrak{C}}$ checks the satisfiability of the constraints at a given state.

Definition 5. *Given a set of deadlock-cycle constraints $\mathfrak{C}$, and a state $St = (S, table)$, check holds, written $\mathsf{check}_{\mathfrak{C}}(St)$, if $\forall t_{L_i,Tk_i,PP} \mapsto \langle N, \mathsf{sync}(p_i, F_i)\rangle \in \mathfrak{C}, fut(F_i, L_j, Tk_j, p_j) \in \mathfrak{C}$, one of the following conditions holds:*

1. $\mathsf{reachable}(t_{L_i,Tk_i,p_i}, S)$
2. $\exists t_{\ell_i,tk_i,pp} \mapsto \langle n, \mathsf{sync}(p_i, f_i)\rangle \in table \wedge fut(f_i, \ell_j, tk_j, p_j) \in S \wedge$
   $(\mathsf{pending}(Tk_j) \in \mathfrak{C} \Rightarrow \mathsf{getTskSeq}(tk_j, S) \neq \epsilon)$

Function $\mathsf{reachable}$ checks whether a given task might arise in subsequent states. We over-approximate it syntactically by computing the transitive call relations from all tasks in the queues of all locations in S. Precision could be improved using more advanced analyses. Function $\mathsf{getTskSeq}$ gets from the state the sequence of instructions to be executed by a task (which is ϵ if the task has terminated). Intuitively, check does not hold if there is at least a time constraint so that: (i) its time identifier is not reachable, and, (ii) in the case that the interleavings table contains entries matching it, for each one, there is an associated future variable in the state and a pending constraint for its associated task which is violated, i.e., the associated task has finished. The first condition (i) implies that there cannot be more representatives of the given abstract cycle in subsequent states, therefore if there are potential deadlock cycles, the associated time identifiers must be in the interleavings table. The second condition (ii) implies that, for each potential cycle in the state, there is no deadlock chain since at least one of the blocking tasks has finished. This means there cannot be derivations from this state leading to the given cycle, hence the derivation can be stopped.

Definition 6 (Deadlock-cycle guided-testing (DCGT)). *Consider an abstract deadlock cycle c, and an initial state St_0. Let $\mathfrak{C} = \phi(c, L_{init}, Tk_{init})$ with L_{init}, Tk_{init} fresh variables. We define DCGT, written $exec_c(St_0)$, as the set $\{d : d \in exec(St_0), deadlock(St_n)\}$, where St_n is the last state in d.*

Example 6. Let us consider the DCGT of our working example with the deadlock-cycle of Example 4, and hence with the constraints $\mathfrak{C}$ of Example 5. The interleavings table at St_5 contains the entries $t_{ini,main,1} \mapsto \langle 0, return \rangle$, $t_{cl,wakeup,21} \mapsto \langle 1, 24 : f_0.block \rangle$ and $t_{ba,cuts,12} \mapsto \langle 2, return \rangle\}$. check$_{\mathfrak{C}}$ does not hold since $t_{L_1,Tk_1,24}$ is not reachable from St_5 and constraint pending(Tk_5) is violated (task *cuts* has already finished at this point). The derivation is hence pruned. Similarly, the rightmost derivation is stopped at St_{11}. Also, derivations at St_4, St_8 and St_{10} are stopped by function deadlock of Theorem 1. Since there are no more deadlock cycles, the search for deadlock detection finishes with this DCGT. Our methodology therefore explores 19 states instead of the 181 explored by the full systematic execution.

Theorem 2 (Soundness). *Given a program P, a set of abstract cycles C in P and an initial state St_0, $\forall d \in exec(St_0)$ if d is a derivation whose last state is deadlock, then $\exists c \in C$ s.t $d \in exec_c(St_0)$. (The proof can be found in App. A)*

6 Experimental Evaluation

We have implemented our approach within the SYCO tool, a testing tool for *concurrent objects* which is available at http://costa.ls.fi.upm.es/syco, where most of the benchmarks below can also be found. Concurrent objects communicate via *asynchronous* method calls and use `await` and `block`, resp., as instructions for non-blocking and blocking synchronization. This section summarizes our experimental results which aim at demonstrating the effectiveness and impact of the proposed techniques. The benchmarks we have used include: (i) classical concurrency patterns containing deadlocks, namely, *SB* is an extension of the sleeping barber, *UL* is a loop that creates asynchronous tasks and locations, *PA* is the pairing problem, *FA* is a distributed factorial, *WM* is the water molecule making problem, *HB* the hungry birds problem; and, (ii) deadlock free versions of some of the above, named *fX* for the *X* problem, for which deadlock analyzers give false positives. We also include here a peer-to-peer system *P2P*.

Table 1 shows, for each benchmark, the results of our deadlock guided testing (DGT) methodology for finding a representative trace for each deadlock compared to those of the standard systematic testing. Partial-order reduction techniques are not applied since they are orthogonal. This way we focus on the reductions obtained due to our technique per-se. For the systematic testing setting we measure: the number of solutions or complete derivations (column Ans), the total time taken (column T) and the number of states generated (column S). For the DGT setting, besides the time and number of states (columns T and S), we measure the "number of deadlock executions"/"number of unfeasible cycles"/"number of abstract cycles inferred by the deadlock analysis" (column $D/U/C$), and, since the DCGTs for each cycle are independent and can be performed in parallel, we show the maximum time and maximum number of states measured among the different DCGTs (columns T_{max} and S_{max}). For instance, in the DGT for HB the analysis has found five abstract cycles, we only found a deadlock execution for two of them (therefore 3 of them were unfeasible), $44\,s$ being the total time of the process, and $15\,s$ the time of the longest DCGT (including the time of the deadlock analysis) and hence the total time assuming an ideal parallel setting with 5 processors. Columns in the group **Speedup** show the gains of DGT over systematic testing both assuming a sequential setting, hence considering values T and S of DGT (column T_{gain} for time and S_{gain} for number of states), and an ideal parallel setting, therefore considering T_{max} and S_{max} (columns T_{gain}^{max} and S_{gain}^{max}). The gains are computed as X/Y, X being the measure of systematic testing and Y that of DGT. Times are in milliseconds and are obtained on an Intel(R) Core(TM) i7 CPU at 2.3 GHz with 8 GB of RAM, running Mac OS X 10.8.5. A timeout of 150 s is used. When the timeout is reached, we write $>X$ to indicate that for the corresponding measure we have got X units in the timeout. In the case of the speedups, $>X$ indicates that the speedup would be X if the process finishes right in the timeout, and hence it is guaranteed to be greater than X. Also, we write X^* when DGT times out.

Our experiments support our claim that testing complements deadlock analysis. In the case of programs with deadlock, we have been able to provide concrete traces for feasible deadlock cycles and to discard unfeasible cycles. For deadlock-free programs, we have been able to discard all potential cycles and therefore prove deadlock freedom. More importantly, the experiments demonstrate that our DGT methodology achieves a notable reduction of the search space over systematic testing in most cases. Except for benchmarks HB and WM which are explained below, the gains of DGT both in time and number of states are enormous (more than three orders of magnitude in many cases). It can be observed that the gains are much larger in the examples in which the deadlock analysis does not give false positives (namely, in SB, UL and PA). In general, the generated constraints for unfeasible cycles are often not able to guide the exploration effectively (e.g. in HB and WM). Even in these cases, DGT outperforms systematic testing in terms of scalability and flexibility. Let us also observe that the gains are less notable in deadlock-free examples. That is because, each DCGT

Table 1. Experimental results: deadlock-guided testing vs. systematic testing

Bm.	Systematic			DGT (deadlock-per-cycle)					Speedup			
	Ans	T	S	$D/U/C$	T	T_{max}	S	S_{max}	T_{gain}	S_{gain}	T^{max}_{gain}	S^{max}_{gain}
HB	35k	32k	114k	2/3/5	44k	15k	103k	34k	0.73	0.9	2.15	3.33
FA	11k	11k	41k	2/1/3	2k	759	3k	2k	5.5	13.7	15.1	22.2
UL	>90k	>150k	>489k	1/0/1	133	133	5	5	>1.1k	>2.5k	>2.5k	>98k
SB	>103k	>150k	>584k	1/0/1	59	59	23	23	>2.5k	>25k	>2.5k	>25k
PA	>121k	>150k	>329k	2/0/2	42	4	12	6	>3.6k	>27k	>38k	>55k
WM	>82k	>150k	>380k	1/0/2	>150k	>150k	>258k	>258k	1*	1.47*	1*	1.47*
fFA	5k	7k	25k	0/1/1	5k	5k	11k	11k	1.61	2.35	1.61	2.35
fP2P	25k	66k	118k	0/1/1	34k	34k	52k	52k	1.96	2.28	1.96	2.28
fPA	7k	7k	30k	0/2/2	4k	2k	9k	4k	1.75	3.33	3.73	6.98
fUL	>102k	>150k	>527k	0/1/1	410	410	236	236	>1k	>2k	>1k	>2k

cannot stop until all potential deadlock paths have been considered. As expected, when we consider a parallel setting, the gains are much larger.

All in all, we argue that our experiments show that our methodology complements deadlock analysis, finding deadlock traces for the potential deadlock cycles and discarding unfeasible ones, with a significant reduction.

7   Conclusions and Related Work

There is a large body of work on deadlock detection including both dynamic and static approaches. Much of the existing work, both for asynchronous programs [6,7] and thread-based programs [11,13], is based on static analysis techniques. Static analysis can ensure the absence of errors, however it works on approximations (especially for pointer aliasing) which might lead to a "don't know" answer. Our work complements static analysis techniques and can be used to look for deadlock paths when static analysis is not able to prove deadlock freedom. Using our method, we try to find a deadlock by exploring the paths given by our deadlock detection algorithm that relies on the static information.

Deadlock detection has been also studied in the context of dynamic testing and model checking [4,9,10,15], where sometimes has been combined with static information [2,8]. As regards combined approaches, the approach in [8] first performs a transformation of the program into a trace program that only keeps the instructions that are relevant for deadlock and then dynamic testing is performed on such program. The approach is fundamentally different from ours: in their case, since model checking is performed on the trace program (that over-approximates the deadlock behaviour), the method can detect deadlocks that do not exist in the program, while in our case this is not possible since the testing is performed on the original program and the analysis information is only used to drive the execution. In [2], the information inferred from a type system is used to accelerate the detection of potential cycles. This work shares with our work that information inferred statically is used to improve the performance of the testing tool, however there are important differences: first, their method developed for Java threads captures deadlocks due to the use of locks and cannot handle wait-notify, while our technique is not developed for specific patterns but works on a general characterization of deadlock of asynchronous programs; their underlying static analysis is a type inference algorithm which infers deadlock types and the checking algorithm needs to understand these types to take advantage of them, while we base our method on an analysis which infers descriptions of chains of tasks and a formal semantics is enriched to interpret them.

References

1. Abdulla, P., Aronis, S., Jonsson, B., Sagonas, K.F.: Optimal dynamic partial order reduction. In: Proceedings of POPL 2014, pp. 373–384. ACM (2014)
2. Agarwal, R., Wang, L., Stoller, S.D.: Detecting potential deadlocks with static analysis and run-time monitoring. In: Ur, S., Bin, E., Wolfsthal, Y. (eds.) HVC 2005. LNCS, vol. 3875, pp. 191–207. Springer, Heidelberg (2006)
3. Albert, E., Arenas, P., Gómez-Zamalloa, M.: Actor- and task-selection strategies for pruning redundant state-exploration in testing. In: Ábrahám, E., Palamidessi, C. (eds.) FORTE 2014. LNCS, vol. 8461, pp. 49–65. Springer, Heidelberg (2014)
4. Christakis, M., Gotovos, A., Sagonas, K.F.: Systematic testing for detecting concurrency errors in erlang programs. In: ICST 2013, pp. 154–163. IEEE (2013)
5. Flanagan, C., Godefroid, P.: Dynamic partial-order reduction for model checking software. In: Proceedings POPL 2005, pp. 110–121. ACM (2005)
6. Flores-Montoya, A.E., Albert, E., Genaim, S.: May-happen-in-parallel based deadlock analysis for concurrent objects. In: Beyer, D., Boreale, M. (eds.) FORTE 2013 and FMOODS 2013. LNCS, vol. 7892, pp. 273–288. Springer, Heidelberg (2013)
7. Giachino, E., Grazia, C.A., Laneve, C., Lienhardt, M., Wong, P.Y.H.: Deadlock analysis of concurrent objects: theory and practice. In: Johnsen, E.B., Petre, L. (eds.) IFM 2013. LNCS, vol. 7940, pp. 394–411. Springer, Heidelberg (2013)
8. Joshi, P., Naik, M., Sen, K., Gay, D.: An effective dynamic analysis for detecting generalized deadlocks. In: Proceedings of FSE 2010, pp. 327–336. ACM (2010)
9. Joshi, P., Park, C., Sen, K., Naik, M.: A randomized dynamic program analysis technique for detecting real deadlocks. In: Proceedings of PLDI 2009. ACM (2009)
10. Kheradmand, A., Kasikci, B., Candea, G.: Lockout: efficient testing for deadlock bugs. Technical report (2013)
11. Masticola, S.P., Ryder, B.G.: A model of ada programs for static deadlock detection in polynomial time. In: Parallel and Distributed Debugging. ACM (1991)
12. Naik, M., Park, C., Sen, K., Gay, D.: Effective static deadlock detection. In: Proceedings of ICSE, pp. 386–396. IEEE (2009)
13. Savage, S., Burrows, M., Nelson, G., Sobalvarro, P., Anderson, T.E.: Eraser: a dynamic data race detector for multithreaded programs. ACM TCS 15(4), 391–411 (1997)
14. Sen, K., Agha, G.: Automated systematic testing of open distributed programs. In: Baresi, L., Heckel, R. (eds.) FASE 2006. LNCS, vol. 3922, pp. 339–356. Springer, Heidelberg (2006)
15. Havelund, K.: Using runtime analysis to guide model checking of java programs. In: Havelund, K., Penix, J., Visser, W. (eds.) SPIN 2000. LNCS, vol. 1885, pp. 245–264. Springer, Heidelberg (2000)
16. Albert, E., Gómez-Zamalloa, M., et al.: Combining Static Analysis and Testing for Deadlock Detection. In: Ábrahám, E., Huisman, M. (eds.) IFM 2016. LNCS, vol. 9681, pp. 409–424. Springer, Heidelberg (2016). http://costa.ls.fi.upm.es/papers/costa/AlbertGI15.pdf

Fuzzing JavaScript Engine APIs

Renáta Hodován[(✉)] and Ákos Kiss

Department of Software Engineering, University of Szeged,
Dugonics tér 13., 6720 Szeged, Hungary
{hodovan,akiss}@inf.u-szeged.hu

Abstract. JavaScript is one of the most wide-spread programming languages: it drives the web applications in browsers, it runs on server side, and it gets to the embedded world as well. Because of its prevalence, ensuring the correctness of its execution engines is highly important. One of the hardest parts to test in an execution environment is the API exposed by the engine. Thus, we focus on fuzz testing of JavaScript engine APIs in this paper. We formally define a graph representation that is suited to describe type information in an engine, explain how to build such graphs, and describe how to use them for API fuzz testing. Our experimental evaluation of the techniques on a real-life in-use JavaScript engine shows that the introduced approach gives better coverage than available existing fuzzing techniques and could also find valid issues in the tested system.

1 Introduction

JavaScript (standardized as ECMAScript [3] but rarely referred to by that name) is the de-facto standard programming language of web browsers, which have evolved into one of the most important application platforms of our days – in which evolution the language played a major role. However, it is not only the client side of the web where JavaScript spreads: it is gaining popularity in server-side scripting as well, thanks to the Node.js framework[1]. And recently JavaScript has penetrated the embedded world as well: several engines (e.g., Duktape[2], JerryScript[3]) and frameworks (e.g., IoT.js[4]) emerged that enable the programming of highly resource-constrained Internet-of-Things devices in JavaScript. Because of the prevalence of the language, ensuring the correctness of its execution engines – both functionally and security-wise – is of paramount importance.

One testing method that has a special focus on security is fuzzing [11] – or fuzz testing, random testing. In fuzzing, a so-called test generator produces totally random or partially randomized ('fuzzed') test inputs in a great volume, which

---

[1] https://nodejs.org/.
[2] http://duktape.org/.
[3] http://www.jerryscript.net/.
[4] http://www.iotjs.net/.

© Springer International Publishing Switzerland 2016
E. Ábrahám and M. Huisman (Eds.): IFM 2016, LNCS 9681, pp. 425–438, 2016.
DOI: 10.1007/978-3-319-33693-0_27

are then given to a program (or system-under-test, SUT) for processing in the hope that some of them cause malfunction. The most easily recognizable errors are crashes, assertion failures, and unhandled exceptions, since they certainly signal a design flaw in the application – quite often flaws that can be exploited by a malicious attacker. Since fuzzing has the potential of uncovering such errors, the technique is often used in internal security testing processes [8].

For a random test generation approach to be useful in practice, it should be able to reach as 'deep' in the SUT as possible, i.e., generate test inputs that are not discarded by early correctness (e.g., syntax or CRC) checks. For some input formats or SUTs, even the simplest, random byte sequence generation or existing test mutation (e.g., bit flipping) techniques may give satisfying results, but as the format gets stricter such approaches tend to scratch the surface of the SUT only. This is the case with JavaScript, too: even fuzzers with knowledge about the language syntax (e.g., AST mutators or grammar-based generators) are mostly exercising the parser of the engine-under-test only (i.e., whether language constructs are correctly recognized and transformed into internal representation). The reason for this is that the execution of these fuzzed inputs often fails because of mismatch between the generated operations and operands.

This is especially true for the application programming interfaces (APIs) exposed by the engines: there are requirements regarding what method can be invoked on what object with which arguments. Gathering this information manually from the standards is both burdensome and error prone. Moreover, both because of different stages in the implementation of (different versions of) the standard and because of different application domains (e.g., web browsers, server side, command line), the APIs exposed by existing engines differ (and will change as they evolve). Thus, automatic means for modeling the exposed API are heavily needed.

Existing approaches [1,10] that try to infer information – e.g., a type system – about JavaScript, however, work on user source code. Since the execution engine itself is rarely written in JavaScript, these methods cannot be used for engine analysis. To deal with the issues outlined above, we present three major novel contributions in this paper: first, we define a graph-based type representation that is suited to describe the API of a JavaScript execution engine with different precisions, then we describe two methods how to build such a graph, and finally, we show an application of the graph representation, i.e., how it can be used in fuzzing.

The rest of the paper is organized as follows: Sect. 2 gives the formal definition of the graph used throughout the paper. Section 3 formalizes API fuzzing based on the introduced graph representation. Section 4 outlines two automated methods to infer information about the API of an engine. Section 5 presents experimental results from a prototype implementation of the graph representation, the analyses, and the fuzzing technique. Section 6 discusses related work, and finally, Sect. 7 concludes the paper and forecasts future work.

2   Graph Representation of Type Information in JavaScript

It is a commonly known feature of JavaScript that although it has the concept of objects, it lacks a strong type system. Some kind of inheritance exists, mimiced by prototypes, but it is a relation between individual objects however. And theoretically, each object can be significantly different in terms of its prototype and members. Nevertheless, objects in practice in an actual execution environment tend to fall into similarity categories or 'types', i.e., they share the same prototype chain and they have members with the same name, which in turn again have the same 'type'. Below, we define a graph, titled the *Prototype Graph* after the prototype feature of the language, that can represent such type information.

Definition 1 (Prototype Graph).   Let a *Prototype Graph* be a labeled directed multigraph (a graph allowing parallel edges with own identity)

$$G = \langle V, E, s, t, l_{prop}, l_{param} \rangle$$

such that

- $V = V_{type} \cup V_{sig}$, set of vertices, where the subsets are disjoint,
  - V_{type} vertices represent 'types', i.e., categories of similar objects,
  - V_{sig} vertices represent 'signatures' of callable types, i.e., functions,
- $E = E_{proto} \cup E_{prop} \cup E_{cstr} \cup E_{call} \cup E_{param} \cup E_{ret}$, set of edges, where all subsets are mutually disjoint,
  - E_{proto} edges represent prototype relation ('inheritance') between types,
  - E_{prop} edges represent the properties ('members') of types,
  - E_{cstr} and E_{call} edges connect callable types to their signatures and represent the two ways they can be invoked, i.e., the construct and call semantics,
  - E_{param} edges represent type information on parameters of callable types,
  - E_{ret} edges represent return types of callable types,
- $s : E \to V$ assigns to each edge its source vertex, under the constraint that $\forall e \in E_{proto} \cup E_{prop} \cup E_{cstr} \cup E_{call} \cup E_{param} : s(e) \in V_{type}$ and $\forall e \in E_{ret} : s(e) \in V_{sig}$,
- $t : E \to V$ assigns to each edge its target vertex, under the constraint that $\forall e \in E_{proto} \cup E_{prop} \cup E_{ret} : t(e) \in V_{type}$ and $\forall e \in E_{cstr} \cup E_{call} \cup E_{param} : t(e) \in V_{sig}$,
- the $\langle V, E_{proto}, s|_{E_{proto}}, t|_{E_{proto}} \rangle$ directed sub-multigraph is acyclic,
- $l_{prop} : E_{prop} \to \Sigma$ labeling function assigns arbitrary symbols ('names') to property edges, under the constraint that $\forall e_1, e_2 \in E_{prop} : s(e_1) = s(e_2) \Rightarrow l_{prop}(e_1) = l_{prop}(e_2) \iff e_1 = e_2$,
- $l_{param} : E_{param} \to \mathbb{N}_0$ labeling function assigns numeric indices to parameter edges, under the constraint that $\forall e_1, e_2 \in E_{param} : t(e_1) = t(e_2) \Rightarrow l_{param}(e_1) = l_{param}(e_2) \iff e_1 = e_2$.

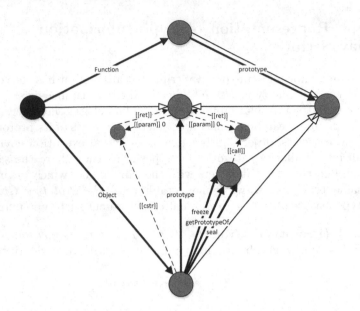

Fig. 1. Example prototype graph manually constructed based on a portion of the ECMAScript 5.1 standard [3, Sects. 15.2, 15.3]. Large and small nodes represent *type* and *sig* vertices respectively. (The single black node on the left represents the type of the global object, however, that is for identification and presentation purposes only.) Thick lines with labels represent *prop* edges, thin lines with hollow arrows represent *proto* edges, while dashed lines with double-bracketed labels represent *cstr*, *call*, *param*, and *ret* edges.

Informally, a prototype graph is a collection of *type* and *sig* vertices connected by six different kind of edges (and several edges can run between two vertices). *Proto* and *prop* edges connect *type* vertices, while the others connect *type* and *sig* vertices in one direction or the other. And finally, member name information and function argument order is encoded in edge labels. (Note, that vertices have no labeling; most information is stored in the existence of and labels of edges.)

As an example, Fig. 1 shows a prototype graph of 6 *type* and 2 *sig* vertices, manually constructed based on a portion of the ECMAScript 5.1 standard. The graph contains the types of `Object`, `Object.prototype`, `Function`, and `Function.prototype` objects, the global object, and also the constructor signature for `Object` and the call signatures for three functions of it.

Finally, we define some useful notations on prototype graphs as follows.

Definition 2 (Notations). Let $G = \langle V, E, s, t, l_{prop}, l_{param} \rangle$ be a prototype graph, where $V = V_{type} \cup V_{sig}$ and $E = E_{proto} \cup E_{prop} \cup E_{cstr} \cup E_{call} \cup E_{param} \cup E_{ret}$, according to Definition 1. Then we introduce the following notations:

- Let $v \xrightarrow[x]{e} v'$, denote the edge e of type x, where $x \in \{proto, prop, cstr, call, param, ret\}$, iff $e \in E_x \wedge s(e) = v \wedge t(e) = v'$.

– Let $v \xrightarrow[X]{e_1 \ldots e_n}{}^* v'$, denote the finite path $e_1 \ldots e_n$ over X type of edges, where $X \subseteq \{proto, prop, cstr, call, param, ret\}$, iff $e_1 \ldots e_n$ is a sequence of edges, with $n \geq 1$, such that $\forall 1 \leq i \leq n : v_i \xrightarrow[x_i]{e_i} v_{i+1} \wedge x_i \in X$, and $v_1 = v \wedge v_{n+1} = v'$.

– Let P_G denote the set of all finite paths in G.

3   Valid API Call Expressions from a Graph Representation

In this section, we present an application of the prototype graph, i.e., JavaScript engine API fuzzing, as motivated in the introduction. Thus, given a built graph, our goal is to generate call expressions that invoke functions on API objects with type-correct arguments. Therefore, we formally define with graph terms how such expressions can look like.

Definition 3 (Function Call Expressions). Let $G = \langle V, E, s, t, l_{prop}, l_{param}\rangle$ be a prototype graph, where $V = V_{type} \cup V_{sig}$, $E = E_{proto} \cup E_{prop} \cup E_{cstr} \cup E_{call} \cup E_{param} \cup E_{ret}$, and $l_{prop} : E_{prop} \rightarrow \Sigma$, according to Def. 1. Let $\Lambda : \mathcal{P}(V) \rightarrow \mathcal{P}(\Sigma_+^*)$ be a function that maps a set of types to a set of literals from an extended alphabet $\Sigma_+ \supseteq \Sigma \cup \{\boxed{\text{new}}, \boxed{.}, \boxed{(}, \boxed{,}, \boxed{)}\}$. Then we define $\Phi_{G,\Lambda} : V_{type} \rightarrow \mathcal{P}(\Sigma_+^*)$ as a function that gives for some selected starting vertex v_0 a set of type-correct call expressions that are available from an object of that type:

$$\Phi_{G,\Lambda}(v_0) = \Gamma_{G,\Lambda}(v_0, V_{sig})$$

$\Phi_{G,\Lambda}$ is given with the help of several auxiliary functions, all of which are defined below:

– The function $\Gamma_{G,\Lambda} : V \times \mathcal{P}(V) \rightarrow \mathcal{P}(\Sigma_+^*)$ gives the set of type-correct expressions available along a set of paths:

$$\Gamma_{G,\Lambda}(v_0, V') =$$
$$\bigcup_{e_1 \ldots e_n \in \Pi_G(v_0, V')} \left(\left(\boxed{\text{new}} \cdot \boxed{(} \right)^{|\{e_i \in E_{cstr}\}|} \cdot \Lambda(\{v_0\}) \cdot \prod_{i=1}^{n} \boxed{)}^{[e_i \in E_{cstr}]} \cdot \gamma_{G,\Lambda}(v_0, e_i) \right)$$

– The function $\gamma_{G,\Lambda} : V \times E \rightarrow \mathcal{P}(\Sigma_+^*)$ gives a set of sub-expressions for a step (i.e., edge) along a path:

$$\gamma_{G,\Lambda}(v_0, e) = \begin{cases} \boxed{.} \cdot l_{prop}(e) & \text{if } e \in E_{prop}, \\[2mm] \boxed{(} \cdot \left(\prod_{i=1}^{n} \boxed{,} \Gamma_{G,\Lambda}(v_0, \nabla_G(v_i)) \cup \Lambda(\nabla_G(v_i)) \right) \cdot \boxed{)} \\[2mm] \quad \text{if } e \in E_{cstr} \cup E_{call}, \text{ where} \\ \quad n = |\{e' : \exists v' : v' \xrightarrow[param]{e'} t(e)\}| \text{ and} \\ \quad \forall 1 \leq i \leq n : v_i \xrightarrow[param]{e_i} t(e) \text{ and} \\ \quad \forall 1 \leq i < n : l_{param}(e_i) < l_{param}(e_{i+1}), \\ \lambda & \text{otherwise.} \end{cases}$$

- The function $\Pi_G : V \times \mathcal{P}(V) \to \mathcal{P}(P_G)$ gives the set of all finite paths from a vertex to a set of vertices over *proto*, *prop*, *cstr*, *call*, and *ret* edges:

$$\Pi_G(v, V') = \left\{ e_1 \ldots e_n : v \xrightarrow[proto,prop,cstr,call,ret]{e_1 \ldots e_n}{}^{*} v' \wedge v' \in V' \right\}.$$

- The function $\nabla_G : V \to \mathcal{P}(V)$ gives the set of all vertices reachable from a given vertex backwards over *proto* edges:

$$\nabla_G(v) = \left\{ v' : \exists e_1 \ldots e_n : v' \xrightarrow[proto]{e_1 \ldots e_n}{}^{*} v \right\}.$$

- The $\cdot$, $\prod$, and power notations denote concatenation of strings (or sets of strings) over an alphabet, and λ is the empty word. The $\prod$ notation with an additional superscript symbol denotes concatenation with a separator symbol:

$$\prod_{i=1}^{n} {}^{\sigma} a_i = \begin{cases} \left(\displaystyle\prod_{i=1}^{n-1} {}^{\sigma} a_i \right) \cdot \sigma \cdot a_n & \text{if } n > 1, \\ \displaystyle\prod_{i=1}^{n} a_i & \text{otherwise.} \end{cases}$$

- $[P]$ denotes the Iverson bracket, i.e., gives 1 if P is true, 0 otherwise.

As visible from the definition above, the graph representation is capable of describing how a property can be accessed (the first case of $\gamma_{G,\Lambda}$), how a function can be parametrized to retrieve a type-correct value (the second case of $\gamma_{G,\Lambda}$), and how a new object can be created with a constructor call (the E_{cstr}-related parts of $\Gamma_{G,\Lambda}$). There is one more way of creating an expression of a given type, however: with literals. Since they fall outside the expressiveness of the graph representation – mostly because a literal is more of a syntactic entity while the concepts in the graph represent components of type information – possible literals of a type (or some types) are represented by the Λ function that complements the graph.

An actual implementation of the above formalism, e.g., a fuzzer, would most probably not generate the (potentially infinite) set $\Phi_{G,\Lambda}(v_0)$ but may choose an arbitrary element from it (and perhaps a different one on every execution). That can be achieved by a random walk on the prototype graph based on the informal concept behind the formal definition: "First walk forward on *proto*, *prop*, *cstr*, *call*, and *ret* edges to a *sig* vertex, then walk backward on *param* and *proto* edges, and so on..." Also, in an API fuzzer, v_0 would most probably be the type of global object, and Λ would map v_0 to a literal referring to the global object.

As an example, below we give some expressions in $\Phi_{G_{ex},\Lambda_{ex}}(v_{ex})$, where G_{ex} is the graph in Fig. 1, v_{ex} is the type of the global object in that graph (marked with black), and $\Lambda_{ex}(V') = \bigcup_{i=1}^{[v_{ex} \in V']} \{ \boxed{\texttt{this}} \}$:

- `this.Object.getPrototypeOf(this.Function.prototype)`,
- `new (this.Object)(this)`.

4   Building a Prototype Graph

The most trivial way of building a prototype graph may seem to be by hand. However, processing web standards manually – not only that of ECMAScript but potentially others as well, e.g., HTML5 DOM bindings – may require huge human efforts and is still heavily error prone, will be hard to maintain, and will not know about any engine-specific extensions. Thus, we outline two automated techniques below.

Both approaches rely on the introspecting capabilities of the JavaScript language: not only can we determine the actual type of every expression at runtime (with the `typeof` operator, e.g., whether it is of primitive boolean, number, or string type, or an object or a function, to name the most important types) but we can enumerate all properties and walk the property chains of all objects (with `Object.getOwnPropertyNames()` and `Object.getPrototypeOf()`), and retrieve the number of the formal parameters of every function (by reading their `length` property). By relying on introspection, the approaches do not require the source code of the engine-to-be-tested making them applicable to any engines.

The first approach, which we will call *engine discovery* in the paper (or just discovery, for short), is a one-time analysis of the engine. It's core idea is to execute a specially crafted JavaScript program inside the engine-to-be-tested using the above mentioned constructs. If this JavaScript program gets access to an object, it can create type descriptor data structures from all values recursively reachable from it by recording property names, and prototype and property relations – and formal argument list lengths for function objects. If this JavaScript program gets access to the global object of the execution environment then it can discover the whole API of the engine. Fortunately, the language standard mandates the existence of that global object (available as `this` in the outmost lexical scope), thus the approach is universal for all engines.

The discovery technique can find the prototypes and properties in the exposed API, but as mentioned above, it has a very limited view of the signatures (parameter and return types) of the functions. Therefore, we propose a second approach to extend the information about functions in the type descriptor data structure: in JavaScript, every object can be modified dynamically, even most of the built-in objects, and this includes the replacement of built-in functions with user-written JavaScript code. Thus, we propose to wrap (or patch) every function found using the discovery technique in a special code that, when called, collects type descriptor information about every parameter before passing them through to the original function, and also collects details about the returned value after the original call finished but before it is given back to the caller. This way the observable behaviour of the wrapped system does not change, but as programs execute in the engine, information about function signatures in the type descriptors can be continuously extended, refined (or, *learned*). Executing official or project-specific JavaScript test suites in such a patched environment is a plausible choice to learn signatures.

The data structures built by the engine discovery and signature learning approaches can be exported from the engine, e.g., in JSON format by using

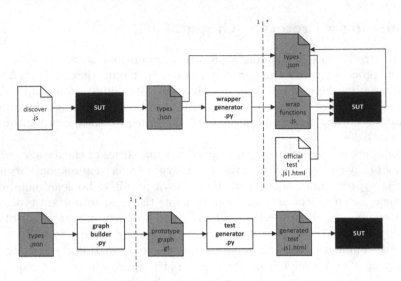

Fig. 2. Architecture overview of the prototype implementation of the graph-based JavaScript engine API fuzzing technique. The black boxes stand for the SUT, white elements are part of the implementation, while gray ones are generated during its execution. Dashed lines separate parts which execute only once from those which run multiple times (changing elements are marked with *).

built-in conversion routines. Then, that information can be easily transformed to the prototype graph format introduced in Sect. 2.

5   Experimental Results

5.1   Tools and Environment

To evaluate the ideas explained in the previous sections, we have created a prototype implementation. The code that discovers the API of the engine and learns signatures from existing tests was written in JavaScript (relying on the introspection capabilities of the language, as described in Sect. 4), while test generator code, execution harness for the engine-under-test, and utility routines were implemented in Python 3, with the help of the graph-tool module[5]. The architecture overview of the prototype implementation is shown in Fig. 2.

As SUT, we have chosen *jsc*, the command line JavaScript execution tool from the WebKit project[6]. The project – checked out from its official code repository at revision 192323 dated 2015-11-11 – was built in debug configuration for its GTK+ port (i.e., external dependencies like UI elements were provided by the GTK+ project[7]), on an x86-64 machine running Ubuntu 14.04 with Linux kernel 3.13.0, with gcc 4.9.2. To enable the investigation of the effects of fuzzing

---

[5] https://graph-tool.skewed.de/.

[6] https://webkit.org/.

[7] http://www.gtk.org/.

on the SUT, we made use of the coverage computation support of the compiler together with the gcov 4.9.2 and gcovr 3.2 tools[8].

Our goal was not only to evaluate the prototype graph-based fuzzing technique on its own but also to compare it to existing solutions. Therefore, we have downloaded jsfunfuzz[9] – with hash 6952e0f dated 2016-01-08 – , one of the few available open source JavaScript fuzzers to act as a baseline for our experiments.

5.2   Graphs

Since in our fuzzing technique the first step is to build a prototype graph, we have applied both previously outlined approaches to *jsc*, i.e., first we have discovered the engine and then learned functions signatures from existing tests. For the latter step, we have used the official JavaScript stress test suite of the WebKit project, executing 3,573 tests in the wrapped engine.

Table 1 shows the size metrics of the built graphs. The most striking difference is in the number of V_{type} vertices. This can be attributed to two factors: first, because of the limited view of the engine discovery on the function signatures, a large number of function objects are considered to be of the same prototype (i.e., only their argument number differentiates between them, and those with the same number of arguments get represented by a single type vertex). With signature learning, however, most of the function objects get represented by a separate type vertex. The second factor in the increase are new types emerging during signature learning either originating from the test suite (e.g., previously unseen literal parameters) or from the engine itself (e.g., natively constructed return values).

Figure 3 shows the prototype graph resulting after the learning step.

Table 1. Size metrics of prototype graphs built for *jsc*. (Signatures were learned from 3,573 official stress tests.)

	pgdiscover	pglearn
$|V_{type}|$	90	2022
$|V_{sig}|$	6	2362
$|E_{proto}|$	83	779
$|E_{prop}|$	670	2297
$|E_{cstr}|$	0	473
$|E_{call}|$	32	2404
$|E_{param}|$	17	83300
$|E_{ret}|$	6	2362

---

[8] http://gcovr.com/.

[9] https://github.com/MozillaSecurity/funfuzz/.

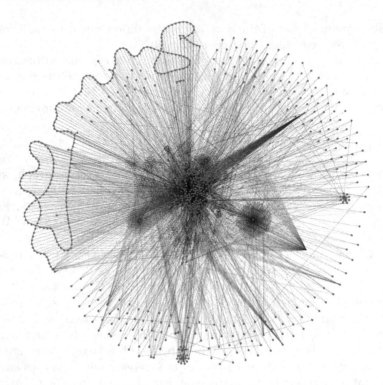

Fig. 3. Prototype graph built for *jsc* with the signature learning technique.

5.3 Evaluation

Once the graphs were built, we have used our test generator implementation to create 50,000 expressions from both, each expression resulting from a path consisting of a maximum of 20 property steps (as defined by $\gamma_{G,\Lambda}$ in Sect. 3). Then, we executed all expressions in *jsc*, one by one, and monitored their results. We took note of all assertion failures and program crashes, and after every 5,000 expressions we also measured the accumulated code coverage of the hitherto executed tests.

For the execution of jsfunfuzz, we used its own framework with the slight modification of adding a periodic code coverage measurement to the system. Jsfunfuzz was written with continuous (or continuously restarting) execution in mind and thus does not support the generation of a given number of expressions. Therefore, we could neither generate one expression per test as with our implementation nor could we execute exactly 50,000 expressions. However, we wanted to keep changes to it to the minimum, therefore we did not alter that behavior. To allow fair comparison, we parametrized jsfunfuzz to restart after every 1 second to generate only a small amount of expressions per test and we stopped the whole framework after the first code coverage measurement past the 50,000 expressions limit (thus finishing with 50,320 expressions).

Table 2 shows the line coverage results of all three fuzzing approaches both with module-level granularity and in total. (We have considered each sub-directory and standalone file of the *JavaScriptCore* build folder of the WebKit project as a separate module.) The results show that the basic engine discovery-based approach does not perform as well as jsfunfuzz in terms of total code coverage (23.31 % compared to 37.25 %), but as soon as we extend our graph with signature information extracted from tests, it improves significantly and gives higher results (44.13 %).

We should also highlight results on three important modules, namely on *runtime*, *yarr*, and *jsc.cpp*. The first contains C++ implementations of core JavaScript language functionality (like built-in functions), while the second contains the regular expression engine of the project. The third module (actually, a single file), is the main command line application, which is a classic JavaScript engine embedder in the sense that it binds some extra, non-standard routines into the JavaScript environment. That is, these are the modules that expose API of native code to the JavaScript space and thus are in our focus. As the table shows, even the simpler engine discovery-based technique can outperform jsfunfuzz in two out of the three modules, and the signature-extended variant gives the best results in all three cases.

For the sake of completeness, we should also mention some modules where the coverage is very low for all techniques. *API* and *bindings* contain API exposed to an embedder: a JavaScript code has no effect on how the engine is linked to its container application (moreover, *bindings* is marked deprecated in the code base, thus won't reach a higher coverage ever). The other modules – i.e., *debugger*, *disassembler*, *inspector*, *profiler*, and *tools* – contain code that are development-related and are also not under the control of the JavaScript code. Thus, these modules cannot be – and are not – the target of JavaScript API fuzzing.

As the ultimate goal of fuzzing is not only to reach good code coverage but also to cause system malfunction, we compared the three techniques on the basis of caused crashes as well. Table 3 shows the total number of observed failures, and since several tests triggered the same problem, the number of unique failures as well. (The uniqueness was determined based on crash backtrace information retrieved with a debugger.) Interestingly, both graph-based fuzzing techniques found the same failures. This also means that even the engine discovery technique with lower total coverage ratio could find more errors than jsfunfuzz. (However, it has to be noted that one of the two crashes caused by jsfunfuzz was not found by the graph-based prototype implementation.)

6 Related Work

Several previous authors tried to handle the weak-typedness of the JavaScript language by creating various type systems. One of the most well-known type systems was introduced by Anderson [1], who gave a formal algebraic definition for types of a language named JS_0 and also described how to perform type inference on such grammars. Other authors extended that work, like Franzen

Table 2. Code coverage results on *jsc* after 50,000 generated expressions (after 50,320 expressions for jsfunfuzz).

Module	Total lines	Covered lines					
		pgdiscover		pglearn		jsfunfuzz	
API	1698	9	0.53 %	9	0.53 %	9	0.53 %
DerivedSources	4546	148	3.26 %	167	3.67 %	312	6.86 %
assembler	2997	1046	34.90 %	2037	67.97 %	2054	68.54 %
bindings	165	0	0.00 %	0	0.00 %	0	0.00 %
builtins	96	63	65.63 %	63	65.63 %	62	64.58 %
bytecode	8578	1650	19.24 %	4196	48.92 %	3320	38.70 %
bytecompiler	4656	2344	50.34 %	2372	50.95 %	2887	62.01 %
debugger	713	3	0.42 %	3	0.42 %	3	0.42 %
dfg	29959	27	0.09 %	11019	36.78 %	9403	31.39 %
disassembler	1033	3	0.29 %	3	0.29 %	3	0.29 %
heap	4221	2517	59.63 %	2671	63.28 %	2373	56.22 %
inspector	3594	0	0.00 %	0	0.00 %	0	0.00 %
interpreter	1336	594	44.46 %	664	49.70 %	648	48.50 %
jit	8919	814	9.13 %	4852	54.40 %	4345	48.72 %
jsc.cpp	926	507	54.75 %	519	56.05 %	240	25.92 %
llint	840	344	40.95 %	424	50.48 %	451	53.69 %
parser	6586	3618	54.93 %	3801	57.71 %	4400	66.81 %
profiler	788	4	0.51 %	4	0.51 %	4	0.51 %
runtime	27112	12115	44.69 %	15101	55.70 %	10648	39.27 %
tools	534	13	2.43 %	13	2.43 %	13	2.43 %
yarr	3538	486	13.74 %	1879	53.11 %	856	24.19 %
TOTAL	112835	26305	23.31 %	49797	44.13 %	42031	37.25 %

Table 3. Number of failures caused in *jsc*.

	pgdiscover	pglearn	jsfunfuzz
total failures	1326	1445	4
unique failures	6	6	2

and Aspinall [4], who also tried to reason about the resource usage of programs with the help of the type system. However, even if designed to be "realistic", JS_0 is only a subset of the complete JavaScript language to make it manageable with respect to formalization.

Other type system and type inference approaches have also been proposed [2,7,13] but all authors focused on the static analysis of applications, not on the API of engines or on the execution engines themselves. Sen et al. have created

Jalangi [10], a dynamic analysis framework for JavaScript but it also deals with user code only with the help of preprocessing and not with the environment the programs run in, just like the static analyses.

The origins of random test generation date back to at least the '70s, when Purdom published his paper about grammar-based sentence generation for parser testing [9]. However, the term fuzzing was coined by Miller in 1988 only, as a result of truly random noise appearing in modem lines, disturbing terminals, and causing programs to crash [12]. Since then, randomized testing has become widespread; a good overview is also given in the work of Sutton et al [11].

The records on JavaScript fuzzing are not that long, but as the importance of the language started raising, the topic gained attention both in academia and industry. Godefroid et al. [5] have presented a whitebox fuzzing technique and experimented with it on the JavaScript interpreter of the Internet Explorer 7. That approach, however, required the symbolic execution of the application and constraint solving in addition. Holler et al. created LangFuzz [6] but that is an almost purely syntax-directed approach, which aims to avoid introducing language-dependent semantic knowledge into the fuzzer, thus LangFuzz has no type representation at all. Closest to our work is the state-of-the-art jsfunfuzz system from Ruderman, which we have chosen to compare our proposed technique against. That system does apply an engine discovery approach similar to ours, but it does not utilize all introspecting possibilities of the language, e.g., does not traverse the prototype chains and completely omits the automated discovery and learning of function signatures (all possible parametrizations are manually specified for the fuzzer).

7 Summary and Future Work

In this paper, we have defined a graph-based formalization of type information in JavaScript, we have shown how to automate the building of such graphs to describe the API exposed by a JavaScript execution engine, and we have also defined an API fuzzing method based on graph terms. According to our knowledge, this paper is the first work to use graph formalization and traversal for type information and related analyses of JavaScript. In addition to the formal definitions, we have also presented the experimental results of a prototype implementation of a JavaScript engine API fuzzer. The results show that the prototype graph based API fuzzing technique can be on par with available solutions in terms of total code coverage and even yield significantly better coverage results in JavaScript API-related modules. Moreover, the implementation triggered real program crashes during the experiments.

We see several potential directions for future work. First of all, we would like to enhance the potential of the API fuzzer. We plan to experiment with changing the formulas of Sect. 3 so that they do not necessarily generate type-correct expressions (e.g., by replacing the occurrences of ∇_G with a function that traverses *proto* edges in both directions instead of forward only). That may (or probably will) cause more generated inputs to be discarded by the engines, but we speculate that it may trigger more intrigued bugs as well. We would also like to evaluate our approach on other SUTs: both on different standalone JavaScript engines and especially on systems that bind external APIs into the JavaScript execution environment, e.g., on web browsers that expose HTML DOM manipulation API to user code. Moreover, we plan to investigate the recently published ECMAScript 6 standard and evolve both the formalizations and the implementation to adapt to any new concepts as needed. Finally, we plan to investigate the potential use cases of the prototype graph outside the fuzzing domain as well.

References

1. Anderson, C.L.: Type inference for JavaScript. Ph.D. thesis, University of London, Imperial College London, Department of Computing (2006)
2. Chugh, R., Herman, D., Jhala, R.: Dependent types for JavaScript. In: Proceedings of the ACM International Conference on Object Oriented Programming Systems Languages and Applications (OOPSLA 2012), pp. 587–606. ACM (2012)
3. Ecma International: ECMAScript Language Specification (ECMA-262), 5.1st edn., June 2011
4. Franzen, D., Aspinall, D.: Towards an amortized type system for JavaScript. In: Proceedings of the 6th International Symposium on Symbolic Computation in Software Science (SCSS 2014). EPiC Series in Computer Science, vol. 30, pp. 12–26. EasyChair (2014)
5. Godefroid, P., Kiezun, A., Levin, M.Y.: Grammar-based whitebox fuzzing. In: Proceedings of the 29th ACM SIGPLAN Conference on Programming Language Design and Implementation (PLDI 2008), pp. 206–215. ACM (2008)
6. Holler, C., Herzig, K., Zeller, A.: Fuzzing with code fragments. In: 21st USENIX Security Symposium, pp. 445–458. USENIX (2012)
7. Jensen, S.H., Møller, A., Thiemann, P.: Type analysis for JavaScript. In: Palsberg, J., Su, Z. (eds.) SAS 2009. LNCS, vol. 5673, pp. 238–255. Springer, Heidelberg (2009)
8. Microsoft Corporation: Security development lifecycle (verification phase). https://www.microsoft.com/en-us/sdl/default.aspx
9. Purdom, P.: A sentence generator for testing parsers. BIT Numer. Math. **12**(3), 366–375 (1972)
10. Sen, K., Kalasapur, S., Brutch, T., Gibbs, S.: Jalangi: A selective record-replay and dynamic analysis framework for JavaScript. In: Proceedings of the 9th Joint Meeting of the European Software Engineering Conference and the ACM SIG-SOFT Symposium on the Foundations of Software Engineering (ESEC/FSE 2013), pp. 488–498. ACM (2013)
11. Sutton, M., Greene, A., Amini, P.: Fuzzing: Brute Force Vulnerability Discovery. Addison-Wesley, Boston (2007)
12. Takanen, A., DeMott, J., Miller, C.: Fuzzing for Software Security Testing and Quality Assurance, chap. Foreword, Artech House (2008)
13. Thiemann, P.: Towards a type system for analyzing JavaScript programs. In: Sagiv, M. (ed.) ESOP 2005. LNCS, vol. 3444, pp. 408–422. Springer, Heidelberg (2005)

Theorem Proving and Constraint
Satisfaction

A Component-Based Approach to Hybrid Systems Safety Verification

Andreas Müller[1]([✉]), Stefan Mitsch[1], Werner Retschitzegger[1],
Wieland Schwinger[1], and André Platzer[2]

[1] Department of Cooperative Information Systems, Johannes Kepler University,
Altenbergerstr. 69, 4040 Linz, Austria
{andreas.mueller,stefan.mitsch,werner.retschitzegger,
wieland.schwinger}@jku.at
[2] Computer Science Department, Carnegie Mellon University,
Pittsburgh, PA 15213, USA
aplatzer@cs.cmu.edu

Abstract. We study a component-based approach to simplify the challenges of verifying large-scale hybrid systems. Component-based modeling can be used to split large models into partial models to reduce modeling complexity. Yet, verification results also need to transfer from components to composites. In this paper, we propose a component-based hybrid system verification approach that combines the advantages of component-based modeling (e.g., reduced model complexity) with the advantages of formal verification (e.g., guaranteed contract compliance). Our strategy is to decompose the system into components, verify their local safety individually and compose them to form an overall system that provably satisfies a global contract, without proving the whole system. We introduce the necessary formalism to define the structure and behavior of components and a technique how to compose components such that safety properties provably emerge from component safety.

Keywords: Component-based development · Hybrid systems · Formal verification

1 Introduction

The hybrid dynamics of computation and physics in safety-critical cyber-physical systems (CPS), such as driver assistance systems, self-driving cars, autonomous robots, and airplanes, are almost impossible to get right without proper formal analysis. To enable this analysis, CPS are modeled using so called *hybrid system models*. At larger scales of realistic hybrid system models, formal verification of monolithic models becomes quite challenging. Therefore, component-based modeling approaches split large models into partial models, i.e., co-existing or interacting components (e.g., multiple airplanes in a collision avoidance maneuver).

Work partly funded by BMVIT grant FFG BRIDGE 838526, OeAD Marietta Blau grant ICM-2014-08600, FWF P28187-N31, and ERC PIOF-GA-2012-328378.

© Springer International Publishing Switzerland 2016
E. Ábrahám and M. Huisman (Eds.): IFM 2016, LNCS 9681, pp. 441–456, 2016.
DOI: 10.1007/978-3-319-33693-0_28

Even though this can lead to component-based models with improved structure and reduced modeling complexity, component verification results do not always transfer to composite systems without appropriate care.

This paper generalizes our previous work [18], which was limited to traffic flow models (i.e., port conditions limited to maximum values, contracts limited to load restrictions, components limited to interfaces and predefined behavior), to a more generic approach to *make hybrid system theorem proving modular on a component level*. The approach exploits component contracts to compose *verified components* and their *safety proofs* to a verified CPS. Differential dynamic logic d$\mathcal{L}$ [21,22], the hybrid systems specification and verification logic we are working with, is already compositional for each of its operators and, thus, a helpful basis for our approach. Reasoning in d$\mathcal{L}$ splits models along the d$\mathcal{L}$ operators into smaller pieces. In this paper, we build compositionality for a notion of components and interfaces on top of d$\mathcal{L}$. We focus on modeling a system in terms of components that each capture only a part of the system's behavior (as opposed to monolithic models) and a way to compose components by connecting their interfaces (as opposed to basic program composition with d$\mathcal{L}$ operators). Component-based hybrid systems verification is challenging because both local component behavior (e.g., decisions and motion of a robot) and inherently global phenomena (e.g., time) co-occur, because components can interact virtually (e.g., robots communicate) and physically (e.g., a robot manipulates an object), and because their interaction is subject to communication delays, measurement uncertainty, and actuation disturbance. Typically, our components are open systems [11], which are described and verified in isolation from other components, separated by interfaces with assumptions about the environment that provide guarantees about the behavior of components. If needed, they can be turned into a closed system [11] by including a model of a specific environment.

This paper focuses on (i) lossless and instantaneous interaction between components (allows uncertainty and delay in dedicated "ether" components, e.g., sense the speed of a car precisely without measurement error), (ii) components without physical entanglement (allows separated continuous dynamics, e.g., robots drive on their own, but do not push each other), and (iii) components without synchronized communication (parallel composition of continuous dynamics, simplification to any sequential interleaving for discrete dynamics, e.g., robots can sense their environment, but not negotiate with each other).

With this focus in mind, we define the structure and behavior of a notion of components and a technique how to compose components such that safety properties about the whole system emerge from component safety proofs (e.g., robots will not collide when staying in disjoint spatial regions). We illustrate our approach with a vehicle cruise control case study.

2   Preliminaries: Differential Dynamic Logic

For specifying and verifying correctness statements about hybrid systems, we use *differential dynamic logic* (d$\mathcal{L}$) [21,22], which supports *hybrid programs* as a program notation for hybrid systems. $d\mathcal{L}$ models can be verified using KeYmaera X [8], which is open source and has been applied for verification of several case studies.[1] The syntax of hybrid programs is generated by the following EBNF grammar:

$$\alpha ::= \alpha; \beta \mid \alpha \cup \beta \mid \alpha^* \mid x := \theta \mid x := * \mid \{x'_1 = \theta_1, \ldots, x'_n = \theta_n \ \& \ H\} \mid \ ?\phi.$$

The sequential composition $\alpha; \beta$ expresses that β starts after α finishes. The non-deterministic choice $\alpha \cup \beta$ follows either α or β. The non-deterministic repetition operator α^* repeats α zero or more times. Discrete assignment $x := \theta$ instantaneously assigns the value of the term θ to the variable x, while $x := *$ assigns an arbitrary value to x. $\{x' = \theta \ \& \ H\}$ describes a continuous evolution of x (x' denotes derivation with respect to time) within the evolution domain H. The test $?\phi$ checks that a condition expressed by ϕ holds, and aborts if it does not. A typical pattern $x := *; ?a \leq x \leq b$, which involves assignment and tests, is to limit the assignment of arbitrary values to known bounds.

To specify safety properties about hybrid programs, $d\mathcal{L}$ provides a modal operator $[\alpha]$. When ϕ is a $d\mathcal{L}$ formula describing a state and α is a hybrid program, then the $d\mathcal{L}$ formula $[\alpha]\phi$ expresses that all states reachable by α satisfy ϕ. The set of $d\mathcal{L}$ formulas relevant for this paper is generated by the following EBNF grammar (where $\sim \ \in \{<, \leq, =, \geq, >\}$ and θ_1, θ_2 are arithmetic expressions in $+, -, \cdot, /$ over the reals):

$$\phi ::= \theta_1 \sim \theta_2 \mid \neg\phi \mid \phi \wedge \psi \mid \phi \vee \psi \mid \phi \to \psi \mid \phi \leftrightarrow \psi \mid \forall x \phi \mid \exists x \phi \mid [\alpha]\phi.$$

Notation: Variables. In $d\mathcal{L}$ (and thus throughout the paper) all variables are real-valued. We use V to denote a set of variables. $FV(.)$ is used as an operator on terms, formulas and hybrid programs returning only their free variables, whereas $BV(.)$ is an operator returning only their bound variables.[2] Similarly, $V(.) = FV(.) \cup BV(.)$ returns all variables (free as well as bound).

Notation: Indices. Throughout this paper, subscript indices represent enumerations (e.g., x_i). Superscript indices are used to further specify the kinds of items described by the respective variables (e.g., v^{out} represents an *output* variable). If needed, a double (super- and subscript) one-letter index is used for double numeration (e.g., x_i^j represents element j of the vector x_i).

3 Modeling and Verification Steps

In this section we present the modeling and verification steps in our component-based verification approach (cf. Fig. 1). To illustrate the steps, we will use an

---

[1] cf. http://symbolaris.com/info/KeYmaera.html.

[2] *Bound variables* of a hybrid program are all those that may potentially be written to, while *free variables* are all those that may potentially be read [23].

example of a vehicle cruise control system, which consists of an actuator component adapting the vehicle speed according to a target speed chosen by a cruise control component. The vehicle moves *continuously*, while the control behavior is described by a *discrete* control part (e.g., choose velocity and acceleration). The goal is to keep the actual velocity in some range $[0, V]$, where V denotes a maximum velocity. Note that we model components fully symbolically, which means that each component represents actually a family of concrete components.

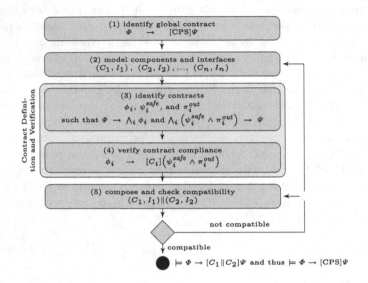

Fig. 1. Steps for component-based modeling and verification

The approach consists of the following steps:

(1) **identify global contract:** Before decomposing the system, it is important to learn what properties the system as a whole should fulfill (e.g., supported by domain experts). The global contract specifies the initial state of the whole system (Φ, e.g., initially the velocity is 0) as well as its overall safety property (Ψ, e.g., the velocity will stay in the desired range).

(2) **model components and interfaces:** Find recurring parts or natural splitting points for implementations (e.g., we split our cruise control system in a cruise controller and an actuator). The number of different components should be kept small, so that the verification effort remains low; still, there have to be sufficiently many components that can be instantiated to assemble the system. Modeling components and their interfaces is a manual effort (e.g., by modeling experts). A component has a behavior, while its interface defines public input ports and output ports, see Definitions 2 and 3 later.

(3) **identify contracts:** For each component and its interface, we identify initial states ϕ_i (e.g., initial target velocity is 0), a safety property ψ_i^{safe} (e.g., actual velocity does not exceed V), as well as an output contract π_i^{out}

(e.g., target velocity is always in the desired range), see Definition 4 later. These properties have to be chosen such that the global contract follows by *refinement* or *dominance* [4]: $\Phi \rightarrow \bigwedge_i \phi_i$ and $\bigwedge_i (\psi_i^{safe} \wedge \pi_i^{out}) \rightarrow \Psi$.

(4) **verify contract compliance:** Verify that components satisfy their contracts formally, in our case (hybrid programs and d$\mathcal{L}$), with KeYmaera X.

(5) **compose and check compatibility:** Construct the system by connecting component ports to compose verified components in parallel, see Definition 5 later. Any component can be instantiated multiple times in the whole system (e.g., instantiate maximum velocity parameters of a cruise control with actual values; connect the controller with the actuator). In order to transfer proofs about components to a global system proof, the compatibility of the components must be checked (see Theorem 1 in Sect. 4.2, which is proved under these compatibility assumptions). Intuitively, the *compatibility check* ensures that the values *provided* for symbolic parameters of an output port of one component instance are *compatible* with the values *required* on a connected input port of the next instance, see Definition 6 later (e.g., the controller cannot demand target speeds outside the target range).

The main result of this process is that the component safety proofs—done for compatible components in isolation—transfer to an arbitrarily large system built by instantiating these components (cf. Theorem 1).

4   Component-Based Modeling

In this section we introduce essential modeling idioms and definitions for the presented steps. Section 4.1 introduces components (cf. step (2)) and their contracts (cf. step (3)). Similarly, Bauer et al. [3] show how a contract framework can be built generically. Section 4.2 introduces composition (cf. step (5)) and ensures that the local properties transfer to the overall system.

4.1   Components and Contracts

Components can observe a shared global state, and modify their internal state.

Definition 1 (Global Variables). *The global variables V^{global} are a set of variables shared by all components. It contains the variable t, which represents the system time, is initially set to 0, and increases linearly with rate 1. None of the global variables can ever be bound in any part of any component.*

In the following paragraphs, we define components, which have a behavior (e.g., how a cruise controller chooses a target velocity), and interfaces, which consist of input ports (e.g., the current velocity received by cruise control) and output ports (e.g., the new target velocity as provided by cruise control). We define the behavior of a component in the canonical order of a control part followed by a plant, which enables the definition of a structured composition operation for components and interfaces.

Definition 2 (Component). *A component C is defined as a tuple*

$$C = (\text{ctrl}, \text{plant}),\ \ where$$

- ctrl *is the discrete control part of a hybrid program (HP) and does not contain continuous parts (i.e., differential equations), and*
- plant *is the continuous part of the form* $\{x'_1 = \theta_1, ..., x'_n = \theta_n \& H\}$ *for* $n \in \mathbb{N}$ *i.e., an ordinary differential equation with evolution domain constraint* H.

The interface of a component consists of input and output ports, which can have contracts (i.e., π^{in} and π^{out}, e.g., value range for the target velocity).

Definition 3 (Interface). *An interface I is defined as a tuple*

$$I = \left(V^{\text{in}}, \pi^{\text{in}}, V^{\text{out}}, \pi^{\text{out}}\right),\ \ where$$

- V^{in} *is a set of input variables,* V^{out} *is a set of output variables,*
- $\pi^{\text{in}} : V^{\text{in}} \to \mathcal{P}$ *specifies an input predicate ($\mathcal{P}$ represents the set of all logical formulas) representing input requirements and assumptions, exactly one per input variable (i.e., input port), accordingly for* $\pi^{\text{out}} : V^{\text{out}} \to \mathcal{P}$,
- $\forall v \in V^{\text{in}} : V(\pi^{\text{in}}(v)) \subseteq \left(V \setminus V^{\text{in}}\right) \cup \{v\}$, *i.e., no input predicate can mention other input variables, which lets us reshuffle port ordering.*

An interface I is called admissible *for a component C, if* $(BV(\text{ctrl}) \cup BV(\text{plant})) \cap V^{\text{in}} = \emptyset$, *i.e., none of the input variables are bound in* ctrl *or* plant.

Consider our running example of the vehicle cruise control, where the actuator component chooses the acceleration according to a target velocity (cf. Fig. 2). As illustrated in Fig. 2a, the component has a single input port to receive a target velocity and a single output port to provide the current velocity.

Figure 2b describes this component and interface formally: The actuator receives a target speed between 0 and V on its single input port v^{tr}_{ac}, cf. (3). It is a time-triggered controller with sampling period ε. The controller chooses the acceleration of the vehicle such that it will not exceed the target velocity until the next run and stores the current system time, cf. (1). The plant adapts

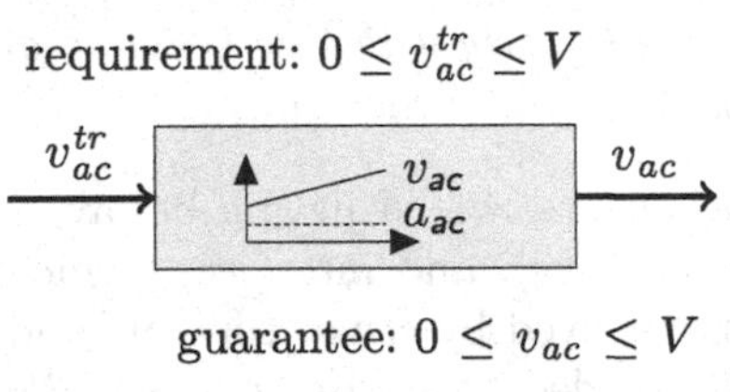

requirement: $0 \le v^{tr}_{ac} \le V$

guarantee: $0 \le v_{ac} \le V$

(a) Actuator illustration

$$ctrl_{ac} \equiv a_{ac} := \frac{v^{tr}_{ac} - v_{ac}}{\varepsilon};\ t^0_{ac} := t \quad (1)$$

$$plant_{ac} \equiv \{v'_{ac} = a_{ac} \ \& \ t - t^0_{ac} \le \varepsilon\} \quad (2)$$

$$\pi^{in}_{ac}(v^{tr}_{ac}) \equiv 0 \le v^{tr}_{ac} \le V \quad (3)$$

$$\pi^{out}_{ac}(v_{ac}) \equiv 0 \le v_{ac} \le V \quad (4)$$

(b) Formal component/interface

Fig. 2. Actuator component/interface example (C_{ac}, I_{ac})

the velocity accordingly and runs for at most ε time to enforce the sampling period, cf. (2). The single output port yields the resulting actual velocity, which still has to be in range between 0 and V, cf. (4).

Definition 4 (Contract). *Let C be a component, I be an admissible interface for C, and ϕ be a formula over the component's variables V, which determines the component's initial state. Let ψ^{safe} be a predicate over the component's variables V, i.e., a property describing the desirable target system state (i.e., a safety property). We define $\psi \stackrel{def}{\equiv} \psi^{\mathrm{safe}} \wedge \Pi^{\mathrm{out}}$, where $\Pi^{\mathrm{out}} \equiv \bigwedge_{v \in V^{\mathrm{out}}} \pi^{\mathrm{out}}(v)$ is the conjunction of all output guarantees. The contract of a component C with its interface I is defined as*

$$\mathrm{Cont}(C, I) \ \equiv \ t = 0 \wedge \phi \rightarrow [(\mathrm{in}; \mathrm{ctrl}; \{t' = 1, \mathrm{plant}\})^*]\psi$$

with input in $\stackrel{def}{\equiv} \left(v_1 := *; ?\pi^{\mathrm{in}}(v_1)\right); \ldots; \left(v_r := *; ?\pi^{\mathrm{in}}(v_r)\right)$ for all $v_i \in V^{\mathrm{in}}$.

As the input predicates are not allowed to mention other inputs, the order of inputs in *in* is irrelevant. We call a component with an admissible interface that provably satisfies its contract to be *contract compliant*. This means, if started in a state satisfying ϕ, the component only reaches states that satisfy safety ψ^{safe} and all output guarantees π^{out} when all inputs satisfy π^{in}.

In our running example of Fig. 2, the actuator component has an output guarantee $\pi^{\mathrm{out}} \equiv (0 \leq v_{ac} \leq V)$ (i.e., the speed must always be in range), and when starting from the initial conditions $\phi \equiv (v_{ac} = 0 \wedge \varepsilon > 0 \wedge V > 0)$ (i.e., vehicle initially stopped) it can provably guarantee safety[3] $\psi^{\mathrm{safe}} \equiv 0 \leq v_{ac} \leq V$.

4.2   Composition of Components

Now that we have defined the structure and behavior of single components and their interfaces, we specify how to compose a number of those components by defining a syntactic composition operator for components. Differential dynamic logic follows the common assumption in hybrid systems that discrete actions do not consume time, i.e., multiple discrete actions of a program can happen instantaneously at the same real point in time. Time only passes during continuous evolution measured through t' in *plant*. Hence, if we disallow direct interaction between the controllers of components,[4] we can compose the discrete *ctrl* of multiple components in parallel by executing them sequentially in any order, while keeping their plants truly parallel through $\{x'_1 = \theta_1, \ldots, x'_n = \theta_n \ \& \ H\}$. Interaction between components is then possible by observing plant output.

Such interaction, which exchanges information between components, will be defined by connecting ports when composing components through their interfaces. The port connections are represented by a mapping function $\mathcal{X}$, which assigns an output port to an input port for some number of input ports. In this paper, we focus on instantaneous lossless interaction, where the input variable

---

[3] Note that in this case the output property and the safety property coincide. This is not necessarily always the case.

[4] Definition 5 restricts how variables between components can be shared.

v instantaneously takes on the value of the output port it is connected to, cf. $v := \mathcal{X}(v)$ in Definition 5. Other interaction patterns can be modeled by adapting Definition 5. For example, measurement with sensor uncertainty Δ is $v := *; \, ? \, (\mathcal{X}(v) - \Delta \leq v \leq \mathcal{X}(v) + \Delta)$, which yields a modified compatibility check.

As we do not require all ports to be connected, the mapping function is a partial function. Ports which are not connected become ports of the composite, while ports which are connected become internal variables.

Definition 5 (Parallel Composition). *Let C_i denote one of n components*

$$C_i = (\mathrm{ctrl}_i, \mathrm{plant}_i) \ \ for \ i \in \{1, ..., n\}$$

with their corresponding admissible interfaces

$$I_i = \left(V_i^{\mathrm{in}}, \pi_i^{\mathrm{in}}, V_i^{\mathrm{out}}, \pi_i^{\mathrm{out}} \right) \ \ for \ i \in \{1, ..., n\}$$

where $\left(V_i^{\mathrm{in}} \cup V_i^{\mathrm{out}} \cup \mathrm{V}(\mathrm{ctrl}_i) \cup \mathrm{V}(\mathrm{plant}_i) \right) \cap \left(V_j^{\mathrm{in}} \cup V_j^{\mathrm{out}} \cup \mathrm{V}(\mathrm{ctrl}_j) \cup \mathrm{V}(\mathrm{plant}_j) \right) \subseteq$ V^{global} *for $i \neq j$, i.e., only variables in V^{global} are shared between components, and let*

$$\mathcal{X} : \left(\bigcup_{1 \leq j \leq n} V_j^{\mathrm{in}} \right) \rightharpoonup \left(\bigcup_{1 \leq i \leq n} V_i^{\mathrm{out}} \right)$$

be a partial (i.e., not every input must be mapped), injective (i.e., every output is only mapped to one input) function, connecting inputs to outputs. We define $\mathcal{I}^{\mathcal{X}}$ as the domain of $\mathcal{X}$ (i.e., all variables $x \in V^{\mathrm{in}}$ such that $\mathcal{X}(x)$ is defined) and $\mathcal{O}^{\mathcal{X}}$ as the the image of $\mathcal{X}$ (i.e., all variables $y \in V^{\mathrm{out}}$ such that $y = \mathcal{X}(x)$ holds for some $x \in V^{\mathrm{in}}$).

$$(C, I) \stackrel{def}{\equiv} ((C_1, I_1) \| ... \| (C_n, I_n))_{\mathcal{X}}$$

is defined as the composite of n components and their interfaces (with respect to $\mathcal{X}$), where

– *the sensing for non-connected inputs remains unchanged*

$$\mathrm{in} \equiv \underbrace{v_k := *; \, ?\pi^{\mathrm{in}}(v_k); \ldots; v_s := *; \, ?\pi^{\mathrm{in}}(v_s)}_{open \ inputs} \ for \ \{v_k, \ldots, v_s\} = V^{\mathrm{in}} \setminus \mathcal{I}^{\mathcal{X}}$$

– *the order in which the control parts (and the respective port mappings) are executed is chosen non-deterministically (considering all the $n!$ possible permutations of $\{1, ..., n\}$), so that connected ports become internal behavior of the composite component*

$$\mathrm{ctrl} \equiv (\mathrm{ports}_1; \mathrm{ctrl}_1; \mathrm{ports}_2; \mathrm{ctrl}_2; ...; \mathrm{ports}_n; \mathrm{ctrl}_n) \cup$$
$$(\mathrm{ports}_2; \mathrm{ctrl}_2; \mathrm{ports}_1; \mathrm{ctrl}_1; ...; \mathrm{ports}_n; \mathrm{ctrl}_n) \cup$$
$$...$$
$$(\mathrm{ports}_n; \mathrm{ctrl}_n; ...; \mathrm{ports}_2; \mathrm{ctrl}_2, \mathrm{ports}_1; \mathrm{ctrl}_1)$$

with $\mathrm{ports}_i \stackrel{def}{\equiv} \underbrace{v_j := \mathcal{X}(v_j); \ldots; v_r := \mathcal{X}(v_r)}_{connected \ inputs} \ for \ \{v_j, \ldots, v_r\} = \mathcal{I}^{\mathcal{X}} \cap V_i^{\mathrm{in}},$

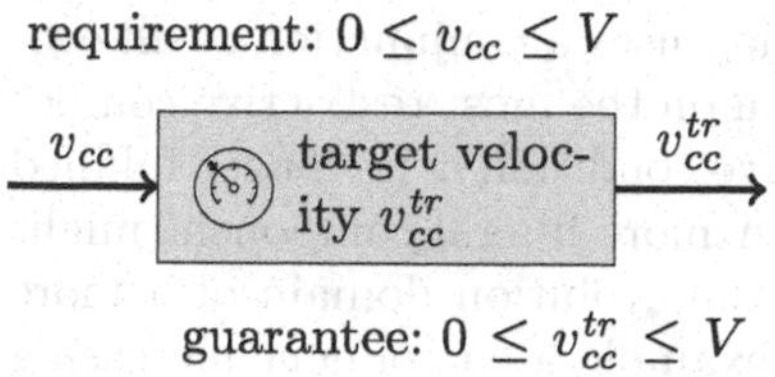

requirement: $0 \leq v_{cc} \leq V$

guarantee: $0 \leq v_{cc}^{tr} \leq V$

(a) Cruise controller illustration

$$ctrl_{cc} \equiv v_{cc}^{tr} := *; \ ?\big(0 \leq v_{cc}^{tr} \quad (5)$$
$$\wedge \ |v_{cc}^{tr} - v_{cc}| \leq \delta_V\big) \quad (6)$$
$$\pi_{cc}^{in}(v_{cc}) \equiv 0 \leq v_{cc} \leq V \quad (7)$$
$$\pi_{cc}^{out}(v_{cc}^{tr}) \equiv 0 \leq v_{cc}^{tr} \leq V \quad (8)$$

(b) Formal component/interface

Fig. 3. Cruise controller component/interface example (C_{cc}, I_{cc})

- *continuous parts are executed in parallel, staying inside all evolution domains*

$$\text{plant} \equiv \big\{ \underbrace{x_1^{(1)\prime} = \theta_1^{(1)}, \ldots, x_1^{(k)\prime} = \theta_1^{(k)}}_{\text{component } C_1}, \ldots, \underbrace{x_n^{(1)\prime} = \theta_n^{(1)}, \ldots, x_n^{(m)\prime} = \theta_n^{(m)}}_{\text{component } C_n}$$
$$\& \ H_1 \wedge \ldots \wedge H_n \big\},$$

- *the respective sets of variables are merged, where* $V^{in} = \bigcup_{1 \leq i \leq n} V_i^{in} \backslash \mathcal{I}^{\mathcal{X}}$, $V^{out} = \bigcup_{1 \leq i \leq n} V_i^{out} \backslash \mathcal{O}^{\mathcal{X}}$, *i.e., ports not connected within the composite component remain input and output variables of the resulting interface,*
- *input port requirements of all interfaces are preserved, except for connected inputs, i.e.,* $\pi^{in} : V^{in} \to \mathcal{P}$ *becomes* $\pi^{in}(v)$, *accordingly for* $\pi^{out}(v)$:

$$\pi^{in}(v) \equiv \begin{cases} \pi_1^{in}(v) & \text{if } v \in V_1^{in} \backslash \mathcal{I}^{\mathcal{X}} \\ \ldots \\ \pi_n^{in}(v) & \text{if } v \in V_n^{in} \backslash \mathcal{I}^{\mathcal{X}} \end{cases} \qquad \pi^{out}(v) \equiv \begin{cases} \pi_1^{out}(v) & \text{if } v \in V_1^{out} \backslash \mathcal{O}^{\mathcal{X}} \\ \ldots \\ \pi_n^{out}(v) & \text{if } v \in V_n^{out} \backslash \mathcal{O}^{\mathcal{X}} \end{cases}.$$

To demonstrate parallel composition in our running example, we first introduce a cruise controller component (cf. Fig. 3). The cruise control selects a target velocity from the interval, but keeps the difference between the current (received) velocity and the chosen target velocity below δ_V (cf. (5) and (6)). That way, the acceleration set by the actuator component is bounded by δ_V / ε (i.e., the vehicle does not accelerate too fiercely). We connect this cruise controller component to the actuator component (cf. Fig. 2), as illustrated in Fig. 4.

Remark 1. Note that verifying the hybrid program for a composite according to Definition 5 would require a proof of each of the $n!$ branches of *ctrl* individually, as they all differ slightly. For a large number of components, this entails a huge proof effort. Previous non-component-based case studies (e.g., [13,16,17]), therefore, chose only one specific ordering. Our component-based approach verifies all possible orderings at once, because the permutations are all proven correct as part of proving Theorem 1 below in this paper.

Remark 2. This definition of parallel composition uses a conjunction of all evolution domains, which resembles synchronization on the most restrictive component (i.e., as soon as the first and most restrictive condition is no longer fulfilled all plants have to stop and hand over to *ctrl*). A more liberal component might be forced to execute its control part because the evolution domain of a more restrictive component did no longer hold. For example a component increasing a counter on every run of its control is then forced to count although its own evolution domain might have allowed it to postpone control. If this is undesired, a component's control can be defined as *ctrl*$_i$ ∪ ?true, which would allow the component to skip when forced to run its control part.

Remark 3. We define this composition operation for any number of components, since it is *not associative*, because the composition of three components results in 3! = 6 possible execution orders, whereas composing two components and adding a third yields only 2! + 2! = 4 of the possible 6 execution orders.

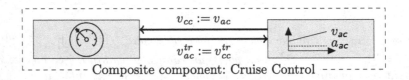

Fig. 4. Cruise control composed of a cruise controller and an actuator by Definition 5. The port connections $\mathcal{X} = \{(v_{cc}, v_{ac}), (v_{ac}^{tr}, v_{cc}^{tr})\}$ replace the input port $v_{ac}^{tr} := *$; $?(0 \leq v_{ac}^{tr} \leq V)$ with an internal port assignment $v_{ac}^{tr} := v_{cc}^{tr}$, provided the compatibility check $[v_{ac}^{tr} := v_{cc}^{tr}] \left(\pi_{cc}^{out}(v_{cc}^{tr}) \rightarrow \pi_{ac}^{in}(v_{ac}^{tr}) \right)$ succeeds, cf. Definition 6, and accordingly for the second port.

Note that Definition 5 replaces the non-deterministic input guarded by a test from Definition 2 with a deterministic assignment that represents instantaneous and lossless interaction between components (i.e., *ports*$_i$), as illustrated in Fig. 4. Hence, the respective output guarantees and input assumptions must match. For instance, a cruise controller component demanding velocities $0 \leq v_{cc}^{tr} \leq 70$ is compatible with an actuator $0 \leq v_{ac}^{tr} \leq 100$, but not the other way around.

Definition 6 (Compatible Composite). *The composite of n components with interfaces* $((C_1, I_1)\|...\|(C_n, I_n))_{\mathcal{X}}$ *is a* compatible composite *iff*

$$\text{CPO}(I_i) \equiv [v := \mathcal{X}(v)]\left(\pi_j^{out}(\mathcal{X}(v)) \rightarrow \pi_i^{in}(v)\right)$$

is valid for all input ports $v \in \mathcal{I}^{\mathcal{X}} \cap V_i^{in}$, *for all interfaces* I_i *and where* I_j *is the interface containing the port that is connected to the input port v of* I_i. *We call* $\text{CPO}(C_i)$ *the* compatibility proof obligation *for the interfaces* I_i *and say the interfaces* I_i *are* compatible *(with respect to* $\mathcal{X}$*) if* $\text{CPO}(I_i)$ *holds.*

In other words, $((C_1, I_1)\|...\|(C_n, I_n))_{\mathcal{X}}$ is a *compatible* composite if all internal port connections are appropriate, i.e., if the guarantee of the output port implies the requirements of the respective input port to which it is connected.

Composite Contracts. Now that we have defined components and interfaces, their contracts, and how to compose them to form larger composites, we prove that the contracts of single components transfer to composites if compatible.

Theorem 1 (Composition Retains Contracts). *Let C_1 and C_2 be components with admissible interfaces I_1 and I_2 that are contract compliant (i.e., their contracts are valid)*

$$\models t = 0 \wedge \phi_1 \rightarrow [(\text{in}_1; \text{ctrl}_1; \{t' = 1, \text{plant}_1\})^*] (\psi_1) \ and \tag{9}$$

$$\models t = 0 \wedge \phi_2 \rightarrow [(\text{in}_2; \text{ctrl}_2; \{t' = 1, \text{plant}_2\})^*] (\psi_2) \tag{10}$$

and compatible *with respect to $\mathcal{X}$ (i.e., compatibility proof obligations are valid)*

$$\models [v := \mathcal{X}(v)] \big(\pi_1^{\text{out}}(\mathcal{X}(v)) \rightarrow \pi_2^{\text{in}}(v)\big) \ and \tag{11}$$

$$\models [v := \mathcal{X}(v)] \big(\pi_2^{\text{out}}(\mathcal{X}(v)) \rightarrow \pi_1^{\text{in}}(v)\big) \tag{12}$$
$$for \ all \ input \ ports \ v \in \mathcal{I}^{\mathcal{X}} \cap V_{1,2}^{\text{in}}.$$

Then, the parallel composition $C_3, I_3 = ((C_1, I_1)\|(C_2, I_2))_{\mathcal{X}}$ satisfies the contract

$$\models t = 0 \wedge (\phi_1 \wedge \phi_2) \rightarrow [(\text{in}_3; \text{ctrl}_3; \{t' = 1, \text{plant}_3\})^*](\psi_1 \wedge \psi_2) \tag{13}$$

with in_3, ctrl_3, *and* plant_3 *according to Definition 5.*

The proof for Theorem 1 can be found in [19], along with a generalization to n components. This central theorem allows us to infer how properties from single components transfer to their composition. As such, it suffices to prove the properties for the components and conclude that a similar property holds for the composite, without explicitly having to verify it. The composite contract states that, considering both pre-conditions hold (i.e., $\phi_1 \wedge \phi_2$), all states reached by the parallel execution of the components, both post-conditions hold (i.e., $\psi_1 \wedge \psi_2$).

5   Case Study: Vehicle Cruise Control

To illustrate our approach, we used a running example of a simple *vehicle cruise control system*. The overall system requirement was to keep the velocity v_{ac} in a desired range $[0, V]$ at all times, i.e., $0 \leq v_{ac} \leq V \rightarrow [CruiseControl]0 \leq v_{ac} \leq V$. We split the system into two components, cf. Fig. 4: an actuator component adapts velocity according to a target v_{ac}^{tr} provided by a cruise control component as v_{cc}^{tr}. If the cruise control component (Fig. 3) provides a valid target velocity to the actuator (i.e., $0 \leq v_{ac}^{tr} \leq V$), the actuator component (Fig. 2) ensures to keep the actual velocity in the desired range (i.e., $0 \leq v_{ac} \leq V$), thus ensuring the overall system property. Additionally, the actuator provides the current velocity on an output port that is read by the controller, acting as a feedback loop.

Following Definition 4, we derive contracts for each component, which consists of initial conditions ϕ (cf. (14) and (15)), safety conditions ψ^{safe} (cf. (16)) and the port conditions (cf. (4) and (8)). Maximum speed $V > 0$ and cycle time $\varepsilon > 0$ must be known. Additionally, the controller initializes $v_{cc}^{tr} = 0$ and $\delta_V > 0$. The actuator restricts the initial velocity to $0 \le v_{ac} \le V$.

$$\phi_{cc} \equiv v_{cc}^{tr} = 0 \wedge \varepsilon > 0 \wedge V > 0 \wedge \delta_V > 0 \tag{14}$$

$$\phi_{ac} \equiv 0 \le v_{ac} \le V \wedge \varepsilon > 0 \wedge V > 0 \tag{15}$$

$$\psi_{ac}^{safe} \equiv 0 \le v_{ac} \le V \tag{16}$$

The set of global variables follows accordingly (cf. Definition 1): $V^{global} = \{\varepsilon, V, t\}$.

After verifying[5] both contracts $Cont(C_{cc}, I_{cc})$ and $Cont(C_{ac}, I_{ac})$, we want to compose the components to get the overall system, using the mapping function $\mathcal{X} = \{(v_{cc}, v_{ac}), (v_{ac}^{tr}, v_{cc}^{tr})\}$. Therefore, we have to check the compatibility proof obligations for both connected ports (cf. Fig. 4). Then the overall system property directly follows from the contract of the actuator component.

Splitting a system into components reduces the model complexity considerably, since a component needs to know neither about the differential equation systems of other components, nor about their control choices. In combined models, we have to analyze all the possible permutations of control choices, while in the component-based approach, by Theorem 1 we can guarantee correctness for all possible sequential orderings, without the proof effort entailed by listing them explicitly.

The benefit of component-based verification becomes even larger when replacing components in a system. For example, we can easily replace the cruise control from Fig. 3 with a more sophisticated controller that takes the target velocity as user input from an additional input port. After verifying the user guided cruise control component, we only have to re-check the compatibility proof obligations. In a monolithic model, in contrast, the whole system including the actuator component must be re-verified.

6   Related Work

CPS Verification. Hybrid automata [2] are popular for modeling CPS, and mainly verified using reachability analysis. Unlike hybrid programs, hybrid automata are not compositional, i.e., for a hybrid automaton it is not sufficient to establish a property about its parts in order to establish a property about the automaton. Techniques such as assume-guarantee reasoning or hybrid I/O automata [14], which are an extension of hybrid automata with input- and output-ports, address this issue. Our approach here shares some of the goals with hybrid

---

[5] All proofs were done in KeYmaera X [8].

I/O automata and also uses I/O ports. But we target compositional reasoning for *hybrid programs*, where the execution order of statements is relevant, so that our approach defines how parallel composition results in interleaving of hybrid programs. Furthermore, we define compositional modeling for hybrid programs such that *theorem proving* of the entire system is reduced to proving properties about the components and *simple composition checks*. Hybrid process algebras (e.g., Hybrid χ [24], HyPA [20]) are specifically developed as compositional modeling formalisms to describe behavior and interaction of processes using algebraic equations. For verification purposes by simulation or reachability analysis, translations from Hybrid χ into hybrid automata and timed automata exist, so even though modeling is compositional, verification still falls back to monolithic analysis. We, in contrast, focus on exploiting compositionality in the proof.

Component-Based CPS Modeling. Damm et al. [5] present a component-based design framework for controllers of hybrid systems with a focus on reaction times. The framework checks connections when interconnecting components: alarms propagated by an out-port must be handled by the connected in-ports. We, too, check component compatibility, but for contracts, and we focus on transferring proofs from components to the system level.

Focusing on architectural properties, Ruchkin et al. [26] propose a component-based modeling approach for hybrid-systems. Although they do not transfer verification results from components to composites, their definitions have been an inspiration for our notion of components. Ringert et al. [25] model CPS as Component and Connector (C&C) architectures using automata to describe solely the discrete behavior. They verify the translated models of single components, but do not provide guarantees about verified compositions.

Interface algebras (cf. [1,9]) are formalisms that separate component-based models into interface models and component models. Similar to our approach, the component model describes what a component does, while the interface model defines how the component can be used. It is often distinguished between interfaces with and without state, where stateful interfaces are usually viewed as concurrent games. Our approach is similar to a stateless interface algebra [1]. Similarly, Bauer et al. [3] show how a contract framework can be built generically. While useful for inspiration, these approaches focus on modeling aspects and do not consider verification.

Verification. Madl et al. [15] model real-time event-driven systems. Their models can be transformed to UPPAAL (cf. [12]) timed automata, restricting the continuous part of their models to time instead of arbitrary physical behavior (e.g., movement). Moreover, their analysis targets the *entire composition* of timed automata, thus defeating the advantages of components for verification.

A field closely related to component-based verification is assume-guarantee reasoning (AGR, e.g., [7,10]), which was originally developed as a device to counteract the state explosion problem in model checking by decomposing a verification task into subtasks. In AGR, individual components are analyzed together

454   A. Müller et al.

with *assumptions* about their context and *guarantees* about their behavior (i.e., a component's contract). AGR rules need to exercise care for circularity in the sense that the approaches verify one component in the context of the other and vice-versa, like Frehse et al. [7] (using Hybrid Labeled Transition Systems as abstraction for Hybrid I/O-Automata) and Henzinger et al. [10] (using hierarchical hybrid systems based on hybrid automata). However, existing approaches are often limited to linear dynamics, cannot handle continuity or use corresponding reachability analysis or model checking techniques. In d$\mathcal{L}$, in contrast, we can handle non-linear dynamics and focus on theorem proving.

In summary, only few component-based approaches handle generic CPS with both discrete and continuous aspects (e.g., [5,15,26]), but those do not yet focus on the impact on formal verification. Related techniques for CPS and hybrid systems verification focus mainly on timed automata, hybrid process algebras, and hybrid automata with linear dynamics or end up in monolithical verification.

7 Conclusion and Future Work

We presented an approach for component-based modeling and verification of CPS that (i) splits a CPS into components, (ii) verifies a contract for each of these components and (iii) composes component instances in a way that transfers the component contracts to a composite contract. Our approach makes hybrid system verification more modular at the scale of components, and combines the advantages of component-based modeling approaches (e.g., well structured models, reduced model complexity, simplified model evolution) with the advantages of formal verification (e.g., guaranteed contract compliance).

Currently, our approach is limited to global properties that are stated relative to the initial system state. Port conditions are only allowed to mention global variables and the port variable itself, which prevents conditions on the change of a port since the last measurement (e.g., how far has a vehicle moved since the beginning vs. how far has it moved since the last measurement). This restriction can be removed with ports that remember their previous value and relate measurements over time. Additionally, we plan to (i) introduce further composition operations (e.g., sensing with measurement errors), (ii) provide further component extensions (e.g., multi-cast ports), and (iii) provide tool support to instantiate and compose components, and to generate their hybrid programs.

References

1. de Alfaro, L., Henzinger, T.A.: Interface theories for component-based design. In: Henzinger, T.A., Kirsch, C.M. (eds.) EMSOFT 2001. LNCS, vol. 2211, pp. 148–165. Springer, Heidelberg (2001)
2. Alur, R., Courcoubetis, C., Henzinger, T.A., Ho, P.: Hybrid automata: an algorithmic approach to the specification and verification of hybrid systems. In: Grossman, R.L., Nerode, A., Ravn, A.P., Rischel, H. (eds.) Hybrid Systems. LNCS, vol. 736, pp. 209–229. Springer, Heidelberg (1993)

3. Bauer, S.S., David, A., Hennicker, R., Larsen, K.G., Legay, A., Nyman, U., Wasowski, A.: Moving from specifications to contracts in component-based design. In: de Lara, J., Zisman, A. (eds.) FASE 2012. LNCS, vol. 7212, pp. 43–58. Springer, Heidelberg (2012)
4. Benvenuti, L., Bresolin, D., Collins, P., Ferrari, A., Geretti, L., Villa, T.: Assume-guarantee verification of nonlinear hybrid systems with Ariadne. Int. J. Robust Nonlinear Control 24(4), 699–724 (2014)
5. Damm, W., Dierks, H., Oehlerking, J., Pnueli, A.: Towards component based design of hybrid systems: safety and stability. In: Manna, Z., Peled, D.A. (eds.) Time for Verification. LNCS, vol. 6200, pp. 96–143. Springer, Heidelberg (2010)
6. Felty, A.P., Middeldorp, A. (eds.): CADE-25. LNCS, vol. 9195. Springer, Switzerland (2015)
7. Frehse, G., Han, Z., Krogh, B.: Assume-guarantee reasoning for hybrid i/o-automata by over-approximation of continuous interaction. In: 43rd IEEE Conference on Decision and Control, CDC, vol. 1, pp. 479–484, December 2004
8. Fulton, N., Mitsch, S., Quesel, J., Völp, M., Platzer, A.: KeYmaera X: an axiomatic tactical theorem prover for hybrid systems. In: Felty and Middeldorp [6], pp. 527–538
9. Graf, S., Passerone, R., Quinton, S.: Contract-based reasoning for component systems with rich interactions. In: Sangiovanni-Vincentelli, A., Zeng, H., Di Natale, M., Marwedel, P. (eds.) Embedded Systems Development, vol. 20, pp. 139–154. Springer, New York (2014)
10. Henzinger, T.A., Minea, M., Prabhu, V.S.: Assume-guarantee reasoning for hierarchical hybrid systems. In: Di Benedetto, M.D., Sangiovanni-Vincentelli, A.L. (eds.) HSCC 2001. LNCS, vol. 2034, pp. 275–290. Springer, Heidelberg (2001)
11. Kurki-Suonio, R.: Component and interface refinement in closed-system specifications. In: Wing, J.M., Woodcock, J., Davies, J. (eds.) FM 1999. LNCS, vol. 1708, pp. 134–154. Springer, Heidelberg (1999)
12. Larsen, K.G., Pettersson, P., Yi, W.: UPPAAL in a nutshell. STTT 1(1–2), 134–152 (1997)
13. Loos, S.M., Platzer, A., Nistor, L.: Adaptive cruise control: hybrid, distributed, and now formally verified. In: Butler, M., Schulte, W. (eds.) FM 2011. LNCS, vol. 6664, pp. 42–56. Springer, Heidelberg (2011)
14. Lynch, N.A., Segala, R., Vaandrager, F.W.: Hybrid I/O automata. Inf. Comput. 185(1), 105–157 (2003)
15. Madl, G., Abdelwahed, S., Karsai, G.: Automatic verification of component-based real-time CORBA applications. In: Proceedings of the 25th IEEE Real-Time Systems Symposium (RTSS), 5–8 December 2004, pp. 231–240. IEEE Computer Society (2004)
16. Mitsch, S., Ghorbal, K., Platzer, A.: On provably safe obstacle avoidance for autonomous robotic ground vehicles. In: Newman, P., Fox, D., Hsu, D. (eds.) Robotics: Science and Systems IX, Technische Universität Berlin, 24–28 June 2013
17. Mitsch, S., Loos, S.M., Platzer, A.: Towards formal verification of freeway traffic control. In: ICCPS, pp. 171–180. IEEE/ACM (2012)
18. Müller, A., Mitsch, S., Platzer, A.: Verified traffic networks: component-based verification of cyber-physical flow systems. In: 18th IEEE Intelligent Transportation Systems Conference (ITSC), pp. 757–764. IEEE (2015)
19. Müller, A., Mitsch, S., Retschitzegger, W., Schwinger, W., Platzer, A.: A component-based approach to hybrid systems safety verification. Technical report CMU-CS-16-100, Carnegie Mellon (2016)

20. Cuijpers, P.J.L., Reniers, M.A.: Hybrid process algebra. J. Log. Algebr. Program. **62**(2), 191–245 (2005)
21. Platzer, A.: Differential-algebraic dynamic logic for differential-algebraic programs. J. Log. Comput. **20**(1), 309–352 (2010)
22. Platzer, A.: The complete proof theory of hybrid systems. In: Proceedings of the 27th Annual IEEE Symposium on Logic in Computer Science, LICS, 25–28 June 2012, pp. 541–550. IEEE Computer Society (2012)
23. Platzer, A.: A uniform substitution calculus for differential dynamic logic. In: Felty and Middeldorp [6], pp. 467–481
24. Schiffelers, R.R.H., van Beek, D.A., Man, K.L., Reniers, M.A., Rooda, J.E.: Formal semantics of hybrid chi. In: Larsen, K.G., Niebert, P. (eds.) FORMATS 2003. LNCS, vol. 2791, pp. 151–165. Springer, Heidelberg (2004)
25. Ringert, J.O., Rumpe, B., Wortmann, A.: From software architecture structure and behavior modeling to implementations of cyber-physical systems. In: Wagner, S., Lichter, H. (eds.) Software Engineering 2013 - Workshopband. LNI, vol. 215, 26 February – 1 March, 2013, pp. 155–170. GI (2013)
26. Ruchkin, I., Schmerl, B.R., Garlan, D.: Architectural abstractions for hybrid programs. In: Kruchten, P., Becker, S., Schneider, J. (eds.) Proceedings of the 18th International ACM SIGSOFT Symposium on Component-Based Software Engineering, CBSE 2015, 4–8 May 2015, pp. 65–74. ACM (2015)

Verifying Pointer Programs Using Separation Logic and Invariant Based Programming in Isabelle

Viorel Preoteasa[(✉)]

Aalto University, Espoo, Finland
viorel.preoteasa@aalto.fi

Abstract. In this paper we present a technique based on invariant based programming and separation logic for verifying pointer programs. Invariant based programs are directed graphs where the nodes are called situations and are labeled by predicates (invariants). The edges are called transitions, and are labeled by guarded assignment statements. We represent the situations using Isabelle's locales. A locale is a theory parameterized by constants and types. The constant parameters are used for modeling the state of the program, and the type parameters are used for obtaining generic programs. The invariants are modeled as locale assumptions (axioms), and the transitions are modeled as locale interpretations. For modeling pointer programs we use separation logic. The final result of this construction is a collection of mutually recursive Isabelle functions that implements the program. We apply this technique to Lindstrom's algorithm for traversing a binary tree without additional memory.

1 Introduction

In this paper we introduce a technique for constructing correct programs manipulating pointers within the *Isabelle/HOL* [21] theorem prover, using *invariant based programming* [1,2] and *separation logic* [22,24,27].

Invariant based programming is an approach to construct a program where we start by identifying the basic *situations* (*pre-* and *post-conditions* as well as *invariants*) that could arise during the execution of the algorithm. These situations are identified before any code is written. After that, we identify the *transitions* between the situations, which will give us the flow of control in the program. The transitions are verified at the time when they are constructed. The correctness of the program is thus established as part of the construction of the program. The program structure in invariant based programs is determined by the information content of the situations, using *nested invariant diagrams*. The control structure is secondary to the situation structure, and will usually not be well-structured in the classical sense, i.e., it is not necessarily built out of

---

This work was partially supported by the Academy of Finland research project 265939.

E. Ábrahám and M. Huisman (Eds.): IFM 2016, LNCS 9681, pp. 457–473, 2016.
DOI: 10.1007/978-3-319-33693-0_29

single-entry single-exit program constructs. We refer to a program constructed in this manner as an *invariant based program* or *invariant diagram*. Detailed explanations and motivating examples for the invariant based programming approach can be found in [1].

Pointer manipulating programs as well as object oriented programs are difficult to get right and even more difficult to verify mainly due to aliasing. For example, in the C language we could have two pointers to integer numbers: int $* x$, $*y$. After the assignment $*x := 7$ we have two possibilities for the value of $*y$. If addresses x and y are different, then $*y$ is unchanged, otherwise $*y$ is 7. We cannot say just by looking at the program $*x := 7$ what will be the effect on $*y$. We can specify that address x and y are different, and they both store the value 1 using the assertion $x \neq y \land *x = 1 \land *y = 1$. If we have more pointer variables, expressing the non-aliasing properties becomes much more involved. Separation logic was introduced for specifying in a more abstract manner non-aliasing properties about pointers. Within separation logic two new predicate operators were introduced: singleton heap ($\mapsto$) and separation conjunction ($*$). The predicate $x \mapsto a$ is true in those computation states where the heap contains exactly one address x, and the value stored at address x is a. The predicate $p * q$ is true in a computation state if we can split the heap such that p is true for one part of the heap and q is true for the second part. For example the predicate $(x \mapsto 1) * (y \mapsto 1)$ is true in a state where the heap contains two distinct addresses x and y, and 1 is stored at both addresses x, and y. Using separation logic, if we know that $(x \mapsto 1) * (y \mapsto 1)$ is true before executing the program $*x := 7$, then after the execution $(x \mapsto 7) * (y \mapsto 1)$ is also true.

Isabelle/HOL is an interactive theorem prover based on higher order logic. Isabelle has a powerful mechanism for creating sub-theories (called *locales*) [3] with a local scope for constants (or parameters), assumptions, definitions and theorems. A locale can *extend* other locales and we may have *locale interpretations*. A locale interpretation is an assignment of specific terms to the locale parameters. As a consequence of this assignment we should prove that the assumptions of the locales are true when the parameters are replaced by these terms.

In [23] we have introduced a technique for representing invariant diagrams in Isabelle using locales. In this paper, we extend the technique from [23] with separation logic for verifying pointer programs. The advantages of this technique are the following: (1) the program and its specification (pre, post conditions and invariants) are expressed using the same powerful language (higher order logic), (2) the transitions correspond directly to *verification conditions (VC)*, (3) the proofs for the transitions are given after the transitions similarly to proofs of lemmas in Isabelle, (4) Isabelle's library of theories is available for specifications, (5) We can use automatic theorem provers, (6) we can use separation logic, (7) we construct a collection of mutually recursive functions in Isabelle implementing the program and we generate executable code from them.

To illustrate our technique, we apply it to Lindstrom's algorithm [17] for traversing a binary tree. The algorithm is non-trivial, and it traverses the tree without any additional memory. The drawback of the algorithm is that it visits every node three times.

There are many implementations of separation logic in different theorem provers, and some implementations in Isabelle [12–15,19,20]. The purpose of this paper is not to introduce yet another representation of separation logic. In fact we use the existing implementation from [12,13]. There are also many mechanical verifications of graph traversal algorithms using various techniques, including separation logic. The purpose of this work is to show how to combine existing techniques as invariant based programming, separation logic, theorem proving, parametric theories (Isabelle locales), and code generation to obtain a powerful tool for developing correct by construction imperative programs. In earlier work [2] we also showed how to combine data refinement with invariant based programming, and we verified the closely related Deutsch-Schorr-Waite graph marking algorithm. The Isabelle theorem prover offers already few alternatives for constructing correct programs, however in all of them the invariants are embedded within the structure of the program, and if the structure changes significantly, then it is difficult to keep the proofs in sync with the verification conditions. We propose an approach where the verification conditions are exactly the program transitions and the proofs are attached to them. In our approach it is possible to name individual invariants and statements of transitions, and use these names in Isar [26] poofs. If we add or remove invariants or statements, the proofs for the unchanged components stay the same due to using of names.

All results presented in this paper have been formalized and proved in Isabelle and are available from http://users.ics.aalto.fi/viorel/Lindstrom.zip.

2 Related Work

Dafny [16] is an automatic program verifier for functional correctness. One problem that we see in this approach is that it uses an automatic theorem prover that only has support for some theories. It is not easy to develop additional theories to support programs on different domains. Because proving the correctness relies only on automation, when proving some verification condition (VC) fails due to its complexity, the user has to tweak the program by adding additional functions until the automated proof succeeds. This tweaking is equivalent to interactively proving the VC, but without an explicit proof language, and it may be much more time consuming than an interactive proof. Dafny does not support separation logic.

Why3 [8] is another platform for program verification. It provides a rich language for specification and programming, called WhyML, and relies on external theorem provers, both automated and interactive, to discharge verification conditions. Why3 comes with a standard library of logical theories and basic programming data structures. It is possible to extend the Why3 library with new theories, however these extensions are axiomatic in nature and practice has shown that this can easily create inconsistencies. Although Why3 supports also interactive theorem provers, the logic from the theorem prover is different from the logic of Why3, and keeping the interactive proofs in sync with the program is not a trivial task [6]. Why3 has some support for separation logic [5].

There are also dedicated automatic provers for verifying programs using separation logic such as Smallfoot [4] and VeriFast [11]. One drawback is the limited expressive power of the assertion language in Smallfoot. VeriFast allows more expressive specification constructs but the user must introduce additional lemma functions to help the automation. This again is a mechanism to add manual proofs for VCs without an explicit proof language.

In [18] the authors report on the automatic verification of Lindstrom's algorithm. This approach can verify some aspects of the functional correctness of the algorithm (all nodes are visited, and at the end the tree is left unchanged) and termination. However this approach is based on some abstraction relations provided by the user, and this requires deep understanding of the algorithm. Assuming that on each visit of a node we apply a function f to the label of the node, we verify that after the traversal, every label is equal to f^3 ($f \circ f \circ f$) applied to its initial value. It does not seem possible to verify this kind of properties about the algorithm using the approach from [18].

In [10] another method based on graph grammar abstraction for automatic verification of Lindstrom's algorithm is presented. Although it seems possible to modify this approach to verify that all nodes are visited 3 times, it does not seem possible to verify that during the traversal the function f^3 is applied to every label.

3   Preliminaries

In this paper we use higher order logic as implemented by the Isabelle theorem prover. We use capital letters $X, Y, \ldots$ for types and small letters to denote elements of these types $x \in X$. We denote by bool the type of Boolean values false and true, and by nat the type of natural numbers. We use $\wedge, \vee, \Rightarrow$, and $\neg$ for the Boolean operations.

If X and Y are types, then $X \to Y$ denotes the type of functions from X to Y. We denote by id : $A \to A$ the identity function $(\forall x \bullet \mathsf{id}(x) = x)$, and we use a small bullet ($\bullet$) for separating the quantified variables in formulas. For $f : X \to Y$, $x \in X$, and $y \in Y$, we define $f[x := y] : X \to Y$ by $f[x := y](x) = y$ and $(\forall z \neq x \bullet f[x := y](z) = f(x))$. Predicates are the functions with Boolean values with one or more arguments (e.g., a predicate with two arguments has signature $X \to Y \to$ bool). If $r, r' : X \to$ bool are two predicates then $r \cap r'$ and is the predicate given by $(r \cap r')(x) = r(x) \wedge r'(x)$. We use $\bot$ and $\top$ as the smallest and greatest predicates: $\bot(x) = $ false and $\top(x) = $ true. We use the notation $X \times Y$ for the Cartesian product of X and Y.

4   Separation Logic

We use an existing implementation in Isabelle of a generic Separation Algebra [12,13] that we instantiate for our verification.

We model the heap storing values from a set V as a partial function from the type of addresses (Address) to values. In Isabelle this corresponds to total functions from Address to Option(V), where Option(V) = V + {none} is the disjoint union of V and {none}. Heap(V) = Address $\rightarrow$ Option(V).

For $h \in$ Heap(V) and $p \in$ Address if $h(p)$ = none then h is not defined in p, otherwise $h(p) \in V$ and h is defined in p. The allocated addresses of a heap h are the addresses in which h is defined: alloc(h) = $\{p \mid h(p) \neq$ none$\}$.

We use the predicates on the heap (Heap(V) $\rightarrow$ bool) as program assertions, and using [13] we have a Separation Algebra structure on Heap(V) that gives us the separation conjunction, and empty heap assertions together with their properties and a number of simplification tactics. Here we give the definitions of the empty heap and separation conjunction for completeness, but they are obtained from [13].

1. Empty heap: emp(h) = (alloc(h) = $\emptyset$)
2. Separation conjunction:
   $(\alpha * \beta)(h) = (\exists h_1\ h_2 \bullet$ alloc(h_1) $\cap$ alloc(h_2) = $\emptyset \wedge h = h_1 + h_2 \wedge \alpha(h_1) \wedge \beta(h_2))$

where $(h_1 + h_2)(p)$ = if $p \in$ alloc(h_1) then $h_1(p)$ else $h_2(p)$.

The predicate emp is true for a heap h if h does not contain any address. The separation conjunction $\alpha * \beta$ is true for h if h can be split in two disjoint heaps h_1 and h_2 such that α is true for h_1 and β is true for h_2.

For an address p and a value v we introduce the predicate *singleton heap* $p \mapsto v$ that is true for a heap h if h contains only the address p and the value stored in p is v: alloc(h) = $\{p\} \wedge h(p) = v$. We assume that $\mapsto$ binds stronger than $*$, i.e. $(p \mapsto v) * \alpha$ is the same as $p \mapsto v * \alpha$.

If α, β and γ are predicates on the heap, $p \in$ Address, and $v, v' \in V$, then following properties are true

$$\text{emp} * \alpha = \alpha * \text{emp} = \alpha \qquad (p \mapsto v) * (p \mapsto v') = \bot \qquad \alpha * \beta = \beta * \alpha$$
$$(\alpha * \beta) * \gamma = \alpha * (\beta * \gamma) \qquad (p \mapsto v * \alpha)(h) \Rightarrow p \in \text{alloc}(h) \qquad \bot * \alpha = \bot$$

The properties involving only emp, $*$, and $\bot$ are available from [13], and the others are direct consequences of the definitions.

We also need a special null address nil $\in$ Address add we define the predicate heap(h) to be true if and only if nil is not allocated in h (h(nil) = none). The predicate heap(h) is a global invariant of our programs.

Next we introduce the operations manipulating pointers. For an address p and a value v, the *address update operation*, denoted $[p] := v$, is a function which takes as parameter a heap h, and returns a new heap h'. If the address p is allocated in h, then h' is h where the value of p is updated to v. Otherwise h' is some arbitrary but fixed element of Heap(V). In this approach, updating unallocated addresses, is not necessarily a fault, but if we update an unallocated address, then we know nothing about the resulting heap. If the predicate heap is an invariant of our program, then after updating an unallocated address, we will not be able to prove that heap holds for the new heap. If a more conservative approach is desired, in which the fact that we access unallocated addresses is a fault, then when updating an unallocated address, we can return the heap which has nil as the only allocated address, and this violates the invariant heap. Formally we have:

$$([p] := v)(h) = (\text{if } p \in \text{alloc}(h) \text{ then } h[p := v] \text{ else } \epsilon(\text{Heap}(V)))$$

where, for a set A, $\epsilon(A)$ is an arbitrary, but fixed, element of A. This operation preserves the global invariant heap.

If p is an address, then the *address look-up operation*, denoted $[p]$, is a function that maps heaps to values. If $h \in \text{Heap}(V)$ then $[p](h)$ is the value of address p in h if p is allocated in h, and it is an arbitrary, but fixed, value of V otherwise.

$$[p](h) = (\text{if } p \in \text{alloc}(h) \text{ then } h(p) \text{ else } \epsilon(V))$$

Here again, if p is not an allocated address in h, then $[p](h)$ is an arbitrary value, but it is not a fault. We can construct meaningful programs which access unallocated address if we ignore the values of these addresses. However, if we want to prove that our application is secure (it does not access arbitrary data from the heap), then we can also use a more conservative approach for this construct. We can design $[p](h)$ to return a pair of a value and a new heap. If the address is allocated, then it returns the value of p and h, otherwise it returns an arbitrary value and the heap with nil as the only allocated address. In this case, if we try to access an unallocated address, then the invariant heap is false for the returned heap.

We can state now some rules for correctness of the heap operations. We state these rules in a format that can be used for invariant based programs.

Theorem 1. *If α is a predicate on heaps, $p \in \text{Address}$, $v, v' \in V$, and $h, h' \in \text{Heap}(V)$, then*

1. $(p \mapsto v * \alpha)(h) \Rightarrow v = [p](h)$
2. $(p \mapsto v * \alpha)(h) \wedge h' = ([p] := v')(h) \Rightarrow (p \mapsto v' * \alpha)(h')$

The first property of this theorem corresponds to the Hoare rule for look-up of an address in separation logic: $\{p \mapsto v * \alpha \wedge x = v'\}\ x := [p]\ \{x = v \wedge p[v' := x] \mapsto v * \alpha\}$ where α does not contain variable x free. The second property of this theorem corresponds to the Hoare rule for address update: $\{p \mapsto v * \alpha\}$ $[p] := v'\ \{p \mapsto v' * \alpha\}$.

5 Pointer Representation of Binary Trees

In this section we introduce the abstract data type of binary trees and we use separation logic to define the pointer representation of these trees. We also introduce the basic results that are needed for proving Lindstrom's tree traversal algorithm.

The *type of (abstract) binary trees* with labels from the set A is defined by the following recursive data type definition:

$$\text{BTree}(A) = \bullet \mid \text{node}(\text{label} : A, \text{left} : \text{BTree}(A), \text{right} : \text{BTree}(A))$$

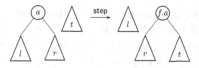

Fig. 1. One step of the traversal algorithm

A binary tree with labels from A can be empty ($\bullet$), or it can be the tree $\mathsf{node}(a, l, r)$ where a is its label, and l, r are the left and right sub-trees. For a non-empty tree t, the functions $\mathsf{label}(t)$, $\mathsf{left}(t)$, and $\mathsf{right}(t)$ return the label, the left sub-tree, and right sub-tree of t, and they return some arbitrary, but fixed, values for the empty tree. In addition we can also define recursively functions on binary trees. We define a recursive function f on binary trees by defining $f(\bullet)$, and by defining $f(t)$ for a non-empty tree t, assuming that we know $f(\mathsf{left}(t))$ and $f(\mathsf{right}(t))$. For example for a function $f : A \to B$ we define recursively the function $\mathsf{map}(f) : \mathsf{BTree}(A) \to \mathsf{BTree}(B)$ which for a tree t returns a new tree t' that has the same structure as t, but the labels t' are obtained from the labels of t by applying the function f. The formal definition of $\mathsf{map}(f)$ has two cases:

$$\mathsf{map}(f)(\bullet) = \bullet \qquad \mathsf{map}(f)(\mathsf{node}(a, l, r)) = \mathsf{node}(f(a), \mathsf{map}(f)(l), \mathsf{map}(f)(r))$$

Lindstrom's algorithm traverses a binary tree stored in memory using pointers, and it does so by using constant space. However, the algorithm visits every node of the tree three times. If on each visit of a node we apply a function $f : A \to A$ to the label of the node, then at the abstract level, the traversal algorithm is equivalent to applying f^3 to every label of the tree, where $f^3 = f \circ f \circ f$. In other words the traversal of the tree t is the same as computing $\mathsf{traverse}(f)(t) := \mathsf{map}(f^3)(t)$. The algorithm traverses the tree in a number of steps, and it uses an additional single node tree. A step of the algorithm is represented in Fig. 1. The basic step takes two binary trees t_0 and t, and if t_0 is nonempty ($t_0 = \mathsf{node}(a, l, r)$), then it returns another two trees l and $\mathsf{node}(f(a), r, t)$. If t_0 is empty ($t_0 = \bullet$), then it returns t and t_0. Formally the step of the algorithm is given by the following definition:

$$\mathsf{step}(f)(\bullet, t) = (t, \bullet) \qquad \mathsf{step}(f)(\mathsf{node}(a, l, r), t) = (l, \mathsf{node}(f(a), r, t))$$

We will prove next that for a suitable natural number n, if we iterate the $\mathsf{step}(f)$ function on a pair of trees (t, t') n times, then we obtain t' and the traversal of t. The *size of the traversal* is the number of steps needed for achieving this and it is given by the following definition:

$$\mathsf{size}(\bullet) = 1 \qquad \mathsf{size}(\mathsf{node}(a, l, r)) = 3 + \mathsf{size}(l) + \mathsf{size}(r)$$

That is for every empty sub-tree of t we need one step, and for every proper sub-tree of t we need 3 steps.

Theorem 2. *If t and t' are binary trees, then $(\mathsf{step}(f))^{\mathsf{size}(t)}(t, t') = (t', \mathsf{traverse}(f)(t))$*

Now, using this theorem, if we iterate the step size(t) number of times, then we obtain the traversed tree. However we do not know size(t) a priori, and calculating it would be as difficult as the original task of traversing the tree. The additional property that we can prove is that if we iterate the function step(id) k times where $k <$ size(t), then the first tree of the result is empty, or its label is in the set of all labels of the original tree t. If we know that t' is not empty, and the label of t' is not among the set of all labels of t, then we can stop applying the step when the label of the first tree is the same as the label of the initial t'.

Theorem 3. *If t and t' are binary trees, $k <$ size(t), and $(u, u') = $ (step(id))$^k(t, t')$, then $u = \bullet$ or label(u) $\in$ set(t), where set(t) is the set of all labels of the tree t.*

In the reminder of this section we use separation logic to define the representation of binary trees in memory using the heap. In this and next sections we will use heaps that can store triples of a tree label from A, and two addresses for the left and right sub-trees (Heap($A \times$ Address $\times$ Address)). We will use binary trees with labels from A and with labels from Address.

If $u \in$ BTree(Address) then plabel(u) = (if $u = \bullet$ then nil else label(u)), and if $x \in$ BTree(A), then the predicate ptree(x, u)(h) is true if the trees x and u have the same structure, all labels of u are distinct and are the allocated addresses in h, and h represents the tree x. Formally we have

ptree($\bullet, u$) = ($u = \bullet$)
ptree(node(a, l, r), u) = ($u \neq \bullet \wedge$ (label(u) $\mapsto$ (a, plabel(left(u)), plabel(right(u)))
    $*$ ptree(l, left(u)) $*$ ptree(r, right(u))))

When representing abstract binary trees using separation logic, usually a predicate is defined on the abstract tree x and an address p, which is true when at address p we have the representation of x. The definition of this predicate uses existential quantifiers for the internal addresses of the tree. In our case it is useful to make these internal addresses explicit for two reasons. Firstly, the termination of the algorithm relies on these addresses. Secondly, we can show that the content of the heap (with respect to the allocated addresses and the structure) is the same after the execution of the algorithm.

Theorem 4. *If $x, y \in$ BTree(A) and $u, v \in$ BTree(Address) then*

1. (ptree(x, u) $* \alpha$)(h) $\Rightarrow$ size(x) = size(u)
2. (ptree(x, u) $*$ ptree(y, v) $* \alpha$)(h) $\Rightarrow$ set(u) $\cap$ set(v) = $\emptyset$

The second property of this theorem states that if the heap contains two abstract binary trees x and y, and some other addresses specified by α, then the two sets of addresses at which these trees are stored are distinct.

6   Invariant Based Program for Lindstrom's Algorithm

We are ready now to introduce the Lindstrom's algorithm for traversing a binary tree as an invariant diagram. The algorithm is represented in Fig. 2.

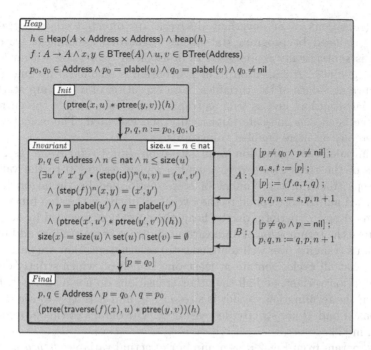

Fig. 2. Lindstrom's algorithm as an invariant diagram

This diagram contains four situations (*Heap*, *Init*, *Invariant*, and *Final*). The situation *Heap* introduces the variables and the invariants that are common to all other situations. We have the heap h, the function f that we apply to the labels, the abstract binary tree x that we are traversing, its corresponding abstract tree u labeled by address, the auxiliary tree y and its corresponding address tree v, and the addresses p_0 and q_0 of the heap representations of the two trees. In order for this algorithm to work, we need to assume that the root address of the auxiliary tree y is not nil ($q_0 \neq$ nil). This is because the termination condition for the algorithm is $p = q_0$, and, while visiting the leaves of the tree x, the variable p will become nil many times before finishing the traversal. The situation *Init* states the precondition of the algorithm, i.e. the heap h contains exactly the two trees x and y at addresses specified in u and v. In addition, the conditions $p_0 =$ plabel(u) and $q_0 =$ plabel(v) assert that p_0 and q_0 are the addresses of the roots of x and y. The situation *Final* states the post-condition of the algorithm. At the end of the algorithm, the heap contains the traversal of the tree x at address $q = p_0$ and the original tree y at address $p = q_0$. The post-condition states also that the structure, and the addresses of the heap are exactly the same, only the labels of the original tree x are changed. The loop invariant is represented in the situation *Invariant*. This invariant states that at current addresses p and q we have two binary trees which are obtained iterating the step function n times on the original trees x and y.

The transitions of an invariant diagram are directed edges between the situations, labeled by program statements – guarded assignment statements. A guard is syntactically represented by a Boolean expression within brackets ($[p \neq q_0 \wedge p \neq \mathsf{nil}]$). A transition from a situation is enabled if its guard is true for the current values of the variables. The execution of a diagram starts from some initial situation, and as long as transitions are enabled in the current situation, one is chosen non-deterministically and executed. The execution stops when there are no more enabled transitions.

The initialization transition from situation *Init* to *Invariant* assigns the addresses of the trees x and y to p and q and it assigns 0 to the variable n which keeps tracks of the number of steps performed by the algorithm. The transitions A and B correspond to the two cases of the of the step function. The transitions A and B perform on the heap the operation specified by step.

To prove the termination of an invariant diagram in general, we add termination variants (ranging over well-founded sets) to situations that are part of loops. We show that all cycles contain at least one transition which strictly decreases the termination variant, and all the other transitions do not increase it. For this algorithm, the termination variant is $\mathsf{size}(u) - n$, and it is easy to see that both transitions A and B are strictly decreasing it. The details of this procedure can be found in [23].

The program from Fig. 2 uses a number of actual variables h, p, q, q_0, p_0, f as well as some specification or ghost variables x, y, u, v, n. In fact the variable n is also used as a proper variable in the transitions A and B. We could have n existentially quantified inside the situation *Invariant*, but if we use this approach, then we cannot use n to prove the termination of this algorithm. Because n occurs only in assignment statements, and it is used only to update itself, we can turn it also into a specification variable. The variables a, s, t are local to the transition A.

The existential quantifier in the situation *Invariant* is used only to name the two components of $(\mathsf{step}(f))^n(x, y)$ and of $(\mathsf{step}(\mathsf{id}))^n(u, v)$. When proving the correctness of the transitions involving this situation, the existential quantifier is eliminated automatically by Isabelle.

7   Isabelle Representation of the Invariant Based Program

In this section we introduce the Isabelle representation of the Lindstrom's algorithm from Fig. 2. More details about this representation can be found in [23].

To represent the situations we use Isabelle locales [3], and to represent nesting of situations we use the locale extension mechanism. Locales are parametric theories with constants and axioms. The constants are used to model the program variables, and the axioms are used to model the invariants.

locale $Heap$ =
    fixes h : Heap.$(A \times$ Address $\times$ Address$)$ and $f : A \to A$
    fixes x, y : BTree.A and u, v : BTree.Address and p_0, q_0 : Address
    assumes $isheap$: heap.h
    assumes $labels\ [simp]$: $p_0 =$ plabel.u and $q_0 =$ plabel.v
    assumes $q_0\_not\_nil\ [simp]$: $q_0 \neq$ nil
locale $Init$ = $Heap$ +
    assumes $trees\_heap$: $(\text{ptree}(x, u) * \text{ptree}(y, v))(h)$
locale $Invariant$ = $Heap$ + $\cdots$
locale $Final$ = $Heap$ + $\cdots$

The definitions of the *Invariant* and *Final* locales follow the same pattern as the definitions of *Heap* and *Init*, and they contain the invariants introduced already in Fig. 2. In locales we can also name the assumptions, and we can declare some of them as automatic simplification rules.

The transitions in the diagram are modeled as locale interpretations:

context $Init$:
    theorem $to\_Invariant$:
        assumes $p = p_0$ and $q = q_0$ and $n = 0$
        shows $Invariant(h, f, x, y, u, v, p_0, q_0, p, q, n)$

That is, if we are in the context of the situation *Init*, and we assign p_0, q_0, and 0 to p, q, and n, then the situation *Invariant* holds for the new values.

context $Invariant$:
    theorem $A\_to\_Invariant$:
        assumes $p \neq q_0$ and $p \neq$ nil
        assumes $(a, s, t) = [p](h)$
        assumes $h' = ([p] := (f.a, t, q))(h)$
        assumes $p' = s$ and $q' = p$ and $n' = n + 1$
        shows $Invariant(h', f, x, y, u, v, p_0, q_0, p', q', n')$

We model transitions that assign new values to existing variables using equalities, and we introduce primed names for the new values of the existing variables. For the heap look-up and update operations, we also need to use explicitly the heap variable. Similar to the assumptions in locales, we can also name the transitions and we can declare them as simplification rules.

The other transitions from Fig. 2 are modeled in a similar manner.

Within locales we can also prove auxiliary lemmas that are useful to prove the theorems for the transitions. For example a property that is useful for proving the transitions A and B and also for termination, is the fact that if we are in the situation *Invariant*, then if $p \neq q_0$ then $n < \text{size}(u)$.

context $Invariant$:
    lemma $less\_size$: $p \neq q_0 \implies n < \text{size}(u)$

We show how to prove the transition A of the diagram (theorem $A\_to\_Invariant$). We assume that all invariants of the situation *Invariant*, are

468   V. Preoteasa

(a) : $\mathsf{heap}(h)$
(b) : $p_0 = \mathsf{plabel}(u) \wedge q_0 = \mathsf{plabel}(v)$
$\qquad \wedge\; q_0 \neq \mathsf{nil}$
(c) : $n \leq \mathsf{size}.u$
(d) : $(\mathsf{step}(f))^n(x,y) = (x',y')$
(e) : $(\mathsf{step}(\mathsf{id}))^n(u,v) = (u',v')$
(f) : $p = \mathsf{plabel}(u') \wedge q = \mathsf{plabel}(v')$
(g) : $(\mathsf{ptree}(x',u') * \mathsf{ptree}(y',v'))(h)$
(h) : $\mathsf{size}(x) = \mathsf{size}(u) \wedge \mathsf{set}(u)\cap\mathsf{set}(v) = \emptyset$
(ta) : $p \neq q_0 \wedge p \neq \mathsf{nil}$
(tb) : $(a,s,t) = [p](h)$
(tc) : $h' = ([p] := (f.a,t,q))(h)$
(td) : $p' = s \wedge q' = p \wedge n' = n+1$

(a') : $\mathsf{heap}(h')$
(b') : $p_0 = \mathsf{plabel}(u) \wedge q_0 = \mathsf{plabel}(v)$
$\qquad \wedge\; q_0 \neq \mathsf{nil}$
(c') : $n' \leq \mathsf{size}(u)$
(d') : $(\mathsf{step}(f))^{n'}(x,y) = (x'',y'')$
(e') : $(\mathsf{step}(\mathsf{id}))^{n'}(u,v) = (u'',v'')$
(f') : $p' = \mathsf{plabel}(u'') \wedge q' = \mathsf{plabel}(v'')$
(g') : $(\mathsf{ptree}(x'',u'') * \mathsf{ptree}(y'',v''))(h')$
(h') : $\mathsf{size}(x) = \mathsf{size}(u) \wedge \mathsf{set}(u)\cap\mathsf{set}(v) = \emptyset$

Fig. 3. (a) Invariant before transition and transition, (b) invariant after the transition

true, and the transition A is enabled. That is, there exists x',y',u',v' such that properties from Fig. 3(a) are true and we have to find x'',y'',u'',v'' such that the properties from Fig. 3(b) are true.

Using lemma *less_size* we obtain that $n' = n+1 \leq \mathsf{size}(u)$, so (c') is proved. (b') and (h') are also true because they are identical to (b) and (h). Because $p \neq \mathsf{nil}$ (ta) and $p = \mathsf{plabel}(u')$ (f) it follows that $u' \neq \bullet$. So there is w,w' such that $u' = \mathsf{node}(p,w,w')$. Because $u' \neq \bullet$ and (g) it follows that $x' \neq \bullet$, so there are also b,z,z' such that $x' = \mathsf{node}(b,z,z')$, and from (g), expanding the definition of ptree we have

(obs_a) : $(p \mapsto (b, \mathsf{plabel}(w), \mathsf{plabel}(w')) * \mathsf{ptree}(z,w) * \mathsf{ptree}(z',w') * \mathsf{ptree}(y',v'))(h)$.

Because of (obs_a), (tb), using Theorem 1, we obtain

(obs_b) : $b = a \;\wedge\; s = \mathsf{plabel}(w) \;\wedge\; t = \mathsf{plabel}(w')$.

If we set $x'' = z$ and $y'' = \mathsf{node}(f(a),z',y')$ then (d') follows from the following derivation:

$\qquad (\mathsf{step}(f))^{n'}(x,y)$
$=\quad \{(td)$ and $(d)\}$
$\qquad \mathsf{step}(f)(x',y')$
$=\quad \{$our observations$\}$
$\qquad \mathsf{step}(f)(\mathsf{node}(a,z,z'),y')$
$=\quad \{$definition of step$\}$
$\qquad (z,\; \mathsf{node}(f(a),z',y'))$
$=\quad \{$instantiations of $x'',y''\}$
$\qquad (x'',y'')$

Similarly, if we set $u'' = w$ and $v'' = \mathsf{node}(p,w',v')$ then (e') is true. From (obs_b) and (td) it follows (f'). We have now only the property (g'), and this can also be proved easily by expanding definitions, and using the heap update rule from Theorem 1.

Although we have to write explicitly the heap parameter h in our specifications, we reason about heap statements as abstract as in classical separation logic. To reason about a look-up statement $v := [p]$ we need to show that the heap before this statement has the structure $(p \mapsto v' * \alpha)$, and then we know that $v = v'$. For the update statement $[p] := v$ we also need to know that the heap has the structure $p \mapsto v' * \alpha$ before the statement, and then after the statement we know that the new heap has the structure $(p \mapsto v) * \alpha$.

8   Isabelle/HOL Function Implementing the Algorithm

Section 7 introduced the invariant based program for Lindstrom's algorithm using Isabelle's locales. This construction, including the supporting formalization (binary trees in this case), should be done by the developer. In this section we show how to construct a collection of Isabelle/HOL mutually recursive functions that implements this algorithm. All steps from this section can be automated.

We introduce a function for each situation, except *Heap*. The function corresponding to a situation implements the execution of the algorithm starting in this situation. The functions are defined in Fig. 4.

Every function has as parameters the variables defined in the corresponding situation. We use all the variables, including the specification ones to be able to prove easily the termination and the correctness property for these functions. At the end of this section we will eliminate the specification parameters. All these functions return a triple (h, p, q) that corresponds to the values of the variables h, p, and q at the end of the algorithm. These functions can be mechanically constructed from the transitions.

$$\text{init\_fun}(h, f, x, y, u, v, p_0, q_0)$$
$$= \text{inv\_fun}(h, f, x, y, u, v, p_0, q_0, p_0, q_0, 0)$$
$$\text{inv\_fun}(h, f, x, y, u, v, p_0, q_0, p, q, n)$$
$$= \text{if } Invariant(h, f, x, y, u, v, p_0, q_0, p, q, n) \text{ then}$$
$$\qquad \text{if } p \neq q_0 \text{ then}$$
$$\qquad \quad \text{if } p \neq \text{nil then}$$
$$\qquad \qquad \text{let } (a, s, t) = [p](h), \; h' = ([p] := (f(a), t, q))(h) \text{ in}$$
$$\qquad \qquad \quad \text{inv\_fun}(h', f, x, y, u, v, p_0, q_0, s, p, (n+1))$$
$$\qquad \quad \text{else}$$
$$\qquad \qquad \text{inv\_fun}(h, f, x, y, u, v, p_0, q_0, q, p, (n+1))$$
$$\qquad \text{else}$$
$$\qquad \quad \text{final\_fun}(h, f, x, y, u, v, p_0, q_0, p, q)$$
$$\quad \text{else}$$
$$\qquad (\epsilon.\text{Heap}, \epsilon.\text{Address}, \epsilon.\text{Address})$$
$$\text{final\_fun}(h, f, x, y, u, v, p_0, q_0, p, q)$$
$$= (h, p, q)$$

Fig. 4. Mutually recursive functions

Because the termination of the recursive call to inv_fun can be proved only assuming that we are in situation *Invariant*, we have to include the expression $Invariant(h, f, x, y, u, v, p_0, q_0, p, q, n)$ in the definition of inv_fun. If this expression is true, then we proceed with the transitions from situation *Invariant*, otherwise we stop returning some arbitrary values. We show later how to eliminate this condition.

The termination of this functions is proved by mechanically constructing a well founded relation on the parameters. The fact that the relation is well founded is proved by using the termination verification conditions. The details of this procedure are presented in [23].

Together with the function definitions from Fig. 4 we obtain also an induction theorem. Using the theorems for the transitions and the induction theorem we can prove the following correctness theorem for these functions.

Theorem 5. *The following properties are true*

$Init(h, f, x, y, u, v, p_0, q_0) \wedge (h', p', q') = \text{init\_fun}(h, f, x, y, u, v, p_0, q_0)$
$\quad \implies Final(h', f, x, y, u, v, p_0, q_0, p', q')$
$Invariant(h, f, x, y, u, v, p_0, q_0, p, q, n)$
$\quad \wedge (h', p', q') = \text{inv\_fun}(h, f, x, y, u, v, p_0, q_0, p, q, n)$
$\quad \implies Final(h', f, x, y, u, v, p_0, q_0, p', q')$
$Final.h.f.x.y.u.v.p_0.q_0.p.q \wedge (h', p', q') = \text{final\_fun}(h, f, x, y, u, v, p_0, q_0, p, q)$
$\quad \implies Final(h', f, x, y, u, v, p_0, q_0, p', q')$

This theorem states that if we are in a situation of the diagram, and we execute the corresponding function, then we end in the final situation. The proof of this theorem can be automated by applying the induction theorem of the recursive functions, and then using the theorems of the transitions.

The last step in our development is to eliminate the specification variables and introduce new functions that can also be executed and translated to code. In general our functions are mutually tail recursive and we can also define them using the partial function mechanism from [25]. Isabelle supports defining partial recursive functions, and [25] extends this mechanism to mutually recursive partial functions. Our example has only one recursive function and we can define it directly as a partial function in Isabelle:

```
partial_function (tailrec) :
    inv_code(h, f, q₀, p, q) =
        if p ≠ q₀ then
            if p ≠ nil then
                let (a, s, t) = [p](h),  h' = ([p] := (f(a), t, q))(h) in
                    inv_code(h', f, q₀, s, p)
            else
                inv_code(h, f, q₀, q, p)
        else
            (h, p, q)
```

Using the well established code generation mechanism of Isabelle [9], from the function inv_code we can generate directly ML, Scala, Ocaml, or Haskell executable code. However we do not know yet that inv_code satisfies the correctness conditions from Theorem 5. Using again the induction theorem and the transition theorems we can prove that under the invariant conditions the functions inv_fun and inv_code are equal:

Theorem 6. *The following properties are true*

$Init(h, f, x, y, u, v, p_0, q_0)$
$\implies$ init_fun$(h, f, x, y, u, v, p_0, q_0)$ = init_code(h, f, q_0, p_0, q_0)
$Invariant(h, f, x, y, u, v, p_0, q_0, p, q, n)$
$\implies$ inv_fun$(h, f, x, y, u, v, p_0, q_0, p, q, n)$ = init_code(h, f, q_0, p, q)

Using Theorems 5 and 6, if we start init_code(h, f, q_0, p_0, q_0) in a state satisfying the properties of the initial situation, then the result of this function satisfies the properties of the final situation, i.e. the tree at address p_0 is traversed three times.

The code generation mechanism employed above does not produce efficient code because it implements the heap structure in a functional manner. However there are solutions available in Isabelle capable of generating efficient imperative code [7,14] for programs using the same heap structure as our invariant programs. The functions that we produce are always tail recursive, and they can be implemented efficiently. Translating from our functional representation from Fig. 4 into another program representation, better suited for imperative code generation, is easy using the induction and the transition theorems. We showed here the inv_code representation suitable for pure functional code generation, and we experimented with another representation. Proving the equivalence of the representations (under the invariant assumptions), is a mechanical task of applying the induction theorem, then expanding the recursive functions one step, and finally applying the transition theorems on all branches.

9   Conclusions

In this paper we have introduced a technique based on separation logic and invariant based programming for constructing correct pointer programs as higher order functions in Isabelle/HOL theorem prover. We applied our technique for a non-trivial algorithm due to Lindstrom for traversing a binary tree without additional memory.

In our approach the developer needs to construct the situations, the invariants, the transitions, and prove the correctness of the transitions. All the other steps regarding the construction of the mutually recursive functions, and their executable variants can be automated.

Acknowledgments. I am grateful to Stavros Tripakis and anonymous reviewers for their useful comments that contributed to the improvement of the final version of the paper.

References

1. Back, R.J.: Invariant based programming. In: Donatelli, S., Thiagarajan, P.S. (eds.) ICATPN 2006. LNCS, vol. 4024, pp. 1–18. Springer, Heidelberg (2006)
2. Back, R.J., Preoteasa, V.: Semantics, proof rules of invariant based programs. In: 26th Symposium On Applied Computing - Software Verification and Testing Track. ACM (2011)
3. Ballarin, C.: Locales: a module system for mathematical theories. J. Autom. Reasoning **52**(2), 123–153 (2014)
4. Berdine, J., Calcagno, C., O'Hearn, P.W.: Smallfoot: modular automatic assertion checking with separation logic. In: de Boer, F.S., Bonsangue, M.M., Graf, S., de Roever, W.-P. (eds.) FMCO 2005. LNCS, vol. 4111, pp. 115–137. Springer, Heidelberg (2006)
5. Bobot, F., Filliâtre, J.-C.: Separation predicates: a taste of separation logic in first-order logic. In: Aoki, T., Taguchi, K. (eds.) ICFEM 2012. LNCS, vol. 7635, pp. 167–181. Springer, Heidelberg (2012)
6. Bobot, F., Filliâtre, J.-C., Marché, C., Melquiond, G., Paskevich, A.: Preserving user proofs across specification changes. In: Cohen, E., Rybalchenko, A. (eds.) VSTTE 2013. LNCS, vol. 8164, pp. 191–201. Springer, Heidelberg (2014)
7. Bulwahn, L., Krauss, A., Haftmann, F., Erkök, L., Matthews, J.: Imperative functional programming with Isabelle/HOL. In: Mohamed, O.A., Muñoz, C., Tahar, S. (eds.) TPHOLs 2008. LNCS, vol. 5170, pp. 134–149. Springer, Heidelberg (2008)
8. Filliâtre, J.-C., Paskevich, A.: Why3 — Where programs meet provers. In: Felleisen, M., Gardner, P. (eds.) ESOP 2013. LNCS, vol. 7792, pp. 125–128. Springer, Heidelberg (2013)
9. Haftmann, F., Nipkow, T.: Code generation via higher-order rewrite systems. In: Blume, M., Kobayashi, N., Vidal, G. (eds.) FLOPS 2010. LNCS, vol. 6009, pp. 103–117. Springer, Heidelberg (2010)
10. Heinen, J., Noll, T., Rieger, S.: Juggrnaut: Graph grammar abstraction for unbounded heap structures. In: Electronic Notes in Theoretical Computer Science, vol. 266, pp. 93–107 (2010)
11. Jacobs, B., Smans, J., Piessens, F.: A quick tour of the verifast program verifier. In: Ueda, K. (ed.) APLAS 2010. LNCS, vol. 6461, pp. 304–311. Springer, Heidelberg (2010)
12. Klein, G., Kolanski, R., Boyton, A.: Mechanised separation algebra. In: Beringer, L., Felty, A. (eds.) ITP 2012. LNCS, vol. 7406, pp. 332–337. Springer, Heidelberg (2012)
13. Klein, G., Kolanski, R., Boyton, A.: Separation algebra. Archive of Formal Proofs, May 2012. http://afp.sf.net/entries/Separation_Algebra.shtml. Formal proof development
14. Lammich, P.: Refinement to imperative/HOL. In: Urban, C., Zhang, X. (eds.) ITP 2015. LNCS, vol. 9236, pp. 253–269. Springer, Heidelberg (2015)
15. Lammich, P., Meis, R.: A separation logic framework for imperative HOL. Archive of Formal Proofs, Nov 2012. http://afp.sf.net/entries/Separation_Logic_Imperative_HOL.shtml
16. Leino, K.R.M.: Dafny: an automatic program verifier for functional correctness. In: Voronkov, A., Clarke, E.M. (eds.) LPAR-16 2010. LNCS, vol. 6355, pp. 348–370. Springer, Heidelberg (2010)
17. Lindstrom, G.: Scanning list structures without stacks or tag bits. Inform. Process. Lett. **2**(2), 47–51 (1973)

18. Loginov, A., Reps, T., Sagiv, M.: Automated verification of the deutsch-schorr-waite tree-traversal algorithm. In: Yi, K. (ed.) SAS 2006. LNCS, vol. 4134, pp. 261–279. Springer, Heidelberg (2006)
19. Nanevski, A., Morrisett, G., Birkedal, L.: Hoare type theory, polymorphism and separation. J. Funct. Program. **18**, 865–911 (2008)
20. Nanevski, A., Vafeiadis, V., Berdine, J.: Structuring the verification of heap-manipulating programs. In: Proceedings of POPL 2010, pp. 261–274. ACM, New York (2010)
21. Nipkow, T., Paulson, L.C., Wenzel, M. (eds.): Isabelle/HOL. LNCS, vol. 2283. Springer, Heidelberg (2002)
22. O'Hearn, P.W., Reynolds, J.C., Yang, H.: Local reasoning about programs that alter data structures. In: Fribourg, L. (ed.) CSL 2001 and EACSL 2001. LNCS, vol. 2142, pp. 1–19. Springer, Heidelberg (2001)
23. Preoteasa, V., Back, R.-J., Eriksson, J.: Verification and code generation for invariant diagrams in Isabelle. J. Logical Algebraic Methods Program. **84**, 37–53 (2015)
24. Reynolds, J.: Separation logic: A logic for shared mutable data structures. In: 17th Annual IEEE Symposium on Logic in Computer Science. IEEE, July 2002
25. Thiemann, R.: Mutually recursive partial functions. Archive of Formal Proofs, Feb 2014. http://afp.sf.net/entries/Partial_Function_MR.shtml, Formal proof development
26. Wenzel, M.: Isar - a generic interpretative approach to readable formal proof documents. In: Bertot, Y., Dowek, G., Hirschowitz, A., Paulin, C., Théry, L. (eds.) TPHOLs 1999. LNCS, vol. 1690, pp. 167–183. Springer, Heidelberg (1999)
27. Yang, H., O'Hearn, P.W.: A semantic basis for local reasoning. In: Nielsen, M., Engberg, U. (eds.) FOSSACS 2002. LNCS, vol. 2303, pp. 402–416. Springer, Heidelberg (2002)

A Constraint Satisfaction Method
for Configuring Non-local Service Interfaces

Pavel Zaichenkov$^{(\boxtimes)}$, Olga Tveretina, and Alex Shafarenko

Compiler Technology and Computer Architecture Group,
University of Hertfordshire, Hatfield, UK
{p.zaichenkov,o.tveretina,a.shafarenko}@ctca.eu

Abstract. Modularity and decontextualization are core principles of a
service-oriented architecture. However, the principles are often lost when
it comes to an implementation of services due to rigid service interfaces.
This paper focuses on a two-fold problem. On the one hand, the interface
description language must be flexible for maintaining service compatibility in different contexts without modification of the service itself. On the
other hand, the composition of interfaces in a distributed environment
must be provably consistent.

We present a novel approach for automatic interface configuration
in distributed services. We introduce a Message Definition Language
(MDL), an interface description language with support of subtyping,
flow inheritance and polymorphism. The MDL supports configuration
variables that link input and output interfaces of a service and propagate requirements over an application graph. We present an algorithm
that solves the interface reconciliation problem using constraint satisfaction that relies on Boolean satisfiability as a subproblem.

Keywords: Service-oriented architecture · Interface configuration ·
Constraint satisfaction · Satisfiability

1 Introduction

For the last decade service-oriented computing (SOC) has been a promising technology facilitating development of large-scale distributed systems. SOC allows
enterprises to expose their internal business systems as services available on
the Internet. On the other hand, clients can combine services and reuse them
for developing their own applications or constructing more complex services.
Although web services continue to play an important role in modern software
development, a service composition is still a key challenge for SOC and web services. Web service composition empowers organizations to build inter-enterprise
software, to outsource software modules, and to provide an easily accessible functionality for their customers. Furthermore, service composition reduces the cost
and risks of new software development, because the software elements that are
represented as web services can be reused repeatedly [1].

© Springer International Publishing Switzerland 2016
E. Ábrahám and M. Huisman (Eds.): IFM 2016, LNCS 9681, pp. 474–488, 2016.
DOI: 10.1007/978-3-319-33693-0_30

Web Service Description Language (WSDL) is an XML-based specification language for describing service interfaces, which is a *de facto* standard in SOC. Functionality and compatible data formats of the service are specified in WSDL in the form of an interface. The names and formats in the interfaces of communicating services must exactly match for interface compatibility. Today the environment in which services are developed and executed has become more open, changing and dynamic, which requires an adaptable and flexible approach to service composition. The choreography wired to specific WSDL interfaces is too restrictive for dependable service composition. The choreography is statically bounded to specific operation names and types, which impedes reusability of compound services and their interaction descriptions.

Reliable and dependable service composition remains a significant challenge today [1, 2]. Services are provided autonomously by various organizations. Developers of applications, particularly safety-critical applications, such as health care, stock trading, nuclear systems, must be able to check soundness and completeness of service composition at early stages. Therefore, model checking and verification of web services is being actively researched today [3, 4].

Web Services Choreography Description Language (WS-CDL) [5] and Web Service Choreography Interface (WSCI) [6] are languages for describing protocols from a global perspective. This approach is based on π-calculus that defines a behavioral semantics for concurrent processes. An application designer writes a global description in WS-CDL or WSCI that should be realizable by local protocols of communicating services. Service interfaces in WS-CDL are specified in WSDL. The relation between service interfaces connected with a communication channel is one-to-one, i.e. there is no way to propagate data format requirements and capabilities across the communication graph if services are not explicitly connected by a channel. Moreover, [7] emphasizes that the existing association between WS-CDL and WSDL does not allow equivalent services with different WSDL interfaces to be part of the choreography.

Session types is another approach based on π-calculus that assures communication safety in distributed systems and in service choreographies particularly [8]. A choreography is defined as a global protocol in terms of the interactions that are expected from the protocol peers and a set of local protocols, one for each peer, which describes the global protocol from the viewpoint of an individual peer. The session types require services to expose their behavior as a protocol. This information is enough to define a communication type system, which is well-suited for verifying runtime properties of the system such as deadlock-freedom, interleaving, etc. The session types essentially rely on behavioral protocols, which in most cases are neither explicitly provided nor can be derived from the code.

In this paper we present a formal method for configuring flexible interfaces in the presence of subtyping, polymorphism and flow inheritance. Our method is based on constraint satisfaction and SAT. In contrast to the approaches based on π-calculus, our method does not require services to define a protocol, but only to specify the data interface. The method is illustrated using an example introduced in Sect. 2.

2 Motivating Example

Our approach for configuring web services is motivated by rapid development of Cloud computing, social networks and Internet of Things, which accelerate the growth and complexity of service choreographies [9,10]. Accordingly, we chose a simple but non-trivial example from one of those areas to illustrate our approach. The same example, known as the *three-buyer use case*, is often called upon to demonstrate the capabilities of session types such as communication safety, progress and protocol conformance [11].

Consider a system involving buyers called Alice, Bob and Carol that cooperate in order to buy a book from a Seller. Each buyer is specified as an independent service that is connected with other services via a channel-based communication. There is an interface associated with every input and output port of a service, which specifies the service's functionality and data formats that the service is compatible with. The interfaces are defined in a Message Definition Language (MDL) that is formally introduced in Sect. 3. Figure 1 depicts composition of the application where Alice is connected to Seller only and can interact with Bob and Carol indirectly. AS, SB, BC, CB, BS, AS denote interfaces that are associated with service input/output ports. For brevity, we only provide AS, SB and BC (the rest of the interfaces are defined in the same manner), which are specified in the MDL as algebraic terms in the following way:

$$AS_{out} = (\text{:request: } \{\text{title: } tv^{\downarrow}\},$$
$$\text{payment: } \{\text{title: } tv^{\downarrow}, \text{money: int, id: int}\},$$
$$\text{share}(x): \{\text{title: } tv^{\downarrow}, \text{money: int}\},$$
$$\text{suggest}(y): \{\text{title: } tv^{\downarrow}\}:)$$
$$SB_{out} = (\text{:response : } \{\text{title: string, money: int}\}$$
$$| \ ct1^{\uparrow}:)$$
$$BC_{out} = (\text{:share}(z): \{\text{quote: string, money: int}\} \ | \ ct2^{\uparrow}:)$$

$$AS_{in} = (\text{:request: } \{\text{title: string}\},$$
$$\text{payment: } \{\text{title: string, money: int}\}$$
$$| \ ct1^{\uparrow}:)$$
$$SB_{in} = (\text{:share}(z) : \ \{\text{quote: string,}$$
$$\text{money: int}\},$$
$$\text{response : } \{\text{title: string, money: int}\}$$
$$| \ ct2^{\uparrow}:)$$
$$BC_{in} = (\text{:share : } \{\text{quote: string, money: int}\}:)$$

$(::)$ delimit a collection of alternative label-record pairs called *variants*, where the label corresponds to the particular implementation that can process a message defined by the given record. A *record* delimited by $\{ \ \}$ is a collection of label-value pairs. Collection elements may contain Boolean variables called *guards* (e.g. x, y or z in our example). A guard instantiated to false excludes the element from the collection. This is the main self-configuration mechanism: Boolean variables control the dependencies between any elements of interface collections (this can be seen as a generalized version of intersection types [12]) The variables exclude elements from the collection if the dependencies between corresponding elements in the interfaces that are connected by a communication channel cannot be satisfied.

$$\text{Alice} \xleftarrow{\;\;\; AS_{out} \quad AS_{in} \;\;\;} \text{Seller} \xleftarrow{\;\;\; SB_{out} \quad SB_{in} \;\;\;} \text{Bob} \xleftarrow{\;\;\; BC_{out} \quad BC_{in} \;\;\;} \text{Carol}$$
$$SA_{in} \quad SA_{out} \qquad BS_{in} \quad BS_{out} \qquad CB_{in} \quad CB_{out}$$

Fig. 1. Service composition in a Three Buyer usecase

Parametric polymorphism is supported using interface variables such as $tv^{\downarrow}$, $ct1^{\uparrow}$ and $ct2^{\uparrow}$ (the meaning of $\uparrow$ and $\downarrow$ is explain in Sect. 3). Moreover, the presence of $ct1^{\uparrow}$ and $ct2^{\uparrow}$ in both input and output interfaces enables flow inheritance [13] mechanism that provides delegation of the data and service functionality across available services.

AS_{out} declares an output interface of Alice, which declares functionality and a format of messages sent to Seller. The service has the following functionality:

- Alice can request a book's price from Seller by providing a title of an arbitrary type (which is specified by a term variable $tv^{\downarrow}$) that Seller is compatible with. On the other hand, Seller declares that a title of type string is only acceptable, which means that $tv^{\downarrow}$ must be instantiated to string.
- Furthermore, Alice can provide a payment for a book. In addition to the title and the required amount of money, Alice provides her id in the message. Although Seller does not require the id, the interconnection is still valid (a description in standard WSDL interfaces would cause an error though) due to the subtyping supported in the MDL.
- Furthermore, Alice can offer to share a purchase between other customers. Although Alice is not connected to Bob or Carol and may even not be aware of their presence (the example illustrates a composition where some service communicates with services that the service is not directly connected with), our mechanism detects that Alice can send a message with "share" label to Bob by bypassing it implicitly through Seller. In order to enable flow inheritance in Seller's service, the mechanism sets a tail variable $ct1^{\uparrow}$ to (:share: {title: string, money: int}:). If Bob were unable to accept a message with "share" label, the mechanism would instantiate x with false, which automatically removes the corresponding functionality from the service.
- Finally, Alice can suggest a book to other buyers. However, examination of other service interfaces shows that there is no service that can receive a message with the label "suggest". Therefore, a communication error occurs if Alice decides to send the message. To avoid this, the configuration mechanism excludes "suggest" functionality from Alice's service by setting y variable to false.

The proposed configuration mechanism analyses the interfaces of services Seller, Bob and Carol in the same manner. The presence of $ct1^{\uparrow}$ variable in both input and output interfaces of Bob enables support of data inheritance on the interface level. Furthermore, the Boolean variable z behaves as an intersection type: Bob has "purchase sharing" functionality declared as an element share(z): {...} in its input interface SB_{in} (used by Seller). The element is related to the element share(z): {...} in its output interface BC_{out} (used by Carol). The relation declares that Bob provides Carol with "sharing" functionality only if Bob was provided with the same functionality from Seller. In our example, z is true, because Carol declares that it can receive messages with the label "share". Note that there could be any Boolean formula in place of z, which wires any input and output interfaces of a single service in an arbitrary way. The existing interface description languages (WSDL, WS-CDL, etc.) do not support such interface wiring capabilities.

Interface variables provide facilities similar to C++ templates. Services can specify generic behavior compatible with multiple contexts and input/output data formats. Given the context, the compiler then specializes the interfaces based on the requirements and capabilities of other services.

The problem being solved is similar to type inference problem; however, it has large combinatorial complexity and, therefore, direct search of a solution is impractical. Furthermore, additional complexity arises from the presence of Boolean variables in general form. Another problem is potential cyclic dependencies in the network, which prevent the application of a simple forward algorithm. In our approach, we define our problem as a constraint satisfaction problem. Then we employ a constraint solver, which was specifically developed to solve this problem, to find correct instantiations of the variables.

3 Message Definition Language and CSP

Now we define a term algebra called Message Definition Language (MDL). The purpose of the MDL is to describe flexible service interfaces. Although we use a concise syntax for MDL terms that is different from what standard WSDL-based interfaces look like, it can easily be rewritten as a WSDL extension.

In our approach, a message is a collection of data entities, each specified by a corresponding *term*. The intention of the term is to represent a standard atomic type such as int, string, etc.; or inextensible data collections such as tuples; or extensible data records [14,15], where additional named fields can be introduced without breaking the match between the producer and the consumer and where fields can also be safely inherited from input to output records; or data-record variants, where generally more variants can be accepted by the consumer than the producer is aware of, and where such additional variants can safely be inherited from the output back to the input of the producer.

3.1 Terms

Each term is either atomic or a collection in its own right. Atomic terms are *symbols*, which are identifiers used to represent standard types such as int, string, etc. To account for subtyping we include three categories of collections: *tuples* that are required to be of a certain arity and thus admit only depth structural subtyping, *records* that are subtyped covariantly (a larger record is a subtype) and *choices* that are subtyped contravariantly using set inclusion (a smaller choice is a subtype). The records and the choices support both depth and width subtyping.

In order to support parametric polymorphism and flow inheritance in interfaces, we introduce term variables (called later *t-variables*), which are similar to type variables. For coercion of interfaces it is important to distinguish between two variable categories: *down-coerced* and *up-coerced* ones. The former can be instantiated with symbols, tuples and records (terms of these three categories are call down-coerced terms), and the latter can only be instantiated with choices (up-coerced terms). Informally, for two down-coerced terms, a term associated with a structure with "more data" is a subtype of the one associated with a structure that contains less; and vice versa for up-coerced terms. We use the notation $v^\downarrow$ and $v^\uparrow$ for down-coerced and up-coerced variables respectively, and v when its coercion sort is unimportant. Explicit sort annotation on variables is useful for simplifying partial order definitions on terms.

We introduce Boolean variables (called *b-variables* below) in the term interfaces to specify dependencies between input and output data formats. The intention of b-variables is similar to intersection types, which increase the expressiveness of function signatures.

A Boolean expression $b \in \mathcal{B}$ ($\mathcal{B}$ denotes a set of Boolean expressions) called a guard is defined by the following grammar:

$\langle guard \rangle$ ::= $(\langle guard \rangle \wedge \langle guard \rangle) \mid (\langle guard \rangle \vee \langle guard \rangle) \mid \langle guard \rangle \rightarrow \langle guard \rangle \mid$
$\quad \neg \langle guard \rangle \mid$ **true** $\mid$ **false** $\mid b\text{-}variable$

MDL terms are built recursively using the constructors: tuple, record, choice and switch, according to the following grammar:

$\langle term \rangle$ ::= $\langle symbol \rangle \mid \langle tuple \rangle \mid \langle record \rangle \mid \langle choice \rangle \mid$ t-variable
$\langle tuple \rangle$ ::= $(\langle term \rangle \, [\langle term \rangle]^*)$
$\langle record \rangle$ ::= $\{[\langle element \rangle [, \langle element \rangle]^* [\,|\, \text{down-coerced t-variable}]]\}$
$\langle choice \rangle$ ::= $(: [\langle element \rangle [, \langle element \rangle]^* [\,|\, \text{up-coerced t-variable}]] :)$
$\langle element \rangle$ ::= $\langle label \rangle (\langle guard \rangle) : \langle term \rangle$
$\langle label \rangle$ ::= $\langle symbol \rangle$

Informally, a *tuple* is an ordered collection of terms and a *record* is an extensible, unordered collection of guarded labeled terms, where *labels* are arbitrary symbols, which are unique within a single record. A *choice* is a collection of alternative terms. The syntax of choices is the same as that of records except for the delimiters. The difference between records and choices is in width subtyping and will become clear below when we define seniority on terms. We use choices to represent polymorphic messages and service interfaces on the top level. Records and choices are defined in *tail form*. The tail is denoted by a t-variable that represents a term of the same kind as the construct in which it occurs.

A switch is an auxiliary construct intended for building conditional terms, which is specified as a set of unlabeled (by contrast to a choice) guarded alternatives. Formally, it is defined as

$$\langle switch \rangle \quad ::= \quad <\langle guard \rangle : \langle term \rangle [, \ \langle guard \rangle : \langle term \rangle]^*>$$

Exactly one guard must be **true** for any valid switch, i.e. the switch is substitutionally equivalent to the term marked by the **true** guard:

$$\langle (\text{false}): t_1, \ldots, (\text{true}): t_i, \ldots, (\text{false}): t_n \rangle = \langle (\text{true}): t_i \rangle = t_i.$$

For example, $\langle (a): \texttt{int}, (\neg a): \texttt{string} \rangle$ represents the symbol $\texttt{int}$ if $a = \text{true}$, and the symbol $\texttt{string}$ otherwise.

3.2   Seniority Relation

For a guard g, we denote as $V^b(g)$ the set of b-variables that occur in g. For a term t, we denote as $V^{\downarrow}(t)$ the set of down-coerced t-variables that occur in t, and as $V^{\uparrow}(t)$ the set of up-coerced ones; and finally $V^b(t)$ is the set of b-variables in t.

Definition 1 (Semi-ground and Ground Terms). *A term t is called semi-ground if $V^{\downarrow}(t) \cup V^{\uparrow}(t) = \emptyset$. A term t is called ground if it is semi-ground and $V^b(t) = \emptyset$.*

Definition 2 (Well-formed Terms). *A term t is well-formed if it is ground and exactly one of the following holds:*

1. *t is a symbol;*
2. *t is a tuple $(t_1 \ldots t_n)$, $n > 0$, where all t_i, $1 \leq i \leq n$, are well-formed;*
3. *t is a record $\{l_1(g_1): t_1, \ldots, l_n(g_n): t_n\}$ or a choice $(:l_1(g_1): t_1, \ldots, l_n(g_n): t_n:)$, $n \geq 0$, where for all $1 \leq i \neq j \leq n$, $g_i \wedge g_j \implies l_i \neq l_j$ and all t_i for which g_i are true are well-formed;*
4. *t is a switch $\langle (g_1): t_1, \ldots, (g_n): t_n \rangle$, $n > 0$, where for some $1 \leq i \leq n$, $g_i = $ true and t_i is well-formed and where $g_j = $ false for all $j \neq i$.*

If an element of a record, choice or switch has a guard that is equal to false, then the element can be omitted, e.g.

$$\{a(x \wedge y): \mathtt{string}, b(\mathtt{false}): \mathtt{int}, c(x): \mathtt{int}\} = \{a(x \wedge y): \mathtt{string}, c(x): \mathtt{int}\}.$$

If an element of a record or a choice has a guard that is true, the guard can be syntactically omitted, e.g.

$$\{a(x \wedge y): \mathtt{string}, b(\mathtt{true}): \mathtt{int}, c(x): \mathtt{int}\} = \{a(x \wedge y): \mathtt{string}, b: \mathtt{int}, c(x): \mathtt{int}\}.$$

We define the *canonical form* of a well-formed collection as a representation that does not include false guards, and we omit true guards anyway. The canonical form of a switch is its (only) term with a true guard, hence any term in canonical form is switch-free.

Next we introduce a seniority relation on terms for the purpose of structural subtyping. In the sequel we use nil to denote the empty record $\{\ \}$, which has the meaning of unit type and represents a message without any data. Similarly, we use none to denote the empty choice $(:\ :)$.

Definition 3 (Seniority Relation). *The seniority relation $\sqsubseteq$ on well-formed terms is defined in canonical form as follows:*
1. *none $\sqsubseteq t$ if t is a choice;*
2. *$t \sqsubseteq$ nil if t is a symbol, a tuple or a record;*
3. *$t \sqsubseteq t$;*
4. *$t_1 \sqsubseteq t_2$, if for some $k, m > 0$ one of the following holds:*
    (a) $t_1 = (t_1^1 \ldots t_1^k), t_2 = (t_2^1 \ldots t_2^k)$ and $t_1^i \sqsubseteq t_2^i$ for each $1 \leq i \leq k$;
    (b) $t_1 = \{l_1^1: t_1^1, \ldots, l_1^k: t_1^k\}$ and $t_2 = \{l_2^1: t_2^1, \ldots, l_2^m: t_2^m\}$, where $k \geq m$ and for each $j \leq m$ there is $i \leq k$ such that $l_1^i = l_2^j$ and $t_1^i \sqsubseteq t_2^j$;

(c) $t_1 = (:l_1^1: t_1^1, \ldots, l_1^k: t_1^k:)$ *and* $t_2 = (:l_2^1: t_2^1, \ldots, l_2^m: t_2^m:)$, *where* $k \leq m$ *and for each* $i \leq k$ *there is* $j \leq m$ *such that* $l_1^i = l_2^j$ *and* $t_1^i \sqsubseteq t_2^j$.

Similarly to the t-variables, terms are classified into two categories: symbols, tuples and records are down-coerced terms and choices are up-coerced terms. The seniority relation for down- and up-coerced terms possesses duality: the element nil is the maximum element for down-coerced terms; on the other hand, none is the minimum element for up-coerced terms. $\mathcal{T}^{\downarrow}$ denotes the set of all down-coerced ground terms, $\mathcal{T}^{\uparrow}$ denotes the set of all up-coerced ground terms and $\mathcal{T} = \mathcal{T}^{\downarrow} \cup \mathcal{T}^{\uparrow}$ is the set of all ground terms. Similarly, $\mathcal{T}_m^{\downarrow}$ denotes the set of all vectors of down-coerced ground terms of length m and $\mathcal{T}_n^{\uparrow}$ denotes the set of all vectors of up-coerced ground terms of length n. If t_1 and t_2 are vectors of terms $(t_1^1, \ldots, t_n^1)$ and $(t_1^2, \ldots, t_n^2)$ of size n, then $t_1 \sqsubseteq t_2$ denotes the seniority relation for all pairs $t_i^1 \sqsubseteq t_i^2$ $(1 \leq i \leq n)$.

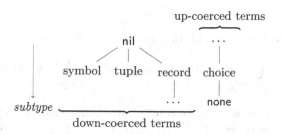

Fig. 2. Two semilattices representing the seniority relation for terms of different categories. The lower terms are the subtypes of the upper ones

Proposition 1. *The seniority relation* $\sqsubseteq$ *is a partial order, and* $(\mathcal{T}, \sqsubseteq)$ *is a pair of meet and join semilattices (Fig. 2):*

$$\forall t_1, t_2 \in \mathcal{T}^{\downarrow}, t_1 \sqsubseteq t_2 \text{ iff } t_1 \sqcap t_2 = t_1;$$

$$\forall t_1, t_2 \in \mathcal{T}^{\uparrow}, t_1 \sqsubseteq t_2 \text{ iff } t_1 \sqcup t_2 = t_2.$$

The seniority relation represents the subtyping relation on terms. If a term t describes the input interface of a service, then the service can process any message described by a term t', such that $t' \sqsubseteq t$.

Although the seniority relation is straightforwardly defined for ground terms, terms that are present in the interfaces of services can contain t-variables and b-variables. Finding such ground term values for the t-variables and such Boolean values for the b-variables that the seniority relation holds represents a CSP problem, which is formally introduced next.

3.3 Constraint Satisfaction Problem for Web Services

We define a substitution, which is used in the definition of the CSP and in the algorithm, as a syntactic transformation that replaces b-variables with Boolean values and t-variables with ground or semi-ground values.

Definition 4 (Substitution). *Let g be a guard, t be a term, $k = |\mathsf{V}^b(g) \cup \mathsf{V}^b(t)|$, and $\boldsymbol{f} = (f_1, \ldots, f_k)$ be a vector of b-variables contained in g and t, and $\boldsymbol{v} = (v_1, \ldots, v_k)$ be a vector of term variables contained in t. Then for any vector of Boolean values $\boldsymbol{b} = (b_1, \ldots, b_k)$ and a vector of terms $\boldsymbol{s} = (s_1, \ldots, s_k)$*

1. *$g[\boldsymbol{f}/\boldsymbol{b}]$ denotes a Boolean value (true or false), which is obtained as a result of the simultaneous replacement and evaluation of f_i with b_i for each $1 \le i \le k$;*
2. *$t[\boldsymbol{f}/\boldsymbol{b}]$ denotes the vector obtained as a result of the simultaneous replacement of f_i with b_i for each $1 \le i \le k$;*
3. *$t[\boldsymbol{v}/\boldsymbol{s}]$ denotes the vector obtained as a result of the simultaneous replacement of v_i with s_i for each $1 \le i \le k$;*
4. *$t[\boldsymbol{f}/\boldsymbol{b}, \boldsymbol{v}/\boldsymbol{s}]$ is a shortcut for $t[\boldsymbol{f}/\boldsymbol{b}][\boldsymbol{v}/\boldsymbol{s}]$.*

Given the set of constraints $\mathcal{C}$, we define the set of b-variables as

$$\mathsf{V}^b(\mathcal{C}) = \bigcup_{t \sqsubseteq t' \in \mathcal{C}} \mathsf{V}^b(t) \cup \mathsf{V}^b(t'),$$

the sets of of down-coerced and up-coerced t-variables as

$$\mathsf{V}^{\downarrow}(\mathcal{C}) = \bigcup_{t \sqsubseteq t' \in \mathcal{C}} \mathsf{V}^{\downarrow}(t) \cup \mathsf{V}^{\downarrow}(t') \text{ and } \mathsf{V}^{\uparrow}(\mathcal{C}) = \bigcup_{t \sqsubseteq t' \in \mathcal{C}} \mathsf{V}^{\uparrow}(t) \cup \mathsf{V}^{\uparrow}(t').$$

In the following for each set of constraints S such that $|\mathsf{V}^b(S)| = l, |\mathsf{V}^{\uparrow}(S)| = m$ and $|\mathsf{V}^{\downarrow}(S)| = n$ we use $\boldsymbol{f} = (f_1, \ldots, f_l)$ to denote the vector of b-variables contained in S, $\boldsymbol{v}^{\uparrow} = (v_1^{\uparrow}, \ldots, v_m^{\uparrow})$ to denote the vector of up-coerced t-variables and $\boldsymbol{v}^{\downarrow} = (v_1^{\downarrow}, \ldots, v_n^{\downarrow})$ to denote the vector of down-coerced t-variables.

Let $\mathcal{C}$ be a set of constraints such that $|\mathsf{V}^b(\mathcal{C})| = l$, $|\mathsf{V}^{\downarrow}(\mathcal{C})| = m$, $|\mathsf{V}^{\uparrow}(S)| = n$ and for some $l, m, n \ge 0$. Now we can define a CSP-WS formally as follows.

Definition 5 (CSP-WS). *Find a vector of Boolean values $\boldsymbol{b} = (b_1, \ldots, b_l)$ and vectors of ground terms $\boldsymbol{t}^{\downarrow} = (t_1^{\downarrow}, \ldots, t_m^{\downarrow})$, $\boldsymbol{t}^{\uparrow} = (t_1^{\uparrow}, \ldots, t_n^{\uparrow})$, such that for each $t_1 \sqsubseteq t_2 \in \mathcal{C}$*

$$t_1[\boldsymbol{f}/\boldsymbol{b}, \boldsymbol{v}^{\downarrow}/\boldsymbol{t}^{\downarrow}, \boldsymbol{v}^{\uparrow}/\boldsymbol{t}^{\uparrow}] \sqsubseteq t_2[\boldsymbol{f}/\boldsymbol{b}, \boldsymbol{v}^{\downarrow}/\boldsymbol{t}^{\downarrow}, \boldsymbol{v}^{\uparrow}/\boldsymbol{t}^{\uparrow}]$$

The tuple $(\boldsymbol{b}, \boldsymbol{t}^{\downarrow}, \boldsymbol{t}^{\uparrow})$ is called a solution.

4   Solution Approximation

One way to solve CSP-WS is to attempt to solve the problem for all possible instantiations of b-variables. We start with considering the simplification when the original problem is reduced to the one without b-variables provided that some vector of Boolean assignments is given.

We use an approximation algorithm that iteratively traverses the meet and the join semilattices for vectors of ground terms $\mathcal{T}_m^{\downarrow}$ and $\mathcal{T}_n^{\uparrow}$, where $m = |\mathsf{V}^{\downarrow}(\mathcal{C})|$ and $n = |\mathsf{V}^{\uparrow}(\mathcal{C})|$, which represent solution approximations for down-coerced and up-coerced terms respectively. The algorithm monotonously converges to a solution if one exists. Informally, the algorithm performs the following steps:

1. Compute the initial approximation of the solution for $i = 0$ as $(a_i^\downarrow, a_i^\uparrow) = ((\text{nil}, \ldots, \text{nil}), (\text{none}, \ldots, \text{none}))$, where the first element in the pair is the vector of top elements from the meet semilattice and the second element is the vector of bottom elements from the join semilattice.
2. Compute $(a_{i+1}^\downarrow, a_{i+1}^\uparrow)$ such that $a_{i+1}^\downarrow \sqsubseteq a_i^\downarrow$ and $a_i^\uparrow \sqsubseteq a_{i+1}^\uparrow$.
3. Repeat step 2 until a chain of approximations converges to the solution, i.e. $(a_{i+1}^\downarrow, a_{i+1}^\uparrow) = (a_i^\downarrow, a_i^\uparrow)$, or a situation where some of the constraints from step 2 cannot be satisfied. Then return the last approximation as the solution or Unsat.

We extend the set $\mathcal{T}_m^\downarrow$ with the element $\bot$, i.e. $\widetilde{\mathcal{T}}_m^\downarrow = \mathcal{T}_m^\downarrow \cup \{\bot\}$, and the set $\mathcal{T}_n^\uparrow$ with the element $\top$, i.e. $\widetilde{\mathcal{T}}_n^\uparrow = \mathcal{T}_n^\uparrow \cup \{\top\}$. Here $\bot$ is defined as the bottom element of the meet semilattice, i.e. $\bot \sqsubseteq a^\downarrow$ for any $a^\downarrow \in \widetilde{\mathcal{T}}_m^\downarrow$, and $\top$ is defined as the top element of the join semilattice, i.e. $a^\uparrow \sqsubseteq \top$ for any $a^\uparrow \in \widetilde{\mathcal{T}}_n^\uparrow$. The algorithm returns $\bot$ or $\top$ if it is unable to find an approximation for some constraints, which, as shown in Theorem 1 below, means that the input set of constraints does not have a solution.

4.1   Approximating Function

In order to specify how the next approximation is computed we introduce the *approximating function* $\mathsf{AF} : \mathcal{C} \times \widetilde{\mathcal{T}}_m^\downarrow \times \widetilde{\mathcal{T}}_n^\uparrow \to \widetilde{\mathcal{T}}_m^\downarrow \times \widetilde{\mathcal{T}}_n^\uparrow$ that maps a single constraint and the current approximation to the new approximation.

The function AF is given below for all categories of terms (except for choices because they are symmetrical to the cases for records and switches that are reduced to other term categories). Let $v^\downarrow = (\overline{v}_1, \ldots, \overline{v}_m)$, $v^\uparrow = (\overline{\overline{v}}_1, \ldots, \overline{\overline{v}}_n)$, $a^\downarrow = (\overline{a}_1, \ldots, \overline{a}_m)$, $a^\uparrow = (\overline{\overline{a}}_1, \ldots, \overline{\overline{a}}_n)$.

If t is a symbol, the given approximation $(a^\downarrow, a^\uparrow)$ already satisfies the constraint:

$$\mathsf{AF}(t \sqsubseteq t, a^\downarrow, a^\uparrow) = (a^\downarrow, a^\uparrow).$$

If t is a down-coerced term and $\overline{v}_l$ is a down-coerced variable, the approximation for $\overline{v}_l$ is used to refine the approximation for variables in t. Therefore, the constraint is reduced to the one with $\overline{v}_l$ as a ground term, which is obtained by substitution $\overline{v}_l[v^\downarrow/a^\downarrow]$:

$$\mathsf{AF}(t \sqsubseteq \overline{v}_l, a^\downarrow, a^\uparrow) = \mathsf{AF}(t \sqsubseteq \overline{v}_l[v^\downarrow/a^\downarrow], a^\downarrow, a^\uparrow).$$

If $\overline{\overline{v}}_l$ is an up-coerced variable and t is an up-coerced term, the case is symmetric to the previous one:

$$\mathsf{AF}(\overline{\overline{v}}_l \sqsubseteq t, a^\downarrow, a^\uparrow) = \mathsf{AF}(\overline{\overline{v}}_l[v^\uparrow/a^\uparrow] \sqsubseteq t, a^\downarrow, a^\uparrow).$$

If $\overline{v}_l$ is a down-coerced variable and t is a down-coerced term, then $\overline{v}_l$ must be not higher than the ground term $t[v^\downarrow/a^\downarrow, v^\uparrow/a^\uparrow]$ in the meet semilattice:

$$\mathsf{AF}(\overline{v}_l \sqsubseteq t, a^\downarrow, a^\uparrow) = ((\overline{a}_1, \ldots, \overline{a}_l \sqcap t[v^\downarrow/a^\downarrow, v^\uparrow/a^\uparrow], \ldots, \overline{a}_m), a^\uparrow).$$

If t is an up-coerced term and $v_l^\uparrow$ is an up-coerced variable, the case is symmetric to the previous one:

$$\mathsf{AF}(t \sqsubseteq v_l^\uparrow, a^\downarrow, a^\uparrow) = (a^\downarrow, (\bar{a}_1, \ldots, \bar{a}_l \sqcup t[v^\downarrow/a^\downarrow, v^\uparrow/a^\uparrow], \ldots, \bar{a}_n)).$$

If t_1 and t_2 are tuples $(t_1^1 \ldots t_k^1)$ and $(t_1^2 \ldots t_k^2)$ respectively, then the constraint must hold for the corresponding nested terms:

$$\mathsf{AF}((t_1^1 \ldots t_k^1) \sqsubseteq (t_1^2 \ldots t_k^2), a^\downarrow, a^\uparrow) = (\prod_{1 \leq i \leq k} a_i^\downarrow, \bigsqcup_{1 \leq i \leq k} a_i^\uparrow).$$

If t_1 and t_2 are records $\{l_1^1\colon t_1^1, \ldots, l_p^1\colon t_p^1\}$ and $\{l_1^2\colon t_1^2, \ldots, l_q^2\colon t_q^2\}$ respectively, two cases must be considered:

- If for all i $(1 \leq i \leq q)$ there exists j such that $l_j^1 = l_i^2$, then the constraint for nested terms $t_j^1 \sqsubseteq t_i^2$ must hold:

$$\mathsf{AF}(\{l_1^1\colon t_1^1, \ldots, l_p^1\colon t_p^1\} \sqsubseteq \{l_1^2\colon t_1^2, \ldots, l_q^2\colon t_q^2\}, a^\downarrow, a^\uparrow) = (\prod_{1 \leq i \leq q} a_i^\downarrow, \bigsqcup_{1 \leq i \leq q} a_i^\uparrow).$$

- Otherwise, the set of labels in t_2 is not a subset of the labels in t_1 and, therefore, $t_1 \sqsubseteq t_2$ is unsatisfiable:

$$\mathsf{AF}(\{l_1^1\colon t_1^1, \ldots, l_p^1\colon t_p^1\} \sqsubseteq \{l_1^2\colon t_1^2, \ldots, l_q^2\colon t_q^2\}, a^\downarrow, a^\uparrow) = (\bot, \top).$$

If $\bar{v}_l$ is a down-coerced variable, t_1 and t_2 are records $\{l_1^1\colon t_1^1, \ldots, l_p^1\colon t_p^1 | \bar{v}_l\}$ and $\{l_1^2\colon t_1^2, \ldots, l_q^2\colon t_q^2\}$ respectively, the constraint can be satisfied only if for every nested term t_i^2 with the label l_i^2 in t one of the following holds: 1) there exists a subterm t_j^1 with equal label in t_1 and $t_j^1 \sqsubseteq t_i^2$ holds, or 2) $\bar{v}_l$ is a record that contains a junior to t_i^2 element with the same label:

$$\mathsf{AF}(\{l_1^1\colon t_1^1, \ldots, l_p^1\colon t_p^1 | \bar{v}_l\} \sqsubseteq \{l_1^2\colon t_1^2, \ldots, l_q^2\colon t_q^2\}, a^\downarrow, a^\uparrow) = (\prod_{1 \leq i \leq q} a_i^\downarrow, \bigsqcup_{1 \leq i \leq q} a_i^\uparrow),$$

where

$$(a_i^\downarrow, a_i^\uparrow) = \begin{cases} \mathsf{AF}(t_j^1 \sqsubseteq t_i^2, a_i^\downarrow, a_i^\uparrow) & \text{if } \exists j : l_j^1 = l_i^2 \\ ((\bar{a}_1, \ldots, \bar{a}_l \sqcap t_i^2[v^\downarrow/a^\downarrow, v^\uparrow/a^\uparrow], \ldots \bar{a}_m), a^\uparrow) & \text{otherwise.} \end{cases}$$

If t_1 is a record $\{l_1^1\colon t_1^1, \ldots, l_p^1\colon t_p^1\}$ or $\{l_1^1\colon t_1^1, \ldots, l_p^1\colon t_p^1 | \bar{v}_l\}$ and t_2 is a record $\{l_1^2\colon t_1^2, \ldots, l_q^2\colon t_q^2 | \bar{u}_r\}$, then the constraint can by substitution be reduced to the previous cases for records:

$$\mathsf{AF}(t_1 \sqsubseteq t_2, a^\downarrow, a^\uparrow) = \mathsf{AF}(t_1 \sqsubseteq t_2[\bar{u}_r/\bar{a}_r], a^\downarrow, a^\uparrow).$$

The function AF has the property of homomorphism, which is important for showing termination and correctness of the algorithm.

Lemma 1 (Homomorphism). *Let* $AF(t_1 \sqsubseteq t_2, a_1^{\downarrow}, a_1^{\uparrow}) = (\overline{a}^{\downarrow}_1, \overline{a}^{\uparrow}_1)$ *and* $AF(t_1 \sqsubseteq t_2, a_2^{\downarrow}, a_2^{\uparrow}) = (\overline{a}^{\downarrow}_2, \overline{a}^{\uparrow}_2)$. *Then*

$$AF(t_1 \sqsubseteq t_2, a_1^{\downarrow} \sqcap a_2^{\downarrow}, a_1^{\uparrow} \sqcup a_2^{\uparrow}) = (\overline{a}^{\downarrow}_1 \sqcap \overline{a}^{\downarrow}_2, \overline{a}^{\uparrow}_1 \sqcup \overline{a}^{\uparrow}_2).$$

The function $AF_{\mathcal{C}}$ is a composition of AF functions that are sequentially applied to all constraints in $\mathcal{C}$ (the order in which AF is applied to the constraints is not important due to distributivity of the semi-lattices):

$$AF_{\mathcal{C}}(a^{\downarrow}, a^{\uparrow}) = AF(t_1^{|\mathcal{C}|} \sqsubseteq t_2^{|\mathcal{C}|}, AF(t_1^{|\mathcal{C}|-1} \sqsubseteq t_2^{|\mathcal{C}|-1}, \ldots, AF(t_1^1 \sqsubseteq t_2^1, a^{\downarrow}, a^{\uparrow}) \ldots)).$$

The sequential composition preserves homomorphism for $AF_{\mathcal{C}}$. In Sect. 5 we tacitly assume that for arbitrary terms the function $AF_{\mathcal{C}}$ is defined in a similar way.

4.2 Fixed-Point Algorithm

Now we present the algorithm (see Algorithm 1) that computes a chain of approximations for the case $V^b(\mathcal{C}) = \emptyset$ that converges to the solution if one exists.

Algorithm 1. CSP-WS($\mathcal{C}$), where $V^b(\mathcal{C}) = \emptyset$

```
1:  i ← 0
2:  (a₀↓, a₀↑) ← ((nil, ..., nil), (none, ..., none))
3:  repeat
4:      i ← i + 1
5:      (aᵢ↓, aᵢ↑) ← AF_C(aᵢ₋₁↓, aᵢ₋₁↑)
6:  until (aᵢ↓, aᵢ↑) = (aᵢ₋₁↓, aᵢ₋₁↑)
7:  if (aᵢ↓, aᵢ↑) = (⊥, ⊤) then
8:      return Unsat
9:  end if
10: return (aᵢ↓, aᵢ↑)
```

Theorem 1. *For any set of constraints $\mathcal{C}$ such that $V^b(\mathcal{C}) = \emptyset$ the following holds: (1) Algorithm 1 terminates after a finite number of steps; (2) CSP-WS for $\mathcal{C}$ is unsatisfiable iff Algorithm 1 return* Unsat.

The proof is given in the extended version of the paper [16].

5   CSP-WS Algorithm

A straightforward algorithm for CSP-WS has to run Algorithm 1 for each of 2^l pairs of the semi-lattices, where $l = |V^b(\mathcal{C})|$. Instead, we present iterative Algorithm 2 which takes the advantage of the order-theoretical structure of the MDL and generates an adjunct SAT problem on the way.

Algorithm 2. CSP-WS($\mathcal{C}$)

```
 1: c ← |C|
 2: i ← 0
 3: B₀ ← ∅
 4: a₀↓ ← (nil, ..., nil)
 5: a₀↑ ← (none, ..., none)
 6: repeat
 7:     i ← i + 1
 8:     (aᵢ↓, aᵢ↑) ← AF_C(aᵢ₋₁↓, aᵢ₋₁↑)
 9:     Bᵢ ← Bᵢ₋₁ ∪     ⋃     (WFC(t₁[v/aᵢ]) ∪ WFC(t₂[v/aᵢ]) ∪ SC(t₁[v/aᵢ] ⊑ t₂[v/aᵢ]))
                    t₁⊑t₂∈C
10: until (SAT(Bᵢ), aᵢ↓, aᵢ↑) = (SAT(Bᵢ₋₁), aᵢ₋₁↓, aᵢ₋₁↑)
11: if Bᵢ is unsatisfiable then
12:     return Unsat
13: else
14:     return (b, aᵢ↓[f/b], aᵢ↑[f/b]), where b ∈ SAT(Bᵢ)
15: end if
```

Let $B_0 \subseteq B_1 \subseteq \cdots \subseteq B_s$ be sets of Boolean constraints, and $\boldsymbol{a}^\downarrow$ and $\boldsymbol{a}^\uparrow$ be vectors of semiground terms such that $|\boldsymbol{a}^\downarrow| = |V^\downarrow(\mathcal{C})|$ and $|\boldsymbol{a}^\uparrow| = |V^\uparrow(\mathcal{C})|$. We seek the solution as a fixed point of a chain of approximations in the form:

$$(B_0, \boldsymbol{a}_0^\downarrow, \boldsymbol{a}_0^\uparrow), \ldots, (B_{s-1}, \boldsymbol{a}_{s-1}^\downarrow, \boldsymbol{a}_{s-1}^\uparrow), (B_s, \boldsymbol{a}_s^\downarrow, \boldsymbol{a}_s^\uparrow),$$

where for every i, $1 \le i \le s$, and a vector of Boolean values $\boldsymbol{b} \in SAT(B_i)$:

$$\boldsymbol{a}_i^\downarrow[\boldsymbol{f}/\boldsymbol{b}] \sqsubseteq \boldsymbol{a}_{i-1}^\downarrow[\boldsymbol{f}/\boldsymbol{b}] \qquad \text{and} \qquad \boldsymbol{a}_{i-1}^\uparrow[\boldsymbol{f}/\boldsymbol{b}] \sqsubseteq \boldsymbol{a}_i^\uparrow[\boldsymbol{f}/\boldsymbol{b}].$$

The adjunct set of Boolean constraints potentially expands at every iteration of the algorithm by inclusion of further logic formulas produced by the set of Boolean constraint WFC (see Fig. 3) ensuring well-formedness of the terms and the set of Boolean constraints SC (see Fig. 4) ensuring that the seniority relations holds. The starting point is $B_0 = \emptyset$, $\boldsymbol{a}_0^\downarrow = (nil, \ldots, nil)$, $\boldsymbol{a}_0^\uparrow = (none, \ldots, none)$ and the chain terminates as soon as $SAT(B_s) = SAT(B_{s-1})$, $\boldsymbol{a}_s^\uparrow = \boldsymbol{a}_{s-1}^\uparrow$, $\boldsymbol{a}_s^\downarrow = \boldsymbol{a}_{s-1}^\downarrow$, where by $SAT(B_i)$ we mean a set of Boolean vector satisfying B_i. Whether the set of Boolean constraints actually expands or not can be determined by checking the satisfiability of $SAT(B_i) \neq SAT(B_{i-1})$ for the current iteration i.

We argue that if the original CSP-WS is satisfiable, then so is $SAT(B_s)$ and that the tuple of vectors $(\boldsymbol{b}_s, \boldsymbol{a}_s^\downarrow[\boldsymbol{f}/\boldsymbol{b}_s], \boldsymbol{a}_s^\uparrow[\boldsymbol{f}/\boldsymbol{b}_s])$ is a solution to the former, where $\boldsymbol{b}_s$ is a solution of $SAT(B_s)$. In other words, the iterations terminate when the conditional approximation limits the t-variables, and when the adjunct SAT constrains the b-variables enough to ensure the satisfaction of all CSP-WS constraints. In general, the set $SAT(B_s)$ can have more than one solution and we select one of them. Heuristics that allows to choose a solution that is better for the given application is left for further research.

Implementation. We implemented the CSP-WS algorithm as a solver in the OCaml language. The input for the solver is a set of constraints and the output

1. $\mathsf{WFC}(t) = \emptyset$ if t is a symbol;
2. $\mathsf{WFC}(t) = \bigcup_{1 \leq i \leq n} \mathsf{WFC}(t_i)$ if t is a tuple $(t_1 \ldots t_n)$;
3. $\mathsf{WFC}(t) = \{\neg(g_i \wedge g_j) \mid 1 \leq i \neq j \leq n \text{ and } l_i = l_j\} \cup \bigcup_{1 \leq i \leq n} \{g_i \rightarrow g \mid g \in \mathsf{WFC}(t_i)\}$
   if t is a record $\{\mathsf{l}_1(g_1): t_1, \ldots, \mathsf{l}_n(g_n): t_n\}$ or a choice $(:\mathsf{l}_1(g_1): t_1, \ldots, \mathsf{l}_n(g_n): t_n:)$;
4. $\mathsf{WFC}(t) = \{\neg(g_i \wedge g_j) \mid 1 \leq i \neq j \leq n\} \cup \{\bigvee_{1 \leq i \leq n} g_i\} \cup \bigcup_{1 \leq i \leq n} \{g_i \rightarrow g \mid g \in \mathsf{WFC}(t_i)\}$ if t is a switch $\langle (g_1): t_1, \ldots, (g_n): t_n \rangle$.

Fig. 3. The set of Boolean constraints that ensures well-formedness of a term t

1. $\mathsf{SC}(t_1 \sqsubseteq t_2) = \emptyset$, if t_1 and t_2 are equal symbols.
2. $\mathsf{SC}(t_1 \sqsubseteq t_2) = \bigcup_{1 \leq i \leq k} \mathsf{SC}(t_i^1 \sqsubseteq t_i^2)$, if t_1 is a tuple $(t_1^1 \ldots t_k^1)$ and t_2 is a tuple $(t_1^2 \ldots t_k^2)$;
3. $\mathsf{SC}(t_1 \sqsubseteq t_2) = \bigcup_{1 \leq j \leq m} \mathsf{SC}_j(t_j^2)$, if t_1 is a record $\{\mathsf{l}_1^1(g_1^1): t_1^1, \ldots, \mathsf{l}_k^1(g_k^1): t_k^1\}$, t_2 is a record $\{\mathsf{l}_1^2(g_1^2): t_1^2, \ldots, \mathsf{l}_m^2(g_m^2): t_m^2\}$ and $\mathsf{SC}_j(t_j^2)$ is one of the following:
   (a) $\mathsf{SC}_j(t_j^2) = \{(g_i^1 \wedge g_j^2) \rightarrow g \mid g \in \mathsf{SC}(t_i^1 \sqsubseteq t_j^2)\}$, if $\exists i: 1 \leq i \leq k$ and $l_i^1 = l_j^2$;
   (b) $\mathsf{SC}_j(t_j^2) = \{\neg g_j^2\}$, otherwise;
4. $\mathsf{SC}(t_1 \sqsubseteq t_2) = \bigcup_{1 \leq i \leq m} \mathsf{SC}_i(t_i^1)$, if t_1 is a choice $(:\mathsf{l}_1^1(g_1^1): t_1^1, \ldots, \mathsf{l}_k^1(g_k^1): t_k^1:)$, t_2 is a choice $(:\mathsf{l}_1^2(g_1^2): t_1^2, \ldots, \mathsf{l}_m^2(g_m^2): t_m^2:)$ and $\mathsf{SC}_i(t_i^1)$ is one of the following:
   (a) $\mathsf{SC}_i(t_i^1) = \{(g_i^1 \wedge g_j^2) \rightarrow g \mid g \in \mathsf{SC}(t_i^1 \sqsubseteq t_j^2)\}$, if $\exists j: 1 \leq j \leq m$ and $l_i^1 = l_j^2$;
   (b) $\mathsf{SC}_i(t_i^1) = \{\neg g_i^1\}$, otherwise;
5. $\mathsf{SC}(t_1 \sqsubseteq t_2) = \{g_i^1 \rightarrow g \mid 1 \leq i \leq k \text{ and } g \in \mathsf{SC}(t_i^1 \sqsubseteq t_i^2)\}$, if t_1 is a switch $\langle (g_1^1): t_1^1, \ldots (g_k^1): t_k^1 \rangle$ and t_2 is an arbitrary term.
6. $\mathsf{SC}(t_1 \sqsubseteq t_2) = \{g_i^2 \rightarrow g \mid 1 \leq i \leq k \text{ and } g \in \mathsf{SC}(t_1 \sqsubseteq t_i^2)\}$, if t_1 is an arbitrary term and t_2 is a switch $\langle (g_1^2): t_1^2, \ldots (g_k^2): t_k^2 \rangle$.
7. $\mathsf{SC}(t_1 \sqsubseteq t_2) = \{\mathsf{false}\}$, otherwise.

Fig. 4. The set of Boolean constraints that ensures the seniority relation $t_1 \sqsubseteq t_2$

is in the form of assignments to b-variables and t-variables. It works on top of the PicoSAT [17] library (although any other SAT solver could be used instead). PicoSAT is employed as a subsolver that deals with Boolean assertions.

6   Conclusion and Future Work

We have presented a new mechanism for choreographing service interfaces based on CSP and SAT that configures generic non-local interfaces in context. We developed a Message Definition Language that can be used with service-based applications. Our mechanism supports subtyping, polymorphism and flow inheritance thanks to the order relation defined on MDL terms. We have presented the CSP solution algorithm for interface configuration, which was developed specifically for this task.

In the context of Cloud, our results may prove useful to the software-as-service community since we can support much more generic interfaces than are currently available. Building services the way we do could enable service providers to configure a solution for a network customer based on services that they have at their disposal as well as those provided by other providers and the customer themselves, with automatic tuning to (locally unknown) non-local requirements.

The next step will be the design of a mechanism for automatic interface derivation from the sources of the services, which can be done in a straightforward manner. This complements as yet unavailable choreography mechanisms that rely on behavioral protocols: automatic derivation of code behavior from the sources is an open problem that presents a considerable challenge.

References

1. Sheng, Q.Z., Qiao, X., Vasilakos, A.V., Szabo, C., Bourne, S., Xu, X.: Web services composition: a decades overview. Inf. Sci. **280**, 218–238 (2014)
2. Dustdar, S., Schreiner, W.: A survey on web services composition. Int. J. Web Grid Serv. **1**(1), 1–30 (2005)
3. Bourne, S., Szabo, C., Sheng, Q.Z.: Ensuring well-formed conversations between control and operational behaviors of web services. In: Liu, C., Ludwig, H., Toumani, F., Yu, Q. (eds.) Service Oriented Computing. LNCS, vol. 7636, pp. 507–515. Springer, Heidelberg (2012)
4. Zheng, Z., Lyu, M.R.: Personalized reliability prediction of web services. ACM Trans. Softw. Eng. Methodol. **22**(2), 12 (2013)
5. Web services choreography description language: web services choreography description language (WS-CDL). https://www.w3.org/TR/ws-cdl-10/
6. Arkin, A., Askary, S., Fordin, S., Jekeli, W., Kawaguchi, K., Orchard, D., Pogliani, S., Riemer, K., Struble, S., Takacsi-Nagy, P., et al.: Web service choreography interface (WSCI) (2002). https://www.w3.org/TR/2002/NOTE-wsci-20020808/
7. Barros, A., Dumas, M., Oaks, P.: A critical overview of the web services choreography description language. BPTrends **3**, 1–24 (2005)
8. Carbone, M., Honda, K., Yoshida, N.: Structured communication-centred programming for web services. In: Nicola, R. (ed.) ESOP 2007. LNCS, vol. 4421, pp. 2–17. Springer, Heidelberg (2007)
9. Bouguettaya, A., Sheng, Q.Z., Daniel, F. (eds.): Advanced Web Services. Springer, New York (2013)
10. Duan, Q., Yan, Y., Vasilakos, A.V.: A survey on service-oriented network virtualization toward convergence of networking and cloud computing. IEEE Trans. Netw. Serv. Manage. **9**(4), 373–392 (2012)
11. Honda, K., Yoshida, N., Carbone, M.: Multiparty asynchronous session types. SIGPLAN Not. **43**(1), 273–284 (2008)
12. Davies, R., Pfenning, F.: Intersection types and computational effects. ACM SIGPLAN Not. **35**(9), 198–208 (2000)
13. Grelck, C., Scholz, S.B., Shafarenko, A.: A gentle introduction to S-Net: typed stream processing and declarative coordination of asynchronous components. Parall. Process. Lett. **18**(02), 221–237 (2008)
14. Gaster, B.R., Jones, M.P.: A polymorphic type system for extensible records and variants. Technical report (1996)
15. Leijen, D.: Extensible records with scoped labels. Trends Funct. Program. **5**, 297–312 (2005)
16. Zaichenkov, P., Tveretina, O., Shafarenko, A.: A constraint satisfaction method for configuring non-local service interfaces. http://arxiv.org/abs/1601.03370
17. Biere, A.: Picosat essentials. J. Satisfiability Boolean Model. Comput. **4**, 75–97 (2008)

Case Studies

Rule-Based Consistency Checking of Railway Infrastructure Designs

Bjørnar Luteberget[1]([✉]), Christian Johansen[2], and Martin Steffen[2]

[1] RailComplete AS (Formerly Anacon AS), Sandvika, Norway
bjlut@railcomplete.no
[2] Department of Informatics, University of Oslo, Oslo, Norway
{cristi,msteffen}@ifi.uio.no

Abstract. Railway designs deal with complex and large-scale, safety-critical infrastructures, where formal methods play an important role, especially in verifying the safety of so-called interlockings through model checking. Model checking deals with state change and rather complex properties, usually incurring considerable computational burden (chiefly in terms of memory, known as state-space explosion problem). In contrast to this, we focus on static infrastructure properties, based on design guidelines and heuristics. The purpose is to automate much of the manual work of the railway engineers through software that can do verification on-the-fly. In consequence, this paper describes the integration of formal methods into the railway design process, by formalizing relevant technical rules and expert knowledge. We employ a variant of Datalog and use the standardized "railway markup language" railML as basis and exchange format for the formalization. We describe a prototype tool and its (ongoing) integration in industrial railway CAD software, developed under the name RailCOMPLETE®. We apply this tool chain in a Norwegian railway project, the upgrade of the Arna railway station.

Keywords: Railway designs · Automation · Logic programming · Signalling · Railway infrastructure · railML · CAD · Datalog

1 Introduction

Railway systems are complex and large-scale, safety-critical infrastructures, with increasingly computerized components. The discipline of railway engineering is characterized by heavy national regulatory oversight, high and long-standing safety and engineering standards, a need for interoperability and (national and international) standardization. Due to the high safety requirements, the railway design norms and regulations recommend the use of formal methods (of various kinds), and for the higher safety integrity levels (SIL), they "highly recommend" them (cf. e.g. [4]). Railways require thoroughly designed control systems to ensure safety and efficient operation. The railway signals are used to direct traffic, and the *signalling component layout* of a train station is crucial to its traffic capacity. Another central part of a railway infrastructure is the so-called

© Springer International Publishing Switzerland 2016
E. Ábrahám and M. Huisman (Eds.): IFM 2016, LNCS 9681, pp. 491–507, 2016.
DOI: 10.1007/978-3-319-33693-0_31

interlocking, which refers, generally speaking, to the ensemble of systems tasked to establish safe, conflict-free routes of trains through stations (cf. [18]).

Railway construction projects are heavy processes that integrate various fields, engineering disciplines, different companies, stakeholders, and regulatory bodies. When working out railway designs a large part of the work is repetitive, involving routine checking of consistency with rules, writing tables, and coordinating disciplines. Many of these manual checks are simple enough to be automated.

With the purpose of increasing the degree of automation, we present results on integrating formal methods into the railway design process, as follows:

– We formalize rules governing track and signalling layout, and interlocking.
– The standardized "railway markup language" railML [19] is used as basis and exchange format for the formalization.
– We model the concepts describing a railway design in the logic of Datalog; and develop an automated generation of the model from the railML representation.
– We develop a prototype tool and integrate it in existing railway CAD software.

We illustrate the logical representation of signalling principles and show how they can be implemented and solved efficiently using the Datalog style of logic programming [21]. We also show the integration with existing railway engineering workflow by using CAD models directly. This enables us to verify rules continuously as the design process changes the station layout and interlocking. Based on railML [19], our results can be easily adopted by anyone who uses this international standard. The work uses as case study the software and the design (presently under development) used in the *Arna-Fløen* upgrade project,[1] with planned completion in 2020. The Arna train station is located on Northern Europe's busiest single-track connection, which is being extended to a double-track connection. The case study is part of an ongoing project in Anacon AS (now merged with Norconsult), a Norwegian signalling design consultancy. It is used to illustrate the approach, test the implementation, and to verify that the tool's performance is acceptable for interactive work within the CAD software.

The rest of the paper is organized as follows. Section 2 discusses aspects of the railway domain relevant for this work. Section 3 proposes a tool chain that extends CAD with formal representations of signalling layout and interlocking. Section 4 presents our formalization of the rules and concepts of railway design as logical formulas amenable for the Datalog implementation and checking. Section 5 provides information about the implementation, including details about counterexample presentation and empirical evaluation using the case study. We conclude in Sect. 6 with related and future work.

2   Background on the Railway Signalling Domain

The signalling design process results in a set of documents which can be categorized into (a) track and signalling component layout, and (b) interlocking specification.

---

[1] www.jernbaneverket.no/Prosjekter/prosjekter/Arna-Bergen.

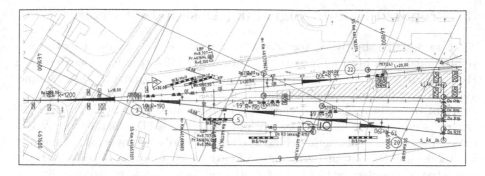

Fig. 1. Cut-out from 2D geographical CAD model (construction drawing) of preliminary design of the Arna station signalling (Color figure online).

Railway construction projects rely heavily on *computer aided design* (CAD) tools to map out railway station layouts. The various disciplines within a project, such as civil works, track works, signalling, or catenary power lines, work with *coordinated CAD models*. These CAD models contain a major part of the work performed by engineers, and are a collaboration tool for communication between disciplines. The signalling component layout is worked out by the signalling engineers as part of the design process. Signals, train detectors, derailers, etc., are drawn using symbols in a 2D geographical CAD model. An example of a layout drawing is given in Fig. 1.

2.1 Interlocking Specification

An interlocking is an interconnection of signals and switches to ensure that train movements are performed in a safe sequence [18]. Interlocking is performed electronically so that, e.g., a green light (or, more precisely, the *proceed aspect*) can only be lit under certain conditions. Conditions and state are built into the interlocking by relay-based circuitry or by computers running interlocking software. Most interlocking specifications use a *route-based tabular* approach, which means that a train station is divided into possible *routes*, which are paths that a train can take from one signal to another. These signals are called the *route entry signal* and *route exit signal*, respectively. An *elementary route* contains no other signals in-between. The main part of the interlocking specification is to tabulate all possible routes and set conditions for their use. Typical conditions are:

- *Switches* must be positioned to guide the train to a specified route exit signal.
- *Train detectors* must show that the route is free of any other trains.
- *Conflicting routes*, i.e. overlapping routes (or overlapping safety zones), must not be in use.

3   Proposed Railway Signalling Design Tool Chain

Next we describe shortly the tool chain that we propose for automating the current manual tasks involved in the design of railway infrastructures (see details in [15]). In particular, we are focused on integrating and automating those simple, yet tedious, rules and conditions usually used to maintain some form of consistency of the railway, and have these checks done automatically. Whenever the design is changed by an engineer working with the CAD program, our verification procedure would help, behind the scenes, verifying any small changes in the model and the output documents. Violations would either be automatically corrected, if possible, or highlighted to the engineer. Thus, we are focusing on solutions with small computational overhead.

3.1   Computer-Aided Design (CAD) Layout Model

CAD models, which ultimately correspond to a database of geometrical objects, are used in railway signalling engineering. They may be 2D or 3D, and contain mostly spatial properties and textual annotations, i.e., the CAD models focus on the *shapes* of objects and *where* to place them. The top level of the document, called the *model space block*, contains geometrical primitives, such as lines, circles, arcs, text, and symbols.

Geometric elements may represent the physical geometry directly, or symbolically, such as text or symbols. However, the verification of signalling and interlocking rules requires information about object properties and relations between objects such as which signals and signs are related to which track, and their identification, capabilities, and use. This information is better modelled by the railway-specific extensible hierarchical object model called railML [17].

3.2   Integrating railML and Interlocking Specifications with CAD Models

CAD programs were originally designed to produce paper drawings, and common practice in the use of CAD programs is to focus on *human-readable* documents. The database structure, however, may also be used to store machine-readable information. In the industry-standard DWG format, each geometrical object in the database has an associated *extension dictionary*, where add-on programs may store any data related to the object. Our tool uses this method to store the railML fragments associated with each geometrical object or symbol. Thus, we can compile the complete railML representation of the station from the CAD model.

Besides the layout, the design of a railway station consists also of a specification for the interlocking. This specification models the behavior of the signalling, and it is tightly linked to the station layout. A formal representation of the interlocking specification is embedded in the CAD document in a similar way as for the railML infrastructure data, using the document's global extension dictionary. Thus, the single CAD document showing the human-readable layout of the train station also contains a machine-readable model which fully describes both the component layout and the functional specification of the interlocking. This allows a full analysis of the operational aspects of the train station directly from a familiar editable CAD model.

3.3   Overall Tool Chain

Figure 2 shows the overall tool chain. The software allows checking of rules and regulations of static infrastructure (described in this paper) inside the CAD environment, while more comprehensive verification and quality assurance can be performed by special-purpose software for other design and analysis activities.

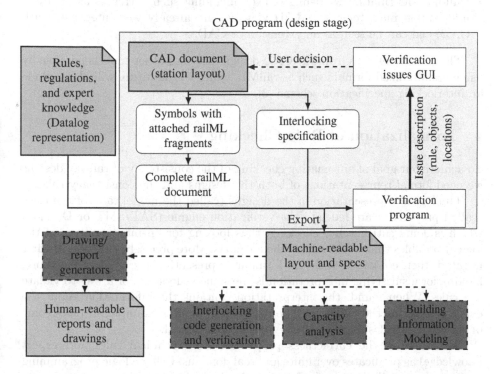

Fig. 2. Railway design tool chain. The CAD program box shows features which are directly accessible at design time inside the CAD program, while the export creates machine-readable (or human-readable) documents which may be further analyzed and verified by external software (shown in dashed boxes).

Generally, analysis and verification tools for railway signalling designs can have complex inputs, they must account for a large variety of situations, and they usually require long running times. Therefore, we limit the verification inside the design environment to static rules and expert knowledge, as these rules require less dynamic information (timetables, rolling stock, etc.) and less computational effort, while still offering valuable insights. This situation may be compared to the tool chain for writing computer programs. Static analysis can be used at the detailed design stage (writing the code), but can only verify a limited set of properties. It cannot fully replace testing, simulation and other types of analysis, and must as such be seen as a part of a larger tool chain.

Other tools, that are external to the CAD environment, may be used for these more calculation heavy or less automated types of analysis, such as:

– Code generation and verification for interlockings, possible e.g. through the formal verification framework of Prover Technology.
– Capacity analysis and timetabling, performed e.g. using OpenTrack, LUKS, or Treno.
– Building Information Modeling (BIM), including such activities as life-cycle information management and 3D viewing, are already well integrated with CAD, and can be seen as an extension of CAD.

The transfer of data from the CAD design model to other tools is possible by using standardized formats such as railML, which in the future will also include an interlocking specification schema [3].

4   Formalization of Rule Checking

To achieve our goal of automating checking of the consistency of railway designs we need formal representations of both the designs and the consistency rules.

The logical representation of the designs (called the model) and of the rules (called properties) are fed into the verification engine (SAT/SMT or Datalog) which is doing satisfiability checking, thus looking for an interpretation of the logical variables that would satisfy the formulas. More precisely, the rules are first negated, then conjoined with the formulas representing the model. Therefore, looking for a satisfying interpretation is the same as looking for a way to violate the rules. When found, the interpretation contains the information about the exact reasons for the violation. The reasons, or counter-example, involves some of the negated rules as well as some parts of the model.

We formalize the correctness properties (i.e., technical rules and expert knowledge) as predicates over finite and real domains. Using a logic programming framework, we will include the following in the logical model:

1. Predicate representation of input document *facts*, i.e. track layout and interlocking.
2. Predicate representation of derived concept *rules*, such as object properties, topological properties, and calculation of distances.
3. Predicate representation of technical rules.

Each of these categories are described in more detail below, after we present the logical framework we employ.

4.1 Datalog

Declarative logic programming is a programming language paradigm which allows clean separation of logic (meaning) and computation (algorithm). This section gives a short overview of Datalog concepts. See [21] for more details. In its most basic form Datalog is a database query, as in the SQL language, over a finite set of atoms which can be combined using conjunctive queries, i.e. expressions in the fragment of first-order logic which includes only conjunctions and existential quantification.

Conjunctive queries alone, however, cannot express the properties needed to verify railway signalling. For example, given the layout of the station with tracks represented as edges between signalling equipment nodes, graph reachability queries are required to verify some of the rules. This corresponds to computing the transitive closure of the graph adjacency relation, which is not expressible in first-order logic [13, Chap. 3]. Adding fixed-point operators to conjunctive queries is a common way to mitigate the above problem while preserving decidability and polynomial time complexity.

The Datalog language is a first-order logic extended with *least fixed points*. We define the Datalog language as follows: *Terms* are either constants (atoms) or variables. *Literals* consist of a *predicate* P with a certain arity n, along with terms corresponding to the predicate arguments, forming an expression like $P(\vec{a})$, where $a = (a_1, a_2, \ldots, a_n)$. *Clauses* consist of a *head* literal and one or more *body* literals, such that all variables in the head also appear in the body. Clauses are written as

$$R_0(\vec{x}) \; :- \; \exists \vec{y} : R_1(\vec{x}, \vec{y}), R_2(\vec{x}, \vec{y}), \ldots, R_k(\vec{x}, \vec{y}).$$

Datalog uses the Prolog convention of interpreting identifiers starting with a capital letter as variables, and other identifiers as constants. E.g., the meaning of the clause $a(X, Y) :- b(X, Z), c(Z, Y)$ is $\forall x, y : ((\exists z : (b(x, z) \land c(z, y))) \rightarrow a(x, y))$.

Clauses without body are called *facts*, those with one or more literals in the body are called *rules*. No nesting of literals is allowed. However, recursive definitions of predicates are possible. In the railway domain, this can be used to define the *connected* predicate, which defines whether two objects are connected by railway tracks:

$$directlyConnected(a, b) :- track(t), belongsTo(a, t), belongsTo(b, t).$$
$$connected(a, b) :- directlyConnected(a, b).$$
$$connected(a, b) :- directlyConnected(a, x), connection(x, c),$$
$$connected(c, b).$$

Here, the *connection* predicate contains switches and other connection types. Further details of relevant predicates are given in the sections below.

Another common feature of Datalog implementations is to allow negation, with *negation as failure* semantics. This means that negation of predicates in rules is allowed with the interpretation that when the satisfiability procedure cannot find a model, the statement is false. To ensure termination and unique solutions, the negation of predicates must have a *stratification*, i.e. the dependency graph of negated predicates must have a topological ordering (see [21, Chap. 3] for details).

Datalog is sufficiently expressive to describe static rules of signalling layout topology and interlocking. For geometrical properties, it is necessary to take sums and differences of lengths, which requires extending Datalog with arithmetic operations. A more expressive language is required to cover all aspects of railway design, e.g. capacity analysis and software verification, but for the properties in the scope of this paper, a concise, restricted language which ensures termination and short running times has the advantage of allowing tight integration with the existing engineering workflow.

4.2   Input Documents Representation

Track and Signalling Objects Layout in the railML Format. Given a complete railML infrastructure document, we consider the set of XML elements in it that correspond to identifiable objects (this is the set of elements which inherit properties from the type `tElementWithIDAndName`). The set of all IDs which are assigned to XML elements form the finite domain of constants on which we base our predicates (IDs are assumed unique in railML).

$$\text{Atoms} := \{a \mid \text{element.ID} = a\}.$$

We denote a railML element with $ID = a$ as element_a. All other data associated with an element is expressed as predicates with its identifying atom as one of the arguments, most notably the following:

– Element type (also called class in railML/XML):

$$track(a) \leftarrow \text{element}_a \text{ is of type } \texttt{track},$$
$$signal(a) \leftarrow \text{element}_a \text{ is of type } \texttt{signal},$$
$$balise(a) \leftarrow \text{element}_a \text{ is of type } \texttt{balise},$$
$$switch(a) \leftarrow \text{element}_a \text{ is of type } \texttt{switch}.$$

– Position and absolute position (elements inheriting from `tPlacedElement`):

$$pos(a, p) \leftarrow (\text{element}_a.\texttt{pos} = p), \quad a \in \text{Atoms}, p \in \mathbb{R},$$
$$absPos(a, p) \leftarrow (\text{element}_a.\texttt{absPos} = p), \quad a \in \text{Atoms}, p \in \mathbb{R}.$$

– Direction (for elements inheriting from `tOrientedElement`):

$$dir(a, d) \leftarrow (\text{element}_a.\texttt{dir} = d), \quad a \in \text{Atoms}, d \in \text{Direction},$$

where Direction $= \{up, down, both, unknown\}$, indicating whether the object is visible or functional in only one of the two possible travel directions, or both.

– Signal properties (for elements of type tSignal):

$$signalType(a,t) \leftarrow (\text{element}_a.\text{type} = t), t \in \{\text{main, distant, shunting, combined}\},$$
$$signalFunction(a,f) \leftarrow (\text{element}_a.\text{function} = f),$$
$$a \in \text{Atoms}, f \in \{\text{home, intermediate, exit, blocking}\}.$$

The *switch* element is the object which connects tracks with each other and creates the branching of paths. A switch belongs to a single track, but contains *connection* sub-elements which point to other connection elements, which are in turn contained in switches, crossings or track ends. For connections, we have the following predicates:

– Connection element and reference:

$$connection(a) \leftarrow \text{element}_a \text{ is of type connection,}$$
$$connection(a,b) \leftarrow (\text{element}_a.\text{ref} = b).$$

– Connection course and orientation:

$$connectionCourse(a,c) \leftarrow (\text{element}_a.\text{course} = c), c \in \{\text{left, straight, right}\}$$
$$connectionOrientation(a,o) \leftarrow (\text{element}_a.\text{orientation} = o),$$
$$a \in \text{Atoms}, o \in \{\text{outgoing, incoming}\}.$$

To encode the hierarchical structure of the railML document, a separate predicate encoding the parent/child relationship is added:

– Object belongs to (e.g. a is a signal belonging to track b):

$$belongsTo(a,b) \leftarrow b \text{ is the closest XML ancestor of } a \text{ whose element}$$
$$\text{type inherits from tElementWithIDAndName.}$$

Interlocking. An XML schema for tabular interlocking specifications is described in [3], and this format is used here with, anticipating that it will become part of the railML standard schema in the future. We give some examples of how XML files with this schema are translated into predicate form:

– Train route with given direction d, start point a, and end point b ($a, b \in$ Atoms, $d \in$ Direction):

$$trainRoute(t) \leftarrow \text{element}_t \text{ is of type route}$$
$$start(t,a) \leftarrow (\text{element}_t.\text{start} = a)$$
$$end(t,b) \leftarrow (\text{element}_t.\text{end} = b)$$

– Conditions on detection section free (a) and switch position (s,p):

$$detectionSectionCondition(t,a) \leftarrow (a \in \text{element}_t.\text{sectionConditions}),$$
$$switchPositionCondition(t,s,p) \leftarrow ((s,p) \in \text{element}_t.\text{switchConditions}).$$

4.3   Derived Concepts Representation

Derived concepts are properties of the railway model which can be defined independently of the specific station. A library of these predicates is needed to allow concise expression of the rules to be checked.

Object Properties. Properties related to specific object types which are not explicitly represented in the layout description, such as whether a switch is *facing* in a given direction, i.e. if the path will branch when you pass it:

$$switchFacing(a, d) \leftarrow \exists c, o : switch(a) \wedge switchConnection(a, c) \wedge$$
$$switchOrientation(c, o) \wedge orientationDirection(o, d).$$

Topological and Geometric Layout Properties. Predicates describing the topological configuration of signalling objects and the train travel distance between them are described by predicates for **track connection** (predicate $connected(a, b)$), **directed connection** (predicate $following(a, b, d)$), **distance** (predicate $distance(a, b, d, l)$), etc. The track connection predicate is defined as:

$$directlyConnected(a, b) \leftarrow \exists t : track(t) \wedge belongsTo(a, t) \wedge belongsTo(b, t),$$

$$connected(a, b) \leftarrow directlyConnected(a, b) \vee (\exists c_1, c_2 : connection(c_1, c_2) \wedge$$
$$directlyConnected(a, c_1) \wedge connected(c_2, b)).$$

Interlocking Properties. Properties such as $existsPathWithoutSignal(a, b)$ for finding elementary routes, and $existsPathWithDetector(a, b)$ for finding adjacent train detectors will be used as building blocks for the interlocking rules.

4.4   Rule Violations Representation

With the input documents represented as facts, and a library of derived concepts, it remains to define the technical rules to be checked. Technical rules are based on [11]. Some examples of technical rules representing conditions of the railway station layout are given below. More details can be found in the technical report [16].

Property 1 (Layout: Home signal [11]). *A* home main signal *shall be placed at least 200 m in front of the first controlled, facing switch in the entry train path.*

See also Fig. 3 for an example. Property 1 may be represented in the following way:

$$isFirstFacingSwitch(b, s) \leftarrow stationBoundary(b) \wedge facingSwitch(s) \wedge$$
$$\neg(\exists x : facingSwitch(x) \wedge between(b, x, s)),$$

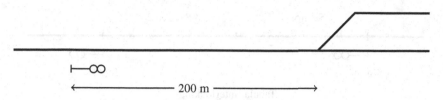

Fig. 3. A home main signal shall be placed at least 200 m in front of the first controlled, facing switch in the entry train path. (Property 1)

$$ruleViolation_1(b, s) \leftarrow isFirstFacingSwitch(b, s) \wedge$$
$$(\neg(\exists x : signalFunction(x, \text{home}) \wedge between(b, x, s)) \vee$$
$$(\exists x, d, l : signalFunction(x, \text{home}) \wedge$$
$$\wedge \, distance(x, s, d, l) \wedge l < 200).$$

Checking for rule violations can be expressed as:

$$\exists b, s : ruleViolation_1(b, s),$$

which in Datalog query format becomes `ruleViolation1(B,S)?`.

Property 2 (Layout: Exit main signal [11]). *An exit main signal shall be used to signal movement exiting a station.*

This property can be elaborated into the following rules:

– No path should have more than one exit signal:

$$ruleViolation_2(s) \leftarrow \exists d : signalType(s, \text{exit}) \wedge following(s, s_o, d) \wedge$$
$$\neg signalType(s_0, \text{exit}).$$

– Station boundaries should be preceded by an exit signal:

$$exitSignalBefore(x, d) \leftarrow \exists s : signalType(s, \text{exit}) \wedge following(s, x, d)$$
$$ruleViolation_2(b) \leftarrow \exists d : stationBoundary(b) \wedge \neg exitSignalBefore(b, d).$$

Property 3 (Interlocking: Track clear on route). *Each pair of adjacent train detectors defines a track detection section. For any track detection sections overlapping the route path, there shall exist a corresponding condition on the activation of the route.*

See Fig. 4 for an example. Property 3 can be represented as follows:

$$adjacentDetectors(a, b) \leftarrow trainDetector(a) \wedge trainDetector(b) \wedge$$
$$\neg existsPathWithDetector(a, b),$$

$$detectionSectionOverlapsRoute(r, d_a, d_b) \leftarrow trainRoute(r) \wedge$$
$$start(r, s_a) \wedge end(r, s_b) \wedge$$
$$adjacentDetectors(d_a, d_b) \wedge overlap(s_a, s_b, d_a, d_b),$$

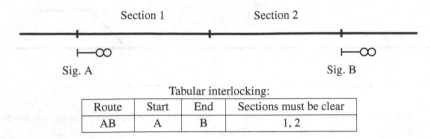

Tabular interlocking:

Route	Start	End	Sections must be clear
AB	A	B	1, 2

Fig. 4. Track sections which overlap a route must have a corresponding condition in the interlocking. (Property 3)

$$rule\ Violation_3\,(r, d_a, d_b) \leftarrow detectionSectionOverlapsRoute(r, d_a, d_b) \wedge$$
$$\neg detectionSectionCondition(r, d_a, d_b).$$

Property 4 (Interlocking: Flank protection [11]). *A train route shall have flank protection.*

For each switch in the route path and its associated position, the paths starting in the opposite switch position defines the *flank*. Each flank path is terminated by the first flank protection object encountered along the path. An example situation is shown in Fig. 5. While the indicated route is active (A to B), switch X needs flank protection for its left track. Flank protection is given by setting switch Y in right position and setting signal C to *stop*. Property 4 can be elaborated into the following rules:

- All flank protection objects should be eligible flank protection objects, i.e. they should be in the list of possible flank protection objects, and have the correct orientation (the *flankElement* predicate contains the interlocking facts):

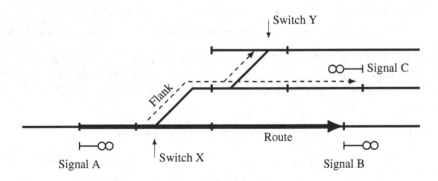

Fig. 5. The dashed path starting in switch X must be terminated in all branches by a valid flank protection object, in this case switch Y and signal C. (Property 4)

$$flankProtectionObject(a, b, d) \leftarrow ((signalType(a, \text{main}) \wedge dir(a, d)) \vee$$
$$(signalType(a, \text{shunting}) \wedge dir(a, d)) \vee$$
$$switchFacing(a, d) \vee$$
$$derailer(a)) \wedge following(a, b, d).$$

$$flankProtectionRequired(r, x, d) \leftarrow trainRoute(r) \wedge start(r, s_a) \wedge$$
$$end(r, s_b) \wedge switchOrientation(x, o) \wedge between(s_a, x, s_b) \wedge$$
$$orientationDirection(o, o_d) \wedge oppositeDirection(o_d, d).$$

$$flankProtection(r, e) \leftarrow flankProtectionRequired(r, x, d) \wedge$$
$$flankProtectionObject(e, x, d).$$

$$ruleViolation_4(r, e) \leftarrow flankElement(r, e) \wedge$$
$$\neg flankProtection(r, e).$$

- There should be no path from a model/station boundary to the given switch, in the given direction, that does not pass a flank protection object for the route:

$$ruleViolation_4(r, b, x) \leftarrow stationBoundary(b) \wedge$$
$$flankProtectionRequired(r, x, d) \wedge following(b, x, d) \wedge$$
$$existsPathWithoutFlankProtection(r, b, x, d).$$

5 Tool Implementation

The XSB Prolog interpreter was used as a back-end for the implementation as it offers tabled predicates which have the same characteristics as Datalog programs [20], while still allowing general Prolog expressions such as arithmetic operations.

5.1 Counterexample Presentation

When rule violations are found, the railway engineer will benefit from information about the following:

- Which rule was violated (textual message containing a reference to the source of the rule or a justification in the case of expert knowledge rules).
- Where the rule was violated (identity of objects involved).

Also, classification of rules based on e.g. *discipline* and *severity* may be useful in many cases. In the rule databases, this may be accomplished through the use of *structured comments*, similar to the common practice of including structured documentation in computer programs, such as JavaDoc (see Fig. 6 for an example). A program parses the structured comments and forwards corresponding queries to the logic programming solver. Any violations returned are associated with the information in the comments, so that the combination can be used to present a helpful message to the user. A prototype CAD add-on program for Autodesk AutoCAD was implemented, see Fig. 7.

504   B. Luteberget et al.

```
%| rule: Home signal too close to first facing switch.
%| type: technical
%| severity: error
homeSignalBeforeFacingSwitchError(S,SW) :-
    firstFacingSwitch(B,SW,DIR),
    homeSignalBetween(S,B,SW),
    distance(S,SW,DIR,L), L < 200.
```

Fig. 6. Structured comments on rule violation expression

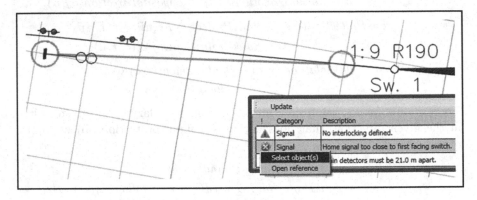

Fig. 7. Counterexample presentation within an interactive CAD environment.

5.2 Case Study Results

The rules concerning signalling layout and interlocking from *Jernbaneverket* [11] described above were checked in the railML representation of the Arna-Fløen project, which is an ongoing design project in Anacon AS (now merged with Norconsult). Each object was associated with one or more construction phases, which we call phase A and phase B, which also correspond to two operational phases. The model that was used for the work with the Arna station (phase A and B combined) included 25 switches, 55 connections, 74 train detectors, and 74 signals. The interlocking consisted of 23 and 42 elementary routes in operational phase A and B respectively.

Table 1. Case study size and running times on a standard laptop.

	Testing station	Arna phase A	Arna phase B
Relevant components	15	152	231
Interlocking routes	2	23	42
Datalog facts	85	8283	9159
Running time (s)	0.1	4.4	9.4

The Arna station design project and the corresponding CAD model has been in progress since 2013, and the method of integrating railML fragments into the CAD database, as described in Sect. 3, has been in use for about one year. Engineers working on this model are now routinely adding the required railML properties to the signalling components as part of their CAD modelling process. The rule collection consisted of 37 derived concepts, 5 consistency predicates, and 8 technical predicates. Running times for the verification procedure can be found in Table 1.

6   Conclusions, Related and Further Work

We have demonstrated a logical formalism in which railway layout and interlocking constraints and technical rules may be expressed, and which can be decided by logic programming proof methods with polynomial time complexity.

Related Work. Railway control systems and signalling designs are a fertile ground for formal methods. See [1,7] for an overview of various approaches and pointers to the literature, applying formal methods in railway design. In particular, safety of interlockings has been intensively formalized and studied, using for instance VDM [9] and the B-method, resp. Event-B [12]. Model checking has proved particularly attractive for tackling the safety of interlocking, and various model checkers and temporal logics have been used, cf. e.g. [5,6,22]. Critically evaluating practicality, [8] investigated applicability of model checking for interlocking tables using NuSMVresp. Spin. The research shows that interlocking systems of realistic size are currently out of reach for both flavors of model checkers. [10] uses *bounded* model checking for interlockings. An influential technology is the verified code generation for interlockings from Prover AB Sweden [2]. Prover is an automated theorem prover, using Stålmarck's method.

The mentioned works generally include *dynamic* aspects of the railway in their checking, like train positions and the interlocking state. This is in contrast to our work, which focuses on checking against static aspects. Lodemann et al. [14] use semantic technologies to automate railway infrastructure verification. Their scope is still wider than this paper in the computational sense, with the full expressive power of OWL ontologies, running times on the order of hours, and the use of separate interactive graphical user interfaces rather than integration with design tools.

Future Work. In the future work with RailComplete AS, we will focus on extending the rule base to contain more relevant signalling and interlocking rules from [11], evaluating the performance of our verification on a larger scale. Design information and rules about other railway control systems, such as geographical interlockings and train protection systems could also be included. The current work is assuming Norwegian regulations, but the European Rail Traffic Management System is expected to dominate in the future.

Finally, we plan to extend from consistency checking to optimization of designs. Optimization requires significantly larger computational effort, and the relation between Datalog and more expressive logical programming frameworks could become relevant.

Acknowledgments. We thank Anacon AS and RailComplete AS, especially senior engineer Claus Feyling, for guidance on railway methodology and philosophy. We acknowledge the support of the Norwegian Research Council through the project RailCons – Automated Methods and Tools for Ensuring Consistency of Railway Designs.

References

1. Bjørner, D.: New results and trends in formal techniques for the development of software in transportation systems. In: Proceedings of the Symposium on Formal Methods for Railway Operation and Control Systems (FORMS 2003). L'Harmattan Hongrie (2003)
2. Borälv, A., Stålmarck, G.: Formal verification in railways. In: Hinchey, M.G., Bowen, J.P. (eds.) Industrial-Strength Formal Methods in Practice. FACIT, pp. 329–350. Springer, London (1999)
3. Bosschaart, M., Quaglietta, E., Janssen, B., Goverde, R.M.P.: Efficient formalization of railway interlocking data in RailML. Inf. Syst. **49**, 126–141 (2015)
4. Boulanger, J.-L.: CENELEC 50128 and IEC 62279 Standards. Wiley-ISTE, New Jersey (2015)
5. Busard, S., Cappart, Q., Limbrée, C., Pecheur, C., Schaus, P.: Verification of railway interlocking systems. In: 4th Internationl Workshop on Engineering Safety and Security Systems (ESSS), vol. 184 of EPTCS, pp. 19–31 (2015)
6. Eisner, C.: Using symbolic model checking to verify the railway stations of hoorn-kersenboogerd and heerhugowaard. In: Pierre, L., Kropf, T. (eds.) CHARME 1999. LNCS, vol. 1703, pp. 97–109. Springer, Heidelberg (1999)
7. Fantechi, A., Fokkink, W., Morzenti, A.: Some trends in formal methods applications to railway signalling. In: Gnesi, S., Margaria, T. (eds.) Formal Methods for Industrial Critical Systems, pp. 61–84. Wiley, New Jersey (2012)
8. Ferrari, A., Magnani, G., Grasso, D., Fantechi, A.: Model checking interlocking control tables. In: Schnieder, E., Tarnai, G. (eds.) FORMS/FORMAT 2010, pp. 107–115. Springer, Heidelberg (2010)
9. Fukuda, M., Hirao, Y., Ogino, T.: VDM specification of an interlocking system and a simulator for its validation. In: 9th IFAC Symposium Control in Transportation Systems Proceedings, vol. 1, pp. 218–223, Braunschweig. IFAC (2000)
10. Haxthausen, A.E., Peleska, J., Pinger, R.: Applied bounded model checking for interlocking system designs. In: Counsell, S., Núñez, M. (eds.) SEFM 2013. LNCS, vol. 8368, pp. 205–220. Springer, Heidelberg (2014)
11. Jernbaneverket. Teknisk regelverk (2015). http://trv.jbv.no/
12. Lecomte, T., Burdy, L., Leuschel, M.: Formally checking large data sets in the railways. In: Proceedings of DS-Event-B 2012: Advances in Developing Dependable Systems in Event-B. In conjunction with ICFEM, 2012, vol. 3(1), pp. 35–43 (2012)
13. Libkin, L.: Elements of Finite Model Theory. Texts in Theoretical Computer Science. An EATCS Series. Springer, Heidelberg (2004)

14. Lodemann, M., Luttenberger, N., Schulz, E.: Semantic computing for railway infrastructure verification. In: IEEE Seventh International Conference on Semantic, Computing, pp. 371–376 (2013)
15. Luteberget, B., Feyling, C.: Automated verification of rules and regulations compliance in CAD models of railway signalling and interlocking. In: Computers in Railways XV. WIT Press (2016) (to appear)
16. Luteberget, B., Johansen, C., Steffen, M.: Rule-based consistency checking of railway infrastructure designs. Technical report 450, January 2016
17. Nash, A., Huerlimann, D., Schütte, J., Krauss, V.P.: RailML - a standard data interface for railroad applications. In: Allan, J., Hill, R.J., Brebbia, C.A., Sciutto, G., Sone, S. (eds.) Computers in Railways IX, pp. 233–240. WIT Press, Southampton (2004)
18. Pachl, J.: Railway Operation and Control. VTD Rail Publishing, Mountlake Terrace (2015)
19. RailML. The XML interface for railway applications (2016). http://www.railml.org
20. Swift, T., Warren, D.S.: XSB: extending prolog with tabled logic programming. Theor. Pract. Log. Program. **12**(1–2), 157–187 (2012)
21. Ullman, J.D.: Principles of Database and Knowledge-Base Systems. CSPP, New York (1988)
22. Winter, K., Johnston, W., Robinson, P., Strooper, P., van den Berg, L.: Tool support for checking railway interlocking designs. In: Proceedings of the 10th Australian Workshop on Safety Critical Systems and Software, pp. 101–107 (2006)

Formal Verification of Safety PLC Based Control Software

Dániel Darvas[1,2]([⊠]), István Majzik[2], and Enrique Blanco Viñuela[1]

[1] CERN – European Organization for Nuclear Research, Geneva, Switzerland
{ddarvas,eblanco}@cern.ch
[2] Budapest University of Technology and Economics, Budapest, Hungary
{darvas,majzik}@mit.bme.hu

Abstract. Programmable Logic Controllers (PLCs) are widely used in the industry for various industrial automation tasks. Besides non-safety applications, the usage of PLCs became accepted in safety-critical installations, where the cost of failure is high. In these cases the used hardware is special (so-called fail-safe or safety PLCs), but also the software needs special considerations. Formal verification is a method that can help to develop high-quality software for critical tasks. However, such method should be adapted to the special needs of the safety PLCs, that are often particular compared to the normal PLC development domain. In this paper we propose two complementary solutions for the formal verification of safety-critical PLC programs based on model checking and equivalence checking using formal specification. Furthermore, a case study is presented, demonstrating our approach.

Keywords: PLC · Model checking · Formal specification · Safety-critical systems

1 Introduction and Motivation

Programmable Logic Controllers (PLCs) are special industrial computers, widely-used for various automation tasks. Although initially PLCs were not specifically targeting safety-critical applications, it is feasible and increasingly accepted to use these controllers in critical settings with some restrictions [9].

Most of the PLCs can be programmed in one of the languages defined by the IEC 61131-3 standard: Instruction List (IL), Structured Text (ST), Ladder Diagram (LD), Function Block Diagram (FBD) and Sequential Function Chart (SFC). The first two languages are textual with different levels of abstraction: ST is a high-level language, while IL is "assembly-like". The last three languages are graphical. As SFC is a special-purpose language for structuring the PLC programs, this paper focuses on the first four languages. Short examples of these four languages can be seen in Fig. 2. These example programs have the same meaning and behaviour, i.e. they provide the same output sequences for the same input sequences.

© Springer International Publishing Switzerland 2016
E. Ábrahám and M. Huisman (Eds.): IFM 2016, LNCS 9681, pp. 508–522, 2016.
DOI: 10.1007/978-3-319-33693-0_32

Safety-Critical PLC-Based Systems. The safety-critical controllers have to fulfil the requirements of the corresponding standards, such as IEC 61508, IEC 61511, or IEC 62061. These standards define different safety integrity levels (SIL) and various requirements and guidelines for the system and the development process. Many PLC vendors produce a special range of hardware complying with the corresponding standards. These so-called fail-safe PLC CPUs (or simply *safety PLCs* in the following) are typically certified up to SIL3 according to IEC 61508-2. Besides the special hardware, the PLC vendors provide special development environments, often with additional restrictions compared to the non-safety-critical PLC programming. For instance, Siemens[1] restricts the developer to use the LD or FBD language with further restrictions, such as no floating-point or compound data types can be used [17], following the recommendations of the IEC 61511-2 standard. Although the hardware of the safety PLCs is special, the hardware differences do not affect the software part. Thus the main particularity of the safety PLCs for us is the restricted programming possibilities, namely the obligation to use restricted LD or FBD language for programming.

Typically, testing is applied to assess and improve the quality of PLC-based applications. In safety-critical settings more precise verification is needed. Formal verification is not widely used yet in the industry, presumably because of its high cost and complexity. However, as the cost of failure is high in safety-critical PLC-based systems, they are good candidates for formal verification. Fortunately, formal verification becomes more and more accessible thanks to the new methods that hide the difficulties from the developers.

The goal of this work is to apply formal verification (model checking and equivalence checking) to safety-critical PLC programs in order to complement the current verification methods, to increase the quality of the programs by finding more faults. However, the goal is not (yet) to prove the correctness of the PLC programs, therefore we will not focus directly on proving the correctness of our methods in this paper. We extend the PLCverif approach [7], already providing a scalable and flexible model checking method adapted to PLC programs, to make it suitable for the verification of safety-critical systems. This involves three main tasks: (1) support for the specific languages used in safety PLCs, (2) development of new reduction heuristics to cope with large safety programs, and (3) introduction of a new verification approach based on complete behaviour specification. Furthermore, we present a case study, where our method proved to be applicable and useful.

Case Study. CERN, the European Organization for Nuclear Research operates a particle accelerator complex, comprising the Large Hadron Collider (LHC).

---

[1] As Siemens is widely-used at our organization, we are using it as an example PLC provider. The languages used in Siemens PLCs are compliant with the IEC 61131 standard, but small syntactic and semantics differences exist. The Siemens variants have different names: instead of IL, ST, LD, FBD, SFC, they are called STL, SCL, LAD, FBD, SFC/GRAPH, respectively. To avoid the confusion, we will use the standard language names for the Siemens variants too, but when a detail is vendor-specific, we will use the Siemens syntax or implementation.

Fig. 1. SM18 Cryogenic Test Facility (©CERN, 2013. CERN-GE-1304099-24)

The high collision energy of the LHC necessitates a strong magnetic field to bend the particle beams, achieved by superconducting magnets. These magnets should be tested before putting them into production. For this, CERN has a unique testing facility (so-called *SM18 Cryogenic Test Facility*) where the magnets can be tested at low temperature (1.8 K, achieved by liquid helium and nitrogen), high currents (14 kA) and vacuum. A photo of the SM18 test hall can be seen in Fig. 1 (4 out of the total 10 test benches are shown in the photo, with a white, shorter quadrupole and a blue, longer dipole magnet currently under test). Testing the magnets is a safety-critical task, as a failure can cause serious damage or injury. Therefore a safety instrumented system is in use to allow or forbid the magnet tests based on whether their preconditions are met. Recently a project started to re-engineer this safety system based on safety PLCs. In this project we have applied formal methods from the beginning of the development.

Structure of the Paper. Section 2 introduces the original PLCverif verification approach, that is not adapted yet to safety-critical PLC programs. Then Sect. 3 defines two extensions, making the method applicable in safety-critical settings. The validation and our experiences on the above-presented case study are discussed in Sect. 4. Section 5 presents the related work on formal verification of PLC programs. Section 6 summarizes and concludes the paper.

2   The Original PLCverif Approach

The PLCverif tool[2] provides a scalable and flexible workflow for the model checking of PLCs [5,7]. It has already proven to be useful for non-safety-critical programs, written in ST language [7]. However, as it does not support the FBD and LD languages, PLCverif cannot be used as it is for the verification of our safety-critical PLC programs.

The original workflow (see Fig. 3) builds on two inputs: (1) the ST source code (created by an engineer) and (2) the requirements formalized using pre-defined

---

[2] http://cern.ch/plcverif/

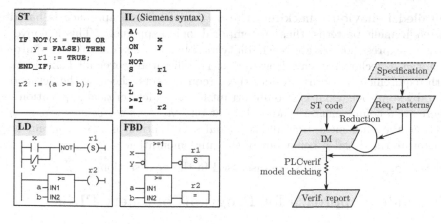

Fig. 2. PLC language examples   **Fig. 3.** Original verification workflow

requirement patterns. A requirement pattern is an English sentence containing gaps to be filled by the user with simple expressions. The meaning of the sentence is formalized using temporal logic, having the same placeholders.

First, the ST source code is parsed and translated to an internal, automata-based *intermediate model* (IM). After, based on the given requirement and generic PLC knowledge, the IM is reduced, preserving the properties to be checked [6]. Then the "PLCverif model checking" step is performed: (a) the reduced IM and the requirement are translated to one of the supported model checker's input format; next (b) the model checker tool is executed; and finally (c) the output of the model checker tool is parsed, analysed and presented to the user in a verification report. At the moment the concrete syntaxes of NuSMV, nuXmv, UPPAAL, BIP and ITS tools are supported.

This method has three main advantages:

- **Scalability.** The automated reductions make the verification of large programs possible.
- **Flexibility.** The usage of IM allows to exchange the model checker tools.
- **Usability.** No special knowledge about formal verification is needed from the user: the input of the PLCverif tool is an ST source code and a filled requirement pattern, and the output is a self-contained verification report.

The PLCverif approach was found to be practical and applicable in real cases [7]. However, to reuse this workflow for the safety-critical PLC programs of CERN, three main extensions are needed.

- **Support for new languages.** The (Siemens) safety PLCs can only be programmed in LD or FBD languages, therefore these languages should be supported by PLCverif.
- **Sustain the scalability.** The newly targeted languages are on a lower abstraction level than the ST language, therefore new, specialized reduction heuristics are needed to cope with verification of the large PLC programs.

– **Detailed behaviour checking.** The original PLCverif approach is based on requirement patterns, thus on temporal logic expressions. This is convenient to express some state reachability problems or general safety requirements in a declarative way. However, it is difficult to cover all behaviours with requirement patterns. Besides these requirements, checking the detailed (step-by-step) behaviour is also important for the safety-critical applications. Therefore a complementary method, built on *behaviour equivalence checking* between the implementation and a formal specification, is more convenient to capture the detailed behaviour of the implementation.

The details of these extensions are discussed in the next section.

3   Extended Approach for Programs of Safety PLCs

This section is dedicated to the extensions of the PLCverif workflow that are necessary to use it for safety-critical PLC programs. Section 3.1 discusses the extensions required to handle the LD and FBD languages. Section 3.2 presents a complementary workflow, built on formal specification and equivalence checking.

3.1   Verification of LD and FBD Programs

The primary need to verify safety-critical PLC programs is the ability to check LD and FBD codes. However, in case of Siemens PLCs, the programs written in graphical languages are not directly accessible, but they can be exported from the development environment as IL code. This solves the problem of parsing LD and FBD languages. However, the abstraction level of IL is even lower than LD's or FBD's, thus it is more difficult to handle IL programs. Our extended workflow can be seen in Fig. 4a, where the new parts are denoted by bold letters.

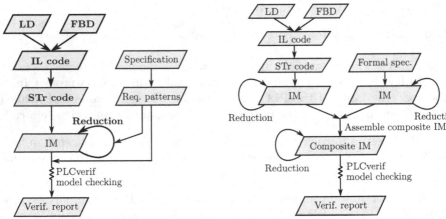

(a) Workflow to check requirements on safety PLC programs

(b) Workflow to check conformance of safety PLC programs

Fig. 4. Extended verification workflows

Handling IL Code Inputs. The ST parser of PLCverif is based on Xtext[3], providing rich tooling for the language defined by a grammar. However, IL cannot be conveniently represented using Xtext. For example, in Siemens IL "A" may be a variable and an AND logic instruction in the same program.

It is resource demanding to implement (1) a parser that can build the abstract syntax tree of the IL language, and (2) a model translator that translates the syntax tree to the intermediate model. Instead of developing these, we have decided to represent IL code as ST code, providing a mapping in an inductive way from each IL instruction to ST instructions. This way the PLCverif model translator does not change, also the instruction-by-instruction mapping can be much simpler than a complete parser in case of the IL language.

The challenge of this mapping is that the IL instructions directly access and modify the different registers[4] of the PLC. For example, the instruction "L var1" stores the contents of Accumulator 1 in Accumulator 2, then it loads the value of variable var1 to Accumulator 1. There is no language element to access the registers directly in ST, making the direct representation of IL code impossible. However, this can easily be solved for verification purposes. We emulate the registers as local ST variables according to a well-defined naming convention, and use it consistently in the ST programs and in the properties to be verified. To avoid the confusion – though it does not require a language extension –, we will use *STr* as language name for programs written in ST where the registers are emulated as local variables. This solution is similar to the one presented in [19]. To distinguish between ordinary variables and the ones representing STr registers, the latter's names start with double underscores.

With this extension, each IL instruction (e.g. bit logic and comparison operations, conversions, jumps, arithmetic instructions, load and transfer instructions) can be represented in STr, by making all implicit effects of the IL instructions explicit in STr. For this purpose, we have identified the semantics of each IL instruction by checking on real PLCs what are the results of the instruction for every possible initial state (i.e. for each valuations of the read registers and variables). The identified semantics of the IL instructions are generic, not specific to our case studies. Some examples for this translation with different complexities are in Table 1. A short description of the used registers is in Table 2[5].

As each IL instruction can be translated into STr, it can be seen inductively that each IL program can be translated into STr as well. In other words, STr can emulate all IL programs, and consequently all FBD and LD programs too. Furthermore, STr can be regarded as a textual concrete syntax of the PLCverif intermediate model (IM), therefore there is no theoretical difference if we translate IL programs to the intermediate model directly or through STr.

---

[3] https://www.eclipse.org/Xtext/

[4] As previously discussed, we use the Siemens notations in this paper. Throughout this paper *registers* are used as a generic term referring to the status bits, accumulators and the nesting stack.

[5] Here we omit the registers not necessary for simple IL programs, such as the BR (binary result), OV (overflow), OS (stored overflow) bits and the address registers.

514   D. Darvas et al.

Table 1. IL to STr transformation examples

IL	STr equivalent
A var1	IF __NFC THEN __RLO:=__RLO AND (var1 OR __OR); ELSE __RLO:=var1 OR __OR; END_IF; __STA:=var1; __NFC:=TRUE;

A(	__nsRLO[8]:=__nsRLO[7]; ... __nsRLO[2]:=__nsRLO[1]; __nsRLO[1]:=__RLO OR NOT __NFC;
	 __nsOR[8] := __nsOR[7]; ... __nsOR[2] := __nsOR[1]; __nsOR[1]:=__OR AND __NFC;
	 __nsFC2[8]:=__nsFC2[7]; ... __nsFC2[2]:=__nsFC2[1]; __nsFC2[1]:=FALSE;
	 __nsFC1[8]:=__nsFC1[7]; ... __nsFC1[2]:=__nsFC1[1]; __nsFC1[1]:=FALSE;
	 __nsFC0[8]:=__nsFC0[7]; ... __nsFC0[2]:=__nsFC0[1]; __nsFC0[1]:=FALSE;
	 __OR:=FALSE; __STA:=TRUE; __NFC:=FALSE;

>I	__OR:=FALSE; __NFC:=TRUE; __RLO:=(__ACCU1<__ACCU2); __CC0:=(__ACCU1>__ACCU2); __CC1:=(__ACCU1<__ACCU2);
L var1	__ACCU2 := __ACCU1; __ACCU1 := var1;

Table 2. Main registers in Siemens PLCs [16]

Register	Purpose
__RLO	*Result of last logic operation.*
__OR	Helper bit for the "and before or" logical operation (O instruction).
__NFC	*Not first computation.* If it is false, the current value of __RLO is not taken into account.
__STA	*Status bit.* Stores the value of a bit that is referenced.
__CC0, __CC1	*Condition codes.* The result of the last comparison or other operations.
__ACCU*	*Accumulators.*
__ns*[]	*Nesting stack.* Temporarily stores register values (__nsRLO, __nsOR) and the last Boolean operation (__nsFC*) while a nested Boolean computation is in progress.

Code Size Blow-Up and Reductions. Representing the registers as local variables allows the inductive mapping of IL programs to the ST language, making possible to reuse the PLCverif workflow and toolchain. However, it raises a new concern: a single IL instruction may read and modify several registers. This causes a significant blow-up, as illustrated in Fig. 5. The original sample IL code contains 4 instructions (Fig. 5a), that can be represented by one single statement in ST (Fig. 5b). However, the IL code translated to STr have 14 variable assignments (Fig. 5c). Note that these assignments represent the storage of (intermediate) results that are not necessarily needed by the subsequent statements. The extremities of this are the nesting Boolean operators (e.g. "A("). They store some intermediate computation results in the so-called nesting stack, therefore a single IL operation might be translated to 40–50 STr assignments (see Table 1).

This blow-up effect can be reduced by developing new automated reduction heuristics, similarly to the ones already included in the PLCverif workflow [6]. The new reductions are similar to the reductions used in optimized compilers.

– *Expression propagation* can help to reduce the number of assignments. For example, the second assignment of line 1 in Fig. 5c can be removed and the

```
1   L a
2   L b
3   >=I
4   = r
```

(a) Source IL code
(Siemens)

```
1   r := (a >= b);
```

(b) Equivalent ST code

```
1   __ACCU2 := __ACCU1;   __ACCU1 := a;
2
3   __ACCU2 := __ACCU1;   __ACCU1 := b;
4
5   __OR := FALSE;   __NFC := TRUE;
6   __RLO := (__ACCU1 <= __ACCU2);
7   __CCO := (__ACCU1 >  __ACCU2);
8   __CC1 := (__ACCU1 <  __ACCU2);
9
10  IF __MCR THEN r := __RLO; END_IF;
11  __OR := FALSE;   __STA := r;   __NFC := FALSE;
```

(c) Generated STr code

Fig. 5. Illustration of code blow-up caused by IL to STr translation

first assignment of line 3 can be replaced by __ACCU2 := a; without modifying the behaviour of the program.

- The *assignments without observable effect* can be removed. For example, the first assignment of line 1 in Fig. 5c can be removed, as its effect is hidden by the first assignment of line 3.
- The non-used variables are deleted by the already existing *cone of influence* reduction. For example, the __CCO and __CC1 variables can be removed, as they are never read in Fig. 5c.
- The expression propagation can result in complex Boolean expressions, that can be reduced by *Boolean factoring* and other *Boolean expression reduction methods*. If the simplified expression refers to fewer variables, these reductions may help the cone of influence reduction. Nevertheless, even if they do not reduce the state space, the Boolean expression simplification makes the other reductions faster and decreases the memory needs.

By using these reduction heuristics, the code in Fig. 5c can be automatically reduced to the one in Fig. 5b, when the registers are not read by any further part of the code. Note that each reduction is applied only if it preserves the properties that are currently under evaluation.

3.2 Verification Based on Formal Specification

The previous approach reused the original pattern-based requirement specification method. This is a suitable way to check state reachability properties expressed by the developer. However, the verification of the detailed behaviour is similarly important in safety-critical systems, for which the original approach is not convenient. Furthermore, there is no guarantee that the verification based on manually extracted requirements covers all important aspects of the code. In extreme cases the verification of these requirements can have an opposite effect: the developer convinces himself based on incomplete requirements that the implementation is correct. Later this might bias the testing process. To avoid this, we provide a complementary verification approach which is more convenient for detailed behaviour verification.

The specification of PLC programs is an important topic, yet there are no widely used behaviour specification methods, especially not formal methods with precise semantics definition. Providing a detailed specification is often too "expensive", and instead of precisely specifying the behaviour, documents written in natural language and informal control tables are used that are easy to misunderstand and difficult to verify. However, as the cost of failure is high in the safety-critical domain, also the behaviour of a safety PLC program is typically simpler. Therefore providing a formal specification may be feasible in these cases.

Previously we have proposed a method called *PLCspecif* [4] for the formal specification for PLC programs. Its aim is to provide a formal, yet convenient way for the PLC developers to describe a detailed, complete behaviour specification of the module or system under development. PLCspecif plugs together different, already used semi-formal description methods, e.g. state machines, data-flow diagrams, truth tables; and assigns a unified formal semantics to them. This helps the development and the verification by providing unambiguous requirements. The semantics of PLCspecif is designed in a way that the specifications can be easily transformed to automaton-based models for formal verification.

If such specification exists for the safety-critical PLC program, we can benefit from it and check directly the equivalence between the implementation and the specification. This workflow is shown in Fig. 4b. The semantics of PLCspecif is given as an automaton construction, that can be directly represented in the IM formalism of PLCverif. Accordingly, two IMs are used in this approach: one to represent the implementation, and another one representing the specification. First, both IMs are reduced independently. In this phase we only use reduction rules that preserve all properties, assuming that they check variable values only at the end of the PLC cycles. Then the two IMs are automatically combined into a composite verification model. This composite verification model is constructed on the basis of the definition of the behavioural equivalence. As the equivalence relation we would like to check requires that for each possible input sequence, the specification and the implementation give the same output sequences, the composite verification model ensures by construction that the two model parts always get the same input values. After, the composite model is reduced again. Then, similarly to the original PLCverif approach, we use one of the supported external model checkers to decide whether the equivalence relation holds, namely, that the corresponding outputs of the two model parts are equal in each step.

4   Validation and Analysis of Applicability

To demonstrate and validate the presented approaches, we recall the SM18 Cryogenic Test Facility's safety controller. The implementation under test in this case is the safety logic of this controller, isolated from the rest of the program that is responsible for the non-safety-critical tasks. The IL code exported from the original LD implementation contains about 9500 instructions. This was translated into approx. 120 000 STr statements, already with some optimizations (e.g. the nesting stack depth was reduced to the necessary amount). The potential state

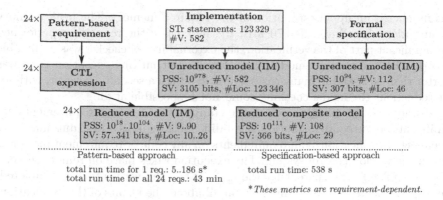

Fig. 6. Key metrics of the example

space (i.e. the cross-product of all contained variable's domain and the possible automata locations in the IM) contains approx. 10^{978} states.

We have applied both previously described formal verification approaches: first the pattern-based, then the specification-based approach. The key metrics and the summary of the two methods can be seen in Fig. 6. For each IM we give the size of potential state space (PSS), the number of variables (#V), the size of the state vector, i.e. the length of binary vector that can represent the current values of all variables (SV), and the number of automata locations (#Loc).

Verification Based on Requirement Patterns. After the successful representation of the safety logic in STr language, we have captured pattern-based requirements from the informal specification provided by the client of the project. As this was the first safety-critical PLC program verification project at CERN, the requirements were extracted by formal methods experts, rather than the PLC program developers. In total 24 different requirements were extracted and formalised using requirement patterns. Some of them are fairly simple, while some others contain references to up to 50 different variables.

In each case the verification was successfully executed, thanks to the requirement-specific and general reductions that reduced both the number of variables and automaton locations. Also, the reductions were able to eliminate all register-representing variables in every case. The typical verification run time of each requirement was 150–170 s, including the model generation, the model reductions and the execution of the external model checker (nuXmv in this case)[6]. In case of some requirements, only a small part of the model was enough for the verification of the given requirement, therefore the reductions were able to eliminate a large part of the IM, resulting a total run time of 4–5 s. The total run time of all verification cases together was 43 min. The peak memory consumption of PLCverif was 2926 MB, however as the implementation is in Java,

---

[6] For all measurements we have used PLCverif 2.0.2 and nuXmv 1.0.1 on Windows 7 x64, executed on a PC with Intel® Core™ i7-3770 3.4 GHz CPU and 8 GB RAM.

this number is an upper estimation of the required memory. The peak memory consumption of nuXmv was 570 MB. In these cases the reductions performed the significant part of the verification, the external model checker was easily able to cope with the reduced model. Even the longest nuXmv execution time was shorter than 30 s, and in many cases it was less than a second. However, without our reductions the model checking could not be possible at all.

As the total run time, as well as the computation resource requirements are significant, an automated solution was built using Jenkins[7], that automatically executes the verification of all requirements on any code or requirement modification in the version control system. The execution takes place on remote servers, this is completely transparent for the user. When the verification is completed, the responsible people are notified by e-mail about the results of the verification.

Verification Based on Formal Specification. To validate the second approach, the formal specification of the magnet test safety logic had to be captured. We did not have a formal specification a priori, the implementation was developed based on a semi-formal specification. As the precise semantics of the client's specification was already clarified during the previous verification process, the creation of the formal specification was relatively simple. Note that PLCspecif provides various tabular description methods, similar to the one used by the customer of the project. As previously discussed, first the PLCspecif specification was automatically translated to intermediate model. Even before reductions, this IM generated from the specification was much smaller than the IM generated from the STr code, as the model size blow-up caused by the explicit representation of PLC registers does not occur in this case. After the reductions, the composite verification model was constructed and reduced. The resulting verification model was larger than the biggest individual verification model generated using the pattern-based approach. Consequently the total run time was longer, approximately 10 min. However, this had to be done only once, while the first approach necessitated 24 verification runs, one for each requirement. Therefore in total the run time of the second approach was more than four times shorter.

Analysis of the Results. After performing the case study we have concluded that the verification was successful, as it was possible to model and verify the critical part of the PLC program. We have applied an iterative workflow: every time the model checking pointed out a problem, we have suspended the verification process until the root cause of the problem was fixed. Then the verification process restarted with the new code version. In total 14 issues were identified. We have classified the problems found into the following main categories:

- 4 *requirement misunderstanding* problems. In these cases the formalization of the requirements pointed out ambiguous or contradictory elements in the specification provided by the customer, overlooked during implementation.
- 3 *functionality* problems. In these cases the problem could have caused unexpected behaviours, but not dangerous situations.

---

[7] https://jenkins-ci.org/

- 5 *safety* problems. In these cases the problem could have caused dangerous situations, i.e. a magnet test might be permitted when it should not.
- 2 *mixed functionality-safety* problems.

All these problems were found before on-site testing of the PLC program. As the (re-)deployment and the PLC's on-site testing is a time-consuming operation, model checking provided an efficient verification method. Furthermore, model checking does not involve the use of real hardware, therefore no dangerous situations can happen contrarily to on-site testing.

As testing in lab and on site provides the state-of-the-practice in the verification of PLC-based systems, we have checked whether the problems identified using formal methods could have been found using the typically applied testing methods. Setting up a test scenario on-site can take up to hours, therefore only the main functionalities and their most critical errors are targeted, potentially omitting problems. Out of the 10 functionality or safety issues, 4 could have been found using testing. In 6 cases it was practically impossible to find the problem using our regular testing approach, as the testing is not exhaustive in practice.

We have performed the pattern-based verification approach first, which identified 12 of the 14 issues. The remaining 2 problems were found using the specification- and equivalence checking-based approach. This shows that the two methods are convenient for different types of requirements, and they can complement each other. The system is now in production for 7 months. So far no major problem was observed in operation caused by mistakes in the safety logic.

Comparison of the Two Approaches. The two presented verification approaches (pattern-based and behaviour specification-based approaches) provide different advantages and disadvantages.

- Using the behaviour specification-based approach, all requirements contained in the original specification are covered, there is no potential user omission in extracting the requirements.
- The pattern-based approach can check properties in a more "declarative" way, i.e. without specifying the complete behaviour and may help the user to find discrepancies between the general expectations and the implementation, or various requirement misunderstandings.
- The verification models generated in the pattern-based approach are often smaller than in the other approach, providing better verification performance. On the other hand, this approach involves multiple verification runs, whereas the specification-based approach needs only one model generation and one model checker execution.
- The integration to the existing development processes is easier in case of the pattern-based approach, as there is no need for a complete formal specification, which does not exist typically and often difficult to be constructed.

5   Related Work

The formal verification, especially model checking of PLC programs was deeply studied in the last fifteen years [13]. Several approaches were developed with

Table 3. Related work

Ref.	Lang.	Real-life applicability	Scalability	Tool	Verifier tool
[2]	IL, ST	●●	●●	+	Arcade
[3]	IL	●	●	−	CaSMV
[8]	ST, ...	●●	●●	−	NuSMV
[10, 20]	FBD	●●	●●●	+	CaSMV
[11]	IL	●●	●●	−	Z3
[12]	SFC	●●	●●	+	SpaceEx
[14]	FBD	●●	●●	−	NuSMV
[15]	LD	●	?	−	UPPAAL
[18]	FBD	●	?	−	UPPAAL
[19]	IL	●	●	−	MiniSat
[7]	ST, SFC	●●●	●●●	+	nuXmv, UPPAAL, ...

Legend ●●●: high, ●●: medium, ●: low; +: exists, −: does not exist

different advantages and capabilities. We summarize the works most relevant to us in Table 3. To investigate the applicability of the methods, we have four main factors to take into account: the set of supported languages, the real-life applicability (how feasible it is to include the method in the normal PLC development workflow), the scalability of the method and whether a supporting tool was developed. It should be noted that the tools are typically not publicly available, except for [2].

For checking applicability, we used the PLCverif approach [7] as a base of comparison. This comparison contains subjective elements, but we claim that PLCverif provides a better real-life applicability than the other methods, as the formal verification-related difficulties are hidden from the user, there is no need to edit directly temporal logic expressions or to invoke model checker tools. The scalability is a similarly important question. We have tried to judge the scalability of each method based on the cited papers. If it was not possible (e.g. there was no presented verification example), we put "?" in the table. We have also included the used verifier tools in the table. It can be seen that [7] was the only approach we have found that provides a generic approach relying on multiple model checkers, depending on the current verification needs.

Since [7] does not provide support for the FBD and LD languages necessary to verify programs of safety PLCs, we decided to extend this method and to benefit from its advantages in the other dimensions.

[19] is a particularly interesting related work. Their approach is similar to ours: they translate the IL code instruction by instruction into a pivot language, that is SystemC in their case. The verification is performed as an equivalence checking between the SystemC representation of the implementation and the specification. However, the scalability of this method is not justified.

Furthermore, the SystemC specification cannot be used directly in our PLC development workflow due to the lack of specific knowledge.

Equivalence checking was already used in different verification settings for PLC programs: [1] applies regression verification between two versions of the implementation. In our work we apply equivalence checking between the formal behaviour specification and the implementation.

6 Summary and Conclusion

In this paper we presented an extension to the PLCverif approach [7] to handle the PLC programs written in FBD, LD or IL language that is necessary to verify safety-critical PLC programs. As [7] already contains methods to handle the ST and SFC languages, the current paper justifies also the claim that PLCverif can be a generic approach handling all five common PLC languages. To cope with the safety-related languages, additional reduction heuristics were introduced. Besides the requirement pattern and model checking-based verification approach, a new approach was drawn up, based on a PLCspecif formal specification and equivalence checking. These two approaches can complement each other.

A case study was presented showing that formal verification can be applied to significantly large, real safety-critical PLC programs. The two formal verification techniques identified several problems and they complemented each other. Many of the problems identified using them could have not been found using the currently used testing techniques. Moreover, the presented approaches helped to identify problems with the requirements, such as ambiguity or contradictions, overlooked by the developers during implementation. Formal verification was applied in the design phase, thus fixing the problems was easier than if they would have been found during on-site testing or in production. Furthermore, model checking and behavioural equivalence checking provided a safe way to check requirements, without any safety risks that might arise during on-site testing.

Acknowledgement. The authors would like to thank the people involved in the presented re-engineering project for their support and cooperation. Special thanks to Roberto Speroni for the cooperation and the continuous feedback.

References

1. Beckert, B., Ulbrich, M., Vogel-Heuser, B., Weigl, A.: Regression verification for programmable logic controller software. In: Butler, M., Conchon, M., Zaïdi, F. (eds.) ICFEM 2015. LNCS, vol. 9407, pp. 234–251. Springer, Heidelberg (2015)
2. Biallas, S., Brauer, J., Kowalewski, S.: Arcade.PLC: a verification platform for programmable logic controllers. In: Proceedings of 27th IEEE/ACM International Conference on Automated Software Engineering, pp. 338–341. ACM (2012)
3. Canet, G., Couffin, S., Lesage, J.J., Petit, A., Schnoebelen, P.: Towards the automatic verification of PLC programs written in instruction list. In: Proceedings of IEEE International Conference on Systems, Man, and Cybernetics, vol. 4, pp. 2449–2454. IEEE (2000)

4. Darvas, D., Blanco Viñuela, E., Majzik, I.: A formal specification method for PLC-based applications. In: Proceedings of 15th International Conference on Accelerator & Large Experimental Physics Control Systems, pp. 907–910. JaCoW, Geneva (2015, in press)

5. Darvas, D., Fernández Adiego, B., Blanco Viñuela, E.: PLCverif: a tool to verify PLC programs based on model checking techniques. In: Proceedings of 15th International Conference on Accelerator & Large Experimental Physics Control Systems, pp. 911–914. JaCoW, Geneva (2015, in press)

6. Darvas, D., Fernández Adiego, B., Vörös, A., Bartha, T., Blanco Viñuela, E., González Suárez, V.M.: Formal verification of complex properties on PLC programs. In: Ábrahám, E., Palamidessi, C. (eds.) FORTE 2014. LNCS, vol. 8461, pp. 284–299. Springer, Heidelberg (2014)

7. Fernández Adiego, B., Darvas, D., Blanco Viñuela, E., Tournier, J.C., Bliudze, S., Blech, J.O., González Suárez, V.M.: Applying model checking to industrial-sized PLC programs. IEEE. Trans. Ind. Informat. **11**(6), 1400–1410 (2015)

8. Gourcuff, V., de Smet, O., Faure, J.M.: Improving large-sized PLC programs verification using abstractions. In: Proceedings of the 17th IFAC World Congress, pp. 5101–5106. IFAC (2008)

9. Greenway, A.: A user's perspective of programmable logic controllers (PLCs) in safety-related applications. In: Redmill, F., Anderson, T. (eds.) Technology and Assessment of Safety-Critical Systems, pp. 1–20. Springer, London (1994)

10. Jee, E., et al.: FBDVerifier: interactive and visual analysis of counterexample in formal verification of function block diagram. J. Res. Pract. Inf. Technol. **42**(3), 171–188 (2010)

11. Lange, T., Neuhäußer, M.R., Noll, T.: Speeding up the safety verification of programmable logic controller code. In: Bertacco, V., Legay, A. (eds.) HVC 2013. LNCS, vol. 8244, pp. 44–60. Springer, Heidelberg (2013)

12. Nellen, J., Ábrahám, E., Wolters, B.: A CEGAR tool for the reachability analysis of PLC-controlled plants using hybrid automata. In: Bouabana-Tebibel, T., Rubin, S.H. (eds.) Formalisms for Reuse and Systems Integration. AISC, vol. 346, pp. 55–78. Springer, Heidelberg (2015)

13. Ovatman, T., Aral, A., Polat, D., Ünver, A.O.: An overview of model checking practices on verification of PLC software. Software & Systems Modeling, 1–24 (2014). doi:10.1007/s10270-014-0448-7. Advance online publication

14. Pavlović, O., Ehrich, H.D.: Model checking PLC software written in function block diagram. In: Proceedings of International Conference on Software Testing, Verification and Validation, pp. 439–448. IEEE (2010)

15. Sarmento, C.A., Silva, J.R., Miyagi, P.E., Santos Filho, D.J.: Modeling of programs and its verification for programmable logic controllers. In: Proceedings of the 17th IFAC World Congress, pp. 10546–10551. IFAC (2008)

16. Siemens: Statement List (STL) for S7–300/S7-400, C79000–G7076-C565-01 (1998)

17. Siemens: SIMATIC Industrial Software SIMATIC safety – Configuring and Programming, A5E02714440-AD (2014)

18. Soliman, D., Frey, G.: Verification and validation of safety applications based on PLCopen safety function blocks. Control Eng. Pract. **19**(9), 929–946 (2011)

19. Sülflow, A., Drechsler, R.: Verification of PLC programs using formal proof techniques. In: Formal Methods for Automation and Safety in Railway and Automotive Systems, pp. 43–50. L'Harmattan, Budapest (2008)

20. Yoo, J., Cha, S., Jee, E.: A verification framework for FBD based software in nuclear power plants. In: Proceedings of the 15th Asia-Pacific Software Engineering Conference, pp. 385–392. IEEE (2008)

CloudSDV Enabling Static Driver Verifier Using Microsoft Azure

Rahul Kumar[1(✉)], Thomas Ball[2], Jakob Lichtenberg[2], Nate Deisinger[2], Apoorv Upreti[3], and Chetan Bansal[2]

[1] Jet Propulsion Laboratory, Pasadena, CA, USA
rahulskumar@gmail.com
[2] Microsoft, Redmond, WA, USA
[3] Facebook, London, UK

Abstract. In this paper we describe our experience of enabling Static Driver Verifier to use the Microsoft Azure cloud computing platform. We first describe in detail our architecture and methodology for enabling SDV to operate in the Microsoft Azure cloud. We then present our results of using CloudSDV on single drivers and driver suites using various configurations of the cloud relative to a local machine. Our experiments show that using the cloud, we are able to achieve speedups in excess of 20x, which has enabled us to perform mass scale verification in a matter of hours as opposed to days. Finally, we present a brief discussion about our results and experiences.

Keywords: Cloud · Verification · Azure · Static analysis · Performance · Parallel · SDV · Scalability

1 Introduction

The last decade has seen a marked increase in the use of formal methods and static analysis in a variety of domains such as software development and systems engineering. Applications of formal methods vary from defect discovery to automated/manual theorem proving for performing analysis and proving system correctness. The Static Driver Verifier tool is one such static analysis tool that enables the discovery of defects in Windows device drivers [8,9]. It is and has been used with great effectiveness to check Windows device drivers for API compliance [7]. Currently, SDV is shipped as part of the Windows Driver Development Kit. As with other program analysis and defect discovery tools, the major issues with SDV are related to the *performance* and *scalability* of the tool. By *performance*, we refer to the total amount of time and memory resources required for performing the verification task (e.g., wall clock time, memory pressure etc.). *Scalability* on the other hand, is the *size of the driver* that we are able to successfully verify by proving the absence or presence of defects with no concern for

R. Kumar and A. Upreti—Work performed while at Microsoft Research India, Bangalore, India.

© Springer International Publishing Switzerland 2016
E. Ábrahám and M. Huisman (Eds.): IFM 2016, LNCS 9681, pp. 523–536, 2016.
DOI: 10.1007/978-3-319-33693-0_33

utilized resources. Small drivers may be completely verifiable by SDV, but still face a performance problem because it takes a long time to completely verify them. For example, for WDM drivers, there are approximately 200 rules that need to be verified for each device driver. The maximum time that each rule can take to be verified is 50 min; thus, resulting in a maximum possible total of 10000 min, or 167 h. Even on a multi-core computer, the verification can possibly span days. For device driver developers, this can be extremely frustrating and negative, possibly resulting in finally not using the tool for verification and losing confidence in static analysis in general. It is important to note that this particular problem can easily get worse if more rules are developed and verified on device drivers. Past experiences of using SDV on larger device drivers proved valuable for understanding the scalability problem that SDV runs into.

We attempt to solve some of these problems by enabling SDV to use a cloud platform such as Microsoft Azure [2]. CloudSDV is a Microsoft Azure based computation system that allows SDV to farm out its verification task to the cloud. Doing so, provides benefits in multiple different areas for both, users as well as developers of SDV:

- *Parallelize.* Multiple verification tasks can be dispatched simultaneously for parallel computation; thus, improving the performance of the verification run.
- *Offline Computation.* By farming out verification tasks to Azure, it is possible to schedule the entire verification of a driver and re-visit the results at a later point.
- *Result storage.* Using Azure, it is now possible to perform better result storage and telemetry for SDV. Results that were previously produced on local machines, are now recorded systematically in the Microsoft Azure cloud for future analysis. Additionally, it also becomes easier to *query* for results in the past, whereas previously, such results would have been lost permanently.
- *Verification as a Service.* Similar to other software services, CloudSDV allows improvements and bug fixes to SDV to be distributed much more easily. Updates can also be distributed with a much higher cadence as opposed to being governed by a less frequent schedule of the parent software (in this case the Windows Driver Development Kit).
- *Scalability.* Moving verification tasks to Azure does not solve the scalability problem in the traditional sense, but does provide the opportunity to verify larger drivers that have been resource intense to verify until now. For example, allowing a much larger timeout for each rule does not significantly increase the total verification time anymore. Rather, only a much smaller penalty is associated with the larger timeout; thus, allowing users to potentially get better results.

The paper is organized as follows. Section 2 gives a brief introduction to SDV. Section 3 gives an overview of the architecture and implementation of CloudSDV. Section 4 presents the results of using CloudSDV on various drivers and test suites. Section 5 presents a brief overview of known related work in this area and Sect. 6 presents a discussion and conclusions.

2   SDV Background

We first present a brief overview of SDV and how it functions. Figure 1 shows a high level overview of how SDV operates.

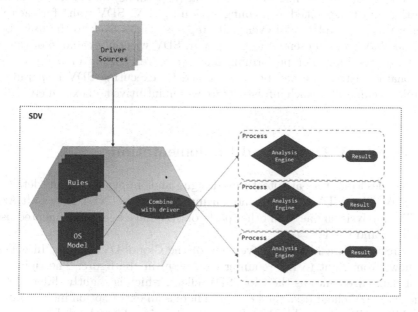

Fig. 1. An overview of the SDV system.

SDV takes as input the sources of the driver under test and optionally, a set of rules that are to be verified on the driver. Given a driver, SDV first ensures that the driver can be compiled correctly. Following this initial compilation, SDV then proceeds to combine the driver sources with the Operating System model and the *rules* that are to be verified on the driver. The Operating System model inside SDV is a set of C source files that model the Windows operating system in a manner that is most useful for performing verification by the analysis engine within SDV. There are two primary parts to the OS model. The *stubs* that provide a demonic model of the kernel APIs that can possibly be called by Windows device drivers, and the *harness* that simulates the operating system and how it would call into the driver to perform functions. The *rules* within SDV express temporal safety properties that drivers must adhere to. These rules are expressed in SLIC, which is a C-like language streamlined to express safety automaton [10]. The result of combining the driver sources with the operating system model and rules is an intermediate binary file that can be consumed by the analysis engine for verification. It should be noted that each rule that is to be verified produces a new unique intermediate file. Thus, for N rules, there are N unique binary files that are created for performing the verification.

Until now SDV has only prepared the work that needs to be performed for verifying the driver. Once the verification files are ready for all the rules, SDV schedules the verification tasks in parallel, limiting the number of concurrent verification tasks to the total number of logical cores available in the local machine. Each verification task is limited to a *timeout* (in seconds) and *spaceout* (in MB) value that can be specified as a configuration to SDV. SDV waits for each verification run to complete and eventually reports results back to the user. Until the CloudSDV work presented in this paper, SDV was only capable of running on a single machine. For performing mass scale verification of many drivers, additional infrastructure had been developed for executing SDV in parallel on multiple machines, but such infrastructure was unintuitive and extremely tedious to use.

3   CloudSDV Design and Implementation

We now describe the architecture, design, and implementation details of CloudSDV. CloudSDV is implemented using C# and the .NET Microsoft Azure API. The analysis engines and other parts of SDV have been implemented using OCaml, C, and C++.

Figure 2 shows a high level overview of the CloudSDV system. In general, time flows from right to left (counter clockwise) in the figure. The right most side of the figure contains the CloudSDV client, which is slightly different from the normal SDV client described earlier. There is an extra option included in the normal SDV client to enable the CloudSDV scenarios. The CloudSDV client can

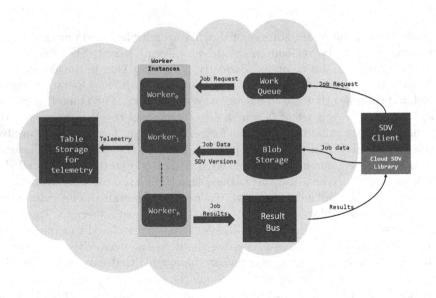

Fig. 2. An overview of the CloudSDV system.

be partitioned into two distinct parts. The first is the CloudSDV library that is a generic library that allows any application to interact with the CloudSDV Microsoft Azure service, and the second, is the SDV client slightly modified to interact with the CloudSDV library. The CloudSDV library provides a generic interface (the compute engine interface) that allows an application to schedule a verification task, upload files and other data for performing a verification task, and retrieve results from the computation platform. Figure 3 illustrates the current implementations of the interface, with the bottom right hand box representing future implementations for other parallelization platforms. Based on the configuration of the application or command line arguments, the CloudSDV client can either choose to perform the verification tasks locally, or using the Microsoft Azure computation platform. In the future, we plan on providing additional implementations that can take advantage of other computation platforms such as clusters, super computers etc. It should be noted that currently, in all cases, the given driver is always compiled on the local machine and all the verification tasks themselves are created on the local machine.

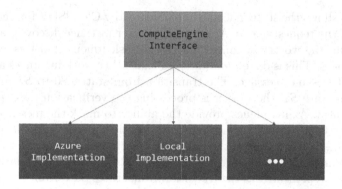

Fig. 3. Various implementations of the compute engine interface.

After the CloudSDV client has compiled the driver and produced the various verification tasks that need to be run, each task is scheduled. This translates to two actions for each verification task: uploading the relevant payload/data to the cloud computation platform, and scheduling the verification task by inserting an entry into the work request queue. The payload/data is uploaded to Microsoft Azure's blob storage [4], which allows storing large amounts of unstructured text or binary data for random direct access. The Azure queuing service is used for storing verification task requests [5]. Each verification task in the queue contains pointers to the data that has been previously uploaded by the CloudSDV client. Within the CloudSDV Azure implementation, there exist CloudSDV worker instances (grouped vertically in the middle of the cloud). The worker instances are responsible for polling the work queue for new verification tasks that have been submitted by CloudSDV clients.

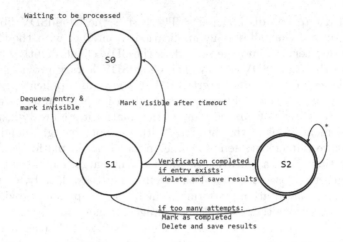

Fig. 4. State machine of the queuing system employed by CloudSDV.

Figure 4 shows the state machine implemented by CloudSDV for dealing with messages in the request queue. As soon as a worker instance discovers a new task in the queue, the worker instances marks the task (queue item) as *invisible* to other instances. This is done *atomically*, so that other work instances are unable to retrieve the same message. The transition from states $S0$ to $S1$ reflects this behavior. In state $S1$, the worker is processing the verification task specified in the queue entry. Azure queues provide the ability to mark the message invisible for a specific time period. For a given *timeout* value specified to CloudSDV, we use *timeout* + 300 seconds as the invisibility period of the entry in the queue. After that time limit has been reached, the entry is automatically marked visible again. This is represented as the transition from states $S1$ to $S0$. This transition is *only* executed in cases where the worker was unable to process the task successfully within the allocated amount of time (due to unknown reasons arising from faulty code or unexpected crashes). In such cases, the result of the worker can be considered lost, and having marked the task as invisible allows us to guarantee processing it again. In the case when the worker successfully processes the verification task, the entry is deleted from the queue permanently, as shown by the transition from states $S1$ to $S2$. State $S2$ is a final state where the entry no longer exists in the queue. We choose *timeout* + 300 seconds as the value of the invisibility period to allow for delays. For example, it may be possible that the verification task completes extremely close to the *timeout* period, in which case, in highly congested network conditions, the delete message from the worker to the Azure queuing system may only arrive after the *timeout* has expired. The additional 300 s (arbitrary choice) buffer allows us to account for this scenario. Even with the additional buffer time, under extreme circumstances it is possible that the entry may be marked visible and then later deleted from the queue by the worker that originally dequeued the entry. In such a case, there is only a side effect if another worker has dequeued the same entry and marked it invisible before the original worker's delete message was processed, but after the Azure queuing system marked the entry as visible. In this particular scenario, the entry is deleted by the original worker and the second worker (after performing the verification) eventually discards its results and proceeds to the next work item in the queue (based on an existence check in the queue). The disadvantage in this scheme is the possibility for redundant processing (at most one extra time), which arises in part due to Azure's at-least-once best effort FIFO queue semantics. In our experience and experiments, we never encountered this situation, which we believe is in part is due to the large buffer we specify in the invisibility timeout period. On the other hand, the advantage of marking items as invisible/visible in the queue is the strong guarantee of always processing all tasks in the queue. Finally, we also impose a limit on the number of times an entry can be dequeued from the queue. Each time an entry is dequeued for processing, we modify the entry and increment the dequeue count. Once the specified limit is reached, the entry is deleted from the queue and the result of that verification task is listed as a `ToolError`. This condition is implemented to account for situations where the tools encounter an irrecoverable deterministic error and workers repeatedly try to complete the same task.

Both the *timeout* and the *spaceout* values are used to limit the amount of time and memory that can be consumed by the verification task on the worker instance. If these values are exceeded, the verification task is ended and the result is marked as a `TimeOut` or `SpaceOut`. These limits are user configurable only on the CloudSDV client. Once a verification task has been submitted to the queue, the configuration of the task can no longer be modified. The space and time restrictions for the verification task are enforced using a monitoring agent on the worker instance.

For each task that is executed, the instance also inserts telemetry data into Azure table storage [6]. Telemetry data is used for performing analysis of CloudSDV. Telemetry data and analysis includes various metrics such as time taken to complete task, average time a task was waiting in the queue before retrieval by a worker, number of times the task was marked visible/invisible etc. Telemetry data is anonymous and used solely for the purpose of studying the system to improve performance, stability, and efficiency.

During the entire time the verification is occurring in the cloud, the CloudSDV client is continuously polling the Result service bus for new available results. The service bus is a commonly accessible storage medium (between workers and CloudSDV client) where workers publish new results to a *topic*. Each topic in the result bus is the unique ID of the CloudSDV client that submitted verification tasks. This ID is made part of the task details, so the workers know where to publish the result. As soon as results are available for any scheduled tasks, the CloudSDV client reports the results to the user and exits. It should be noted that there is extremely little difference (regarding GUI and console output) in the experience the end user gets when using CloudSDV relative to just using the SDV client, which is considered a positive aspect of the CloudSDV system.

3.1 CloudSDV and SDV Versions

A salient feature provided by CloudSDV is the ability to use different versions of the core SDV product. This feature is especially useful for development and testing of new SDV versions, where one is interested in comparing two versions of SDV against each other. The feature enables SDV developers (analysis engine, rule, operating system model) to upload their custom versions of SDV to the Azure blob storage and run experiments on a mass scale very quickly. Using existing infrastructure, the developers are then able to regress their current results against saved baselines.

To enable multiple version support, each component of CloudSDV must be aware of the specific version being used. The CloudSDV client can be configured to specify the SDV version that is to be used for the verification. Each verification task that is created from that client, will also contain the same version string that is to be used for verification. In the Azure cloud, when each worker instance starts processing a new task request, it first checks to see if the SDV version specified is present on the worker instance or not. If present, the worker instance switches to using the specified SDV version and completes the task. If not present, the worker instance first downloads the specified SDV version from CloudSDV's private blob store. If the version cannot be found in the blob store, the worker instance marks the verification task as completed and provides an error code as the final result.

SDV developers (infrastructure, OS model, analysis engines, and rules) are provided special access and instructions for uploading their private versions of SDV.

3.2 CloudSDV Monitor

As part of the CloudSDV infrastructure, we also implemented a simple CloudSDV monitoring tool that allows us to monitor the current state of a CloudSDV deployment. Figure 5 shows a screen shot of the CloudSDV monitor. Our goal is to have the monitor serve as a one stop location for administrators to view/modify the status of CloudSDV. The monitor is deployed as a Microsoft Azure application itself. As configuration, it takes the list of CloudSDV deployments to monitor. Currently we have two deployments in Asia and US. Given a deployment, the CloudSDV Monitor shows basic information about the deployment, the number of current active workers, and the status of the task queue. Each entry in the queue is either currently being verified (shown in Tasks list) or waiting to be verified (shown in Pending list). For each entry, we display the globally unique identifier for the task, the name of the driver, the rule being verified on the driver, the version of SDV requested the submission time, and the exact command that is to be used for performing the verification task. Future versions of the monitor are intended to be more interactive and enable administrators to perform operations on individual tasks or the entire deployment itself.

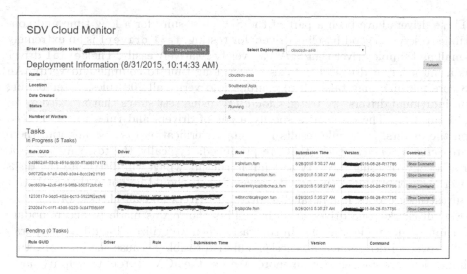

Fig. 5. Screen shot of the CloudSDV monitor.

3.3   Autoscale

To minimize costs incurred on a regular basis, the CloudSDV system always operates with a default of two worker instances. Along with the default 2 workers, we use the Autoscale [3] feature of Microsoft Azure to adjust to incoming verification tasks. The Autoscale feature is configured to increase the number of active workers based on the size of the queue. Since Azure monitors the length of the queue at fixed intervals (CloudSDV uses an interval of 10 min), any time the length of the queue exceeds the configured limit, a certain number of new instances of the workers are created (CloudSDV specifies this number as 50). This process can potentially repeat itself until an upper limit of the total number of worker instances is reached (for CloudSDV this limit is 200). It should be noted that the new worker instances created are not immediately available; it can take anywhere up to 10 min for the workers to be fully functional and available, although, in practice we observe that all the new worker instances are available between 2 and 3 min. Further, each worker once activated has no SDV versions available to it. Rather, a new worker lazily acquires SDV versions as new tasks from the queue are processed. All results presented in this paper are using the Autoscale feature as described here. We believe it would be interesting to repeat the experiments with different configurations of the Autoscale feature, or to disable Autoscale and always have 200 instances available. We plan on doing such experiments in the future.

4   Results

We now present our test methodology and results of using the CloudSDV system. To test CloudSDV, we first selected two drivers that vary in size and complexity.

These drivers have been a part of the SDV test suite for a long time and continue to serve as good baseline drivers for testing. `fail_driver1` is an extremely small and simple driver that SDV can verify relatively easily. The `serial` driver is a much larger driver that takes a very long time to compile and verify. An 8 core machine may take 6 h to compile and verify all 200 rules. After testing on individual drivers, we tested CloudSDV using test suites that are also available in SDV. The test suites specify a set of drivers and rules to be checked on the drivers. Each rule results in a single verification task, so in total, there are *drivers × rules* checks that are produced. Typically, the test suites can be run locally, or using the SDV test infrastructure which will distribute the tasks over a set of machines (managed personally). It should be noted that SDV test infrastructure does not parallelize over all drivers and all checks, rather only over all checks, one driver at a time. This choice was made to accommodate for infrastructure limitations. In contrast, when we utilize CloudSDV, we parallelize over all drivers and all checks. This is possible because the infrastructure limitations are not relevant anymore. We use the JOM [1] tool to help us parallelize over all drivers. Figure 6(a) illustrates the parallelism as implemented with CloudSDV, and Fig. 6(b) illustrates the parallelism as implemented by the SDV test infrastructure. Each dashed line followed by a solid line is one driver being compiled and then verified.

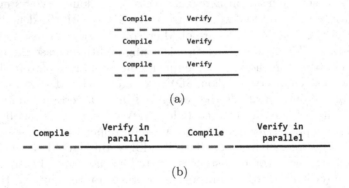

Fig. 6. A visualization of the parallelism schemes implemented in (a) CloudSDV and (b) the SDV test infrastructure.

Table 1 shows the results of using CloudSDV on various drivers and test suites. The Local run is performed using an Intel(R) Xeon(R) CPU with 64 logical cores with a total of 64 GB of memory. The same machine is also used as the CloudSDV client machine for utilizing the CloudSDV cloud (for compilations and submitting tasks to the cloud). For each driver and test suite, we list the total number of drivers and checks to be performed on the driver along with the time taken (`hh:mm`) when using the local machine and when using a maximum of 20, 100, and 200 worker instances in the CloudSDV cloud.

Table 1. Results of using CloudSDV for various drivers and test suites.

Driver/Suite	Drivers	Checks	Local	Azure20	Azure100	Azure200
fail_driver1	1	192	00:55	00:58	00:59	00:56
serial	1	192	01:56	02:09	01:57	01:56
sdv_regress	2	26	00:25	00:22	00:22	00:18
svb-ITP	28	5040	27:26	08:11	02:20	02:08
sdv_bugbash	91	16380	101:06	18:19	05:10	04:31

For fail_driver1, where each verification task is at most 3 s (as measured in the past on a local machine), the local verification run completes in approximately 55 min. Most of that time is spent creating the 192 different verification tasks, 1 for each rule. Utilizing CloudSDV is actually ineffective in this case because each verification check has to be transported to the cloud before it can be completed. The additional overhead of transporting and waiting for results creates a *slowdown*, irrespective of how many worker machines are utilized. For the serial driver, we again notice the same behavior, where scheduling tasks on the CloudSDV cloud results in no significant improvement. Again, this can be explained by making the observation that the majority of the work being performed in verifying these drivers is the compilation and creation of the tasks as opposed to the actual execution of the verification tasks. The sdv_regress test suite consists of 2 drivers which take a total of 25 min to verify on the local machine. This is the first time we observe any improvement when using CloudSDV to verify the drivers. Using 20 workers, we see that the run only takes 22 min, and using 100 and 200 worker instances, the total time taken is again 22 min and 18 min respectively. Since there are only a total of 26 tasks produced by this suite, we don't observe any significant speedup when going from 20 to 100 workers. For the svb-ITP case, we observe that there is much more speedup in going from the local run to using 20 and 100 workers. This is because the total number of tasks (5040) produced is much greater than in any of our experiments before this. Since the total number of checks is still not significant enough for completely utilizing the 200 workers, we don't see any significant speedup when going from 100 to 200 cores. For our last test suite, we picked sdv_bugbash, which is by far the largest test suite in terms of the number of checks it produces. The local run takes more than 4 days to complete. Using even 20 workers produces over a 5x speedup. Furthermore, CloudSDV's true value is shown when we move to 100 and 200 cores where we observe speedups of 17.5x and 22.5x respectively. As seen in the results, the speedup when moving from 100 to 200 cores is modest. This is because all the compilation is still being performed on a single machine, which does require a significant amount of time and space resources. We suspect that it is possible to get even more speedup by using multiple machines for compilation and adding even more workers.

Table 2 shows statistics for time spent by a single verification task in the queue. These results were gathered over a total of 3858 checks. As shown in the

Table 2. Statistics for time spent by a task waiting in the queue.

Mean	Median	Standard Deviation	Minimum	Maximum
24.87 s	11.51 s	27.35 s	1 s	91 s

table, on average, a verification task spends around 25 s waiting in the queue before a worker starts to process the task. This number can prove to be too high if the verification task itself is trivial and does not require much time to be processed and completed. On the other hand, for much larger tasks that require significantly more time to complete, the time spent waiting in the queue proves to be trivial and has no noticeable impact on the entire time taken for verifying the driver. The maximum time any task spent waiting in the queue was 91 s, which is a direct result of the Microsoft Azure Autoscale feature. This happens when all worker instances are busy with a task and the tasks in the queue are waiting either for new instances to be created or for an existing worker instance to poll the queue for a new task.

5   Related Work

In the past, parallel techniques for model checking have been explored in great depth. [18] specifically focused on parallelizing the Murphi model checker for speeding up the exploration of states and also possibly achieving higher scalability by exploring more states and verifying larger models. Kumar et. al. present work in [17] that performs load balancing of parallel model checking algorithms. Work presented in [11] investigates how to perform LTL model checking in a distributed environment. Work presented in [16] also aims at taking advantage of availability of greater resources and computation power.

Given the body of work in parallel model checking, and the rise of static analysis as a more practical solution for certain problems, it was only a matter of time before the case for static analysis in the cloud was made [12]. To this effect, [13] presents work that ports the CPAChecker to the Google App-Engine and exposes the abilities through API as well as a web interface. To our knowledge, this work is the closest to the work presented in this paper but has key differences. Primarily, the work in [13] focuses on using the Google App-Engine in a Platform as a Service (PaaS) setting, while our work is focused on using Microsoft Azure in a Infrastructure as a Service (Iaas) setting. Due to this primary difference, porting the verification technologies involved no effort in CloudSDV, whereas [13] had to make significant changes to CPAChecker for it to function correctly using the Google App-Engine.

Cloud based testing services have also become more practical and popular. [14,15] present cloud based frameworks and environments for performing automated testing.

The work presented in this paper focuses on taking an existing static analysis and verification tool (SDV) and making it available to the users through the cloud in an effort to offload the computational resources required to perform the verification, speedup the verification task, and possibly scale to larger problems.

6   Conclusion

We have presented a method for parallelizing the SDV verification tool using Microsoft Azure. The architecture and implementation make use of core concepts provided by Microsoft Azure (blobs, queues, workers, Autoscale etc.). Using the CloudSDV implementation, we were able to perform large scale verification of drivers and SDV test suites in a sound and consistent manner. Our results show that the CloudSDV implementation is extremely performant and scalable. At *worst*, CloudSDV performs as well as a local verification run, and in the *best* case, CloudSDV is capable of delivering extremely large amounts of speedup. We conclude that the observed speedup is directly proportional to the amount of verification checks that can be submitted to the CloudSDV system. From our current experiments and results, we observe that CloudSDV is extremely effective for large test suites containing a lot of verification tasks, but not as effective for single drivers.

Currently, the CloudSDV implementation is being evaluated for integration with the primary SDV product that is shipped with the Windows Driver Kit. The evaluation is primarily for the purpose of exposing the CloudSDV service to driver developers, both internal and external.

As future work, we plan on performing more experiments with different configurations of the Autoscale feature to identify a possible *sweet spot*. We also plan on investigating the potential to make the CloudSDV client asynchronous (remove polling) and *offline*, where one can schedule jobs and exit the CloudSDV client (not be required to have the client running continuously). Finally, we intend to study the system in greater detail to identify possible bottlenecks and improve performance, especially in the area of payload transport and create techniques that can positively impact the single driver case.

Acknowledgments. We would like to thank B. Ashok and Vlad Levin for their valuable input and support of this work.

References

1. Jom. https://wiki.qt.io/Jom
2. Microsoft azure. https://azure.microsoft.com/en-us/
3. Microsoft azure autoscale. https://msdn.microsoft.com/en-us/library/Hh680945%28v=PandP.50%29.aspx
4. Microsoft azure blob storage. https://msdn.microsoft.com/library/azure/dd179376.aspx
5. Microsoft azure queue storage. http://azure.microsoft.com/en-us/documentation/articles/storage-introduction/
6. Microsoft azure table storage. https://azure.microsoft.com/en-us/documentation/articles/storage-table-design-guide/

7. Microsoft DDI compliance rules. http://msdn.microsoft.com/en-us/library/win-hardware/ff552840.aspx
8. Microsoft Static Driver Verifier. http://msdn.microsoft.com/en-us/library/windows/hardware/ff552808.aspx
9. Ball, T., Cook, B., Levin, V., Rajamani, S.K.: SLAM and static driver verifier: technology transfer of formal methods inside Microsoft. In: Boiten, E.A., Derrick, J., Smith, G.P. (eds.) IFM 2004. LNCS, vol. 2999, pp. 1–20. Springer, Heidelberg (2004)
10. Ball, T., Rajamani, S.K.: Slic: a specification language for interface checking (of C) (2002)
11. Barnat, J., Brim, L., Ročkai, P.: Scalable multi-core LTL model-checking. In: Bošnački, D., Edelkamp, S. (eds.) SPIN 2007. LNCS, vol. 4595, pp. 187–203. Springer, Heidelberg (2007)
12. Barnett, M., Bouaziz, M., Fahndrich, M., Logozzo, F.: A case for static analyzers in the cloud (position paper)
13. Beyer, D., Dresler, G., Wendler, P.: Software verification in the google App-engine cloud. In: Biere, A., Bloem, R. (eds.) CAV 2014. LNCS, vol. 8559, pp. 327–333. Springer, Heidelberg (2014)
14. Candea, G., Bucur, S., Zamfir, C.: Automated software testing as a service. In: Proceedings of the 1st ACM symposium on Cloud computing, pp. 155–160. ACM (2010)
15. Ciortea, L., Zamfir, C., Bucur, S., Chipounov, V., Candea, G.: Cloud9: a software testing service. ACM SIGOPS Oper. Syst. Rev. 43(4), 5–10 (2010)
16. Holzmann, G.J., Joshi, R., Groce, A.: Swarm verification. In: Proceedings of the 23rd IEEE/ACM International Conference on Automated Software Engineering, ASE 2008, pp. 1–6. IEEE Computer Society, Washington, DC (2008)
17. Kumar, R., Mercer, E.G.: Load balancing parallel explicit state model checking. Electron. Notes Theoret. Comput. Sci. 128(3), 19–34 (2005)
18. Stern, U., Dill, D.L.: Parallelizing the murφ verifier. Formal Methods Syst. Des. 18(2), 117–129 (2001)

Author Index

Printed in the United States
By Bookmasters